A DICTIONARY OF BATTLES

A DICTIONARY OF BATTLES

1816–1976

Brigadier Peter Young
with Brigadier Michael Calvert

MAYFLOWER BOOKS
NEW YORK

All rights reserved under International and
Pan American Copyright Convention. Published in the
United States by Mayflower Books, Inc., New York,
New York 10022.

Originally published in Great Britain by New English
Library, Barnard's Inn, Holborn, London, EC1N 2JR.

Library of Congress Cataloging In Publication Data
Young, Peter (Brigadier)
1. Title
2. A Dictionary of Battles (1816-1976)

ISBN 0-8317-2260-6

Printed in Great Britain by Thomson Litho,
East Kilbride, Scotland.
Bound by Hunter and Foulis, Edinburgh, Scotland.

FIRST AMERICAN EDITION 1978

Contents

Acknowledgements

I am in duty bound to acknowledge the very kind assistance of a number of helpers in the construction of this volume. Foremost among them is my friend Brigadier Michael Calvert, DSO, who has followed a distinguished career as a fighting soldier, with a second as a military historian and commentator. His team of researchers has included Stephen Clissold; Captain Adrian Northey, CBE, DSC, RN; Major Leslie Clinton-Robinson, MBE; John William Buchan; Ian Walker, MBE; Alison Michelli; Tony Calvert; Michael Clarke; Leonard Robinson and Ian Wheeler. I am grateful to them for their diligence and energy, and for the time they have generously devoted to this project.

I would like to thank Richard Natkiel for the excellent maps which complement the text.

Author's Preface

This work, which will eventually comprise four volumes, has been planned as a comprehensive study of military operations, on land, by sea and in the air, since the earliest times. The word 'battle' has been given a fairly wide interpretation, for sieges, amphibious landings, single-ship actions, and a variety of other operations are included.

The importance of a military operation cannot be measured solely by the size of the forces engaged: a raid, such as Vaagso (27 December 1941), or an ambush, may have an effect out of all proportion to the forces engaged. It has seemed reasonable, for example, to include actions which have been emblazoned on the colours and appointments of regiments or corps of the various armies of the world, despite the fact that these may vary in importance from epoch-making battles such as Waterloo or the Somme to long-forgotten fights such as Lincelles or the storming of the Malakand Pass.

The descriptions of the various battles are on the whole brief. We have endeavoured to strike a balance between full-length accounts of battles, such as are found in the official histories, and a brief chronology like that in Haydn's *Dictionary of Dates.* In each case we have endeavoured to show clearly where the action was fought; its precise date; the aim of the respective commanders; the forces at their disposal; what took place; the casualties; and the effect of the engagement on future operations and upon the development of the art of war - if any.

A word of warning: these volumes do not set out to be a complete body of the art military. The development of strategy, tactics and weapons is touched on every now and then, but rather *en passant* than with any intention of giving comprehensive information as to the characteristics of weapons, or the formations adopted at various periods. At the same time it is conceived that the reader will wish to know that there is evidence that cannon were used at the battle of Crécy (1346), and that shrapnel shells were first employed at the capture of Surinam (1804). In the latter instance the operation offers little else of interest or instruction!

And now another word of warning! Accounts of battles are woefully imprecise. It is not only that generals, and even admirals, in their dispatches and their memoirs seldom strive to show with blinding clarity what errors they fell into, what principles of war they neglected or even how they managed to get themselves into a confounded muddle. No, it is sometimes that there are extant no accounts at all! Who has ever read the Saxon Official History of the Battle of Senlac? For the highly unimportant battle of Ripple (13 April 1643), which is only mentioned here because the author lives on the battlefield, there are but two accounts. The Parliamentarian account gives some useful information. The Cavalier one is a garbled account in *Mercurius Aulicus,* the Royalist weekly, of what various participants wrote in letters describing their adventures. In a case of this sort one is compelled to fall back on inherent military probability, knowledge of the ground, and a vivid imagination. The opinion of the great Duke of Wellington was that

'You might as well try to write the history of a ball as of a battle'. Who can remember next day precisely with whom they danced the previous evening?

Put not your trust in strength returns. Who can say with confidence how many men Picton, whose division had been bitterly engaged at Quatre Bras, led into action at Waterloo? Put not your trust in war diaries: these too are not infallible. After the battle of Le Câteau (1914) a gunnery officer sent in the diary of his battery, which had been in the thick of it. 'Beg to submit a Nil return' was all he wrote. Magnificent, but not very helpful to the poor historian.

It follows that these volumes are intended as a guide to the annals of the art of war. We have striven for perfection, but in the nature of things we cannot hope to have achieved it. But at least we may claim to have approached our task without bias. We do not believe that the Japanese are always cruel, the French invariably undisciplined, the Italians unduly timorous, the Germans heavy-handed, or the British unflinchingly heroic. In war there are never enough heroes to go round.

P. Y.
Ripple, 1976

SECTION ONE

EUROPE 1816–1914

See Map Section, nos 1–8

ACROPOLIS, THE (Greece)   War of Greek Independence   May-30 June 1821, 1822, 1827-33
Fought between the Greeks and the Turks.
Besieged in turn by the Greeks (1821 and 1822) and the Turks (1827-33).
Battle: In May 1821 the surviving Moslem inhabitants of Athens took refuge in the Acropolis, which was relieved by Omar Vrioni on 30 June. In 1822 it fell to the Greeks who massacred the garrison.

On 25 August 1826 Reshid Pasha took Athens at the first assault, and at once laid siege to the Acropolis, which was held by one Gouras. A first attempt to relieve the place was made by the French colonel, Fabvier, who was repulsed at Chaidari. The death of Gouras (13 October) rendered the situation desperate, but his heroic wife carried on the struggle, inspiring the garrison with her courage.

On 5 February General Gordon had dug in on the hill of Munychia, near the Piraeus and, supported by fire from the *Karteria* (Captain Hastings), had held his position. When Admiral Lord Cochrane and Major-General Sir Richard Church arrived they made a general attack on the Turkish camp near the monastery of St Spiridion (25 April) cutting off Reshid from his vanguard at the Piraeus. The Albanian troops in the monastery surrendered two days later, and were massacred by the Greeks. On 5 May Karaiskakis was killed in a skirmish, with a consequent fall in Greek morale, for he was a brave and wily leader. Next day a general assault was launched, but Reshid's cavalry caught the Greeks advancing across the open in no known formation. They took to their heels, and their English officers, after trying in vain to stop them, were compelled to take to the warships. Church hung on to Munychia until 27 May, when he sent the garrison of the Acropolis instructions to capitulate. The garrison marched out with the honours of war on 5 June.
Result: The Turks, albeit briefly, regained their power over continental Greece.

ACS (Hungary)   Hungarian Rising   2 July 1849
Fought between the Hungarians under General Arthur von Görgey, and the Russo-Austrian army under Prince Windischgrätz.
Strength: Hungarians 25,000; Allies —? But greater in number than the Hungarians.
The Allied attack against the entrenchments of the Hungarians outside Komorn (qv) was repulsed, as was the Hungarians' simultaneous assault on the Allied left flank, which they tried unsuccessfully to turn.
The battle was indecisive.

ADRIANOPLE VII (Turkey)   First Balkan War   3 February-26 March 1913
Fought between the Bulgarians and the Turks.
When an armistice was agreed between Bulgaria and Turkey, the Bulgarians kept troops in the area of Constantinople (Istanbul) and of Adrianople (Edirne), 130 miles NW. Adrianople was ceded to the Bulgarians in the armistice and the Turkish nationalists under Enver Bey, determining to keep the town, overthrew the government of Mohammed V and occupied it. The Bulgarians invested the place

and it was forced to capitulate on 26 March. In May a peace treaty was signed in London.

During the Second Balkan War Turkey reoccupied and kept Adrianople.

AKHALTSKHE (USSR)   Ottoman Wars   27 August 1828
Fought between the Russians under General Count Ivan Feodorovich Paskievich. and the Turks under Achmet Pasha.

Strength: Russians 11,000 (13½ infantry battalions, 8 squadrons regular cavalry, and 6 squadrons cossacks) with 50 guns; Turks 40,000 (mostly undisciplined irregulars).

Aim: Paskiewich intended to take Akhaltskhe as a preliminary to attacking Erzurum, the capital of the vilaret of Anatolia.

Battle: A three week lull followed the storming of Kars. Then on 24 July Paskievich began his advance on Akhaltskhe. After a difficult march through unknown country the Russians took Achalkalaki (5 August) and on 8 August sat down before the fortress of Akhaltskhe. After a three-week siege the Russians stormed the place on 27 August. The Russian losses were 618 killed and wounded and the Turks 5,000 killed or severely wounded.

Result: With the frontier fortresses of Kars and Akhaltskhe in his hands, Paskievich was in a position to resume the advance into Anatolia.

ALADJA DAGH (ALACA-DAG) E Turkey   Russo-Turkish War   15-18 October 1877
Fought between the Russians under General Count Mikhail Loris-Melikov, and the Turks under General Ahmet Muhktar Pasha.

Aim: The Russians advancing through the Caucasus sought to push the Turks back before them.

Battle: The position taken up by the Turks on the Aladja Dagh was very strong but their troops' morale was low owing to previous defeats at Great Yahni and Borluk Dagh. The Russians clinched the victory when, after a heavy bombardment, they charged and overran the Turk positions. The Turks fell back on to Kars (qv). The Russians pursued, and engaged the Turks, forcing them to take refuge under the city walls.

Casualties: Turks 6,000 killed and wounded, 12,000 prisoners, 22 guns; Russians 1,500 killed and wounded.

Result: The Russian objective was achieved.

ALCOLEA (Spain)   Deposition of Isabella II   28 September 1868
The authoritarian and unpopular rule of Isabella II brought revolution in 1868.

E of Cordoba on the Guadalquivir River the two opposing forces met and the rebels under Francisco Serrano won a decisive victory. Isabella fled to France the following day and a provisional government ruled Spain until the accession of King Amadeo I in 1871. The search for a ruler of the country was a contributory cause of the Franco-Prussian War.

ALMA (USSR)   Crimean War   20 September 1854
Fought between the Allies under General Lord Raglan and Marshal Armand
Saint-Arnaud, and the Russians under Prince Alexander Menshikov.
Strength: Allies 56,000 (British 26,000, French 30,000) with 126 guns; Russians
37,000, including 3,400 cavalry and 2,600 artillerymen with 106 guns.
Aim: The Allies intended to besiege Sebastopol. They had landed at Old Fort at
the NW base of the Crimean peninsula, 30 miles north of Sebastopol, and marched
on that fortress. They were halted by the Russians at the river Alma.
Battle: Menshikov disposed his command in three sectors:

		cavalry	battalions	men	guns
Left	Major-General Kiriakov	—	24	10,000	20
Centre	Major-General Prince Gorchakov	—	12	10,000	16
Right	Major-General Kvetzenski	3,400	16	13,000	70
	TOTAL	3,400	52	33,000	106

The Russian position was a strong one. Menshikov's left was refused so as to be
out of range of the Allied fleet. The position, from left to right, ran first along a
ledge above the river, then via Telegraph Height to Kourganie Hill, where the Great
Redoubt mounted 14 heavy guns from Sebastopol. The Russian battalions averaged
about 800, and were usually massed in columns of four companies.

The Allies were drawn up with the French on the right and the British on the
left. After a preliminary cannonade, and some skirmishing, at about 2.30pm Lord
Raglan ordered his infantry to advance, which they did with ceremonial precision.
The river did not stop them, though it disordered the ranks, and after fierce
fighting, they carried the Great Redoubt. The French, thanks partly to the
ineptitude of a divisional commander, Prince Napoleon, were very slow to start,
and by 3pm only four battalions had crossed the river. Raglan, setting an extra-
ordinary example by his *sang froid*, rode through the gap between the two Allied
armies, and established his observation post and 2 guns upon a prominent knoll
which was actually within the Russian lines. This was a considerable surprise to
some of his opponents who, not unnaturally, supposed that the French were at
least up level with him.

The Russians counter-attacked against the British, but their unwieldy columns
were repulsed by the line, and Kourganie Hill was taken. Meanwhile the French
had fought their way on to the plateau. Kiriakov covered the withdrawal of the
Russians. The Allies failed to launch their cavalry in pursuit.

CASUALTIES

	British	French	Russians
Killed	362	60	1,807
Wounded	1,640	c 500	2,820
Prisoners	—	—	1,082?
TOTAL	2,002	560	5,709

Result: After their victory the Allies were able to advance and lay siege to the great fortress and naval base of Sebastopol. Had they lost the battle they must have quit the Crimea. In that sense the Alma was the decisive battle of the War. The tactics employed by both sides were virtually those of the Napoleonic Wars. Of the generals Raglan, who had left an arm at Waterloo, did rather well; Saint-Arnaud who was dying of cholera did practically nothing; whilst Menshikov succeeded in proving that he was no tactician.

ALSEN (Denmark)   Schleswig-Holstein War   28 June 1864
Fought between the Danes and the Prussians.
Aim: The Prussians sought the surrender of the island.
Battle: After the fall of Dybböl the Danish garrison took refuge on the island of Alsen. The Prussians crossed from the mainland in boats on the night of 29 June and, under heavy fire, stormed and carried the Danish entrenchments, compelling the defenders to surrender.
Result: This was the last action of the War. By the Treaty of Vienna King Christian IX of Denmark ceded to Prussia and Austria his rights over Schleswig-Holstein and the little Duchy of Lauenburg. The friction arising from this uneasy condominium was a cause of the war between the victors which broke out in 1866.

AMIENS I (France)   Franco-Prussian War   27 November 1870
Fought between the French under General Faure and the Prussians under General Baron Edwin von Manteuffel.
Battle: After the fall of Metz (qv), the Prussians advanced towards Paris (qv), forcing the French back before them. The French were forced to abandon the city with a loss of 1,383 killed and wounded and 1,000 missing. Prussian losses were 76 officers and 1,216 men.
Result: The Prussians were able to continue their advance.

ANCONA (Italy)   Italian Wars of Independence   September 1860
Fought between the Piedmontese under Admiral Count Carlo Pellione di Persano and General Enrico Cialdini, and the Papal troops under General Louis Lamoricière.
Strength: Piedmontese 13 warships + 9,000 men; Papal troops 6,000.
Aim: The Piedmontese sought to beat the Papal troops out of Ancona, whither they had retreated after their defeat at Castelfidardo (qv).
Battle: The town was attacked by land and sea, and Persano forced the boom which guarded the harbour. After a week's resistance the place capitulated (29 September).
Result: Umbria and the marches were now in the power of Piedmont.

ANTWERP II (Belgium)   Liberation of Belgium   October 1830-23 December 1832
Fought between the Dutch under Lt-General Baron David Hendrik Chassé and Belgian insurgents, supported, eventually, by a French army, 60,000 strong, under Marshal Count Maurice-Etienne Gérard.

Aim: Since 1814 Holland and Belgium had formed the Kingdom of the Netherlands. The aim of the Belgians was to win their independence.

Battle: Following the outbreaks at Brussels from 25 August onwards, Belgium was declared independent, and Antwerp was the only place of importance which remained in the hands of the Dutch. At the end of October an insurgent army was welcomed by the populace, and Chassé withdrew the Dutch garrison into the citadel. He then bombarded the city for two days, destroying houses and merchandise. This did not improve the Belgians' opinion of the Dutch.

The great powers endeavoured in vain to bring about a cessation of hostilities, and the Dutch clung to Antwerp. On 18 November 1832 Gérard laid siege to Antwerp, and after a gallant defence, in which the city sustained further damage, Chassé made an honourable surrender on 23 December.

Result: By the Treaty of London (19 April 1839) Holland and Belgium became independent.

ASPROMONTE (Italy)   Italian Wars of Independence   29 August 1862
Fought between the Redshirts under Giuseppe Garibaldi and Italian troops under the Marchese Giorgio Guido Pallavicini-Trivulzio.

When the unification of Italy occurred, Rome, abetted by France, refused to be annexed. Garibaldi came out of retirement to raise popular support against the papacy. Crossing from Sicily to Calabria with 1,000 followers he marched on Rome in defiance of the Italian government.

Battle: Fearful of French intervention, Victor Emmanuel II sent a force against Garibaldi to prevent him reaching Rome. They met at Aspromonte in the S Appenines. Garibaldi ordered his men not to fire but his undisciplined Sicilian volunteers loosed off a volley or two. After a short action, during which Garibaldi was severely wounded, the Redshirts were defeated and laid down their arms, Garibaldi being among those captured. He was imprisoned in the fortress of Varignano.

Result: Five weeks later, the Italian government granted an amnesty. However, the affair had made the Rattazzi ministry so unpopular that it was compelled to resign.

BALACLAVA (USSR)   Crimean War   25 October 1854
Fought between the Russians under General Liprandi and the Allies under General Lord Raglan.

Strength: Russians 25,000; Allies (British 2 weak cavalry brigades, the 93rd Foot (550 strong) and 100 invalids; Turks 1,100). The Allies were later reinforced by: British 1st and 4th infantry divisions; French 2 infantry brigades and the Chasseurs d'Afrique.

Aim: The Russians intended to capture the landlocked harbour of Balaclava, the base of the British army taking part in the siege of Sebastopol.

Battle: Before dawn the Russians advanced and at about 6am they stormed six redoubts on the Causeway Heights, mounting naval 12-pounders. The Turkish defenders fled.

The Russian cavalry were stopped in front of Balaclava by Major-General Sir Colin Campbell and the 93rd Foot, the 'thin red line'.

Next some 500 sabres of the Heavy Brigade, under Brigadier-General the Hon James Scarlett, then routed some 3,000 Russian cavalry by an astonishing charge, which cost 78 casualties.

Thanks to indifferent staff work the Light Brigade (607 sabres) under Brigadier-General Lord Cardigan followed this up with a charge against 30 Russian guns supported by both infantry and cavalry. Only 198 returned unhurt. Their withdrawal was helped by a brilliant charge by the *Chasseurs d'Afrique,* which silenced the Russian guns on the Fedukhine Heights.

By this time reinforcements had arrived and the Russians drew off.
Result: The Russians did not attain their object.
Note: General Pierre Bosquet is reputed to have said of the charge of the Light Brigade 'C'est magnifique, mais ce n'est pas la guerre.' The exploit was also commemorated by Tennyson in his poem 'The Charge of the Light Brigade'.

BAPAUME (France)   Franco-Prussian War   3 January 1871
Fought between the French under General Louis Faidherbe and the Prussians under General August Karl von Goeben.
Aim: The French objective was to raise the siege of Peronne.
Battle: The action was indecisive, but the Prussians gained a strategic advantage as the French were compelled to give up their plan to relieve Peronne. French losses were 53 officers and 1,516 men killed and wounded and 550 prisoners. Prussian losses were 52 officers and 698 men killed and wounded.

Faidherbe's army was destroyed on 19 January at St Quentin (qv).

BEAUMONT (France)   Franco-Prussian War   30 August 1870
Fought between the French under General de Failly and the Prussians under the Crown Prince of Saxony.

After Marshal le Comte de MacMahon had crossed part of his force over the Meuse at Douzy, Prussians on both banks began to force the French north towards Sedan (qv). At Beaumont, the 5th French Corps d'Armée met the 4th and 12th Prussian Army Corps where the Prussians surprised the French in their cantonments. The French were driven back to Monzon with a loss of 4,800 men and 42 guns. Prussian losses were 3,500.

Prussian pressure drove the French north-westward towards Sedan where they were disastrously defeated.

BEAUNE-LA-ROLANDE (France)   Franco-Prussian War   28 November 1870
Fought between the French under General Crouzat and the Prussians under the Grand Duke of Mecklenburg.
Strength: French 60,000; Prussians 9,000.
Aim: The French sought to drive the Prussian 10th Corps from their position

at Beaune-la-Rolande.
Battle: The Prussians fought brilliantly, and despite their superior numbers the French failed to dislodge them from their position, and were compelled to with-draw with a loss of 8,000. Prussian losses were 37 officers and 817 men.
Result: The victory led to the German capture of Orléans.

BELLEVUE (France)   Franco-Prussian War   18 October 1870
Fought between the French under Marshal Achille Bazaine and the Prussians under Prince Frederick Charles.

After the battle of Gravelotte (qv), the French withdrew into Metz (qv) where they were besieged. Bazaine made an unsuccessful attempt to break through the Prussian lines, and was driven back into the city with a loss of 64 officers and 1,193 men. Prussian losses were 75 officers and 1,703 men.

Metz capitulated on 27 October.

BILBAO I (Spain)   First Carlist War   9 November-25 December 1836
Fought between the Carlists and the Cristinos.
Aim: The Carlists sought the reduction of the town of Bilbao. Don Carlos, brother of the late King Ferdinand VII, had been deprived of his Salic-law right to the throne of Spain because Ferdinand had bequeathed it to his daughter, Isabella, under the regency of his widow, María Cristina. Don Carlos led a revolt.
Battle: The small Cristino garrison lost some suburbs to the Carlists, but recaptured them in a sortie. General Baldomero Espartero, Conde de Luchana, at the head of 18,000 Cristinos, made several unsuccessful attempts to relieve the garrison and finally compelled the Carlists' retreat on 25 December with the loss of all their 25 guns. Cristino losses in the attack were 714, and during the siege losses amounted to 1,300.

BOMARSUND (Finland)   Crimean War   16 August 1854
Fought between the British and French under Vice-Admiral Sir Charles Napier, and the Russians.
Aim: The Allies sought to launch a maritime offensive against Russia.
Battle: The Allied fleet under Napier bombarded the Russian fortress of Bomarsund, on Ahvenanmaa Island in the Gulf of Bothnia. A landing party composed of 10,000 Frenchmen seized the fortress on the same day but the offensive progressed no further. The French General, Baragney d'Hilliers, regarded by the Emperor Napoleon III as the victor of Bomarsund, was made a Maréchal de France as a result of this action.

When a second, similar offensive the following year also failed, the Allies concentrated their operations against Sebastopol (qv).

The first Victoria Cross awarded was to Charles Davis Lucas 'for having thrown overboard a live shell', on 20 June 1854, when HMS *Hecla* was bombarding the principal fort, which mounted 80 guns, at a range of only 500 yards. The shell exploded before it hit the water.

BRESCIA (Italy)   Italian Rising   31 March-1 April 1849
The town was overrun by Italians during the uprising and the small Austrian
garrison was shut up in the citadel. The Italians threw up barricades in the streets
and on 31 March the Austrians, 4,000 strong, stormed the town. Entering by the
Porta Torrelunga, they fought their way from barricade to barricade until, by the
evening of 1 April, all resistance had ended. The Austrians had 480 killed and many
wounded.
    Following the victory, General Baron Julius von Haynau ordered so many
executions that he became known as the Hyena.

BUZENVAL (France)   Franco-Prussian War   19 January 1871
Fought between the French under General Louis Trochu and the Prussians.
Battle: During the siege of Paris several sorties were attempted by the defenders,
commanded by Trochu, President of the Government of National Defence and
governor of the city.
    Advancing under cover of fog, the French took up a position in the Park of
Buzenval, occupying St Cloud, which they maintained throughout the day. Other
positions along the line were not held, however, and the force at St Cloud,
finding themselves unsupported, retired, abandoning the positions that had been
captured. French losses were 189 officers and 3,881 men. Prussian losses were
40 officers and 570 men.
Result: The capital surrendered on 28 January.
Note: The action is also known as the Battle of Mont Valérien.

CALAFAT (Romania)   Crimean War   February-May 1854
Fought between the Russians under General Aurep and the Turks under
Ahmed Pasha.
Strength: Russians 40,000; Turks 30,000.
Aim: The Russians sought to beat the Turks out of their entrenchments.
Battle: The Russians invested the position and assaulted it time after time, always
being beaten back by the Turks. In May the Russians withdrew, having suffered
losses of 20,000 through disease and privation, as well as in battle. The Turks
lost 12,000.
Result: The Russians did not achieve their objective.

CALATAFIMI (Sicily)   Italian Wars of Independence   15 May 1860
Fought between the Redshirts under Giuseppe Garibaldi and the Neapolitans
under General Landi.
Strength: Garibaldi 1,000 Redshirts + −? Picciotti; Neapolitans 4,000.
Aim: After the failure of the alliance of Piedmont and France, Garibaldi landed
in W Sicily to assist in an uprising against Austrian-dominated Naples.
Battle: Garibaldi attacked the Neapolitans at Calatafimi and, despite their superior
numbers and their strong position, drove them back with heavy loss. Garibaldi's
losses were 18 killed and 128 wounded.

Result: Garibaldi went on to occupy Palermo (qv) twelve days later.

CASTELFIDARDO (Italy)   Italian Wars of Independence   18 September 1860
Fought between the Papal troops of Pius IX under General Louis Lamoricière, and
the Piedmontese under General Enrico Cialdini.
Strength: Papal troops 8,000; Piedmontese 35,000.
Aim: On 7 September Giuseppe Garibaldi occupied Naples. His next objective was
Rome (qv). This alarmed Count Camillo Cavour, who feared French intervention.
Battle: A Piedmontese army was sent south and entered Papal territory (11
September). It crushed the pontifical army under Lamoricière at Castelfidardo.
Result: Lamoricière, rallying 300 infantry, retreated to Ancona (qv). The
Piedmontese marched south to join with Garibaldi against the Neapolitan army of
Francis II. Naples and Sicily elected to throw in their lot with Piedmont.

CHERNAYA (USSR)   Crimean War   16 August 1855
Fought between the Russians under General Prince Mikhail Gorchakov, and the
Allies under General Aimable Pelissier and General the Marchese di La Marmora.
Strength: Russians 2 corps; Allies 37,000 (French and Sardinians).
Aim: The Russian field army intended to relieve Sebastopol, which was besieged
by the Allies.
Battle: The corps of Generals Liprandi and Read attacked the heights above
Traktir Bridge with the greatest determination, but were compelled at the end of
the day to draw off, baffled. The Russians lost 260 officers and 8,000 men. The
Allies 1,700.
Result: The Russians lost their last chance of saving Sebastopol.

CHETATE (Romania)   Crimean War   6-9 January 1854
Fought between the Russians under General Fischbuch and the Turks under
Ahmed Pasha.
Strength: Russians 6,000; Turks 6,000.
Aim: The Turks sought to capture Chetate.
Battle: On 6 January the Turks attacked the Russian advanced post in the village.
In heavy fighting, the Russians were gradually forced back and the Turks took the
village. The Russians lost 3,000 killed or wounded and many prisoners. The Russians
made several attempts to regain the village and on 9 January General Anrep brought
up 20,000 men from Cragova. They failed to gain their objective, however, and
lost another 2,000 men in the process. Turkish losses during the three days'
fighting were about 1,000.

CHEVILLY (France)   Franco-Prussian War   30 September 1870
Fought between the French under General Vinoy and the Prussians under General
Ludwig Karl von Tümpling.
    Paris (qv) was invested by the Prussians on 20 September 1870. Several sorties
were made by the French. The 6th Prussian Army Corps repulsed an attack by the

Parisians who lost 74 officers and 2,046 men. Prussian losses were 28 officers and 413 men killed and wounded.

The siege of Paris continued. The city capitulated on 28 January 1871.

CHIOS (Greece)   Greek War of Independence   18-19 June 1822
Konstantinos Kanaris took two fireships into the middle of a Turkish squadron, and succeeded in burning the Turkish flagship with her crew of 3,000.

This exploit was received with joy in the Christian countries supporting Greece.

COLOMBEY (France)   Franco-Prussian War   14 August 1870
Fought between the French under Marshal Achille Bazaine and the Prussians under General Count Helmuth von Moltke.

After having beaten the French three times in as many days, the three Prussian armies of von Moltke continued their advance in order to harass the retreating French.
Battle: Four miles east of Metz, at Colombey, the Prussian 1st Army under General Karl Friedrich von Steinmetz overtook the retreating enemy. The Prussians attacked here and at Borny and Courcelles and on all three fronts the French managed to hold their positions, although two divisions were routed. French losses were 7,000. The Prussians suffered casualties of 222 officers and 5,000 men.
Result: The retreat on Verdun, though seriously delayed by the action, was continued by the French.

COULMIERS (France)   Franco-Prussian War   9 November 1870
Fought between the French under General Louis d'Aurelle de Paladines and the Prussians under General von der Tann.

After the destruction of all the regular armed forces of France, the people of the provinces rose in revolt against the occupying army. A force raised at Tours marched on Coulmiers, west of Orléans, and encountered a Bavarian corps. The Bavarians held their position for most of the day, but fell back at the end having lost 576 killed and wounded, while 800 of their men, 2 guns and an ammunition column were captured. French losses were about 1,500.

This was the only victory won by a French provincial force.

CUSTOZA I (Italy)   Italian Wars of Independence   23-5 July 1848
Fought between the Austrians under Field-Marshal Joseph Radetzky and the Piedmontese under King Charles Albert.
Strength: Austrians 100,000; Piedmontese 70,000, including volunteers from other Italian states.
Aim: Charles Albert, meaning to besiege Mantua, one of the four fortresses of the Quadrilateral, had strung out his army on a 45-mile front from Santa Giustina to Sommacampagna so as to cover the operation.
Battle: Radetzky concentrated opposite the Piedmontese centre at Sona and Sommacampagna and broke it (23 July), though the Piedmontese fell back in good

order and assembled 25,000 men at Villafranca. On 24 July they counter-attacked and retook the heights at Custoza and Sommacampagna. Next morning Radetzky, having massed half his army opposite a quarter of his enemy's, attacked again. He was completely victorious.
Result: Radetzky pursued with vigour and, winning the action of Volta (26-7 July), drove the Piedmontese back across the Mincio. The Austrians reoccupied Milan without fighting, and with Charles Albert back in his own domain, the first campaign for Italian liberty ended in total failure.

CUSTOZA II (Italy)   Italian Wars of Independence   24 June 1866
Fought between the Italians under General the Marchese di La Marmora and the Austrians under the Archduke Albert.
Strength: Italians 80,000; Austrians 74,000.
Aim: The Austrian government of Franz Josef I held Venice, and the kingdom of Italy under Victor Emmanuel II sought to force the Austrians to relinquish the city.
Battle: The Italian army advanced across the Mincio towards Verona which the Austrians were covering. The Italians had to march through hilly country which broke up their columns so that they descended to the plain of Custoza, 11 miles SW of Verona, piecemeal, enabling the Austrians to defeat them in detail. The Italians were driven back south. Austrian losses were 4,650 killed and wounded. Italian losses were 720 killed, 3,112 wounded and 4,315 captured.
Result: Although the Italians lost the battle, Franz Josef ceded Venice to Italy because of his preoccupation with the war against Prussia.

DOLNI-DUBNIK (Bulgaria)   Russo-Turkish War   1 November 1877
Fought between the Russians under General Osip Gurko and the Turks.
Aim: The Russians sought the capture of the redoubt of Dolni-Dubnik on the outskirts of Plevna (qv), as the possession of it by them would make the investment of Plevna complete.
Battle: Two divisions of Russian guards advanced on the redoubt which was surrendered with little resistance, the Turks retiring to Plevna.
Result: The Turks were now completely encircled in Plevna and the Russian objective was achieved.

DOMOKOS (Greece)   Greek War of Independence   17 May 1879
Fought between the Turks under Edhem Pasha and the Greeks under the Crown Prince of Greece.
Strength: Turks 60,000; Greeks 40,000.
Aim: The Greeks sought to drive the Turks out of Greece.
Battle: Five Turkish divisions clashed with the Greeks who held their ground until late in the evening when their right flank was turned. This was the only advantage that the Turks gained, but both sides were prepared to renew the fight the following day. The Crown Prince, however, discovered that the retirement of his right flank had rendered his position untenable, so he was forced to withdraw overnight.

Greek losses were 600 killed and wounded. Turkish losses were 1,800.
Result: The Greek objective was not achieved.

DYBBÖL (DÜPPEL) (W Germany)   Schleswig-Holstein War   30 March-18 April 1864

Fought between the Prussians under Prince Frederick Charles and the Danes.
Strength: Prussians 16,000; Danes 22,000.

The duchies of Schleswig and Holstein were the subject of an alliance between Prussia and Austria early in 1864 when Prince Otto von Bismarck made an agreement with Franz Josef I which would end the friction between Prussia and Denmark. The Prussian general, Count Helmuth von Moltke, sent an army into the duchies, whereupon the Danish troops of Christian IX fell back to the fortress of Dybböl (Düppel), on the east coast. The fortress was protected by an outer chain of ten redoubts. Prince Frederick Charles invested the fortress and opened the first parallel on 30 March. On 17 April, after heavy bombardment, an assault on six of the redoubts was launched and all were taken after short resistance. The fortress and remaining redoubts surrendered the following day. Prussian casualties totalled 1,201. Danish losses were 4,814, including 3,605 prisoners.

The Danes fled to the island of Alsen (qv) and the Prussians pressed on into Denmark. Christian gave up the duchies under the Peace of Vienna, signed on 30 October, and Prussia absorbed Schleswig while Holstein went to Austria. The Austrian territory inside Prussian land caused trouble that would lead to war between the Allies within the next two years.

The Schleswig-Holstein War was the first of Bismarck's three wars which would create the German Empire.

FORBACH   see SPICHEREN

GAETA (Italy)   Italian Wars of Independence   3 November 1860-13 February 1861

Fought between the Neapolitan army under Francis II and the Italian army of unification under General Enrico Cialdini.
Aim: The reduction of the fortress of Gaeta where Francis had set up his government of the Two Sicilies.
Battle: Giuseppe Garibaldi, having occupied Naples, pursued Francis towards Gaeta, beating him back from the line of the river Volturno which he tried to hold. Garibaldi occupied Capua on 1 October. Joined by the Piedmontese army, the army of unification invested the town which was strongly held. The French fleet, though ostensibly neutral, prevented a sea attack on the town, but when they withdrew in January the siege was tightened and Gaeta finally capitulated on 13 February.
Result: Francis abdicated and went into exile, ending the rule of the Neapolitan Bourbons. The first Italian government was set up, but Rome (qv), which was not included in the new nation, continued to make trouble.

GARIGLIANO III (Italy) Italian Wars of Independence October 1850
Italian Patriots under Colonel Enrico Cialdini fought the Neapolitans under Francis II. The Patriots sought to crush dissidents, and achieved their object.

GISIKON (Switzerland) Sonderbund Civil War 23 November 1847
Fought between the Federals (Diet) under General Guillaume Henri Dufour and the troops of the Roman Catholic cantons (Lucerne, Uri, Schwyz, Unterwalden, Zug and Fribourg), the Sonderbund, under Colonel J. U. von Salis-Soglio.
Strength: Federals 100,000 in 7 divisions with 260 guns; Sonderbund 79,000, mostly infantry, few guns. Of these, perhaps 70,000 Federals and 40,000 of the Sonderbund were engaged.
Aim: Dufour aimed to crush the rebellion.
Battle: The troops of the Sonderbund, strongly positioned at Gisikon, near Lake Zug, were attacked by the Federals, who drove them from their position with comparatively small loss to either side. Casualties suffered by the Federals were 78 killed, 260 wounded; and by the Sonderbund, 50 killed and 175 wounded.
Result: The Federals entered Lucerne the next day and the Civil War, which had lasted only twenty days, was brought to an end.

GOITO (Italy) Italian Wars of Independence 30 May 1848
Fought between the Piedmontese under Lt-General Bava and the Austrians under General Count Wratislaw.
On 18 March the Milanese rose against Austrian domination, and soon Venice and all the great cities of Lombardy were in revolt.
Strength: Austrians 15 battalions, 8 squadrons and 33 guns; Piedmontese 23 battalions, 24 squadrons and 43 guns.
Battle: The Italians got the better of the engagement, and the Austrians were compelled to withdraw. The Austrians lost 618; the Piedmontese 362.
Result: In consequence of this and other setbacks Field-Marshal Joseph Count Radetzky withdrew the Austrian forces behind the river Adige and regrouped.

GORNI-DUBNIK (Bulgaria) Russo-Turkish War 24 October 1877
Fought between the Russians under General Osip Gurko and the Turks under Achmet Hefzi Pasha.
Battle: The Russians, investing the fortress of Plevna (qv), systematically reduced its satellite forts. The 2nd Division of the Russian Guard under Gurko attacked the Turks and drove them out after heavy fighting. Turkish losses were 1,500 killed and wounded and 53 officers and 2,250 men captured, including the Pasha. Russian losses were 3,300 killed and wounded (including 116 officers of the Guard).
Result: The Russians strengthened their hold on Plevna.

GRAVELOTTE AND MARS-LA-TOUR (France) Franco-Prussian War 16 and 18 August 1870
Fought between the Prussians under General Count Helmuth von Moltke and the

French under Marshal Achille Bazaine.

Strength: Prussians 187,000 with 732 guns (1st and 2nd Armies of the North German Confederation); French 113,000 with 520 guns (Army of the Rhine).

Battle: The Germans were advancing cautiously on a broad front against Bazaine, who was about to fall back from the fortress of Metz. On 14 August Prince Frederick Charles (2nd Army) made contact with the French outposts, at the moment when the Emperor Napoleon III, believing the position at Metz to be untenable, had ordered Bazaine to withdraw and join up with Marshal MacMahon at Châlons.

Von Moltke now ordered General Karl Friedrich von Steinmetz (1st Army) to mask the fortress of Metz whilst the 2nd Army, advancing westwards on Verdun, should cut off the French retreat. The Prussians thought that Bazaine had indeed escaped to Verdun, and were surprised when on 16 August they ran into the French 2nd Corps, south of Vionville. Lt-General Konstantin von Alvensleben (3rd Corps) soon realised, however, that he was faced with Bazaine's whole army. Undismayed he boldly threw every available man into an attack, which took Vionville and cut the French escape route to the W. Bazaine could still have broken through towards Verdun, but, obsessed with the idea that he should keep open his communications with Metz, he concentrated on his left wing round Rezonville and fought a mainly defensive battle. The Prussian 10 Corps arrived about 3.30pm to reinforce Alvensleben. German cavalry attempted to turn the French right and a tremendous cavalry mêlée ensued. In the dusk the Prussians were able to consolidate their positions.

Bazaine, his forces in disorder, decided that he must give up his attempt to reach Verdun, and on 17 August, abandoning many wounded and quantities of stores, withdrew to a strong position a few miles W of Metz. Moltke brought the whole of the 2nd Army and 2 corps of the 1st Army wheeling up so that by evening they were facing north on a line Rezonville-Mars-la-Tour.

When the battle began on 18 August the Germans did not appreciate that the French army was on their right flank. The 9th Corps attacked Amanvillers, the French centre, believing that it had found an open flank. It met with a bloody repulse. The Guard Corps attacking St Privat was halted by Marshal François Certain Canrobert (6 Corps) with dreadful slaughter. But at Rancourt, on the extreme French right, the Royal Saxon Corps did find the flank, and in the dusk Canrobert fell back on Metz.

On their left the French held Steinmetz all day, and towards evening some of his troops, crowded into the Mance ravine, broke in panic. Now, if ever, was the time for a French counter-attack, which might have opened the road to Verdun and cut the Germans' communications, but Bazaine was not the man to command it. That night he withdrew under the guns of the fortress of Metz. The Prussians lost 20,000; the French 12,800.

Result: It could be argued that the French had won the battle, but that Bazaine had conceded the victory to his enemy. He had locked up his army, which was still intact, in a fortress, where it was cut off from the rest of France, and where on

27 October 1870 he was to surrender.

GREEK INDEPENDENCE, WAR OF   1821-33
Fought between the Greeks and the Turks.
Aim: The Greeks fought to throw off Ottoman domination and establish an independent kingdom.
  The struggle fell into three periods:
1   1821-4. The Greeks and numerous European volunteers waged a successful war against the Sultan's forces.
2   1824-7. The disciplined forces of Mehemet Ali, Pasha of Egypt, turned the tide against the Greeks.
3   1827-33. The great European powers, France, Great Britain and Russia, intervened on behalf of the Greeks whose object was achieved.
Phase 1: On 2 April 1821 Archbishop Germanos raised the standard of the cross at Kalavryta in the Morea, and a general rising took place. The Ottoman army was engaged in operations against Ali Pasha of Iannina, and the Greeks early won command of the sea, because the Turkish fleet had been manned largely by Greek seamen.

  Germanos, with an army of peasants armed with primitive weapons, took the town of Patras, and massacred its Moslem inhabitants, save those who fled to the citadel which held out until 1828.

  In the south the Mavromichales clan took Kalamata and Theodorus Kolokotrones, a brigand, captured Karytaena. In both places the infidels were slaughtered. With these successes the revolt spread until soon Turks survived only in the fortified towns.

  In April Boeotia and Attica rose, and in May the Moslem inhabitants of Athens were compelled to take refuge in the Acropolis. One by one most of the fortresses of the Morea fell, and everywhere the Turks were butchered, until in September Kolokotrones stormed Tripolitsa, capital of the vilayet. Regardless of age or sex 2,000 prisoners were slain in cold blood.

  Meanwhile Omar Vrioni, after inflicting a number of reverses upon the Greeks, had relieved the Acropolis (30 June). Mohammed Pasha, marching to his support, was routed at Mount Oeta, and the campaign ended with the Turks retreating into Thessaly.

  In March 1822 the Turks exterminated the prosperous Greek community on the island of Chios (Scio). Now Christians everywhere espoused the cause of Greece. The exploit of Konstantinos Kanaris (18-19 June) in burning the Turkish flagship off Chios was hailed with joy.

  In the spring of 1822 two Turkish armies advanced S: the first under Omar Vrioni along the west coast, the second, under Ali Pasha Dramali, into Boeotia and Attica. Omar was halted by the earthworks of Missolonghi. Dramali, having avenged the massacre of the Turkish garrison of the Acropolis, moved across the Isthmus of Corinth to relieve Nauplia. At his approach most of the Greek government, assembled at Argos, fled in panic, but a few hundred men held the castle of Larissa, and checked Dramali, whilst Kolokotrones assembled an army. Their fleet failed to supply the Turks, and so on 6 August they retreated. The Greeks ambushed them in the pass of Dervenaki, threw them into confusion with a hail of boulders and cut them to pieces. At Missolonghi a surprise attack was repulsed (6 January 1823), compelling Omar Vrioni to beat a retreat to the north.

One way and another the campaign had been a disaster for the Turks. The Greeks for their part fell to fighting amongst themselves. Luckily for them the Ottoman Admiral Khosrev, unduly impressed by Kanaris' fireships, was unenterprising. He contented himself with relieving beleaguered fortresses, among them Patras and Modon.

Mustai Pasha led an army down the west coast, but on 21 August 1823 his camp was surprised by Marko Botzaris, who was killed. The Greeks failed to exploit this success and Mustai laid siege to Anatoliko, a small town a few miles NW of Missolonghi, but on 23 December 1823 he was forced to abandon the siege and retreat N.

In the eastern theatre Kolokotrones' guerilla tactics were, eventually, too much for Yussuf Pasha.

At this juncture Lord Byron arrived bringing with him the first loans raised in Europe amongst those who sympathised with Greek aspirations. With the Turks repulsed the Greeks were now able to indulge in a second civil war to decide how the money should be shared. Kolokotrones, attacking the government forces, was defeated and imprisoned.

Phase 2: Sultan Mahmud now - albeit reluctantly - called in Mehemet Ali Pasha of Egypt, whose army and navy were relatively well-organised and disciplined. His son-in-law, Hussein Bey, had landed in Crete in June 1823, and by April 1824 had reduced the island which served henceforth as a Turkish base of operations.

On 19 June Ibrahim Pasha sailed from Alexandria, effecting a junction with Khosrev off Budrun on 1 September. Two indecisive engagements followed (5 and 10 September) and on 16 November the Greek Admiral Andreas Vokos Miaoulis succeeded in preventing Ibrahim getting his transports to Crete. But then his captains, clamouring for their arrears of pay, dispersed and Ibrahim, who had retired to Rhodes, was able to reach Suda Bay unopposed (5 December). On 24 February 1825 he landed 4,000 infantry and 500 cavalry at Modon in the Morea. Once more he was unopposed. On 21 March he laid siege to Navarino.

The Greeks, who affected to despise the Egyptians, had a nasty shock at Krommydi (qv) on 19 April 1825. Ibrahim completely defeated their attempt to relieve Navarino, which fell in consequence, as did Pylos. Struck with terror, the government had to bring Kolokotrones out of prison to lead their army. But Ibrahim proved a match for the guerillas and, seizing Tripolitsa, made it his base, systematically devastating the surrounding country.

Another Turkish army under Reshid Pasha, a capable and resolute officer, advanced and on 7 May 1825 began the second siege of Missolonghi (qv), where in September Ibrahim joined him. Missolonghi fell on 23 April 1826.

Reshid Pasha was now able to advance on Athens, take the city, and besiege the Acropolis (qv). During the long siege Georgios Karaiskakis continued the struggle in the mountains. His victory at Distomo (February 1827) over Omar Vrioni gave the Greeks control of the whole country save for a few Turkish garrison towns.

Phase 3: The Allies, besides providing a fresh loan, sent Admiral Lord Cochrane and Major-General Sir Richard Church to command the Greek forces. The relief of the Acropolis was their first object. On 25 April 1827 Cochrane led an attack on the Turkish position near the monastery of St Spiridion, and isolated Reshid's vanguard at the Piraeus. The monastery surrendered two days later and the Greeks massacred the Albanian garrison. Karaiskakis' death, in a skirmish on 5 May, had a bad effect on Greek morale. A general assault next day on the main Turkish camp ended in panic, and on 5 June the defenders of the Acropolis were compelled to surrender. Only the jealousy of Reshid and Ibrahim prevented a Turkish reconquest of the Morea. The Greek factions fell out once more, and at Nauplia two forts actually bombarded each other across the town! Ibrahim Pasha, after a period of inactivity, renewed his systematic devastation of the countryside. The Powers, therefore, intervened to enforce an armistice. (Treaty of London, 6 July 1827.) Ibrahim declined to evacuate the Morea without a direct order from the Sultan, and thereupon the Allied fleet went into action at Navarino (qv) (20 October 1827). This victory and the pressure of the two campaigns of the Russo-Turkish War (1828-9) put an end to the struggle. By the Treaty of London (7 May 1832) Greece became an independent kingdom.

GROCHOW (Poland)   Polish Revolt   25 February 1831
Fought between the Russians under General Count Hans von Diebitsch and the Poles under Prince Michael Radziwill.
Strength: Russians 100,000; Poles 90,000.

The Treaty of Vienna (1815) put most of Poland under Russian control. Inspired by the revolution in Paris in 1830, Polish patriots expelled the Russian garrison and proclaimed their independence.

A Russian army marched on Warsaw. At Grochow, an eastern suburb on the right bank of the Vistula, the Russians met a Polish force. In a fierce engagement the two sides fought themselves to a standstill, leaving the Poles a strategic victory. Polish casualties were less than those of their opponents, being 5,000 killed or wounded. Russian losses were 10,000.

HALLUE (France)   Franco-Prussian War   23-4 December 1870
Fought between the French under General Louis Faidherbe and the Prussians under General Baron Edwin von Manteuffel.
Strength: French 40,000; Prussians 22,500 from the 1st Army.
Aim: While the Prussian army besieged Paris (qv), campaigns went on to subdue French resistance elsewhere.
Battle: Manteuffel, released by the surrender of Metz (qv), marched NE mopping up minor fortresses. He attacked the French entrenched on the heights above the

little river Hallue, near Amiens, but failed to carry the position, and after the attack was repulsed Faidherbe went over to the offensive, but without decisive results. French losses were 1,000+ and 1,300 prisoners. Prussian losses were 927 killed and wounded.
Result: Faidherbe, who considered that his troops could only succeed if they took their objective at the first rush, withdrew his army intact.

HATVAN (Hungary)   Hungarian Rising   2 April 1849
Fought between the Austrians under Marshal Count Franz von Schlick and the Hungarians.
Strength: Austrians 15,000; Hungarians 15,000.
   The Austrians attacked the 7th Hungarian Corps and, after a fierce fight, were totally defeated.

HERNANI I (Spain)   First Carlist War   29 August 1836
Fought between the British Legion under General Sir George de Lacy Evans and the Carlists.
Aim: The British Legion fought on the side of the Cristinos to crush the Carlist rebellion.
Battle: The Carlists won the action.
Result: The British objective was not achieved.

HERRERA (Spain)   First Carlist War   23 August 1837
Fought between the Carlists under Don Carlos, with General Moreno in actual command, and the Cristinos under General Buerens.
Aim: The Carlists sought to march on Madrid, which the Cristinos sought to prevent.
Battle: The Cristinos sought to make a junction with General Espartero who had 20,000 men, but Carlos attacked him before this was achieved and severely defeated him. Cristino losses were 50 officers and 2,600 men killed and wounded. The Carlists' losses were about 900.
Result: Carlos marched to within 12 miles of Madrid, when the appearance of Espartero forced him to retire.

INKERMAN (USSR)   Crimean War   5 November 1854
Fought between the British and French under General Lord Raglan and General Aimable Pelissier, and the Russians under Prince Alexander Menshikov.
Strength: Allies 16,000 (British 8,500, French 7,500) with 56 guns; Russians 42,000 with 106 guns.
Aim: The Russians sought to break the allied siege of Sebastopol (qv).
Battle: At dawn, Menshikov led a large-scale sortie to the east of the city where the Allies were only thinly deployed at the mouth of the Chernaya River (qv). The action was closely contested, consisting chiefly of small hand-to-hand fights in dense fog, much of the action taking place round Sandbag Battery where alone the Russians lost about 1,200 men. The arrival of General Pierre Bosquet's

division gave the Allies the victory and the Russians retired, having lost 15,187 men.
Raglan's losses were 2,640, Pelissier's 1,465.
Result: The siege of Sebastopol continued.

CASUALTIES

	British	French	Russians
Killed	660	132	4,978
Wounded	1,980	1,333	10,209
TOTAL	2,640	1,465	15,187

IOÁNNINA (JANINA) (Albania)   First Balkan War   5 March 1913
Fought between the Greeks and the Turks.

Bulgaria and Serbia agreed to an armistice two months after the outbreak of the war, but Montenegro and Greece continued to fight. The Greeks invested Ioánnina (Janina) on the Albanian frontier in 1912 and, although the Turkish garrison was cut off from outside relief, it resisted stubbornly until forced to capitulate in March 1913.

The war was ended by an armistice the following month.

IRUN (Spain)   First Carlist War   18 May 1837
Fought between a Cristino and British force under General Sir George de Lacy Evans, and the Carlist garrison.
Strength: Cristinos/British 10,000; Carlists 4,000.
Aim: The reduction of the Carlist garrison.
Battle: Evans arrived before Irun and summoned the town to surrender. Upon receiving a negative reply an assault was ordered, and by 11pm the fortress was taken at small cost to the assailants.
Result: The Cristino objective was achieved.

ISASZCQ (Hungary)   Hungarian Rising   6 April 1849
Fought between the Hungarians under General Arthur von Görgey and the Croats under General Josip Jelacic od Buzima (Jellachich).
Strength: Hungarians 42,000; Croats 27,000.
Aim: Hungary sought to beat the Croatians and proclaim itself a republic.
Battle: The Hungarian 1st Corps under Klapka was driven from the field, but the rest of the Hungarian army stood its ground throughout the day and the armies bivouacked on the field overnight. On the following day, however, the Croats retired and the Hungarians claimed a victory.
Result: The Hungarians proclaimed a republic, but on 9 August, the Russians and Austrians defeated them at Timisoaca (TEMESVÁR) and the country was made part of the Austrian Empire.

JIČIN (GITSCHIN) (Czechoslovakia)   Seven Weeks' War   29-30 June 1866
Fought between Prussians belonging to the 1st Army under Prince Frederick
Charles; and Saxons and Austrians under Crown Prince Albert of Saxony and
General Eduard Count Clam-Gallas respectively.
Strength: Prussians 16,000 (2 divisions); Austrians and Saxons 30,000 (7 infantry
brigades, 1 cavalry division) with 56 guns.
Aim: The Crown Prince of Saxony believed that Feldzeugmeister Ludwig August
von Benedek intended him to hold Jičin, and would support him.
Battle: The Prussians advanced on the town from two directions. The 3rd Division
(Lt-General August Leopold Count von Werder) from the W and the 5th Division
(Lt-General Ludwig Karl von Tümpling) from the N. The Crown Prince of Saxony
had made his dispositions so as to take every advantage of the terrain, and, after
three hours fighting, the Prussians had made no impression. By 7.30pm Tümpling
had used up his reserves, whilst Prince Albert still had some. Then a message
arrived from Benedek ordering the Austrians and Saxons to withdraw and join
him. With the armies locked in heavy fighting this was not easy. Soon the roads
in front of Jičin were clogged with vehicles and men. Prince Albert and Clam-Gallas
wisely left a brigade to hold the town and cover the withdrawal of the remainder.
    At about 11pm Pomeranian Fusiliers from von Werder's division broke into the
town, and Clam-Gallas departed. His command disintegrated. The Saxons, however,
drove out the Pomeranians and then withdrew in good order to Smidar. The Saxons
lost 27 officers and 586 men; the Austrians 184 officers and 4,714 men; and the
Prussians 71 officers and 1,482 men.
    General von Tümpling, who was hit in the arm, received a congratulatory
message from Prince Frederick Charles: 'It is fine when a Prussian general bleeds.
It brings the army luck.' Unfortunately Tümpling's comments are not recorded.
    Result: After their defeat at Jičin the Austrians, from Benedek downwards,
began to suspect that the war was lost. Clam-Gallas was relieved of his command.

KAPOLNA (Hungary)   Hungarian Rising   26-7 February 1849
Fought between the Hungarians under a Polish refugee, General Henryk Dembinski,
and the Austrians under Prince Alfred Candidus Ferdinand zu Windischgrätz.
Strength: Hungarians 45,000; Austrians 15,000.
Aim: The Austrians sought to quell the Hungarian Rising.
Battle: Four Hungarian divisions engaged General Count Franz von Schliek's
corps and held their own on 26 February, though on the following day they retired
unmolested, when the Austrians captured their key position at Kapolna.
Result: The battle was bloody and indecisive. Dembinski retreated and was replaced
as commander-in-chief by an officer of proven ability, General Arthur von Görgey.

KARS I (Turkey)   Ottoman Wars   5 July 1828
Fought between the Russians under General Count Ivan Feodorovich Paskievich
and the Turks under Emin Pasha.
Strength: Russians 12,000 (15 infantry battalions in 3 brigades, 8 squadrons

regular cavalry, and 7 squadrons cossacks) with 70 guns; Turks 18,000 (including 3,000 cavalry) with 165 guns and mortars.

Aim: The Russians declared war on 28 April 1828 and took the field both in the Balkans and in the Caucasus. Paskievich's immediate object was to capture the fortress of Kars.

Battle: Paskievich crossed the Turkish frontier on 26 June, and began his advance. On 1 July he cleared the suburbs of Kars, preparatory to laying siege to the fortress. At dawn on 5 July the Russian batteries opened a heavy fire on the western walls and under its cover the Russian infantry stormed into the place. The Russian casualties were 600 killed and wounded; the Turks 3,500 killed and wounded and 1,500 prisoners.

At 8am on 6 July the Turks showed the white flag.

Result: By the terms of the capitulation the fortress and its citadel were surrendered, with all the war material therein. Emin Pasha and the captured troops were sent to Russia. The irregulars, some 11,000, were dispersed to their homes. The Russians' spoils included 151 guns, 33 flags and quantities of powder and stores. Paskievich was able to continue his advance.

KARS II (Turkey)   Crimean War   June-28 November 1855
Fought between the Russians, 25,000 strong, under General Mikhail Mouraviev and the Turks under Major-General Sir William Fenwick Williams, an artillery officer, who was a *ferik* (lieutenant-general) in the Turkish army and a pasha.

Aim: With the main Allied forces besieging Sebastopol (qv), Czar Alexander II was able to operate more freely to the south. He sent an army into the Caucasus and the Turks fell back into Armenia.

Battle: At Kars, Ottoman troops under Williams made a stand against the Russians who assaulted the garrison on 29 September. The attack was repulsed and a relief force was sent under Omar Pasha. On 28 November the Russians stormed the town again and the garrison, weakened by starvation, surrendered.

Result: The offensive was halted at this point because of the threatened intervention of Austria in the war. The Czar signed preliminary peace terms with the British, French and Turks.

KARS III (Turkey)   Russo-Turkish War   17 November 1877
Fought between the Russians under General Count Mikhail Loris-Melikov and the Turks under General Hussein Pasha.

While the main Russian offensive struck through the Balkans, a secondary column thrust through the Caucasus. On the night of 17 November the Russians stormed Kars, in Armenia, the attacking force being led by General Lazarev. The eastern forts were all captured and Hussein led an attempt to break out from the west of the town. The bulk of his troops were driven back, but he escaped with some officers. The town then surrendered. Of 24,000 in the garrison, 2,500 were killed, 4,500 wounded and 17,000 captured along with 303 guns. Russian losses were 2,273.

The Turkish commander in the area, General Ahmed Muhktar Pasha, was forced to withdraw to Erzurum on the Upper Kara Su (W Euphrates). The Turks withdrew from the area altogether the following year.

KERCH (USSR) (Sea of Azov)   Crimean War   24 May 1855
After the arrival in April of General Aimable Jean Jacques Pélissier, a dynamic French general who had been successful in the Algerian Wars, and who replaced General Canrobert, the Allied effort in the Crimea became more aggressive. Pélissier helped organise a naval operation, the object of which was to obtain control of the Sea of Azov and thus threaten and cut Russian communication from the mainland to the Crimean peninsula. It was first necessary to seize control of the Straits of Kerch, the entrance to the landlocked Sea of Azov.

A joint Franco-British military force was landed near Kerch and the town was soon taken. The British contingent was commanded by Lt-General Sir George Brown.

Naval domination of the Sea of Azov cut one of the Russians' main lines of communication and materially assisted in the fall of Sebastopol a few months earlier, but this indirect approach to victory was never fully exploited, mainly owing to the British commanders: Lord Raglan and General Sir James Simpson's objection to any diversion from the head-on attack against the fortress.

KIRK-KILISSA (KIRKARELI) (Turkey)   First Balkan War   25 October 1912
Fought between the Turks and the Bulgarians.

At the outbreak of war, Sultan Mohammed V of Turkey ordered an offensive against the Bulgarians in Thrace. The Bulgarians met the Turks at Kirk-Kilissa (Kirkareli), 35 miles east of Adrianople, and drove them back with heavy losses. At the same time, a Turkish army was fielded against Serbia.

KISSINGEN (West Germany)   Seven Weeks' War   10 July 1866
Fought between the Prussians under General Eduard Vogel von Falckenstein and the Bavarians under General Zoller.

As part of the Prussian offensive against the S German Allies of Austria, Falckenstein's army beat the Hanoverians at Langensalza (qv) and then massed against the remaining Allies. At Kissingen, the Prussians attacked the Bavarians and beat them out of the town with heavy loss.

The Prussian objective was achieved.

KIZIL-TEPE (Turkey)   Russo-Turkish War   25 June 1877
Fought between the Russians under General Count Mikhail Loris-Melikov and the Turks under Ahmed Muhktar Pasha.
Aim: The Turks sought to relieve the siege of Kars (qv).
Battle: A superior force to that of the Russians attacked the besiegers and defeated them, forcing them to raise the siege.
Result: The Turkish objective was achieved.

KOMORN (KOMARNO) (Czechoslovakia)   Hungarian Rising   26 April 1849
Fought between the Hungarians under General Arthur von Görgey and the Austrians.
Aim: The Hungarians sought to relieve the besieged fortress of Komorn.
Battle: Early in the morning two Hungarian corps under Generals Gyorgy Klapka and Janos Damjanich surprised the Austrian entrenchments, taking 200 men and 6 guns. The Austrians retired, unpursued.
Result: The Hungarians had achieved their object: the fortress was relieved.

KROMMYDI (Greece)   Greek War of Independence   19 April 1825
Fought between the Egyptians under Ibrahim Pasha and the Greeks under Captain Skourti, a naval officer.
Strength: Egyptians 2,400 (2,000 regular infantry, 400 cavalry) with 4 guns; Greeks 7,000 (including Albanians and irregular Bulgarian cavalry).
Aim: Ibrahim was besieging Navarino, which Skourti was sent to relieve.
Battle: Ibrahim came upon Skourti at Krommydi, and at their first rush his fellahin infantry stormed the Greek entrenchments with the bayonet. The Greeks fled in disorder. Egyptian losses were light. The Greeks, who left 600 killed, may well have lost as many as 2,000 from all causes.
Result: Pylos and Navarino fell. Public clamour compelled the terror-stricken Greek government to release Theodoros Kolokotrones from prison to head their army once more.

KULEVCHA (Bulgaria)   Ottoman Wars   11 June 1829
Fought between the Russians under General Count Hans von Diebitsch and the Turks under the Grand Vizier, Mustafa Reshid Pasha.
Strength: Russians 50,000; Turks 40,000.
Aim: While the Russians besieged Silistria (qv) on the right bank of the Danube, a two-pronged offensive was launched into Turkey, General Count Ivan Feodorovich Paskievich driving through the Caucasus and Diebitsch moving S through the Balkans, 40 miles W of Varna (qv).
Battle: Diebitsch trapped a Turkish army in the Kulevcha defile and attacked. The Turks lost 5,000 men and all their guns before they could extricate themselves, Reshid Pasha escaping with difficulty.
Result: Diebitsch marched rapidly to Adrianople (qv) which he seized on 20 August, having outmanoeuvred the Turks by the speed of his advance. With the Russians only 130 miles from Constantinople Mahmud II sued for peace.

KUMANOVO (Yugoslavia)   First Balkan War   24 October 1912
Fought between the Turks and the Serbians.
    At the same time as they were opposing the Bulgarians in Thrace, the Turks launched an offensive against the Serbians in Macedonia. A Serbian army of King Peter I Karageorgevich met the Turks at Kumanovo, 15 miles NE of Skoplje, and in a three-day battle drove them back. Continuing their advance the Serbians took

Monastir (Bitolj) on 18 November. An armistice was concluded on 3 December.

LANGENSALZA (East Germany)   Seven Weeks' War   27 June 1866
Fought between the Prussians under General Eduard Vogel von Falckenstein and
the Hanoverians under George V of Hanover.
Strength: Prussians 12,000; Hanoverians 12,000.

    As a result of the partitioning of Schleswig-Holstein in 1864, war broke out
between Prussia and Austria in 1866. Hanover, Bavaria, Saxony and most other
German states sided with Austria. General Helmuth von Moltke, Chief of General
Staff in the Prussian army, sent most of his forces into Bohemia to attack
the Austrians. Nineteen miles NW of Erfurt the van of the Prussian army met and
attacked the Hanoverian army, but, in a hard-fought battle, was repulsed with a
loss of 2,000. Hanoverian losses were 1,392. Vogel von Falckenstein brought the
rest of his 50,000 troops up and the Hanoverians, greatly outnumbered, were
forced to lay down their arms (29 June).
Result: George V abdicated and Hanover was annexed by Prussia.

LE BOURGET (France)   Franco-Prussian War   27 October 1870
Fought between the French and the Prussians.

    During the siege of Paris (qv) several sorties were made by the defenders. To the
NE of Paris the French attacked towards Le Bourget, which they carried. They
held the position for three days before being driven out by the Prussian Guard
Corps with a loss of 1,200 prisoners. Prussian losses were 34 officers and 344 men.
The Prussians attacked in open order, thus reducing their casualties.

    The siege of Paris continued until the city capitulated on 28 January 1871.

LE MANS (France)   Franco-Prussian War   10-12 January 1871
Fought between the French under General Antoine Chanzy and the Prussians
under Prince Frederick Charles.
Strength: French 150,000; Prussians 50,000 (4 corps and 4 cavalry divisions).
Battle: After the destruction of the French regular army, several improvised armies
took the field against the Prussians.

    The Prussians, pushing westward, converged on Le Mans, 117 miles SW of
Paris, where the resolute Chanzy fought hard for three days. He was only compelled
to retreat by the misconduct of his Breton *mobiles,* who not only fled from their
position when the German infantry appeared, but succeeded in transmitting their
panic to troops in the reserve camps of instruction. Chanzy drew off towards
Laval, having lost 10,000 casualties, 20,000 prisoners, 17 guns and supplies.
Prussian casualties totalled 200 officers and 3,200 men.
Result: Chanzy, reinforced by a new corps, rebuilt his army and was soon at the
head of 156,000 men. He was planning an offensive against the 40,000 Germans
in and around Le Mans when, to his chagrin, he heard of the capitulation of Paris.
'We have France still', he told his staff, but the populace had become apathetic
and he was compelled to submit.

LISSA   see   VIS

LOFTCHA (Bulgaria)   Russo-Turkish War   3 September 1877
Fought between the Russians under Prince Imeretinsky and the Turks under Adil Pasha.
Strength: Russians 20,000; Turks 15,000.
Aim: The Russians sought to beat the Turks out of Loftcha.
Battle: An attack on the Turkish positions was made by 5,000 men under General Mikhail Skobelev, who was later reinforced to 9,000 men. The Turkish positions were carried and the Turks were driven out of Loftcha with a loss of 5,200 killed. Russian losses were 1,500 killed and wounded.
Result: The Russian objective was achieved.

LOIGNY-POUPREY (France)   Franco-Prussian War   1 December 1870
Fought between the Prussians under the Grand Duke Frederick William of Mecklenburg and the French under General Louis-Baptiste d'Aurelle de Paladines.
Strength: Prussians 34,000; French 90,000 (The Army of the Loire).
Battle: The Prussians won a complete victory. French losses were 18,000 killed or wounded and 9 guns. Prussian losses were 4,200.
Result: After heavy fighting, the Prussians retook Orléans on 4 December, thus severing the two wings of the French army under Chanzy (West) and Bourbaki (East).

LÜLEBÜRGAZ (Turkey)   First Balkan War   28-30 October 1912
Fought between the Bulgarians and Turks.
Aim: Having stopped the offensive of the Turks in Thrace at Kirk-Kilissa (qv), the Bulgarians took the offensive themselves and attacked the Turks at Lüleburgaz, 85 miles NW of Constantinople (Istanbul).
Battle: In a fierce battle lasting three days, the Turks were driven back to a fortified line across the peninsula near the Bosporus at Catalca. Here the Bulgarians attacked again, but were repulsed. Total Bulgarian losses were 15,000, to the Turks' 30,000 killed or wounded.
Result: With Russian mediation, the Bulgarians agreed to an armistice on 3 December.

MAGENTA (Italy)   Italian Wars of Independence   4 June 1859
Fought between the French and Piedmontese under General le Comte de Mac-Mahon, and the Austrians under General Count Eduard von Clam-Gallas.
Strength: French/Piedmontese 49,500; Austrians 53,000.
Aim: A secret treaty with France had assured Piedmont of help from Louis Napoleon III in the struggle of the Italians to expel the Austrians from their country and to unify it. The 2nd French Corps d'Armée and the Piedmontese marched east across the Ticino River into Austrian-held Lombardy. The Austrians mobilised.
Battle: The two armies met at Magenta and, despite poor command, the French

gained a victory over the Austrians in a confused engagement. The Austrians withdrew towards the Quadrilateral (Mantua, Peschiera, Verona and Legnano) and the Allies entered Milan in triumph. French losses were 4,000 killed and wounded and 600 missing. Austrian losses were 5,700 killed and wounded and 4,500 missing.
Result: The Allied offensive gained the upper hand.

MALAKOV (Sebastopol) (USSR)   Crimean War   8 September 1855
Fought between the Russians and the French under General Pierre Bosquet.
Strength: Russians 10,000; French 30,000.
Aim: The capture of the fort of Malakov which formed part of the southern defences of Sebastopol (qv).
Battle: After a three-day bombardment of the fort, the French charged the position from their trenches which were 30 yards away from their objective. Three columns took part in the operation which was carefully planned and was the only manoeuvre of the war to go perfectly. Details such as the ease of mounting the assault from the trenches were checked. It was perhaps the first time in military history that an assault had been governed by the synchronisation of watches; the attack began at midday. The French gained the outer wall and took the inner defences where the Russians, taken by surprise, fought hand-to-hand combat for possession of every point of the fort. The fort was in French hands by nightfall.
Result: Although a simultaneous assault on the Redan (qv) fort by the British was repulsed, the French were able to fire on the Russians from Malakov and drive them out. The capture of Malakov resulted in the fall of Sebastopol.

MALNATE   see VARESE

MARS-LA-TOUR   see GRAVELOTTE AND MARS-LA-TOUR

MELEGNANO (Italy)   Second War of Italian Independence   8 June 1859
Fought between the French under Marshal Achille Baraguey d'Hilliers and the Austrians under Field-Marshal Lieutenant Ludwig August Ritter von Benedek.
Strength: French: The 1st and 2nd Corps; Austrians: The rearguard of the 8th Corps.
Aim: The French were exploiting their victory at Magenta (qv).
Battle: Baraguey d'Hilliers sent General Patrice MacMahon (2nd Corps) to turn the Austrian right, whilst he himself (1st Corps) engaged their position frontally. MacMahon's army made slow progress through the vineyards surrounding the village. However, at about 6pm Baraguey d'Hilliers delivered a brusque frontal attack, which dislodged Benedek who managed, none the less, to withdraw safely. The French had about 1,000 killed and wounded; the Austrians lost 1,484 including about 1,000 prisoners.
Result: The French lost contact with the Austrians who were able to retire quietly and reorganise behind the River Mincio.

MENTANA (Italy)   Italian Wars of Independence   3 November 1867

Fought between the Garibaldians under Giuseppe Garibaldi and the French under General Kanzler.
Strength: Garibaldians 10,000; French 5,000 + 1,500 Papal Zouaves.

In 1866 Napoleon III withdrew the last of the French troops in Rome (qv), whereupon Italian patriots under Garibaldi promptly undertook a march on the city. Because Pope Pius XI's troops were too weak to withstand an attack, the French sent more troops back into the city in October 1867. The King of Italy disowned Garibaldi.

The forces met NE of Rome, and the French and Papal troops drove the Patriots back from position after position until they were thoroughly beaten. The Zouaves fought particularly well and the use of breech-loading centre-fire rifles also played a part in the French success. Allied losses were 182, of which 144 were Zouaves. Garibaldians lost 1,100 killed and wounded and 1,000 prisoners. Garibaldi was captured and sent to the island of Caprera.

In 1870 the Franco-Prussian War forced Louis Napoleon to withdraw his troops from Rome, whereupon it was stormed by patriots and later made the country's capital.

METZ (France)   Franco-Prussian War   18 August-27 October 1870
Fought between the French under Marshal Achille Bazaine and the Prussians under Prince Frederick Charles.
Strength: French 170,000; Prussians 250,000.

After the French defeat at Gravelotte and Mars-la-Tour (qv) Bazaine retreated into Metz, which was promptly invested.

When Napoleon III led a relief force to the Moselle on 31 August, Bazaine ordered a sortie. The French gained some ground before being beaten back the following day with a loss of 3,000 men. Prussian losses were less than 3,000. The French defeat at Sedan (qv) the same day ended all hope of early relief, but new armies were being raised in the provinces and Paris had not fallen when Bazaine capitulated on 27 October. Three marshals, 6,000 officers and 173,000 men surrendered with him, and the Prussians took 56 eagles, 622 field-guns, 72 mitrailleuses, 876 pieces of fortress artillery and 300,000 rifles.

Bazaine was court-martialled (1873) under the Third Republic. The death sentence was commuted to twenty years' imprisonment. He escaped (1874) and lived in exile in Spain until his death in 1888.

MILAZZO (Italy)   Italian Wars of Independence   20 July 1860
Fought between the Redshirts under Giuseppe Garibaldi assisted by local volunteers, and the Neapolitans under General Bosco.
Aim: The Redshirts sought to bring about the unification of Italy.
Battle: Having driven the Neapolitans out of NW Sicily, Garibaldi pursued them to Milazzo, a fortified seaport where the Neapolitans were strongly entrenched. The Redshirts attacked the position and, turning it, routed the troops, who fell back to Messina.

Result: The victory enabled Garibaldi to cross the strait to the mainland the following month and march on Naples.

MISSOLONGHI (Greece)   Greek War of Independence   July 1822-February 1823 and 7 May 1825-23 April 1826
Fought between the Greeks and the Turks.
Strength: Reliable figures are not available, but generally speaking the Greeks could dispose of about 7,000 men, and the Turks of some 11,000.
Aim: The Turks intended to reduce the port, which stands on the northern shore of the Gulf of Patras guarding the entrance to the Gulf of Corinth.
Battle: In the first siege the stubborn resistance of the garrison, under Alexandros Mavrokordatos, behind its earthworks, eventually compelled Omar Brionis Pasha to abandon the operation.

The second siege. Reshid Pasha bribed the Albanians to remain neutral, passed the Makryneros defile unopposed and invested the town. In September he was joined by Ibrahim Pasha and his Egyptians, and they gradually wore down the defenders, taking the outlying forts. On the night 22-3 April 1826, the garrison, rendered desperate by starvation and disease, risked all on a desperate sortie, but untrained troops are useless for night operations. Misunderstanding their orders, the Greeks fell into confusion and retreated. The Turks seized their opportunity and rushed into the town with them. A remnant of the defenders escaped into the forests of Mount Zygos, but few survived.

Lord Byron's death at Missolonghi occurred on 19 April 1824, between the two sieges.
Result: The fall of Missolonghi, as much as anything, persuaded the great powers, France, Great Britain and Russia, to intervene in Greece. Its immediate effect was to free Reshid Pasha to overrun eastern Greece.

MODENA REVOLUTION (central Italy)   February 1831
Ciro Menotti convened a meeting of revisionists in Modena who wished to form a league of constitutional states in central Italy. Francis IV, King of Modena, who at first supported the constitutionalists, decided to change sides and sent his troops to capture the plotters. The Constitutionalists resisted the troops for some hours until the army brought up artillery. All of the Constitutionalists, including many wounded, were taken prisoner.

MONTEBELLO II (Italy)   Italian Wars of Independence   20 May 1859
Fought between the Austrians under Feldmarschall-Lieutenant Graf Stadion, and the French and Piedmontese under General Élie-Frédéric Forey.
Strength: Austrians 8,000; Allies 8,000.
Aim: The Allied forces of France and Piedmont sought to beat the Austrians out of Italy.
Battle: The French attacked the Austrians and beat them, driving them back to Stradella. The Austrian losses were 1,423. The Allies lost 723.

Result: The immediate French objective was achieved.

MONTENEGRO (SW Yugoslavia)   Turkish Invasions   1852-3; 1861
Fought between the Turks and Montenegrins.
1852-3: A Turkish force under Omar Pasha invaded Montenegro, but withdrew when threatened by Austria.
1861: The Turks under Omar Pasha invaded Montenegro anew and swiftly overran the country, forcing her to acknowledge Turkish suzerainty.

MONT VALÉRIEN   see BUZENVAL

MORELLA (Spain)   First Carlist War   23 May 1840
Fought between the Carlists under General Ramon Baldomero Cabrera and the Cristinos under General Espartero.
Strength: Carlists 4,000; Cristinos 20,000.
Aim: The Cristinos sought the reduction of the Carlist garrison.
Battle: The Carlist veterans attempted to break out of the town through the enemy lines, but the plan was betrayed and the Cristinos met him and drove him back into Morella, which was surrounded. Cabrera, however, with some of the garrison cut his way out of the town.
Result: This was the last stronghold of the Carlists and its fall took place after the end of the Carlist War. The Cristino objective was achieved.

MORTARA (Italy)   Italian Wars of Independence   21 March 1849
Fought between the Piedmontese under the Duke of Savoy (later Victor Emmanuel II) and General Darando, and the Austrians under Field-Marshal Joseph Radetzky.
Aim: When the truce was renounced by Charles Albert, the Austrians immediately took the field.
Battle: The main Austrian army under Radetzky advanced to Mortara, which the Piedmontese had taken no steps to fortify. The guard was lax and the town was taken by surprise, the Piedmontese being driven out by the Austrians with a loss of 500 killed and wounded, with 2,000 men and 5 guns captured. Austrian losses were 300.
Result: Charles Albert took steps to launch a counter-offensive, which ended at Novara (qv).

MÜNCHENGRÄTZ (MNICHOVO HRADIŠTÉ) (Czechoslovakia)   Seven Weeks' War   28 June 1866
Fought between the Prussians under Prince Frederick Charles and the Austrians under General Count Eduard von Clam-Gallas.
Strength: Prussians 140,000; Austrians 20,000.
   When the war broke out in June the Prussian Chief of Staff, General Count Helmuth von Moltke, sent four armies to deal with the Austrians and their Allies.

All four marched south, one to engage the armies of Hanover and Austria's other Allies in S Germany, the other three to converge on Bohemia. From around Torgau the Army of the Elbe, 45,000 strong, under General Karl Herwarth von Bittenfeld, moved on Dresden where an outnumbered Saxon corps withdrew into Bohemia to link up with the main Austrian army of the north which was massing there under General Ludwig von Benedek.

The Army of the Elbe now linked up with the Prussian 1st Army under Prince Frederick Charles and the force moved through the Bohemian mountains NE of Prague. At Münchengrätz (Mnichovo Hradiště) the Prussians encountered a forward corps of the Austrian army under Clam-Gallas. In a skirmish, the Austrians suffered a loss of 300 killed and wounded and 1,000 captured, before retreating to Jičin (qv), where the Prussians drove them back farther. Clam-Gallas was relieved and Benedek ordered a general withdrawal towards the upper Labe (Elbe), between Sadowa (qv) and Königgrätz.

NACHOD (Czechoslovakia)   Seven Weeks' War   27 June 1866
Fought between the Prussians under General Karl Friedrich von Steinmetz and the Austrians under General Ramming, as part of the skirmishing action preceding the Battle of Münchengrätz (qv).

The 5th Prussian Corps, considerably outnumbered by the Austrian cavalry, beat Ramming, forcing the Austrians to withdraw. The Austrians suffered heavy casualties. Prussian losses were 900, but they took 2,000 men prisoner and captured 5 guns.

The Austrians were forced to retreat farther by the Battle of Münchengrätz the following day.

NAGY-SARLO (Hungary)   Hungarian Rising   19 April 1849
Fought between the Hungarians under General Arthur von Görgey and the Austrians.
Strength: Hungarians 25,000; Austrians 10,000.

The Austrians endeavoured to prevent the Hungarians from constructing bridges over the Gran River, but they were defeated and the Hungarians were able to bridge the river as planned.

NAVARINO (Greece)   Greek War of Independence   20 October 1827
Fought between the Allied fleets of Britain, France and Russia under Vice-Admiral Sir Edward Codrington, Rear-Admiral Henri-Daniel de Rigny and Rear-Admiral le Comte de Heyden respectively, and the Turkish-Egyptian fleet under Tahir Pasha.
Strength: British 3 ships of the line + 4 frigates, French 4 ships of the line + 1 frigate, Russians 4 ships of the line + 4 frigates; Turks and Egyptians 3 ships of the line + 19 frigates + approx 50 other vessels; guns: Allies 1,294; Turks 1,962.
Aim: Hearing that Ibrahim was carrying out operations ashore, Codrington, the senior commander, sailed into the harbour where the Turkish-Egyptian fleet was at anchor in a horseshoe formation. The Allies followed Codrington with the

intention of crippling the enemy fleet while it lay at anchor.
Battle: The Allies dropped anchor in the midst of the Turkish-Egyptian fleet and a Turkish ship fired on a British dispatch boat, killing an officer and some men. The British opened fire on the enemy, and the Allies did likewise. Despite the fact that the Turkish-Egyptian fleet was protected by shore batteries, the Allies inflicted heavy loss on the enemy, 60 vessels being destroyed either by the Allies or fired by their own crews, the remainder being driven ashore. Allied losses were 272 killed and wounded, while Turkish losses were over 4,000 men. The action was the last to be fought between wooden sailing ships. British and French sailors had not fought on the same side since the Battle of Sole Bay, in 1672.
Result: The London Protocol recognised Greek independence in March 1829.

NICOPOLIS IV (NIKOPOL) (USSR)   Russo-Turkish War   16 July 1877
Fought between the Russians under General Nikolai Krüdener and the Turks.
Aim: After the fall of Svishtov (qv) the Russians moved on to capture Nicopolis as a prelude to the siege of Plevna (qv).
Battle: After a two-day bombardment, the 9th Russian Army Corps captured the town with a loss of 1,300 killed and wounded. The garrison of 7,000 Turks surrendered.
Result: The Russian objective was achieved and Plevna was now besieged.

NOISSEVILLE (France)   Franco-Prussian War   31 August 1870
Fought between the French under Marshal Achille Bazaine and the Prussians under Prince Frederick Charles.

After the Battle of Gravelotte (qv), the French retired into Metz (qv) where they were besieged by the 1st and 2nd Prussian Armies. Several sorties were made in an attempt to break out of the encirclement. The French attacked the Prussian lines and gained some ground which they held throughout the day. On 1 September the attack was renewed, but with no success, and the French were forced back into Metz with a loss of 145 officers and 3,379 men. Prussian losses were 126 officers and 2,850 men.

The town of Metz capitulated on 27 October 1870.

NOVARA II (Italy)   First War of Italian Independence   23 March 1849
Fought between the Piedmontese under Charles Albert and General Albert Chrzanowski, and the Austrians under Field-Marshal Joseph Radetzky.
Strength: Piedmontese 47,000; Austrians 45,000.
Aim: After the truce collapsed the Austrians seized the fortress of Mortara (qv) in Lombardy. The Piedmontese sought to retaliate.
Battle: In a manoeuvre similar to the one Napoleon carried out at Marengo, Radetzky defeated the Piedmontese after a fierce fight which ended when the Piedmontese, who were ill-disciplined beside the Austrian forces, fled the field in disorder.
Result: When, a week later, the town of Brescia, 54 miles NE of Milan, was subdued,

Charles Albert abdicated in favour of his son, Victor Emmanuel, later to become the first King of Italy. Under the peace treaty which was signed on 9 August, an indemnity of 65 million francs was to be paid to Austria.

OFEN (Hungary)   Hungarian Rising   4-21 May 1849
Fought between the Hungarians under General Arthur von Görgey and the Austrians under General Hentzi.

The fortress was held by an Austrian garrison under Hentzi. After an unsuccessful assault the Hungarians under Görgey laid siege to the fortress on 4 May. Several other assaults were made, all of which failed, but it was finally taken by storm on 21 May. Hentzi was mortally wounded.

OLTENITZA (USSR)   Crimean War   4 November 1853
Fought between the Turks under Omar Pasha and the Russians.
Aim: Owing to a diplomatic quarrel Czar Nicholas I found the opportunity to declare war on Turkey and to occupy Wallachia, which was a Danubian principality of Turkey. The Turks marched northwards to counter-attack.
Battle: At the confluence of the Arges and the Danube the Turks met and defeated the Russians, making use of their superior numbers. The Russians were driven north.
Result: The victory gave the Turks their first triumph over the Russians for more than a hundred years. France and Britain, who did not want to see the balance of power shift in the Middle East, both sent fleets to the Mediterranean to aid Turkey, since Russia was trying to gain control of the straits into the Black Sea.

OSTROLENKA (USSR)   Crimean War   November 1853
The Turks under Omar Pasha sought to beat the Russians out of the Danubian principalities which they had invaded. The Turks, who were superior in numbers, compelled the Russians to retreat northwards.

OTTOMAN WAR WITH SERBIA AND MONTENEGRO   1876
Fought between the Serbs and the Montenegrins under Russian leadership, and the Turks under Suleiman Pasha.

Christian insurrections in Herzegovina and Bosnia (1875) were cruelly put down by the Turks and led to a declaration of war by Serbia and Montenegro. Serb forces including Russian volunteers were defeated at Alexinatz on 1 September and Djunis on 29 October.

Russia, in favour of the pan-Slav movement in the Balkans, began to mobilise along the southern frontiers.

PALERMO (Italy)   Italian Wars of Independence   26-7 May 1848
Fought between Garibaldians under Giuseppe Garibaldi and the Neapolitans under General Lanza.
Strength: Garibaldians 750+; Sicilian Picciotti 3,000; Neapolitans 18,000.
Aim: The Garibaldians sought to capture the city of Palermo.

Battle: Garibaldi surprised one of the gates into the city of Palermo which was garrisoned by Neapolitans under Lanza. The Picciotti fled at the first shot, but the Garibaldians penetrated the town where the citizens rose in their support. Garibaldi erected barricades and severe fighting ensued, after which the Neapolitans surrendered, having suffered heavy losses.

Result: The last of the Neapolitan troops were withdrawn 20 June, and Garibaldi's objective was achieved.

PALESTRINA (Italy)   Italian Wars of Independence   9 May 1849
Fought between the Italian Patriots under Giuseppe Garibaldi and the Neapolitans under King Ferdinand.

Strength: Patriots 4,000; Neapolitans 7,000.

Aim: The Neapolitans sought to put down the rising by the Patriots.

Battle: In a fierce engagement lasting three hours the Neapolitans were totally routed. Garibaldi was wounded in the action.

Result: The Neapolitan objective was not achieved.

PALESTRO (Italy)   Italian Wars of Independence   30 May 1859
Fought between the Piedmontese under General Enrico Cialdini and the Austrians under General Stadion.

Aim: The Austrians sought to prevent the advance of the Piedmontese army whose aim was the expulsion of the Austrians from Italy.

Battle: The Austrians attacked the Piedmontese as they crossed the Sesia, but the Piedmontese repulsed the assault and completed their passage, attacking the Austrians in turn, whom they drove out of Palestro with considerable loss.

Result: The Austrian objective was not achieved.

PARIS II (France)   Franco-Prussian War   20 September 1870-28 January 1871
Fought between the French under General Louis Trochu and the Prussians under General Count Helmuth von Moltke.

Strength: French 400,000; Prussians 146,000 (total strength available, 240,000) with 240 siege guns.

Aim: After the defeat and capture of Napoleon III at Sedan (qv), the Prussians moved on to besiege Paris which was encircled by the Army of the Meuse under the Crown Prince of Saxony to the north and the 3rd Army under Crown Prince Frederick William to the south.

Battle: On 8 October General Léon Gambetta escaped from Paris by balloon to rally support in the provinces while Trochu organised a series of sorties. On 29 November the Great Sortie took place when the French attacked across the Marne to the SE before being repulsed by the Prussians with a loss of 5,236. Prussian losses were 2,091. Another sortie at Le Bourget (qv), NE of the city, was beaten back with a loss of 2,000+. Prussian losses were less than 500. Bombardment commenced on 27 December and continued for three weeks, during which time 12,000 shells fell on the city, taking 97 lives and wounding 278. French resistance in the provinces had been crushed by mid-January and, with only eight days of food left, Paris capitulated on 28 January. French military casualties totalled 28,450, of which less than 4,000 had been killed. Total Prussian losses were 16,000 killed and wounded.

Result: Peace terms were accepted by the provisional republican government on 1 March and, prior to that, William I was proclaimed Emperor of Germany in the Hall of Mirrors in the Palace of Versailles.

PELLSCHAT (Bulgaria)   Russo-Turkish War   30 August 1877
Fought between the Russians under General Zotov and the Turks.
Strength: Russians 20,000; Turks 25,000 with 50 guns.
Aim: The Turks sought to break out from the Russian encirclement of Plevna (qv).
Battle: In a sortie from Plevna, the Turks attacked the Russian lines in front of Poradim, but all their assaults were repulsed with a loss of 3,000 killed and wounded. Russian losses were 1,000.
Result: The Turkish objective was not achieved.

PENA CERRADA (Spain)   First Carlist War   21 June 1838
Fought between the Carlist garrison under General Gergue and the Cristinos under General Espartero.
Strength: Carlists 3,000; Cristinos 19,000.
Aim: The reduction of the Carlist garrison.
Battle: Espartero shelled the fortress for seven hours, after which he stormed and carried the heights outside the town and dispersed the Carlists who had held them. Six hundred men and all Carlist guns were captured. The garrison was then abandoned.
Result: The Cristino objective was achieved.

PERED (Hungary)   Hungarian Rising   21 June 1849
Fought between the Hungarians under General Arthur von Görgey and the Austrians and Russians under Prince Windischgrätz.
Strength: Hungarians 16,000; Austrians/Russians 25,000.
   The Austrians and Russians attacked the Hungarian position and after heavy fighting drove the Hungarians out with the loss of about 3,000.

PHARSALUS II (Greece)   Turko-Greek War   6 May 1897
Fought between the Greeks under the Crown Prince, Constantine, and the Turks under Edhem Pasha.
   The Turks sought to drive the demoralised Greek army out of the town. The Greeks were entrenched in front of Pharsalus (Thessaly) and three Turkish divisions drove them back after slight resistance. Both Greek and Turkish losses were about 250. Little more action was seen in the war. Czar Nicholas II intervened to prevent the total collapse of the Greek defence, since, on the Epirus front, the Greeks had been equally unsuccessful in their attempts to drive the Turks back.

A peace treaty was signed in September and Crete, the cause of the war, was placed in international control.

PHILIPPOPOLIS II (Bulgaria)   Russo-Turkish War   17 February 1878
Fought between the Russians under General Osip Gurko and the Turks under Fuad Pasha and Shakir Pasha.
Aim: The Russians sought to capture the town.
Battle: The Turks were outnumbered and, though they made a stubborn defence of the approaches, they were beaten back and forced to retreat with a loss of 5,000 killed and wounded, and 2,000 men and 114 guns captured. Russian losses were 1,300.
Result: The Russian objective was achieved.

PIROT (Yugoslavia)   Serbo-Bulgarian War   26-7 November 1885
Fought between the Serbians under King Milan I and the Bulgarians under Prince Alexander.
Strength: Serbians 40,000; Bulgarians 45,000.
After being defeated at Slivnica (qv), the Serbians fell back NW behind their own border to Pirot. The Bulgarians pursued. On 26 November the Bulgarians stormed Pirot and took it after desultory fighting. In a dawn attack on the following day, the Serbians retook the town, but Alexander rallied his troops and had retaken Pirot by the evening. The Serbians held a position south of the town until nightfall. The intervention of Austria brought about an armistice at dawn the following day. Bulgarian losses were 2,500; Serbian casualties totalled 2,000.
A peace treaty was signed on 3 March 1886.

PLEVNA (PLEVEN) (Bulgaria)   Russo-Turkish War   20 July-10 December 1877
The Russians, under Grand Duke Michael, King Carol I of Romania and General Frants Totleben, besieged the Turks under Marshal Osman Nuri Pasha.
Strength: Russians 100,000; Turks 30,000.
Aim: After the Russians had captured the fortresses of Svishtov and Nicopolis (Nikopol) (qqv), they moved south into what is now Bulgaria. They sought the capture of the major Ottoman fortress at Plevna.
Battle: The action incorporates four battles. On 20 July a rash attack on the fort was made by the van of the Russian army under General Nikolai Krüdener (6,500 men). The attack, which was made on the north and east defences, was beaten back with a loss of 2,000 men and two-thirds of the officers. Krüdener led a second assault on the city with 30,000 men. The attack was made by two divisions, one under General Schakovsky on the east, and one under Krüdener on the Gravitza redoubt on the north. Schakovsky had overall command. Krüdener's attack was repulsed, but Schakovsky carried two of the E redoubts. The Turks counter-attacked, however, and recaptured the positions, forcing the Russians to retire all along the line. Their losses were 169 officers and 7,136 men (2,400 being left dead on the field). On 11 and 12 September the Russian army of investment under

Grand Duke Michael, now 95,000 strong, attacked Plevna on three sides. Two redoubts on the SW were captured by a force under General Mikhail Skobelev on 11 September, but the Turks recaptured them in a counter-attack. An attack on the Omar Tabrija redoubt was also repulsed. The Russians lost 20,000 men in the two days, the Turks about 5,000. The Russian investment remained tight despite the firm resistance. Command of the Russian army passed to Carol I and Totleben. Relief of the garrison was impossible and Osman tried to break out on 10 December with 25,000 men and 9,000 convalescents and wounded in carts. The Turks crossed the Vid before the Russians could bring up reinforcements and Osman charged and carried the first line of Russian entrenchments on a 2-mile line before Totleben could organise a counter-attack which, when it came, drove the Turks back across the river in confusion and during which Osman was severely wounded. The Turks made another stand on the far side of the river, but were again beaten back into Plevna. That evening the garrison capitulated. The Turks lost 5,000 in the sortie, the Russians 2,000.

Result: The Russians resumed their advance through the Balkans while a second column moved through the Caucasus.

PLOVDIV (Philippopolis) (Bulgaria)   Russo-Turkish War   17 January 1878
Fought between the Russians under General Osip Gurko and the Turks under Suleiman Pasha.

After Plevna (qv) fell to the Russians and the Turks failed to take the Schipka Pass (qv), the Turkish front on the Balkans became very precarious. Sofia fell to the Russians in January, whence Gurko marched SE to Plovdiv on the river Maritsa. The city was stormed and taken by the Russians, the outnumbered Turks being routed. Suleiman Pasha lost 4,500 killed or wounded and 2,000 prisoners. Russian losses were 1,200.

The Russians continued to advance and the Turks retreated down the Maritsa valley, abandoning Adrianople to a column under General Mikhail Skobelev. When they had almost reached Constantinople, Britain intervened by sending a fleet to enforce mediation. Russia agreed to an armistice on 31 January and the Treaty of San Stefano was signed on 3 March.

PODOL (Czechoslovakia)   Seven Weeks' War   26 June 1866
Fought between the Prussians under Prince Frederick Charles and the Austrians under General Count Eduard von Clam-Gallas.
Aim: Helmuth von Moltke, Prussia's Chief of Staff, sent three armies into Bohemia to deal with the Austrian army there which was advancing to meet its adversary.
Battle: The van of the Prussian force met the Austrian army at Podol, out of which it was driven after severe fighting. The Austrians suffered heavy casualties and lost 500 prisoners. Prussian losses are not known.
Result: The action formed a prelude to Münchengrätz (qv), where a battle took place two days later.

PUENTA DE LA REYNA (Spain)   Second Carlist War   6 October 1872
Fought between the Carlists under General Ollo and the Republicans under General Moriones.
Strength: Carlists 50,000; Republicans 9,000.

   After a hard fight the Republicans were defeated and driven from the field by a bayonet charge. Carlist losses were 113. The Republicans lost many more.

REDAN, THE (Sebastopol, USSR)   Crimean War   8 September 1855
Fought between the British under Sir William Codrington and the Russians.
Strength: British 4,900; Russians 4,000.
Aim: The capture of the fort which formed part of the southern defences of Sebastopol (qv).
Battle: The troops of the British 2nd and Light Divisions took part in the attack on the ramparts, which they gained. They were unable to consolidate their position and were eventually driven back in confusion with heavy loss. The capture of the Malakov fort (qv) by the French forced the Russians out of the Redan, however, and they retired during the night. British losses were 2,184 killed and wounded.
Result: The capture of the Redan and the Malakov led to the fall of Sebastopol.

RIETI (Italy)   Italian Wars of Independence   7 March 1821
Fought between the Neapolitans under General Guglielmo Pepe and the Austrians.
Strength: Neapolitans 10,000; Austrians 80,000.
Aim: The Austrians sought to crush the rebellion.
Battle: The Neapolitans attacked the advanced guard of the Austrian army; but when that was reinforced by the main body, the rebels were overwhelmed and driven from the field.
Result: The Austrians restored Ferdinand IV to the throne; he had been forced out of Naples in 1820 by the liberal group. Pepe was banished under penalty of death. The Austrian objective was achieved.

ROMANIAN REBELLION   Spring 1907
Fought between the Romanian peasants and the Romanian government.

   The Romanian peasants rose against the government which had taken over communal land for private capitalisation of the European wheat market. The rebellion began in the north of the country and quickly spread south and west. Bands of roving peasants were speedily subdued and the army was called in, bombarding villages into submission. In a little over a month, 11,000 people were killed and the rising was quelled.
Result: The peasants did not achieve their objective.

ROME VIII (Italy)   Italian Wars of Independence   30 April-2 July 1849
Fought between the French under General Nicolas Oudinot and the Republicans under Giuseppe Garibaldi.
Strength: French 20,000; Republicans 20,000.

Aim: On 9 February 1849 Rome was declared a republic by Giuseppe Mazzini and others. Among the garrison were 5,000 of Garibaldi's men. Pope Pius IX had fled to Gaeta (qv) but a French expeditionary force was sent to restore him.

Battle: Oudinot landed at Civitavecchia and, five days later, a force of 8,000 attacked Rome at the Porta San Pancrazio. The Republicans, under Garibaldi, repulsed them with a loss of 300 killed and wounded and 500 prisoners. Republican losses were 100. Oudinot was reinforced, and attacked again on 3 June with 20,000 men, but was again repulsed though the Garibaldians lost heavily: 2,000 men including 200 officers. Oudinot then laid siege to the city and opened a bombardment. The Republicans surrendered on 2 July.

Result: When the Garibaldians marched out of Rome the French attacked the force and killed, captured or dispersed it. Garibaldi escaped and made his way to Venice.

SADOWA/KÖNIGGRÄTZ (HRADIC KRÁLOVÉ) (Czechoslovakia) Seven Weeks' War 3 July 1866

Fought between the Prussians under Prince Frederick Charles and the Austrians under General Ludwig von Benedek.

Strength: Prussians 220,000; Austrians 205,000 with 600 guns.

The Prussian Chief of Staff, General Count Helmuth von Moltke, sent three armies into Bohemia, employing the first large-scale use of telegraph and railways in Europe.

Battle: The army of Prince Frederick Charles with that of the Elbe under Karl Herwarth von Bittenfeld engaged the Austrian van at Münchengrätz (qv) and Jičin (qv). The Austrians began to retreat SE towards Königgrätz (Hradic Králové) on the Upper Labe (Elbe). The Austrians retreated so slowly that the Prussians caught up with them at Sadowa, 65 miles east of Prague, before Benedek could cross the river. It was intended that Prussia should pin down the enemy while awaiting the arrival of the 3rd Army under Crown Prince Frederick William to come up from Silesia on the left flank. When the 7th division under General Eduard von Fransecky attacked on the morning of 3 July, however, a battle was precipitated. Outnumbered by the Austrians, the Prussians were beaten back all along the 7-mile front. The arrival of the Crown Prince was delayed because a broken telegraph held up his orders, but, when he arrived at 2pm, he launched a strong attack on the Austrian right and, breaking it, carried the hill at Chulm which was the key to the strong Austrian defensive position. Benedek counter-attacked with cavalry, but made no impression and, under cover of heavy artillery fire, the Austrians withdrew. Austrian losses totalled 40,000, half of whom were captured, and 174 guns. Prussian losses were 9,000.

Result: The battle cost Franz Josef all his military resources and he signed a peace treaty on 26 July. The battle thus ended the second of the wars undertaken by Bismarck from which came the German Empire. It may thus be ranked as one of the decisive battles of history.

The Prussian victory was in part owing to their use of the needle-gun, a centre-fire, breech-loading rifle with a rapid rate of fire which could be loaded from a prone position, impossible with the Austrian muzzle-loading weapons.

ST PRIVAT   see GRAVELOTTE

ST QUENTIN II (France)   Franco-Prussian War   19 January 1871
Fought between the French under General Louis Faidherbe and the Prussians under General August von Goeben.
Strength: French 40,000; Prussians 33,000.
Aim: Faidherbe's army was the last of the provincial French forces which remained in the field along the Upper Somme. Its objective was the relief of the siege of Paris (qv).
Battle: At St Quentin the French were completely defeated, losing 3,000 killed and wounded, 9,000 prisoners and 6 guns. Prussian losses were 96 officers and 2,304 men.
Result: The defeat of this army meant that there was no hope left for the relief of Paris which capitulated on 28 January.

SAN SEBASTIAN II (Spain)   First Carlist War   February/June 1836
Fought between the Cristino and British legion garrison under Colonel Wylde, and the Carlists under General Sagastibelza.
Aim: The reduction of the garrison by the Carlists.
Battle: The siege was not very vigorous, constant fighting taking place between the outposts, but no major assault being undertaken. In June, the appearance of General Sir George de Lacy Evans with 10,000 British and Cristino troops, who occupied the advanced Carlist positions, forced the Carlists to withdraw.
Result: The Carlist objective was not achieved.

SANTAREM II (Portugal)   Portuguese Civil War   18 February 1834
Fought between the Portuguese Loyalists under General Duque João Carlos de Saldanha and the Miguelists under Dom Miguel.
Aim: When Pedro IV succeeded to the throne of Portugal he was already Emperor of Brazil; therefore he handed the throne to his nine-year-old daughter Maria de Gloria. His brother, Dom Miguel, who had already attempted to restore absolute monarchy in Portugal, now usurped the throne while Maria fled first to England, then Brazil. The British sent Sir Charles Napier to aid the Loyalists.
Battle: Forty-three miles up the Tagus River, the Loyalists forced a showdown, in which the troops of Dom Miguel were decisively beaten.
Result: Miguel relinquished all claim to the Portuguese throne.

SAPRI (S Italy)   Insurrection   June 1857
Carlo Pisarane with a small band of Patriots landed and attempted to start an insurrection in the Kingdom of the Two Sicilies. The attempt failed and Pisarane and many others were killed at Sapri. Giuseppe Garibaldi's Thousand regarded

Pisarane and his massacred band as their precursors.

SARKNAY (Hungary)   Hungarian Rising   30 December 1848
Fought between the Austrians under Prince Windischgrätz and the Hungarians
under General Perczel.

   The Sarknay defile protected the line which General Arthur von Görgey had
elected to hold, but when the Austrians attacked Perczel there, the Hungarians
fled without putting up much resistance, thus forcing Görgey to retire.

SCHIPKA PASS (Bulgaria)   Russo-Turkish War   21 August 1877-9 January
1878
Fought between the Russians under General Darozhinsky and the Turks under
Suleiman Pasha.
Strength: Russians 7,000; Turks 25,000.
Aim: The Turks on successive occasions sought to drive the Russians from their
positions astride the Schipka Pass.
Battle: Beginning on 21 August, the Turks attacked the Russian positions and
drove the Russians farther and farther back from their defences until they were
on the point of being completely defeated. At this stage reinforcements arrived
and, counter-attacking, they regained their lost positions at a cost of 4,000,
including Darozhinsky. Turkish losses totalled 11,500. Fighting ended on 26
August. On 16 September Suleiman renewed the offensive, the Turkish ranks
having been reinforced to 40,000. He attacked the Russian position on Mount St
Nicholas, but the attack was repulsed with a loss of 3,000 men. Russian losses were
31 officers and 1,000 men. The Russian forces were increased and by 8 January
1878 they numbered 60,000, commanded by General Joseph Radetsky. The
Turkish forces were now commanded by Vessil Pasha. General Mirsky attacked
the Turks in their entrenchments with 25,000 men and drove them out of their
positions. Vessil Pasha surrendered the next day with 36,000 men and 93 guns.
Russian losses were 5,000.
Result: The Turkish objective was not achieved.

SCHWECHAT (suburb SE of Vienna)   Hungarian Rising   30 October 1848
Fought between the Austrians under Prince Windischgrätz and the Hungarians
under General Moga.

   When, in 1848, the Hungarians rose in revolt against the Austrian Empire of
Ferdinand I, a rebel force marched on Vienna, while inside the city sympathisers
threw up barricades. Windischgrätz, Imperial Commander in Bohemia, marched
on the rebels with a force of Austrian regulars, and at Schwechat the Hungarians
were routed on 30 October after making but feeble resistance all along the line.
The Hungarians suffered heavy losses.

   The following day, in conjunction with General Josip Jelacic od Buzima
(Jellachich), Governor of Croatia, Windischgratz bombarded Vienna into
submission. The following month, Ferdinand was persuaded to abdicate in

favour of his nephew, Franz Josef I.

SEBASTOPOL I (USSR)   Crimean War   28 September 1854-9 September 1855
Fought between the Allies under General Lord Raglan and General François
Canrobert, and the Russians under Prince Alexander Menshikov.
Aim: The Allies sought to reduce the city of Sebastopol.
Battle: When the Allies - British, French and Turks - beat the Russians at the Alma
(qv) River, they went on to Sebastopol, which they bombarded on 17 October,
from which time it was under almost continual fire until the end of the siege. The
Allies were too few in number to take the town by storm so a regular siege was
begun. At the same time the British fleet under Sir Edmund Lyons blockaded the
harbour, leaving the Russians only the difficult northern route by which they
could obtain supplies. The Russian Chief Engineer, Count Frantl Totleben,
constructed strong fortifications and, while the bombardment of both sides cost
many lives, no lasting damage was done to the siege-works. The Czar, Alexander II,
sent forces to relieve the city, but they failed at Balaclava (qv), and a sortie
resulting in the Battle of Inkerman (qv) was also beaten back. Another Russian
attack on the Chernaya River (qv) the following year also failed. During the
winter both sides suffered terrible hardships. The Russians had difficulty getting
supplies through the northern route and the artillery bombardment hit both the
army and civilians alike. The French commissariat was better organised than the
British, and Canrobert took over administration in the British sector to alleviate
the suffering. Here fuel, clothing and supplies were scarce, a storm having sunk
30 transports at Balaclava which had held most of the remaining British supplies.
A cholera epidemic took many lives. The situation was reported and the story
caused the fall of Lord Aberdeen's government and the arrival of Florence
Nightingale who organised nursing and relief work from Uskudar across the
Bosporus from Constantinople. In the spring several assaults on the town were
repulsed. On 5 September General Pélissier, who now commanded the French,
successfully stormed Malakov (qv), the fortification at the SE of the city. The
British under General Sir James Simpson (who had replaced Raglan on the latter's
death) captured the Redan (qv) fortification on the south of the city, but lost it
again, suffering over 2,000 casualties. Prince Mikhail Gorchakov, who had succeeded Menshikov, now abandoned Sebastopol, blowing up the defences and sinking the
Russian ships in the harbour. Towards the end of the Allied bombardment the
Russians lost as many as 3,000 men a day.
Result: This was the last engagement of the war. Peace was signed at the Congress
of Paris on 30 March 1856. Russian influence in E Europe had been checked.

SEDAN (France)   Franco-Russian War   1 September 1870
Fought between the French under Napoleon III and the Prussians under General
Count Helmuth von Moltke.
Strength: French 130,000 with 564 guns; Prussians 200,000 with 774 guns.
   When Marshal Achille Bazaine withdrew the French army of 170,000 into the

fortress of Metz (qv), only one French force was left in the field. This was commanded by Marshal le Comte de MacMahon and it lay at Chalons-sur-Marne. Louis Napoleon took personal command of the force and marched NE towards Metz with the object of relieving the town, even at the expense of leaving Paris (qv) vulnerable. Moltke had already blockaded Metz, however, and he now formed a new force - the Army of the Meuse - which was sent to attack towards Chalons. Louis Napoleon's army was forced to move north, away from Metz, on 29 August. *Battle:* The French retired to Sedan instead of returning to defend Paris. The 3rd Prussian Army under Crown Prince Frederick William moved from its march on Paris to the north of the town, while the Army of the Meuse under the Crown Prince of Saxony moved up on the south. The French army was trapped. On 1 September the French tried to fight their way out, but the Prussian lines held at a cost of 9,000 killed and wounded. French losses were 3,000 killed, 14,000 wounded and 20,000 captured. MacMahon and Louis Napoleon both surrendered, the former being wounded. The action is notable for the desperate charge made by the Chasseurs d'Afrique, who were destroyed, and their commander, General Margueritte, killed. The following day, General Emmanuel de Wimpffen, who had taken over from MacMahon, completed the capitulation, handing over 82,000 men. The Prussians also took 419 guns, 139 fortress guns and 66,000 rifles. They lost 460 officers and 8,500 killed and wounded in the operation, and 6,000 horses. *Result:* The Prussians marched on Paris. The surrender led to Louis Napoleon's dethronement and the proclamation of a republic in Paris. It was one of the worst defeats in French history.

SEVASTOPOL   see SEBASTOPOL

SHKODËR (SCUTARI) (Albania/Yugoslavia)   First Balkan War   1912-22 April 1913
Fought between the Montenegrins and the Turks.
   Montenegro was the first of the Balkan powers to declare war on Turkey, followed by Bulgaria, Serbia and Greece. Under Nicholas I, the Montenegrins laid siege of Shkodër (Scutari), now on the borders of Yugoslavia and NW Albania. Although Bulgaria and Serbia agreed to an armistice on 3 December, Montenegro and Greece continued the war and, on 22 April, the Montenegrins stormed the city despite the protests of their Allies who had assigned the city to Albania.
   Shkodër was yielded to the Albanians by Nicholas I after the intervention of Austria.

SILISTRIA II (Bulgaria)   Crimean War   20 March-22 June 1854
Fought between the Turks assisted by Captain Buller and Lieutenant Nasmyth, and the Russians under Field-Marshal Ivan Paskievich.
Aim: After their victory at Sinop (qv) and their defeat at Oltenitza (qv) the Russians besieged the Turkish fortress on the south bank of the Danube in what is now Bulgaria.
Battle: Though the Russians made repeated assaults on the city it held out, despite

the fact that no Turkish relief force was sent to its aid. The Russians finally withdrew on 22 June, having lost 10,000 men.
Result: The Russians refused to accede to requests that they evacuate the Turks' Danubian principalities within a month and, as a result, the British and French both declared war, thus beginning the Crimean War.

SINOP (Turkey)   Crimean War   30 November 1853
Fought between the Russian fleet under Admiral Pavel Nakhimov and the Turkish fleet under Admiral Russein.
Strength: Russians 6 ships of the line + 3 frigates + several smaller vessels; Turks 7 frigates + 3 corvettes + 2 steamers.
Aim: The Russians sought to destroy the Turkish fleet.
Battle: The Russians trapped the Turks in the harbour at Sinop. Though the Turks fought to the end, they were outnumbered and outgunned and were totally destroyed, along with the harbour installations, by a fierce bombardment. The engagement lasted six hours. Turkish losses were 4,000. Only 400 men escaped the massacre, almost all wounded.
Result: The British and French sent their fleets to Constantinople (Istanbul) in an effort to preserve the balance of power.
Remarks: One of the main reasons the Russian attack was so successful was that much of the damage was inflicted by shell-guns. It was the first appearance of this new type of naval ordnance.

SKALITZ (Czechoslovakia)   Seven Weeks' War   28 June 1866
Fought between the Prussians under General Karl Friedrich von Steinmetz and the Austrians under General Ramming.
   A skirmishing party was detached from the main Austrian army, as was one from the Prussian force. Both were engaged in the Battle of Münchengrätz (qv). The 5th Prussian Army Corps met the 6th and 8th Austrian Corps at Skalitz and beat them out of the town, which they then occupied, taking 4,000 prisoners and 8 guns.
Result: The Prussian position was consolidated.

SLIVNICA (Bulgaria)   Serbo-Bulgarian War   17 19 November 1885
Fought between the Serbians under King Milan I and the Bulgarians under Stefan Stambulov.
Strength: Serbians 28,000; Bulgarians 10,000 (reinforced to 15,000 after first day).
Aim: Seven years after its independence from Turkey, Serbia went to war with Bulgaria, demanding compensation from that country for the annexation of E Rumelia.
Battle: Nineteen miles NW of Sofia the two armies clashed. The Bulgarians made an attack on the Serbian left on 17 November in order to distract attention from the weakness of their own left which was vulnerable, although the position held was a strong one from the viewpoint of frontal attack. The Bulgarian attack was

repulsed but the left was reinforced overnight, so that when the Serbians attacked there the following day they were beaten back. A frontal attack was also repulsed. On 19 November Serbian attacks were likewise repulsed and by mid-afternoon they were in full retreat. The Bulgarians pursued. The Serbians lost 2,000, the Bulgarians 3,000.
Result: The Serbians retreated across their own border and the Battle of Pirot (qv) followed.

SOLFERINO (Italy)   Second War of Italian Independence   24 June 1859
Fought between the Austrians under Emperor Franz Josef with General Scholick, and the French and Piedmontese under Napoleon III and Victor Emmanuel II with Marshal le Comte de MacMahon, and Generals Emmanuel de Wimpffen, Adolphe Niel and Baraguey d'Hilliers.
Strength: Austrians 120,000 with 451 guns; Allies 118,600 with 320 guns.
Aim: After their defeat at Magenta (qv) the Austrians fell back east across Lombardy. Pursued by the Allies, they stopped at Solferino, 5 miles in front of the Mincio River, and entrenched on a series of hills. The Allies sought to beat them from their position.
Battle: In a confused action where the high command exercised little control, the superiority of the French generals and troops won the day. The French attacked the heights which were taken by the corps of MacMahon and d'Hilliers. An attack on the French left was held off by Niel's corps and at nightfall Franz Josef was forced to retire, his centre having been broken. A rearguard action by General Ludwig von Benedek saved the Austrian army from total rout. Allied losses were 18,000, 4,000 of which came from the Piedmontese corps of 25,000. Austrian losses were 22,000 killed and wounded.
Result: Napoleon III, sickened by the slaughter, signed a truce with Austria by which Lombardy was ceded to France who in turn allowed it to be annexed to Piedmont. France received Nice and Savoy. Franz Josef retired beyond the Mincio.
Remarks: The sufferings of the casualties here and at Magenta helped to lead to the founding of the International Red Cross in 1864.

SPICHEREN (Moselle, France)   Franco-Prussian War   6 August 1870
Fought between the French under General Charles-Auguste Frossard and the Prussians under General Karl Friedrich von Steinmetz.
Strength: French 28,000; Prussians 35,000.
   At the outbreak of the Franco-Prussian War a French corps raiding along the border captured the city of Saarbrücken, but were forced to retreat before the advance of one of the three Prussian armies launched by General Helmuth von Moltke against Napoleon III. In a confused and hotly contested fight the French were finally routed and retreated to Metz (qv). The action is chiefly memorable for the storming of the Rote Berg by a company of the 39th Regiment and four companies of the 74th Regiment under General von François, who was killed. The troops maintained their position against heavy odds throughout the afternoon.

The Germans lost 223 officers and 4,648 men. French losses were 4,000. The action is also known as the Battle of Forbach, after a village near Spicheren.

On the same day, another French force was defeated at Wörth (qv).

SVISHTOV (Bulgaria) Russo-Turkish War 26 June 1877
Fought between the Russians under General Mikhail Dragomirov and the Turks.
Aim: The main Russian army under Grand Duke Nicholas marched into Romania following the Russian declaration of war on Turkey. They sought the capture of the Turkish fortresses as a prelude to an attack on Plevna (qv).
Battle: After crossing the van of the army over the Danube in boats, Dragomirov made a swift attack towards Svishtov, 14 miles east of Nicopolis (qv), during the night. The garrison was completely surprised and surrendered the following day when assaulted by the Russians under General Mikhail Skobelev. Russian casualties were less than 1,000.
Result: The objective being achieved, the Russians moved upstream to attack Nicopolis.

TASHKESSEN (Taskesen) (NE Turkey) Russo-Turkish War 28 December 1877
Fought between the Russians under General Kourlov and the Turks under Valentine Baker Pasha.
Strength: Russians 12,000; Turks 2,000.
Aim: In order to cover the withdrawal of Shakir Pasha from the Shandurnik Heights, Baker fought a rearguard action.
Battle: A Russian division under Kourlov made repeated and determined attacks on the Turkish position throughout the day, but they were withstood by the greatly inferior force. Baker withdrew having lost 800 men. Russian losses were 32 officers and 1,000 men.
Result: The Turkish objective was achieved.

TEMESVAR (Hungary) Hungarian Rising 9 August 1849
Fought between the Austrians under Marshal Baron Julius von Haynau and the Hungarians under General Henryk Dembiński.

Following the success of the Hungarian revolt, the diet proclaimed a republic on 13 April 1849. Czar Nicholas I was alarmed by this development and sent an army under Field-Marshal Ivan Paskevich (Prince of Warsaw) to support the Austrians. This army advanced on Hungary from the north while Haynau moved in from the west. Hungarian resistance crumbled under the pressure.

In this, the last stand made by the Hungarians during the revolt, they were completely routed and dispersed. On 13 August, General Arthur von Görgey surrendered his army to the Russians at Villagos.

Dembiński and Lajos Kossuth, the Governor-President, fled to Turkey. Görgey was interned by the Austrians. Nine rebel generals were hanged by Haynau (the Hyena), and four others were shot, all at Arad. Hungary was absorbed totally into the Austrian Empire, although after the Seven Weeks' War in 1866 it became part of a dual monarchy with Austria. The action is also known as the Battle of Timisoaca.

Lajos Kossuth was responsible for raising a Hungarian National Army of 200,000 by his fiery zeal and condemnation of Austrian rule. His famous declaration of independence sent a thrill of inspiration throughout Europe. In September 1848 he became Commander-in-Chief and practically dictator, but although he inspired the rank and file he was ignorant of military matters and unable to get on with his generals, and his strategy must be held responsible for the Hungarian defeat. However, he is the hero of Hungary. He remained in exile in England but died in Turin on 20 March 1894, having been deprived of his nationality. Later he was buried in Budapest.

TIMISOACA   see TEMESVAR

TRAUTENAU (Czechoslovakia)   Seven Weeks' War   27 June 1866
Fought between the Prussians under General von Bonin and the Austrians under General Gablenz.
Aim: Three Prussian armies were all converging on Bohemia. The Austrians sought to halt their advance.
Battle: The 10th Austrian Corps met the 1st Prussian Army Corps which was on the march. The Prussians attacked and were at first successful, but the Austrians then counter-attacked in force, forcing the tired Prussians to retreat. Prussian losses were 1,227 killed and wounded. Austrian losses were 5,732.
Result: The setback did not prevent the Prussians from continuing their march.

TURBIGO (Italy)   Italian Wars of Independence   3 June 1859
Fought between the French under Marshal le Comte de MacMahon and the Austrians under General Count Eduard von Clam-Gallas.
Aim: The Austrians sought to halt the advance of the Allied army.
Battle: The Austrians attacked the van of the French army while 4,000 more troops assaulted the main French army as it crossed the bridge over the canal near the Ticino. Severe fighting ended with both attacks being repulsed by the French.
Result: The Austrian objective was not achieved.

TYRNAVOS (Greece)   Turko-Greek War   20-1 April 1897
Fought between the Greeks under the Crown Prince (later Constantine I) and the Turks under Edhem Pasha.
Strength: Greeks 45,000; Turks 58,000.
Aim: Sultan Abdul Hamid II believed that the Greek government of George I had fermented anti-Turkish feeling in Crete, and declared war on Greece on 17 April.
Battle: In Thessaly the Ottoman General had massed his troops, where the Greeks had also collected to protect the frontier. On 18 April the Turks advanced along the front and the Greeks fell back to Tyrnavos, 10 miles NW of Larissa, where

they stood stubbornly. The Turks threatened both Greek flanks after two days, however, and on 23 April the Greeks began a retreat which soon turned into a rout. *Result:* The Greeks retreated to Pharsalus (qv).

VARESE (Italy)   Second War of Italian Independence   25 May 1859
Fought between the Garibaldians under Giuseppe Garibaldi and the Austrians under General Urban.
Strength: Garibaldians 3,000; Austrians 5,000.
Aim: Garibaldi sought to beat the Austrians out of Italy.
Battle: After severe fighting the Austrians were repulsed with considerable loss. The action is also known as the Battle of Malnate.
Result: Garibaldi's objective was achieved.

VARNA II (Bulgaria)   Ottoman Wars   July-12 October 1828   5 August-11 October 1829
Fought between the Turkish garrison and the Russians under General Count Hans von Diebitsch.
Strength: Turks 20,000; Russians 35,000.
Aim: The reduction of the garrison of Varna, which was one of several fortresses blocking the Russian advance into Turkey after they had crossed the Danube in a spring offensive.
Battle: The town was invested by the Russians in July, but it was strongly held by the troops of Mahmud II. An attempt to relieve the town by forces under Omar Vrione Pasha failed and the Russians stormed and carried the fortress on 11 October 1828.
Result: The Russians were able to continue their march into Turkey the following year.

VELENEZE (Hungary)   Hungarian Rising   29 September 1848
Fought between the Hungarians under General Moga and the Croats under General Josip Jelacic od Buzima (Jellachich).
   The action produced no decisive result and was followed by an armistice. But on 3 October the Hungarians, who were certain that they had won a victory, invaded Austria and marched towards Vienna whose population rose in revolt in support of the Hungarian rebels. Marshal Alfred zu Windischgrätz, who had successfully quashed a Czech uprising in Bohemia in the same year with great brutality, turned on the Vienna insurgents and suppressed them. He then repelled the Hungarians and drove them out of the country back to Hungary.
   But these revolts caused Emperor Ferdinand I of Austria, who had promised constitutional reforms and the relaxation of unduly suppressive measures throughout his empire, to resign in favour of his nephew Franz Joseph on 2 December 1848.

VELESTINOS (Greece)   Turko-Greek War   5 May 1897
Fought between the Turks under Hakki Pasha and the Greeks under

Colonel Smolenski.
Strength: Turks 17,000; Greeks 9,000.
Aim: The Turks sought to drive the Greeks from their entrenchments at Velestinos.
Battle: The Turks attacked the strong position which the Greeks held throughout the day. The line of retreat was threatened, however, and Smolenski withdrew after nightfall to Volo, where he embarked the troops on 7 May.
Result: An armistice was signed on 18 May. Greece paid an indemnity of £3½ million.

VELLETRI II (Italy)   Naples-Roman Republic War   19 May 1849
Fought between the Garibaldians under General P. Roselli and the Neapolitans under King Ferdinand.
Strength: Garibaldians 1,100; Neapolitans 12,000.
    The Garibaldian army sought to capture the town of Velletri. Their van attacked the town which put up little defence. The Neapolitans evacuated the place during the night and so the Garibaldians were able to occupy it and thus achieved their object, though they failed to follow up their advantage.

VENICE (Italy)   Italian Wars of Independence   20 July-28 August 1849
Fought between the Venetians under Daniele Manin and the Austrians under Field-Marshal Joseph Radetzky.
Aim: The Austrians sought the reduction of the city which had proclaimed itself the Republic of St Mark on 22 March 1848 under the presidency of Daniele Manin.
Battle: When all other Italian uprisings had been crushed, Radetzky turned his whole force against Venice which was the only rebel to remain. A heavy bombardment, a cholera epidemic and starvation forced the Venetians to surrender.
Result: Manin fled in exile to Paris. All revolts in Italy were now suppressed by Radetzky.

VILLIERS (France)   Franco-Prussian War   30 November 1870
Fought between the French under General Ducrot and the Prussians.
    During the siege of Paris (qv), which lasted from September 1870 until January 1871, several attempts were made by the French to break through the Prussian lines. An attack was made against the Württembergers at Villiers by a determined party under Ducrot. Although the French gained ground to begin with, the operation ended on 3 December when they were beaten back into the city with a loss of 424 officers and 9,053 men. Prussian losses were 156 officers and 3,373 men.
    Further sorties were executed before the capitulation.

VIONVILLE   see GRAVELOTTE AND MARS-LA-TOUR

VIS (Yugoslavia)   Italian Wars of Independence   20 July 1866
Fought between the Italians under Admiral Count Carlo di Persano and the Austrians under Admiral Wilhelm von Tegetthoff.

Strength: Italians 10 ironclads; Austrians 7 ironclads + some wooden vessels.
Although Franz Josef ceded Venice (qv) to the Italians, fighting did not end and
the war shifted to the Adriatic where the Austrian fleet challenged the Italian off
Vis or Lissa (by which the battle is sometimes known). The Austrians attacked in
a wedge formation with the flagship at its apex. The Italian fleet, which was
steaming across the Austrians' bows, was broken and Tegetthoff rammed and sank
the Italian flagship. A mêlée ensued, which ended when the Italians were driven off.
Result: The embryonic Italian navy was almost destroyed, but Franz Josef had by
then lost the Seven Weeks' War with Prussia and, weakened, could not pursue
aggression with Italy.

VOLTURNO (Italy)   Italian Wars of Independence   1 October 1860
Fought between the Redshirts under Giuseppe Garibaldi and the Neapolitans
under Afan de Riva.
Strength: Garibaldi Redshirts 20,000; Neapolitans 40,000.
   The Neapolitans, seeking to prevent the capture of Capua by Garibaldi,
attacked his position in front of the town, but they were repulsed after a hard
fight. Redshirt casualties were 2,023 killed and wounded. Neapolitan losses were
400 killed and 2,070 captured.
   Garibaldi went on to capture Capua.

WAIZAN (Hungary)   Hungarian Rising   10 April 1849
Fought between the Hungarians under General Damjanics and the Austrians under
Generals Götz and Jablonowski.
Strength: Hungarians 7,000; Austrians 25,000.
   The 3rd Hungarian Corps attacked two Austrian brigades, driving them out of
Waizan. The Austrian losses were heavy, and included General Götz.

WEISSENBURG (W Germany)   Franco-Prussian War   4 August 1870
Fought between the French under General Charles Abel Douay and the Prussians
under Crown Prince Frederick William.
Strength: French 4,000; Prussians 25,000.
   When a dispute arose over a German candidate for the throne of Spain,
Napoleon III declared war on Prussia. Three armies were promptly fielded and
sent towards France. Forty miles north of Strasbourg, the 3rd Army under
Frederick William attacked Weissenburg which was held by a portion of Marshal
le Comte de MacMahon's command. This was the first engagement of the war. The
town was stormed and carried in six hours with a loss of 1,500. French casualties
were 2,300, including the death of Douay.
   MacMahon pulled his forces back for a stand at Wörth (qv).

WÖRTH (W Germany)   Franco-Prussian War   6 August 1870
Fought between the French under Marshal le Comte de MacMahon and the
Prussians under Crown Prince Frederick William.

Strength: French 37,000 with 101 muzzle-loading guns; Prussians 77,000 with 234 rifled, breech-loading guns.

After beating the French out of Weissenburg (qv), the Prussian 3rd Army marched SW towards Wörth where MacMahon had concentrated French forces to block the invasion. The Prussians attacked at dawn with artillery support which was markedly superior to the French counterpart. French use of centre-fire rifles and mitrailleuses enabled them to withstand the attacks of the Prussians, however, for eight hours. The Cuirassier Division of General Bonnemain was cut to pieces when it charged Prussian infantry near Elsasshausen. When MacMahon had lost a third of his force he retreated behind the Vosges, having lost 10,000 killed and wounded, 6,000 prisoners and 28 guns as well as 5 mitrailleuses. German losses were 489 officers and 10,153 men.

The Prussians pursued slowly. On the same day, the French were also defeated at Spicheren (qv).

ZEIM (Turkey)   Russo-Turkish War   20 April 1877
Fought between the Russians under General Count Mikhail Loris-Melikov and the Turks under Ahmed Muhktar Pasha.

While a primary thrust was undertaken through the Balkans, a secondary force was sent by Russia through the Caucasus. Melikov attacked the Turkish entrenchments at Zeim, but was repulsed with considerable loss.
Result: The Russian objective was not achieved.

SECTION TWO

SOUTHERN ASIA INCLUDING AFGHANISTAN, BANGLADESH, BURMA, CEYLON, INDIA, NEPAL, PAKISTAN, PERSIA, TIBET

See Map Section, nos 8 and 9

AFGHAN CIVIL WAR   January-October 1929
Fought between the followers of Habibullah Ghazi and those of Mohammed
Nadir Khan (Nadir Shah).

Following the abdication of the Amir after a tribal insurrection, a bandit chief,
Habibullah Ghazi, captured Kabul (qv). Mohammed Nadir Khan captured and
executed him, however, following which he went on to reform the army, aided by
the British, and to restore a degree of stability in Afghanistan.

AFGHAN WAR, THIRD   May-November 1919
After the assassination of the Amir Habibullah on 19 February, his successor, the
Amir Amanullah Khan, declared Afghanistan independent. A jihad (holy war) was
then declared and Afghan troops crossed the border into India near Landi Khana
and occupied Bagh. On 6 May war was declared in Afghanistan and general
mobilisation began.

An Anglo-Indian force under Major-General Fowler was immediately sent
through the Khyber Pass to Landi Kotal and on 11 May drove the invaders out of
Bagh. Continuing through the pass, the expedition entered Afghanistan and pushed
on to Dacca while Jalalabad (qv) and Kabul were bombed. However, the main
Afghan threat had developed in the south where the Commander-in-Chief,
Mohammed Nadir Khan, a future Amir, was thrusting down the Kurram valley
with a force about 10,000 strong. However, he was repulsed at Thal by a column
under Brigadier-General Reginald Dyer, who had been concerned in the Amritsar
(qv) riots.

While this action was continuing, on 31 May Amanullah asked for an armistice
and a nominal peace was achieved by the Treaty of Rawalpindi, signed on
8 August 1919. Under this treaty Britain agreed to renew her recognition of the
independence of Afghanistan but at the same time ceased to continue providing
subsidies. This short war left the North-West Frontier in a great state of unrest
and guerilla warfare in the Waziristan (qv) region continued for some years.

AGRA III (Uttar Pradesh, India)   Indian Mutiny   2 August 1857
Fought between the British under Brigadier-General E. H. Greathed and mutineers
at Agra.
Strength: British 2,600, Rebels 7,000.
Aim: After the fall of Delhi (qv) a column under Brigadier-General Greathed was
ordered to relieve Agra, the headquarters of the civil government of the North-West
Frontier Provinces, and then move on to Cawnpore (qv).
Battle: The British garrison at Agra made a sortie from the fort against a force of
rebels encamped 4 miles from the city. The Kutahs, who formed part of the
British party, deserted to the side of the rebels and the British, under pressure and
short of ammunition, were beaten back and retired into the fort. In October
Greathed's column of four battalions and two cavalry regiments came upon a force
of some 7,000 rebels near Agra and dispersed it after a fight in which the mutineers
held their own at first, but afterwards collapsed. Then, on 11 October, Greathed

entered Agra without opposition and left the city on the 14th on the road to Cawnpore.
Result: Agra was relieved.

AHMED KHEL (Afghanistan)   Second Afghan War   19 April 1880
Fought between the British under General Sir Donald Stewart and the Ghilzis.
Strength: British 6,000; Ghilzis 15,000.
Aim: The Ghilzis sought to attack a British force on its way from Kandahar to Ghazni (qqv).
Battle: The British were attacked by a horde of 3,000 Ghazis (religious fanatics), whom they repulsed with great loss to the enemy. The rest of the force was defeated and beaten back, leaving 1,000 dead on the field. British losses were 17.
Result: The British were able to resume their march to Ghazni.

ALIWAL (Punjab, India)   First Sikh War   28 January 1846
Fought between the British under Major-General Sir Harry Smith, a veteran of the Peninsula and Waterloo, and the Sikhs under Runjur Singh.
Strength: British 12,000; Sikhs 20,000.
Aim: The Anglo-Indian army sought to push the Sikhs back towards the Sutlej River.
Battle: The Sikhs were entrenched between the Punjab villages of Aliwal and Bhundri, a mile in front of the Sutlej. Smith attacked with infantry and drove them out of Aliwal despite stubborn counter-attacks. With strong cavalry and artillery support, the British rolled up the Sikh line and Smith, leading the last charge in person, drove them headlong over the difficult ford of the broad Sutlej. British losses were 580 killed and wounded. Sikh losses were 3,000 killed, wounded or missing and 67 guns - all they had - besides their camp, baggage, stores of ammunition and supplies of grain.
Result: Aliwal was a notable success, as it showed that with proper handling of troops the Sikhs could be thoroughly defeated, and they were now forced to retire behind the Sutlej. The Duke of Wellington told the House of Lords: 'I never read an account of any affair in which an officer has shown himself more capable than this officer did of commanding troops in the field.'

AMRITSAR (Punjab, India)   13 April 1919
Religious conflicts between Moslems and Hindus after the First World War, together with Mahatma Gandhi's passive non-co-operation with the government, resulted in open rebellion in the Punjab.
  Disturbances of great violence broke out in Amritsar 20 miles from Lahore on 11 April 1919 and several Europeans were killed in a riot the following day. Brigadier-General Reginald Dyer, commanding the garrison of some 1,200 British and Indian troops, marched through the city and at nineteen points a proclamation was read out forbidding processions or meetings. On 13 April an unarmed crowd of at least 25,000 had assembled in an open space in the Jallianwala Bagh in

defiance of the order and the meeting was to be addressed by the leading agitators in the city. Dyer marched a party of 90 Indian troops to the Bagh and opened fire on the crowd, killing 379 and wounding 1,208.
Result: Dyer was to state later before the Hunter Committee that he had no alternative but to take strong measures in the circumstances, and that his action saved the Punjab from bloody revolt and all India from a second Mutiny. However, the incident aroused British public opinion. Dyer was denounced in the Commons but the Lords upheld his action and controversy still continues.

AONG (Uttar Pradesh, India)   Indian Mutiny   15 July 1857
Fought between the British relief force under Brigadier-General Sir Henry Havelock and a band of mutineers.
Strength: British/Sikhs 1,130 with 8 guns; Rebels 3,000.
Aim: To disperse the rebel force dug in in front of the village of Aong *en route* to Cawnpore (qv).
Battle: The rebels were strongly entrenched in front of the village with 2 9-pounder guns. The British moved forward under artillery cover and drove the enemy infantry before them, seeing which the rebel cavalry immediately withdrew, leaving large quantities of stores and baggage behind. Havelock's shortage of cavalry prevented a pursuit.
Result: After a rest the column proceeded on its way to Cawnpore.

ARRAH (Bihar, India)   Indian Mutiny   25 July-3 August 1857
Fought between the mutineers under Kur Singh and the British and Sikhs under Mr Boyle and the relief column under Major Vincent Eyre.
Strength: British 16+ Sikh police 60+ Eyre's force 216 with 3 guns; Rebels 2,500.
Aim: Near the eastern limits of the Mutiny, in the town of Arrah, 35 miles west of Patna, the fortified house of a Mr Boyle was besieged by three Indian regiments led by Kur Singh, the Raja of Jagderpur.
Battle: The defenders beat off all assaults until the house, already mined by the enemy, was relieved in the nick of time by a force consisting mainly of the 5th Fusiliers led by Eyre, after desperate fighting. This defence was one of the most courageous actions of the Indian Mutiny. General Sir James Outram strongly recommended Eyre for the VC, but he did not get the award.

ASHTI (Maharashtra, India)   Third Mahratta War   25 February 1818
Fought between the British under Brigadier-General Michael William Smith and the Mahrattas under the Peshwa, Baji Rao.
Strength: British 3,000; Mahrattas 10,000 cavalry.
Aim: The British sought to crush the Mahratta forces under the Peshwa of Poona.
Battle: The Peshwa fled before the action began, leaving his most courageous and experienced commander Gokla with 10,000 horse to cover the general retreat. The advancing British were suddenly attacked by 2,500 Mahratta cavalry, but on being charged by the 22nd Dragoons they turned and fled in the direction of the

main army, leaving their leader Gokla dead on the field.
Result: The Peshwa became a fugitive and his dominions were annexed. He died
in exile near Cawnpore (qv). His adopted son, Dundhu Panth, inherited some of
his estates and became Nana Sahib of the Mutiny, famous for his massacre of
British women and children at Cawnpore (Kanpur).

ASIRGHAR (Madhya Pradesh, India)   Third Mahratta War   18 March-6 April
1819
Fought between the British under General Sir John Malcolm and Brigadier-General
Sir John Doveton, and the Mahrattas under Jaswunt Rao, and the Pindari Chitus.
Strength: British 11,000 with 17 guns; Mahrattas 6,000.
Aim: The British sought the reduction of this formidable Mahratta stronghold,
defended by a large garrison and mounting 100 guns.
Battle: The British force invested the fortress on 18 March and on 21 March the
garrison was driven into the upper citadel. The British then opened up a bombardment with heavy guns which continued until the garrison surrendered on 6 April,
1,200 Arab mercenaries being allowed to march out. The enemy losses of 43 killed
and 95 wounded were considerably less than the British, who lost 323 killed
and wounded.
Result: The fall of Asirghar, the siege of which had been watched by the whole of
India, produced a profound political effect and brought the war to a dramatic
conclusion, and order was at last restored in central India.

AZIMGHUR (Bihar, India)   Indian Mutiny   15 April 1858
Fought between the British under General Sir Edward Lugard and the Dinapore
mutineers under Kur Singh.
Strength: British 2,500; Rebels 13,000.
Aim: Late in March 1858 General Sir Colin Campbell received news that one of
the rebel leaders in Bihar had driven a small force under Colonel Milman into
Azimghur and was besieging the town. Campbell sent off a column under Lugard
to relieve the garrison.
Battle: After defeating a rebel force of some 4,000 near the village of Tigra and
capturing both their guns, Lugard was by 14 April within 7 miles of Azimghur.
Kur Singh had drawn up his troops along the banks of a small river at the head of
a bridge of boats. He managed to hold the bridge long enough to enable his force
to retire across the Ganges to make for Jagdispur. By this time his army had
suffered heavy casualties and had been reduced to 2,000 men without artillery,
and Kur Singh himself was fatally wounded.
Result: Kur Singh's brother Amar Singh continued to carry on a guerilla war until
his final defeat in October 1858, when he escaped to Nepal.

BADULI-KI-SERAI (Uttar Pradesh, India)   Indian Mutiny   8 June 1857
Fought between the British under Lt-General Sir Henry Barnard and the mutineers.
Strength: British 3,500 with 2 guns; Rebels 30,000 with 30 guns.

Aim: After the outbreak of the Mutiny in Meerut in May 1857 the mutineers proceeded to capture Delhi (qv). A small force of British stationed at Ambala was dispatched to join up with a force from Meerut under Major-General Sir Archdale Wilson to invest and recapture Delhi.

Battle: About 6 miles from Delhi a body of mutineers was strongly entrenched at a place called Baduli-ki-Serai. The rebels were driven from their position after a sharp engagement and lost all their guns.

Result: The British force proceeded to the old military cantonments outside Delhi on the Ridge.

BANDA (Uttar Pradesh, India)   Indian Mutiny   19 April 1858
Fought between the British under Brigadier-General Whitlock and the mutineers under the Nawab of Banda.

Strength: British 1,000; Rebels 7,000.

Aim: The British sought to disperse a force of rebels near the town of Banda, some 50 miles south of Cawnpore.

Battle: After a sharp engagement the rebels were routed.

Result: The British objective was achieved, although the Nawab escaped.

BANGLADESH WAR (E Pakistan)   2 December 1971-17 December 1971
Fought between the Pakistan army, navy and air force on two main fronts, with the E Pakistan forces under command of Lt-General Amin Abdullah Khan Niazi and General Farman Ali (military adviser to the Governor of E Pakistan), all headed by President Yahya Khan of Pakistan, and the Indian armed forces under President Giri, the Prime Minister Indira Gandhi, the Chief of Staff General Sam Manekshaw, with General Aurora as Commander of the Indian forces attacking Bangladesh, and supported by the Mukhta Bahini under Sheikh Mujibur Rahman.

India had already fought two wars with Pakistan and one with China. It seemed to her essential to weaken Pakistan by detaching E Pakistan from W Pakistan, an apparently practical idea as, although of the same religion, they were ethnically far apart. So India actively supported the separatist movement headed by Sheikh Mujibur Rahman who, on 26 March 1971, declared E Pakistan independent of W Pakistan. W Pakistan quickly sent reinforcements by sea, the air route being forbidden by India, to deal with the widespread unrest. Tales of atrocities by W Pakistan troops were widely disseminated throughout India and the world by Indian sources. Meanwhile Indian construction engineer regiments speeded up the building of strategic roads to the E Pakistan border and contact was made with representatives of the Mukhta Bahini, the pro-Indian and anti-W Pakistani guerillas. By December 1971 the stage was set for invasion coupled with an internal revolt by the Mukhta Bahini. The weather had been dry since October and the paddy-fields were mostly capable of taking tanks.

On 2 December 1971 Indian troops crossed the E Pakistan frontier. Pakistan immediately put into effect its plan to eliminate the Indian air force and at dawn on 3 October attacked very many airfields including Srinagar and Avantipur

(Kashmir), Amritsar, Faridkot, Ambala, Agra, Johdpur and others in the east, but failed to destroy the IAF, since they were alerted and all aircraft were concealed in concrete covered bunkers. On the same day Indian army forces, taking advantage of their superior strength, and guided and supported by the guerillas, attacked E Pakistan from five main directions (Comilla sector, Sylhet, Mymensingh, Ranjpur-Dinajpur, and Jessore) and bypassed and isolated the main Pakistan garrisons. The Pakistani Razakars, a paramilitary force, were of little use apart from eliminating a number of traitorous guerillas. Aircraft from the IN carrier *Vikrant* bombed Cox' Bazar and Chittagong repeatedly while the IAF bombed the capital, Dacca, every half hour. Many of the E Pakistani units murdered their W Pakistan officers as soon as the invasion started and this, naturally, threw the Pakistan forces into confusion.

General Aurora's forces, avoiding the main highways and advancing across country along previously reconnoitred routes and accompanied by engineers with the requisite Bailey bridges for crossing the numerous large rivers, rapidly advanced from five directions on Dacca until, on 14 December 1971, Aurora's guns were shelling the city and his aircraft attacking with rockets. General Niazi suggested a cease-fire, but Manekshaw would only negotiate with Farman Ali.

Western front: On the western front the Pakistanis attacked vigorously in Kashmir at Chhamb, west of Jammu, and the Indian forces were driven back. A second offensive at Poonch, further south, resulted in a stalemate. On the Punjab front an extensive tank battle was fought in which 45 Pakistani General Patton tanks were destroyed, proving the British Centurion, manned by the Indians, a far better tank. The Indians counter-attacked on the Sind front towards Karachi, but after achieving some penetration in this desert country, were soon held.

Air war: After the PAF had failed to destroy the IAF on the ground, the latter, with their superior numbers, quickly established superiority, their ratio of sorties being 5 to 1. Both countries claimed that hundreds of civilians were killed by bombing, but this was especially evident near Karachi docks.

Sea war: The Indian Navy quickly took advantage of their superior strength. Early on, a task force sank the Pakistan destroyers *Khaiber* (formerly HMS *Cadiz*), *Shah Jehar* (formerly HMS *Charity*) and 2 minesweepers. The Pakistan submarine *Ghazi* was sunk in the Bay of Bengal on the night of 3/4 December, but another Pakistani submarine got revenge by sinking the Indian frigate *Khukri* on 9 December in the Arabian Sea. Some British and neutral vessels were stopped as the Indian navy blockaded Pakistan.

Cease-fire: The Pakistan army in E Pakistan, 10,000 strong, surrendered at 5.30pm on 16 December. A cease-fire was agreed on the western front at 8pm on 17 December.

Figures for casualties are from Indian sources:

	INDIA		PAKISTAN	
	E front	W front	E front	W front
Killed	1,047	1,426	} 5-6,000	1,500
Wounded	3,042	3,611		3,500

CASUALTIES TABLE (CONTINUED)

Missing	89	2,149	6-7,000
Prisoners			10,000
Tanks		73	246
Aircraft		45	94
Warships		1 frigate	2 destroyers
			2 submarines
			2 minesweepers
			16 gunboats

Results of war: On 12 January 1972 Sheikh Mujibur Rahman became Prime Minister of the new state of Bangladesh with a population of 71,316,517. After a few years of civil disturbance, famine and flood, he was overthrown by an army-backed *coup* on 14 August 1975, in the course of which he happened to be killed. The new President was Khonder Mostaque Ahmed, who had more sympathy with Pakistan than his predecessor, but he was in turn overthrown in a *coup* on 7 November 1975. The country was then governed by a Chief Martial Law Administrator (CMLA), Mr Justice A. M. Sayem, with three DCMLAs to assist him.

BAREILLY (Uttar Pradesh, India)   Indian Mutiny   6 May 1858
Fought between the British under General Sir Colin Campbell and the mutineers under Khan Bahadur Khan.
Strength: British 8,000; Rebels 30,000 infantry + 6,000 cavalry + 40 guns.
Aim: The defeat of the large force of rebels operating in the province of Rohilkhand. Campbell planned to send four divisions against the rebel groups converging by different routes on their main centre at Bareilly, thus sweeping them into a net.
Battle: The combined British force reached Faridpur on 4 May, then only a day's march from Bareilly. Khan Bahadur Khan decided to meet the British outside the town and set up his artillery on some sandhills commanding the approaches. When the British advance commenced, however, the rebels abandoned their first line of defence and fell back on the town itself. The subsequent battle was notable for the savage attack of a force of some 130 Ghazis (religious fanatics), all of whom were killed before the advance could proceed. When night fell Khan Bahadur Khan quietly evacuated the town, leaving only a small rearguard. In the morning when Campbell's artillery opened up on the town there was no reply; all the rebels had gone.
Result: The failure of the British to maintain the momentum of their original attack resulted in large rebel groups escaping, requiring further military effort before the province was finally brought under control.

BASHIRATGUNJ (Uttar Pradesh, India)   Indian Mutiny   29 July 1857
Fought between the British under Brigadier-General Sir Henry Havelock and a force of mutineers.

Strength: British/Sikhs 850; Rebels 2,000.
Aim: About 15 miles along the road from Cawnpore to Lucknow (qqv) the rebels occupied a strong defensive position in the walled town of Bashiratgunj which it was necessary to overcome.
Battle: The rebels were heavily entrenched behind earthworks protected by large buildings in the town and at the rear was a large sheet of water over which the road was carried on a causeway. Havelock marched his men round the town in a flanking movement and so frightened the defenders that after a short engagement they fled.
Result: Although having beaten the rebels twice in one day the British force was now reduced to 850 effectives, having lost 88 killed and wounded and many casualties from cholera. Havelock had also used up one-third of his artillery ammunition and accordingly decided to return to Cawnpore to leave his sick and wounded and receive reinforcements before going on to Lucknow. On two further occasions with small additions to his force Havelock was to disperse concentrations of rebels at Bashiratgunj.

BETWA (Madhya Pradesh, India)   Indian Mutiny   1 April 1858
Fought between the British under Lt-General Sir Hugh Rose and the rebels under Tantia Topi.
Strength: British 1,500 (500 Europeans); Rebels 22,000 with 28 guns.
Aim: Tantia Topi was advancing to the relief of Jhansi (qv), besieged by the British, and it was decided to attack his force on the line of the Betwa River.
Battle: Rose detached a third of the besieging troops and divided this force into two columns, the first under Brigadier C. S. Stuart and the second under his own command. Tantia Topi taking the initiative attacked Rose's column which was barely 900 strong. However, the British charged the rebels on both flanks with their cavalry, throwing them into confusion. As the flanks retired the centre, seeing the infantry advancing with the bayonet, broke and fled. The enemy left upwards of 1,500 dead and wounded on the field and all their guns were captured, together with two rebel standards.
Result: Having lost his artillery, Tantia Topi decided not to try to hold a line on the Betwa and fled to Kalpi (qv), leaving Rose free to continue the siege of Jhansi, which was stormed and captured on 5 April 1858.

BEYMAROO (Afghanistan)   First Afghan War   23 November 1841
Fought between the British under Brigadier-General John Shelton and Afghans under Akbar Khan.
Strength: British 4,500; Afghans 10,000 horse + 15,000 foot.
Aim: On 2 November 1841 the Afghans rose against the British and murdered the Resident. The occupying forces under Major-General William Elphinstone were unable to control the situation and were pinned down in their cantonments outside the city. The Afghans had overrun the village of Beymaroo from which the British obtained food supplies and it was necessary to regain the position.

Battle: A detachment of the British force including the Queen's 44th Foot attempted to dislodge the Afghans posted round the village but took only one gun which soon became useless through overheating. The Afghan cavalry attacked, driving the British back down the hill in disorder with many casualties.

Result: The defeat on the Beymaroo hills finally destroyed the will to resist of General Elphinstone who had been ill for some time and precipitated the decision to evacuate Kabul (qv).

BHURTPORE II (Madhya Pradesh, India) Third Mahratta War 28 December 1825-18 January 1826

Fought between the British under General Lord Combermere and the garrison of Jats, Pathans and Rajputs.

Strength: British 27,000 with 112 siege-guns; Jats/Pathans/Rajputs 25,000.

Aim: The Governor-General Lord Amherst had decided that the usurper Doorjan Sal must be deposed; and the Commander-in-Chief Lord Combermere led a large force from Agra (qv) to besiege the fortress.

Battle: The siege commenced on 28 December with a heavy bombardment and on 16 and 17 January respectively mines were exploded under two bastions with devastating effect. Major-General T. Reynell was placed in command of the three assault columns which the next day stormed through the breaches against a desperate defence put up by the garrison. The 14th Foot (the Old Bucks) particularly distinguished themselves and it is said that the whole front rank of its Grenadier Company were awarded the Waterloo Medal. It is reported that 13,000 of the defenders were killed or wounded and 135 guns captured, together with immense treasure. Outside the town the cavalry under Brigadier Sleigh captured over 6,000 fugitives including Doojan Sal. British losses were under 1,100.

Result: The prestige gained as a result of this victory was immense, quite obliterating memories of General Gerard Lake's repulse at Bhurtpore in 1805. The troops taking part were granted a large proportion of the prize money amounting to some £480,000.

BITHUR (Uttar Pradesh, India) Indian Mutiny 16 August 1857

Fought between the British under Brigadier-General Sir Henry Havelock and a force of mutineers.

Strength: British 1,100 with 8 guns; Rebels 4,000 with 4 guns.

Aim: Whilst back at Cawnpore (qv) Havelock had been informed that a force of rebels had concentrated at Bithur a few miles to the NW and that it was essential to disperse them to clear the Delhi (qv) road.

Battle: The rebels lay in front of the town behind a plain covered with dense plantations and interspersed with villages. The British attacked in two echelons, one from the right and the other from the left, each supported by artillery. Though the rebel infantry were soon scattered, their guns continued to discharge heavy fire until they were finally taken at the point of the bayonet.

Result: Unable to pursue the rebels owing to his lack of cavalry, Havelock returned to Cawnpore the following day.

BURMESE REBELLION   1930-2
The world economic crisis, which lowered the price of rice and resulted in considerable hardship to the peasantry in Burma, produced conditions favourable to a native uprising with a view to overcoming British rule. A multitude of small jungle-based gangs of malcontents under leaders known as Bohs sprang into being, the most important being the Galen Army, some 1,500 strong, led by Saya San who had some military skill. The movement spread and by May 1931 most of Burma south of Prome was involved. At the outset of the rebellion the only military forces available to act in support of the police were two battalions of British infantry, one Indian battalion and two battalions of Burma Rifles. Reinforcements of six battalions from India, coupled with the establishment of a special intelligence branch, led to co-ordinated jungle drives by mobile columns being introduced with considerable success. In July 1931 Saya San was captured and before the end of the year the back of the rebellion was broken. A small uprising in January 1932, which was immediately suppressed, led to the re-establishment of law and order by the spring of that year.

BUSHIRE (BANDAR-E-BŪSHEHR) (Iran)   Persian War   10 December 1856
Fought between the British expeditionary force under Major-General Foster Stalker and the Persian garrison.
Strength: British 5,670 (2,270 Europeans); Persians 5,000.
Aim: On 1 November 1856 war was declared on Persia as a result of the Persian occupation of the city of Herat (qv), 600 miles east of Teheran, which menaced the North-West Frontier of India. An expeditionary force supported by men-of-war of the Indian navy commanded by Admiral Sir Henry Luke landed in the area of Bushire (Bandar-e-Būshehr) on 7 December 1856.
Battle: After the capture of the old Dutch fort at Reshire (qv) the British force advanced towards the town of Bushire which was being heavily bombarded by the navy off-shore. One by one the Persian batteries in the town were silenced and a breach was made in the defensive wall at the SW angle. On the approach of the British columns led by General Stalker the Governor surrendered, hauling down the Persian flag. Following this action, eight regiments of the British and Indian armies were authorised to bear the battle honour 'Bushire', although none had incurred a single casualty.
Result: As the British cabinet had decided to extend the operations in Persia to capture the town of Mohammerah (qv) at the head of the Gulf, the expedition was reinforced with a second division and the Sind cavalry, and a new commander, Lt-General Sir James Outram, was appointed to supersede Major-General Stalker, who later committed suicide.

CAWNPORE I (KANPUR) (Uttar Pradesh, India)   Indian Mutiny   6-25 June 1857
Fought between the British garrison under Major-General Sir Hugh Wheeler and

the mutineers under Nana Sahib.
Strength: British 240; Rebels 3,000.
Aim: The intention of the rebels was to annihilate the garrison at Cawnpore (Kanpur) and women and children who totalled 375.
Battle: Wheeler had prepared a defensive position around two large barrack buildings which was not adequately protected by strong earthworks. On 6 June the rebels surrounded the entrenchments and commenced to bombard it. By 23 June the ammunition was almost gone, starvation stared the garrison in the face, and on 26 June the survivors, about 450, surrendered on the promise of a safe passage to Allahabad. On 27 June, as the garrison with the women and children marched towards the river to board the boats, they were fired on by the mutineers and those still on the bank were massacred by order of Nana Sahib, only four survivors escaping to tell the tale. About 200 women and children were then herded into a small house known as the Bibighur.
Result: This tragic event was later described as 'so foul an act of treachery the world had never seen'. It was to be bitterly avenged at the engagement in December of the same year.

CAWNPORE II (KANPUR) (Uttar Pradesh, India)   Indian Mutiny   26 November 1857
Fought between the British garrison of Cawnpore (Kanpur) under Major-General Sir Charles Windham and the Gwalior contingent of mutineers under Tantia Topi.
Strength: British 1,200 infantry + 100 cavalry + 12 guns; Rebels 2,500 infantry (advance force) + 500 cavalry + 6 guns.
Aim: Learning of the advance of the Gwalior contingent in the direction of Cawnpore, Windham decided on a strong sortie to intercept them.
Battle: On 24 November, leaving a small force to guard the Cawnpore defences, Windham moved out towards the Pandu Nadi where he was engaged by the advance force of the rebels. The enemy were put to flight and 3 guns captured. However, Tantia Topi's main force of about 20,000 troops with 40 guns was nearer than Windham had supposed and the British were forced back into the entrenchment, having lost 300 men and large quantities of baggage and stores.
Result: The sortie had been of small practical success and the rebels now threatened to destroy the bridge of boats across the Ganges used by the British.

CAWNPORE III (KANPUR) (Uttar Pradesh, India) Indian Mutiny   6 December 1857
Fought between the British under General Sir Colin Campbell and the Gwalior contingent of mutineers under Tantia Topi.
Strength: British 5,000 infantry + 600 cavalry + 35 guns; Rebels 25,000 with 40 guns.
Aim: During the night of 29/30 November Campbell's force from Lucknow (qv) came in to Cawnpore (Kanpur) with a large convoy of sick and wounded. Arrange-

ments were then made for the refugees to be sent on to safety at Allahabad and at last, on 6 December 1857, Campbell was free to deal with Tantia.
Battle: The rebels had taken up a strong position including the town of Cawnpore itself and extending through an open plain down to the Ganges. Campbell delivered his main attack on the rebels' position on the plain, which was completely successful. The enemy was routed and pursued by cavalry, infantry and light artillery as far as the fourteenth milestone on the Kalpi (qv) road. Whilst these operations were going on General Sir William Rose Mansfield, Campbell's Chief of Staff, had moved on the rebels' left and routed the forces of Nana Sahib. The rebels suffered heavy losses and the British captured 19 guns with less than 100 casualties.
Result: The saving of Cawnpore and the rout of Tantia Topi formed the turning-point of the Mutiny. Henceforth the British were no longer struggling for their position in India; they were merely putting down a rebellion. The way was now clear for the final capture of Lucknow.

CHANDA (Nagpur, Maharashtra, India)   Third Mahratta War   9-11 May 1818
Fought between the British under Colonel Adams and the forces of the Bhonsla of Nagpur.
Strength: British 4,000 + 2,000 irregular cavalry + 25 guns; Mahrattas 3,000.
Aim: The British sought the reduction of the garrison of Chanda.
Battle: The fortress was one of the main strongholds of the Bhonsla of Nagpur. After two days of bombardment it was stormed and carried, Mahratta losses being some 200 killed, including the Commandant. British casualties were only 14 killed and 56 wounded.
Result: The capture of Chanda was a serious setback for the Nagpur forces.

CHARASIA (Afghanistan)   Second Afghan War   6 October 1879
Fought between the British under Major-General Sir Frederick Roberts and the Afghans and Ghilzyes.
Strength: British 6,500; Afghan/Ghilzyes 15,000.
Aim: After the accession of Yakub Khan, the British Envoy, Major Sir Louis Cavagnari, and his staff and escort of Guides arrived in Kabul (qv) on 24 July 1879. It soon became evident that Yakub Khan could not control his own people and on 3 September Cavagnari and his staff and escort were murdered by the mob. Roberts was accordingly instructed to resume command of the Kabul Field Force and advance on Kabul. The Afghans mustered at Charasia, 6 miles south of Kabul, to oppose the British.
Battle: Roberts's column, now reduced to 4,000 by garrisons on the line of communications, was composed of excellent troops, the British element being armed with the new Martini-Henry rifle. Although the Afghans were entrenched in a strong position, Roberts skilfully dislodged them by a flanking movement followed by a cavalry pursuit, and by nightfall the enemy had fled with severe losses. It was in this engagement that Major White, the future defender of

Ladysmith, won the VC. Enemy losses were 300 and British casualties less than 100 killed and wounded.
Result: On 10 October 1879 Roberts occupied Kabul. Two days later Yakub Khan came to see him, offering to abdicate and saying that he 'would rather be a grass-cutter in the English camp than ruler of Afghanistan'. He was allowed to retire to India, Roberts taking over the administration of Kabul with the rank of lieutenant-general.

CHILIANWALA (Pakistan)   Second Sikh War   13 January 1849
Fought between the British under Lt-General Sir Hugh Gough and the Sikhs under Sher Singh.
Strength: British 12,000 with 60 guns; Sikhs 40,000 with 62 guns.
Aim: The Sikhs sought to halt the British advance into W Punjab.
Battle: After being repulsed in his attempt to cross the Chenab River at Ramnagar (qv) Gough moved upstream, where he crossed, encountering little opposition. Five miles from the Jhelum River the Sikhs held the village of Chilianwala in considerable strength to block the British advance. Gough drew up his forces in two divisions with cavalry on the flanks and the artillery distributed along the front; unfortunately for the British, however, the jungle and scrub reduced the effect of the artillery. Both sides then attacked simultaneously and eventually, after a hard and evenly contested fight, the Sikhs retired from the field, taking with them some guns and three regimental colours. Sikh losses were of the order of 8,000 and the British casualties were 2,338 killed and wounded. This was perhaps the hardest battle ever fought by the British in India and the Sikhs had held Gough to what was virtually a drawn contest.
Result: British losses were so heavy that, coupled as they were with lack of water, Gough was compelled to retire and re-form his forces, thus rendering the action indecisive. There is little doubt that, owing to lack of directions from the top, British attacks in this action were badly co-ordinated throughout, giving the Sikhs every advantage. When news of the engagement reached England an unreasoning clamour was raised against Gough's 'Tipperary tactics' and he was replaced by General Sir Charles Napier. In the meantime, however, Gough had decisively crushed the Sikhs at Gujarat (qv).

CHINHUT (Pakistan)   Indian Mutiny   30 June 1857
Fought between garrison troops of Lucknow (qv) under Sir Henry Lawrence, Chief Commissioner of Oudh, and mutineers under Barhat Ahmed.
Strength: British 300 with 10 guns; Rebels 6,300 with 16 guns.
Aim: To intercept mutineers advancing on Lucknow, then at Chinhut, about 10 miles away.
Battle: The force under Lawrence himself was badly handled and part deserted to the enemy. The remainder came under heavy attack and were obliged to fall back on Lucknow in disorder and with considerable loss.
Result: This was a misjudged sortie which resulted in great loss of British prestige

and the subsequent investment of Lucknow.

CHITRAL (N Pakistan)   Chitral (Malakand) Campaign   March-April 1895
Fought between the garrison under Captain C.V.P. Townshend and the Chitralis/
Pathans under Umra Khan.
Strength: British garrison 400; Chitralis/Pathans 10,000.
Aim: On 1 January 1895 the Mehta (Prince) of the state of Chitral was shot dead
by his half-brother Amir-ul-Mulk and the usurper aided by a neighbouring Pathan
ruler Umra Khan besieged the British Agent in the fort in Chitral town, 200 miles
north of Peshawar (qv). Two separate relief expeditions, the 1st Division under
General Sir Robert Low from Peshawar and a small force of 400 Pioneers under
Colonel J. G. Kelly from Gilgit, were ordered to advance on Chitral to relieve
the garrison.
Battle: The fort which was only 80 yards square with walls 25 feet high was
gallantly held by the small garrison under Captain Townshend of the Central
India Horse, later to be the defender of Kut-el-Amara. From 7 March onwards
repeated attacks by hordes of tribesmen were driven off until on 19 April the
garrison was relieved by Colonel Kelly and his column. After great hardships they
had crossed the Shandur Pass at 12,400 feet to reach Chitral a few days before
the advance brigade of the main relief force under Brigadier-General Gatacre.

   The Viceroy, Lord Elgin, called it 'a glorious episode in the history of the Indian
Empire and its army'.

DARGAI (Pakistan)   Tirah Campaign   20 October 1897
Fought between the British expedition commanded by General Sir William
Lockhart and the Afridis.
Strength: British 2,000; Afridis 5,000.
Aim: During the North-West Frontier campaigns of 1897 two divisions under Sir
William Lockhart penetrated the Tirah country, the home of the Afridis and
Orakzais. This was the largest frontier expedition ever mounted involving all told
some 35,000 men.
Battle: The heights of Dargai, 50 miles from Peshawar, were held by a large force
of Afridis. It was a difficult feature with a narrow, exposed approach and several
attempts at assault were made by units of General Yeatman Briggs's column
without success. Colonel Mathias commanding the Gordons said to his men:
'Highlanders, the General says the position must be taken at all costs. The Gordons
will take it.' He then ordered officers and pipers to the front and the pipes set up
'Cock of the North' followed by 600 cheering Highlanders. The artillery doubled
their supporting fire and the heights were taken by assault, with the loss of 300
men killed and wounded.
Result: Having forced the Arhanga Pass the British column reached the tribal
centre, Bagh, where they burned the homesteads and destroyed the groves, after
which surrender terms were imposed on the Afridi chiefs. Lockhart then returned
to India after a campaign which had cost several million pounds but not

more than 800 casualties.

DELHI V (India)   Indian Mutiny   8 June-20 September 1857
Fought between the British under Major-General Sir Archdale Wilson and the Indian mutineers in Delhi.
Strength: British 12,000 with 22 guns; Rebels 40,000 with 40 guns + 114 guns mounted on the walls.
Aim: The reduction of the rebel garrison by the British.
Battle: With the arrival of the siege train and reinforcements from the Punjab under Brigadier-General John Nicholson, it was decided to attempt storming the city. On 8 September Wilson opened fire with the breaching batteries and four storming parties of about 1,000 men each took up position. On the morning of 14 September the assault began and by nightfall the city had been entered from all breaches. Fighting, however, was to continue for six days before the city was finally in the hands of the British. Losses were severe, amounting to 4,000, of whom rather more than half were European. Brigadier-General Nicholson was among the dead.
Result: The rebel hold on Delhi and the surrounding country was broken decisively.

ERZURUM (Turkey)   Turko-Persian War   1821
Fought between the Turkish army under the Pasha of Baghdad and the Persians under Prince Abbas Mirza.
Strength: Turks 52,000; Persians 30,000.
Aim: A combination of Russian intrigue and the open Turkish protection of rebel tribesmen fleeing from Azerbaydzhan precipitated war between Turkey and Persia.
Battle: Abbas Mirza moved his forces west into Turkey in the Lake Van region. In retaliation the Turks moved east into Persia but were repulsed. The campaign ended with the Battle of Erzurum, where the Persians under Abbas Mirza defeated the Turks.
Result: Peace was finally restored by the Treaty of Erzurum in 1823, under which both sides agreed to maintain the *status quo.*

FATEHPUR (Uttar Pradesh, India)   Indian Mutiny   12 July 1857
Fought between the British under Brigadier-General Sir Henry Havelock and a force of mutineers.
Strength: British/Sikhs 1,130 with 8 guns; Rebels 3,500 with 12 guns.
Aim: The British relief column under Havelock left Allahabad on 7 July *en route* to Cawnpore (qv) and was opposed by a force of rebels at Fatehpur, which it was necessary to disperse.
Battle: The rebels were established in a strong position in the village but were vigorously attacked by the British infantry, ably supported by a battery of 8 guns under Captain Maude, RA. The enemy broke and fled leaving all 12 guns in the hands of the British, whose casualties had been negligible.
Result: After occupying Fatehpur, which was set fire to by the Sikhs, Havelock

proceeded on the road to Cawnpore.

FEROZESHAH (Punjab, India)   First Sikh War   21-2 December 1845
Fought between the British under Lt-General Sir Hugh Gough and the Sikhs
under Lal Singh.
Strength: British 18,000 with 65 guns; Sikhs 20,000 with 108 guns.
Aim: The British sought to beat the Sikhs from their entrenchments.
Battle: After beating the Sikhs at Mudki (qv), Gough went north in the E Punjab
where he came upon the Sikhs entrenched in a strong position outside Ferozeshah.
The Governor-General of India, Sir Henry Hardinge, was present and volunteered
to serve as Second-in-Command under Gough. Disagreement between the two men,
however, prevented the British from attacking the Sikh lines until nearly dusk.
Repeated assaults were driven back, but after a hard battle the Sikhs fell back,
the 3rd Light Dragoons charging right through the enemy's entrenchments to cut
down their gunners. As darkness had now fallen, however, Gough ordered a
withdrawal, as it was impossible to distinguish friend from foe. The British were
shelled in their positions all night and the next morning the struggle continued
with renewed intensity, and only after desperate fighting were the Sikhs compelled
to retreat at the point of the bayonet. The exhausted British were then threatened
by the approach of a fresh Sikh army some 30,000 strong under Tej Singh, which
unaccountably failed to press home an attack and soon retreated. Sikh losses
exceeded 7,000 men and British were 694 killed and 1,721 wounded, whilst 75
Sikh guns were captured.
Result: It was asserted that Tej Singh's failure to mount an attack on the weakened
British forces was due to treachery; but, be that as it may, the British had been
within an ace of being toppled from their position of supremacy in India.

GANDAMAK (Afghanistan)   First Afghan War   13 January 1842
Fought between the remnants of the retreating British force under Major-General
William Elphinstone and the Afghans and Ghilzyes.
Aim: The final destruction by the Afghan tribesmen of the remaining officers
and men of Elphinstone's army evacuating Kabul (qv).
Battle: At dawn on 13 January 1842 after emerging from the Jugdulluk Pass the
small band, now reduced to about 20 officers and men, found themselves at
Gandamak with the enemy gathering round again. They had no more than two
rounds of ammunition apiece. The majority were slaughtered, the only prisoners
taken being Captain Souter of the 44th Foot, who saved the regimental colours by
tying them round his waist, and 4 privates of the regiment.
Result: Of the 18,000 soldiers and civilians who started out from Kabul on
6 January 1842 the only one to reach Jalalabad (qv) was Surgeon Brydon, as
portrayed in Lady Butler's famous painting, 'The Remnants of an Army' (1881),
now in the Tate Gallery, London.

GEOK TEPE (USSR)   Conquest by Russia   8-17 January 1881
Fought between the Russians under General Mikhail Skobelev and the Tekkes.
Strength: Russians 10,000; Tekkes 30,000.
Aim: After the Russo-Turkish war (1877-8), Czar Alexander II decided to conquer
the Tekke tribe in what is now Turkmen SSR. The tribe's fortress of Geok Tepe
was besieged by a Russian column on 9 September 1878.
Battle: Although the Russians bombarded the place, they were unable to take it.
A second attempt to reduce the fortress was made three years later when, on 8
January 1881, Skobelev surrounded the garrison. On 17 January the Russians
stormed the defences, killing 6,000 of the garrison. Another 8,000 were killed
during the pursuit.
Result: The resistance of the Tekkes was at an end.

GHAZNI (GHUZNEE) (Afghanistan)   First Afghan War   23 July 1839
Fought between the Afghan garrison under Haider Khan, the son of Dost
Mohammed Khan, and the British under General Sir John Keane.
Strength: Afghans 3,000; British Bengal Army 9,500 + Shah Shuja's levies 6,000.
Aim: The British sought the reduction of this hitherto impregnable fortress which
barred the way to Kabul (qv).
Battle: Having left their siege guns at Kandahar (qv) the British blew the main gate
with a charge of 900 pounds of gunpowder and the storming column under
Brigadier-General Robert Sale carried the fortress with the loss of only 17 killed
and 165 wounded. The garrison lost 1,200 killed, 300 wounded and 1,500 prisoners.
Result: The capture of Ghazni demoralised the Afghans, and Dost Mohammed
with a few devoted followers fled to the Hindu Kush. On 7 August 1839 the
British entered Kabul and placed Shah Shuja on the throne. Dost Mohammed later
gave himself up and was given asylum in Ludhiana, near Delhi. Afghanistan was
to be under British rule for the next three years.

GHOAINE (Afghanistan)   First Afghan War   30 August 1842
Fought between the British under Major-General William Nott and the Afghans
under Shemsuddin, Governor of Ghazni.
Strength: British 6,000; Afghans 12,000.
Aim: The Afghans sought to block the British, who were marching from
Kandahar to Ghazni (qqv).
Battle: The Afghans were totally defeated, losing all their guns, tents and baggage.
Result: The British continued the advance to Ghazni.

GORARIA (Madhya Pradesh, India)   Indian Mutiny   23-4 November 1857
Fought between the British under Brigadier-General Stuart and the acting Agent
in central India, Sir Henry Durand, and a force of mutineers.
Strength: British 1,500 with 9 guns; Rebels 15,000 with 16 guns.
Aim: The suppression of the rebel outbreak in central India under the command
of the Mogul prince, Firuz Shah, and concentrated in the Mandisur area.

Battle: On 22 November the rebels had taken up a position covering the approaches to Mandisur (Mandesar). A brisk barrage from Stuart's artillery followed by a cavalry charge drove the rebels to take refuge in the town. A report to the effect that a large force of rebels was in the neighbourhood of the village of Goraria led Stuart to launch an attack on their position before they could come to the assistance of the mutineers in Mandisur. The village, in spite of heavy artillery bombardment, was stubbornly defended and it was not until late afternoon on 24 November that the defenders were finally dislodged. While the British were engaged at Goraria, Firuz Shah and about 2,000 men evacuated Mandisur and the British were too exhausted to follow them.

Result: The prompt and decisive action of the British under the direction of Sir Henry Durand had prepared the way for the final campaign in central India, which was to be commanded by Lt-General Sir Hugh Rose with conspicuous success.

GUJARAT (W Punjab, Pakistan)   Second Sikh War   21 February 1849
Fought between the British under Lt-General Sir Hugh Gough and the Sikhs under Sher Singh.

Strength: British 24,000 with 96 guns (including 3 heavy batteries); Sikhs 50,000 + 59 guns + Afghans 1,500 cavalry.

Aim: Since Chilianwala (qv) Gough had been reinforced by General William Whish's force and siege guns after the fall of Multan (qv) and the Sikhs by a force of Afghan cavalry. This was to be the final test of strength between the two armies.

Battle: For the first time in the campaign Gough had powerful artillery at his disposal and opened the battle with a heavy bombardment, steadily outgunning the Sikh artillery. The infantry then advanced, breaking the Sikh lines, and cavalry attacks on both flanks dispersed the enemy into overwhelming flight. The Sikhs lost more than 2,000 and all their guns, while British losses were only 92 killed and 682 wounded. The battle had undoubtedly been decided by artillery.

Result: This battle ended the Sikh uprising. The enemy was relentlessly pursued, Rawalpindi, Attock and Peshawar (qv) all falling into the hands of the British, and upwards of 20,000 Sikhs surrendering and laying down their arms. The Punjab was now formally annexed and with it the Koh-i-noor (Mountain of Light) diamond which had been in the possession of Ranjit Singh. It was sent to England to be set in the imperial crown.

GWALIOR II (Madhya Pradesh, India)   Indian Mutiny   17-20 June 1858
Fought between the British under Lt-General Sir Hugh Rose and the rebels under Tantia Topi and the Rani of Jhansi.

Strength: British 5,000; Rebels 10,000 with 2 guns.

Aim: After their defeat at Kalpi (qv) the last rebel stronghold south of the Jumna, Tantia Topi and the Rani decided to take over the great fortress of Gwalior, 60 miles south of Agra (qv), from the Maharaja Scindhia and occupy it as a base. They defeated the Maharaja's troops and Tantia Topi proclaimed the Nana Sahib as Peshwa in the fort at Gwalior.

Battle: Although Rose was due to hand over his command to his successor he decided that immediate action was called for and on 5 June he set out from Kalpi. After defeating large concentrations of rebels at Morar and Kotah-ke-Serai (qqv) Rose advanced on the town of Gwalior, which was defended by large rebel forces. After a short engagement the enemy were put to flight and by nightfall the British had occupied the whole city save for the massive fortress still in rebel hands and approachable only from the NE side. On the morning of 20 June the fort was taken by the intrepid action of a small detachment of 25th Bombay Native Infantry led by Lieutenants Rose and Waller after a desperate fight during which Rose, a relative of Sir Hugh, was killed. Waller was awarded the VC.

Result: With the capture of Gwalior the main central Indian campaign ended and Rose relinquished his command to Brigadier-General Robert Napier (later Lord Napier of Magdala). Tantia Topi fled with the Rao Sahib and the Nawab of Banda and eluded capture until April 1859 when he was betrayed to the British, court-martialled, found guilty and hanged. The Rao Sahib too was betrayed in 1862 and hanged. Another leader, the Moslem Firuz Shah, managed to escape the net, to die penniless in Mecca in 1877.

So ended the Indian Mutiny.

HERAT II (Afghanistan)   Perso-Afghan Wars   22 November 1837-4 June 1838
Fought between the Afghan garrison under Yar Mohammed and the Persian army.

Aim: The Persian Shah, Mohammed, sent an army into Afghanistan to capture the town of Herat which was on the Indian trade route.

Battle: The siege was somewhat desultory and on 4 June a major assault was beaten back with a loss to the attackers of more than 1,500. An interesting feature of the siege was the presence in Herat of a young Irish artillery officer, Eldred Pottinger, who had arrived in the city in Eastern dress and stayed to help organise the defences and rally the natives.

Result: After the failure of their main attack the Persians lingered on until 9 September when they withdrew under pressure from the British.

HYDERABAD (Pakistan)   Sind (Scinde) Campaign   24 March 1843
Fought between the British under General Sir Charles Napier and the Baluchis under Amir Shir Mohammed, the Lion of Mirpur.

Strength: British 5,000 (including 1,500 cavalry) with 19 guns; Baluchis 26,000 with 15 guns.

Aim: Colonel James Outram, the British Resident in Hyderabad, had been attacked by a Baluchi mob but had escaped up the Indus in an armed steamer to join Napier. It was now necessary to occupy the city.

Battle: Following the British victory at Miani (qv) Napier collected reinforcements and moved down the line of the river Indus. On 24 March the Anglo-Indian force attacked Hyderabad, capital of Sind. Although the British were heavily out-numbered, the city was stormed under cover of a heavy artillery bombardment and the Baluchis were routed, 5,000 being killed.

Result: Soon afterwards the Amir surrendered and Sind was annexed. Napier is said to have sent a signal to the Governor-General, Lord Ellenborough, containing the single word 'Peccavi' (I have sinned). A week later he was appointed Governor of Sind and was in due course responsible for constructing the port of Karachi, which replaced Hyderabad as the capital.

INDIA   Chinese Invasion   20 October-21 November 1962
Chinese aggressive tactics along the Himalayan border had led to repeated clashes between Chinese and Indian troops. Then on 20 October 1962 Chinese columns made massive unprovoked attacks on Indian positions in various areas and in the east all Indian resistance north of the Brahmaputra valley was overcome. In November, having gained all the border regions they had claimed, the Chinese suddenly withdrew to lines which would ensure they retained these areas, and then on 21 November they declared a cease-fire. Pandit Nehru rejected the Chinese terms for settling the dispute but, as the Indians had no desire to resume the offensive, the Chinese achieved *de facto* control of large areas of the border. Before the fighting ended some 3,213 Indian soldiers had been made prisoner, later to be returned. Total casualties are not known.

The unreadiness of the Indian army for war as was shewn in this campaign led to the downfall of Nehru's leftist Defence Minister, Krishna Menon. One reason for the Chinese superiority was that their rifle- and gun-sights were zeroed for the heights (up to 18,000 feet) where they fought, while the Indians, coming up from the plains, did not zero their weapons to take into account the rarefied atmosphere, and so fired high and left the Chinese unscathed.

INDO-PAKISTAN WAR   5 August-22 September 1965
This war arose out of violations of the cease-fire, beginning on 5 August when, in the regions of Jammu and Kashmir (qv), armed civilians crossed from Pakistan to India for combat. On 14 August the Pakistanis attacked across the Jammu border in battalion strength. In order to seal entry routes, on 28 August the Indians closed the Haji Hir Pass. On 1 September the Pakistanis launched a tank attack with air cover across the border between Pakistan and Jammu. The Indian air force retaliated. On 6 September the Indians drove across the border into the Lahore section of W Pakistan. Two further thrusts were made the following day, one into Sialkot from Jammu and one from Rajasthan into Sind. The tank battles which ensued were some of the heaviest since the First World War.

Fighting ended on 22 September following a United Nations Security Council resolution and both sides withdrew to the positions they had occupied on 5 August. Indian losses during the war were 2,759 killed, 7,636 wounded and 1,500 missing; and in addition 80 tanks and 28 aircraft. Pakistani losses were estimated at 5,800 killed or wounded, as well as 475 tanks and 73 aircraft. The British Centurion tank had proved superior to any other make engaged in the war.

The Tashkent Agreement of 10 January 1966 laid down that both sides were henceforth to settle their disputes peacefully.

IPI, FAKIR OF   North-West Frontier   1936
During the 1930s fighting on the North-West Frontier reached possibly its highest pitch of intensity, to a large extent owing to the energetic leaders found by the tribes. Of these Mirza Ali Khan, known as the Fakir of Ipi, was perhaps the most determined and resourceful and certainly the most troublesome. He was Imam of a small mosque in Ipi, a hamlet near the town of Bannu in the Lower Tochi valley in Waziristan (qv), and a fanatical hater of all infidels. In 1936 he found a cause in what became known as the 'Islam Bibi' case, in which the wife of a Hindu merchant in Bannu was abducted by a Waziri. The husband sued in the Bannu court for restoration of conjugal rights and won his case. This led to violent protests from the tribes and within a matter of days their leader, the Fakir of Ipi, had organised a widespread revolt among the Waziris. Heavy fighting ensued over a wide area and by 1937 over 30,000 Anglo-Indian troops were in the field trying to curb the Fakir's activities but with little practical success. The Fakir led his *lashkars* with great skill and, when hard pressed, they would merely cross the nearby Durand Line - marking the Afghanistan Frontier - to rest and re-form and then advance into action again. From the British point of view operations were also hampered by the restrictions placed on air action which enabled the tribesmen to disperse before bombing could take place.

The Fakir had built himself a hide-out in a remote valley at Arsalkot, near the Afghan border among the Tori Khel tribe, and in 1937 a punitive expedition was sent to the area, resulting in the collapse of Tori Khel resistance but in failure to capture the Fakir, who remained as elusive as an eel.

Casualties in all the operations in Waziristan were considerable and the Indian army lost 163 killed and several hundreds wounded. It was during this period when extensive operations took place against the Mohmands and later the Waziris that Field-Marshal Sir Claude Auchinleck acted as a brigade commander.

The Fakir of Ipi was to remain a thorn in the flesh of the British for many years and in 1940 he was still causing great unrest in the Bannu area. When he died in 1960 he was described by a Pakistan official as 'a vicious old man, twisted with hate and selfishness' but he nevertheless was honoured with an obituary in *The Times* which described him as 'the inspiration and the general of revolt' and as 'a doughty and honourable opponent'. Without doubt he was one of the great guerilla commanders of history.

The Fakir caused infinite trouble to the Indian authorities over a very difficult period and it is almost certain that he was at times subsidised by Soviet Russia. The cost of all the Frontier operations in which he and other tribal leaders were involved was enormous, totalling between 1924 and 1939 £112 million.

JALALABAD (Afghanistan)   First Afghan War   11 March 1842-18 April 1843
Fought between the British under Brigadier-General Sir Robert Sale and the Afghans under Akbar Khan.
Strength: British 2,000; Afghans 6,000.
Aim: The Afghans sought to annihilate the British garrison.

Battle: After the massacre of Major-General William Elphinstone's force in the Khoord-Kabul and Jugdulluk (qqv) Passes the Afghans under Akbar Khan went on to besiege Jalalabad. An assault by the entire Afghan army was repulsed and a regular investment then started. In January 1843 Brigadier-General Wilde attempted to relieve the fortress, but was repulsed in the Khyber Pass and forced to retreat to Peshawar (qv). The garrison made several successful sorties and on 7 April drove Akbar Khan from his entrenchments with considerable loss in both men and guns. The siege was then raised and all chance of a reinvestment ended when Major-General Sir George Pollock stormed the Khyber Pass and arrived at Jalalabad with a strong relieving force. The Governor-General, Lord Ellenborough, referred to the defenders of Jalalabad as 'that illustrious garrison'.
Result: The way was now clear for the return to Kabul to avenge the massacre of Elphinstone's forces.

JAWRA ALIPUR (Madhya Pradesh, India)   Indian Mutiny   20 June 1858
Fought by the British under General Sir Charles Napier and the rebels under Tantia Topi.
Strength: British 800; Rebels 4,000.
Aim: While Lt-General Sir Hugh Rose was occupying Gwalior (qv) his successor-designate Napier was left behind at Morar (qv) to cut off the enemy retreat.
Battle: Early in the morning of 20 June Napier moved off with his small force of cavalry and horse artillery to intercept and destroy the enemy retreating after their defeat at Morar. He caught up with rebels holding a strong position at Jawra. Under rebel artillery fire Napier charged with his whole force. After a brief resistance the rebels broke and fled, hotly pursued. They lost 400 dead, 25 guns and all their ammunition, elephants and stores.
Result: Napier later joined Rose at Gwalior, subsequently taking over command of the Central Indian Field Force.

JHANSI (Uttar Pradesh, India)   Indian Mutiny   21 March-5 April 1858
Fought between the British under Lt-General Sir Hugh Rose and the mutineers under the Rani of Jhansi.
Strength: British 4,500; Rebels 11,000.
Aim: The widowed Rani of Jhansi had been refused by the Governor-General the succession for her adopted son and in consequence became the bitter enemy of the British. On 7 June 1857 the Europeans in the fort had surrendered on promise of safe conduct but all 64 were then massacred on the Rani's orders. It was essential to the British that Jhansi be captured and the Rani deposed.
Battle: When Rose finally left his base at Saugor (qv) on 3 March on the long road to Jhansi, 125 miles north, he found it necessary first to subdue a number of hill forts barring the route, the main one at Madanpur. This successfully accomplished he pressed on to Jhansi and by 21 March his main force lay before the city, dominated by an immensely strong fort flying the Rani's flag. On 24 March Rose commenced bombarding the city, but his plans for the assault had to be postponed

when news came that the rebel general Tantia Topi was hurrying to the relief of the city. After defeating the rebel relief force at Betwa (qv) Rose returned to the siege of Jhansi. By 2 April a breach had been made in the city walls and, despite fierce resistance from the rebels, by 5 April the city and fort were finally captured. The Rani, however, had managed to elude the attackers and escaped to Kalpi (qv), where she was joined by Tantia Topi. It was estimated that rebel losses including civilians exceeded 5,000, whilst British losses were relatively small, totalling 343 killed and wounded.

Result: Although all rebel resistance in the Jhansi area had been overcome, the Rani's escape resulted in the continuance of the campaign in the Central Provinces for another twelve months.

In retaliation for the women and children who had been murdered by the Rani, although these families had been placed in her safe keeping, many of the British troops, affected by that betrayal, took the soldiers of the Rani up a limestone prominence rising out of the plain and hurled them 800 feet down a precipice. This is still named 'Retribution Hill'.

During the 1941-5 Japanese war in Burma Subhas Chandra Bose formed the 'Indian National Army' to fight for the Japanese against the British. A small force of his women soldiers was called The Rani of Jhansi Regiment.

JUGDULLUK (Afghanistan) First Afghan War 12 January 1842
Fought between the remnants of the retreating British force, under Brigadier-General Anquetil, and the Afghans and Ghilzyes.

Aim: The destruction of the remnants of the British force, now reduced to 120 men of the 44th Foot and 25 gunners, apart from the rabble of camp followers.

Battle: In this grim defile the Kabul (qv) force was practically annihilated. At the summit of the pass the Afghans had blocked the way with barriers of prickly holly-oak. As officers and men sought to clear the barriers the waiting Afghans poured in a deadly fire and then charged with scimitar and knife. When the pass was finally cleared there were only 20 officers and 45 European soldiers left.

Result: The remnants of the force struggled towards Jalalabad (qv).

JVP REVOLT (Ceylon/Sri Lanka) 5-23 April 1971
The Janata Vimukhti Peramuna (JVP or People's Liberation Front), led by Rohan Wijeweera, launched an abortive revolt, starting on 5 April 1971, with a view to overthrowing the government and establishing a more liberal and equitable régime. The JVP consisted mainly of young, unmarried, well-educated unemployed Sinhalese who were appalled at the way Mrs Sirima Bandaranaike was managing the country. Later, government and some foreign propagandists tried to assert that these young revolutionaries had Communist views - but this was not so.

As revolutionaries they held out for nearly three weeks, about 20,000 of them, but the government was supported by Britain, the US, Soviet Russia, China and India, which sent helicopters and advisers to help track the insurgents down. By 25 April the main revolt was over. A witch-hunt assisted by the strange assortment of nations continued throughout the year and, by April 1972, 13,433 of the JVP were detained and attempts were being made to rehabilitate them. Also the major powers vied with each other to try and win Ceylon to their side by easy loans, with military and naval missions, and by means of other busybodies.

The main party with a grievance are the Indian Tamils who are being deported, according to plan, to India.

KABUL (Afghanistan)   First Afghan War   6 January 1842
Fought between the British under Major-General William Elphinstone and the Afghan insurgents under Akbar Khan, son of the deposed Amir, Dost Mohammed Khan.
Strength: British 4,500; Afghans 16,000 horse + 15,000 foot.
Aim: After three years in Kabul the British position became untenable following a rising led by Akbar Khan. After lengthy negotiations it was agreed that the British would be allowed to evacuate the city and retire to Jalalabad (qv), a distance of 90 miles. Accordingly 4,500 British and Indian troops with their families and 12,000 camp followers left Kabul on the morning of 6 January in deep snow and bitterly cold weather. During the retreat the force was continually harassed by the Afghans and the wild Ghilzye tribesmen and, apart from a handful of prisoners, the whole force was massacred except for one man, Surgeon William Brydon, who reached Jalalabad on 13 January. Shah Shuja, who had been placed on the throne in place of Dost Mohammed, was amongst those killed.
Result: The pursuing Afghans were finally stopped at Jalalabad by a strong Anglo-Indian defence under Brigadier-General Sir Robert Sale.

KALPI (Uttar Pradesh, India)   Indian Mutiny   19-23 May 1858
Fought between the British under Lt-General Sir Hugh Rose and the mutineers under the Rao Sahib, nephew of Nana Sahib, the Rani of Jhansi and the Nawab of Banda.
Strength: British 4,000; Rebels 11,000.
Aim: The British sought the reduction of the rebel-held town of Kalpi on the River Jumna, 102 miles NE of Jhansi (qv) and 46 miles SW of Cawnpore (qv).
Battle: In front of the town the rebels had constructed an elaborate defence system. The rear of the town lay upon the Jumna, with the fort sited on a precipitous rock overlooking the river. On 19 May batteries were set up by the British on both sides of the river and the bombardment of the town commenced. However, on 22 May, the garrison made two determined sorties on the main British position near the village of Golawli which forced them to retire. A strong counter-attack, led personally by Rose and including the famed Camel Corps, supported by intense artillery fire, then drove the rebels back into the town. This action was one of the fiercest of the Mutiny, owing, it is thought, to the leadership and tactics of the Rani.

At nightfall Rose decided to break off the attack until the following day, as his troops had suffered severely from the heat. But, on resuming operations the next morning, no further opposition was encountered, the rebels having fled during the night.

Result: As the next day, 24 May, was Queen Victoria's birthday, the Union Jack was ceremoniously hoisted over the fort to mark what Rose confidently believed to be the end of the campaign. However, the rebel leaders were to continue the struggle from Gwalior (qv).

KANDAHAR IV (Afghanistan)   Afghan Tribal Wars   29 July 1834
Fought between the followers of Shah Shuja and the army of Dost Mahommed Khan, his successor, and Kohandil Khan.
Aim: Shah Shuja, expelled Amir of Afghanistan, sought to take the city of Kandahar.
Battle: The Shah's troops assaulted the city but were repulsed by the forces of Dost Mahommed.
Result: Shah Shuja's followers were dispersed.

KANDAHAR V (Afghanistan)   Second Afghan War   1 September 1880
Fought between the British under Lt-General Sir Frederick Roberts and the Afghans under Ayub Khan.
Strength: British 10,000; Afghans 25,000.
Aim: After the disastrous British defeat at Maiwand (qv) the garrison at Kandahar was besieged by the Afghan army under Ayub Khan. As the newly appointed Amir, Abdur Rahman Khan, had arrived in Kabul (qv), it was decided that Roberts should proceed to the relief of Kandahar.
Battle: With one cavalry and three infantry brigades, 18 mountain-artillery guns and nearly 8,000 camp followers, Roberts set out from Kabul on 8 August 1880 with no base or line of communications on a march across mountains and deserts which captured the imagination of the world. The total distance of 313 miles was covered in twenty-two days, with no fighting *en route* but not without serious casualties owing to sickness. Roberts arrived at Kandahar to find that Ayub Khan had raised the siege and taken up a strong position near Dubba, 2 miles to the NW of the city. Here he was decisively defeated by the British. When the 92nd Highlanders and 2nd Gurkhas charged their position at the point of the bayonet the Afghans broke and fled, leaving 1,200 casualties behind. British losses were only 40 killed and 228 wounded, extremely small for so decisive a victory.
Result: Ayub Khan's army was irretrievably smashed and this action ended the war. Ayub Khan fled to Herat in the north and Abdur Rahman assumed undisputed power as Amir, retaining friendly relations with successive Indian viceroys. By April 1881 all British forces in Afghanistan had been withdrawn.

KAREN REVOLT (Burma)   August 1948-March 1950
With the object of achieving an autonomous state the Karens revolted and gained control of part of central Burma, and on 14 June 1949 proclaimed their independence with their capital at Toungoo on the Sittang River. Continuing south they

80 SECTION TWO: SOUTHERN ASIA

cut the Mandalay railroad and were within artillery range of Rangoon (qv) itself. A strong counter-offensive mounted by government forces under General Ne Win pushed the rebels back and on 19 March 1950 Toungoo was recaptured, after which the Karen revolt virtually collapsed. However, government forces had still to cope with communist rebels (Red Band and White Band) operating in deep jungle and it was not until 1954 that law and order were re-established in most parts of Burma.

KASHMIR (India)   November 1947-December 1949
In October 1947 the Hindu Raja of Kashmir's decision that his state should join India precipitated an uprising of the predominantly Moslem population who wished to be associated with Pakistan. Indian troops were sent in to Kashmir to quell the disturbances which led to intensive hostilities. In November Pakistani troops crossed the border into Kashmir to assist the Moslem rebels, thus creating a state of undeclared war between Pakistan and India.

On 1 January 1949 United Nations mediators brought about a truce along the fighting line in Kashmir.

On 26 January 1957 India finally annexed Kashmir, but tension did not cease and in 1965 serious attacks by both sides across the cease-fire line took place as part of the larger Indo-Pakistan War (qv).

KHAMBA RESISTANCE MOVEMENT (Tibet)   1950-74
Fought between the Khamba tribesmen of E Tibet under Gompo Tashi Andrustang and Gyalo Thondup, supported by the USA, and the Chinese regular army which occupied Tibet (qv) in October 1950.

The Chinese occupation of the whole of Tibet in October 1950 met with only token resistance, but Gompo Tashi Andrustang, a rich Tibetan businessman, decided to organise the latent resistance of the independent-minded and warlike Khamba tribesmen in E Tibet, south of Chamdo. With Gyalo Thondup, a respected Khamba leader, he contacted the CIA, which arranged for men to be trained in the guerilla school in Taiwan. Serious resistance started on 17 March 1959 when the Dalai Lama fled to India. The CIA arranged for supplies of arms, accompanied by trained guerillas, to be dropped by parachute to the Khamba by aircraft operating from Taiwan. During the Chinese invasion of India (qv) in 1962, one of these aircraft was shot down by the Burmese and crash-landed in Thailand.

The main guerilla base was in the Mustang valley at the base of the 27,000-foot mountains of Annapurna and Dhaulagiri near the Nepalese frontier. By 1969 the Americans started to lose interest in their Khamba allies as their détente with China proceeded. The guerillas were now being trained by the Indian army at Dehra Dun, but their commander in the field was now Baba Yeshi, who feared the Indians as much as the Chinese. The Americans also introduced a new leader, Wangdu, a nephew of Gompo Tashi, who had been trained in Taiwan. A split occurred between Baba Yeshi and Gyalo Thondup. After the Americans deserted the Tibetan guerillas Yeshi was the only Khamba leader who continued to resist.

In August 1974 the Nepalese army moved into the Mustang valley, disarmed most of the guerillas and, after a brief chase, killed Wangdu. Yeshi went into hiding and, by autumn 1974, the Khamba resistance was over.

The Chinese suffered about 3,000 casualties, and the Khamba about 3,000.

KHELAT (Afghanistan)   First Afghan War   13 November 1839
Fought between the Baluchi garrison under Mehrab Khan and the British under Brigadier-General Thomas Willshire ('Tiger Tom'), a veteran of the Peninsular War.
Strength: Baluchis 2,000; British 1,300 with 6 guns.
Aim: A punitive expedition against the Khan for acts of treachery committed during the passage of the main British force from Kandahar to Kabul (qv).
Battle: The fortress was almost as formidable as Ghazni (qv), but after the main gates had collapsed under a bombardment from only 200 yards' range, the British storming columns surged forward and the citadel was taken with the loss of only 37 killed and 107 wounded. Baluchi losses were 400 killed and 2,000 prisoners. Mehrab Khan with eight of his chief ministers and generals died in the fighting.
Result: A new Khan was installed and later the Governor-General gave authority for Khelat to be annexed to the kingdom of Afghanistan.

KHOJAK PASS (Afghanistan)   First Afghan War   28 March 1842
Fought between the British under Brigadier-General Sir Richard England and the Afghans.
Strength: British 3,500; Afghans 5,000.
Aim: The British sought to relieve the garrison at Kandahar (qv), under Major-General William Nott.
Battle: Without waiting for the rest of his brigade, England marched into the pass with 500 men. His force was defeated with a loss of 100 killed and wounded and they were forced to retire to Quetta. On 26 April, however, he again set out, this time with a force of four battalions and a battery of horse artillery. He was met in the Khojak Pass by a support column sent from Kandahar and joined up with Major-General William Nott on 10 May.
Result: Nott's force was augmented in readiness for the eventual march on Kabul.

KHOOSH-AB (Iran)   Persian War   8 February 1857
Fought between the British expeditionary force commanded by General Sir James Outram and the Persians under the Commander-in-Chief, Sooja-ool-Moolk.
Strength: British 4,000 infantry + 400 cavalry + 18 guns; Persians 6,000 infantry + 800 cavalry + 18 guns.
Aim: On arriving at Bushire (qv) on 27 January 1857 Outram found that the Persians had formed an entrenched camp at Borasjoon, 46 miles inland, with the object of launching an attack against the British position.
Battle: On 3 February, leaving some 2,000 troops to garrison Bushire, Outram set out towards Borasjoon. On arriving before the camp the Persian army was seen to be retreating towards the hills to the north, whereupon the British force occupied the Persian camp. As a pursuit was not practicable, Outram decided to return to

Bushire, but at midnight on 7 February the Persians attacked the rearguard - which, however, held steady. On the following morning the Persian army, 6,000 strong, was seen near the walled village of Khoosh-Ab flanked by groups of cavalry. At first light the 3rd Bombay Light Cavalry charged a square formed by the Persian infantry, the 'unbreakable square' they had learnt from the British, and destroyed it, two of their officers being awarded the VC. Then on the advance of the British infantry the entire Persian front broke and fled, leaving 700 dead on the field. British losses were only 19 killed and 64 wounded.
Result: The Persian army was thoroughly disheartened by this defeat, and the Commander-in-Chief, who had fled well in advance of his troops, was suspended. The British returned to Bushire to prepare for the next phase of the campaign.

KINEYRE (Central Pakistan)   Second Sikh War   18 June 1848
Fought between Pathan mercenaries led by Lieutenant Herbert Edwardes aided by Bhawalpuris under their Nawab, Futteh Mohammed Khan, and the Sikhs under Rung Ram.
Strength: Pathans 3,000 + Bhawalpuris 12,000; Sikhs 8,000.
Aim: In April 1848 Mulraj, the Governor of Multan, had murdered 2 British envoys and raised the standard of revolt in SW Punjab. Edwardes was a young District Officer stationed at Dera Fateh Khan on the river Indus watching the Afghan frontier. He immediately levied a force of Pathans and Baluchis and arranged for aid from the Moslem Nawab of Bhawalpur.
Battle: The Bhawalpuris took the offensive, but their attack on the Sikh defences in front of Multan (qv) was repulsed. The arrival of Edwardes with artillery support turned the tables and a second assault on the Sikh entrenchments carried the position, driving the enemy out with a loss of 500. Many more casualties were inflicted during the flight to Multan. The victors lost 300 men.
Result: The Allied force under Edwardes pressed on towards Multan.

KIRKEE (Maharashtra, India)   Third Mahratta (Pindari) War   5 November 1817
Fought between the British under Colonel Burr and the Mahrattas under Baji Rao, Peshwa of Poona.
Strength: British 2,800; Mahrattas 25,000 horse + 10,000 foot.
Aim: Large areas of central India had been devastated by the Pindaris, recruited from the irregular followers of the Mahratta princes who took advantage of the situation to renew the offensive against the British. The Peshwa attacked and burnt the British Residency in Poona.
Battle: The British force of four regiments, three of them Sepoy, moved out of their entrenchments at Kirkee on the outskirts of Poona and were charged by hordes of Mahratta cavalry. The troops stood firm and the attack was repulsed with the loss of some 500 Mahrattas. British losses were 86 killed and wounded.
Result: The British position was consolidated.

KIROVABAD (USSR)   Russo-Persian War   26 September 1826
Fought between the Russians under General Ivan Paskievich and the Persians under Abbas Mirza.
Strength: Russians 15,000; Persians 30,000.
Aim: In the frontier conflict, Nicholas I opened up new aggression in 1825, seeking to push the Persians back from frontier territories they held.
Battle: At Kirovabad (Gandzha), 110 miles south of Tiflis, the two armies met, and, though the Persians were initially successful, the Russians gained a decisive victory, the first of the campaign.
Result: In 1828 the Treaty of Turkmanchai was signed, in which Shah Fath Ali ceded most of Persian Armenia to Russia.

KOREGAON (Maharashtra, India)   Third Mahratta War   1 January 1818
Fought between a small British force of mainly Indian troops under Captain Staunton and the Mahrattas under the Peshwa, Baji Rao.
Strength: British 800; Mahrattas 20,000.
Aim: The Mahrattas aimed to drive the British from their position 17 miles NE of Poona.
Battle: Captain Staunton had occupied the village and organised its defence, but the enemy quickly surrounded the place with their horse and infantry. Though heavily outnumbered the British held their ground all day in an heroic defence and when, after dark, reinforcements under Brigadier-General Smith approached, the Peshwa retired with a loss of 600 men. British losses were 275, including 5 out of 8 officers.
Result: The British were able to continue their offensive against the Mahrattas.

KOTAH (Rajasthan, India)   Indian Mutiny   22-30 March 1858
Fought between the mutineers of the Raja of Kotah and the British under Major-General Sir Frederick Roberts.
Strength: Rebels 5,000; British 1,500.
Aim: The British sought the reduction of the town which was seized by rebels during the Mutiny.
Battle: The Raja held the citadel and he joined the British. After a short bombardment, the city was stormed on 30 March 1858.
Result: The British regained control of the town.

KOTAH-KE-SERAI (Madhya Pradesh, India)   Indian Mutiny   17 June 1858
Fought between a British column under Brigadier-General Michael William Smith and a rebel force led by the Rani of Jhansi.
Strength: British 3,500; Rebels 10,000.
Aim: The Rani had been entrusted with the defence of the east side of Gwalior (qv) and determined on a bold offensive to drive the British back from their position at Kotah-ke-Serai, 5 miles south of Gwalior.
Battle: On arriving at Kotah-ke-Serai on the morning of 17 June, Brigadier-

General Michael William Smith saw the rebels in considerable strength on the heights between his position and Gwalior and decided to attack at once. He first advanced his Horse Artillery, silencing the enemy's guns, and then sent the infantry in to the attack, the final charge of the 95th Regiment putting the rebels to flight. Smith then brought his cavalry forward and launched a squadron of 8th Hussars against some 300 rebel cavalry, putting them to flight. It was during this charge that the Rani, dressed as a cavalry leader, was cut down by a Hussar.

Result: Although there are conflicting stories as to the exact circumstances in which the Rani met her death, and her body was never found, there is no doubt that in the words of Lt-General Sir Hugh Rose himself the rebels had lost 'their bravest and best military leader', a most colourful personality with considerable martial qualities.

KUNCH (Uttar Pradesh, India)   Indian Mutiny   6 May 1858
Fought between the British under Lt-General Sir Hugh Rose and the rebel forces under Tantia Topi.
Strength: British 4,000; Rebels 10,000.
Aim: The rebel intention was to intercept the British force on its way to capture Kalpi (qv). The place chosen for the stand was Kunch, a town 42 miles south of Kalpi with a strong series of defences.
Battle: Hearing from his spies that Tantia Topi had concentrated his troops in the centre of the defensive position in preparation for a frontal attack by the British, Rose decided to turn the rebel flanks. On 6 May, on approaching the town, the British artillery commenced to bombard the rebel defences, driving them into the town itself. The infantry stormed the town and drove the rebels out along the Kalpi road, leaving 600 men killed with 15 guns captured. The casualties in Rose's force amounted to 62 killed and wounded, with 45 casualties from sunstroke.
Result: The British were too exhausted by the heat to keep up the pursuit of the enemy, but the road to Kalpi was now open.

KURDISTAN REBELLION (Iraq)   12 March 1974-6 March 1975
Fought between the Pesh Merga, the military wing of the Democratic Party of Kurdistan (DPK) under the old rebel, Mullah Mustafa Barzani, his son Driss Barzani and Habib Karim, General Secretary of the DPK, and the Iraqi armed forces under Field-Marshal Ahmad Hasan al Bakr, President of the Republic and Supreme Commander of the Armed Forces.
Strength: Pesh Merga 20,000 (maximum); Iraqis 100,000 (23 combat brigades involved) + 10,500 with 218 combat aircraft.

The aim of the DPK was to form an autonomous free state of Kurdistan in Iraq, which had been promised them in the peace agreement signed on 11 March 1970 which had brought the previous civil war to an end.

By March 1974 the Iraqi government's plans for Kurdish autonomy had not been fulfilled. Mustafa Barzani renewed military operations on 12 March, occupying the whole Turkish border - which he closed - and half the Iran frontier. Iraqi forces retaliated by bombing. Marshal Grechko visited Baghdad on 23 March to confirm Russian support. Many atrocities ensued on both sides. The Kurds were supported across the frontier by Iran, which provided them with artillery and anti-tank missiles. As to refugees, 130,000 fled to Iran and 5,000 to Turkey. In April 1974 an Iraqi brigade was ambushed and suffered over 500 casualties, including 230 who surrendered. The Pesh Merga then invaded the plains but were driven back by tanks. In August 1974 the Iraqis launched a two-pronged offensive by two infantry divisions supported by armour and air against Choman, the Kurd capital. The Kurd irregulars suffered badly during the winter of 1974/5.

On 6 March 1975 President Houari Boumedienne of Algeria announced after an OPEC meeting that the Shah of Iran and Mr Sadam Hussein Takriti, Vice-President of the Iraqi Revolutionary Command Council, had signed an agreement to 'eliminate entirely the conflict between two brotherly countries'. The Kurdish revolt promptly collapsed and an amnesty was offered to Kurds returning to Iraq.

Casualties suffered by Iraqi forces were 3,500, by the Pesh Merga 4,000, while there were 3,000 civilian casualties.

LUCKNOW I (Uttar Pradesh, India)   Indian Mutiny   19-26 September 1857
Fought between the British relief force under Brigadier-General Sir Henry Havelock and Major-General Sir James Outram, and the mutineers under the Nana Sahib.
Strength: British 1,700 (garrison) + 3,179 (relief force) + 3 batteries of guns; Rebels 60,000.
Aim: The object was the relief of the British garrison and their families in the Residency compound in Lucknow.
Battle: At the outbreak of the Mutiny rebel Sepoys marched on the Residency at Lucknow, which was put in a state of defence and the garrison and civilians took refuge in it under command of Sir Henry Lawrence, the Chief Commissioner for Oudh. Unfortunately Lawrence was killed on 2 July when a shell burst in his room, and command was then assumed by Brigadier-General John Inglis. A relief force under Havelock and Outram left Cawnpore (qv) on 19 September 1857. Their way was barred by a strong force of rebels at Mangalwar, driven from its position by a cavalry charge commanded personally by Outram, killing 120 and capturing 2 guns. On 23 September the relief column encountered a strong force of 10,000 infantry and 1,500 cavalry entrenched in the vicinity of the Alumbagh (the 'Garden of the World'), 4 miles south of Lucknow. The force was decisively beaten and was soon in full retreat. The British then established a base in the Alumbagh which they were to retain.

On the morning of 25 September the relief force divided into two brigades, crossed the Charbagh bridge and fought its way from strongpoint to strongpoint through the city to reach the Residency which, after five long months, was at last relieved. The cost was heavy and, of the 2,000 men who had marched out of the Alumbagh that morning, 31 officers and 504 men had been killed or wounded, and the garrison had suffered 483 casualties, including Lawrence.
Result: In effect the relief force now pinned down in the Residency had merely

reinforced the garrison, and the siege by the mutineers in possession of the main city continued. Outram therefore had no alternative but to hold on and await relief.

LUCKNOW II (Uttar Pradesh, India)   Indian Mutiny   11-26 November 1857
Fought between the British relief force under General Sir Colin Campbell, the new Commander-in-Chief, and the mutineers under Nana Sahib.
Strength: British 3,400 (relief force) with 8 heavy naval guns; Rebels 60,000.
Aim: The final relief of the garrison at Lucknow and withdrawal from the Residency.
Battle: With very little opposition the force, which included the Naval Brigade under command of Captain William Peel, RN, reached Alumbagh on 12 November. With further reinforcements and including the garrison in the fortress, Campbell now had 5,000 men and 49 guns, and proceeded to divide the force into five brigades for the assault. On the 14th the attack began and on the 16th the Secunderbagh, a high-walled enclosure of strong masonry, was stormed with a loss of 2,000 of the rebels. After reducing a number of other strongpoints in the city, the final relief of the Residency was achieved. On 19 November the evacuation of women and children began. Leaving a force of 4,000 men with 25 guns as a garrison for the Alambagh, under Outram, to await Campbell's return and the resumption of the offensive against the rebels holding Lucknow, Campbell then returned to Cawnpore (qv).
  Unfortunately Havelock, who was already weak and ill, was struck with severe dysentery on the 23rd and was buried at the Alambagh on 26 November.
Result: The garrison and civilians in the Residency had at last been safely evacuated and were brought back to Cawnpore, whilst a strong base for future operations against the rebels in Lucknow had been established.

LUCKNOW III (Uttar Pradesh, India)   Indian Mutiny   9-17 March 1858
Fought between the British under General Sir Colin Campbell and the mutineers under Nana Sahib holding the city of Lucknow.
Strength: British 31,000 with 104 guns and mortars; Rebels 100,000.
Aim: The final capture of Lucknow from the rebels.
Battle: Campbell's force now included 9,000 Gurkhas sent by Jang Bahadur, the ruler of Nepal, and commanded by Brigadier Sir Thomas Harte Franks and also some powerful naval guns from HMS *Shannon.* On 1 March Campbell had reached the Alumbagh, joining up with Outram's garrison, and proceeded to organise the attacking force into four divisions. The enemy had made great efforts to prepare the defences of Lucknow based on the many large buildings in the city whilst the main streets had all been barricaded. On the morning of 2 March the attack began and it was to continue until 21 March, by which time all the strongpoints in the city stubbornly held by the rebels had been captured, including the Residency. British losses were comparatively small: 127 officers and men killed and 595 wounded.

Result: With this action, operations in Lucknow and its environs ended. Unfortunately, however, large numbers of the rebels had been allowed to escape and consequently the campaign in Oudh was protracted for over another year 'by the fugitives . . . occupying forts and other strong positions, from which they were able to offer resistance to our troops until towards the end of May, 1859' (Lord Roberts).

MAHARAJPUR I (Uttar Pradesh, India) Gwalior Campaign   29 December 1843.
Fought between the British under General Sir Hugh Gough and the Mahrattas under Bhagerat Rao Sandhia.
Strength: British 10,000 with 40 guns; Mahrattas 18,000 with 100 guns.
Aim: On the death of the Maharaja Scindhia of Gwalior a dispute arose as to the succession and the Mahratta army took over control, and it was necessary for the British to re-establish their authority.
Battle: Gough, the Commander-in-Chief in India, advanced with an army of 20,000 divided into two wings, one under himself and the other under General Sir John Grey. The Mahrattas held a strong position in Gwalior (qv), but the British were unaware of its exact location until they came under intense artillery fire. The batteries were stormed at the point of the bayonet in the teeth of a hail of grape-shot and the Gwalior infantry were routed with a loss of 3,000 killed and wounded and 56 guns. British losses were 106 killed and 684 wounded.
Result: After this victory and that on the same day at Paniar (qv) Gough marched on to Gwalior, entering the Mahratta capital on 4 January 1844.
    This campaign was remarkable in that the Governor-General, Lord Ellenborough, had accompanied the army together with several ladies, not apparently anticipating serious fighting.

MAHARAJPUR II (Uttar Pradesh, India)   Indian Mutiny   16 July 1857
Fought between the British under Major-General Sir Henry Havelock and the mutineers under Nana Sahib.
Strength: British 1,130 with 8 guns; Rebels 5,000 with 4 guns.
Aim: To dislodge the rebel force under Nana Sahib from its strongly entrenched position across the Grand Trunk Road near the village of Maharajpur, some 7 miles from Cawnpore (qv).
Battle: The Nana's position was extremely strong, well supported by artillery, and a frontal attack by so small a force as Havelock's would have been doomed to failure. He accordingly decided to turn the position by a left flanking movement, which was completely successful, and after a fiercely fought engagement the infantry drove the enemy from their entrenchments in headlong rout.
Result: The first real battle of the Mutiny had been fought and won. The next day, with only 800 European troops left, Havelock entered Cawnpore, to learn that all the women and children held in the Bibighur had been slaughtered by the mutineers before they left the city and their mangled remains flung down a well.

MAHIDPUR (Rajasthan, India)   Third Mahratta War   21 December 1817
Fought between the British under Lt-General Sir Thomas Hislop and the Mahrattas
under Baji Rao II, the Peshwa, and Jaswant Rao Holkar of Indore.
Strength: British 5,500; Mahrattas 30,000 horse + 5,000 foot + 100 guns.
Aim: The Mahrattas were entrenched behind the river Sipra and the British sought
to drive them from their strong position.
Battle: The British crossed the Sipra under heavy fire and the infantry then charged
straight at the enemy's guns. Their onslaught was irresistible and the Mahrattas
fled with a loss of some 3,000 casualties and 76 guns. Enormous quantities of
stores including Holkar's regalia fell into British hands. British losses were 174
killed and 621 wounded.
Result: Holkar's forces were pursued and dispersed and the Peshwa surrendered on
2 June 1818. This marked the end of Mahratta power in central India and the
beginning of the paramountcy of the East India Company.

MAIDAN (Afghanistan)   First Afghan War   14 September 1842
Fought between the British under Major-General William Nott and the Afghans
under Shems-ud-din.
Strength: British 6,000; Afghans 12,000.
Aim: The British sought to drive the Afghans from their position.
Battle: Nott attacked the Afghans who occupied a strong position on the heights
commanding the road to Kabul (qv). The British carried the position and drove
the Afghans off with heavy loss.
Result: The British objective was achieved.

MAIWAND (Afghanistan)   Second Afghan War   27 July 1880
Fought between the British under Brigadier-General G. R. S. Burrowes and Durani
tribesmen under Ayub Khan.
Strength: British 2,500 with 6 guns; Afghans 25,000.
Aim: Ayub Khan, brother of Yakub Khan, the Amir of Afghanistan, rose in revolt
against the British and led a large force of Durani tribesmen towards Kandahar
(qv), which was held by General James Primrose with 4,000 men. Not realising how
dangerous the menace had become Primrose detailed a force of 2,500 under
Brigadier-General Burrowes to deal with the advancing Afghans.
Battle: On 14 July the Afghan contingent provided by the Governor of Kandahar
deserted *en masse* to Ayub Khan and Burrowes's position became serious. On
26 July it was reported that Ayub Khan was at Maiwand, 11 miles from the British
position, intending to cut off the road to Kandahar. Burrowes accordingly set off
at dawn on 27 July to intercept him. He launched an attack across a ravine into
an open plain, but could make no progress against the Afghan artillery and was
forced to retire, with the tribesmen swarming all round him. The 66th Regiment
alone preserved discipline and twice the main body of the regiment made a stand
to cover the retreat. Finally about 100 men stood at bay in an enclosure surrounded
by the whole Afghan army, where they all perished to a man. British losses

amounted to 970 killed and 168 wounded.

Result: During the night the survivors of Burrowes's force struggled back to Kandahar, having suffered a major defeat redeemed only by the heroic display by the 66th Regiment. At the base of the memorial stone representing the 'Maiwand Lion' in Reading, England, is an inscription with these words: 'History does not record a finer example of courage and devotion to duty than that displayed by the Royal Berkshire Regiment.'

MAKHWANPUR (Nepal)   Gurkha War   27 February 1816

Fought between the British under Major-General Sir David Ochterlony and the Gurkhas.

Strength: British 2,000 with 1 gun; Gurkhas 2,000.

Aim: After Almorah (25 April 1815) Gurkha resistance deteriorated and peace negotiations were opened. They were not concluded, however, and in February 1816 Ochterlony marched towards Katmandu with a force of 20,000 men. The village of Makhwanpur formed part of the British advance position in the mountains and was attacked by the Gurkhas.

Battle: The defenders were under heavy pressure until the arrival of reinforcements enabled them to drive off their assailants with considerable loss, at least 500 Gurkhas being killed. British losses were 220.

Result: This was the last engagement of the Gurkha War. Consternation ensued in Katmandu and the peace terms, now considerably stiffer than before, were ratified without further delay. Thus ended the first and last Gurkha War.

MALAKAND I (Pakistan)   Chitral Campaign   3 April 1895

Fought between the British under General Sir Robert Low and the Chitralis

Strength: British 15,000; Chitralis 12,000.

Aims: On news being received that the Mehta (Prince) of Chitral was besieging a British force in the fort of Chitral (qv) in the North-West Frontier, a relief column consisting of the 1st Division under General Low set out from Peshawar (qv). The Chitrali tribesmen held the entrance to the Malakand Pass in strength in an effort to stop the British advance.

Battle: Low launched two infantry battalions against the extreme right of the enemy position, under cover of a concentration of 20 mountain guns. Two more battalions then attacked the main enemy position and the tribesmen broke and fled, pursued by the cavalry. The Chitralis suffered casualties of 2,000 killed or wounded and 10,000 were dispersed. British losses were only 69 men killed or wounded.

Result: The road to the Swat valley was now open and after a number of smaller engagements the forward brigade under Brigadier-General Gatacre reached Chitral on 23 April, only to find that the small relief force from Gilgit of four hundred Pioneers with 2 guns under Colonel Kelly had already arrived.

MALAKAND II (Pakistan)   Malakand Campaign   2 August 1897
Fought between the British Malakand Field Force under General Sir Bindon Blood
and Pathan tribesmen under the Mullah of Swat.
Strength: British 2,000; Pathans 12,000.
Aim: In July 1897 a holy man known as the Mullah of Swat roused the Pathan
tribesmen of the North-West Frontier to attack the forts at Chakdara and Malakand
guarding the route to the British outpost at Chitral (qv). Brigadier-General
Meiklejohn, the Garrison Commander, called for reinforcements and the Malakand
Field Force was formed, comprising two brigades commanded by Meiklejohn and
Brigadier-General Jeffrey respectively and divisional troops under General Sir
Bindon Blood.
Battle: On arrival at Malakand on 1 August Blood found that the Pathans were
strung out in a semicircle to the north of the camp. The key to their position was
a rocky peak high up to the right. An early morning flanking attack to capture
this height on 2 August was brilliantly successful and the enemy were completely
routed with great loss. The route to Chakdara was now open.
Result: After several other engagements the leaders of the tribesmen made a
token surrender. On 12 October Blood led his column out of the valley *en route*
for India. Out of a total strength of 1,200 they had lost 33 officers and 249 men
killed or wounded. The punitive campaign had left the Pathans subdued but
resentful. Young Winston Spencer Churchill, who took part in the campaign both
as an officer and a war correspondent, was mentioned in dispatches and wrote
the financially successful *The Story of the Malakand Field Force.*

MIANI (MEANEE) (Pakistan)   Sind (Scinde) Campaign   17 February 1843
Fought between the British under General Sir Charles Napier and the Baluchis
under the Amirs of Sind.
Strength: British 2,600 with 19 guns; Baluchis 20,000 with 15 guns.
Aim: Owing to the misgovernment of their country by the three Amirs of Sind
(now Pakistan), the Governor-General, Lord Ellenborough, decided on their
deposition and ordered Napier to annex the country.
Battle: The British advanced into Lower Sind with a force which included the
22nd Foot, to find the Baluchi army supported by artillery drawn up in a strong
position in the bed of the Fuleli River near Miani, 6 miles north of Hyderabad (qv).
For four hours the 22nd Foot, drawn up along the edge, exchanged volleys at 10
yards' range with the enemy, who could not get at them. At last, after having lost
2,000 killed and some 3,000 wounded, the Baluchis gave way and fled the field.
British losses were 256 killed and wounded.
Result: The British column resumed its march towards Hyderabad.

MINHLA (Burma)   Third Burma War   17 November 1885
Fought between the British under Major-General Sir Harry Prendergast, a veteran of
the Mutiny, and the Burmese under Thibaw Min.
Strength: British army 9,000 with 67 guns + British navy 600; Burmese 20,000.

Aim: Alarmed by the growing French involvement in Burmese affairs since the accession of King Thibaw in 1878, coupled with his increasingly ineffectual rule, the British government sent an ultimatum on 22 October 1885 which was not accepted.

Battle: On 1 November a British amphibious force moved up the Irrawaddy River from Thayetmo in 55 river steamers and barges manned by the Royal Navy. The only serious opposition was encountered at Minhla which had been strongly fortified by two Italian experts. Prendergast landed several battalions armed with light mountain guns in the dense jungle before the town, which was eventually stormed after stubborn resistance from the Burmese. On 27 November, when the flotilla was within sight of Ava, a message was received from the King agreeing to surrender. The following day troops landed at Mandalay and the short war was over.

Result: Burma was annexed as a province of British India on 1 January 1886. King Thibaw and his wife Queen Supayalat were exiled to Bombay. There followed ten years of guerilla warfare in the forest before Burma could be said to be pacified. Even after 1895 banditry and dacoitry were rife.

MOHAMMERAH (KHORRAMSHAHR) (Iran)   Persian Wars   26 March 1857
Fought between the British expeditionary force under Lt-General Sir James Outram and the Persians under Prince Khanzler Mirza.

Strength: British 4,000; Persians 13,000.

Aim: As the capture of Bushire (qv) and the Battle of Khoosh-Ab (qv) had not forced the Shah to surrender, it was decided to extend operations by the capture of Mohammerah at the head of the Gulf beyond Abadan.

Battle: The small town of Mohammerah lay on the Karun River just above its junction with the Shat-al-Arab, the confluence of the Tigris and Euphrates. The Persians had large batteries protected by enormous earthworks in the area in front of the town, which was further protected by an army of about 13,000. The British force was supported by warships of the Indian navy which, anchoring in line ahead, opened fire on the Persian fortifications, gradually silencing the shore batteries. The troops were then landed from their transports and marched towards the town; but as the British advanced so did the Persians retreat, so that when the invaders reached the camp the enemy had gone, leaving enormous loot behind. Persian losses were 300 men and all their baggage, British casualties no more than 41.

Result: Mohammerah was the last battle of the war. By the terms of the treaty of peace the Shah agreed to withdraw his troops from Herat (qv) and not to interfere in the internal affairs of Afghanistan. This was 'John Company's' last war, for, after the Indian Mutiny which was soon to follow, the East India Company ceased to exist and Queen Victoria became Empress of India.

MOPLAH REBELLION (Kerala, S India)   1921-2
The Moplahs are a undeveloped race of about 1½ million Moslems of Arab origin

who live in the Malabar coastal area in India. They are fanatical Moslems who
settled in the area in the eighth century A D and are difficult to control. Indian
Congress agitation succeeded in fermenting serious trouble in the area and in
August 1921 riots broke out and isolated bodies of police and some European
planters were murdered. There was only a small detachment of the Leinster
Regiment at Calicut available to cope with the situation. This force had to be
reinforced by one British, two Indian and one Gurkha battalions, and another of
Chins. The climatic conditions in dense jungle with heavy rainfall rendered operations particularly arduous and, at times, necessitated the use of artillery as a
psychological noise weapon, but without much effect. Most of the fighting was hand
to hand, in which the Chin-Kachin battalion of the Burma Rifles excelled in jungle
country similar to their own. The province of Kerala formed after Partition has
since maintained its reputation for disorder and defection.

MORAR (Madhya Pradesh, India)   Indian Mutiny   16 June 1858
Fought between the British under Lt-General Sir Hugh Rose and a rebel force
under Tantia Topi.
Strength: British 4,000; Rebels 8,000.
Aim: The rebel force was attempting to bar the way of the British column to
Gwalior (qv).
Battle: On the morning of 16 June cavalry reconnaissance revealed a large body
of rebels drawn up before the town of Morar, not far from Gwalior, with strong
forces of infantry supported by cavalry and artillery. Rose's cavalry was unable
to operate effectively, owing to the ground being pitted with ravines, and the
action developed into a hand-to-hand struggle between the enemy and the British
infantry, in which the 71st Highlanders suffered heavy casualties. Eventually,
however, the rebels were put to flight, hotly pursued by the Light Dragoons.
Result: Rose's column joined that of Brigadier-General Michael William Smith
to the investment of Gwalior.

MUDKI (Punjab, India)   First Sikh War   18 December 1845
Fought between the British under Lt-General Sir Hugh Gough and the Sikhs under
Tej Singh.
Strength: British 12,000 with 42 guns; Sikhs 16,000 with 22 guns.
Aim: On the death of Ranjit Singh power eventually passed to two ministers, Lal
Singh and Tej Singh, who, however, were unable to control the Khalsa, the 60,000-
strong Sikh army trained by French and Italian officers. In late 1845 the Khalsa
forces crossed the Sutlej River into British territory and war became unavoidable.
Battle: The first battle took place at Mudki, where the British after a long march
were surprised by Tej Singh who attacked late in the afternoon. Gough immediately
pushed forward the Horse Artillery with 30 6-pounder guns and the cavalry,
directing the infantry to move forward in support. The battle was hotly contested
and it was only after the capture of the enemy's guns that the infantry were able
to drive the Sikhs from the field. Enemy losses were considerable, including 17
guns, and British casualties were 872 killed and wounded. Amongst the dead were

Generals McGaskill and Sir Robert Sale, the latter being the defender of Jalalabad (qv) in the First Afghan War.
Result: The Sikhs retired to a strong position at Ferozeshah (qv) where, three days later, Gough attacked them again.

MULTAN (W Punjab, Pakistan)   Second Sikh War   July 1848-22 January 1849
Fought between the Sikhs under Dewan Mulraj and the British under Lieutenant Herbert Edwardes and General William Whish.
Strength: Sikhs —?: British 15,000 (under Edwardes) + 16,000 regulars + 17,000 mercenaries (under Whish) + 64 guns.
Aim: The reduction of the garrison of Multan.
Battle: Edwardes besieged the town of Multan in July 1848 and, after an ineffectual bombardment, he was obliged to raise the siege on 22 September. On 27 December the siege was renewed by General Whish. The bombardment was taken up again and the city was stormed and pillaged on 2 January 1849. The garrison retreated into the citadel, which surrendered on 22 January. British losses during the siege were 210 killed and 910 wounded. Prize agents, soldiers and the British seized gold and silver worth £5 million.
Result: The fall of the city enabled Whish to join Lt-General Sir Hugh Gough in the field. The part taken in these operations by young Lieutenant Edwardes was quite remarkable, and Lawrence said of him that 'since the days of Clive no man had done as Edwardes'.

MUSA BAGH (Uttar Pradesh, India)   Indian Mutiny   19 March 1858
Fought between the British under Lt-General Sir James Outram and the mutineers under Huzrat Mahul, Begum of Oudh, and her son.
Strength: British 4,000; Rebels 10,000.
Aim: The mutineers headed by the Begum of Oudh occupied the Musa Bagh, a fortified palace with gardens and courtyards set in open wooded country about 4 miles NW of Lucknow (qv), and it was essential to the British to evict them.
Battle: After some difficulty in breaching a wall leading to the Musa Bagh, Outram opened fire on the rebel position and before long they streamed out and fled. However, Brigadier Campbell, in command of the cavalry, took no action to stop them and the majority escaped.
Result: The countryside around Lucknow was now free of major concentrations of rebels.

NAGA REBELLION (Nagaland, E India)   March 1955-December 1962, 1968-
Fought between the Naga Nationalist Organisation (NNO), later called the Naga National Council (NNC) with the Naga Federal Army (NFA) as the military wing, under A. Z. Phizo (exiled), General Kaito Sema (assassinated) and General Mowu Angami (surrendered 16 March 1969), and their successors, and the Indian army.
  The Nagas originally wanted a separate, independent state. In the peace treaty in 1963 Nagaland was set up as a separate state in the Republic of India. The NNO in 1963 gained twenty-three seats, but this did not give them a majority.

The NNO maintained close contact with China and in 1969 fighting again broke out. On 7 June 1969 a battle was fought at Jotsama, 8 miles from Kohima, in which the Nagas suffered 150 casualties and had 24 prisoners taken, while the Indians lost 29 killed. Fighting continued. A neighbouring tribe, the Kuki, revolted in April 1969, as did the Mizos who invaded Manipur briefly also in 1969. The Nagas attacked the Lumding railway in Assam. Phizo tried to gain sympathy by visiting the USA and then settled in London. In late 1969 Mr Mhiasui assumed leadership of the NNO. The Chinese continued to send instructors and arms to the rebels, which the Indians tried fairly successfully to intercept. In February 1974 Mr Vizol formed a Naga government supporting the Indian constitution, and then visited Phizo in London. The peace offer was rejected. Incidents had increased to about 100 a year, and during 1975 45 members of the security forces and 27 civilians were killed.

The very difficult terrain bordering on a practically unadministered district of Burma, through which supplies are sent from China which wishes to weaken India, now an ally of Russia, postulates that the revolt will simmer on.

NAGPUR (Maharashtra, India)   Third Mahratta War   16 December 1817
Fought between the British under Brigadier-General John Doveton and the Mahrattas under the Bhonsla of Nagpur.
Strength: British 3,500; Mahrattas 7,000 infantry + 14,000 cavalry + 64 guns.
Aim: Following the action at Sitibaldi (qv) Doveton's division moved to reinforce Colonel Hopeton Scot and take Nagpur.
Battle: The Mahratta force attacked the British as they approached Nagpur, but they were repulsed and pursued for 5 miles by the cavalry and had 64 guns captured. British casualties did not exceed 141. The Arab mercenaries - about 3,000 attached to the Mahratta force - withdrew into the citadel, where they offered strong resistance. They surrendered on 24 December following an assault by the Royal Scots and the Berar Infantry, in which the British lost a further 300.
Result: This action completed the destruction of the Nagpur force, resulting in the deposition of the Bhonsla.

NAJAFGARH (Haryana, India)   Indian Mutiny   24 August 1857
Fought between the British under Brigadier-General John Nicholson and a force of mutineers under Mohammed Bukat Khan.
Strength: British 2,500 with 16 guns; Rebels 6,000.
Aim: Nicholson's force with a siege train was approaching Delhi (qv) to reinforce the investing troops, now under Major-General Sir Archdale Wilson, when a large contingent of rebels sallied forth from Delhi to intercept it.
Battle: The rebels had taken up a position extending for 2 miles from the village of Najafgarh but could not withstand the strong attack by Nicholson's cavalry and infantry. They were decisively defeated with the loss of 800 men and all their guns. British losses were 23 men killed and 70 wounded.
Result: Nicholson's column proceeded to join the main besieging force.

NEPALESE CIVIL WAR   March-December 1961
In January 1961 King Mahendra banned all political parties following the dissolution of parliament in the previous month. This takeover by the King was very unpopular and civil disturbances on a large scale ensued. Although quelled by December 1961, unrest continued throughout the country as the King implemented his plans for a democracy with himself at its head, chairing the council of ministers.

PANDJEH (Afghan border)   Russo-Afghan Conflict   30 March 1885
Fought between the Afghans under Amir Abdur Rahman Khan and the Russians under General Komarov.
Strength: Afghans 1,000 infantry + 900 cavalry + 8 guns; Russians 4,000 with 8 guns.
Aim: Following their policy of expansion towards India, the Russians in 1884 annexed the Merv oasis only 130 miles north of Afghanistan, and moved south to occupy the Pandjeh oasis, only 30 miles from the frontier. Abdur Rahman Kahn accordingly moved troops into the disputed area.
Battle: The Afghan force crossed the left bank of the Kushk, where they were attacked by the entire Russian column and forced back across the river. A charge of Cossacks completed their rout and inflicted heavy losses.
Result: The Russians now occupied the Pandjeh oasis. This incident brought Britain and Russia very close to war, but eventually a Joint Commission succeeded in negotiating an agreed frontier line which Abdur Rahman Khan accepted without demur. The Durand Line, which subsequently delineated the whole length of the frontier, still holds today.

PANDU NADI (Uttar Pradesh, India)   Indian Mutiny   15 July 1857
Fought between the British relief column under Brigadier-General Sir Henry Havelock and the mutineers barring the way to Cawnpore (qv).
Strength: British/Sikhs 1,130 with 8 guns; Rebels 2,000.
Aim: To seize the masonry bridge across the Pandu Nadi, a river now swollen by the rains, before the mutineers could blow up the bridge.
Battle: The British made a forced march during the hottest time of the day and came under fire from artillery entrenched near the bridge. However, the bridge was taken undamaged and by nightfall all the troops and baggage wagons were across.
Result: The next day the march to Cawnpore was continued.

PANIAR (Madhya Pradesh, India)   Gwalior Campaign   29 December 1843
Fought between the British under General Sir John Grey and the Mahrattas.
Strength: British 10,000; Mahrattas 12,000 with 40 guns.
Aim: General Grey led the left wing of Lt-General Sir Hugh Gough's army advancing towards Gwalior (qv).
Battle: This action was similar to that at Maharajpur (qv). After a heavy artillery bombardment by the Mahratta batteries, the British stormed the enemy position

and the Mahrattas were totally routed.
Result: Grey's column then proceeded to join Gough's army and march on Gwalior.

PEGU (S Burma)   Second Burma War   18 November 1852
Fought between the British expeditionary force under Lt-General Henry Thomas Godwin and the Burmese.
Strength: British 1,000; Burmese 5,000.
Aim: Concerned at the slow progress of the war, the Governor General, Lord Dalhousie, decided that reinforcements were required to bring the total force up to 2 divisions, totalling 20,000. They arrived in Rangoon (qv) in September 1852.

Battle: After occupying Prome on 9 October, Godwin himself had a force of 1,000 men to take Pegu town, 55 miles north of Rangoon. After landing in thick mist below the town on 21 November the force marched through the jungle to take the place by storm the following day. On 20 December Lord Dalhousie proclaimed the annexation of the whole of Pegu Province. Early the following year an internal revolt in the Burmese capital of Amarapura near Mandalay had dethroned King Pagan Min and set up his half-brother, Mindon Min in his place. The latter tacitly acknowledged the annexation of Pegu but refused to sign a treaty to embody it.
Result: A cease-fire was finally declared on 30 June 1853 and ended what *The Times* declared was 'an inglorious war'.

PEIWAR KOTAL (Afghanistan)   Second Afghan War   2 December 1878
Fought between the British under Major-General Sir Frederick Roberts and the Afghans under Sher Ali Khan.
Strength: British 3,200 with 13 guns; Afghans 18,000 with 18 guns.
Aim: Owing to the increasingly friendly relations between the Afghan Amir, Sher Ali Khan, and the Russians, it was decided to insist on the reception of a British envoy in Kabul (qv). The British mission was refused passage through the Khyber Pass and it was decided to resort to force. Accordingly Roberts, in command of the Kurram Field Force, was instructed to occupy Kabul.
Battle: Robert's column advancing up the Kurram valley found itself opposed by a strong force of Afghans in an almost impregnable position on the Kotal at the head of the valley supported by guns which had been dragged into position on the heights. Leaving Brigadier Cobbe with the main force to engage the enemy front, Roberts himself led a force of 1,300 men with a mountain battery on a right flanking movement during the night of 1 December, completely surprising and dispersing the Afghans the following morning, when they fled, leaving 18 guns behind. British losses were 20 killed and 78 wounded.
Result: The column pressed through the Kurram valley to the crest of the Shutargardan Pass. As thence to Kabul there were no military obstacles, the Amir fled. He died the following year, to be succeeded by his son Yakub Khan. All British demands were then conceded, including the acceptance of a British envoy in Kabul.

PESHAWAR (North-West Frontier Province, Pakistan)   1930
In 1930 agitation among the Pathans together with the activities of the 'Redshirts',
a Moslem organisation led by one Abdul Gaffar, caused serious disaffection in the
city of Peshawar and on 23 and 24 April rioting broke out. The police were
insufficient to maintain order and the hesitation of the authorities to use force
had the effect of encouraging hill tribesmen to attack border posts. The most
serious effect was seen in Tirah, where 5,000 Afridis concentrated with the intention of attacking Peshawar, and operations against them lasted for some months.
On 16 August martial law was proclaimed throughout the whole Peshawar district.
Continuous military pressure led to discouragement among the tribesmen, and the
whole affair subsided as quickly as it had begun.

RAMNAGAR (Pakistan)   Second Sikh War   22 November 1848
Fought between the British under Lt-General Sir Hugh Gough and the Sikhs under
Sher Singh.
Strength: British 12,000; Sikhs 35,000.
Aim: The British sought to force a crossing at the Chenab River. Gough was
advancing from Lahore into W Punjab where the Sikhs had tried to overthrow the
regency of Sir Henry Lawrence, imposed after the First Sikh War.
Battle: Gough met the Sikhs who were deployed opposite Ramnagar and, on
trying to force a crossing of the river, was repulsed by heavy artillery fire and
fierce resistance. The attempt was made by a brigade group under Brigadier-General
Sir Colin Campbell with a force of cavalry under Brigadier-General Cureton who
was killed in the action. British losses were heavy.
Result: Gough withdrew to wait for reinforcements from General William S.
Whish besieging Multan (qv), but when that siege dragged on Gough decided to
advance once more.

RANGOON (Burma)   Second Burma War   12-14 April 1852
Fought between the British expeditionary force under Lt-General Henry Thomas
Godwin, and the Burmese.
Strength: British 6,000; Burmese 20,000 with 90 guns.
Aim: Continued friction between British interests and the Burmese government,
caused by the latter's infractions of the 1826 Treaty of Yandaboo, led to the
launching of an amphibious expedition escorted by a fleet of men-of-war commanded by Admiral Austen.
Battle: Godwin commenced the campaign by occupying Martaban at the mouth of
the Salween River on 5 April, before proceeding to attack the new city of Rangoon,
which included the heavily fortified Shwedagon Pagoda. After a prolonged bombardment both from the naval vessels in the river and from batteries taken ashore,
the storming party, including the 18th Foot (Royal Irish Regiment) and the 80th
Foot (South Staffs) assaulted the Pagoda. After heavy fighting the enemy were

driven out at the point of the bayonet and fled in all directions. In the three days' fighting from 12 to 14 April, the British lost 17 killed and 132 wounded.
Result: Godwin proceeded to take Bassein on the Irrawaddy Delta, after which the campaign was interrupted by the monsoon season which lasted until October.

RESHIRE (Iran)   Persian War   7 December 1856
Fought between the British expeditionary force under Major-General Foster Stalker and the Persian garrison.
Strength: British 5,670; Persians 5,000.
Aim: When the British expeditionary force landed near Bushire (qv) on 5 December 1856, they found the Persians holding a redoubt at Reshire in an old Dutch fort, which it was necessary to take before they advanced on Bushire itself.
Battle: The walls of the fort were composed of heaped-up sand which rendered the British artillery fire harmless. The fort was then stormed by the 64th Regiment and two Bombay Infantry battalions and, after a desperate fight inside, the Persians poured out of the fort and fled to the hills. British losses were 9 killed, including Brigadier Stopford of the 64th, and 31 wounded.
Result: The approach to Bushire was now unopposed.

SABRAON (SOBROAN) (E Punjab, India)   First Sikh War   10 February 1846
Fought between the British under Lt-General Sir Hugh Gough and the Sikhs under Runjur Singh.
Strength: British 20,000; Sikhs 30,000 with 70 guns.
Aim: After Aliwal (qv) the Sikhs fell back on Sabraon, their last position on the British side of the Sutlej River, and Gough decided to attack with his main army.
Battle: The Sikhs occupied a strongly entrenched position in a bend in the river, but made the mistake of standing with the river immediately in their rear. On 9 February Gough massed 3 batteries of heavy guns facing the enemy's right front and on the following morning hostilities commenced with thunderous cannonades. from both sides. Gough then launched feigned attacks on the Sikh right and centre and pushed the left back. After a desperate attack the British infantry, suffering heavy losses, surged into the entrenchments. Gough then ordered the cavalry under General Sir Joseph Thackwell to sweep through the enemy's entire camp, the 3rd Light Dragoons particularly distinguishing themselves. The bridge of boats across the river was partially destroyed by gunfire and large numbers of the enemy were driven into the river and drowned trying to escape. Sikh losses were 8,000 and 67 guns were captured, whilst British losses were 320 killed and 2,063 wounded.
Result: This was the final battle of the First Sikh War and with it the power of the Sikh army, the Khalsa, appeared to be completely broken. The Governor-General, Sir Henry Hardinge, described the victory as 'one of the most daring ever achieved'. The Punjab now became a British Protectorate and Colonel Henry Lawrence was appointed Resident.

SADULAPUR (W Punjab, Pakistan)   Second Sikh War   3 December 1848
Fought between the British under Lt-General Sir Hugh Gough and the Sikhs under
Sher Singh.
Strength: British 7,000 with 32 guns; Sikhs 20,000.
Aim: The British sought to push the Sikhs back to enable them to advance into
W Punjab.
Battle: After being repulsed at Ramnagar (qv), Gough dispatched a force under
General Sir Joseph Thackwell to cross the Chenab River and turn the Sikh left.
The action which followed was not decisive, but the Sikhs retired and Gough
claimed it as a British victory. The Sikhs took up a position on the Jhelum River
at Chilianwala (qv) which was stronger than the position they had previously
occupied.
Result: Gough did not consider his force sufficient to attack the Sikhs until he
had received reinforcements from General William Whish besieging Multan (qv).

SAUGOR (Madhya Pradesh, India)   Indian Mutiny   3 February 1858
Fought between the British under Lt-General Sir Hugh Rose and the rebels under
the Rajah of Bahpur.
Strength: British 4,500; Rebels 8,000.
Aim: On assuming command of the Central India Field Force, Rose had received
disquieting news regarding the 170 European women and children sheltering in the
fort at Saugor, about 200 miles south of Cawnpore (qv), with a small garrison of
68 European artillerymen, and determined to relieve the place.
Battle: About 30 miles from Saugor stood the town of Rathgarh dominated by a
strong fort, which it was necessary to secure. The walls were breached on 28
January, when the rebels fled. After defeating a further concentration of mutineers
at Barodia, 15 miles from Saugor, Rose reached the town on 3 February and
relieved the garrison.
Result: After clearing the countryside of a number of rebel groups, Rose made
Saugor his base in preparation for the next stage in his campaign, the advance on
Jhansi (qv), 12 miles north.

SHERPUR (Afghanistan)   Second Afghan War   23 December 1879
Fought between the British garrison of Kabul under Lt-General Sir Frederick
Roberts and the Afghans under Mohammed Jan.
Strength: British 6,500; Afghans 100,000.
Aim: When the British expeditionary force had occupied Kabul (qv) following the
assassination of the British Envoy, Sir Louis Cavagnari, they were assailed on all
sides by hordes of hostile tribesmen. After a number of engagements in the
surrounding hills, Roberts decided to concentrate his force within the safety of
the cantonments at Sherpur just outside the city. The Afghans then reoccupied
Kabul and prepared to attack.
Battle: Just before dawn on 23 December vast hordes of Afghans advanced with
scaling ladders, attempting to penetrate the cantonment defences. Fortunately for

the British, Roberts was in possession of Mohammed Jan's plan for the assault, brought in by a spy, and was able to take effective counter-measures. Attack after attack was beaten off and by 10 am the Afghans had had enough and were streaming back in disorder. Roberts then launched the cavalry to cut their line of retreat. It was estimated that 3,000 Afghans were left dead on the field.

Result: Arrangements were now made for the return of Abdur Rahman Khan to Kabul, where he was proclaimed Amir on 30 July 1880.

SHOLAPUR (Maharashtra, India)   Third Mahratta War   10 May 1818
Fought between a body of British cavalry under Brigadier-General Theophilus Pritzler and the remnant of the Peshwa's army.
Strength: British 4,000; Mahrattas 7,500 with 90 guns.
Aim: The British sought to crush the last remnants of the Peshwa's forces.
Battle: The Mahratta chief, Gompat Rao, had taken up a position under the walls of Sholapur with a force comprising 850 horse, 1,200 Arab mercenaries and 4,300 other infantry supported by 14 pieces of artillery. Inside the fortress was a garrison of 1,000. The British cavalry mounted a strong attack on the Peshwa's forces and completely dispersed them, with more than 1,000 Mahratta dead left on the field. On 15 May Sholapur surrendered with 37 guns and 39 field pieces. British losses were 102 killed and wounded.
Result: All further opposition to the British was crushed.

SIND (Pakistan)   Hur Revolt   1942-3
While major disturbances were taking place in 1942 throughout India following the arrest of the Congress leaders, including Gandhi and Nehru, serious troubles were also arising in other parts of the subcontinent. Amongst these was the menacing situation created by the Farqi Hurs in Upper Sind. These people were of Baluchi extraction and belonged to a fanatical Moslem sect, followers of the Pir Pagaro, a religious leader who had a large shrine at Pir-Jo-Goth (literally, the House of the Pir) in north Sind. Their activities had no connection whatever with the Moslem League or with Congress. As early as March 1942 it became clear that the position in Upper Sind was becoming increasingly unstable, the Hurs committing murder and robbery on a considerable scale. They attacked their victims with small hatchets and created a widespread reign of terror which succeeded in demoralising the police. At the height of their activities their toll of murders reached as many as 600 a month.

On 16 May a large band of Hurs wrecked the Karachi-Lahore mail train in Upper Sind and an Indian infantry battalion was ordered up to protect the line. Shortly afterwards martial law was declared over a wide area and three Indian infantry battalions and a flight of Lysander (reconnaissance) aircraft were placed under command of Major-General Richardson to assist police action. For the next six months punitive columns operated against the Hur gangs in the desert areas to the north and in the Makki Dand swamps in the south, until finally the Hurs were crushed and scattered.

Early in the operations the leader, Pir Pagaro, had been captured. He was a ruthless murderer and it is possible he was subsidised by the Germans to foment trouble, but there is no evidence of any Communist influence. He was said to have amassed a fortune of some £200,000, although it was never found. After considerable delay he was eventually brought to trial, convicted and sentenced to death. An appeal to the Viceroy for clemency was rejected and in due course, on 17 March 1943, he was hanged. In order to avoid the possibility of his being regarded as a religious martyr and his burial place becoming a shrine, his body was taken in a Royal Indian Navy warship and buried in an unmarked grave in the uninhabited island of Astola, off the Makran coast.

SITIBALDI (Maharashtra, India)   Third Mahratta War   26 November 1817
Fought between the British garrison under Colonel Hopeton Scot and the Mahrattas under the Bhonsla of Nagpur.
Strength: British 1,400; Mahrattas 18,000 with 36 guns.
Aim: Seeing the renewed conflict between the British and Baji Rao, the Bhonsla of Nagpur decided to attack the Europeans also.
Battle: Scot, who was in command of the troops at Nagpur (qv) on the outbreak of hostilities, withdrew his force to the fortified hill of Sitibaldi outside the town. The British position was naturally strong and, although the Nagpur forces attacked repeatedly, none of their drives was successful. Despite this, the enormous disparity in numbers placed the British in considerable difficulty. The Bengal Cavalry under Captain Fitzgerald took every opportunity to harass the enemy and finally, charging some Nagpur infantry recoiling after another unsuccessful assault on the British position, turned their retreat into a rout, ending the eighteen-hour battle. The British losses were 106 killed and 244 wounded.
Result: The Bhonsla was deposed although his dynasty continued to reign until the Mutiny.

SUDDASAIN (W Punjab, Pakistan)   Second Sikh War   1 July 1848
Fought between a force of Bhawalpuris and Pathan mercenaries under Lieutenant Herbert Edwardes, and the Sikhs under the Dewan Mulraj.
Strength: Mercenaries 18,000; Sikhs 12,000.
Aim: The Sikhs sought to repel the mercenaries' advance on Multan (qv).
Battle: The Sikhs attacked the mercenaries but, largely owing to Edwardes's superior artillery, they were beaten back and defeated.
Result: The Sikhs were forced to retreat into the town of Multan, where they were to be besieged for the next six months.

TALNEER (Maharashtra, India)   Third Mahratta War   17 February 1818
Fought between the garrison of Arabs and the British under Lt-General Sir Thomas Hislop.
Strength: Arabs 300; British 5,500.
Aim: The occupation of the fortress of Talneer.

Battle: Under the treaty signed on 6 January, Jaswant Rao Holkar surrendered the fortress at Talneer to the British. However, when General Hislop arrived to take possession, the Commandant refused to hand it over and fired on the British forces. Fire was returned and on the afternoon of the same day the place surrendered. Owing to a misunderstanding, the entire garrison was drawn up by one of the gates and, when 2 officers and some Sepoys went forward to take the surrender, they were cut down. The garrison was then taken with no quarter given, every man being killed and the Commandant hanged.

Result: The British gained possession of the fortress in accordance with the terms of the peace treaty.

TIBET   Younghusband Expedition   1903-4

In 1902 there were persistent rumours of a secret treaty between Russia and Tibet, connived at by the Chinese government. The Viceroy of India, Lord Curzon, was concerned that a hostile Tibet could upset the peace of northern India and cause unease along the Himalayan frontier. It was accordingly decided to send a mission to Lhasa headed by Colonel Francis Younghusband to force the Dalai Lama to accept a British representative.

The mission duly arrived at Gyantse but was not met by the expected Tibetan representatives. Before proceeding further, arrangements were made for a strong military escort and some 3,000 men and 7,000 followers under Brigadier-General J. MacDonald were transported across the Himalayas to Tuna, 50 miles inside Tibet. When in January 1904 the expedition was about to advance it was confronted by a large Tibetan force. Younghusband warned the Tibetan general he would not fire unless attacked. However, a shot was fired on the Tibetan side followed by a fierce attack mainly with swords. The British then opened fire and within ten minutes the affair was over with at least 300 Tibetans dead and as many wounded.

After only one more serious engagement, when a further 300 Tibetans were killed, opposition evaporated, and the mission reached Lhasa. After two months' deliberations, an Anglo-Tibetan convention was signed, including settlement of frontier problems, the establishment of trading arrangements and the payment of an indemnity.

TIBET   Chinese Invasion   October 1950-April 1959

After the victory of the Communist forces in China under Mao Tse-tung in September 1949 Chinese propaganda, claiming their intention to 'liberate' the Tibetan people, was intensified and they stated that the new Panchen Lama supported their aims.

Despite appeals by the Tibetan government to world opinion for assistance, the Chinese, claiming ancient rights of suzerainty, launched a large-scale attack on 7 October 1950 in the Chamdo region in E Tibet. The untrained and inexperienced Tibetan troops were quickly overwhelmed and resistance was soon virtually at an end. At the same time a force of Chinese troops from Khotan crossed the mountains and entered NW Tibet, taking the undefended western part of the country completely by surprise.

In November 1950 the Tibetans sent two appeals to the United Nations for help but none was forthcoming. By the end of that month Chinese forces were strongly established and in April 1951 a Tibetan delegation from Lhasa began negotiations in Peking, which ended in the signing of a Sino-Tibetan Convention agreeing to the 'peaceful liberation of Tibet'. The Dalai Lama was permitted to remain as a figurehead in Lhasa.

During the next few years widespread revolts continued despite fierce Communist repressive measures, and by 1954 most of the 40,000 rebels had been killed or executed.

A further rebellion in 1959 was suppressed by the Chinese and the Dalai Lama then fled to India, where he was granted political asylum in April that year.

The Khamba resistance movement (qv) in Eastern Tibet continued until 1973 when, deserted by the American CIA and the Nepalese, they gave up. But incipient discontent throughout the country continues in spite of, or because of, large-scale settlement of Chinese throughout the area. But benefits of the occupation include the construction of roads to China and India, vast irrigation schemes and, in general, more technology which is levering the Tibetans away from a priest-ridden society and into the modern world.

UNAO (Uttar Pradesh, India)   Indian Mutiny   29 July 1857
Fought between the British under Brigadier-General Sir Henry Havelock and the mutineers.
Strength: British 1,500 with 10 guns; Rebels 6,000 with 20 guns.
Aim: After relieving Cawnpore (qv) Havelock decided to leave a garrison of 300, which was all he could spare, and press on to Lucknow (qv).
Battle: At Unao, a village 8 miles NE of Cawnpore, Havelock encountered a strong rebel force occupying a position with its flanks protected by swamps. The only alternative was a frontal attack, which was carried out by the 78th Foot and the Fusiliers, whilst the 64th Foot stormed the village itself, capturing all the enemy's guns. A further large body of mutineers with artillery then approached the village, but they were scattered by heavy artillery and small-arms fire, leaving some 300 dead and 15 guns.
Result: After a short pursuit, Havelock's force continued its advance towards Lucknow.

WAZIRISTAN CAMPAIGN   November 1919-March 1920
After the conclusion of the Third Afghan War a number of North-West Frontier posts in isolated positions in Waziristan were evacuated and this led to the desertion of over 1,000 of the South Waziristan Militia. The Mahsuds and Wazirs thereupon openly defied the government and began raiding on a large scale. In November 1919 a force of 8,500 troops entered Waziristan by the Takki Zam valley. The two infantry brigades contained no British units and some of the battalions had no previous experience of Frontier fighting, and their initial attacks on Mahsud

strongpoints such as Mandanna and Janbola were repulsed with heavy losses. Reinforcements had to be brought up until eventually the punitive expedition numbered 30,000 under the command of Major-General S. H. Climo. After a number of fiercely contested engagements, on 6 March 1920 the column reached the Mahsud capital, Kaniguram. This campaign has been described as the most desperate and costly in the history of the Frontier. When peace was restored British losses had totalled 2,286.

After this campaign it was decided not to withdraw but to occupy central Waziristan. In January 1923 a fortified camp was constructed at Razmak large enough to hold 10,000 men, and new ring roads were constructed, linking up other forts such as Wana in the region. Although tribal warfare still continued from time to time the situation became more under control.

SECTION THREE

AFRICA, ARABIA AND MADAGASCAR

See Map Section, nos 8, 10 and 11

ABU HAMED (Sudan)   British Sudan Campaigns   7 August 1897
A Sudanese brigade with 2 guns of the Royal Artillery, commanded by Major-General Sir Archibald Hunter, stormed the Dervish entrenchments outside Abu Hamed. The Mahdists were driven out and the garrison in the town retreated with heavy losses including their commander, Mohammed Zain, who was captured. The Egyptians lost 80 men, including 4 British officers.

ABU KLEA (Sudan)   British Sudan Campaigns   17 January 1885
Fought between the British under Brigadier-General Sir Herbert Stewart and the Mahdists.
Strength: British 1,800; Mahdists 10,000.
Aim: In order to relieve Gordon who was besieged in Khartoum (qv), a relief column under General Sir Garnet Wolseley set out from Cairo in October 1884.
Battle: The force marched up the Nile to N Sudan where Wolseley ordered a Camel Corps under Stewart to march across country instead of following the river which made a wide meander to the east. At a caravan stop, 63 miles SW of Ed Damer, Stewart encountered a force of Mahdists. The Sudanese were repulsed in a fierce hand-to-hand battle in which they lost more than 1,000 killed. Anglo-Egyptian casualties were 168, including Stewart himself, who was mortally wounded.
Result: The corps fought its way back to the Nile and on 24 January began moving up-river to Khartoum under Lord Charles Beresford. They arrived on 28 January, two days after the town had been stormed by the Mahdists.

ABU KRU (Sudan)   British Sudan Campagins   19 January 1885
The British, 1,200 strong, formed in a square, were attacked near the Nile by a huge host of Mahdists. Still in formation, the British moved towards the river, successfully repelling all attacks until they reached it. British losses were 121.
    The action is also known as the Battle of Gubat.

ABYSSINIA (ETHIOPIA)   1805-87
In 1805 Abyssinia was visited by a British mission. In 1830 Protestant missionaries, notably Dr Ludwig Krapf, the discoverer of Mount Kenya, and Bishop Samuel Gobat, were received at the court.
    In 1838 the missionaries were obliged to leave. In the middle of the nineteenth century Theodore Kassa, an adventurer of great ability, acquired power in Amhara, proclaimed himself Emperor Theodore III and conquered Shoa. For a time the great Theodore ruled wisely, but owing to supposed slights received from the British government he turned against the British consul and other British officials and imprisoned them in chains. This action necessitated the sending of an expedition in 1868, under General Sir Robert Napier (later Field-Marshal Lord Napier of Magdala). Magdala was attacked and captured by Napier on 13 April 1868, whereupon Theodore, deserted by his followers, killed himself.
    After Theodore's death, Prince Kassai, the chief of Tigr'é, became Negus, and

in 1872 was crowned as Johannes II (John of Tigr'é), while Menelek, the son of the former ruler of Shoa, became chief of that province. War with the Khalifa occurred in 1887, when Gondar was sacked and burned down.

ABYSSINIA (ETHIOPIA)   Italian Invasion   1935-6

On 3 October 1935 the Italians invaded Ethiopia without a declaration of war. Supported by artillery and air cover, they captured Adowa on 6 October. On 7 October the League of Nations declared Italy to be an aggressor and debated the imposition of sanctions. On 8 November the Italians took the fortress of Makalle. Although the League did impose sanctions (18 November), it proved incapable of applying them and the Italians were able to operate unhindered. Even so, their initial offensive under General Emilio de Bono lost impetus. Between December 1935 and April 1936 there was a lull in field activities while Field-Marshal Pietro Badoglio reorganised the expeditionary force. During April and May the Italians used bombs and poison gas against a terrified enemy whose army was medieval, and Badoglio moved forward against only slight opposition. On 5 May Addis Ababa was taken and Emperor Haile Selassie fled. Ethiopian resistance crumbled.

On 9 May Italy annexed Ethiopia which was added to Eritrea and Italian Somaliland, to form Italian East Africa. The King of Italy, Victor Emmanuel III, became Emperor of Ethiopia. Germany, Austria and Hungary recognised the conquest at once, while France and Britain did so a year later. During the Second World War the British drove the Italians out of Ethiopia and restored Haile Selassie to his throne.

ABYSSINIAN WAR WITH THE MAHDI   1884

Fought between the Abyssinians and the Mahdists.

King John II sent troops to help the British withdrawal from Gallabat and Kassal.

ACCRA I (Ghana, W Africa)   First Ashanti War   1824

Fought between the Ashantis and the British under General Sir Charles McCarthy.

Strength: Ashantis 10,000; British 1,000.

Aim: The British sought to crush the uprising by the Ashantis who were attempting to overrun the coastal tribes.

Battle: The Ashantis surrounded and routed the British. McCarthy was killed.

Result: The British sent for further reinforcements to crush the uprising.

ACCRA II (Ghana, W Africa)   First Ashanti War   1825

Fought between the Ashantis and the British.

Strength: Ashantis 15,000; British 400 + 4,600 native auxiliaries.

Aim: The British sought to force the retreat of the Ashantis who were moving against Cape Coast Castle.

Battle: The Ashantis were defeated.

Result: Kumasi (qv) was captured in 1874 and the country was annexed in 1901.

ACRE IV (Israel)   Egyptian Revolt against the Turks   3 November 1840
The growing power of Egypt caused concern in Europe. In 1839 the Egyptians
had destroyed the Turkish forces at Nizib (qv) and captured the Turkish fleet at
Alexandria. The Turkish Sultan Mahmud II had died, leaving his sixteen-year-old
son, Abdul-Medjid I, powerless against the might of Egypt in Syria. Britain, Austria,
Prussia and Russia now intervened, though opposed by France.

Admiral Stopford took an Allied fleet (British and Turkish) into the E Mediterranean and on 3 November the town of Acre (then in Syria) was bombarded.
When the defences had been reduced the town was stormed, while the Egyptian
forces under General Ibrahim Pasha, son of Mohammed Ali, evacuated first Acre
itself and then the whole of Syria.

In 1841 Mohammed Ali agreed to return the Turkish fleet and to abandon all
claim to Syria in exchange for hereditary sovereignty in Egypt.

ADEN (Yemen)   1839
Fought between the Arabs and the British under Major T. M. Bailie.

With the advent of steam, the port of Aden grew in importance as a coaling
station. Commodore Haines of the Indian Marine was sent to negotiate with the
Arab ruler of Aden for the use of the port, and the British gained virtual control
of the town in 1835 in return for a cash subsidy and the promise of protection.

By 1838, however, disputes had arisen necessitating the presence of a garrison
in the town. A small force was sent, since violence was not anticipated. Part of the
1st Bombay Fusiliers and the 24th Bombay Native Infantry were to make up the
garrison while the Royal Navy vessels *Volage* and *Cruiser* stood by, along with a
squadron from the Indian Marine. The Arabs refused to allow the troops to land
and also declined to supply them with food or water. The fortifications of the
town were then shelled and, under covering fire, the troops landed and occupied
the town, which had been abandoned. The Arabs had taken refuge in one of the
forts where they flew a white flag. After a while they surrendered. An incident
during the parley caused the loss of 16 men killed or wounded, the only casualties
apart from a wounded midshipman.

During November another attempt was made by the Arabs to take the town, but
this and one other attack the following May were repulsed.

ADOWA (Ethiopia)   Italian-Ethiopian War   1 March 1896
Fought between the Italians under General Oreste Baratieri and the Ethiopians
under King of Kings, Menelek II.
Strength: Italians 20,000; Ethiopians 80,000.
Aim: The Italian protectorate over Ethiopia (Abyssinia) was overthrown by
Menelek, whereupon King Umberto I of Italy sent troops there. The Italians
suffered setbacks and the Italian Premier, Francesco Crispi, ordered Baratieri to
fight and win a major battle in order to restore prestige.
Battle: Eighty miles south of Asmara, Eritrea (an Italian colony), the Italians
encountered a large force of Ethiopians which virtually wiped out their army in

massed attacks. The dead were more fortunate than the prisoners. It was one of the worst defeats ever suffered by a European power.

Result: Baratieri resigned from the army and Crispi's cabinet fell. Italy sued for peace and signed the Treaty of Addis Ababa on 26 October, recognising the independence of Ethiopia.

Benito Mussolini's invasion of Ethiopia in 1935 was in part an act of vengeance for Adowa.

AGORDAT (Sudan)   Italian Sudanese Campaign   21 December 1893
Fought between the Mahdists under Ahmed Ali and the Italians under General Arimondi.

Strength: Italians 2,200; Mahdists 11,500.

Battle: The Mahdists invaded Italian territory and were routed with the loss of about 3,000 men. Italian losses were 13 as well as 225 tribesmen killed and wounded.

ALEXANDRIA IV (Egypt)   Egyptian Revolt   11-12 July 1882
Fought between the British and French under Admiral Frederick Beauchamp Seymour, and the Egyptians under Colonel Arabi Pasha.

Strength: British and French 8 warships + 5 gunboats; Egyptians – ?.

When in 1875 Benjamin Disraeli bought the Suez Canal shares held by the Egyptian Khedive Ismail Pasha, Britain joined with France in the control of the canal and administration of the finances of Egypt. Six years later, Arabi Pasha led a revolt against the European powers.

In order to guard the western entrance to the Nile River, Arabi Pasha began to construct forts at Alexandria. When asked by the British government to cease work, he refused and it was decided to shell the port. France refused to co-operate. On 11 July Seymour's fleet opened fire on the forts, continuing to bombard them until the evening of 12 July, by which time they were destroyed. The garrison evacuated the city, which was occupied by a landing party.

Result: The Suez Canal remained secure in European hands.

ALGIERS (EL DZEJAIR) II (Algeria)   1816
Fought between the British and Dutch under Admiral Lord Exmouth and Admiral van Capellan, and the Algerian garrison under the Bey of Algiers.

Strength: British 19 warships + Dutch 6 warships; Algerians 500 guns.

Aim: The British and Dutch sought the abolition of Christian slavery in the dominions of the Bey of Algiers.

Battle: After an eight-hour bombardment in which the forts and a large part of the city were destroyed, the Bey gave way and acceded to the demands. Allied losses were 885 killed and wounded. Algerian losses were over 6,000 including civilians.

Result: The Allied objective was achieved.

AMATOLA MOUNTAIN (Griqualand East, S Africa)   Kaffir Wars   1846
Fought between the Kaffirs under Sandili and the British and Cape troops under
Colonels Campbell and Somerset.
Aim: The Kaffirs mainly of the Xosi tribe sought to prevent further British and
Boer colonial encroachment.
Battle: The British advanced about 3,000 strong against about 6,000 Kaffirs.
Sandili was defeated, but he broke back and attacked the baggage train of the
British and captured it, a success that forced them to retire.
Result: Neither side fully achieved their objective.

AMOAFUL (Ghana, W Africa)   Second Ashanti War   31 January 1874
Fought between the British under General Sir Garnet Wolseley and the Ashantis.
Aim: The British sought to crush the Ashanti uprising.
Battle: The British advanced with 5,000 men and 12 guns against about 20,000
Fanti tribesmen. After a hotly contested fight, the Ashantis were defeated at a
cost to the British of 16 officers and 174 men killed and wounded, particularly
heavy losses being suffered by the 42nd Regiment which led the attack (9 officers
and 105 men).
Result: The British went on to storm Kumasi (qv).

ANGOLAN CIVIL WAR (SW Africa)   1975-
Fought between the MPLA (Popular Movement for the Liberation of Angola) led
by Agostinho Neto and supported by Russian advisers and 12,000 Cubans with
tanks, aircraft and rocket launchers; and the ill-armed FNLA (National Front for
the Liberation of Angola) led by Holden Roberto supported by Zaire and about 300
(mainly British) mercenaries; and UNITA (National Union for the Total Independence of Angola) under Dr Jonas Savimbi, initially supported by a S African
motorised brigade.
    Beset by troubles at home, the Portuguese revolutionary government, failing to
get agreement amongst the insurgent factions to whom they could hand over,
evacuated all its troops and left Angola on 11 November 1975. But before the
Portuguese moved out, the struggle for power had started in earnest. UNITA, led
by southern protestants, quickly gained ascendancy in the heavily populated
Benguela plateau, obtaining support from underprivileged white settlers and
mesticos as well as from the southern tribes. Savimbi asked for help from the
S Africans, and a brigade about 1,500 strong which had moved into S Angola to
protect the Cunene River Irrigation Project and to help prevent the transfrontier
Ovambos from spreading their incipient revolt further, moved up the coast to
within 100 miles of the capital, Luanda. The S Africans thought that they were
acting in conjunction with the USA through their CIA representatives in Zaire who
were supporting the FNLA forces in the north.
    The FNLA also advanced, to within 50 miles of Luanda, and the situation
looked black for the Russian-supported MPLA. Then Russian sources revealed to
the American public the extent of the US commitment, supported by the usual

propaganda. The American public panicked and pressure was brought to bear on US President Ford to disown the actions of the CIA in Zaire and Angola. This was done. The morale of the FNLA collapsed in spite of some most courageous actions by mostly British mercenaries who tackled Cuban-manned Russian T 34 and T 54 tanks almost bare-handed. By April 1975 Russian advisers and a Cuban division had started to pour into Luanda. Luanda was saved for communism. The FNLA were, within the year, defeated, dispersed and the remnants driven over the Zaire border.

The S Africans, who had done very well militarily, immediately came under criticism from the world press and in the United Nations, once the US had defected from their obligations. Under this stress S Africa withdrew her forces to a 50 mile *cordon sanitaire* in front of the SW Africa (Namibia) border. UNITA could not stand alone and Savimbi decided to revert to a pattern of guerilla warfare. The Cuban armoured units, with the MPLA in attendance, rapidly overran all the towns of S Angola.

By 1 March 1976 the Russian-backed Cubans, now numbering about 20,000 and supported by MiG fighters and an immense amount of armour and supplies, occupied, with the MPLA, 90 per cent of the territory, especially along the Portuguese newly built all-weather road network and airfields. Pockets of resistance continued. Recruiting for the MPLA was stepped up and Communist propaganda teams proliferated. The S Africans meanwhile held the Cunene Dam area and the frontier on either side, with the equivalent of one infantry division supported by some armour. They were also taking steps to revive UNITA's guerilla war capability, but this depended on their morale and motivation. There were no immediate signs of the Cubans taking any military action against the S African military forces.

All white southern Africa felt threatened by these events, but so did Zambia, Tanzania, Botswana and Malawi. The Chinese tightened their economic grip on Tanzania and awaited events. Britain made an attempt to settle the Rhodesian problem. NATO and the EEC discussed extending their defence agreements to the S Atlantic, but no positive steps were taken. But the most important result was the further loss of faith in the US by her Allies. Having seen the US, in turn, let down her allies in China, Vietnam, at Suez, in India, in Kurdistan and elsewhere, the NATO allies especially wondered, when it came to the test, whether the US, which did not revere treaties in the way the older nations of the world did, would honour her commitments. The USA lost further credibility over Angola and the Russians gained accordingly.

ANGOLAN INDEPENDENCE MOVEMENTS (SW Africa)   February 1961-15 October 1974

Fought between the MPLA (Popular Movement for the Liberation of Angola) led by Agostinho Neto, an orthodox Maoist trained at Coimbra University, the FNLA (National Front for the Liberation of Angola), led by Holden Roberto, brother-in-law of President Mobutu of Zaire, and UNITA (National Union for the Total

Independence of Angola) led by Dr Jonas Savimbi, a Protestant graduate of Freiburg and Lausanne Universities, and the Portuguese.

The fighting started with a bloody uprising in the coffee-growing district of Carmona in N Angola in February 1961 when only six infantry companies provided the total military garrison of the colony. This revolt was much affected by the chaos in neighbouring Congo and especially by the turmoil in the copper-mining province of Katanga. From the outset atrocities by Bakongo tribesmen, similar to those in the Congo, such as cutting men, women and children in half lengthways by circular saws, took place coupled with violent retribution by white colonists and rival tribesmen. The Portuguese quickly reinforced their garrison until a peak was reached with a total of 50,000 whites and 10,000 black soldiers in 1972.

The Carmona uprising was rapidly brought under control but resulted in an exodus from the area of 300,000 refugees, some to the Congo (Zaire) and the remainder to Luanda. The revolutionary movements in the north soon split into two. The FNLA, backed by Mobutu with bases in Zaire, remained amongst the forested hills between Carmona and the coast. Holden, on the other hand, made a deal with the President of Zambia, Dr Kenneth David Kaunda and formed secure bases in Zambia from which he raided into E Angola. His line of communications along which he obtained arms, ammunition and explosives stretched through Zambia and Tanzania to Dar-es-Salaam which was the main port of Chinese supply. Neto obtained his arms mainly from Russia through Brazzaville, Congo.

UNITA was the only guerilla organisation to operate wholly within Angola itself, concentrating in Savimbi's home territory of Bié (Silva Porto) and Moxico in central Angola, where, because they often clashed with the more menacing MPLA, they were surreptitiously given some support by the Portuguese.

By 1972 the FNLA were driven back to the Zaire border after their numbers had been considerably reduced by attrition, leaving only a few remnants in the heavily forested Uige district. The move of the MPLA to Zambia was not a success and their efforts in E Angola were severely limited by the vigorous opposition of the energetic General José Bettancourt Rodriguez, commander of E Angola, who proved himself to be the outstanding counter-insurgent commander of this war. He had previously been a reforming but unpopular Minister of Defence during President Antonio d'Oliveira Salazar's rule.

As the constructive and liberal resettlement, road building (1500 kilometres of bitumen road per year), education and *aldeamento* (created village) programme progressed, all these movements declined and by 1973 there was very little guerilla activity in Angola, apart from continued subversion and recruitment by the Russian-backed MPLA in Luanda and other large towns where their main strength lay, as was shewn later. Decolonisation was progressing at a rapid rate when the Lisbon government fell, owing mainly to economic factors brought on by their colonial wars, Marxist subversion of dissatisfied young army and naval officers and pressure from certain socialist governments in Europe.

The Portuguese revolutionary government, beset by troubles at home, after vainly making attempts to form an African régime representative of all the insurgent parties to whom they could hand over, got out on 11 November 1975 and left the Angolans to fight it out for themselves. This caused an exodus of over 300,000 whites from Angola, those remaining siding with the pro-West UNITA.

Civil war between the Russian-backed MPLA on the one hand, and the now Western-supported FNLA and UNITA on the other, broke out (ANGOLAN CIVIL WAR).

Strength during insurgency (maximum): MPLA 10,000; FNLA 6,000; UNITA 3,000 (all figures exclude men under training in China, the USSR and elsewhere); Portuguese 60,000 (including 10,000 local Angolans).

Casualties: Portuguese 4,000 killed, very many sick; insurgent forces 25,000; civilians 50,000.

ARAB-ISRAELI WARS   see JERUSALEM IX, SINAI PENINSULA, SIX DAY WAR, WAR OF ATTRITION

ASHANTI (Ghana, W Africa)   Ashanti Uprising   April-July 1900
The repulse of an ill-advised attempt to obtain possession of the Golden Stool, the emblem of royalty, led to a general rebellion in Ashanti in April 1896 and the Residency of Kumasi was besieged.

Brigadier-General James Willcocks was thereupon selected to lead a relief force comprising the Ashanti Field Force, 1,952 strong, formed from the West India Regiment, the West African Frontier Force, the Central African Frontier Regiment and the West African Regiment. In July Willcocks advanced against fierce opposition and appalling difficulties, pushing inland from the coast to Kumasi. He gained his objective on 15 July at a cost to his own men of 122 killed and 733 wounded.

ASHANTI WARS   1821-31; 1873-4; 1893-4; 1896
Great Britain waged four wars against the Ashantis, in the years 1821-31, 1873-4, 1893-4 and 1896.

The First Ashanti War began in 1821 when, after some trouble about the right of protection over the Fantis and other tribes, a small British force under Major-General Sir Charles MacCarthy entered Ashanti. This force was routed, and Sir Charles was killed at Essamako. The British crushed the Ashantis at Dodowah (qv) in August 1826. In 1831 the Ashantis came to terms. Their King undertook to recognise the protectorate of Britain over all the tribes between the river Prah and the sea.

In 1873 the Second Ashanti War started. In January the Ashantis invaded territory under British protection and, the Fantis having been beaten in battle, General Sir Garnet Wolseley was sent out. He advised a punitive expedition, and he himself marched on Kumasi (qv), fighting at Amoaful (qv) on 31 January 1874, at Bekwai, and before Kumasi, which he entered on 4 February. The town was set alight, and Wolseley's army, stricken with sickness, retired five weeks before an auxiliary force under Major-General Sir John Glover, arrived. Glover found Kumasi deserted. The Ashanti King, Kofi Karikari, then asked for peace and renounced all claims on the protected territory.

The Fourth Ashanti War in 1896 arose mainly out of King Prempeh's refusal to observe the terms of the treaty of 1874. A composite force under General Sir Francis Scott advanced upon his capital in December 1895. Kumasi was entered on 17 January 1896, and Prempeh taken, a prisoner, to the Gold Coast. The success of this bloodless campaign was largely owing to the elaborate preparations made for the army's transport and to the speed with which Sir Francis Scott acted.

ATBARA (Sudan, NE Africa)   British Sudan Campaigns   8 April 1898
Fought between the British under Major-General Sir Herbert Kitchener, sirdar of the Egyptian Army, and the Mahdists under the Mahdi's successor, Kalifa Abdullah.
Strength: British 15,000; Sudanese 18,000.
Aim: The British withdrew from the Sudan after the death of General Gordon at Khartoum (qv), but the increased activity of France, Belgium and Italy in Africa prompted Britain to undertake the reconquest of the country for Egypt.
Battle: Kitchener advanced south, building a railway as he went. He captured Dongola and Abu Hamed (qv) in 1897 and reached Atbara in the spring of the following year. Here, where the Nile tributary of the Atbara joins the river, the Mahdists had taken up a strong position behind a *zariba* (stockade). Kitchener attacked the position and routed the Sudanese despite being outnumbered heavily. Anglo-Egyptian casualties were 570, while 6,000 Sudanese (one-third of the force) were killed or captured.
Result: Kitchener continued his advance up the Nile.

AX (Cape of Good Hope, S Africa)   Kaffir Wars   1846-7
The Kaffirs attacked both British and Boer settlements in protest against land encroachment between the Keiskama and Great Kei Rivers. The rising was put down by the British after a campaign lasting twenty-one months.

BASUTO WARS OF THE ORANGE FREE STATE (S Africa)   1858-68
In 1858 the Basutos under King Mosheshu began to resist Boer encroachment. Hostilities were desultory, but between 1864 and 1866 the Boers successfully annexed large regions of Basutoland. The Basutos continued to resist, but after another war the Orange Free State annexed more land in 1867-8. Britain then annexed Basutoland to prevent further Boer expansion.

BELMONT (Cape Province, W Africa)   Second Boer War   23 November 1899
Fought between the Boers and the British under General Lord Methuen.
Strength: Boers 3,000; British 8,000.
Aim: The British sought to beat the Boers from their strong position in the hills near Belmont.
Battle: With seven battalions of infantry including Guards and Highlanders and a regiment of cavalry, Methuen launched a frontal attack which carried the position with a loss of 28 officers and 270 men. Boer losses were 30 killed and wounded

and 50 prisoners.
Result: Methuen continued his advance towards Magersfontein (qv), where he was decisively defeated on 11-12 December.

BENI BOO ALLI (Persian Gulf)   Destruction of Arab Pirate Strongholds   1821
Fought between the Arabs and the British under Major-General Sir Lionel Smith.

A force under Smith, supported by the vessels *Topaze, Liverpool, Eden* and *Curlew,* landed at Beni Boo Alli where the Arabs had recently beaten a native force sent against them. Amongst those killed in that engagement were 400 Sepoys and 5 British officers. Under cover of the guns of the fleet, the troops landed without opposition. After a fierce fight, the stronghold of the Joassma tribe was taken on 2 March. The Imam of Muscat tried to induce the tribes to come to terms, but on 10 March a strong attack was made on the British camp and, although the Arabs were beaten off, elements of the British force suffered heavy casualties. The fleet then destroyed the forts and vessels of the pirates and the Arabs were persuaded to send hostages to Bombay against their good behaviour.

BEREA (Cape Province, S Africa)   Kaffir Wars   20 December 1852
Fought between the British under General Cathcart and the Basutos under Moshesh.
Strength: British 2,500; Basutos many thousands.
Aim: The Kaffirs sought to drive the British back, since they had reduced the power of the tribal chiefs.
Battle: Though heavily outnumbered, the British held their ground for a day, but retreated to their entrenchments on the Caledon on the day after the engagement. British losses were 37 killed and 15 wounded.
Result: The Kaffir objective was not achieved.

BLOEMFONTEIN (Orange Free State, S Africa)   Second Boer War   13 March 1900
Fought between the British under General Lord Roberts and the Boers.

After the British victory at Paardeberg (qv), where 4,000 Boers surrendered, Roberts crossed the Orange River and launched an offensive against the Boers in the Orange Free State.

Roberts, heavily reinforced, marched on Bloemfontein, capital of the Free State. On 13 March the British stormed the city and drove the Boers out. Continuing north, the British arrived at and besieged Kroonstad on 12 May. On 24 May the Orange Free State was annexed to Britain. However, the fighting continued for another year, until 31 May 1902.

The British force by that time numbered about 250,000. Their losses in the war were 5,774 killed, 22,829 wounded and over 20,000 who died of disease. The total number of Boers under arms was about 95,000, of whom about 4,000 were killed and 40,000 taken prisoner. In January 1902 there were 121,965 Boers in the concentration camps. About 12,000 of these died of disease (mainly typhus), owing to their lack of knowledge of sanitation and inadequate provision made by the British medical services.

BLOOD RIVER (Zululand, Natal, S Africa)   Boer-Zulu War   16 December 1838
Fought between the Boers under Andries Pretorius and the Zulus under Dingaan.
Strength: Boers 500; Zulus 10,000.
Aim: Dutch colonists who moved north, away from British rule at the Cape, came into conflict with the Zulus, who massacred the Boer leader Piet Retief and 60 followers in Natal and went on to destroy Durban. Under Pretorius, the Boers made a stand along Blood River.
Battle: The Boers repulsed repeated attacks by the Zulus, finally routing them with a loss of 3,000.
Result: The Boers founded the Republic of Natal around the town of Pietermaritzburg.
Remarks: This action is also known as the Battle of Dingaan's Bay.

BOER FRONTIER WAR WITH THE BANTUS   1834
The Bantu tribes (chiefly Xhosa), angered by Boer encroachments, invaded the frontier regions. They were repulsed, but with difficulty.

BOOMPLAATS (Orange Free State, S Africa)   Orange Free State War   29 August 1848
Fought between the British under Lt-General Sir Harry Smith and the Boers under Andries Pretorius.
Strength: British 1,000; Boers 1,000.
Aim: When the British Cape Colony annexed Natal in 1844 it also claimed the territory to the west between the Orange and Vaal Rivers.
Battle: The Boers in the area revolted and, led by Pretorius, marched against the British. At Boomplaats they were defeated by forces under General Smith. Total casualties were less than 100.
Result: The British then set up the Orange River Sovereignty, but in 1854 they withdrew south of the Orange River, allowing the Boers to establish the Orange Free State.

BULAWAYO (Rhodesia, central Africa)   British Conquest of Matabeleland   23 October 1893
When gold was discovered in the S Rhodesia area of Mashonaland, white settlers moved into the area. Safe transit was granted to the S Africa Company of Cecil Rhodes by Lobengula, Chief of the Matabeles, but in 1893 he led an uprising against both the British and the Mashonas.
   On 23 October, near the Matabele capital of Bulawayo, 380 miles north of Pretoria, the British cut down the rebels with machine-gun fire. They went on to occupy Bulawayo, on 4 November, the revolt ending two months later with the death of Lobengula.

BURNS HILL (Cape Province, S Africa)   Kaffir Wars   1847
The British sought to arrest Sandili, the chief of the Xhosas, but, heavily outnumbered, were defeated and compelled to retreat. In 1877 Sandili again opposed the British, this time leading the Gaikas, but was defeated.

CASTILLEJOS (Morocco, N Africa)   Spanish-Moroccan War   1 January 1860
Fought between the Spanish under General Prim and the Moors.
Aim: The Spaniards sought to gain access to the road to Tetuan (qv).
Battle: A strong force of Moors was defeated after a hard fight.
Result: The road to Tetuan was opened, thus achieving the Spanish objective.

COLENSO (Natal, S Africa)   Second Boer War   15 December 1899
Fought between the British under General Sir Redvers Buller and the Boers under General Louis Botha.
Strength: British infantry 11,250 (15½ battalions) + mounted infantry 1,325 + cavalry 836 + guns 44; Boers 4,000-5,000.
Aim: In order to take the offensive against the Boers, Buller deployed his army on three fronts, two of which were defeated, in the second week in December, before Buller took the third column to the relief of Ladysmith (qv).
Battle: Fourteen miles south of Ladysmith Buller came upon the Boers at Colenso holding the far (left) bank of the Tugela River, with some 4,000 to 5,000 men. On 15 December the British launched a frontal assault on the Boer position. Despite British gallantry, the position was not taken and Buller called off the attack, having lost 71 officers and 1,055 men, the Irish Brigade suffering about half this total. Ten guns fell into the hands of the Burghers. Buller retained no reserve and for this reason, if no other, his conduct of the battle is open to serious criticism.
Result: In consequence, General Lord Roberts took over command of the British forces in S Africa, with General Lord Kitchener as his Chief of Staff, though Buller retained his command on the Natal front.

COLONIAL WARS IN AFRICA   1899-1914
Continuous wars were fought in Africa in this period to 'pacify' the colonies.
1899-1920, Somaliland (NE Africa): Operations against Mohammed ben Abdullah, the 'Mad Mullah' who waged constant war with the British, Italians and Ethiopians. He was an able desert warrior and his raids ended only with his death.
1899-1902, (Second) Boer War (S Africa).
1900 March-November, Ashanti Uprising (qv): Ashantis in the Gold Coast (Ghana) besieged Kumasi (qv) before British troops suppressed the revolt.
1900, Chad (Republic of Chad): At the Battle of Laknta on 22 April the Arab raider and slave-trader Rabah Zobeir was defeated.
1900, N Sahara: In May the French completed their conquest of the oases of the N Sahara after long-drawn-out warfare.
1900-3, Nigeria (W Africa): The British completed their conquest of the north of the country.

1902, Angola (W Africa): An uprising in Angola was put down by the Portuguese.

1903, German SW Africa: A Hottentot uprising.

1904, Nigeria (W Africa): There was an insurrection in the south of the country.

1904-5, Cameroons (W Africa): An insurrection in the country was suppressed by the Germans.

1904-8, German SW Africa: A rebellion, led by the Herero tribe, was joined by many of the Hottentots. The Herero leaders were Makarero, Hendrik Witboi and Mosengo. General von Trotha was defeated, but the new Governor von Lindquest put down the rebellion with the aid of more administrative reforms. Prince Bernhard von Bülow was the minister in charge in Berlin. The rebellion spread into Angola.

1905, French Congo (Equatorial Africa): An uprising.

1905, German E Africa: Maji-Maji uprising in Tanganyka, in which 120,000 Africans were killed by the Germans.

1906, Sokoto (W Africa): There was a religious insurrection in Sokoto, N Nigeria.

1907, S Angola (W Africa): An uprising of the transfrontier Ovambos took place, inspired mainly by the rebellion of the Herero tribe in German SW Africa. It was successfully suppressed, but not before a column of Portuguese were ambushed and 250 killed.

1908-9, Mauritania (W Africa): The French conquered the country.

1909-11, Wadai (Central African Republican): The French conquered this mountainous region of E Chad.

1914-15, S Africa: From October 1914 to February 1915 Boer extremists led by General Christiaan De Wet and others protested against the Union of S Africa's declaration of war against Germany. Louis Botha, Prime Minister and former Boer General, suppressed the rising with the help of Jan Christiaan Smuts, a former commando leader.

CONSTANTINE (E Algeria)   French Conquest of Algeria   6-12 October 1837
The French under Marshal G. M. D. Damrémont besieged the Berbers under Hadji Ahmad in a fortress of great natural strength.
Strength: French 10,000; Berbers 15,000.

   In the autumn of 1836 the fortified city of Constantine was invested by 7,000 French under Marshal Comte Bertrand Clauzel. The French had occupied Algiers in 1830 but the town of Constantine, 200 miles to the east, had held out. Clauzel had no siege artillery and was therefore obliged to assault the city. He was repulsed with heavy loss.
Battle: In the autumn of 1837 Constantine was besieged by French and Algerian troops under Damrémont. The siege was laid on 6 October, and by 12 October a breach had been made and an assault was ordered. Damrémont himself was killed at the outset and it was his successor, General Valée, who commanded the storming of the city, which fell on 13 October.
Result: The French were now more or less secure along the Algerian coast.

DAHOMEY-FRENCH WARS (W Africa)   1851-94

The natives of Dahomey are mostly pure Negroes. Despite savage customs and frequent tribal wars, in which women often bore arms, Dahomey was a well-organised kingdom by the reign of Gezo. The French signed a commercial treaty with the country in 1851, and set up a protectorate in 1863. Finally, in 1892, the French under General Alfred Dodds defeated the Dahomians after a second war and deposed their King.

France annexed the country in 1894, but uprisings continued until 1899.

DALMANUTHA (Transvaal, S Africa)   Second Boer War   21-8 August 1900

Fought between the British under General Lord Roberts and General Sir Redvers Buller and the Boers under General Louis Botha.

Aim: The British sought to drive the Boers from their positions along a 30-mile front which stretched from Belfast to Machadodorp, covering the Delagoa Bay Railway.

Battle: The British attacked on the west under Roberts and on the south under Buller. In the seven-day attack, the Boers were driven from all their positions, so that when Buller entered Machadodorp on 28 August the line was in British hands. President Paul Kruger fled to Delagoa Bay. British losses during the operation were 500.

Result: The British objective was achieved.

DIAMOND HILL (Transvaal, S Africa)   Second Boer War   11-12 June 1900

Fought between the British under General Lord Roberts and the Boers under General Louis Botha.

Strength: British 17,000 with 70 guns; Boers 15,000.

Aim: The British sought to drive the Boers from their strongly entrenched position 15 miles from Pretoria.

Battle: The British attacked the Boer line which was so extended that three separate actions were in progress at the same time. The Boers were driven from their positions and the British lost 25 officers and 137 men killed or wounded in the action.

Result: The British objective was achieved.

DINGAAN'S BAY   see BLOOD RIVER

DODOWAH (Ghana, W Africa)   First Ashanti War   1826

Fought between the Ashantis and the British under Colonel Purdon.

Aim: The British sought to crush the Ashanti uprising.

Battle: The rebel force, though it fought bravely, was defeated with heavy loss.

Result: The British objective was achieved.

DOORNKOP (Transvaal, S Africa)   Jameson's Raid, Second Boer War
1 January 1896
Fought between the Boers under General Piet Cronje and the British under Dr Leander Starr Jameson.
Strength: Boers — ?; British 740.
Aim: The British sought to overthrow the Transvaal régime of President Paul Kruger in Johannesburg (qv), and several British leaders planned a revolt.
Battle: It was decided that the attack should be supported by a raid from Bechuanaland. Cecil Rhodes, head of the British South Africa Company in S Rhodesia and Prime Minister of Cape Colony, tried to call off the attack at the last minute. Jameson, however, had left Mafeking (qv) on 29 December 1895, and on 1 January was intercepted by Piet Cronje at Krugersdorp, 20 miles west of Johannesburg. Jameson escaped with the survivors but was captured on 2 January at Doornkop.
Result: Jameson was handed over to the British for trial and received a short prison sentence. The failure of the attack led Rhodes to resign as Premier. Kaiser William II sent a congratulatory telegram to Kruger on his success and thus precipitated a diplomatic crisis between Britain and Germany.

DRIEFONTEIN (Orange Free State, S Africa)   Second Boer War   10 March 1900
Fought between the Boers under General Christiaan De Wet and the British under General Lord Roberts.
Aim: The Boers were covering Bloemfontein (qv) and the British sought to beat them from their position.
Battle: The Boer front, which extended seven miles, was attacked frontally by Major-General Kelly-Kenny's division and on the left by General Tucker's division. The Boers were driven from their positions and the road to Bloemfontein opened to the British. The Boers left over 100 dead on the field. British losses were 424 killed or wounded.
Result: The British objective was achieved.

DUNDEE   see TALANA HILL

EGYPTIAN WAR WITH ABYSSINIA (ETHIOPIA)   1875-9
Khedive Ismail Pasha ruled Egypt under the suzerainty of the Sultan of Turkey.
    Ordered by the Turks to expand east in 1865 the Egyptians occupied Suakin (qv) and Massawa, thus threatening to cut off Abyssinia (qv) from the sea. Harar and neighbouring seaports were occupied in 1872-5 and King John II of Abyssinia declared war. The Egyptian forces were nearly wiped out at Gundet on 13 November 1875 and another Egyptian expedition was defeated at Gura on 25 March 1876.
    On 25 June 1879 Ismail was deposed by the Sultan in favour of his son, Mohammed Tewfik.

EGYPT/UNITED ARAB REPUBLIC, INTERNAL UNREST   1945-52
Anti-British feeling resulted in the abrogation of all treaties with Britain on 27 October 1951. The end of British military occupation was also demanded. Britain began to withdraw from the UAR, but rioting broke out at Port Said and Ismailia, threatening the Suez Canal. Britain was obliged not only to refrain from pulling out, but had also to engage in military action to halt the unrest.

After the 1939-45 war, press censorship was abolished in Egypt and anti-British feeling ran high. Negotiations to free the UAR of British control collapsed over the problem of the Sudan. The British naval base at Alexandria had been closed and British forces were concentrated in the Suez Canal. When the Egyptians abrogated the treaty between the two countries, thus forestalling the presentation of new treaty proposals, Mustafa el-Nahas Pasha, the Prime Minister, also asked Parliament to declare Farouk King of the Sudan. The unilateral move was condemned by Britain, who wanted Sudanese autonomy, and she was supported by France and the USA. As tension grew and the situation worsened violence against British troops (now reinforced) increased. On 25 January 1952 the British police barracks at Al Isma'iliyah (Ismailia) were attacked. The strong British defence inflicted heavy losses on the Egyptians. In the general civil unrest, Egyptian police were often involved in actions against the British. On the evening of 26 January rioting broke out in Cairo, in which 400 foreign buildings were attacked, many families were made homeless and several Britons murdered before fighting stopped. Nahas Pasha was forced out of office and Egypt fell into political chaos until General Abdul Nasser organised the *coup* on 22 July 1952 which altered the course of history in the Middle East.

ELANDSLAAGTE (Natal, S Africa)   Second Boer War   21 October 1899
Fought between the Boers under General Koch and the British under General Sir John French.
Aim: The British sought to drive the Boers from the strong position they occupied on high ground near the Ladysmith-Dundee Railway.
Battle: The Boer drive to Ladysmith (qv) was dogged by British attempts to halt their advance. With three battalions and five squadrons and 12 guns, the British attacked the Boer position. The Boers were driven out of their position by the British infantry and the Imperial Light Horse (dismounted) with a loss of 250 killed and wounded and 200 prisoners, of whom Koch was one. The British lost 35 officers and 219 men.
Result: The Boer advance was delayed.

ELANDS RIVER (Natal, S Africa)   Second Boer War   4 August 1900
Fought between the Australians under Colonel Hore and the Boers.
Strength: Australians 400; Boers 2,500 with 6 guns.
Battle: On 4 August the Australians, in an exposed kopje with no water nearer than half a mile away, were surrounded by the Boers. Their Maxim gun became unserviceable and an attempt by General Sir Frederick Carrington to relieve them

failed. They held out, however, and when General Lord Kitchener relieved them on 15 August they had lost 75 killed and wounded and nearly all their horses. In the eleven-day siege 1,800 Boer shells had fallen on the Australian lines.
Result: The Boer objective was not achieved.

EL OBEID (Sudan, NE Africa)   British Sudan Campaigns   1 November 1883
Fought between the British and Egyptians under General William Hicks (Hicks Pasha) and the Mahdists under Mohammed Ahmed.
Strength: Anglo-Egyptians 10,000; Mahdists 70,000.

The Sudan had been conquered by Mohammed Ali of Egypt earlier in the century and had suffered from misrule since. Mohammed Ahmed proclaimed himself Mahdi and led a revolt against Egypt.
Aim: As Egypt was a British protectorate, Hicks led an Egyptian expedition into the Sudan to quell the revolt.
Battle: Two hundred and twenty miles SW of Khartoum (qv) the Mahdists surrounded the Anglo-Egyptian force, which tried for three days to break out of the defile in which they were trapped. By 4 November the last of the defenders had been massacred, including Hicks.
Result: The British withdrew from the Sudan.

EL TEB (Sudan, NE Africa)   British Sudan Campaigns   4 February 1884
Fought between the British under Valentine Baker (Baker Pasha), and the Mahdists under Osman Digna.
Strength: British 3,500; Mahdists 12,000.

After the Sudanese victory at El Obeid (qv), William Gladstone decided to evacuate British forces from the Sudan. One Egyptian column under Baker Pasha was ambushed near Suakin (qv) on the Red Sea. The Anglo-Egyptian force tried to fight its way out, but it was virtually destroyed - 2,000 casualties being inflicted on the Sudanese. Baker Pasha was one of the survivors.

The Mahdists sought to press home their advantage, but another battle at El Teb on 29 March resulted in their repulse. The victory was gained by 4,000 Anglo-Egyptian troops under General Sir Gerald Graham.
Result: The evacuation of the Sudan continued.

ENSLIN   see GRASPAN

ERITREAN REVOLT (E Africa)   1968-
Fought between the ELF (Eritrean Liberation Front) plus the rival guerilla faction, the PLF (Popular Liberation Front), against the Ethiopian government forces.

After the Italian army in Eritrea and Ethiopia (Abyssinia) had in 1941 been defeated by the British, the Eritreans were encouraged to join quasi-Christian Ethiopia as one federated country. But most Eritreans, especially the Moslems, resented this. Armed rebellion started in 1968, led by Osman Saleh Sabbe. Support was obtained from Guinea (Conakry), Senegal, Mauritania, Egypt and Algeria, and later from Colonel Mu'ammar al-Qadhafi (Khadaffi) of Libya who, in May 1973, presented the insurgents with a large quantity of arms, ammunition and explosives. When the Emperor Haile Selassie was deposed on 12 September 1974, and federation under the crown was meaningless, the revolt gained support from most Eritreans. A disastrous drought and famine in 1974, coupled with revelations of government corruption, made the situation much worse.

Full-scale rebellion in Eritrea continues with the Ethiopian army, half-heartedly backed by the USA, deploying over two divisions in an attempt to suppress it. Indiscriminate bombing by the Ethiopian air force has done nothing but gain more support for the guerillas. The outlook is bleak.

FERKEH (FIRKET) (Sudan, NE Africa)   British Sudan Campaigns   7 June 1896
Fought between an Anglo-Egyptian force under General Lord Kitchener and the Mahdists under Emir Hamada.
Strength: Anglo-Egyptians 9,500; Mahdists 4,000.

Kitchener took an Egyptian force with a British horse battery on a night march to the Mahdist camp where he surprised the Mahdists and drove them out after two hours' fighting, killing 1,500 and capturing 500. Of 62 emirs in the camp, 44 fell and 4 were taken. Egyptian losses were 20 killed and 81 wounded.

GRASPAN (Cape Province, S Africa)   Second Boer War   25 November 1899
Fought between the British under General Lord Methuen and the Boers.
Strength: British Methuen's division + naval brigade 400; Boers 400.
Aim: The British sought to beat their opponents from the strong position they occupied.
Battle: The key to the Boer position was a high kopje which was attacked both frontally and on the flank and carried with a loss of nine officers and 185 men, of whom three officers and 86 men were marines whose complement was 200. Boer commando losses were 25.
Result: The British objective was achieved.

The action is also known as the Battle of Enslin.

GUAD-EL-RAS (Morocco)   Spanish-Moroccan War   23 March 1860
Fought between the Spanish under Marshal Leopoldo O'Donnell and the Moors.
Strength: Spanish 25,000; Moors 20,000.
Aim: The Spanish sought to quell a Moorish uprising.
Battle: The Spanish attacked the Moors who were strongly entrenched behind the Guad-el-Ras. The Moors were routed.
Result: The Spanish victory ended the war.

GUBAT   see ABU KRU

GUINEA-BISSAU INSURGENCY (W Africa)   1959-24 September 1974
Fought between PAIGC (African Party for the Independence of Guinea and Cape Verde Islands) under Amilcar Cabral and his successor, Aristides Pereira, and the Portuguese armed forces under General António Spínola and finally General José Bettancourt Rodrígues.

The revolt in this tiny, multi-tribal colony (about the size of Wales) was at all times assisted by its neighbours Guinea (Conakry) and Senegal and supported by Soviet Russia and Cuba. The colony is low-lying, very unhealthy and a highly unpopular military station. It has no worthwhile attributes apart from an all-weather bomber airfield. Service in Guinea-Bissau was a direct cause of low morale of certain sections of the army which led to the soldiers' revolt in Lisbon.

The guerilla war was desultory and consisted mainly of raids across the frontier from Guinea and Senegal. The Portuguese under Spinola started a comprehensive redevelopment and decolonisation programme, but it came too late. This great and expensive effort by Spínola to improve the economy and raise the standard of living had some effect, which caused a rift between the mulatto Cape Verdean leadership and the Conakry-backed African Guineans, resulting in the assassination of Amilcar Cabral in January 1973, for which six PAIGC leaders were executed by their own régime.

Cabral's demise led to an increase in Russian influence and the supply of Strella heat-seeking, anti-aircraft missiles. In 1973/4 these Strellas shot down a number of helicopters on which the Portuguese depended for supply and communication. The Portuguese had been loath to give up Bissau, in spite of its lack of viability, for fear of a domino effect in her other colonies (which did in fact happen). But soon after Bettancourt Rodrígues came from Angola to take over from Spínola, the latter on his return to Portugal deposed the Lisbon government. Guinea-Bissau was granted complete independence on 10 September 1974, when Aristides Pereira took over as President. The Cape Verde Islands were given the opportunity for separate development and the chance of a referendum for complete independence. The practically waterless island of Sal has a superb airport, the possession of which would allow air domination of the central Atlantic.
Strength during insurgency (maximum): PAIGC 5,000, mostly in camps in Senegal and Guinea (Conakry) - other cadres were being trained in Russia and Cuba; Portuguese 20,000.
Casualties 1959-74: PAIGC 2,000; Portuguese 1,000 battle casualties + 30,000 sick, hospitalised and evacuated home.

HAFIR (Sudan, NE Africa)   British Sudan Campaigns   September 1896
Fought between the Mahdists and the British under General Sir Herbert Kitchener.

Following the action at Ferkeh (qv) in June 1896 in which the British worsted a force of encamped Mahdists, another battle took place at Hafir. The action was decisive and opened the road to Dongola to the British.

HASHIN (Sudan, NE Africa)   British Sudan Campaigns   20 March 1885
Fought between the British under General Sir Gerald Graham and the Mahdists under Osman Dinga.
Strength: British 8,000; Mahdists 12,000.
   The British defeated a detachment of Osman Dinga's army with a loss of 1,000 killed. British losses were 48 killed and wounded.

INGOGO (Cape Province, S Africa)   First Boer War   8 February 1881
Fought between the British and the Boers.
Aim: The British sought to beat the Boers from their position.
Battle: A British column of five companies of infantry, 4 guns and some cavalry attacked the Boer position, but was repulsed with a loss of 139 killed and wounded. Boer losses were admitted to be 14.
Result: The British objective was not achieved.

INHLOBANE MOUNTAIN (Natal, S Africa)   Zulu War   28 March 1879
Fought between the Zulus and the British under Colonel Redvers Buller and Colonel Russell.
Strength: Zulus 15,000; British 1,300.
Aim: The British sought to beat their opponents out of their kraal.
Battle: The Zulus were in a strong kraal which the British attacked. After severe fighting the British were repulsed with heavy loss.
Result: The British objective was not achieved.

ISANDHLWANA (Natal, S Africa)   Zulu War   22 January 1879
Fought between the British under Colonel Durnford and the Zulus under Matyana.
Strength: British 1,800; Zulus 20,000.
   Although Britain recognised Cetewayo as King in 1872, the Zulus began to build up strength to invade neighbouring colonies.
Aim: Six companies of the 24th Regiment, two guns and a small force of Natal volunteers were sent to disarm the Zulus.
Battle: At Isandhlwana the force was overwhelmed and massacred by Zulus armed with only assegais. Of the regular force, 26 officers and 600 men were killed and 24 officers and a large number of volunteers were also killed from the colonial force.
Result: The British objective was not achieved. This was the last occasion on which British colours were carried into action as Queen Victoria, after this defeat, disapproved of their being hazarded.

ISLY (Morocco, N Africa)   French-Algerian Guerilla War   14 August 1844
Fought between the French under Marshal Thomas Bougeaud and the Algerians and Moroccans under Sultan Abd-el-Rahman, with Abd-el-Kader attacking Bougeaud's communications.
Strength: French 10,300; Algerians/Moroccans 45,000.

Abd-el-Kader, the great Arab guerilla leader, had resisted the French conquest of Algeria since 1832. The French had made two treaties with him to try and limit their conquest to the coastal strip, which was all that they wanted as long as the Arab tribes in the interior were friendly. Finally the great counter-insurgent commander and administrator General Thomas Bougeaud, who had taken part in counter-insurgent operations during the Peninsular War and who had earlier experience of the war in Algeria, was sent out to conquer the whole of Algeria. He instituted new methods which gradually developed the area with roads, defended villages and local militia, whilst his regular forces operated against Abd-el-Kader in a series of mobile columns. Gradually Bougeaud's methods drove the guerillas back as they captured and destroyed the crops, overran their arsenals and cut their communications to Morocco and the coast. In December 1843 Abd-el-Kader was forced to retreat over the Moroccan border and operate from a safe sanctuary there. This led to friction between the French and the Moroccans. Admiral the Prince de Joinville bombarded Tangier and Mogador to try and bring the Emperor of Morocco into line. Bougeaud also moved over the border to Oudjda. Abd-el-Kader, in true guerilla fashion, did not oppose the regular French forces but attacked their communications.

Eventually the Moroccan Emperor could restrain his army no longer. On 12 August 1844 a Moorish army of 45,000 men, mostly horsemen under Sultan Abd-el-Rahman, concentrated to attack the French forces under Bougeaud, consisting of 8,500 infantry, 1,400 cavalry, 16 guns and 400 friendly Arab militia at Isly. The French veterans, toughened to a peak of durability and fitness by their operations against Abd-el-Kader, easily overcame the Arab horsemen, and defeated them decisively. The Moors lost 1,500 dead.

Abd-el-Kader did not allow his 2,000 guerillas to get mixed up in this mêlée, as he wanted to keep his 'army in being'. But by the Moroccan treaty with the French he lost his safe base and it was the beginning of the end for him. After three more years of operations, on 22 December 1847, he eventually gave himself up to the Duc d'Aumales, Bougeaud's successor. Bougeaud was made Duc d'Isly, retired in 1847, his work done, and died of cholera in France in 1849. Abd-el-Kader was eventually awarded the Grand Cross of the Légion d'Honneur by Napoleon III for his work in Syria and granted a pension of 100,000 francs per year. He died in 1883 aged 76.

ITALO-TURKISH WAR   2 September 1911-15 October 1912
Italy declared war in order to conquer Libya and, by gaining a foothold in N Africa, to provide a counterbalance to the French colonies of Algeria, Tunisia and Morocco.

29-30 September: The Italians bombarded Preveza, on the Epirus coast, and sank several Turkish torpedo boats.

3-5 October: The Italians bombarded Tripoli, forcing the Turks to evacuate the city. The Italians then landed a naval force which seized the capital. Meanwhile, on 4 October, Tobruk was occupied.

11 October: The Italian expeditionary force reached Tripoli, relieving the naval force there. Landings were also made at Homs, Derna and Benghazi. Turkish resistance was only sporadic.

1911-12: The Turks spread propaganda among the Moslem population of Libya which persuaded the cautious Italian General, Carlo Caneva, to confine his activities to the coastal area of the country. Stalemate resulted.

16-19 April 1912: The Italian navy appeared at the mouth of the Dardanelles. Fearing an invasion, the Turks closed the straits and the Italians promptly withdrew.

May: The Italians seized Rhodes and other Dodecanese islands.

July-October: The Italians moved inland in Libya, systematically increasing their control in the country. Two battles at Derna and Sidi Bilal (near Zanzur) were decisive Italian victories over the outnumbered Turks.

15 October: The threat of war in the Balkans forced Turkey to sue for peace. Libya, Rhodes and the Dodecanese were ceded to Italy in the Treaty of Ouchy. Military action in the war did not enhance Italian prestige, since opposition was so slight. The Siwa Oasis in SE Libya remained in the possession of King Idris of Libya until the 1930s.

JAMESON'S RAID   see DOORNKOP

JERUSALEM IX (Israel and Jordan)   Arab-Israeli Wars   15 May-17 July 1948
Fought between the Arabs and the Israelis.

At midnight on 14 May the British mandate over Palestine ended and the UN partitioned the country to form the State of Israel. Immediate fighting broke out between the Israelis and the Palestinians, aided by Arabs from Egypt, Jordan, Syria, Lebanon and Iraq. The Israeli troops came from the Hagana, an underground defence organisation which had been formed during Britain's mandate over Palestine.

The Jews fought off Arab attacks, but the Arabs cut off the supply road from Tel Aviv to Jerusalem and besieged the latter city. A few supplies reached the city over a newly constructed route known as the Burma Road. Military defences within the city were under the command of Colonel David Shaltiel of the Hagana (replaced by Colonel Moshe Dayan on 4 August) and the chief civil officer was Dov Joseph, who was later to become Military Governor. The Old City was soon isolated by Arab attacks, and on 18 May the Jews in this section surrendered to Abdullah el Tel, the local commander of the Arab Legion. As a result, 340 Jewish soldiers were captured and about 1,300 people, mainly women and children, were moved into the New City for safety.

On 11 June a cease-fire was agreed in Israel, but no peace terms could be agreed and fighting resumed on 9 July. Another truce, secured on 17 July in Jerusalem, became effective all over Israel two days later. Of 25,000 Arabs in Israel, about 5,000 had become casualties during the fighting.

Despite the cease-fire, Jerusalem was occasionally shelled, and fighting in other parts of the country sometimes broke out, but the situation was quiet by the end of the year. On 7 September the chief United Nations mediator, Count Bernadotte of Sweden, was assassinated in Jerusalem, supposedly by the Jewish terrorist group called the Stern Gang or Lohmei Herut Yisrael. One of the main points over which negotiations stuck was the UN resolution calling for the internationalisation of Jerusalem. On 2 February 1949 the city was incorporated into the State of Israel and was made into the capital in 1950, thus thwarting the UN scheme.

An armistice was agreed with each of the Arab nations bordering Israel; but no peace treaties were signed, since the Arabs refused to recognise Israel. In Jerusalem itself the boundary between Israel and Jordan remained roughly where it had been on cessation of fighting at the start of the second truce: along a line separating the Old City from the New.

JIDBALLI (Somalia)   Somali Expedition   10 January 1904
Fought between the Somalis and the British under Major-General Sir Charles Egerton.
Strength: Somalis 5,000; British 1,000.
Battle: With a small British and native force, Egerton attacked the Somali camp and after a short, sharp action the Somalis were driven out of their position and pursued for 12 miles by the cavalry. The Somalis lost 1,000 in the fight and pursuit. British losses were small.

JIDDA (Hejaz, Saudi Arabia)   Establishment of Saudi Arabia   January-23 December 1925
Fought between the Hejaz under Sherif Hussein ibn-Ali and the Wahabis under Ibn Saud, Abd-al-Azis III.
In 1916 ibn-Ali proclaimed Arabian independence and became the first King of the Hejaz. By 1924 he had provoked the opposition of the fanatical Wahabi sect in the Nejd. The Wahabis forced Hussein ibn-Ali to abdicate in favour of his son, Ali ibn-Hussein on 3 October 1924. On 13 October Ibn Saud occupied Mecca, and in January 1925 he besieged the last Hejaz stronghold, Jidda, Mecca's port which lies 46 miles west of the city. Jidda surrendered on 23 December, four days after the abdication of Ali ibn-Hussein.
On 8 January 1926 Ibn Saud proclaimed himself King of Hejaz and Nejd. The kingdom was named Saudi Arabia in 1932.

JOHANNESBURG (Transvaal, S Africa)   Second Boer War   31 May 1900
Fought between the British under General Lord Roberts and the Boers under General Louis Botha.
After the Orange Free State was annexed Roberts crossed the Vaal River into the Transvaal, still a Boer stronghold. Botha fell back north, the British pursuing. On 17 May Mahon relieved the siege of Mafeking (qv) and a fortnight later Johannesburg was stormed. The British drove 34 miles north to take Pretoria on 5 June and, on 10 June, General Sir Redvers Buller forced passes in the Drakens-

berg Mountains to invade Transvaal from Natal, the two armies linking at Vlakfontein on 4 July. Formal Boer resistance ceased at this point and Transvaal was annexed while its President, Paul Kruger, fled to Europe.

Boer leaders, amongst whom were Botha, Jacobus Delarey, Christiaan De Wet, James Hertzog, Jan Christiaan Smuts, prolonged the war with guerilla activity until General Lord Kitchener crushed resistance by erecting barbed-wire fences, blockhouses and concentration camps and forming 64 mobile columns of mounted infantry from British yeomanry, colonial cavalry and local militia. The Boers accepted British sovereignty at Vereeniging, 35 miles south of Johannesburg, on 31 May 1902. (See BLOEMFONTEIN for details of casualties during the war.)

KAFFIR WARS (S Africa)   1850-78
Fought between the British and Boers, and the Kaffirs.

There were two wars within this period, the more serious outbreaks of tribal conflict which had already been going on for seventy-five years accompanying the development of Cape Colony. Most of the operations were undertaken by volunteer units of British and Boers.
Eighth Kaffir War, 1850-3: The war resulted from the Cape Governor, Lt-General Sir Harry Smith, reducing the power of the native chiefs in the eastern area within the Cape Colony. After the rising had been quelled, the Kaffirs (mainly Xhosas), believing that their actions would call back their ancestors to help drive out the white invaders, slaughtered their cattle and destroyed their crops in 1856-7. The result was almost total self-destruction, as nearly two-thirds of them died of starvation.
Ninth Kaffir War, 1877-8: A generation later, when their strength had been built up again, a second war was fought. This was the last of the Kaffir wars and the British, suppressing the uprising, annexed all Kaffraria.

KAMBULA (Natal, S Africa)   Zulu War   29 March 1879
Fought between the Zulus and the British under Colonel Henry Wood.
Strength: Zulus 20,000; British 2,000 (including native auxiliaries).
Aim: The Zulus sought to beat the British out of their lager.
Battle: Three Zulu impi attacked the British position, but were repulsed with heavy loss and pursued for 7 miles. British losses were 81 killed and wounded.
Result: The Zulu defeat almost broke the power of their king, Cetawayo.

KAREE (Orange Free State, S Africa)   Boer War   29 March 1900
Fought between the Boers and the British under Major-General Tucker.
Aim: The British sought to drive the Boers from the line of hills they were holding 18 miles north of Bloemfontein (qv).
Battle: A British division under Tucker drove the Boers from their entrenchments with a loss to the British of 10 officers and 172 men killed or wounded.
Result: The British objective was achieved.

KASSASSIN (Egypt)   Egyptian Revolt   28 August 1882
Fought between the British under General Sir Gerald Graham and the Egyptians under Colonel Arabi Pasha.

The British position was attacked by Arabi, and Graham maintained a defensive position throughout the day. In the evening, however, the British heavy cavalry under Colonel Sir Baker Russell charged the Egyptians who broke and fled. British losses were only 11 killed and 68 wounded.

KHARTOUM (Sudan, NE Africa)   British Sudan Campaigns   12 March 1884-26 January 1885
Fought between the British under General Charles Gordon and the Mahdists under Mohammed Ahmed.

Gordon arrived in the Sudan on 18 February 1884 to carry out the Anglo-Egyptian evacuation. Instead of proceeding, however, he decided to defend the country against the Mahdist dervishes and sent to London for reinforcements. While the government hesitated to comply, Gordon evacuated 2,500 women, children and wounded from Khartoum at the confluence of the White Nile and Blue Nile.

On 12 March Gordon was trapped in a fort north of the city by the Mahdists and thereafter directed the defence of Khartoum by the Egyptians. A relief expedition under General Sir Garnet Wolseley set out from Cairo in October, but the fortifications of Khartoum were stormed and carried by the Mahdists on 26 January when every defender, including Gordon, was killed.

The van of Wolseley's force arrived two days later. The relief force withdrew into Egypt.

KHARTOUM (Sudan, NE Africa)   British Sudan Campaigns   1898
Khartoum was founded in 1830 by Mohammed Ali, but it was destroyed by the Mahdists on 26 January 1885, when General Gordon, who made it his head-quarters, was murdered. In 1898, after the Battle of Omdurman (qv), the British recaptured the town. Omdurman was the Mahdist capital. In the Second World War Khartoum was to be the main base for the forces which, in 1941, conquered Eritrea and freed Abyssinia.

KIMBERLEY (Cape Province, S Africa)   Boer War   15 October 1899-15 February 1900
Fought between the Boers under Commandant Marthinus Pretorius Wessels and later under General Piet Cronje, and the British.
Strength: Boers 8,000-10,000; British 4,000.
Aim: The Boers sought the reduction of the town of Kimberley.
Battle: The town was defended by a garrison and armed civilians and was bombarded continuously from the time of its investment. The garrison held out, however, until it was relieved by 5,000 cavalry under General Sir John French. British losses during the siege were 18 officers and 163 men.

Result: The Boer objective was not achieved.

KIRBEKAN (Sudan)   British Sudan Campaigns   10 February 1885
Fought between the British under General Earle and the Mahdists.
Strength: British 1,000; Mahdists 9,000.
Aim: The British sought to beat the Mahdists out of their entrenchments on the heights of Kirbekan.
Battle: The British stormed and carried the heights, totally routing the Mahdists who fled with heavy loss. British losses were 60, among whom was Earle.

KONYA (KONIAH) (Turkey)   Mohammed Ali's First Rebellion   1832
Fought between the Turks under Raschid (Reshid) Pasha and the Egyptians and Syrians under General Ibrahim Pasha. Mohammed Ali had helped the Turks in the Greek War of Independence (1820-30) and wanted some spoils. When he was not given any he marched through Syria and attacked the Turks in Anatolia at Konya.

After fierce fighting the Turks were totally defeated and fled in disorder. Raschid was severely wounded and captured. In desperation at this defeat Turkey called on Russia for assistance. Alarmed at an alliance between Russia and Turkey which threatened the whole balance of power in the Near East, France and Britain, at the Convention of Kutahia, called a halt to the rebellion by persuading the Sultan of Turkey to cede Syria and Adana to Egypt. This whetted the appetite of Mohammed Ali who was a good, but ambitious, soldier.

Later Britain and France quarrelled over the outcome, France taking Turkey's part. Turkey invaded Syria in 1839 but was again defeated by Ibrahim Pasha, Ali's general, at the Battle of Nezib. Meanwhile the Turkish fleet, setting out to invade Egypt, surrendered in Alexandria harbour. The British intervened, made the Egyptians give back the Turkish fleet, made Ibrahim evacuate Syria and, in exchange, organised the Straits Convention whereby the great powers agreed that the Bosporus and Dardanelles be closed in times of peace to all foreign warships.

KORNSPRUIT   see SANNA'S POST

KUMASI (Ghana, W Africa)   Second Ashanti War   4 February 1874
Fought between the British under General Sir Garnet Wolseley and the Ashantis under Kofi Karikari.
Strength: British 2,500; Ashantis — ?

The tribal kingdom of Ashanti made war on the British Gold Coast intermittently during the nineteenth century. The second war began in 1873. In order to crush the rebellion, Wolseley led an expedition to Kumasi (Coomassie), 115 miles NW of Accra (qv).

After fighting at Amoaful (qv) and Bekwa, Sir Garnet entered Kumasi on 4 February 1874 as the retreating Fantis set it on fire. Wolseley's little army, now sick with malaria and lacking supplies, retreated for five weeks to the coast, while Sir John Glover's relieving force reached Kumasi and found it deserted. Kofi

Karikari sued for peace and renounced all claims on the territory which became a British protectorate.

LADYSMITH (Natal, S Africa)   Second Boer War   2 November 1899-27 February 1900
Fought between the Boers under General Petrus Joubert and the British under General Sir George White.
Strength: Boers 10,000; British 12,000.

Despite British attempts to prevent it, the Boers succeeded in investing the town of Ladysmith at the beginning of November.
Battle: The Boers, who had plenty of heavy ordnance, carried out a continuous bombardment, but on 6 January a picked force under Commandant Villiers, backed up by several thousand Boer marksmen posted on the heights, attacked the British lines at Waggon Hill and Caesar's Camp. The battle lasted all day, and though the defenders were under pressure, they held their ground until nightfall when the Boers withdrew, having lost 800 men. From this time on, the Boers fell once more to bombarding the town, which was relieved on 27 February by General Sir Redvers Buller. As well as death by disease, the garrison lost 89 officers and 805 men, more than half of whom fell in the attack on Waggon Hill and Caesar's Camp.
Result: The Boer objective was not achieved.
Remarks: From the British point of view these sieges of Ladysmith, Kimberley and Mafeking (qqv) engaged a large number of Boers who would have been much more dangerous and harder to defeat if they had been operating in the open or in guerilla fashion as was shown later. These British garrisons acted as 'honey-pots' to attract the Boers where they could eventually be destroyed.

LANG'S NECK (Transvaal, S Africa)   First Boer War   28 January 1881
Fought between the British under General Sir George Colley and the Boers under General Petrus Joubert.
Strength: British 1,000; Boers 500.
Aim: Boers in the Transvaal revolted in order to establish their own republic and besieged a small British garrison in the area. Colley moved inland to relieve the British.
Battle: At the pass of Lang's Neck, in the Drakensberg Mountains, the Boers took up a strong position to block the British path. Colley attacked, but was repulsed with a loss of 198 killed and wounded. Boer losses were 14 killed and 27 wounded.
Result: The British objective was not achieved.

LEBANESE CIVIL WAR   1975-
Fought between the Maronite Christian Phalangists under Pierre Gemayyel and Camile Chamoun, and a confederation of Moslem factions under the Druse Chieftain, Kamal Jumblatt, with the Lebanese government under the Christian President, Suleiman Franjieh, and Moslem Prime Minister, Rachid Karamé, trying

to remain neutral.

The apparent aim of the Christian Phalangists is to keep Lebanon from becoming involved in the Arab-Israeli conflict, whereas Moslem factions, egged on by the PLO (Palestine Liberation Organisation) under Yasser Arafat and possibly Russian influence, want to enrol Lebanon in the Arab side. Other factors including greed, Israeli plotting, PLO desire to capture money and bullion in the banks, and even less savoury motives, fuel the flames.

After at least twenty cease-fires and a loss of over 8,000 lives the country was brought to an uneasy stability in February 1976 by the entry of units of the Palestine Liberation army and the Syrian army which joined with the Lebanese army to keep the peace. About 400,000 refugees out of a population of less than 3 million fled the country.

The Christians, February 1976, hold most of Beirut and the coastline north, excluding Tripoli. The Moslems hold all the mountainous hinterland as far as the common frontiers with Syria and Israel, and the small ports of Tyre, Sidon and Damour, as well as Tripoli. After further bloody fighting in March, April and May and in spite of Franjieh's resignation in May, there appears to be no sign of a durable peace. In early June Syrian forces started to move in again ostensibly to restore order but the outcome is not yet clear.

The fact that no major power with interests in the area has, as yet, overtly intervened is significant. The official status given to the powerful PLO has alarmed the Israeli government and is yet another setback to their ambitions.

LINDLEY (Orange Free State, S Africa)   Second Boer War   23-7 May 1900
Fought between the British under Colonel Spragge and the Boers under General Piet De Wet.
Strength: British 500; Boers 200.

The Boers besieged a force of British yeomanry in Lindley which, after four days, surrendered.

MAFEKING (Cape Province, S Africa)   Second Boer War   October 1899-17 May 1900
Fought between the Boers under General Piet Cronje and the British under Colonel Sir Robert Baden-Powell.
Strength: Boers 5,000 (later reduced to 2,000); British 700.

On the outbreak of war General Petrus Joubert launched an offensive in W Transvaal under Cronje who marched on Mafeking on the Bechuanaland border of the Transvaal, 160 miles west of Pretoria.
Battle: The Boers assaulted the town, which Baden-Powell held with 700 men and 600 armed civilians. After the unsuccessful attack, Cronje settled down for a regular siege. Although there was continuous bombardment, only one attempt was made to attack the town again. By this time, Cronje had withdrawn 3,000 of his men to fight elsewhere, leaving the siege in the hands of Lieutenant Snyman. On 12 May 1900, 300 Boers under Sarel Eloff got behind the defences, but were

surrounded and forced to surrender. On 17 May the siege was relieved by Sir Bryan Mahon's cavalry. Boer losses during the siege were 1,000, and British losses 273.

Result: The Boer objective was not achieved. Apart from the casualties the siege was to the strategical advantage of the British as the Boers would have been much more dangerous if they had remained mobile.

Baden Powell (later Lord) founded the Worldwide Boy Scout movement based on his scouting experiences in South Africa and elsewhere.

MAGDALA (Ethiopia, NE Africa)   British Invasion of Ethiopia (Abyssinia)   13 April 1868

Fought between the Ethiopians under Ras Kassa (Emperor Theodore) and the British under General Sir Robert Napier.

Theodore, who seized the throne of Ethiopia in 1855, ruled ruthlessly. In 1864 he threw the British Consul, Charles Cameron, into prison and the envoy sent to negotiate his release in 1866 was similarly treated, being imprisoned at Magdala in the north-central region of Ethiopia.

Aim: Napier led a punitive expedition of Anglo-Indian forces into Ethiopia in 1868, recruiting further strength from dissident local chiefs.

Battle: The British stormed into Magdala on 13 April and the garrison fled. Theodore committed suicide. Napier released the prisoners and, after destroying the fortress, withdrew.

Result: Ethiopia lapsed into anarchy.

MAGERSFONTEIN (Cape Province, S Africa)   Second Boer War   11 December 1899

Fought between the Boers under General Piet Cronje and the British under General Lord Methuen.

Strength: Boers 9,000; British 15,000.

After the British victory at Modder River (qv) Methuen continued his advance on besieged Kimberley (qv), driving the defeated Boers before him.

Aim: At Magersfontein the Boers halted their retreat and took up a strong position to make a stand against the British.

Battle: Methuen deployed his division for an attack and sent the Highland Brigade on a night march to turn the Boers' flank. The Brigade, however, came under heavy fire before they reached their position and, being still extended, suffered heavy casualties - 57 officers and 700 men, including their brigadier, General Wauchope, who was wounded. The rest of the attack also collapsed and the British withdrew, having made no impression on the Boer position. Total British losses were 68 officers and 1,011 men. Boer losses were admitted to be 320, but were probably heavier.

Result: The British objective was not achieved. This disastrous defeat had serious repercussions in Britain and the government decided to send out more competent commanders such as General Lord Roberts and General Lord Kitchener.

MAJUBA (Transvaal, S Africa)   First Boer War   27 February 1881
Fought between the British under Sir George Colley and the Boers under General Petrus Joubert.
Strength: British 647; Boers 500.
Aim: The Boers sought to drive the British from their position on top of Majuba Hill.
Battle: The British post was stormed by a party of young Boers while the fire from the British was overcome by a body of specially chosen marksmen. The British were driven from their position with heavy loss, particularly during the retreat down the hillside. British casualties totalled 223 killed and wounded, including Sir George Colley who was killed, and 50 prisoners. Boer losses were small.
Result: Peace was concluded soon after this action.

MANDINGA-FRENCH WARS (Ivory Coast, W Africa)   1885-6; 1894-5; 1898
Fought between the French and the Mandinga during the time of French colonial expansion in W Africa.
First Mandinga War, 1885-6: The French defeated the Mandinga under Samori, who ruled over the Ivory Coast tribes, and in 1889 established a protectorate.
Second Mandinga War, 1894-5: Samori refused to accept French control and the French were unable to re-establish the protectorate.
Third Mandinga War, 1898: The French defeated and captured Samori, completely breaking the power of the Mandinga on 29 September.

MODDER RIVER (Cape Province, S Africa)   Second Boer War   28 November 1899
Strength: Boers 9,000; British 15,000.
Aim: With the aim of relieving Kimberley (qv), General Lord Methuen marched his 1st Division into the Orange Free State.
Battle: At the Modder River, an eastern tributary of the Vaal River, the British encountered a force of Boers under General Piet Cronje, in a strong position both sides of the river. Early on 28 November the British launched an attack and found the Boers in greater strength than expected. The attack was pressed, however, and by nightfall the Boer position had been turned. British losses were 24 officers and 460 men. Boer casualties were about the same.
Result: Cronje withdrew westward towards Magersfontein. The British pursued.

MOROCCO, BORDER WAR WITH ALGERIA   13-30 October 1963
Fought between the Algerians and the Moroccans.
    After a long period of tension and border incidents, war broke out along the disputed border area of the Atlas Mountains and the Sahara. A cease-fire was arranged by Emperor Haile Selassie of Ethiopia and President Modibo Keita of Mali.

MOZAMBIQUE REVOLT (E Africa)   1965-75

Fought between the Portuguese and Frelimo (Mozambique Liberation Front) under Dr Eduardo Mondlane and (after his murder) his successor, Samora Machel.

After years of plotting and subversion both by Russian and Chinese Communist agents and by 'liberal' Protestant missions supported by President Julius Kambarage Nyere of Tanzania, a full-scale revolt broke out amongst the trans-frontier Makonde tribesmen in the far north of Mozambique. Although serious and well supported by training camps in Tanzania, a limitless supply of weapons from Russia and China passing through the main base port of Dar-es-Salaam and also Mtwara, reinforcements trained in guerilla and political warfare in Russia and China, the revolt was held, and finally brought within bounds, by the wise Portuguese General, Kaulza di Arriaga in 1970. But when Mondlane was assassinated by the extreme Maoists in 1969, the Russian influence declined and Frelimo, now commanded by the Maoist Samora Machel, were advised to diminish their activities in the Makonde and Niassa districts and take the offensive in Tete province where the great Cabora Bassa hydro-electric scheme was being built by the Portuguese and S Africans. To achieve this Frelimo relied on President Nyere's goodwill, although President Kamuzu Banda of Malawi was against attracting Communist revolutionaries into the area. The Chinese advisers also stated that it was unlikely that the war could be won in the jungles of Africa, but, if they could be given bright young Africans who had actually fought, they would take them to China and turn them into such fine political propagandists that they could be sent to London, Washington, Paris and Stockholm and win the war there.

The combination of four years' infiltration of Tete province, the political isolation of Portugal achieved by the African propaganda units based on the Maoist network in the West and the subversion of the metropolitan army caused the collapse of the Portuguese government despite the fact that the troops in Mozambique remained undefeated after gaining a fair success in Operation Gordian Knot, launched by Kaulza di Arriaga against the Makonde guerillas north of Muede in 1971. But the Portuguese had to rely more and more on helicopters and other aircraft for communications and supply. As in Vietnam, as soon as the guerillas received Russian Strella missiles, the Portuguese lost air superiority, and a number of aircraft were shot down, including one carrying diplomats accredited to Lisbon and the British Air and Naval Attaché in May 1973. The fact that the guerillas from then on had more sophisticated weapons of all sorts than the Portuguese was a major morale factor.

In 1975 the Lisbon revolutionary government evacuated Mozambique and, in Lorenzo Marques (Maputo), handed over control to the Frelimo régime headed by Samora Machel as President.

The British government's ten-year blockade of Beira, to prevent oil reaching Rhodesia through the Beira-Salisbury pipeline, gave support and comfort to the Communist Frelimo revolutionary movement. Apart from the warlike Makonde tribesmen in the far north this movement never had much support throughout the rest of the territory, and was violently opposed by the Macuas who occupied a large area of north central Mozambique.

Strength: metropolitan Portuguese forces 35,000 (maximum in 1972/3) + local Portuguese forces 20,000; Frelimo 8,000 (maximum actively engaged) + in training in Tanzania, Russia, China etc 10,000 (ready to replace casualties) + civilian supporters 100,000

Casualties(1965-75): Portuguese army 3,500; Frelimo 10,000; civilians 50,000.

Strategic results: Mozambique is still tied, especially through the continued development of the Cabora Dam project, to the S African economy on which, for some time, it must depend. But Africa now has a Communist state on the Indian Ocean. The defence and very survival of Rhodesia is now threatened by a 700-mile frontier over which hostile ZAPU (Zimbabwe African People's Union) and ZANU (Zimbabwe African National Union) guerillas, supported by a communist régime, can operate. But the new state is made up of mutually antagonistic tribes. Civil war is a likelihood especially if it were to the advantage of S Africa, which at the present it is not. Britain's pro-revolutionary, anti-S Africa policy in southern Africa appears to be the worst choice possible in regard to her own interests.

NICHOLSON'S NEK/FARQUAR'S FARM (Natal, S Africa)   Second Boer War 29 October 1899

Fought between the Boers under General Petrus Joubert and the British under General Sir George White.

Aim: In face of the Boer advance on Ladysmith (qv) the British garrison came out to try and halt the Boers.

Battle: Joubert held a position which covered about 8 miles and the British attacked in three columns. The left column was detached to hold a position at Nicholson's Nek, but was overwhelmed and surrendered. The Boers also launched a strong attack on the British right and, having no heavy guns to answer the Boer ordnance, White ordered a retreat. The manoeuvre was aided by the arrival of 2 naval guns under Captain Hedworth Lambton and was effected in good order. British losses were 317 killed and wounded and 1,068 missing. Boer losses were small.

Result: The British objective was not achieved. White retreated after this disaster into Ladysmith where his force was invested.

NIZIB (N Syria)   Egyptian Revolt against Turkey   24 June 1839

Strength: Turks 30,000; Egyptians – ?

After Mohammed Ali, Viceroy of Egypt, had taken Syria from the Turks, he continued to threaten Mahmud II with total withdrawal from the Ottoman government.

Aim: The Turks under Hafiz Pasha marched into N Syria to end the rebellion.

Battle: General Ibrahim Pasha, son of Mohammed Ali, commanded the Syrian-Egyptian force. His superior artillery shattered the Turkish ranks, so that one infantry charge drove them from the field. Captain Helmuth von Moltke, a Prussian military adviser to Turkey, came under fire for the first time during this action.

At the time the aged Marshal Soult said that the three greatest soldiers in the world were all Mohommedans - Mohammed Ali in Egypt, Abd-el-Kader in Algeria and Schamyl the Avar in the Caucusus.

OMAN INSURGENCY IN DHOFAR (SE Arabia)   1963-76

Fought between the PFLO (Popular Front for the Liberation of Oman) under its President Ahmed Samaid Da'ib and Salim Ahmed Said al-Ghassani (alias Talal Sa'ad); and the Sultan of Oman's armed forces (SAF) led by British seconded officers, under first, Sultan Said bin Taimur and, from July 1970, his son, Sultan Qaboos, the 14th Al Bin Sa'id, ruler of Oman, and supported by a squadron of British SAS (Special Air Service) and, latterly, an Iranian brigade.

The broad aim of the PFLO, and later the NDFLOAG (National Democratic Front of the Liberation of Oman and Arab Gulf States), was to overcome and depose the sultans of the oil-rich Gulf states and form them into a Russian-satellite People's Federated Republic. Britain's long and potentially dangerous involvement was to secure the defeat of the PFLO and ensure the independence of the Gulf states because of the crucial strategic importance of the area. This involvement required the utmost finesse, diplomatic skill and optimum economy of force to prevent the insurgency from spreading and becoming a great power contest and at the same time eliminate Communist influence. By February 1976 it can be said that Britain had succeeded in her aim and Russia had suffered defeat.

After years of indeterminate guerilla fighting, the war took a decisive turn for the better for the Sultan's armed forces when Sultan Said was deposed in 1970 and his son Qaboos succeded to the throne. Qaboos enthusiastically supported a socio-economic coupled with a military offensive against the insurgents who were operating from safe bases in the People's Democratic Republic of Yemen (PDRY).

Apart from a series of long-awaited reforms, two imaginative interlinked engineering operations contributed decisively to the successful termination of the insurgency. The first was the completion of the Midway Road, which ran from Salalah on the coast to Thamarit (Midway), by SAF engineers and contractors in December 1973. This road was later patrolled by an Iranian brigade. The second engineering aid to the campaign was the construction of the Hornbeam Line. This was similar to the Morice Line constructed by the French in the Algerian War (1954-62) between Algeria and Tunis to exclude well-trained guerillas from joining the fray. Like the Morice Line, the Hornbeam Line consisted of a heavy barrier of barbed wire, anti-personnel mines, unattended ground sensors and manned platoon positions, all supported by long-range artillery. This line successfully isolated the insurgents in the central and eastern sectors and deprived them of supplies. The SAS, SAF and the Iranians then mopped them up.

This engineering offensive was supported by an intensive propaganda campaign linked with a comprehensive resettlement, land-reform and pacification plan throughout the disaffected area. The Iranians, although militarily very useful, inevitably stirred up old fears and tensions so, having done their job, in 1974 they withdrew.

Since 1970, 433 members of the PFLO were killed and over 1,000 surrendered.

By 1976 the revolt was over. In PDRY (S Yemen) there are signs that the Arabs of the Hadhramaut wish to secede from the Communist régime in Aden and form an independent state of their own. This would ensure a buffer zone to protect the Dhofar.

This success has been a most important gain for the West, achieved mainly by British arms and clever diplomacy. The success has, certainly for a time, removed the communist threat to the Gulf oil states and will allow Muscat and Oman to develop her own resources in peace.

OMDURMAN (Sudan)   British Sudan Campaigns   2 September 1898
Fought between the British and Egyptians under General Sir Herbert Kitchener, and the Mahdists.
Strength: Anglo-Egyptians 26,000; Mahdists 45,000.

Kitchener, whose orders were, as given him by the British Government, to reconquer the Sudan and restore Anglo-Egyptian rule, advanced up the Nile, beating back Mahdist resistance wherever he met it, and arrived at Omdurman at the end of August 1898. The town lies on the left bank of the Nile, opposite Khartoum (qv), where the Mahdists had established their capital under the Khalifa, Abdullah et Taaisha.
Battle: Kitchener attacked Omdurman with his force, about a third of whom were British, and although the Mahdists fought fiercely, they were routed, with the loss of 15,000 men. They were pursued by detachments of the British army, whose casualties were only 500. The Khalifa escaped into the province of Kordofan where he was caught and killed the following year.
Result: The battle ended the reconquest of the Sudan, which was thereafter ruled by a condominium of Britain with Egypt. In November of the same year the French crisis which had penetrated the Upper Nile at Fashoda (Kodok) was settled.

PAARDEBERG (Orange Free State, S Africa)   Second Boer War   18-27 February 1900
Fought between the Boers under General Piet Cronje and the British under General Lord Kitchener and General Lord Roberts.
Strength: Boers 5,000; British 20,000.
Aim: The British sought to relieve Kimberley (qv).
Battle: Roberts launched an offensive against the Boers who were entrenched south of the town. Sending a cavalry column under General Sir John French on a wide circling manoeuvre, he succeeded in the relief of the town, forcing the Boers to retreat, their rear being now threatened. Cronje retreated to the dry bed of the Modder River (qv), 23 miles SE of Kimberley. The British pursued. As the British approached the Boer laager, Roberts, who was ill, turned his command over to Kitchener, who ordered an assault on the Boer position. Four infantry brigades with four batteries launched the attack which, owing to lack of cover, was beaten back with a loss of 1,000. Arriving, Roberts called off the assault and, having surrounded the Boers, opened a bombardment which lasted until 27 February when

Cronje, who had refused to leave the wounded and his train though he could have broken out with his 4,000 mounted men, was starved into surrender. British losses were 98 officers and 1,437 men. Boer prisoners amounted to 3,000 Transvaalers and 1,100 Free Staters as well as 6 guns.

Result: The simultaneous relief of Ladysmith (qv) meant that the initiative in the war had now passed to the British.

PERSIAN GULF   1819

Fought between the Joassma tribe and the British under Major-General Sir W. Grant Keir.

Arabian pirates, having been quelled once in 1809 by Sir Lionel Smith, began to prey on shipping in the Persian Gulf. The Joassma tribe was the chief cause of the trouble and it was decided to send an expedition against them.

The force was taken to the area by HMS *Liverpool,* accompanied by several cruisers of the East India Company. On 24 November the force assembled at the Island of Larrack in the Persian Gulf while Grant Keir went on in the *Liverpool* to Ras-el-Khima, the pirates' stronghold, to reconnoitre. Attempts to negotiate with the Joassma through the Imam of Muscat were unsuccessful and the force proceeded to Ras-el-Khima, where it disembarked without encountering opposition. The fort had been strengthened since 1809 and Grant Keir borrowed 24-pounder guns from the *Liverpool* to put into his shore batteries. Before the bombardment began, the Arabs made several sorties, but when the batteries opened fire in earnest, resistance fell. Within twenty-four hours 1,200 32- and 24-pound shot were fired into the fort. On 9 December a breach was declared practicable, but when preparations to storm were made on 10 December it was found to be deserted. The Imam informed the British that the pirates had retreated to another stronghold, Rhams, up the coast, but this was also deserted in favour of the hill fort of Zaya, inland. Two British corps and some artillery succeeded in destroying Zaya by 18 December.

PIETER'S HILL (Natal, S Africa)   Second Boer War   19-27 February 1900

Fought between the British under General Sir Redvers Buller and the Boers.

Aim: The position was attacked by the British in the course of their fourth attempt to relieve Ladysmith (qv).

Battle: On 19 February Hlangwane was captured by the British, ensuring their command of the Tugela, which they crossed on 21 February. An advance was made on 22 February by the Irish Brigade which, when the British had reached the line of Pieter's Hill, attacked up the hill on 23 February. They entrenched themselves close to the Boer lines but could not dislodge them until, on 27 February, Buller turned the Boer left and a general assault took the position. British losses during the operation were 1,896 killed or wounded.

Result: The British went on to relieve Ladysmith.

REDDERSBERG (Cape Province, S Africa)   Second Boer War   3 April 1900
Fought between the British and the Boers under General Christiaan De Wet.

Five companies of British infantry were surrounded by a force of 500 Boers with 3 Krupps guns. After twenty-four hours the British surrendered, owing to the lack of water, having lost 4 officers and 43 men killed and wounded. British prisoners totalled 470, including wounded. The Boer losses were 1 officer killed and 6 burghers wounded.

RHODESIAN GUERILLA INCURSIONS (central Africa)   1966-76
Fought between guerilla units of ZAPU (Zimbabwe African People's Union) under the Soviet-inclined Joshua Nkomo and their rivals ZANU (Zimbabwe African National Union) led by the Reverend Ndabaningi Sithole whose movement is Peking aligned; and the *de facto* Rhodesian government forces under Mr Ian Smith and Lt-General Peter Walls.

ZANU was formed in 1961 and, after being outlawed, moved its headquarters to Lusaka in Zambia. Transfrontier guerilla operations started in 1967 by Africans trained in Tanzania and Russia. ZANU, founded in 1963, started similar operations in 1966 from Zambian bases, with guerillas trained in Algeria, China, Czechoslovakia and Ghana. These sporadic forays over the border achieved little, as the Rhodesian African did not sympathise with them and good intelligence allowed them to be rounded up quickly.

Rhodesia's professional army and police force (trained for paramilitary operations) total 11,500, and are supported by a 10,000-strong territorial army and 35,000 police reservists. A small but efficient air force, especially designed for the purpose, supports the counter-insurgent forces.

In 1974 ZAPU's strength was estimated at 2,000 and ZANU at 600, but there has been heavy recruiting since that date and both insurgent forces have developed more sophisticated methods of winning over tribesmen. During the ten years ending in 1975, 493 guerilla infiltrators have been killed at a loss of 50 of the white and black Rhodesian security forces.

Since Mozambique was granted its independence Rhodesian forces have been faced with a new 700-mile-long frontier to protect. A 'Morice' line, similar to that constructed between Algeria and Tunis by the French in 1954-62, and by the British, Muscat and Iranian forces in Oman, of heavy barbed-wire fence and anti-personnel mines, unattended ground sensors and manned platoon positions, is being constructed. The population which was living near the frontier has been removed and resettled in defended villages in the hinterland.

In 1976 guerilla forces up to 20,000 strong threatened to raid across the long Mozambique border and Mr Smith ordered a further call-up. The Angolan Civil War (qv) has naturally stiffened the resolve of nearly all Rhodesians to protect their frontiers and not sink into similar anarchy, but to reach instead towards some more peaceful solution.

RIETFONTEIN (Natal, S Africa)   Second Boer War   24 October 1899
Fought between the British under General Sir George White and the Boers.
Strength: British 4,000; Boers 5,000.
Aim: The British sought to allow the retreat of Colonel Yule's force from Dundee to continue uninterrupted. The Boers aimed to prevent a planned withdrawal.
Battle: The Boers occupied a range of hills 7 miles from Ladysmith (qv), where they were attacked by White. The action was indecisive and the British retired into Ladysmith with a loss of 111 killed and wounded.
Result: The British objective was achieved, as Colonel Yule was able to withdraw unmolested.

RORKE'S DRIFT (Natal, S Africa)   Zulu War   22 January 1879
Strength: British 139 (the majority belonging to a company of the 24th Foot; Zulus about 4,000.
    After destroying the British force at Isandhlwana (qv) the Zulus went on the same night to attack the post of Rorke's Drift on the Tugela River. The defenders, under Lieutenant Chard, RE, and Lieutenant Gonville Bromhead (24th), beat off an all-night attack with rifle fire. Many acts of bravery were performed, notably the evacuation of the hospital which the Zulus had fired. The Zulus retired at daylight leaving some 400 dead on the field. British losses were 25 killed and wounded. The post was not a strong one, and its defence against so large a force was remarkable. Eight Victoria Crosses (including Chard and Bromhead) and nine Distinguished Conduct Medals were awarded to the garrison.
    Lt-General Lord Chelmsford in his dispatch reported that had it not been for the 'fine example and excellent behaviour' of Chard and Bromhead the defence 'would not have been conducted with that intelligence and tenacity which so essentially characterised it'. Both won the VC and promotion to captain and brevet major. In truth their post was not a strong one, and their defence against so large a force of valiant warriors was truly astonishing.

SANNA'S POST (Orange Free State, S Africa)   Second Boer War   31 March 1900
Fought between the British under General Broadwood and the Boers under General Christiaan De Wet.
    A force of 6,000 British cavalry and two Royal Horse Artillery batteries were ambushed by De Wet who had 1,500 men under his command, of which only 350 took part in the ambush. The guns were entering a donga when the Boers opened fire. Four guns of Q Battery succeeded in getting clear. They opened fire and continued firing until only 10 men were left standing. Broadwood managed to get his men out of the ambush, but British losses were 19 officers and 136 men killed or wounded, 426 men and 7 guns captured and all their convoy was taken. De Wet lost 2 men wounded. General Colville's column heard the firing, but did not go to the aid of the ambushed men.
    Lord Roberts was also in Bloemfontein, only 17 miles away, with 60,000 men under his command. Yet in spite of the sound of guns being audible for four

hours, no one appeared to think of sending reinforcements to Broadwood. There was no enquiry at this dereliction of duty until after the war when a Royal Commission was set up to investigate all the shortcomings of the British Army in the war in South Africa. Its findings caused great reforms in organisation, training and tactics which led to the British Army being better trained and probably more ready for war when it came in 1914 than ever before or since.

The action is also known as the Battle of Kornspruit.

SENEKAL (Orange Free State, S Africa)   Second Boer War   29 May 1900
Fought between the British under General Rundle and the Boers under General de Villiers.
Aim: The British sought to drive the Boers from their strong position on the Biddulphsberg.
Battle: The attack was made while a bush-fire raged about the men and although superior in numbers the British failed to take the position, losing 177 men killed or wounded. Many of the wounded were burnt to death by the fire. The Boer losses were slight. But the Boer commander, General de Villiers, died of wounds.
Result: The British objective was not achieved.

SHANGANI RIVER (Rhodesia, central Africa)   Matabele War   3 December 1893
A small British force under Major Allen Wilson was attacked by the Matabele under King Lobengula. They took up defensive positions on the river Shangani and fought on until every man was killed.

This action is intertwined with the legends of the Rhodesian white settlers and may be a foretaste of their defensive stubbornness if ever serious black/white trouble breaks out in the country.

SIERRA LEONE (W Africa)   1898
The colony of Sierra Leone began with the cession of a strip of land to Captain John Taylor on 22 August 1788, to provide homes for the liberated slaves. Periodically additions were made to the colony, and in 1807 the peninsula of Sierra Leone was ceded by its native ruler.

In 1896 a protectorate was established over the hinterland, after its boundaries had been fixed by agreement between Great Britain and France on 21 January 1895.

In 1928 slavery was abolished and over 200,000 slaves were freed.

SINAI PENINSULA (E Egypt)   Arab-Israeli Wars   29 October-4 November 1956
Fought between the Israelis under General Moshe Dayan and the Egyptians, and also known as the 'war of the hundred hours'.

Ever since the creation of the State of Israel there had been border tension between the new country and her Arab neighbours. The tension had manifested itself in border clashes during the first eight years of the country's existence, but in 1956 the tension flared into open conflict following a political act on the part of the Egyptian government. On 26 July President Gamal Abdel Nasser nationalised the Suez Canal, an action which was condemned by Britain and France who called for international control of the waterway.

Military action, however, came from the Israelis when, on 29 October, ten brigades of the small but well-trained army invaded the Sinai peninsula under Dayan. Only two ill-prepared Egyptian divisions were in the area to resist the sudden move and they offered only slight resistance to the advance. Meanwhile, the British and French air forces began to bomb Egyptian airfields on 31 October prior to sending in airborne troops, who seized Port Said and Port Fuad at the northern end of the canal five days later. Although Britain and France claimed merely to be enforcing the cease-fire between Israel and Egypt, world opinion was outraged, probably believing that the real objective was control of the Suez Canal. By 4 November the Israelis had stopped all military action, having overrun all the peninsula at a cost of 1,000 casualties, including 172 killed. Egyptian losses were thousands of prisoners, hundreds of tanks, self-propelled guns and trucks and quantities of ammunition and supplies. The British and French also ceased their activity and a United Nations force was sent to the area when the Anglo-French force withdrew in December.

The Israelis withdrew from Sinai three months later, restoring the previous *status quo.*

SIX DAY WAR   Arab-Israeli Wars   5-10 June 1967
Fought between the Israelis and the Egyptians, Jordanians and Syrians.

After two wars between the Arabs and Israelis since the creation of the State of Israel in 1948, both of which were technically won by the Israelis, no peace agreement had been signed. Egypt, Jordan and Syria continued to build up military forces, as did Israel. On 17 May 1967 President Gamal Abdel Nasser demanded and received the withdrawal of the United Nations Emergency Forces from the Gaza Strip and on 22 May he closed the Gulf of Aqaba to Israeli shipping which was already unable to use the Suez Canal. Faced with the blockade, the Israelis decided to attack in what was half self-defence and half conquest.

On the morning of 5 June Israel, led by Premier Levi Eshkol, the Defence Minister Moshe Dayan and the Chief of Staff Yitzhak Rabin, mobilised. The Israeli air force flew in a wide arc over the Mediterranean to Egypt where 384 aircraft were destroyed in the air and on the ground (chiefly the latter). Having thus won complete mastery of the air, Israeli armoured columns moved into the Gaza Strip and spread west to the Sinai peninsula (qv), advancing towards the Suez Canal in three columns. One objective was Sharm el Sheikh at the mouth of the Gulf of Aqaba. The Egyptian army was retreating on all fronts after three days of fighting. On 7 June a naval force took Sharm el Sheikh. To the east, Jordanian tank units were defeated from the air, the Old City of Jerusalem (qv) was occupied and Israeli units attacked the Jordanian army west of the Jordan River. Bethlehem, Hebron, Jericho, Nablus, Ramallah and Jenin were all taken. King Hussein of

Jordan agreed to the cease-fire proposed by the UN on 7 June. Egypt agreed on 8 June, and Syria on 9 June. Having won mastery of the heights, strongly fortified, along the border with Syria on 9-10 June, Israeli armour and infantry advanced 12 miles into Syria and took the garrison town of Kuneitra, 12 miles from Damascus, before the cease-fire took effect on 10 June. Minor skirmishes took place during the following days. Israel had magnified itself to four times its territorial size in eighty hours of fighting. The UAR lost between 80,000 and 100,000 men killed, wounded or taken prisoner, most of them being captured along with 800 Russian tanks, 10,000 lorries and hundreds of guns. In addition, 258 MiG jets, 60 Ilyushin bombers and 28 Hunters of the UAR air forces were destroyed. Jordanian casualties totalled 12,000-15,000 out of 55,000. Israeli losses were claimed to be only 61 tanks, 679 men killed and 2,563 wounded.

The capture of Sharm el Sheikh opened the Gulf of Aqaba and Straits of Tiran to international shipping.

Skirmishing still continued along the Arab-Israeli borders during a period of conflict called the War of Attrition (qv) and an Egyptian offensive in 1973 on the Jewish Feast of Yom Kippur (qv) provoked a major clash between the two forces once again.

SOUTH AFRICAN GUN WAR   1880-1
When the Basutos were ordered by the British to surrender their arms, they rebelled. The revolt was suppressed.

Lesothe (Basutoland) was annexed by Cape Colony in 1871 without sufficient consultation. The Cape Government attempted to impose direct rule on the people; the hut tax was doubled, leading to minor outbreaks of violence and increasing uneasiness. When, in 1880, the government tried to disarm the people, the revolt flared into war. Peace was established in 1883 and Lesothe became a crown colony the following year.

SOUTH-WEST AFRICA (NAMIBIA)   Revolt in Ovamboland   September 1965-
Fought between SWAPO (South West African People's Organisation) under Sam Nujoma, and the Republic of S Africa's armed forces.

In 1975 the total number of trained SWAPO guerillas numbered about 400. Owing partly to the civil war in Angola, S Africa had, by February 1976, about one division (15,000 men) deployed in Ovamboland and an area 50 miles north of the border.

The Ovambo tribal area stretches north and south of the Angola/SW African border. The Cunene River which rises near Nova Lisboa (Huambo) forms part of the border. Prior to Angolan independence, the S Africans were combining with the Portuguese to develop large irrigation works and hydro-electric schemes on the Cunene in order to develop Ovamboland and raise the standard of living. In 1965 SWAPO formed a training base at Kazungula in Zambia and other recruits went to Ghana, Russia, Algeria, N Korea, China and Egypt for training. On 26 August S African police rounded up 16 guerillas at Ongulumbashe. Further clashes occurred in the Caprivi Strip, and between 1967 and 1971 more guerillas were killed or rounded up and brought to trial. After SWAPO representatives visited London, New York and other capitals in Europe and Africa to gain political support, overt operations increased, and the hasty Portuguese evacuation of Angola encouraged them further. The outbreak of the Angolan Civil War (qv) forced the S Africans to take sterner measures and put the country on to a war footing. But the final aim appears to be to grant the whole of Ovamboland, including its Angolan component, independence, its economic viability being supported by the series of Cunene River hydro-electric and irrigation schemes, under S African protection. This would provide a buffer state to prevent the Angolan conflagration from spreading south.

Casualties (approximate) over the last ten years: SWAPO 220 killed + 400 detained; S Africa 35 killed.

The Russian and Cuban military support of the MPLA faction in the Angolan Civil War is likely to make the whole area of increasing geopolitical and strategic importance. Meanwhile SWAPO resistance continues.

SPANISH SAHARA (W SAHARA) INCIDENT (W Africa)   December 1975-February 1976

When the head of the Spanish State, General Francisco Franco, died, King Hassan II of Morocco saw the opportunity of enlarging his dominions and improving his economy. He organised a demonstration march, partly led by himself, of 200,000 Moroccans into the northern border of Spanish Sahara. Negotiations resulted in an agreement whereby this mainly desert area, the size of England but with a nomadic population of only 60,000, would be jointly administered by Morocco and Mauritania. The rich nitrate deposits (reputedly the richest in the world and developed by the Spanish and Krupps) at Bucrâa would be exploited by a joint Spanish-Moroccan consortium. This pleased everyone except President Houari Boumedienne of Algeria, who laid a tenuous claim to the area and supported Polisario, a vague, ephemeral guerilla organisation purporting to represent some of the more remote nomadic bedouins.

Late in January 1975 an Algerian military column, claiming to be an escort for a food convoy to some indigent Arabs, entered the Saharan territory and was severely mauled by Moroccan regulars, who caused about 200 casualties. It would be difficult at any time for the Algerians to mount a sustained offensive across such barren country.

The economic attractions of the area include, besides the nitrate deposits, excellent fishing grounds off the Saharan coast at present being exploited by Korean, Japanese, Russian and Taiwanese fishing fleets and factory ships; and fabulously rich iron-ore deposits, estimated at 3,000 million tons at Gara Djebilet, near Tindouf, on the short Algerian-W Saharan border.

SPION KOP (Natal, S Africa)   Second Boer War   22-4 January 1900

Fought between the British under General Sir Redvers Buller and the Boers under

General Louis Botha.
Strength: British 24,000; Boers 5,000
Aim: Although Buller was replaced as Commander-in-Chief by General Lord Roberts, he retained command on the Natal front and in January 1900 launched a second attempt to relieve Ladysmith (qv).
Battle: The British fought their way across the Tugela on 19 January when General Sir Charles Warren's division also began to turn the Boer right. In successive days, the Boers were driven back from ridge to ridge until in a night attack on 22 January Warren captured the centre of the Boer position at Spion Kop, 24 miles SW of Ladysmith. An attempt to bring artillery up the steep slopes failed and the brigade holding the position lost heavily during 23 January. At nightfall that day, Colonel Thorneycroft, who had replaced General Woodgate on the latter's death, ordered a withdrawal, and on 24 January Buller decided to recross the Tugela. British losses during the operation were 87 officers and 1,647 men. Boer losses were slight.
Result: Buller's objective was not achieved. British troops had by now lost confidence in Buller and in November 1900 he returned to England and in spite of his long series of defeats, was given command of Aldershot district. But, a year later, he made an indiscreet speech claiming that he, not Roberts nor Kitchener, was the real victor in South Africa, and he was forced into retirement.

STORMBERG (Cape Province, S Africa)   Second Boer War   10 December 1899
Fought between the British under General Gatacre and the Boers.
    As part of the three-pronged offensive launched by General Sir Redvers Buller, Gatacre advanced on Stormberg with a column totalling 3,000 from Cape Colony. The Boers had advanced as far as 70 miles from Queenstown where Gatacre found them.
    The British undertook a night march on the Boer position but, being misled by guides, they came under heavy fire from the Boers and before they could retire they had lost 89 killed or wounded, 600 prisoners and 3 guns. The Boer losses were comparatively slight.
    This was the first of three defeats in what was to be known as 'Black Week', the others being Colenso and Magersfontein (qqv).

SUAKIN (Sudan, NE Africa)   1885
Suakin was occupied by the Egyptians when their power was extended over the Sudan. In the neighbourhood several battles were fought against the forces of the Mahdi. In 1884 Osman Digna with his dervishes wiped out a contingent of 500 Egyptians moving from Suakin to Sinkat. Valentine Baker Pasha was sent to Suakin with a brigade of 3,600 Egyptians but was badly defeated by Osman Digna and his 'Fuzzy Wuzzies', who then captured Tokar and Sinkat. General Sir Gerald Graham, with a mixed force of British infantry, cavalry and seamen, defeated Osman Digna on 29 February and 13 March 1884, the Mahdist forces losing over 2,000 killed.

The British decided to build a railway from Suakin to Khartoum (qv) and a further series of battles took place as the railhead advanced, including one outside Suakin where Osman Digna lost 1,000 men. When 5,000 dervishes attacked General Sir John McNeill's force at Tofrek (qv), later named McNeill's Zareba, on 22 March, 1,500 were killed in twenty minutes, mostly by the Gatling guns.

When the plan for the reconquest of the Sudan was revived twelve years later, Osman Digna was still in the field, having taken part in the Battle of Omdurman (qv) in 1898. He was finally captured in January 1900 and sent to Rosetta, Egypt. From there he was sent to Wadi Halfa, where he lived comfortably in exile until he died at the age of eighty-five.

TALANA HILL (Natal, S Africa)   Second Boer War   20 October 1899
Fought between the Boers under General Lukas Meyer and the British under General Symons.
Strength: Boers 4,000; British 4,000.
Aim: The British sought to beat the Boers from the heights of Dundee.
Battle: The British attacked the strong position and dislodged the Boers with a loss of 300. The British lost 19 officers and 142 men killed and wounded plus 331 prisoners- a detachment of cavalry and mounted infantry which was surrounded by a superior force of Boers and forced to surrender.
Result: Although the British objective was achieved, Symons was mortally wounded and the thrust on Ladysmith (qv) was not halted.
The action is also known as the Battle of Dundee.

TAMAI (SUDAN)   British-Sudan Campaigns   13 March 1884
Fought between the British under General Sir Gerald Graham and the Mahdists under Osman Dinga.
Strength: British 4,000; Mahdists 20,000.
The British in square formation attacked the Mahdist camp. The first square was broken by the Mahdists who took the naval guns, but the second square came up to support the first and the Mahdists were beaten back. The British recovered their guns, losing 10 officers and 204 men killed or wounded. Mahdist losses were over 2,000 killed.

TANANARIVE (Malagasy Republic   French Conquest of Madagascar   30 September 1895
Fought between the French under General Jacques Duchesne and the Hova under Queen Ranavalona III.
Strength: French 15,000; Hova − ?
Aim: For three centuries the French had been trying to conquer Madagascar. In 1895 the Third Republic launched an expedition in order to establish the French on the island.
Battle: Duchesne landed at Majunga on the NW coast in February. Disease and transport problems hampered the progress of the expedition, but a column was

sent SE into the interior towards the capital, Tananarive. The French opened a bombardment outside the city on 30 September, and Ranavalona immediately surrendered.
Result: General Joseph Galliéni became Governor of the new colony in 1896 and native resistance was suppressed. Galliéni was to be one of the great French colonial administrators.

TEL-EL-KEBIR (Egypt)   Egyptian Revolt   12 September 1882
Fought between the British under General Sir Garnet Wolseley and the Egyptians under Colonel Arabi Pasha.
Strength: British 17,000; Egyptians 22,000.
Aim: Following the British occupation of Alexandria (qv), a force was landed in Lower Egypt to quell the nationalist rising led by Arabi Pasha.
Battle: The British marched inland and after a night march across the desert, they came upon the Egyptians in Tel-el-Kebir, a village near Zagazig. The British stormed and took the Egyptian trenches with a loss of 339 killed or wounded. Egyptian losses were heavy.
Result: Continuing south, Wolseley entered Cairo on 15 September. Arabi was captured and exiled and the revolt quelled. Joint British and French rule over Egypt now came to an end.

TEL-EL-MAHUTA (Egypt)   Egyptian Revolt   24 August 1882
The Egyptians attempted to block the advanced guard of the British force under General Sir Gerald Graham as it made its way to Kassassin (qv). After making only a weak attack they were driven off with heavy loss.

TETUAN (Morocco, N Africa)   Spanish-Moroccan War   4 February 1860
Fought between the Spanish under Marshal Leopoldo O'Donnell and the Moors.
Strength: Spanish 30,000; Moors 40,000.
Aim: The Spanish sought to beat the Moors out of their entrenchments around Tetuan.
Battle: The Spanish stormed and carried the Moorish entrenchments.
Result: Three days later the town of Tetuan was entered by the Spanish.

TOFREK (Sudan, NE Africa)   British Sudan Campaigns   22 March 1885
Fought between the Sepoys and British under General Sir John McNeill and the Mahdists.
Strength: British Sepoys 3 battalions + British 1½ battalions; Mahdists 5,000.

Thanks to indifferent scouting by the 5th Lancers the British were surprised in their *zariba* (stockades) by the Mahdists. Although one of the Sepoy regiments broke and fled and the *zariba* was forced by the Mahdists, the rest of the British force held its ground and, after twenty minutes' fighting, the Mahdists were repulsed with a loss of over 2,000 killed. British losses were 294 combatants and 176 camp followers killed, wounded or missing.

TRANSVAAL CIVIL WAR (S Africa)   1862-4
The Boers under Commandant Marthinus Wessels Pretorius and Commandant Paul Kruger quelled the insurgents.

TRINKITAT (Sudan, NE Africa)   British Sudan Campaigns   29 March 1884
Fought between the British under General Sir Gerald Graham and the Mahdists under Osman Dinga.
Strength: British 4,000; Mahdists 6,000.
   The Mahdists were completely defeated after a fierce fight lasting five hours. One hundred and eighty-nine British were killed or wounded. Mahdist losses were about 2,000.
   The action is also known as the Battle of El Teb.

UGANDA, RELIGIOUS WARS (E Africa)   1885-9
Fought between the Catholics under King Mwanga and the Moslems.
   Although the wars were between the Catholics and Moslems to begin with, after Mwanga's victory over the Moslems in 1889 disputes between Catholics and Protestants broke out.
   Mwanga's predecessor, Mutesa, had allowed missionaries into the country in an attempt to try and stop the slavers' attacks from the north. Although without military experience, the missionaries became involved with the politics of the country and, on Mwanga's succession, their influence spread rapidly. Mwanga, jealous of the Christians' influence, attempted to expel them, but was himself deposed in 1888, while the missionaries and their converts were shortly afterwards forced out by the Moslem Baganda who was aided by the Arabs.
   Mwanga was restored in 1889 with the aid of the Catholic and Protestant Bagandas, who later quarrelled amongst themselves.

ULUNDI (Natal, S Africa)   Zulu War   4 July 1879
Fought between the British under General Lord Chelmsford and the Zulus under Cetewayo.
Strength: British 5,000; Zulus 20,000.
Aim: The Zulu uprising in S Africa was successful at first, but the British launched a counter-offensive, marching to Ulundi, 115 miles NE of Durban, where the headquarters kraal of Cetewayo was situated.
Battle: The kraal was guarded by men divided into impis (regiments). The British attacked and defeated the Zulus, breaking the power of the tribe. One thousand five hundred Zulus were killed. The British lost 15 killed and 78 wounded.
Result: Cetewayo was pursued and captured on 28 August, which brought the Zulu War to an end. Zululand was eventually incorporated into the Republic of S Africa.

VAAL KRANZ (Natal, S Africa)   Second Boer War   5-7 February 1900
Fought between the British under General Sir Redvers Buller and the Boers under General Louis Botha.
Strength: British 20,000; Boers 7,000.

Aim: After his failure to relieve Ladysmith (qv) in January at Spion Kop (qv), Buller launched a third relief attempt.

Battle: On 5 February Buller forced a crossing of the Tugela River and, under cover of a feint attack at Brakfontein on the Boer right, seized Vaal Kranz which lay SW of Ladysmith. The Boers counter-attacked for two days, but the British held the village. Further progress proved impossible, however, and on 7 February Buller once again withdrew across the Tugela. British losses were 374. Boer casualties were considerably less.

Result: Buller's objective was not achieved, but this was the last major victory for the Boers.

WAR OF ATTRITION (Israeli-occupied territory, Egypt, Lebanon and Syria)
March 1969-August 1970

Fought between the Egyptians under President Gamal Abdel Nasser, the Syrians and the PFLP (Popular Front for the Liberation of Palestine) guerilla forces under Yasir Mohammed Arafat, and the Israelis.

The so-called War of Attrition was initiated by President Nasser of Egypt in March 1969. In the previous Arab/Israeli wars he had seen how unmilitary the Arab forces were compared with the Israelis, many of whose commanders had fought on either side in the 1939-45 war. So Nasser initiated a series of operations to 'blood' his troops, give them practical exercise of their more sophisticated weapons and to create one or two heroes whom others might be tempted to emulate. He arranged with Yasir Arafat that the Palestine guerillas based on Syria and Jordan should do the same, as only by experience of military operations and raids could the youthful Fedayeen guerillas develop from an irregular, ill-disciplined group into an effective and dangerous raiding force representing occupied Palestine and which was eventually recognised by the United Nations.

Operations during the period included the Egyptian bombardment of the Israeli Bar-Lev line along the east bank of the Suez Canal as it was being constructed, and Israeli reprisals by aerial bombing and raids by parachutists and commandos deep into Egypt and along the Gulf of Suez. The Palestine Fedayeen guerilla raids reached a crescendo during 1969 not only against targets in Israel (90 raids against bridges, railway lines and military camps inflicting 650 Israeli casualties for only 9 guerillas killed) but also against Jews or Jewish property in many countries of the world. The Israelis retaliated with terrorist raids by bomber aircraft against ill-defined guerilla camps in the Lebanon, which was too weak to hit back.

The Israelis also helped stoke up rivalry between King Hussein of Jordan and the Fedayeen which led to the eviction, after heavy casualties, of most of the Arab guerillas from Jordan into Syria and Lebanon.

The guerillas' methods and skill improved greatly during this period until they became both a military and political force to be reckoned with and recognised by all participants in the conflict. Meanwhile both Syria and, especially, Egypt were testing their strength against the Israeli forces and keeping them mobilised which the Israelis could ill afford to be for any length of time as their army was nearly entirely composed of civilians who had businesses to run. So it became a form of economic warfare. Deep penetration raids by the Israeli Air Force continued to April 1970 until the development of an Egyptian SAM 2 surface-to-air missile defence system along the canal and in the Egyptian hinterland made such raids too expensive.

In July 1970 Nasser agreed to the proposed Israeli cease-fire which started on 7 August.

Result: The Egyptian and Arab forces generally improved their military prowess beyond all recognition and the Israelis had to ask the USA for much more sophisticated weaponry to match the Russian weapons which Egyptians and Syrians had received and learned to use. Israeli retaliatory raids against Egyptian and Lebanese territory were counter-productive as it made them lose their poor oppressed image in the world. They therefore lost the propaganda battle and the world sympathised with and understood better the Arab and Palestine viewpoint.

On 28 September 1970 President Nasser died having achieved his aims of uniting the Egyptians and Arabs, turning them into good soldiers with a good tradition in modern warfare, and setting up a respected, effective guerilla organisation prepared to liberate Israeli-held Palestine.

WEPENER (Natal, S Africa)   Second Boer War   9-25 April 1900
Fought between the British under Colonel Dalgety and the Boers under General Christiaan De Wet.
Strength: British 1,700; Boers 1,000.
Aim: The Boers sought the reduction of the garrison.
Battle: The Boers invested the town with a strong force which was superior in both artillery and men to the British men of the Colonial Division. The Boers made many fierce attacks on the British trenches, but they did not succeed in taking the town, which held out until it was relieved by General Rundle. British losses during the siege were 300 killed or wounded. The Boers lost five killed and thirteen wounded.
Result: The Boer objective was not achieved.

YOM KIPPUR WAR   Arab-Israeli Wars   6-24 October 1973
(Also know as War of Atonement or October War)
Fought between Israel under Mrs Golda Meir (Prime Minister), Moshe Dayan (Minister of Defence), Lt-Gen David Elazar (Chief of Staff), Rear-Admiral Benjamin Telem (Navy), Major-General Shmuel Gonen (Sinai front), Major-General Yitzhak Hofi (Golan Heights), Major-General Arik Sharon (counter-attack force), Major-General Israel Tal (VCoS), General Benjamin Peled (Air Force); and the Egyptians under Anwar El Sadat (President and Prime Minister), General Ahmed Ismail (Minister of War), and Lt-General Saad Shazli (Chief of Staff); Syrians under President Hafez Assad, Mustafa Tlas (Defence Minister); Jordanians under King Hussein; Iraq; Libya; Saudi Arabia; and the Palestine Liberation Organisation (PLO) under Yasser Arafat.

Ever since the Six Day War (qv) Israel had been harassing Egypt and Syria by bombing raids as well as land and seaborne raids in retaliation for operations by the PLO (al Fatah guerillas). The PLO was well led by Yasser Arafat, a business-man who had given up a prosperous business in Kuwait to devote himself to the Palestinian cause and so was revered and admired for his selflessness throughout the Arab world. The situation could not last and President Sadat of Egypt decided with President Assad of Syria to make a concerted surprise attack on Israel in an effort to drive the Israelis back to the internationally agreed 1946 treaty line.

Strength: Israelis (army): 95,000 regulars + 180,000 reserves: 10 armoured brigades with 1,700 tanks (including 600 British Centurions, 200 Shermans, 250 locally built Ben Gurions) + 18 infantry brigades + brigades and 5 paratroop units + 3 artillery brigades with 350 self-propelled guns + (air force): 20,000 men with 355 aircraft + reinforcements from USA (95 5-4E Phantoms, 35 Mirage 111-B/C fighter-bomber interceptors, 160 A-4E/4 Skyhawks, 23 Mystère IV-A fighter-bombers, 24 Barak and 18 Super-Mystère B-2 interceptors) + (navy): fleet included 14 Saar Class patrol boats with Gabriel missiles; *Egyptians* (army): 260,000 with 1,850 tanks (1,650 T-54/55s, 100 T-62s, 100 T-34s [medium], all from Russia) + (missile defence system): 130 SAM sites (SA-2 and SA-3 launchers, SA-6s and SA-7s) + ZSU-23mm quadruple cannons, RPG-7 anti-tank unguided rockets and Sagger anti-tank wire-guided weapons + (air force): 23,000 men with 426 aircraft + (navy): 12 Osa-type missile boats + 10 submarines + 6 advanced-type torpedo boats + 20 regular torpedo boats + 3 destroyers + 2 frigates + minesweepers and landing craft + *Syrians* (army): 120,000 regulars + 200,000 reserves with 1,270 tanks + 1,000 armoured personnel carriers + 75 self-propelled guns + (air force): 10,000 men with 326 aircraft + (navy): 3 Osa-type and 6 Komar-type missile boats + 1 : torpedo boats + 2 minesweepers + *Jordanians* (army): 68,000 with 420 medium tanks + (air force): 52 aircraft (32 Hunter fighters, 20 F-104A interceptors) + *Iraqis* (army): 90,000 with 900 tanks (T-54/55s) + (air force): 180 aircraft (60 Su-7s, 90 MiG-2s, 30 MiG-17s) + *Libyans'* supply of 44 aircraft (35 Mirage 111s, 9 FA interceptors).

The campaign was fought on two fronts, the Sinai and the Golan Heights, with considerable air and naval activity but with the Jordan front remaining quiescent and the PLO remarkably inactive.

SINAI FRONT

The Israelis had fortified a $40 million Bar-Lev defensive line on the east bank of the Suez Canal, whose garrison was commanded by Major-General Shmuel Gonen. At 14.05 on 6 October 1973, 1,000 Egyptian guns bombarded the Bar-Lev Line for fifty-three minutes. Ten Egyptian brigades, suitably equipped, then crossed the canal. General Ahmed Ismail had launched two armies across the canal: the 2nd Army (three infantry and one armoured divisions) between Kantara and Ismailia, and the 3rd Army (two infantry and one armoured) south of the Bitter Lakes and near Suez itself. Surprise was complete. The troops were equipped with Sagger anti-tank missiles and RPG-7 rocket launchers. The bridgeheads were protected against air attack by SA-2 and SA-3 missiles west of the canal, and SA-6s on the bridgehead with conventional S-60 anti-aircraft guns and 23mm ZSU 23-4 cannons. The Israeli air force counter-attacked strongly but suffered heavy casualties from this defence. Gonen launched a tank attack but was severely repulsed, losing 140 tanks. General Ismail consolidated to allow the Israelis to shatter themselves on his missile defence. This they proceeded to do.

GOLAN FRONT

At 13.58 on 6 October the Syrians started their attack with a series of air strikes on the Israeli defences, followed swiftly by an attack of 2,000 tanks of the 5th, 7th, and 9th Syrian Mechanised Divisions, of which 600 were Russian-built T-54s and T-55s. In reserve were the 1st and 3rd Armoured Divisions with a further 1,000 tanks including some T-60s. Accompanied by infantry, the Syrian attack overcame all resistance, captured Qneitra that evening and regained most of the Israeli-held Syrian territory. They paused on 7 October, as there was supposedly no hurry. They were on the verge of descending on to the Jordan plains. However on 10 October the Israelis had gathered enough reserves to counter-attack and drove the Syrians back over their starting line towards Damascus. Reinforced by Iraqis, Jordanians, and Saudi Arabians, the Syrians were starting to push the depleted Israeli forces back again, when the war finished on 24 October.

SINAI FRONT

By 7 October the Egyptians had extended the depth of their bridgehead on the east bank to 6 miles. The missile barrier was sufficient to prevent the IAF from causing much harm, in spite of severe casualties to themselves. General Ismail wanted to wait before a further advance, but an appeal from the Syrian army on 12 October forced his hand. A further advance began at dawn on 13 October. This gave the Israelis their chance. In the afternoon of 13 October the Israelis managed to cut behind the 1,000 advancing Egyptian tanks which were heading for the Giddi Pass. The USA were providing Israel with hundreds of tanks, aircraft and guns to retrieve their initial losses and to counter the huge Russian airlift of weapons to Syria. At this crucial period General Arik Sharon was ordered to cross the canal just north of the Bitter Lakes and to attack the Egyptians in the rear. It was to some extent a 'forlorn hope' but it won the war. Sharon, risking everything, crossed successfully at Chinese Farm and wheeled behind the Egyptian communications across the canal. This threw their whole force into jeopardy.

The international situation, with the two major powers helping either side, had become so grave that all participants and apprehensive oil-starved neutrals on the touchline were glad to find an excuse to stop. A cease-fire was agreed between the Israelis and Egyptians on 22 October and with the Syrians on 24 October. A neutral zone was agreed upon on both fronts which was to be manned by a United Nations Emergency Force of 7,000 troops. Within a few months it numbered 4,289, including contingents from Austria (387), Canada (1,037), Finland (620), Indonesia (34), Ireland (268), Panama (425), Peru (497), Poland (447) and Sweden (624). Ghana promised a further 600.

NAVAL OPERATIONS

The most significant lesson learnt from the Yom Kippur War was not the success of anti-tank guided weapons nor that of the unguided RPG-7. Nor was it the very evident vulnerability of aircraft to SAM missiles in spite of electronic counter-measures. It was the technical success of the Osa-type surface-to-surface missile boats (which were originally smuggled in from France). In the Battle of Latakia, on the night of 6/7 October, 5 Israeli missile boats accompanied by the INS *Reshef* engaged 1 Syrian minesweeper and 3 missile boats. All 3 Syrian missile boats were sunk. This was the first purely naval missile battle in history.

A similar IN sweep on the same night in Egyptian waters was not so successful but, as a result, 1 Egyptian missile boat was sunk by the IAF. But on the night 8/9 October, 6 IN missile boats engaged 4 Egyptian boats which were attacking them. After an exchange of missiles, 3 Egyptian craft were sunk.

The Israeli navy continued its aggressive activity throughout the war, including bombarding harbour and oil installations in Syria and Egypt, sinking naval and merchant vessels including, by mistake, the 12,000-ton Soviet supply ship, *Ilya Machnikov,* and using frogmen to attack ships in harbour. In the Red Sea and the Gulfs of Suez and Aqaba the naval activity centred upon the disruption of oil supplies and destruction or seizure of oil installations.

The Egyptian and Syrian navies launched 52 missiles at sea-going IN ships, but caused only 3 killed and 24 wounded. The IN sank 19 naval vessels including 10 missile boats. Naval warfare, certainly in narrow seas, was entering a new era.

THE AIR WAR

The Israeli terror attacks on Syria and Egypt which mounted in crescendo between the Six Day War (5-10 June 1967) and October 1972 fully alerted the UAR to their vulnerability to air attack. So they shopped around for a counter. The Russians provided them with an efficient counter-measure with the provision of SAM 2 and 3 missiles, mobile SAM 6s which could follow the battle and hundreds of SAM 7 portable Strella missile launchers deployed down to infantry-company level. These anti-aircraft measures were supported by conventional weapons such as the Russian multi-barrelled ZSU. The immediate result was that the IAF, in its efforts to contain the Egyptian offensive, suffered enormous losses which were only made up by a major United States effort of convoying new aircraft from Germany to Israel, and across the Atlantic via the Azores, completely equipped with the latest electronic defensive devices which the Americans had previously refrained from selling to the Israelis. Her NATO Allies kept well clear of this partisanship (apart from Portugal, which had no option), not wishing to escalate this war any further in case it might spread. Britain and France also clearly remembered the 1956 Suez War when their ally, the United States, intervened on the side of Egypt against them. The US argument for her active participation in this war was that Russia was overflying Yugoslavia and Greece with an enormous airlift of weapons to Syria.

The danger of these rival airlifts and the escalation in the supply of sophisticated arms to these few, comparatively insignificant countries did more than anything to make the great powers bring the war to an end before it could spread.

True casualties figures have been difficult to assess, since both sides remained

in a state of war and naturally wished to conceal their losses. Estimated losses
are: Israel 4,100 killed or wounded; Egypt 7,500 killed or wounded; Syria 7,300
killed or wounded. Claims by either side of tanks and aircraft destroyed are so
diverse as to make conjecture useless. But, for certain, the Israeli/Egyptian tank
battles were waged by more armoured vehicles than were ever deployed in one
battle at El Alamein or in France or Russia, and the losses were proportionately
higher owing to guided and unguided anti-tank rocket missiles. This war may mark
the end of the offensive power of the tank generally and it may envisage a return
to a period when the defence is stronger than the capability of the offensive.

ZULULAND CIVIL WARS (Natal, S Africa)   1818-19; 1883-4
The first war of 1818-19 was fought between the followers of two rival chiefs -
Dingiswayo and Zwide. Zwide killed Dingiswayo and, after fierce fighting, was
himself killed by Shaka, a protégé of Dingiswayo.

When Cetewayo was restored to his throne on 29 January 1883, quarrels
between rival chiefs again turned into war, and in December of that year Cetewayo
was overthrown by Zibelu who, in turn, was soon deposed by Cetewayo's son,
Dinizulu.

SECTION FOUR

THE FAR EAST AND THE ANTIPODES

See Map Section, nos 12–14

ANKING (Anhwei Province, E central China)   T'ai P'ing Rebellion   10 August-
5 September 1861
After being held by the T'ai P'ing for nine years, and having withstood several
sieges, Anking fell on 5 September 1861 to the Chinese Imperial forces under the
great counter-insurgent commander General Tseng Kuo-fan. T'ai P'ing forces were
commanded by General Yeh Yün-lai.
Strength: Government forces 160,000; T'ai P'ing forces 130,000.
   Each side suffered about 30,000 casualties.
Result: Anking was henceforth used as a base for the government's attack on the
T'ai P'ing capital of Nanking.
   Tseng Kuo-fan, one of China's most illustrious generals, was the general mainly
responsible for the defeat of the T'ai P'ing in the field of battle owing to his
tenacity of purpose, incorruptibility, military genius and strength of character.
The core of his force was usually the Hunan Braves from the province of Hunan.
He has been condemned by left-wing Chinese writers as a traitor who fought for
the Manchu dynasty.

AN LAO VALLEY (S Vietnam)   Vietnam War   25 January-February 1966
Fought between the N and S Vietnamese and US forces.
Strength: N Vietnamese 10,000; S Vietnamese 19,000 + US 20,000.
Aim: Since 1954 the Viet Cong had held the coast of the S China Sea from Qui
Nhon north along Route 1 almost to Chu Lai. The Americans sought to clear the
Binh Dinh plains of Viet Cong in an operation that brought with it some of the
heaviest fighting of the war.
Battle: The centre of the battle was An Lao valley, which lies 280 miles NE of
Saigon, and it was towards this area that the first wave of 12,000 troops drove on
25 January. The US 1st Cavalry, S Vietnamese Airborne and S Korean marines
undertook this, the first divisional attack of the war, known as Operation White
Wing. On 28 January they were reinforced with 5,000 US marines and 2,000
S Vietnamese troops who attacked towards An Lao from the south and west in
Operation Double Eagle, a large-scale pincer movement. The battle lasted three
weeks, during which time 1,800 N Vietnamese were killed. Several hundred
S Vietnamese and US casualties were suffered.
Result: Most of the N Vietnamese troops in the area, estimated at between two
and four regiments, escaped into the hills to the west.

A SHAU (S Vietnam)   Vietnam War   9 March 1966
Fought between the N and S Vietnamese, the latter with some US support.
Strength: N Vietnamese 3,000; S Vietnamese 360 (Montagnard and Nung) + 17
(Green Berets).
   The Communist take-over of S Vietnam seemed to be checked by the increased
military strength in that country in 1965, but a sudden attack on the Special
Forces camp at A Shau opened the hostilities once again. The camp at A Shau,
55 miles west of Da Nang and 360 miles north of Saigon, consisted of a triangular

log fortress 480 feet square. It lay only 3 miles from the Laotian border. Viet Cong infiltration weakened the camp, which was not supported from the air because of bad weather. After thirty-nine hours the camp fell, the first to do so since the Viet Cong stormed Dak Sut in the highlands of the interior, 290 miles north of Saigon, on 19 August 1965. Helicopters lifted 200 defenders out during and after the Communist attack, including 12 of the Special Forces men, and others were thought to have escaped into the jungle. During the battle 3 fighter aircraft and 3 helicopters were lost by the Americans.

BIAS BAY (KWANGTUNG)   Sino-Japanese Incident   12 October 1938
The Japanese controlled the coast of China from Shanghai (qv) to the north. But much oil and supplies were entering China through the great port of Canton, which had only recently (1937) been connected to Hankow and the interior by railway. The Japanese decided to close this supply line.
    On 12 October 1938 the Japanese landed two infantry divisions, one tank brigade and marines at Bias Bay, just east of Hong Kong, a well-known resort of pirates, and advanced inland. Canton fell on 21 October.

BRUNEI REVOLT (AZAHARI'S REBELLION) (NW Borneo)   December 1962
The revolt, led by Sultan Azahari in an attempt to take power, was brought under control by the 17th Gurkha Division, commanded by Major-General Sir Walter Walker, supported by the Royal Navy, including the RM Commandos off HMS *Albion,* the cruiser *Tiger* and destroyer *Cavalier.* British units taking part included the KOYLI (King's Own Yorkshire Light Infantry), Greenjackets and Queen's Own Highlanders. The 22nd SAS followed through the infantry in order to track down the rebels so as to destroy them in their jungle sanctuaries.

CAMBODIA   1841–5
Cambodia revolted against Vietnamese rule and asked Siam for help. P'ya Bodin, the ageing Siamese leader, took an army into Cambodia where there followed four years of fierce fighting in which the Siamese obtained an advantage. In 1845 a compromise peace was agreed, in which Siam and Vietnam were to have a joint protectorate over Cambodia, Siam being the dominant partner.

CHANGSHA (Hunan Province, central China)   T'ai P'ing Rebellion   11 September-30 November 1852
Fought between the Imperial government forces under Chiang Chung-yüan and Tso Tsung-t'ang (who later became a great general), and the T'ai P'ing under Hsiao Ch'ao-kuei, Li K'ai-fang and Lin Feng-hsiang.
    Hsiao, appointed the 'Western King', was an impatient general. As soon as he reached the great metropolitan city of Changsha, he launched a fierce attack. The defenders were surprised and were in dire straits when a marksman from the walls of the city sighted Hsiao in his conspicuous yellow robes on a hill from which he was directing the assault, and killed him.

Hsiao's death was an irreparable loss to the movement, as he was an outstanding strategist and brave leader. Hung Hsui-ch'uan and Yang Hsui-ch'ing on hearing of his death quickly brought up their armies to capture Changsha. But by this time the famous Banner men and the Green Standards had entered the city and joined the defence.

The T'ai P'ing with their Kwangsi miners drove tunnels under the walls and tried to mine the gates, but Tso Tsung-t'ang drove counter-mines to forestall them. The siege continued but the T'ai P'ing lacked reserves and heavy guns.

On 30 November, under cover of a rainstorm, the T'ai P'ing crossed the Hsiang River and on 3 December captured I-yang, where they obtained 1,000 boats with which they crossed the Tungking lake and, on 13 December, captured Yochow (now Yoyang). There they appointed an admiral from amongst the best of the river traders and, from there on, used the river of central China as their main communication.

The three-month siege of Changsha was a failure. But it was the habit of the T'ai P'ing, when they met an obstacle, to move like water around it. Changsha was attacked in 1853 by one of the T'ai P'ing's greatest, an almost invincible general, Shih Ta-k'ai. Here he met the Imperial forces' greatest counter-insurgent, General Tseng Kuo-fan who waged not only a military but a cultural, political and religious war against the neo-Christian T'ai P'ing.

Changsha was saved but the great cities of Wuchang, Hankow and Hanyang were, during the next few years until 1858, lost and won again - then lost and again won by Tseng's counter-insurgent force, the Hunan Braves.

CHEMULPO (INCHON) (S Korea)   Russo-Japanese War   8 February 1904
Fought between the Japanese under Vice-Admiral Hikonojo Kamimura   and   the Russians.
Strength: Japanese 4 cruisers; Russians 1 cruiser + 1 gunboat.
Aim: The Russians sought to prevent the landing by the Japanese of troops at Chemulpo (Inchon) where they were being carried by troopships protected by Japanese cruisers.
Battle: After a short, fierce action the Russian cruiser, after suffering serious damage, was blown up to avoid capture. The gunboat was destroyed by gunfire. Russian losses were 504 killed and wounded. The Japanese suffered no material damage.
Result: The Russian objective was not achieved and the Japanese went on to land their troops and occupy Inchon.

CHINA I   Sino-Japanese War   7 July 1937–7 December 1941
Fought between the Chinese under Chiang Kai-shek and the Japanese.

At the beginning of the twentieth century, some Japanese leaders wished to expand their territorial ownership to the Asian mainland and China became their objective as it became clear that the country was having internal difficulties concerning unification and nationalism. As unrest in China increased, the

Japanese sent troops in under the pretext of helping to establish order. On 18 September 1931 Japanese troops in Mukden attacked Chinese police in Manchuria, using this fracas as a pretext to occupy the province. In February 1932 the Japanese set up a puppet state called Manchukuo, but the situation remained dormant until 1937 when Japan's intentions became clear. On 7 July of that year they clashed with Chinese troops at the Marco Polo Bridge in Lukouchiao, outside Peking (Peiping), and used the incident to launch an attack aimed at subduing all China, although there was no declaration of war. The Japanese strategy was to capture all ports, thus shutting off China from any foreign aid, and then to destroy the Chinese field armies. Chiang, on the other hand, sought to avoid a pitched battle and thus to wear the Japanese down. The invaders poured into N China from Manchukuo (Manchuria) and occupied Peking on 28 July, followed by Tientsin on 29 July.

Shanghai, China's chief port and largest city, was attacked by land, sea and air on 13 August and the Chinese resisted until 8 November, when 200,000 Japanese troops drove them out. Soochow fell on 20 November, Hangchow, to the south, on 24 December. At the same time, the Japanese marched up the Yangtze Kiang to attack Nanking, the capital. Chiang moved his headquarters 600 miles to Hankow, one of the triple cities of Han (Wuhan), and the capital was removed to Chungking. When Nanking fell on 13 December, the Japanese ravaged the place, massacring 40,000 civilians. This act, coupled with the bombing of undefended towns and the sinking of the US gunboat *Panay* in the Yangtze on 12 December, outraged world opinion. By the end of the year, however, Japan held most of N China (except Tsingtao), part of Inner Mongolia and the important Chinese cities at the mouth of the Yangtze Kiang.

In 1938 the Japanese launched three drives. The first was from the north, marching south to the Yellow River (Hwang-Ho) to take Kaifeng on 6 June. The Chinese scored their only major victory in this sector when, between 31 March and 9 April, Chinese troops under General Li Tsung-jen routed two Japanese divisions at Taierchwang (qv). The second drive was along the south coast where the Japanese took Amoy on 10 May and Canton on 21 October. The third thrust was in central China, where Japan moved up both banks of the Yangtze Kiang to take Hankow on 25 October. Twelve divisions were needed for the capture of this railway junction.

Chiang's policy had made its mark on the Japanese by 1939, for they had found that they could not win a quick victory over the Chinese, who would not stand and fight, but that they constantly harassed the flanks, rear and communications of their invaders. Even in areas where Japanese dominance was supreme, it was only in cities and along railways that control was rigidly enforced. The Japanese set up a puppet government in Nanking in order to exploit what resources were in their control, but the Chinese refused all peace overtures. Chiang at that time had the desultory co-operation of Mao Tse-tung and the Communists. The Japanese, however, instituted a severe blockade of both the air and the coast, while Chunking and other major points were subjected to bombing.

Supplies were so effectively cut off that China was unable to launch a counter-offensive. In order to try and appease the Japanese, the British closed the Burma Road, the Chinese chief but meagre supply route overland. The USA had made much talk of helping the Chinese but to this date had taken no positive steps to do so. The road ran for 1,500 miles from Rangoon through Lashio, Burma to Kunming in Yunnan Province. When the Japanese seized the Indo-Chinese air bases, however, the Burma Road was reopened.

Britain opened up a guerilla warfare training school in Burma near the Chinese frontier and sent training cadres with supplies of special guerilla stores into China to keep the Chinese guerillas active and tie down more Japanese on the continent of Asia. This was before Pearl Harbor. The USA allowed Major-General C.L. Chennault to form a squadron of American volunteer pilots called the Flying Tigers to assist these guerilla operations. The British missions penetrated within a few miles of Shanghai and helped sustain the morale of the Chinese by showing that they were not entirely deserted.

Military operations by the Japanese were halted by these efforts, while the Japanese settled down to try to bring under control and administer that part of China which they now occupied. The outbreak of the Second World War found Chiang concentrating on guerilla warfare tactics as a means of weakening the Japanese forces on the mainland of China. In the meantime he was confident that the Western nations would become embroiled in a war with Japan so that China would at last have active allies.

Japanese reports say that 800,000 Chinese casualties resulted from the invasion to 500,000 Japanese, but during 1940 to 1941 the economic gains were largely offset by the necessity to maintain an army of occupation amounting to 1,000,000 men, used mainly in a counter-insurgency rôle. Japan then turned its attention south and east, seeking to enlarge its territory at the expense of the British, Dutch and Americans. When the Japanese attacked the British and Americans on 7 December 1941 the Chinese 'incident' merged into the Second World War.

CHINESE CIVIL WARS   1 January 1916-25 December 1936
Civil strife not legally recognised as war, but in which hundreds of thousands of soldiers and millions of civilians died from battle, disease and starvation, was practically continuous in China from the republican opposition to Yüan Shih-k'ai's effort to re-establish the monarchy in 1916, through the Tuchan wars from 1918 to 1925, to the termination of the anti-Communist wars at the Sian Agreement following on Chiang Kai-shek's capture by Chan Hsueh-liang in 1936.

This period saw the rise of Chiang Kai-shek and his ex-intelligence officer Mao Tse-tung and the latter's epic 'Long March' with the remannts of his Communist forces from Hunan in central southern China, through the 'grasslands' bordering on Tibet, to safety at Sian in Shensi.

Chan Hsueh-liang's acceptance of Chinese nationalism, against the advice of the Japanese, was one of the main causes of Japan's invasion of Manchuria in 1931 (MANCHURIAN HOSTILITIES).

CHINESE REVOLUTION   October 1911-February 1912
An armed insurrection broke out in Wuchang, on the Yangtze in central China, in October 1911 against the Manchu dynasty ruling from Peking. This ended in February 1912 with the deposition of the child-Emperor by Marshall Yüan Shih-K'ai who had joined the movement, and the establishment of the Republic of China on 12 February 1912.

The priests of Tibet who did not believe in democracy took the opportunity of driving out the Chinese garrison and settled down under the traditional rule of the Dalai Lama and Panchen Lama.

CHIN-T'IEN I (Kwangsi Province, S China)   T'ai P'ing Rebellion   4 November 1850
Fought between the T'ai P'ing under Yang Hsiu-ch'ing and the Manchu Imperial forces under the Governor of Kwangsi, Cheng Tsu-ch'in.

This was the first battle fought by the T'ai P'ing. The two T'ai P'ing leaders Hung Hsui-ch'üan and Feng Yun-shan had been preaching in the village of Chin-t'ien, just south of their sanctuary in Thistle Mountain, when the provincial forces heard of it and surrounded the village. Hung and Feng armed the villagers with weapons hidden in a pond and held off the government troops while Yang Hsiu-ch'ing, who had been sick, created a 'miracle' by getting up, raising his followers and rescuing Feng and Hung, killing about 200 of the government forces.

CHIN-T'IEN II (Kwangsi Province, S China)   T'ai P'ing Rebellion   1 January 1851
After Chin-t'ien I (qv), when the government forces were defeated, thousands flocked to join the T'ai P'ing, the God-worshippers. They consisted mainly of Hakka charcoal burners, iron-ore and tin-miners, smugglers, farmers and watermen, and numbered 20,000 to 30,000, under Yang Hsiu-ch'ing, their army commander.

Against the opinion of the leader of the T'ai P'ing movement Hung Hsiu-ch'üan, Yang decided to defend Chin-t'ien. He made the villagers reflood the rice-fields, wherein he concealed aboriginal bowmen. He prepared his defences on a long low ridge north of the village. The T'ai P'ing repulsed the first two government attacks, which were harried all the while by the tribesmen. On the third assault the T'ai P'ing broke and fled down a narrow path between some cliffs and a river leading back to Thistle Mountain, with the regular forces in pursuit. Yang then sprung his ambush as a hail of musket-fire, reinforced with hand-made grenades, was ejected on to the packed ranks of the government forces. The regulars lost 2,000 casualties before they extricated themselves, at little loss to the T'ai P'ing.

This battle was celebrated from thereon on the tenth day of the 12th moon (11 January 1851) as the first day of the *T'ai-p'ing T'ien-kuo,* or Heavenly Kingdom of Great Peace, during which 50 million Chinese lost their lives.

CHONG-JIN (CHONG-JU) (Korea)   Russo-Japanese War   April 1904
Fought between the Russians under General Mischtchenko and the Japanese.

The van of the Japanese army came into contact with a force of Cossacks whom, after a short struggle, they drove back, occupying Chong-jin. Losses on both sides were slight.

This was the first land engagement of the war.

CH'UAN-CHOU (TAO-CHOU) (Kwangsi Province, S China)   T'ai P'ing Rebellion 20 May-3 June 1852

Fought between the T'ai P'ing under their religious leader Hung Hsui-ch'uan and the Manchu government forces under the overall command of the Imperial Commissioner Sai-Shang-a.

After giving up the siege of Kweilin in Kwangsi Province the T'ai P'ing moved down-river to attack Ch'uan-chou (Tao-chou). Hung's great friend and adviser, Feng Yun-san, one of the main originators of the T'ai P'ing, was killed by a marksman from the walls of Ch'uan-chou while he was being carried past, dressed in yellow robes, in his palanquin. Hung's teaching until now was to try to win over the inhabitants and never to resort to terrorist tactics. But he was so shaken by the loss of his friend that he drove his troops on, against the advice of his best general, Yang Hsui-ch'ing, to capture the town. For a fortnight the T'ai P'ing attacked, suffering severe casualties. When they finally broke in they spent three days massacring the inhabitants, thus sullying their reputation as Christians in the eyes of the Western powers. This was one reason given by France and Britain for not assisting them against the Emperor of China.

CHU PONG-IA DRANG RIVER (S. Vietnam)   Vietnam War   14-21 November 1965

Fought between US forces and the Viet Cong.

Aim: As part of the US policy of seeking out and destroying Communist forces, a battalion of the 1st Cavalry Division (Airmobile) landed by helicopter at the base of Chu Pong Mountain, near the border with Cambodia on 14 November.

Battle: Here they encountered the 66th N Vietnamese Regiment, which attacked the Americans for four days until by 17 November the perimeter defences round the helicopter landing zone, called X-Ray, were made secure by the American forces. Tactical planes flew 260 sorties, supported by B-52 bombers from Guam. During this phase of the action 890 Communists were known to have been killed. Moving north, 500 air cavalrymen crossed the Ia Drang River, only to encounter another force of N Vietnamese soldiers. After two days of fierce fighting the Americans were relieved by S Vietnamese paratroopers. In the two battles 2,200 Communists died, while 240 Americans were killed and 470 wounded.

DIEN BIEN PHU (Laos)   French-Vietnamese War   13 March-8 May 1954

Fought between the Vietminh under Ho Chi-minh and General Vo Nguyen Giap, and the French under General Henri Navarre.

Strength: Vietminh 70,000; French 15,000.

After the surrender of Japan in 1945, control of the Indo-Chinese colony of Vietnam theoretically reverted to France. Ho Chi-minh, a Marxist leader, proclaimed a Vietminh republic, however, and, backed by Russia and China, prepared to assert his claim against the French-supported government under the Head of State, Bao Dai. A civil war was raging by the end of 1946 which lasted for seven years, thanks to the dedication of Vietminh guerillas who received much aid from the Chinese. Then, late in 1953, the French Commander-in-Chief in the Far East (who had succeeded General Raoul Salan), decided to draw the Vietminh into a pitched battle in which European heavy weapons would prove decisive. The ground Navarre chose was a valley in the NW of the country, 11 miles long and 3 wide, called Dien Bien Phu (which, translated, literally means 'big frontier administrative centre'). On 20 November the entrenched camp was garrisoned by twenty battalions of infantry commanded by Colonel (later General) Christian de la Croix de Castries in an operation called Castor.

The Communists saw through this manoeuvre and immediately launched a series of diversionary attacks in Laos and Vietnam which drew French strength away from Dien Bien Phu and, having lured the French from their positions, they then quietly withdrew from the other fronts and collected in the hills around the fortress, massing the 308th, 312th, 316th and 351st Divisions. At the same time, General Vo Nguyen Giap surrounded the fortress with 200 pieces of artillery. On 13 March an attack was launched under heavy artillery fire. The two French airstrips were soon out of commission and the garrison could thereafter only be supplied by airdrop. The French fought back as well as they could with such a shortage of ammunition, but the Vietminh drew steadily nearer by digging trenches ever closer to the fortress. The French artillery fire was so ineffective that the artillery commander, Colonel Charles Piroth, committed suicide. There were ten separate French strongpoints. One by one, these were overrun until, on 7 May, the three centre points were taken and the fortress fell into Vietminh hands. On 8 May, the last surviving point, Isabelle, fell. French losses were 2,293 killed and 5,134 wounded, most of the latter being marched to prison camps, making a total of 10,000 prisoners taken.

Although Vietminh losses were much higher, they had made the country untenable for the French, and two months later an international conference partitioned the country at the 17th Parallel. The territory to the north became the Democratic Republic of Vietnam, and that to the south the Republic of Vietnam.

The strategy of putting up a 'honeypot' which would attract Giap's ill-armed forces into the open so that they could be destroyed by the better trained and armed French regulars could be considered a wise and well-tried strategem. But the French underestimated the strength and resolution of their opponents and the choice of the 'honeypot' and the tactics in its defence were not well carried out. But the French did make the Vietminh lose very many men. This battle may be numbered as one of the decisive battles of history for the effect it had on international opinion.

DONABEW (BURMA) First Burma War 7 March 1825
Fought between the British under General Sir Stapleton Cotton and Sir Archibald Campbell and the Burmese under Maha Bandoola.
Strength: British 700; Burmese 12,000.
Battle: The British stormed three stockades, but only one was carried, the other two holding out until the arrival of Campbell, who began shelling the positions, which the Burmese then evacuated. Maha Bandoola was killed.
Result: The British objective was achieved.

EUREKA STOCKADE (Ballarat, NSW, Australia) Miners' Uprising 3 December 1854
Conflict between the gold miners of Ballarat under the Irish engineer, Peter Lalor, and the Governor of New South Wales, Sir Charles Hotham.

The miners felt that the police were interfering overmuch in their attempts to see that all diggers had a licence to dig, and that they were not getting justice in the courts. The miners, who had an Englishman, a Welshman, an Irishman and a German amongst their leaders, adopted the flag of the Southern Cross on a blue background as their emblem; then, collecting weapons and pikes, they built the Eureka Stockade as a form of peaceful protest. The State troopers over-reacted and early on Sunday morning, 3 December 1854, when about 150 miners were on duty in the stockade, 280 soldiers and police attacked, killing 22 miners. In this incident 6 government men were also killed.

Some of the miners were tried for treason, but a sympathetic jury refused to convict. Reforms were instituted and the licensing system was abolished. The flare-up of armed violence was the result of maladministration of the gold-fields. Eureka Stockade from that time gained a place in Australian political folklore.

FUSHIMI (Honshu Island, Japan) Japanese Revolution 1868
Fought between the troops of Aizu and Kuwana under the Shogun, Yoshinobu and the anti-foreign clans of Satsuma and Choshu. The latter gained a complete victory and in 1869 the new 'Imperial System' was established.

GATE PAH (N Island, New Zealand) Second Maori War 27 April 1864
Fought between the British under General Cameron and the Maoris.
Strength: British 1,700; Maoris 300.
Aim: The British aimed to capture a Maori stockade.
Battle: British soldiers and bluejackets attacked the Maori stockade, storming it after a short bombardment. Six hundred men got inside, but they were repulsed. The following day it was found that the stockade had been evacuated. British losses were 14 officers and 98 men killed and wounded, whilst only 30 Maoris were found dead or wounded in the stockade.
Result: The British objective was achieved.

GREAT JAVA WAR   1825-30.
The last native prince, Prince Dipo Negara, led a revolt against Dutch rule. The rebellion took five years to quell after continuous guerilla warfare in which 15,000 Dutch soldiers were killed. Javanese losses are unknown.

HANYANG AND HANKOW (Hupeh Province, central China)   T'ai P'ing Rebellion   23-9 December 1852
Fought between the Imperial forces and the T'ai P'ing forces under Yang Hsui-ch'ing and Shih Ta-k'ai.

   After the repulse at Changsha (qv) Yang moved north and formed a fleet in the Tungting lake, which emptied into the Yangtze Kiang. In this 1,000-ship fleet he moved his army north under the naval command of T'ang Cheng-ts'ai. Yang captured Hanyang on 23 December 1852 and Hankow on 29 December. In both cases the cities' defences were facing landward, thus making waterborne assault comparatively simple.

   Shih Ta'kai, who was the technical brain of the operation, with the use of great iron chains, built a bridge of boats over the 1,000-metre-wide Yangtze, which allowed Yang to change direction with the result that he surprised the Imperial garrison in Wuchang. The T'ai P'ing 1,000-strong battalion of Thistle Mountain miners from Kwangsi drove tunnels under the walls and destroyed the city gates, and Wuchang was captured on 12 January 1853. This was the first provincial capital to be captured by the T'ai P'ing, and the way now lay open down the Yangtze to Nanking and the sea.

   The T'ai P'ing, with their wives and children, now numbered 500,000.

HENZADA (Burma)   Revolt in Burma   August 1937
In August 1937 the Karen population in the Henzada area, 100 miles NW of Rangoon, revolted. The revolt was suppressed by the British and Indian garrison of Burma. The direct cause of the revolt was the Government of Burma Act which gave the Burmese a constituent assembly and a measure of self-government but did not make sufficient provision for the militant minorities of Karens, Kachins, Chins, Shans, etc.

HONE HEKE'S WAR (N Island, New Zealand)   First Maori War   1844-6
Hone Heke was a missionary-educated Ngapuhi Maori of the Bay of Islands country. Owing mainly to economic difficulties when the Bay of Islands ceased to be important with the rise of other ports in the Island, Hone Heke cut down and burned a British flagpole on a hill above Kororeka as a symbolic act on 8 July 1844. This was an act of rebellion which the Governor of New Zealand, Captain Robert R. Fitz Roy, RN, a brilliant but emotionally unstable officer (he eventually committed suicide), quickly suppressed. Heke revolted again in January 1845, signifying his displeasure by twice cutting down the offending flagpole. He was joined by Kawiti, chief of a neighbouring tribe, so that their total strength was 700 fighting men. Fitz Roy responded by ordering a blockhouse to be built to

defend the flagpole. On 11 March 1845, as soon as it was built, the Maoris promptly captured the blockhouse and not only cut down the flagpole for the fourth time but sacked the town of Kororareke, causing the garrison and inhabitants to flee to Auckland.

Governor Fitz Roy sent in one regular British battalion accompanied by a Maori force. Heke beat them twice. Fitz Roy was recalled and Captain George Grey was sent from Australia to take over. Grey decided that the way to defeat the Maoris was to single out their principal *pa* or stockade and to attack and demolish it. This not only acted as a honey-pot to attract the Maori warriors to its defence, but its destruction was acknowledged as a final defeat. So with three British battalions (Northamptons, Manchesters and Wiltshires) and artillery Heke's principal *pa* (stockade), called Ruapekapeka (Bats' Nest) was attacked and destroyed on 11 January 1846. Heke acknowledged defeat and gave no more trouble.

HUKBALAHAP (Luzon, Philippine Islands)   Rebellion in the Philippines 1948-54
When Japan occupied the Philippine Islands American missions were sent to organise guerilla resistance in the hills. When the Philippines were reoccupied by the US forces and the Philippines were granted independence, it was before the spirit of resistance in the mountains of Luzon and in many of the islands had been fully brought under control. The Hukbalahap insurgents operated from central Luzon and numbered about 5,000. They were eventually brought under control by a counter-insurgent force numbering 25,000 under President Ramón Magaysay who used the traditional counter-insurgent methods of opening up the area with roads, land reform, defended villages, local militia, new schools, new markets and light industries, as well as mobile light flying columns supplied and supported by air, to do so.

HWAI-HAI (Kiangsu and Honan Provinces, China)   Chinese Civil War   7 November 1948-12 January 1949
Fought between the Nationalists under Liu Chih and the Communists under Ch'en Yi.
Strength: Nationalists 500,000 comprising 5 army groups + 7 full-strength divisions + 1 armoured corps + miscellaneous other units; Communists 500,000. Following the Nationalists' defeats at Kaifeng and Tsinan (qqv) a third great battle was building up in east-central China between the Lunghai Railway and the Hwai River. Liu massed a Nationalist force here which included General Chiang Kai-shek's prized Armoured Corps, commanded by his second son, Chiang Wei-kuo, while to the north and west a Communist force of similar size was gathered by Ch'en Yi, one of Mao Tse-tung's best commanders.

PLA columns isolated the battlefield, encircling the Nationalists, and then cut off and destroyed Chiang's units piecemeal. Chiang rushed reinforcements into the area in a futile effort to stop the crushing defeat, but by 12 January the fighting was ended with 350,000 Nationalists annihilated. Liu Chih and Chiang Wei-kuo escaped by plane from Hsuchang (Hsuchow), but two top Nationalists were killed and another two captured. Tientsin, to the north, fell on 15 January and Peking (Peiping) on 21 January. East from Hwai-Hai the road lay open to the Nationalist capital of Nanking.

This is one of the great battles of modern history.

INCHON (S Korea)   Korean War   15 September-1 October 1950
Fought between the Communists and the S Korean and US forces.
Aim: In August the US 8th Army and S Korean forces checked Communist advances in the Korean Peninsula at the Pusan Perimeter in the SE. Meanwhile, General Douglas MacArthur, United Nations Supreme Commander, prepared an offensive to strike at the right rear of the N Korean army.
Battle: On 15 September 10 Corps (newly organised and consisting of 1st Marine and 7th Infantry Divisions) under General Edward Almond made an amphibious landing at Inchon, the port of Seoul on the west coast of the peninsula. Following two days of naval bombardment, the 1st Marines under General Oliver Smith took the small off-shore island of Moontip (Wolmi-do) on the morning of 15 September and stormed the beaches later the same day. The force then began to move inland, meeting little N Korean resistance. Kimpo airfield, to the north, was taken on 17 September, the same day that the 7th Infantry began to come ashore. As the Americans deepened and widened their beachhead, Seoul came under attack. On 16 September the US 8th Army, which was 140,000 strong, moved out of the Pusan Perimeter and NW towards Seoul. N Korean lines, stretched thinly along their front, began to collapse. On 26 September the two US forces linked near Osan and cut off parts of eight Communist divisions in the SE. On 28 September Seoul was liberated, although isolated street fighting continued. By 1 October US and S Korean forces were in the region of the 38th Parallel. The first Republic of Korea (ROK) unit crossed the boundary that day. Under the authorisation of the UN, General Walton Walker's troops (the 8th Army) did the same eight days later.
Result: The S Korean and US objective was achieved.

INDONESIA-MALAYSIA WAR   April 1963-June 1966
Fought between the combined forces of Malaysia, Britain, Australia and New Zealand under the successive commands of General Sir Walter Walker and Major-General George Lea against Indonesian guerillas and regular forces invading British N Borneo and Sarawak.

This campaign continued on from the attempted take-over on 8 December 1962 of Brunei (qv) by an Indonesian-supported revolutionary movement under Sultan Azahari. The 970-mile common frontier was easily penetrable. Walker's tactics were to try to obtain advance warning of the movement of these penetration forces from the Border Scouts and 22 SAS (Special Air Service) and then strike them hard with a mobile reserve on the few roads near the coast, with close-support air strikes. Some counter-penetration also took place and much small-boat action. The Indonesians possessed faster motor gunboats - which had been sold to them by the British - than the Royal Navy possessed, but their maintenance was not good.

The conflict escalated in late 1964 when the Indonesian regulars crossed the frontier. The British made full use of their technical superiority in helicopters and fire-power, accompanied by political action. The total Allied strength, including local forces and Malayan regiments, rose to over 30,000, including eight Gurkha battalions and the two Royal Marine Commandos, who bore the brunt of the fighting. The conflict died away when, on 12 March 1966, power was taken away from President Mohammed Achmed Sukarno and General Soeharto took over executive control of Indonesia and suppressed an attempted Communist Chinese *coup* in Java and elsewhere. On 1 June 1966 a provisional agreement was signed at Bangkok, and the confrontation ended when the foreign ministers signed a formal agreement on 11 August at Djakarta.

Mr Denis Healey, as British Defence Minister, stated in the House of Commons that this campaign 'in the history books will be recorded as one of the most efficient uses of military force in the history of the world'. British casualties were 19 killed and 44 wounded, while Gurkha casualties were 40 killed and 83 wounded. The Indonesians, on the other hand, lost 2,000 killed.

INDONESIAN CIVIL WAR   1950-61

There was constant unrest, turmoil and violence in Indonesia, particularly on Sumatra and Celebes, in the period beginning in the late 1940s and lasting until 1961.

On 27 December 1949 the Netherlands granted Indonesia its independence as the United States of Indonesia. On 16 December Mohammed Achmed Sukarno was elected its first President, with Mohammed Hatta as the first Prime Minister. On 17 August 1950 the Republic of Indonesia was proclaimed. The Dutch retained control of Irian Barat, (Dutch New Guinea), and the Indonesians objected to this, finally dissolving their union with the Netherlands in 1954 and expelling all Dutch citizens from Irian Barat. Diplomatic relations were severed in 1960. Objections throughout the islands erupting into violence had, in 1957, caused Sukarno to declare martial law in order to implement his plans for 'Guided Democracy'.

INDONESIAN CRISIS   October 1965-January 1966

In October 1965 elements of the armed forces and armed political factions attempted a military *coup d'état* to overthrow President Mohammed Achmed Sukarno's régime. After intense jockeying for position and power, mainly in Java, loyalist forces won the day, but the powers of Sukarno were reduced so that he became an impotent figurehead. General Soeharto took over power. The anger of the country at the failure of the ignominious confrontation with Britain, coupled with the revelations of Sukarno's corrupt rule, was directed against suspected Communist (especially Chinese) elements amongst the civilian population. Estimates of the numbers killed reached 500,000, and tens of thousands were thrown into prison or exiled on remote islands.

The result was a victory for the Western powers against Communist attempts to bring Indonesia into the Eastern bloc. Passage from the Pacific to the Indian Ocean was now assured in time of war.

INDONESIAN WAR OF INDEPENDENCE   1945-50

Indonesia had been occupied by the Japanese for four years and ideas of independence had been fomented. When the Japanese surrendered, British and Indian forces under Lord Louis Mountbatten's command occupied what was still called the Dutch East Indies in order to disarm the Japanese and restore Dutch control. But on 17 August 1945 Mohammed Achmed Sukarno and Mohammed Hatta, in a joint declaration, declared the independence of the Republic of Indonesia, with Sukarno as President.

On 14 October 1945 conflict started between the Indonesian People's Army and occupation troops of the British and Dutch armies. On 29 November British troops captured the rebel capital of Surabaya.

By the summer of 1946 British troops were being withdrawn as the Dutch increased their strength to 130,000 combatants. The Indonesian forces totalled over 500,000, mostly in Java and Sumatra. In November 1946 with the Cheribon Agreement, the Dutch recognised *two* republics - the Indonesian Republic consisting of Java, Sumatra and Madura, and the United States of Indonesia including Borneo, Celebes, Sunda and the Molucca Islands. Both states would have dominion status under the Netherlands crown.

But the Nationalists were not content and declared the Independence of West Java on 4 May 1947 (Java's total population numbered 45 million, four times that of Holland). Fighting continued between about 100,000 troops on each side, many Indonesians fighting on the Dutch side. On 19 December 1948 Dutch airborne troops seized Jogjakarta, the W Javan capital. After intervention by the United Nations, by November 1949, Dutch troops had withdrawn and the Indonesian Republic, covering all of the Dutch East Indies apart from Dutch New Guinea, had been granted full sovereignty by Holland.

Dutch casualties were 25,000 killed and wounded, while the Indonesians lost 80,000.

On 15 August 1950 Sukarno was (for the second time) proclaimed President of the Republic of Indonesia. Colonel Abdul Haris Nasution had been the principal architect of the Indonesian resistance. He later became Chairman of the Joint Chiefs of Staff and the Minister of Defence in 1959.

JAVA WAR   see GREAT JAVA WAR

KAGOSHIMA (Kyushu Island, Japan)   Satsuma Rebellion   18 August 1877

Fought between the rebels under Saigo Takamori and the Imperialists under Prince Taruhito.
Aim: The rebels sought to break out of their besieged lines.
Battle: Undertaking a forced march, the rebels succeeded in getting through the

lines of the Imperialists and seizing the city of Kagoshima, but the Imperialist army pursued and the rebels stood and fought for ten days, at the end of which time they quitted the city and retired to Shirogama. Both sides suffered heavy losses.
Result: The rebels did not achieve their objective.

KAIFENG (Honan Province, central China)   Chinese Civil War   19 June 1948
Fought between the Nationalists under Chiang Kai-shek and the Communists under Ch'en Yi, Liu Po-ch'eng and Ch'en Keng.
Strength: Nationalists 250,000; Communists 200,000.

During the early stages of the encirclement of Mukden (qv) by the PLA (People's Liberation Army), Mao Tse-tung launched another offensive in east-central China. Yenan, the Communist headquarters in Yensi Province which was taken by the Nationalists in March, was retaken in April. The Communists then moved 200,000 men SE towards the Lunghai Line in N Honan Province, their objective being the city of Kaifeng, defended by Chiang's Nationalists.

Although the Nationalists were in theory greater in number than the Communists, many desertions weakened the forces under Chiang. On 19 June the PLA assaulted and took Kaifeng which had in it huge quantities of stores (much of them US supplies). The city was abandoned a week later, showing the Communist intention to destroy their enemies rather than to gain territory.

KAIPING (Hopeh Province, N China)   Sino-Japanese War   10 January 1895
Fought between the Chinese and the Japanese under General Nogi.
Aim: The Japanese sought to beat the Chinese from their position.
Battle: The Chinese were strongly entrenched in a position which the Japanese attacked. In a fight lasting three hours, the Japanese brigade drove the Chinese from their position, though the latter fought better than usual and inflicted 300 casualties on the Japanese.
Result: The Japanese objective was achieved.

KAMARUT (S Burma)   First Burma War   8 July 1824
Fought between the British under General Sir Archibald Campbell and the Burmese under Tuamba Wangyee.
Aim: The British sought to drive the Burmese from their stockades.
Battle: A small force under Campbell stormed the stockades held by 10,000 Burmese and carried them. Burmese losses were 800 killed, including Tuamba Wangyee.
Result: The British objective was achieved.

KEMENDINE (S Burma)   First Burma War   10 June 1824
Fought between the British under General Sir Archibald Campbell and the Burmese.

Strength: British 3,000; Burmese 3,000.
Aim: The British sought to beat the Burmese out of their stockades.
Battle: Campbell stormed the stockade and beat the Burmese out of them with heavy loss.
Result: The British objective was achieved.

KHALKHIN-GOL (Outer Mongolia)   Hostilities between Japan and the USSR
May-August 1939
The Japanese army, having overrun Manchuria, allowed some of its ambitious officers a free hand to press on and test the Mongolian defences. After a minor clash between Japanese and Russian-officered Mongolian forces, the Japanese claimed certain regions occupied by Russian troops. The confrontation grew until the Japanese deployed the equivalent of four divisions against General Vasily K. Blücher's force of four infantry divisions, two Mongolian cavalry divisions, three tank brigades, two motorised brigades and one airborne brigade, including a major proportion of Mongolian units. The Soviet commander on the spot, General Georgi Zhukov, was to make his name on Russia's western front. Zhukov attacked and drove back the Japanese. The Japanese lost about 53,000 casualties and the Russians over 10,000 killed and wounded.

The dispute was settled by a treaty on 15 September 1939.

The Mongolians still claim that they were the first to defeat the Japanese in a land battle. This considerable battle passed almost unnoticed in the Western press, which at the time was concerned only with events in Europe. Both sides gained a healthy respect for each other and the Japanese maintained ten good divisions in Manchuria throughout her 1941-5 war, which she could ill spare.

KIUKIANG (N Kiangsi Province, central China)   T'ai P'ing Rebellion
18 February 1853
After the capture of Wu-hsüeh (qv) the T'ai P'ing general Shih Ta-k'ai, the Assistant King, took the provincial city of Kiukiang on 18 February and Anking (qv), the capital of Anhwei Province, on 24 February. The Governor, Chiang Wench'ing, had intended to fight, but his troops deserted him as the vast swarm of T'ai P'ing advanced down the river. The T'ai P'ing captured 100 cannon as well as vast quantities of silver and supplies.

The T'ai P'ing had now overrun three highly populated provinces within one month and the route to Nanking lay open.

KOKEIN (S Burma)   First Burma War   12 December 1824
Fought between the British under General Sir Archibald Campbell and the Burmese under Maka Bundala.
Strength: British 1,800; Burmese 20,000.
Aim: The British sought to beat the Burmese out of their stockades.
Battle: The British stormed two large stockades and captured them.
Result: The British objective was achieved.

KUMAMOTO (W Kyushu Island, Japan)   Satsuma Rebellion   22 February-
14 April 1876
Fought between the Satsuma rebels under Saigo Takamori and the Imperialists
under General Tani Tateki.
Strength: Rebels 40,000; Imperialists 50,000
Aim: The rebels sought to reduce the town of Kumamoto which was held by an
Imperialist garrison.
Battle: Although many Samurai deserted to the rebels, the garrison was gallantly
held by the Imperialists and many attempts were made to relieve the siege. The
Imperial army under Prince Taruhito advanced on the town. In March Saigo was
attacked in the rear by an Imperialist force under General Kuroda, but the siege
was maintained. When the garrison was nearly starving, on 14 April Kuroda
brought up every available man and succeeded in driving off the rebels, thus
raising the siege.
Result: The rebels' objective was not achieved.

LIAOYANG (E Liaoning Province, NE China)   Russo-Japanese War
25 August 1904
Fought between the Japanese under Field-Marshal Marquis Iwao Oyama and the
Russians under General Alexei Kuropatkin.
Strength: Japanese 100,000; Russians 100,000.
    After the Japanese crossed the Yalu River (qv) on 1 May, they pressed NW to
the railway running north from Port Arthur (qv). When they reached the railway,
they encountered greater Russian resistance and at Liaoyang, where the Russians
had massed most of their forces, the two armies met.
Battle: The Japanese army was organised in seven divisions and these clashed with
Russian troops on a broad front. The battle speedily became a series of inconclusive skirmishes which continued for six days, the Japanese gaining little ground
while engaged in fierce localised fighting. On 1 September the Russians launched
two days of counter-attacks which the Japanese only checked by the commitment
of all their reserves. On 3 September Kuropatkin withdrew north, having suffered
16,500 casualties to the Japanese 23,500.
Result: This was the first great land battle of the war and it left the Japanese with
the strategic advantage.

MALAYAN EMERGENCY   1948-60
In 1946 the population of Malaya (Malaysia) consisted of about 45 per cent
Malayans, 45 per cent Chinese and 10 per cent Indians. During the Japanese War
the Chinese Communists operated against the Japanese and so were, to a certain
extent, supported by the British, while the Malays remained supine.
    After taking part in the Victory Parades in Hyde Park, London, Chin Peng - who
had been awarded a Military Cross - and his fellow Malay/Chinese guerillas
found on their return that the Malay sultans were going to be given power in
Malaya and the large minority of hard-working Chinese would not only be

second-class citizens but were to be defranchised. Chin Peng and his Communist colleagues used this real grievance amongst the Malayan Chinese to start a revolt.

The Chinese guerillas had learnt their trade against the Japanese and so were good. It took a maximum of 170,000 government troops nine years to bring the guerillas down to manageable proportions so that Malaya could be granted her independence in August 1957, and a further three years before the emergency was declared at an end. In the charter of independence the Malayan Chinese were given the vote and equal citizenship with the Malays. Only a few Malays fought on the guerilla side. So it can be said that the principles for which Chin Peng and his colleagues fought were attained, although their Communist ideological aims were not.

The main architects of the government success were Lt-General Sir Harold Briggs who produced the Briggs Plan, and General Sir Gerald Templer, the Director of Operations, who put the Briggs Plan into effect. He was succeeded in 1954 by the dynamic and highly intelligent Lt-General Sir Geoffrey Bourne who vigorously put an end to the emergency and laid the foundations for a more peaceful future for Malaya.

The Chinese guerillas never exceeded 7,000 actively engaged, as this was the optimum number their leader, Chin Peng, considered necessary and which could be supplied. But they had trained cadres always ready to fill gaps caused by casualties and disease, so that their numbers, until near the end, never fell below about 5,000. The helicopter came into its own during this campaign as a support, casualty clearance and liaison vehicle.

The casualties suffered during twelve years from 1948-60 by the British and government forces were (killed): British army 350, Gurkhas (exclusive of British officers) 159, Malays 128, Malay Police 1,346, civilians 2,473 killed and 810 missing. And of the guerillas 6,710 known killed, 1,287 captured, 2,702 voluntarily surrendered, while those who remained in the jungle in 1960 numbered 500.

In 1973 Chin Peng was still operating, at times vigorously, from an area on the Malay/Thailand border in Pahang. In that year he said that he would cease operating if he could come out safely and be able to put up one candidate of his own in each constituency throughout Malaysia. This request was refused. In the period 1942-76, a total of thirty-four years, he had operated almost continuously from his jungle sanctuaries, which must surely come near to the record for an active operational life of a guerilla leader.

MANCHURIAN HOSTILITIES   18 September 1931-31 May 1933
Japanese armed forces streamed across the border from Korea to occupy the three eastern provinces of Manchukuo (Manchuria) following an alleged murder of a Japanese officer by Chinese soldiers. There was no legal state of war between China and Japan and diplomatic relations were never severed. The Tangku Truce on 31 May 1933 brought an end to hostilities, with the Japanese in occupation of Manchuria.

In this conflict the Japanese lost 10,000 killed, and the Chinese 50,000 killed.

MAORI TRIBAL WARS (New Zealand)   1821-38

These conflicts were mainly brought about by Hongi, Chief of the Ngapuhi tribe who owned the Bay of Islands (the red-light district of New Zealand at that time), and his successor Te Waharoa of the Ngati-Awa, who had acquired guns from the British and wished to improve their material power through the barrel of a gun. Hongi himself was an excellent shot. Between 1821 and 1827 he practically devastated the Maori world in the north of N Island, but was fortunately accidentally shot in the back by one of his own men.

Te Waharoa was an adversary of Hongi's. In his efforts to counter Hongi's marksmen and superiority in weapons he designed magnificent fortifications, in the building of which the Maoris were adept. These stockades, or *pas* were to prove the bane of the British regiments in the Maori Wars. He fought the Arawa people of the Rotorua hot spring country. On his death in 1839 Te Whero Whero (King Potatau) of the Waikatos sought to dominate the island. His main enemies were the Taranaki under Te Rauparaha centred on Mount Egmont, who obtained the help of the white migrants and their artillery. Te Rauparaha with some of the Taranaki were forced to cross the Cook Strait to S Island where, with their guns and new-found skills, they in turn harried the Ngaitahu people of S Island.

These twenty years of tribal warfare initiated by the white settlers and their guns caused the death of over 20,000 Maori warriors out of a total population of 200,000 in 1820. The fighting, subsequent massacres and the disturbance of their tribal way of living rapidly caused a decline, so that by 1840 the number of Maoris was about 100,000 in N Island and between 10,000 and 15,000 in S Island.

MAORI WAR, FIRST, (New Zealand)   1843-9

By the treaty of Waitangi in 1840, Great Britain assumed the sovereignty of New Zealand and guaranteed the Maoris possession of their lands and fisheries. However, friction soon arose between the British settlers and the Maoris over the ownership of land, resulting in skirmishes and ambuscades between the colonists armed with guns and the Maoris armed with spears and axes and only a few firearms. These guerilla skirmishes lasted for five years and became known as the First Maori War. The war was said to have ceased when a final settlement of most of the boundaries was agreed.

MAORI WAR, SECOND (central N Island, New Zealand)   1860-72

This conflict was between discontented Maori tribesmen on the one hand and British troops, local militia and 'loyal' Maoris who supported the government, on the other. In 1864 British troops were gradually withdrawn and all further police action was carried out by local forces and Maori loyalists. One reason for the withdrawal of the British troops was because they tended to sympathise with the hostile Maoris whose courage they admired and from whom they learnt a lot.

The Maori Wars which occurred from March 1860 to February 1872 were a loosely linked series of outbursts of bush-fighting in different parts of N Island.

There was never any general Maori uprising and individual tribes fought discontinuously throughout the period. The main campaigns were: Taranaki, 1860-1 and 1863; Waikato and Bay of Plenty, 1863-4; Taranaki-Wanganui, 1864-6 and 1868-9; and Urewara Mountains, 1868-72. In no engagement were there more than a few hundred on each side. The total losses by death on the government side, including loyal Maoris, did not exceed 700 during these twelve years. The hostile Maoris lost about 2,000 killed. General Platt was the first Commander but was replaced by General Sir Duncan Cameron in March 1863. His successor was General Sir Trevor Chute. But the most successful counter-insurgent commander was Colonel G.S. Whitmore who had seen service in S Africa. Te Koote Rikirangi in the Urewara Mountains was the outstanding rebel leader, strategist and tactician of the Maoris and caused more trouble than all other Maori chieftains put together. He himself was not a chief, but a charismatic personality. In 1872 he was finally allowed by the Governor, Sir George Bowen, to 'retire' in peace.

Much of the fighting consisted of the destruction of the well-built *pas* (stockades) by artillery or sapping. But once the colonial troops, beginning in 1863, learnt the art of bush warfare, they could pursue the Maoris into the forest and, with their superior weapons and cohesion, defeat them there. So, in the later campaigns, bush warfare predominated.

One aspect of these wars was the lack of bitterness engendered, with the result that, when hostilities finally ceased in 1872, the two nations settled down together without racial animosity, to develop the country together.

MIAO REBELLION (SW China)   1855-72

The Miao tribesmen had been forced back by the Chinese over the centuries from the plains of southern China to live in the forested mountainous province of Kweichow and the adjoining border areas of Hunan, Kwangsi, Yunnan and Szechwan. The immediate cause of their revolt was the T'ai P'ing Rebellion (qv) and the taxes the provincial governors levied in order to raise armies to suppress it. The Miao had previously revolted against the Manchu invaders in the years 1733 and 1735-7.

A herb-peddler, Chang Hsiu-mei led the rebellion against the tax collectors and was assisted by the White Lotus Society. The army of the White Lotus was called the Colour-marked army as their units wore white, red, or brown headgear and jackets, with appropriate flag. All these rebels supported the great T'ai P'ing general Shih Ta-k'ai who, with 200,000 troops, had broken away from the T'ai P'ing and overran the province of Kweichow in September 1859 in search of a sanctuary which he could make his own.

After Shih's defeat by the Hunan Braves under Hsi Pao-t'ien in 1864, the Miao reverted to guerilla warfare from the deep, foggy jungles. It was not until 1868 that the White- and Brown-marked armies were dispersed. But Chang Hsiu-mei counter-attacked into the province of Hunan in order to divert the Hunan Braves back to their homeland. But the provincial and Imperial forces surrounded Chang and defeated him. The rebels retreated to the mountain fastnesses where, by

means of an economic blockade, they were all brought to heel by 1872.
  Casualties, including civilians, were about 1½ million.

MUKDEN I (SHENYANG) (Liaoning Province, NE China)   Russo-Japanese War
21 February-6 March 1905
Fought between the Japanese under Field-Marshal Marquis Iwao Oyama and
the Russians under General Alexei Kuropatkin.
Strength: Japanese 300,000; Russians 310,000.
Aim: After winning the battle of Shaho River (qv), the Japanese built up their
strength for an offensive against the Russians and marched north into Manchuria
to where they lay, on a 47-mile front around Mukden (Shenyang).
Battle: The Japanese attacked the Russian position and pushed slowly forward in
what became a battle of attrition. On 6 March Oyama sent both his flanks forward
so that the town of Mukden was surrounded. By 10 March the Japanese had completely encircled the town, but the Russians had withdrawn farther north and
escaped the trap. Japanese casualties during the battle were 50,000. Russian losses,
out of a force about the size of the Japanese, were 90,000.
Result: Kuropatkin was relieved of command - but the main action of the war
was now at sea.

MUKDEN II (SHENYANG) (Liaoning Province, NE China)   Chinese Civil War
23 December 1947-1 November 1948
Fought between the Nationalists under Wei Li-huang and the Communists under
Lin Piao.
Strength: Nationalists 400,000; Communists 200,000.
Aim: By the end of 1947 almost all of Manchuria lay in the control of the
Communist People's Liberation Army (PLA). The next objective was Mukden
(Shenyang), the main city of S Manchuria.
Battle: On 23 December five PLA columns, supported by artillery, were con-
verging on Mukden. On 1 February 1948 General Chiang Kai-shek sent Wei to the
city to assume command of the NE Bandit-Suppression Headquarters. Five more
Communist columns were sent to besiege the city. Throughout the year the siege
strengthened, and on 12 September 30,000 PLA troops began to cut the Liaosi
corridor, the only land route still open from Manchuria. In October General
Liao Yao-hsiang attempted to break out of the encirclement with three Nationalist armies and other odd units. By the end of the month, Lin's forces had killed or
captured the entire command, while Wei escaped by air. On 1 November the 53rd
Army and the 207th (Youth) Division, the sole surviving defenders of Mukden,
surrendered to the Communists. Mukden's seaport, Yunghow, fell four days
later.
Result: All Manchuria was now in Communist control.

NAM DONG (South Vietnam)   Vietnam War   6 July 1964
Fought between the S Vietnamese Allied forces and the Viet Cong.

Strength: Allies (South Vietnamese 311, Nung 60, US 12); Viet Cong 800-900.

Armed camps were set up throughout S Vietnam as a protection against guerilla attacks and one of these, Nam Dong, which lay in the NW, stood near the junction of the borders between S Vietnam, N Vietnam and Laos. The force inside was commanded by Captain Roger Donlon.

At 2 am on 6 July a Communist attack was launched with a heavy barrage of mortars, under cover of which the Communists overran the S Vietnamese at the edge of the camp to reach the centre of the perimeter defences. In a fierce fight, the Viet Cong were repulsed in an attack after daylight. US casualties were 2 killed and 8 wounded (including Donlon). For his part in the action at Nam Dong Donlon was the first man to be awarded the Congressional Medal of Honor in the Vietnam War.

NANKING I (Kiangsu Province, S China)   T'ai P'ing Rebellion   8-19 March 1853
The T'ai P'ing under Shih Ta-k'ai, the Assistant King, advancing down the Yangtze with about 100,000 soldiers, reached the outskirts of Nanking (Nanjing) on 8 March 1853.

The defence of Nanking was left to Lu Chien-ying and Hsiang-hou with between 20,000 and 40,000 Manchu soldiers. After attacking the 40-feet-thick walls day and night for eleven days the T'ai P'ing captured Nanking on 19 March by digging walls and planting mines. Shih Ta-k'ai proclaimed: 'In every district through which we have passed the people have welcomed us as they would reasonable showers, and the inhabitants have reacted as if they were delivered from the greatest calamity. In Nanking the people oppose us and must suffer accordingly.' Within a few days 50,000 Manchus, including their commanders, were put to the sword.

Within two years and two months since it had started the rebellion, like an avalanche, had swept through S China. The next objective should have been Shanghai and an outlet to the sea and Western help. But the leaders had no experience with Westerners who, they thought, would welcome them as fellow-Christians. Shanghai had an international settlement, so the T'ai P'ing paused to negotiate. But the Manchu were more wily at diplomacy than battle. They poisoned the ears of the Western nations against the rebels. So an opportunity was lost.

The T'ai P'ing, after further conquests and a great revival, lost its impetus and gradually declined. The chance of making China a quasi-Christian state was lost, and the great ideas of land reform and peasant regeneration, which was really what the agrarian revolution was all about, had to wait another 100 years.

NANKING III (Kiangsu Province, S China)   Chinese Civil War   22 April 1949
Fought between the Nationalists under General Chiang Kai-shek and the Communists under Mao Tse-tung.

After the defeat of the Nationalists at Hwai-Hai (qv) and the loss of Manchuria,

Chiang was left more or less powerless against the PLA (People's Liberation Army) in the rest of China. Attempts to negotiate a peace treaty failed, however, and on 20 April PLA columns crossed the Yangtze Kiang to the south. The Nationalist government fled Nanking and set themselves up successively at Canton, Chungking and Chengtu.

On 22 April the Communists stormed into Nanking and captured the city. Shanghai, to the east, fell on 27 May, and all further resistance collapsed before the advance of the PLA.

On 1 October the Chinese People's Republic formally took over the government at Peiping, which was renamed Peking, and in December Chiang Kai-shek with other Nationalist leaders of the Kuomintang dictatorship fled to Formosa, leaving the country under firm Communist control.

NANKING CAMPAIGN, THE GREATER (Kiangsu Province, S China)   T'ai P'ing Rebellion   November 1853-9 August 1856
Fought between the main T'ai P'ing forces under the Eastern King and Commander-in-Chief Yang Hsiu-ch'ing, and the Emperor's forces under Hsiang Jung, Ch'i-shan and Te-hsing-a.
Strength: T'ai P'ing 2½ million; Imperial forces 2½ million.

Various estimates have been given of the respective strengths of the two forces. These are always difficult to assess in Chinese armies, as in every Chinese unit there are trained but unarmed men who carry out administrative duties and coolie work like digging but who act as first-line reinforcements to the fighting troops as casualties occur.

The aim of the T'ai P'ing forces was to defeat the Imperial forces in the Great Camps of Kiangnam and Kiangpei, which exerted a stranglehold on their capital at Nanking. The Imperial forces' aim was to retain this siege of Nanking in order to weaken the régime until such time as they could train and bring to bear overwhelming forces against Nanking. Nanking was in a state of siege off and on from 1853 to 1864. The circumference of the defences of Nanking was 30 miles and Hsiang Jung had insufficient forces to surround the city.

After a two-month battle, on 26 December 1853 the Imperial forces under Te-hsing-a captured the rich city of Yangchow. Yang Hsui-ch'ing drove his men to counter-attack. In 1854 the Imperial troops from the Great Camps attacked the T'ai P'ing at Pukow, and in 1855 they dug a deep trench to encircle them at Kwachow and then besieged the town. Yang counter-attacked from Chinkiang and Nanking, relieved Kwachow and recaptured Yangchow on 5 April 1856. Yang then tried to draw the Imperial forces from their defended camps by attacking Ning-kuo in Anhwei Province and launching an offensive in Kiangsu. Hsiang Jung fell into the trap by sending out relief forces. Yang then ordered Shih Ta-k'ai, who had returned from his western offensive, to hurry back to Nanking and attack the Great Camps. Shih dealt Hsiang Jung a crushing defeat at Tan-yang in August 1856 and captured the two Great Camps. On 9 August Hsiang Jung was killed. The T'ai P'ing military power had now reached its zenith.

Casualties during these three years were probably about 4 million on each side. About 40 million Chinese were killed during the whole rebellion, of which about 20 million were soldiers.

As a result of his military success Yang thought he was divine and attempted a *coup d'état*. Hung Hsui-ch'üan, the Heavenly King, however, summoned his generals and assistant kings to his aid, and on 2 September 1856 Yang, along with 30,000 of his family and followers, was murdered. The Western King, Wei Ch'ang-hui, who was mainly responsible for these murders, in turn tried to seize power by attempting to murder the Heavenly King's most reliable and successful general, Shih Ta-k'ai. So in November 1856 the heads of Wei Ch'ang-hui and 200 of his adherents were cut off by order of the Heavenly King. (See T'AI P'ING REBELLION).

NANKING SIEGE (Kiangsu Province, S China)   30 May 1862-19 July 1864
Fought between, on the one hand, the Chinese Imperialist forces under Tseng Kuo-fan and his brother Tseng Kuo-ch'üan, British naval and military forces, a Franco-Chinese corps and the 'Ever Victorious Army' under Major C. C. Gordon, RE, and on the other the T'ai P'ing forces inside Nanking under the overall command of the Celestial King Hung Hsui-ch'üan, Ch'en Yü-ch'eng, Li Shih-Hsien and Hung Jen-kan, and an external field force of 300,000 under Li Hsui-ch'eng. This latter army was repeatedly reinforced.
Strength: Chinese Imperialists 2 million + British/French/Indian 15,000 with modern artillery and naval forces; T'ai P'ing 1½ million.

Tseng Kuo-fan wanted to take Nanking unaided, but the Emperor through his Regency was forced to agree to the Western powers being represented.

Tseng made his base at Yü-hua-t'ai under the walls of Nanking on 30 May 1862. Some great battles were fought between Nanking and Shanghai in which the Ever Victorious Army, first under the command of the American soldier of fortune, H. A. Burgevine (Ward had been wounded) and then under his successor Major Gordon, were heavily involved. Li Hung-chang's Anhwei army captured Kiating on 24 October 1862, and defeated the T'ai P'ing general T'an Shao-kuang at Tsingpu on 13 November, where casualties on both sides numbered 50,000.

Gordon, operating with Ch'eng Hsüeh-ch'i's Anwhei army and having reorganised the Ever Victorious Army, fought at Taitsang on 2 May 1863, Kunshan on 1 June and Soochow on 4 December, all of which were captured.

In the meantime in September 1862 Li Hsui-ch'eng moved with 300,000 men from the environs of Shanghai, set up base and attacked Tseng Kuo-ch'üan at Yü-hua-t'ai, from where he was besieging Nanking. Li attacked Tseng for forty-nine days using enormous quantities of shells, mines and ammunition, but was fought to a standstill, both sides suffering a great number of casualties from hunger, pestilence and exhaustion, apart from battle losses.

Li then tried his favourite tactic of creating a diversion elsewhere to draw Tseng away from Nanking. He moved west on to Anking and Yangchow, but could make no headway against the redoubtable Tseng Kuo-fan who was at last, after years of fighting, seeing his way to winning.

Tseng Kuo-ch'üan redoubled his efforts to capture Nanking, so Li was called back by the Heavenly King, Hung Hsui-ch'üan, and was faced with a further campaign in 1864 in the disease-ridden marshy lowlands around Nanking.

Li tried to persuade Hung to break out of the siege with 500,000 men and march through the Nien Rebellion (qv) areas to Shensi in NW China or to join the Moslem rebels in W China, but Hung insisted on staying on in his capital which was now starving and 'living on grass'. Hung, the Heavenly or Celestial King, suddenly became ill and died on 1 June 1864, and his son Hung T'ien-huei-Sei took over. After a last great battle Nanking fell on 19 July 1864, having withstood a two-year siege. Battle casualties and casualties from disease numbered about 2 million on each side. Nanking was sacked for three days, during which 100,000 rebel soldiers and 200,000 civilians were killed. Li Hsui-ch'eng and Hung's son were later captured and executed.

The remaining T'ai P'ing princes and generals fought on for a few years with troops loyal to them in varying fashion, always moving inland, taking great towns and abandoning them, until they, their forces and fighting spirit petered out, wasted away, and died. Alternatively they joined up with some of the other great revolts which the T'ai P'ing Rebellion (qv) had instigated, such as the Nien, Triads and Panthay (qqv) risings, or the Moslem revolts in the west. Many who surrendered were promptly executed and the Imperial government was quite ruthless in their eradication of every vestige of the T'ai P'ing revolt.

Historians estimate that between 30 million and 50 million people were killed or died during the thirteen years of this revolt.

As a result, the development of China was put back at least fifty years, and China was to remain a non-Christian society. By intervention the Western powers laid the foundations of an economic domination of China for eighty years. The Western nations, all of whom had played a double-dealing game and had spurned the hand of friendship held out by the quasi-Christian T'ai P'ing, won few Christian friends.

NIEN REBELLION (central China)   1854-68

The Nien rebels sought to overthrow the Manchu Emperor and restore the Ch'ing dynasty.

The Nien-fei of Anhwei and Hunan provinces of central China were the successors of the White Lotus Rebellion of 1796-1820, whose members, after the failure of the rebellion, had gone home still deeply imbued with the discipline of a revolutionary movement. The Nien remained as one of China's many subversive secret societies.

When the Nien bandits heard of the T'ai P'ing Rebellion (qv) and the latter captured Anking (qv) in February 1853, they stepped up their own activities and started to come out into the open and attack cities. From 1854 to 1857 the Nien allied with the T'ai P'ing and assisted the Northern Expeditionary Force against the Manchu Emperor commanded by Lin Feng-hsiang, including sending him 7,500 soldiers as reinforcements. The Nien leaders at this time were Chang Lo-hsing and Liu Fe-lang (Hungry Wolf) Liu. Between 1857, after the Imperial forces had beaten the Northern Expedition, and 1863, the Nien commanders, Kung Te and Sun Kuei-hsin, still co-operated with the T'ai P'ing. But after the Heavenly King, Hung Hsiu-ch'üan, died and the Imperial forces sacked Nanking in July 1864, there was a realignment. The Nien became dominant and in one battle the Manchu Emperor's best general, Seng-ko-lin-ch'in, was killed. But when the great Imperial counter-insurgent commander Tseng Kuo-fan took a hand, the eastern Nien were suppressed in January 1868 and the western Nien in August the same year. The Nien had overrun eight provinces, with a population numbering over 100 million. Civil and military casualties are estimated at about 4 million.

NIKKO (Honshu Island, Japan)   Japanese Revolution   1868
Fought between the supporters of the Shogun under Otori Keisuke and the Imperial army under Saigo Takamori.
    The rebels were completely defeated and they fled to the castle of Wakamatsu.

NINGPO (Chekiang Province, SE China)   T'ai P'ing Rebellion   10 May 1862
On 10 May 1862 British and French forces under Captain Roderick Dew joined by the American Frederick T. Ward's Foreign Rifle Corps, (later called the 'Ever Victorious Army') attacked and recaptured the seaport of Ningpo (Ningbo) (see OPIUM WAR) from the T'ai P'ing rebels with the loss of 200 men and inflicting over 1,000 casualties.

NORTH KOREA   Korean War   8 October-15 December 1950
Fought between the Communists and the S Koreans and Americans. After crossing the 38th Parallel in October, the American 8th Army under General Walton Walker and S Korean units drove north, meeting only slight resistance from the shaken N Korean Communists.
    On the left (west coast), the United Nations Supreme Commander, General Douglas MacArthur, sent in 1 Corps under Lt-General Frank Milburn along the Kaesong-Sariwon-Pyongyang axis. Pyongyang, the N Korean capital, fell on 19 and 20 October. On the east coast, Major-General Edward Almond's 10 Corps, independent of the 8th Army, landed behind the ROK units which had crossed the parallel first and reached the Yalu River boundary with Manchuria, 100 miles up-stream, on 26 October. 1 and 10 Corps now moved north, pushing N Korean forces back before them. All UN troops were ordered to close up to the Yalu River and 135,000 Communist prisoners were taken, adding to the total of 200,000 already killed, wounded or missing. The only military problem left for the UN forces seemed to be adequate logistic support, but late in October a new danger appeared in the form of Chinese Communists who had crossed the Yalu River unbeknown to the UN and ROK forces. They entered the fighting north of the Chongchon River near the dividing line between the two American forces in the centre of the peninsula. The first unit to receive an attack from them was the ROK 2 Corps which, being attacked on the night of 25 October, was driven south

of the Chongchon. Only a quarter of the ROK 7th Division's 3,500 men escaped the Chinese assault. On 1 November the first Russian MiG-15 jet aircraft appeared over N Korea to contest American air superiority. The Chinese did not press their advantage and MacArthur decided to extend further his weak and already over-extended lines of communication by attacking all along the Yalu front on 24 November. On the night of 25 November 300,000 Chinese troops, the 3rd and 4th Field Armies under Generals Chin Yi and Lin Piao, struck at the weak link between Walker's 8th Army and Almond's 10 Corps on the right (E). Of these, 180,000 Chinese hit Walker's inland (right) flank and caused it to cave in. In the fighting that followed, all of 1, 9 (John Coulter) and ROK 2 Corps were forced back with the loss of much of their artillery. On 1 December 3,000 of the 7,000 men in the US 2nd Infantry Division were killed or wounded in an ambush near the Chongchon River. Pyongyang was evacuated on 5 December and the retreat all along the 50-mile front continued until the end of the month when the line was stabilised near the 38th Parallel. To the east, the 1st Marines under Major-General Oliver Smith were cut off at the Choshin Reservoir by 120,000 Chinese troops. The Americans fought their way to the coast at Hungnam, whence they were evacuated by ship on 15 December. The S Koreans and Americans suffered 7,500 casualties, half of which were from frost-bite, but it is estimated that 37,000 casualties were inflicted on the Communists. Elements of 10 Corps were also shipped aboard here and at Wonsan, to the south.

The massive intervention by China had prevented the almost certain conquest of N Korea by the UN. By the end of 1950 the Chinese had reversed the situation, despite a staggering number of casualties, and had pushed the line back to the 38th Parallel.

OPIUM WAR   First China War   1839-42
Following disagreements between Chinese officials and British merchants at Canton, particularly concerning the import of opium from India, the Chinese took action against the European community. The Chinese destroyed stocks of the drug believed to be worth £3 million.

In 1840 a force of 4,000 men, some regulars and some native troops of the East India Company, under Lt-General Sir Hugh Gough were escorted into Chinese waters by a British naval squadron. The island of Chusan at the mouth of Hang-chow Bay was occupied and, moving south, the squadron blockaded Hong Kong and Canton.

On 26 February 1841 a British amphibious operation was launched, which took the Pearl River fortifications of the Bogue forts, the key to Canton. Following this, the flotilla moved up the Pearl River. On 24 May an amphibious assault on Canton was followed by the storming of the forts surrounding the port. Following the fall of the city, a temporary peace was restored. From August to October 1841 the British expeditionary force moved up the coast of China. Amoy was bombarded and captured on 26 August and Ningpo (Ningbo) fell on 13 October. When the British ceased their operations during the winter, the troops suffered severely from poor logistic support, contrasting with their effective combat operations. Sometimes as much as half the British force was suffering from disease; many transports were not fit to go to sea and a number foundered in typhoons. Food and medical supplies were short. The Admiralty and War Office, however, paid little attention to these problems, since China was on the other side of the globe and the British East India Company was making a profit. In 1842 the British carried out operations on the Yangtze Kiang. Shanghai was captured on 19 June and, moving up-river, the British took the great city of Chinkiang-foo on 21 July. With Nanking threatened, the Chinese sued for peace. On 29 August the Treaty of Nanking was signed, requiring China to cede Hong Kong, to open the treaty ports of Canton, Amoy, Foochow (Minhow), Ningpo and Shanghai to British trade, and to pay an indemnity of $20 million.

PAGAHAR   First Burma War   1825
Fought between the British under General Sir Archibald Campbell and the Burmese under Zaya-Thayan.
Strength: British 1,300; Burmese 15,000.
   The Burmese did not make a stand but fled the field, their general being the first to go. The encounter, the only pitched battle of the war, was therefore almost bloodless, and the British achieved their object.

PANTHAY REVOLT (Yunnan Province, W China)   1855-73
The Moslem inhabitants of Yunnan, who constituted a strong minority, were dissatisfied with their treatment by Manchu officials. They had revolted in 1818-19, 1826-8 and 1834-40 but, after being suppressed, were treated more harshly. They saw the T'ai P'ing Rebellion (qv) of the Hakkas as an opportunity to carry out a successful revolt based on the copper mines in eastern Ch'u-hsiung, where large numbers of Moslems worked.
   The revolt had a religious head Ma Te-hsin and a military leader Tu Wen-hsiu (Sultan Seleiman) who was highly educated and of great energy and reputation. Ma, like the T'ai P'ing leader Hung, set up the Peaceful Kingdom of the South (P'ing-nan-kuo), whose laws were morally strict.
   The Manchu counter-insurgent commander was Ts'en Yü-ying - from that fount of military commanders, Kwangsi Province. Tu had seized the western city of Tali, and in 1857 drove off Tsen's attempt to recapture it. The provincial capital Kunming was besieged by Ma Ju-lung, a strict Mohammedan who had been on the traditional pilgrimage to Mecca. Outnumbered, Ts'en returned to Kwangsi to obtain a new army. He raised the siege of Kunming in 1859 and carried out a policy of 'pardon and pacification' which won over both Ma Ju-lung and Ts'en, whose forces were incorporated into the Imperial army. Ma became a brigadier-general and the counter-insurgent commander, Ts'en, acting Lieutenant-Governor of Yunnan in 1861.
   In 1863 the revolt flared up again, and Ts'en Yü-ying was defeated at Tali. Ts'en withdrew to eastern Yunnan, where he practised a hearts-and-minds policy

to win over the people whilst he retrained his army. In 1864 the Emperor promoted him and ordered him to wipe out all rebels in the provinces of Yunnan, Szechwan and Kweichow. The Moslem leader Tu, now master of all western Yunnan, was besieging Kunming and drawing supplies from Burma. He also asked for aid from Britian, sending his son to England.

For seven years the war continued until Ts'en's policy of winning over the population, coupled with constant military pressure on the rebels, prevailed. In 1871 Tu Wen-hsui agreed to be beheaded on condition his followers were spared. However, dressed in royal robes, he took poison before the execution. He blamed his defeat on the failure of the T'ai P'ing Rebellion which released battle-trained veterans to fight him.

Military casualties suffered by each side were between 500,000 and 1 million, and the provincial population was reduced from 8 million to 3 million, 5 million having been killed or having moved away.

PEKING III (China)   Boxer Rebellion   20 June-14 August 1900
European seizure of Chinese territory aroused strong anti-foreign feeling in China. Groups of youths (encouraged by the Dowager Empress Tz'u Hsi) formed a secret organisation called the Society of Harmonious Fists (the so-called Boxers). The outbreaks of violence which followed prompted an international expedition, led by Admiral Sir Edward Hobart Seymour, to go to Tientsin where they were fired upon by the Taku forts. In Peking, the Boxers murdered the German Minister, Baron von Ketteler, and beseiged the foreign legations on 20 June.

A six-nation expeditionary force landed at Tientsin on 14 July. The legations in Peking were relieved on 14 August after a fighting march of 80 miles NW from the point of departure.

On 7 September 1901 the Boxer Protocol was signed by twelve nations, making peace with China.

PLEI ME (S Vietnam)   Vietnam War   19-27 October 1965
Fought between the Viet Cong and N Vietnamese, and the S Vietnamese and Americans.
Strength: Viet Cong and N Vietnamese 6,000; S Vietnamese 400 + 12 US special Forces.

One of the largest Communist offensives of the war took place against the triangular fort of Plei Me which lay 20 miles from the Cambodian border. Held by Montagnards, the fort was attacked for a week continuously by Viet Cong and N Vietnamese under cover of mortar and recoilless rifle-fire. On the second day of the attack, 250 S Vietnamese Rangers were dropped inside the garrison by helicopter to reinforce the troops there. A relief force was sent out from 2 Corps headquarters at Pleiku, but it was checked by a Communist ambush. US Sky-raiders made 600 sorties to aid the defenders who were supplied by parachute drops from transport planes. The fort held out until 27 October when part of the US 1st Cavalry Division (Airmobile) were dropped by helicopter north of the fort, thus raising the siege. The Communists withdrew west into Cambodia, having lost 850 killed and 1,700 wounded. Nine of the US Special Forces had been killed or wounded.

PORT ARTHUR (LUSHUN) I (S Liaoning Province, NE China)   Sino-Japanese War   21 November 1894

Fought between the Japanese under General Count Iwao Oyama and the Chinese.
Strength: Japanese 10,000, Chinese 9,000.
Aim: As part of their combined land and sea offensive, the Japanese sought the reduction of the Chinese naval base of Port Arthur (Lushun).
Battle: The Japanese attacked the base with a naval bombardment followed by a land assault. Chinese resistance was slight before they withdrew up the Liaotung Peninsula. Japanese losses were 270 killed and wounded.
Result: The Japanese objective was achieved.

PORT ARTHUR II (S Liaoning Province, NE China)   Russo-Japanese War 8 February 1904-2 January 1905

Fought between the Japanese under Admiral Heihachiro Togo and General Count Maresuke Nogi and the Russians under Admiral Stepan Makarov and General Anatoli Stësel.
Strength: Japanese 30,000 with 16 warships; Russians 40,000 with 6 battleships + 10 cruisers.

On the night of 8 February the Japanese attacked the Russian fleet lying in the harbour with torpedo boats and damaged 2 battleships and a cruiser which were beached at the mouth of the harbour. Opening a bombardment, they damaged another Russian battleship and 4 more cruisers at a loss to themselves of 58 killed and wounded, mainly in torpedo boats. Russian losses were 56 killed and wounded. War was declared two days later and Makarov took command of the Russian fleet from Vice-Admiral Stark, instigating sorties against the Japanese who were now blockading the port. On 13 April the Russian flagship *Petropavlosk* struck a mine and sank with a loss of 700 lives, including Makarov. At the same time the battleship *Pobieda* and a destroyer were also torpedoed, but they contrived to reach the harbour safely. After this defeat, the Russian fleet remained in the harbour for several months. On 2 May the Japanese sent a fleet of merchant steamers into the harbour, accompanied by the torpedo flotilla. Eight vessels succeeded in reaching the outer harbour and two of them broke the boom guarding the entrance to the inner harbour, being then blown up by their commanders in the fairway. Several other vessels were sunk near the harbour entrance. The Japanese rescued 42 men from the crews of the merchantmen, whose complement had been 179 officers and men.

On 5 May Japanese land forces were put ashore under the protection of Togo's naval guns. The force, in five divisions, was commanded by Nogi, who sent the bulk of his men under General Yasukata Oku to attack the heights of Nanhan which were defended by the Russians. The Russians under Stësel repulsed eight assaults on the position on 26 May and the Japanese pulled back in order to allow their own naval guns to bombard Nanhan from Kiuchan Bay. On the following day the Japanese stormed and carried the hill on the Russian left, to find one-sixth of the 3,000 defenders dead on the field. The Japanese lost 4,500, but they took 78 guns and had now surrounded the Russians in Port Arthur, and by 1 June their investment lines were complete. They began to shell the Russian ships in the harbour and the fleet, now led by Admiral Vilgelm Vitgeft, ran the gauntlet of the blockade and sailed into the Yellow Sea. On 10 August, however, the Japanese pursued and drove them back into Port Arthur, Vitgeft being killed in the sea battle. An attempted junction between this fleet and the one blockaded in Vladivostock was therefore thwarted.

Nogi continued to harass the Russians manning their strong defences in the hills around the town and, despite the fact that 13,000 Japanese were incapacitated by illness and wounds each month, they persisted until, on 5 December, they captured the key position known as 203-metre Hill. The possession of this height enabled the Japanese to bombard the Russian fleet in the harbour with accuracy and the 4 battleships left were sunk. On 2 January 1905 Stësel surrendered the port to the Japanese who had lost 58,000 killed and wounded and 34,000 sick during the siege.

Elsewhere the Japanese had been equally successful in overpowering the Russians.

PUSAN PERIMETER (S Korea)   Korean War   25 June-11 August 1950
Fought between the United Nations forces and the Communists.
Strength: UN forces 180,000 (ROK 91,500, US 87,000, British 1,500); Communists 280,000.
Following the intervention of China into the war in Korea, the UN thrust beyond the 38th Parallel was pushed back and, on 25 June, the Communist forces broke out of their lines behind the 38th Parallel at eleven points. Spearheaded by T-34 Russian-built tanks, the Communists moved into the Republic of Korea, forcing the S Korean army of General Chae Byong Duk back before them. Seoul fell in three days to the N Koreans under General Chai Ung Chai. The Han River was bridged on 30 June and 1 Corps moved down the west of the peninsula, 2 Corps to the east. General Douglas MacArthur flew US troops in from Japan under the auspices of the UN. First to take the field against the Communists were 700 men from the 24th Infantry Division under Colonel Charles Smith at Osan, 20 miles south of Seoul, on 5 July. But they lacked effective anti-tank weapons and were unable to make any impression on the weighty advance. In the first attack 150 Americans were lost, killed, wounded or missing. General William Dean, Commander of the 24th Infantry, sent his forces into a series of delaying actions along the Seoul-Taejon-Pusan axis as they arrived. The retreat continued, however. Taejon fell on 20 July and Dean was wounded and later captured. On 13 July General Walton Walker assumed command of the US 8th Army in Korea, the ranks of which were soon swelled to include the 1st Cavalry, 25th Infantry and 2nd Infantry Divisions as well as their marines. Although the Americans had superiority of both air and sea, by 5

August the 8th Army was pushed back as far as the Naktong River. Pohang, 63 miles NE of Pusan, fell on 11 August and the 8th Army dug in in a perimeter around the vital port of Pusan, to the SE, for a desperate defence.

In their drive south, the N Koreans had suffered 58,000 casualties, and they now began to attack the perimeter defences, securing several bridgeheads across the Naktong in the west. Taegu, 55 miles NW, and Masan, 29 miles west, were both seriously threatened by the Communists but Walker, with his interior line position, was able to shift reserves to areas most in need and by the end of the month all Communist penetrations had been blocked or thrown back. During September the fighting along the perimeter indicated a gradual diminution of N Korean power. From Japan, MacArthur planned an amphibious attack behind the Communist lines in the Seoul area.

PYONGYANG (N Korea) Sino-Japanese War.   16 September 1894
Fought between the Japanese under General Marquis Michitsura Nodzu and the Chinese.
Strength: Japanese 14,000; Chinese 12,000.
Aim: The Japanese opened the war by attacking the Chinese garrison in Pyongyang, then known as Heijo, with the intention of taking the town.
Battle: They assaulted the town and routed the Chinese, who were less well disciplined and badly armed, with heavy loss to the Chinese. Japanese losses were 650 killed and wounded.
Result: The Japanese objective was achieved.

QUEMOY-MATSU (Islands off Foochow, Fukien coast, China)   Bombardments 1954-62
During tension between Communist and Nationalist Chinese forces, the latter based in Formosa (Taiwan) and supported by the USA, the off-shore islands of Quemoy and Matsu became a bone of contention. These islands had been heavily garrisoned by the Nationalists under Generalissimo Chiang Kai-shek in the hope that they could be used as a jumping-off site for a future invasion of China. The Communists had no navy or airforce so the islands were fairly safe from capture. But the Communists brought up siege artillery and started an incessant bombardment to reduce the garrisons into submission. The Nationalists countered with heavier guns, built deep underground fortifications and evacuated all civilians. The bombardments continued off and on for eight years, which was good gunnery practice and welcome to the armaments manufacturers, but nothing was achieved but an impasse.

The dispute ended in a cessation of shelling by both sides.

SHAHO RIVER (Liaoning Privince, N China)   Russo-Japanese War   October 1904
Fought between the Russians under General Alexei Kuropatkin and the Japanese under Field-Marshal Marquis Iwao Oyama.

After the Battle of Liaoyang (qv), which ended indecisively owing chiefly to the exhaustion of the armies, the Russians retreated north. The Japanese pursued. At the Shaho River, 15 miles south of Mukden (Shenyang), the Russians halted to make a stand. In mid-October Kuropatkin launched an attack against the Japanese, but, as had happened at Liaoyang, fighting on the 40-mile front deteriorated into a series of fierce skirmishes which were halted by the rains, whereupon both sides dug in behind barbed wire for the winter.

No decisive conclusion was reached.

SHANGHAI (Kiangsu Province, China)   Sino-Japanese Incident.   8 August-13 December 1937

The 'Chinese incident' started on 7 July 1937 when the Japanese clashed with Chinese troops at the Marco Polo Bridge at Lukouchiao, near Peking. The Japanese followed this up with a full-scale invasion of China, but hoped to confine operations to the north. General Chiang Kai-shek wanted to involve the Western powers and so, on 8 August, attacked the Japanese segment of the International Settlement of Shanghai and drove the few Japanese forces back on to the docks and beaches of the Woosung River. The Japanese were quickly reinforced by marines and naval ships which, anchored a few yards off-shore, fired point-blank at the Chinese street fighting on the banks of the river. The *Idzumo,* an old British cruiser sold to the Japanese, was the centre of resistance and the Chinese tried to float electric mines to blow it up, but failed.

The International Settlement was protected by a British brigade under the command of Major-General Telfer Smollett, an American marine regiment and Dutch and Italian contingents. The French had a brigade in the French settlement. As the fighting increased and spread as both the Chinese and Japanese sent in reinforcements, the shells and bombs landed in the Settlements. The Chinese tried to sink the *Idzumo* with 1,000-pound bombs, previously bought from the British, and during the beginning of a typhoon one bomb landed in the Avenue Edward VII and killed 1,123 people, mostly Chinese.

During the first eight weeks of the fighting the Japanese toe-hold on the bank of the Woosung narrowed down in places to only about 50 yards wide. Fighting was continuous and fierce alongside the British sector, and about 30 British troops were inadvertently killed. By October the Japanese had gathered a sufficient naval force and amphibious vessels to land two divisions on the south bank of the Yangtze Kiang near Woosung. By this time the Chinese had 500,000 men on the delta between Soochow and Shanghai.

For about two more weeks the Japanese were stuck on their beachheads. But then, using the same tactics as General Charles Gordon had pioneered when operating in this area against the T'ai P'ing 100 years before, they penetrated the Chinese defences by using their amphibious craft and forsaking the roads. Using the innumerable waterways as a means of advance the Japanese turned the Chinese flanks and penetrated their centre, reaching the S limits of the International Settlement at Bubbling Well Road. A Japanese division landed in Hangchow Bay, where the Japanese used landing craft from whaling ships, thus predating the British and American LSTs, and completed the defeat of the Chinese. The Chinese in the delta area numbered 500,000 and the Japanese over 200,000. The Japanese then turned their attention to Nanking, which they captured on 13 December 1937, and followed this up by a massacre of the inhabitants.

The Chinese are said to have lost over 200,000 casualties during these five months of fighting and the Japanese 50,000. It was the first modern battle in which mechanised landing craft, tanks, aerial bombardment and close air support were used, but very little notice was taken of the reports sent to Europe and America by military observers on the spot, so the Western Allies went to war tactically unprepared.

SHANGHAI I (Kiangsu Province, China)   T'ai P'ing Rebellion   18 August 1860
The T'ai P'ing had had a series of setbacks in early 1859 when Anking (qv) and Pukow had been captured by the Imperialist forces, and some of the best generals of the Nien Rebellion (qv) had changed sides and were operating against them. But the T'ai P'ing General, Li Hsui-ch'eng, recovered Pukow in November 1859 and captured Hangchow between 19 and 23 March 1860. This forced the Imperialist army, which was attacking the T'ai P'ing capital Nanking, to send reinforcements to Hangchow. Li then defeated the weakened main army after a great battle in May 1860 in which the Imperial commanders Ho-ch'in and Chang Kuo-liang were amongst the 80,000 Imperialists who were killed.

The T'ai P'ing military command then decided to attack Shanghai in order to draw forces away from Anking and other areas where the great counter-insurgent commander Tseng Kuo-fan was making headway. The T'ai P'ing leaders had no wish to attack their Western co-religionists whom they wanted as allies, but could not get the British, French and Americans to understand this. General Li Hsui-ch'eng was ordered by the Celestial King, Hung Hsiu-ch'üan, to occupy Shanghai. Li took Changchow on 26 May, Wusih on 30 May and Soochow (about 50 miles south of Shanghai) on 2 June 1860. An attack on Yangchow was repulsed. Li did everything he could to prevent unnecessary destruction, as he wanted to win the people over to his side and impress the Western nations with his Christian forbearance.

Li then wrote to the British Minister in Shanghai, Frederick Bruce, telling him of the necessity of occupying Sungkiang and Shanghai. But Bruce, who was strongly anti-T'ai P'ing, decided to intervene in the war on the Imperialists' side.

The International Settlement in Shanghai, consisting of representatives of traders from the Western powers, formed the Foreign Rifle Corps on 2 June 1860 under Frederick T. Ward, an American soldier of fortune who had seen service in central and S America. This force, which never numbered over 3,000 men, came to be known as the 'Ever Victorious Army'.

Li Hsui-ch'eng occupied Sungkiang on 1 July 1860 and followed this up by sending letters to the representatives of Britain, France and the USA asking them to remove their troops and ships from Shanghai in case they might be hurt or damaged. On 18 August Li and Hung Jen-kan advanced on Shanghai along three routes with 50,000 troops. The Chinese Imperialist troops were driven back, but when the T'ai P'ing met the artillery and rifle-fire of British marines, Indian Infantry and French forces, they were repulsed with heavy losses. The T'ai P'ing withdrew. Ward's forces were maintaining internal security in the city and were not engaged. The British and French forces received about £160,000 from the Chinese Imperial government for defending Shanghai at the same time as they were attacking them in Tientsin and Peking.

SHANGHAI II (Kiangsu Province, China)   T'ai P'ing Rebellion   17 June-30 August 1862

After Ningpo (qv) had changed hands twice and the British Admiral, Sir John Hope, had brought his naval squadron down from the Gulf of Chihli to 'settle the T'ai P'ing problem', The T'ai P'ing military command decided that it was necessary to treat the Western powers as enemies.

The T'ai P'ing Kwangsi Generals Huang Ch'eng-chung and Fan Ju-tseng took Ningpo on 9 December 1861 and Li Hsui-ch'eng took Hangchow, the capital of the Province of Chekiang, on 29 December. Thirty thousand Imperialist troops were brought down the Yangtze from Anking (qv) by the British navy to the neighbourhood of Shanghai. Admiral Sir John Hope having been wounded, a British/French military and naval task force was formed under Captain Borlase, RN, with the object of capturing Chapu, near Shanghai, in which they were successful on 17 April. Borlase, with 3 12-pounders, about 250 British, Frederick T. Ward's 'Ever Victorious Army', 550 French with 5 howitzers and a contingent of the Imperial army, then took Kiating on 1 May, Tsingpu on 12 May and attacked without success Taitsang and Kunshan, all within the vicinity of Shanghai. Li reacted strongly and, with 10,000 veterans, defeated the British/French/Chinese force at Taitsang (21 May) Kiating (26 May) and Tsingpu (2 June), all of which he recaptured.

Li then attacked Shanghai on 17 June, but was repulsed by the Imperial Anhwei army which the Royal Navy had brought in, losing 3,000 casualties. Li attacked again on 18 August and reached Bubbling Well, within 3 miles of the Shanghai docks. But the superior fire-power of the Allied artillery caused him heavy casualties. Then the Celestial King called for help from Nanking which was under heavy attack by Tseng Kuo-ch'üan's Hunan Braves. As Li started to withdraw, the Western powers began to intervene in earnest. At a third Battle of Kiating there were 2,000 British, 800 French and 1,400 soldiers of the Ever Victorious Army with heavy artillery assisting 20,000 Anhwei troops, coupled with supporting fire from naval ships.

At the Battle of Nanjao, on 17 May 1862, Li Hsui-ch'eng was faced with 12,000 Imperialist Anhwei troops, supported by 427 British sailors, and 950 British, 690 Indian, 775 French and 1,000 English-trained Chinese troops under Ward, totalling 3,842 regulars and 30 guns. Li was forced to withdraw. The French Admiral, Protet, was killed in the action. The French avenged his death by massacring every man, woman and child in the town of Nanjao when it was recaptured.

Li Hsui-ch'eng was now ordered by the Heavenly King to give up his attack on Shanghai and hurry back to rescue Nanking, and on 19 June he started to move.

The upshot was Shanghai was saved for the Chinese Imperialists and the Western powers.

SHIROGAWA (Honshu Island, Japan)   Satsuma Rebellion.   24 September 1876
Fought between the rebels under Saigo Takamori and the Imperial army under Prince Taruhito.

In this engagement the last remnants of the rebel army were practically annihilated, most of the leaders of the revolt were killed and, after the battle, Saigo committed *hara-kiri* on the field.

SIAM-VIENTIANE WAR   1826-9
In 1826 King Chao Anou, with the Vientiane (Laotian) army in three columns, invaded Siam. The force came within 30 miles of Bangkok before the Siamese, who had been taken by surprise, mobilised under P'ya Bodin and then halted and repulsed the invaders. The invasion had taken place because Chao Anou wished to free his country from Siam, having, however, maintained good relations with that country until Siamese troubles with the British gave Vientiane its opportunity.

Siam reciprocated by invading Vientiane (Laos). In the week-long battle of Nong-Bona-Lamp'on in 1827, the Siamese forced a passage of the Mekong River, destroying the Vientiane (Laotian) army and forcing Chao Anou to flee east to Vietnam. The Siamese went on to lay waste the capital, Vientiane, and to destroy large areas of country, deporting entire populations to regions of their own country which had been depopulated by Siamese wars with Burma. Vientiane was annexed in 1828. In 1829 Chao Anou returned to Vientiane with a Vietnamese army, which was defeated and scattered. Chao Anou himself was captured.

SINKIANG, MOSLEM REVOLT (central Asia)   1865-77
Yakub Beg (1820-77) was born in Khokand. Having obtained military experience against the advancing Russians in Turkestan, and seeing the outlying provinces of China weakened by the great T'ai P'ing Rebellion (qv), he crossed the border into Chinese Sinkiang in 1865 to carve out an empire for himself. He was a strict Mohammedan whose laws he enforced at pain of death. He quickly raised an army and founded his kingdom over the vast area from the Pamirs to Lob Nor in 1870. His revolt attracted a number of defeated Chinese Moslems who paid allegiance. In 1873 the Sultan of Turkey, Abdul-Aziz, made Yakub Beg the Amir of Kashgaria.

The British and Russians, playing the 'Great Game' for central Asia, both decided to woo him. The British sent a mission and opened a legation in 1873. Russia countered by occupying the khanates of Khokand, Bokhara and Khiva, also in 1873, and recognised Yakub Beg as Lord of Moslem Sinkiang. Yakub could now obtain arms from Britain, Russia and Turkey - which he did, as he feared an attack from the regenerated Chinese.

General Tso Tsung-t'ang, who had earned a well-deserved reputation for his counter-insurgent successes, with a well-stocked army of 100,000 advanced and captured Urumchi in northern Sinkiang on 6 November 1876. Yakub Beg turned to the British minister in Peking for help and asked for the creation of a Chinese vassal state under British protection. General Tso told the British to come over and he would talk, but Tso continued his advance. The Russians saw no future in helping Yakub and diverted their grain caravans to the Chinese. When Tso captured Turfan, on 16 May 1877, Yakub Beg gave up and died.

Tso Tsung-t'ang was noted for his ruthlessness and by 1878 all of Turkestan was recovered, but it was said that 50 per cent of the Moslems were killed. In 1884 the huge area was incorporated into the Chinese Empire and named Sinkiang or New Dominion. Today, with the advent of railways, oil discoveries, nuclear ranges and the development of coal, iron and steel, Sinkiang is becoming industrialised.

SON-TAY (N Vietnam)   Tongking War   14-16 December 1883
Fought between the Chinese under Lin Yung Ku and the French under Admiral Coubert.
Strength: Chinese 25,000 (including 10,000 'Black Flags'); French 7,000 + 7 gunboats.
Aim: The fortress of Son-Tay was attacked on 14 December by the French who sought its surrender.
Battle: The outer defences were taken on the first day and the garrison was forced to retreat into the citadel. The Chinese made a sortie during the night which surprised the French, but their attack was repulsed after heavy fighting. On 16 December the French stormed and carried the citadel. French losses were 92 officers and 318 men killed and wounded. Chinese losses were about 1,000.
Result: The French objective was achieved.

SUNGARI RIVER (NE China)   Chinese Civil War   January-June 1947
Fought between the Nationalists under General Chiang Kai-shek and the Communists under Mao Tse-tung.
Strength: Nationalists 500,000; Communists 270,000.
   At the beginning of the year the PLA (People's Liberation Army) launched an offensive against Nationalist troops in N Manchuria, attacking south against Nationalists across the frozen Sungari River. In January three PLA columns crossed the river, making for Changchun, but after two weeks of fighting they were driven back across the river once more. On 21 February another attack was made and again it was beaten back. Between 8 and 15 March a third attack was repulsed. The successive assaults had reduced the Nationalist bridgehead considerably, however, and when in May the Communists launched the largest attack yet made in the war, amounting to four columns, the Nationalists were

driven back before the thrust into central Manchuria. By the end of June this offensive was also checked, but Nationalist casualties were very high. Chiang's garrisons at Changchun, Yungki and Mukden had almost become isolated because the Communist offensive had wrecked lines of communication between the cities.

The initiative in Manchuria had now passed into Mao's hands.

SZEPINGKAI (Kirin Province, NE China)   Chinese Civil War   18 March–20 May 1946

Fought between the Nationalists under General Sun Li-jen and the Communists under Mao Tse-tung.
Strength: Nationalists 70,000; Communists 110,000.

When the Communists under Mao found that Chiang Kai-shek's Nationalists had occupied Mukden on 15 March, they seized the key rail junction on the S Manchuria Railway at Szepingkai (Ssupingchieh), 70 miles north of Mukden, in order to forestall the expected advance of the Nationalists into central Manchuria.

The New Nationalist 1st Army under Sun attacked the Communists on 16 April. In the first pitched battle of the Civil War, the Nationalists drove the Communists from their position by 20 May.

The Nationalists occupied Changchun, 70 miles north, five days later. On 3 May, however, the last of the Soviet troops in N Manchuria had been withdrawn and Maoist forces were in firm control of land north of Changchun. On 7 June the Communist negotiator, Chou En-lai, agreed to an armistice with Chiang which continued until 30 June while the US General, George Marshall, tried and failed to negotiate a permanent truce.

TAIERCHWANG (Anhwei Province, E China)   Sino-Japanese Incident April 1938

Fought between the Chinese under General Li Tsung-jen advised by General von Falkenhausen and his German mission, and two Japanese divisions.
Strength: Chinese 250,000; Japanese 60,000.

General von Falkenhausen had been trying to lead the Japanese into a trap and at last succeeded in April when two Japanese infantry divisions precipitately advanced to Taierchwang. Falkenhausen persuaded the Kwangsi General Li Tsung-jen to surround the Japanese with vastly superior forces, but waited five days before he could persuade him to attack. During this time Falkenhausen, according to his ADC, sat on a stool in his tent and refused to talk to anyone except Li. Li eventually attacked and destroyed one Japanese division completely and dealt very severely with the other, capturing most of its transport and guns. This was a famous victory as it was the only clear-cut one gained by the Chinese in eight years of fighting. Japanese casualties were 20,000 killed, and Chinese 35,000 killed and wounded.

Falkenhausen's mission, numbering over 300 officers and technicians, stayed on in China, in spite of Japan joining the Axis, until early 1942, when it was withdrawn at the request of the Japanese.

T'AI P'ING NORTHERN EXPEDITION (N China)   13 May 1853-31 May 1855
Fought between the T'ai P'ing rebel army under Lin Feng-hsiang, Li K'ai-fang and
Chi Wen-yüan, supported by the Nien (qv) rebels of Hunan, Anhwei and Shantung
under Chang Lo-hsing; and the Imperial Manchu forces under Sheng-pao and the
great Manchu cavalry commander Seng-ko-lin-ch'in.
Strength: T'ai P'ing 70,000 + 7,500 regulars reinforcements + Nien 100,000
guerillas; Manchu's government forces 500,000 during the two years.
Aim: The object of the Northern Expedition was to overrun China north of the
Yangtze Kiang, capture Peking and convert the people to the T'ai P'ing form of
Christianity.
Campaign: Owing to the easy success enjoyed by the T'ai P'ing in the Yangtze
valley, they were over-confident, and this expedition was badly planned and
badly supported.

The rebels achieved initial success by advancing the 300 miles from Pukow
(13 May 1853) on the Yangtze to K'usi-te where, on 13 June, Lin easily defeated
the Hunan provincial forces, killing 3,000. But north of the Yangtze the country is
flat and dry with extremes of temperature and few rivers, so that the S Chinese
Hakkas were not in their element, whereas it was suitable for Manchu cavalry.

The T'ai P'ing had difficulty crossing the Huang Ho (Yellow River) because
all boats had been removed or destroyed so the rebels were diverted west to
Kung-hsien, where they crossed in coal boats. Their reports to Nanking fell into
the hands of the Imperialists, who could now anticipate their movements. The
rebels waited for two months, besieging Huai-ch'ing just north of the Huang Ho
which they required as a base, but failed to capture the town. The Imperialists
in Peking were greatly disturbed at the invasion and, as the rebels moved on into
Shansi, the Manchu general Sheng-pao was directed on to them. However, the
rebels continued in a great arc - Chü-wo, Hung-tung, then east to Wu-an, north to
Luan-ch'eng and then east again to Shen-chou, which is 150 miles south of Peking.
The rebels fought Sheng-pao to a standstill on 12 September at P'ing-yang. Both
sides considered they were in dire straits and Lin appealed to Hung Hsui-ch'üan
at Nanking for reinforcements. On 6 February 1854 7,500 men were sent due
north towards Peking under Huang Sheng-tsai and Tseng Li-ch'ang.

Meanwhile the rebels were having great trouble with Seng-ko-lin-ch'in's
Manchurian cavalry. But they defeated them at Ch'ing-hai and Tu-liu-chen on
29 October 1853, where they were within 50 miles of their target, Peking. They
had marched 1,400 miles, all their communications to Nanking had been cut
off, the wintry weather with sub-zero temperatures was something they had
never before experienced and they were operating in an unfavourable element.
Yet the fact that all this time they were still full of fight and continued to
advance is put down by European observers on the spot 'to the great religious
beliefs of the T'ai P'ing leaders'.

However, the T'ai P'ing Northern Expedition had shot its bolt. An attack by
Sheng-pao on 23 December was repulsed, but on 5 February the T'ai P'ing started
their retreat and disintegration. They retired to Fou-ch'eng on the Grand Canal

and held it for two months from 9 March to 5 May awaiting the reinforcements from Nanking. These reinforcements under Huang reached Lin-ch'ing, 70 miles south of Fou-ch'ing, on 12 April. Although helped by the Nien rebels, contrary counsels arose. But, led by Tseng Li-ch'ing, the T'ai P'ing reinforcements attacked Sheng-pao's forces. After a ten-day action the town of Lin ch'ing was finally captured by the government forces. There the reinforcements were again defeated by the Manchu cavalry, broken up and irretrievably dispersed.

Lin Feng-hsiang and Li K'ai-fang, hearing of this collapse, themselves retreated the 70 miles to Lin-ch'ing. At this town, Lin Feng-hsiang fought a desperate action with Seng-ko-lin-ch'in, while farther east Li K'ai-fang was besieged at Kao-t'ang by Sheng-pao. Nanking sent further reinforcements but they were defeated and destroyed. Lin Feng-hsiang was wounded, captured by the Manchurian cavalry leader and later executed in Peking. The latter then turned with his cavalry to help Sheng-pao against the redoubtable Li. Li escaped south along the Grand Canal but, during the next eight weeks, fighting hard all the time and with his men being picked off, his physical and moral strength dwindled and he finally surrendered on 31 May 1855 with his last 500 men. They were sent to Peking for decapitation.

Thus ended the Northern T'ai P'ing Expedition. The T'ai P'ing forces sustained casualties of 80,000, the Nien rebels 50,000, and the government forces 250,000.

Result: Although the T'ai P'ing were to recover and wage war for another ten years, their initial drive was at last stopped, and many of their finest and most accomplished generals, experienced officers and tough men from Kwangsi had been eliminated. From this time on it was unlikely that the whole of China would become Christian under Hung Hsui-ch'üan.

T'AI P'ING REBELLION (China) 1851-64

The T'ai P'ing Rebellion started at Thistle Mountain, near Kuei-p'ing, in China's southernmost province, Kwangsi. It was a quasi-Christian, religious-cum-agrarian revolt, whose core were the Hakkas, the original inhabitants of China, and was directed against Confucianism and the alien Manchu Emperor at Peking. Moving along the rivers, as the Hakka are great sailors, its initial 70,000-strong crusade spread rapidly northward, gathering adherents from the peasants as it went to Kweilin, Wuchang and Hankow and then down the Yangtze Kiang to capture Nanking on 19 March 1853 which the religious leader, Hung Hsui-ch'üan the Heavenly King, made his capital. He had enforced a strict puritanical regime on his followers. But he had lost two of his greatest generals and administrators in battle on the way, Fen Yün-shan and Hsiao Ch'ao-Kuei, who held the balance of power amongst his immediate coterie. But the great Generals Yang Hsiu-ch'ing and Shih Ta-k'ai were still serving him. General Hung took an expedition towards Peking, which failed. But General Shih recaptured all the western Yangtze Kiang cities such as Hankow and Wuchang between 1853 and 1855. General Yang remained as Hung's Chief of Staff. However, he defeated the greatest army the Emperor had ever put into the field, at Kiangnan, between 5 April and 9 August 1856, when each side numbered over 2½ million. This went to Yang's head and he tried to seize power by a *coup d'état*.

Hung Hsui-ch'üan appealed to the Western King, Wei Ch'ang-hui, for help and also to Shih Ta-k'ai. Before Shih had returned Wei massacred Yang Hsiu-ch'ing, his family and 30,000 of his followers and then plotted to seize power himself. So the Heavenly King asked Shih to deal with Wei. Shih cut off Yang's head and the heads of 200 of his most important followers.

Shih Ta-k'ai was appalled at all this court plotting and the way Hung himself had become soft and decadent and surrounded with a harem - all the things that he had preached against. So he decided to go away and seize a peaceful, luscious province of his own. He was a great general, never having been defeated. He took away 200,000 of the T'ai P'ing's best troops, conquered, in turn, twelve provinces of China between Shanghai and Tibet but, after six years, his following dwindled and he finally surrendered at Cheng-tu, in Szechwan, where the governor of the province cut off his head.

The T'ai P'ing had a great revival in the period 1856-61, but mostly in the Yangtze basin and delta. The Emperor's counter-insurgency forces improved in spite of a war with France and Britain in 1858-60.

The T'ai P'ing had hoped to gain support from the Christian Western powers but their politics and agrarian reforms which they were putting into effect were too liberal for the mercenary China-coast traders. The International Settlement in Shanghai raised a small force (the Foreign Rifle Corps - *Yang-ch'iang-tui)* of 3,000 Chinese, commanded by an American soldier of fortune Frederick T. Ward, which came to be known as the 'Ever Victorious Army'. This was later taken over by Major Charles (Chinese) Gordon, RE, of later Khartoum fame. This force helped protect the Shanghai settlement and later co-operated with the Emperor's huge armies, which eventually defeated the T'ai P'ing armies and besieged Nanking. Hung Hsui-ch'üan died on 1 June 1864 and so did not see the fall and sack of Nanking (qv) on 19 July.

British and French naval forces had become embroiled in the war more than once, especially in Admiral Sir James Hope's Yangtze expedition of 13 February 1861 to 10 May 1862. The Emperor's forces produced a great and wise counter-insurgent commander in General Tseng Kuo-fan whose famous force of highly trained Hunan Braves were his mainstay. He went on to defeat the Nien Rebellion (qv) and, in spite of not being a Manchu general, he remained the Emperor's greatest general until 1871, campaigning throughout China.

Historians estimate that between 30-50 million Chinese were killed in the T'ai P'ing Rebellion. It was one of the world's greatest convulsions and came within an ace of converting China to a form of Christianity. Chinese communism blossomed forth in the same area where the T'ai P'ing Rebellion grew, and both Sun Yat Sen and Mao Tse-tung learnt much from the mistakes made. Karl Marx stated that the idea of the Indian Mutiny originated amongst Indian Sepoys who had been stationed in Shanghai and who had learnt the T'ai P'ing doctrine.

TAKU FORTS (Hopeh Province, N China)   Second China War   25 June 1859-21 August 1860.
Fought between the British under Captain Vansittart, RN, and Lt-General Sir James Hope Grant and French, and the Chinese.
Strength: British 11 gunboats with 600 Royal Marines (25 June), 11,000 (21 August) + French 7,000 (21 August); Chinese 300 (25 June), 500 (21 August).
Aim: The Western powers sought to induce the Chinese Emperor Wen-tsung, Hsien-feng, to grant trade concessions.
Battle: On 25 June the British attacked the forts mounting 600 guns at the mouth of the Peiho River, when 11 light-draught gunboats unsuccessfully attempted to put shore batteries out of action. At 5 pm a force of marines and bluejackets was put ashore, but in a severe fight they were beaten back to the boats with a loss of 68 killed and 300 wounded. The gunboat crews suffered heavy casualties and 6 boats were sunk or disabled. On 21 August after a short bombardment, the N fort was stormed by 2,500 British and 400 French. The other forts surrendered without further resistance. Losses were: Allies, 21 killed and 184 wounded; Chinese, 400.
Result: The immediate objective of the Allies was achieved, and Grant marched on Peking - 80 miles distant - which he entered on 12 October.

TANSARA SAKA (Honshu Island, Japan)   Satsuma Rebellion   1876
The rebels, who occupied a very strong position, were attacked by the Imperial army under Prince Taruhito and, after fierce fighting, were driven out with heavy loss. The Imperialists also suffered heavily.

TAYEIZAN (Tokyo, Japan)   Japanese Revolution   4 July 1868
Fought between the followers of the Shogun, Yoshinobu (Hitotsubashi), last of the Tokogawa shoguns, and the Imperialists.
A revolution was brought about by the conflict between the pro-foreign and anti-foreign parties in Japan. Those wishing to restore the central power of the Emperor forced the resignation of Yoshinobu, ending 700 years of feudal military rule.
The followers of the Shogun made their last stand in Tokyo, then called Edo, at the Tayeizan temple in the Park of Uyeno. After a brisk fight they were defeated and the Imperialists were left with total control of the Shogun's capital.
The new Emperor, Meiji (Mutsuhito), moved his capital from Kyoto to Tokyo. The action is also known as the Battle of Tokyo. The Meiji period ushered in an era of rapid Westernisation and industrial development throughout Japan.

TE-LI-SSU (Liaotung Peninsula, N China)   Russo-Japanese War   14-15 June 1904
Fought between the Russians under General Baron de Stakelberg and the Japanese under General Yasukata Oku.

Strength: Russians 35,000; Japanese 40,000.

Aim: The Japanese sought to beat the Russians from their position.

Battle: On 14 June the Japanese attacked the Russians who held their ground throughout the day at a cost of 350 killed or wounded. On 15 June the Japanese renewed the attack, and this time the Russian left was turned and they retreated in disorder after a fierce fight. Two batteries of artillery were completely cut to pieces. The Russians left 1,500 dead on the field and lost 300 prisoners and 14 guns, total losses being about 10,000 in the operation. Japanese losses were 1,163 in the two days.

Result: The Japanese objective was achieved.

THIRTY-EIGHTH PARALLEL (Korea)   Korean War   1 January 1951-27 July 1953

Fought between the United Nations forces under General Matthew Ridgway and the Communists under General Lin Piao.

Strength: UN forces 768,000; Communists 1 million.

Following the entry of Chinese Communist forces into the Korean War, by the end of 1950 the UN forces into N Korea were driven back to the 38th Parallel. Ridgway, who had replaced General Walton Walker after the latter's death in a road accident on 23 December 1950, deployed the UN forces in three corps across the width of the Korean Peninsula. From left (W) to right, these were: 1 under Lieutenant-General Frank Milburn, 9 under Lieutenant-General John Coulter and 10 under Major-General Edward Almond and 1, 2 and 3 S Korean Corps which held the east of the line. At the start of the battle, 365,000 men from eighteen different countries making up the UN forces stood against 485,000 Communists under General Lin Piao and the N Korean Head of State, Kim Il Sung.

After an all-night mortar and artillery attack, the Communists, mainly Chinese, attacked the UN position. 1 and 9 Corps received the brunt of the assault and were slowly driven back, although they inflicted very heavy casualties on the Communists. On 4 January Inchon and Seoul were evacuated. To the east, 10 Corps abandoned Wonju on 10 January during their retreat south. By 24 January a stubborn ground defence aided by strong air support stabilised the line about 75 miles south of the 38th Parallel. A counter-attack was launched by Ridgway to the north the following day. The UN forces ground forward all along the front which had now ceased to be clearly defined. The battle was more one of attrition than of position but the Communists were slowly forced back. To the west, Inchon and Kimpo Airfield were recovered on 10 February, the latter being the base of the F-86 Sabrejets which had gained supremacy in the air over MiG-15s. East of this, Seoul was bypassed and then retaken on 14 March without opposition being encountered. At this time General Peng Teh-huai replaced Lin Piao as the supreme Chinese commander in Korea and during March Ridgway's advance recrossed the 38th Parallel all along the front except in the extreme west. This state of affairs led to a disagreement between General

Douglas MacArthur, Supreme Commander, and President Harry S. Truman since the former wanted to enlarge the scope of the war by attacking Chinese bases in Manchuria and the latter wished to limit the fighting to Korea. MacArthur was replaced by Ridgway on 11 April and General James Van Fleet took command of the 8th Army.

Meanwhile the Communists were amassing more troops, armour and artillery within the Iron Triangle for a counter-offensive. The Iron Triangle, an open plateau bounded by Chonwon, Kumhwa and Pyongyang, was a vital road junction and staging area situated near the centre of the peninsula 20-30 miles north of the 38th Parallel. On the night of 22 April, the Communists launched an offensive which hit Seoul hardest but stretched east from that city to the coast of the Sea of Japan. For a week, mainly at night, 350,000 Communists drove forward, but though the UN troops were forced back, a line was stabilised by 1 May which ran from north of Seoul in the west to a point north of the 39th Parallel. The Communists then halted their attacks in order to reinforce their ranks, which had taken heavy casualties, and to resupply. Regrouping, they surged forward again on the night of 15 May, this time against the east of the UN line. In the centre, the ROK 3 Corps was wiped out and the UN 10 Corps on its flank was forced to withdraw south of the 38th Parallel. The offensive was checked by a determined defence undertaken by the US 2nd Infantry, 1st Marine and 3rd Infantry Divisions. By 20 May the line was quiet once more. On 21 May the 8th Army counter-attacked all along the line and the Communist force, exhausted and over-extended, gave ground steadily so that all ground lost to the Communists during the spring offensives was regained. By 11 June the UN forces had reached the Chonwon-Kumhwa base of the Iron Triangle, while a region called the Punchbowl near Sohwa to the east was being mopped up. By 15 June the front was 20 miles north of the 38th Parallel except in the extreme west. Since the offensive of 22 April the Communists are believed to have suffered over 200,000 casualties, while UN losses were markedly fewer. On 10 July 1951 hostilities ceased in favour of peace talks, which proved difficult, particularly on the issue of repatriation of prisoners.

When talks collapsed in August Van Fleet continued the offensive designed to fragment the enemy, but most energy on both sides was spent in improving defensive positions, the resumption of talks at Panmunjon having the effect of scaling down the offensives to a series of small defensive operations. The 40th and 45th Cavalry replaced the 24th and 1st Cavalry during the winter and the only action in 1952 and the early part of 1953 consisted of patrolling, outpost skirmishing and artillery and air attacks (the latter nearly all by US planes). These activities kept the war going and the casualty rate rising, although no tactical changes or improvements occurred. General Mark Clark replaced Ridgway as UN Supreme Commander during this time and General Maxwell Taylor took command of the 8th Army. Both sides sent in reinforcements. Between 20 and 26 April 1953 sick and wounded prisoners were repatriated in Operation Little Switch.

On 27 July, an armistice was signed ending overt hostilities, after which the 8th Army reverted to strengthening the defensive line along the 38th Parallel pending permanent peace.

TIMORESE CIVIL WAR (Indonesia area)   August–December 1975

Fought between the Revolutionary Front for the Independence of Timor (FRETILIN) under the Communist-orientated Sr Francisco Xavier do Amaral (a former Jesuit priest), and the Democratic Union of Timor (UDT), also known as MAC (Anti-Communist Movement), the Timorese Democratic People's Union (APODETI) and some splinter groups under the Chief Executive Officer of APODETI, Sr Arnaldo dos Reis Araiyo.

FRETILIN wanted to form a Communist state of E Timor allied to Russia. The UDT and APODETI, supported by Indonesia and the USA, wanted re-union with Indonesia. Both sides were ill-equipped and ill-trained.

After the Lisbon government had given independence to its African territories in 1975, there was no possibility of holding the colony of E Timor. The UDT staged a *coup* on 11 August 1975. Civil War between FRETILIN and UDT broke out on 20 August. FRETILIN bombarded the capital, Dili, with mortars on 22 August. The big exodus of refugees into Indonesian W Timor started. By 1 September FRETILIN claimed control of the whole of E Timor. Massacres were reported by both sides. The Indonesian navy moved into Timor waters in mid-September and there were clashes on the border on 28-30 September. Five Australian television journalists were killed by FRETILIN. Gough Whitlam, Prime Minister of Australia at that time, appeared well disposed towards FRETILIN. In November 1975 his government was thrown out and a caretaker government of Australia was installed. On 13 December Malcolm Fraser was elected Prime Minister by a large majority.

On 7 December 1,000 Indonesian parachutists, supported by a naval bombard-ment and a landing by marines, seized Dili, and then on 7 December Maubara and on 11 December Baucau were occupied, in each case aided by UDT and APODETI irregulars. On 28 December the off-shore island of Atauro (where the Portuguese had temporarily tried to maintain a form of government) was occupied, as was the enclave of Ocussi Ambeno. The occupation of E Timor was complete by 1 February and Sr Arnaldo dos Reis Araiyo (then aged sixty-two) formed a government.

Result: The possibility of a Russian naval base being established at a strategic point between the Pacific and the Indian Oceans was eliminated. The course of operations shows the efficacy of swift, bold action by a small high-quality force before the escalation of civil war and the development of an international trouble-spot.

TOBA (Honshu Island, Japan)   Japanese Revolution   1868

Fought between the troops of Aiza and Kuwana under the Shogun, Yoshinobu (Hitotsubushi), and the army of Satsuma and Choshu.

The Shogun was completely defeated and was forced to abandon his invasion of

Satsuma and to return to Yedo by sea where, shortly afterwards, he surrendered to the Imperial army.

TOKYO see TAYEIZAN

TOU MORONG (S Vietnam)   Vietnam War   5-7 June 1966
Fought between the N and S Vietnamese.

Before the monsoon, the Communists were threatening the isolated outpost of Tou Morong, which lay in the central highlands in the Province of Kontum. The position was held by a S Vietnamese unit and General Willard Pearson, who commanded the US 1st Brigade of the 101st Airborne Division, launched a three-pronged offensive to relieve the force.

On 5 June three combat battalions converged on Tou Morong: the 1st Battalion of the US 327th Infantry in the NE, a S Vietnamese Ranger Battalion from the NW and the 42nd Battalion of the S Vietnamese regular army (ARVN) from the SW. The operation, known as Hawthorne, encountered little opposition at this stage. At 2 am on 7 June, however, the Communists attacked the American position north of Tou Morong. They were repulsed in a seven-hour fight, at the end of which 85 Viet Cong were dead. The 502nd Infantry and 5th Cavalry now came in to support the attack which was pressed and the Allies began to encircle the 24th N Vietnamese Regiment. During the next six days and nights over 1,200 Communists were killed or wounded, while the Allies' casualties reached only 10 per cent of that total.

With 27,000 rounds of artillery and 473 air sorties, the operation to relieve Tou Morong had turned into a major victory over the Communists in Kontum Province.

TRIAD OCCUPATION (Kiangsu Province, China)   T'ai P'ing Rebellion
7 September 1853-17 February 1855
The Triads, a Chinese secret society whose aim was to drive out the Manchu Imperialists and restore the Ming dynasty, had linked their organisation, which stretched all over S China, with the T'ai P'ing. Their principal leader, Liu Li-ch'uan, was an interpreter for the Western merchants and also a physician who treated the poor free of charge. The Shanghai branch of the Triads was called the Small Sword Society. On 7 September 1853 they seized control of the great city, threw open the jail and distributed $5000,000 of Imperial tribute.

In a few months they had captured Pao-shan, Kiating and other towns in the Yangtze delta. The T'ai P'ing capital was at Nanking, farther up-river, but because they were engaged in internecine quarrels at that time, and also had two expeditions away, one towards Peking and the other to Wuhan, they missed the opportunity of taking over Shanghai with all its Western contacts and superb outlet to the sea. By this failure the T'ai P'ing probably lost their chance of being considered respectable and being recognised by the Western powers instead of being treated as rebels, and so lost their chance of taking over the whole of China and converting it to their form of agrarian Christianity.

The Imperial court in Peking did its best to ridicule and denigrate both the Triads and the T'ai P'ing, and to sow seeds of mistrust between these southern societies and the Western powers. In this they were successful. Where the Imperial armies had hopelessly failed, their diplomacy and intrigue succeeded.

TSINAN (JINAN) (Shantung Province, N China)   Chinese Civil War   14-24 September 1948.
Fought between the Nationalists under General Chiang Kai-shek and the Communists under Mao Tse-tung.
Strength: Nationalists 80,000; Communists 120,000.

After the Communists had taken Kaifeng (qv), the Communists moved on the NE city of Tsinan (Jinan) which lies on the Yellow River. The PLA (People's Liberation Army) attacked the Nationalist garrison there on 14 September and after ten days of fighting the Nationalist force disintegrated. Few became casualties, a large number simply defecting to the Communist side and weakening Chiang's position.

Further Nationalist defeats now loomed ahead.

TSUSHIMA (Tsushima Strait)   Russo-Japanese War   27-8 May 1905
Fought between the Russians under Admiral Zinovi Rozhdestvensky, and the Japanese under Admiral Heihachiro Togo.
Strength: Russians 45 warships (including 7 battleships and 6 cruisers); Japanese 45 warships.

Japanese domination of the war prompted the Russian Czar, Nicholas II to send his Baltic fleet to the Far East. Approaching through the E China Sea, the Russians arrived on 27 May and met the Japanese fleet which had greater speed and fire-power and whose men were more highly trained. Japanese ships, with a speed of 16 knots, bore down on the slower Russian fleet (10 knots) and sailed across the bows of the van of the Russians. The fleets engaged early in the afternoon and in half an hour one Russian battleship was sunk, another was crippled and the Russian line was broken. Three more battleships were sunk by nightfall. The Russians then made for the cover of Vladivostock, but were pursued by the Japanese with destroyers and torpedo boats. During the night 3 more Russian ships were sunk and pursuit continued the following day until all but 12 of the Russian ships had been sunk, captured or driven ashore. Rozhdestvensky was wounded and captured during the pursuit. Japanese losses were only 3 torpedo boats.

In the greatest naval battle since Trafalgar the Russians were demoralised into seeking peace terms, which were negotiated by President Theodore Roosevelt during that year.

USSURI RIVER (CHANGKUFENG HILL) (USSR)   Russo-Japanese Incident
11 July-10 August 1938
A clash between Japanese forces which had entered Manchuria and Russian forces
under General Vasily Blücher occurred at Changkufeng Hill where the Tumen and
Ussuri Rivers meet. It was a drawn battle as neither side had orders to attack - and
the whole incident was probably the result of bad map reading by the Japanese
who did not know the area. The Russians retained possession of the hill, which
they fortified. Casualties were about 2,000 on each side.

UTSONOMIYA (Honshu Island, Japan)   Japanese Revolution   1868
The followers of the Shogun, Yoshinobu (Hitotsubushi), under Otori Keisuke
were completely defeated by the Imperialists under Saigo Takamori.

VAN THUONG PENINSULA (S Vietnam)   Vietnam War   30-1 August 1965
Fought between US forces and the Viet Cong.
Strenght: US 5,000; Viet Cong 700.
Aim: When the United States began to increase military aid to S Vietnam the
Communists started a build-up of troops in the Van Thuong peninsula, south of
the major US air base of Chu Lai. Operation Starlight was undertaken to remove
the threat that these forces represented.
Battle: General Lewis Walt's 3rd Marine Division carried out the operation. One
company blocked the exit leading north out of Van Thuong, and two companies
blocked the south exit. Three other companies then landed by helicopter west of
the peninsula, thus trapping the Communists against the sea, where the American
fleet enjoyed complete superiority. On 30 August 5,000 marines moved in on the
surrounded Viet Cong troops and a fierce fight ensued, lasting all that day and
night. By the afternoon of 31 August the marines reached the beaches at the east
end of Van Thuong, wiping out the last of the resistance on the peninsula. Three
hundred dead Viet Cong were counted and many more were certainly killed, buried
by bombing sorties. US losses were 50 killed and 150 wounded.
Result: The immediate US objective was achieved.

VIETNAM WAR   1961-72
Fought between the Vietnamese and the Viet Cong.
   Following the defeat of the French at Dien Bien Phu (qv) in 1954, Vietnam was
divided into two countries along the 17th Parallel, land to the north becoming a
one-party Communist state and land to the south becoming a democratic republic
with an assembly elected by universal suffrage. The S Vietnamese government of
President Ngo Dinh Diem was subjected to guerilla attacks from Viet Cong and,
although there were only 25,000 guerillas in the field, the S Vietnamese steadily
lost ground. In order to try and maintain the balance of power in the countries,
the US sent economic aid to S Vietnam and a 685-man advisory mission. By 1962
the number of advisers and technicians had grown to 11,000, but the Communists,
aided by Russia and China, still held the upper hand. On 2 November 1963 Diem

was overthrown and killed in a military *coup,* and the succession of unstable governments which followed helped to worsen the military situation. By 1963 16,000 US personnel were in Vietnam and many were now actively engaged in fighting the guerillas. In 1964 US military personnel in Vietnam grew to 23,000, and on 5 August American aircraft bombed N Vietnam for the first time. On 8 February 1965 bombing was instituted on a regular basis, but the Viet Cong attacks also increased in size from battalion to regimental strength. In 1965 the first US combat unit landed at the northern base of Da Nang; in March 3,500 men of the 9th Marine Brigade arrived, and on 28 July that year President Lyndon Johnson announced his intention of supporting the Vietnamese. By the end of the year 190,000 US soldiers were in Vietnam, including these units: 1st Cavalry Division (Airmobile) near An Khe; 1st Infantry Division and 173rd Airborne Brigade at Bien Hoa; 1st Brigade of the 101st Airborne Division at Phan Rang; and the 3rd Marine Amphibious Force at Da Nang and Chu Lai. Added to these were S Korea's Tiger Division at Qui Nhon, 5,000 marines at Tuy Hoa, a Royal Australian Regiment of 1,200 men and a New Zealand artillery battery. All these forces were commanded by General William Westmoreland, the US Supreme Commander, who had his headquarters in Saigon.

Helicopters made their first major rôle in a battle in history when about 1,800 of them served as transports and weaponries. The US 7th Fleet lay just offshore and aircraft from the 2nd Air Division (later the 7th Air Force) as well as B-52s of the 3rd Air Division from Guam supplemented these land forces. The S Vietnamese army grew to 600,000 men with 6,500 American advisers under Premier Nguyen Cao Ky who took office on 19 June 1965. The S Vietnamese army was divided into four corps, numbered from north to south, Saigon being in the area of 3 Corps. It was estimated that 215,000 Viet Cong and 10,000 N Vietnamese regulars opposed this force. By the end of 1965 6,928 US combat casualties had been suffered, including 1,241 killed, and S Vietnamese losses were 11,327 killed and 23,009 wounded. Since 1 January 1961 therefore, total combat losses were as follows: US 1,484 killed, 7,337 wounded; S Vietnamese 30,427 killed, 63,009 wounded; N Vietnamese and Viet Cong 104,500 killed, 250,000 wounded.

Bombing was halted by President Johnson on 24 December 1965 as a means towards bringing about a truce. No agreement was reached, however, and bombing was resumed on 31 January 1966. During that year the 4th, 9th and 25th Infantry Divisions landed in Vietnam, which helped to raise the total of US troops in the country to 389,000. S Vietnamese strength grew to 750,000 fighting men during the year, and 2,000 Filipino troops joined the forces in the field. Communist strength also increased from about 250,000 at a rate of 7,000 a month, of which 4,500 infiltrated S Vietnam along the Ho Chi-minh Trail, the rest being drafted from Viet Cong-controlled areas. Ground action during this year was chiefly to seek out and destroy Communist forces. In Operation Hastings, between 15 July and 5 August, 5,000 marines and a S Vietnamese force of equal size attacked and destroyed the 324th N Vietnamese Division (8,000-10,000 men) just south of the demilitarised zone along the 17th Parallel. Marine losses were about 10 per cent. It was estimated that 1,882 Viet Cong were killed (882 bodies were actually counted) and 15 captured, while 1,209 sorties were flown in support of the assault, the highest number of strikes flown in the war until then. On 15 October Operation Attelboro was launched against the Communist-held War Zone C, 45-65 miles NW of Saigon, near the Cambodian border. Between then and 25 November 25,000 Americans killed 1,101 men, chiefly from the Viet Cong 9th Division and the 101st N Vietnamese Regiment. US casualties were said to be light.

Air battles during the year were the greatest to date. On 12 April a raid was made on Mugia Pass, the main supply route from N Vietnam through Laos to S Vietnam, in which 1,400,000 tons of bombs were dropped. On 23 April the first air battle over N Vietnam took place when two MiG-21s and 14 MiG-17s engaged 14 Phantoms. On 31 May what was reported as the largest air raid of the war was carried out on the Yen Bay arsenal, 75 miles NW of Hanoi. It was set on fire and 25 out of 30 batteries were said to have been knocked out at a cost of 2 Thunderbolts. The scope of bombing targets widened on 29 June when US carrier aircraft (A-4 Skyhawks and F-4 Phantoms) and land-based planes (F-105 Thunderchiefs) attacked Hanoi and Haiphong, destroying most of the N Vietnamese petroleum storage tanks. The N Vietnamese protested about the bombing of civilian targets. On 20 August the N Vietnamese claimed that 132 US aircraft had been shot down since 17 July, and by the end of the year 468 aircraft and 4 helicopters had been lost over N Vietnam and 150 planes and 251 helicopters over S Vietnam - compared to a total of 165 aircraft for the whole of 1965.

1966 was the first full year of combat for US troops. 5,047 Americans were killed in action; 55,000 Communists were killed, while 20,000 more defected to the south. In 1967 the Americans invaded the Communist-held Mekong Delta south of Saigon when, on 6 January, Operation Deckhouse Five was launched. Initially, 4,000 marines landed by sea and air in a region believed to hold about 100,000 Viet Cong. On 8 January a larger American offensive was launched against the so-called Iron Triangle, a Communist stronghold 20-30 miles north of Saigon. In Operation Cedar Falls, which lasted three weeks, 30,000 troops penetrated the triangle from three sides. Units involved included 1st and 25th Infantry Divisions, 196th Light Infantry Brigade, 173rd Airborne Brigade and the 11th Armoured Cavalry Brigade. The third and final offensive that year was an invasion of War Zone C, an area of 1,000 square miles 75 miles NW of Saigon. On 22 February 30,000 troops under General Jonathan Seaman began Operation Junction City. During 1967, the port of Haiphong was reduced to ruins by bombing.

By January 1968 the Allied forces were made up as follows: S Vietnamese 732,000, US 485,000, S Korean 48,000, Australian 8,000, New Zealand 450, Thai 2,500, Filipino 2,100. And during 1968 the casualty figures were as follows: S Vietnamese 10,997 killed or wounded, US and others 9,300 killed or wounded; Viet Cong and N Vietnamese 38,794 killed, 6,991 captured. Saigon was fired upon with rockets during the first half of the year, especially between 28 May and 11

June. Forty fell on the city on 4 June and 16 on 7 June, killing or wounding over 1,000 civilians. Between June and August fighting took place in the central highlands, and on 18 August the Viet Cong launched an offensive near the Laotian and Cambodian borders in order to secure their supply routes. After 15 October President Johnson stopped the bombing of N Vietnamese territory.

In 1969 President Richard M. Nixon began a process of devolvement, withdrawing 25,000 American troops by 8 June and a further 35,000 by 15 December. By 15 April 1970 50,000 more were withdrawn, and further withdrawals were scheduled. However, another offensive was launched by a task force of S Vietnamese troops and 5,000 US infantry on 1 May 1970, when bombing attacks and tanks and artillery thrust 30 miles into S Cambodia in an attempt to surround and annihilate Viet Cong bases, including an important suspected command headquarters. In February 1971 a similar move took place against bases in Laos.

Dr Henry Kissinger, President Nixon's adviser, negotiated a peace treaty which came into effect in 1972 and by that time all US forces had been withdrawn. Nevertheless, violations of the cease-fire persisted and Viet Cong guerilla activity continued unceasingly until finally the Communists overran the S Vietnamese, occupying Saigon on 1 May 1975. Since that time the whole of Vietnam has come under Communist control.

The chief battles in the Vietnam War were as follows:
1964: Nam Dong (qv).
1965: Van Thuong peninsula, Plei Me and Chu Pong-Ia Drang River (qqv).
1966: An Lao Valley, A Shau and Tou Morong (qqv).
1967: Hill 881, Locninh, Dak To and Hill 875.
1968: Khe Sanh (21 January-7 April), Tet Offensive (30 January-24 February), Hue (31 January-24 February) and Saigon (3 January-23 February).

WAKAMATSU (KITAKYUSHU) (N Kyushu Island, Japan)   Japanese Revolution 22 September 1868
The last stand of the Shogun's followers was made at the Castle of Wakamatsu (Kitakyushu) which was stormed by the Imperialists, and all resistance to the new régime was finally broken.

WATIGAON (S Burma)   First Burma War   15 November 1825
Fought between the British under Brigadier-General McDonell and the Burmese under Maha Nemyo.
Aim: The British sought to beat the Burmese into submission.
Battle: The British force, which consisted of four Indian regiments, advanced in three columns but, failing to keep close enough, they were repulsed with a loss of 2000, including McDonell.
Result: The British objective was not achieved.

WEIHAI-WEI (Shantung Province, N China)   Sino-Japanese War   4-9 February 1895

Fought between the Japanese under General Count Iwao Oyama and the Chinese under Admiral Ting Ju-ch'ang.

Aim: The victorious Japanese moved to attack the Chinese mainland. Their objective was Weihai-Wei on the Shantung peninsula.

Battle: The Chinese fleet was in the harbour which was protected by a boom across the mouth. The Japanese cut this and attacked the fleet with 10 torpedo boats. One battleship was sunk at a cost of 2 torpedo boats, and over the next days 4 torpedo boats sank 3 Chinese ships. Land batteries were set up by the Japanese and another battleship was sunk. On 12 February Admiral Ting surrendered the port and, with his principal officers, committed suicide.

Result: The Japanese occupied Weihai-Wei and in April forced China to accept the Treaty of Shimonoseki.

WESTERN RECONQUEST (China)   T'ai P'ing Rebellion   19 May 1853-19 December 1856

A Western Reconquest under the Assistant King, Shih Ta-k'ai was launched on 19 May 1853 to recover the areas over which the T'ai P'ing had traversed but not truly conquered in the Upper Yangtze. Shih's great opponent was the neo-Confucian, Tseng Kuo-fan, who trained a strong provincial militia to oppose the rebels. He is now condemned by left-wing writers as a traitor to China as he supported the Manchu Emperor.

Shih advanced up the Yangtze with close on 100,000 men and over 1,000 junks and sampans. He captured Anking on 10 June, and on 24 June reached Nanchang, which was defended by Chiang Chung-yüan. Shih's brother brought reinforcements from Nanking but had to bypass Nanchang, as it proved too stubborn. Kiukiang was occupied on 26 September and Hankow and Hanyang during the period 20 October to 6 November. A great battle was fought at Lu-chou in Anhwei Province where the Imperial governor Chiang Chung-yüan, was killed on 24 January 1854. The T'ai P'ing army moved west again to recapture Hankow and Hanyang for the third time. Yochow was captured on 27 February and Siangtan on 24 April.

As Shih moved to capture Changsha, which he had failed to do in 1852, Tseng Kuo-fan intervened. Tseng had trained a small, hard-hitting force of 5,000 marines, 12,000 soldiers and a flotilla of 240 boats, with a good organisation for resupply.

His first victory was at Siangtan on 1 May, when he drove the T'ai P'ing back to Yochow which he captured on 25 July. After a great battle he recaptured the city of Wuchang on 14 October 1854 and won another victory at T'ien-chia-chen in December. But early in 1855 his advance was stopped by the T'ai P'ing general Lin Ch'i-jung at Kiukiang, which he held until 1858.

Shih Ta-k'ai fought back and the tide turned in favour of the T'ai P'ing. In a naval battle he burnt 100 of Tseng's boats on the P'o-yang Lake. Tseng then suffered a further naval defeat on the Yangtze. On 3 April Shih retook Hankow, Hanyang and Wuchang, holding them until 19 December 1856. At this time the whole area, 300 miles on either side of the Yangtze from Wuchang to Nanking, was under T'ai P'ing control.

WU-HSÜEH (Hupeh Province, central China)   T'ai P'ing Rebellion   15 February 1853
The T'ai P'ing vanguard, comprising both army and navy elements advancing down the Yangtze Kiang under Ch'in Jih-kang and Lo Ta-kang after the capture of Wuchang, attacked Wu-hsüeh on 15 February 1853. The Governor-General Lu Chien-ying had been sent by the Emperor to supervise the town's defence. The T'ai P'ing vanguard dealt the Imperial forces a crushing blow. The Manchu brigade commander committed suicide and another was killed. Lu ran away, ditched his flagship and fled by boat to Nanking, where the Emperor dismissed him.
    The T'ai P'ing continued their rapid advance down the Yangtze.

YALU RIVER I (NE China/N Korea)   Sino-Japanese War   17 September 1894
Fought between the Japanese under Admiral Yugo Ito and the Chinese under Admiral Ting Ju-ch'ang.
Strength: Japanese 10 cruisers + 2 gunboats; Chinese 2 battleships + 8 cruisers.
Aim: The Japanese sought to attack the Chinese fleet as it emerged from the mouth of the Yalu River.
Battle: The Chinese steamed out in line abreast and were met by the Japanese attacking in line ahead, Ito using his faster ships to circle round the Chinese ships. Two Chinese ships withdrew before coming into action and two more were fired and retired. The rest of the Chinese fleet fought until sundown, when Ito called off the attack. The Chinese retired to Port Arthur (qv). Japanese losses were 294 killed and wounded, of whom 107 fell in the flagship *Matsushima.* The *Chiyada,* next in the line, was untouched. Chinese losses are not known.
Result: The Japanese objective was achieved.

YALU RIVER II/KIU LIEN CHENG (NE China/N Korea)   Russo-Japanese War
1 May 1904
Fought between the Japanese under General Count Tamemoto Kuroki and the Russians under General Zasulich.
Strength: Japanese 40,000; Russians 7,000.
Aim: While the Russians were being blockaded in Port Arthur (qv) a land offensive was prepared by the Japanese in Korea.
Battle: The troops were landed at Jinsen (Chemulpo), whence they moved north. General Alexei Kuropatkin, having concentrated his forces at Liaoyang, sent only a small force to guard the Yalu River, which the Japanese reached on 1 May. A crossing was forced at Gishu (Wiju), where only weak opposition was encountered. The following day the Japanese attacked the Russian position at Kiu Lien-Cheng

and drove the defenders out with a loss of 4,000 killed and wounded, 30 officers and 500 men prisoners, and 48 guns. Japanese losses totalled 898 killed and wounded.

Result: Kuroki pressed on into Manchuria.

The battle received widespread attention in the West, as it was the first time that an Eastern army using Western weapons and tactics had beaten a Western force.

YUNG-AN (MENGSHAN) (Kwangsi Province, S China)   T'ai P'ing Rebellion
25 September 1851

Fought between the T'ai P'ing army under Hsiao Ch'ao-kuei and Feng Yun-shan, and the Manchu government forces under the overall command of the Imperial Commissioner Sai-shang-a, Hsiang Jung, Commander of the Hunan army of the Green Standard, and Wu-lan-t'ai, Commander of the Kwangtung army.

Sai-shang-a had been sent by the Emperor to co-ordinate operations against the T'ai P'ing, but he could not get co-operation between the two provincial armies of Hunan and Kwangtung. The T'ai P'ing suddenly raised the siege of Kuei-p'ing, changed direction and attacked Yung-an. In order to draw the garrison out as they had no siege train, they attacked, feigned defeat and ambushed the government forces as they streamed out in pursuit. The T'ai P'ing occupied Yung-an until April 1852.

Although this was not a major battle it was important to the T'ai P'ing, since it was in Yung-an that their leaders developed their social philosophy and military organisation which helped them to conquer half China.

SECTION FIVE

AMERICAN CIVIL WAR

See Map Section, nos 15 and 16

ALABAMA VERSUS *KEARSARGE* (English Channel off Cherbourg)   American Civil War   19 June 1864
Fought between the Confederates under Commander Raphael Semmes on the *Alabama* and the Federals under Captain Winslow on the *Kearsarge.*
Strength: Confederates 149 with 7 guns; Federals 163 with 8 guns.

Both ships were raiding enemy vessels on the high seas; the *Alabama* finally returning to Europe where, on 11 June, she requested permission to enter Cherbourg in order to overhaul. The *Kearsarge,* at Flushing, was cabled with the information and arrived outside Cherbourg three days after the *Alabama* had entered port.

The *Alabama* sailed out to meet the *Kearsarge* after the latter had been escorted outside territorial waters by a French warship. The *Alabama* opened fire at a range of 2,000 yards and the two ships then gradually closed in, moving in concentric circles, until they were 600 yards apart. The *Kearsarge* benefited from more accurate gunnery and after an hour the *Alabama*'s engines received a direct hit. Semmes tried to get his ship out under sail, but the vessel was sinking. She struck her colours and hoisted a white flag before going down by the stern at 12.30 pm. Semmes and about 40 crewmen were taken aboard by an English yacht, *Deerhound,* which had witnessed the battle. Most of the others were taken by the *Kearsarge,* except for about 12 men who were killed. Union losses were 1 killed and 2 wounded.

ANTIETAM CREEK (Maryland)   American Civil War   17 September 1862
Fought between the Federals under General George McClellan and the Confederates under General Robert E. Lee.
Strength: Federals 75,000; Confederates 41,000.

After the Confederate victory at Bull Run II (qv) Lee turned north to invade Maryland. Half his army (six divisions) under General Thomas (Stonewall) Jackson was to attack Harper's Ferry (qv), the capture of which would open a supply line down the Shenandoah valley. McClellan, with the Army of Virginia absorbed into his own, moved forward only slowly, although he knew that Lee, to his front, was still disorganised, his army widely scattered. The Federals moved to occupy Turner's Gap in South Mountain (qv) which they found held by Confederates under Generals Daniel Hill and James Longstreet. The battle for the gap was won by the Federals, the Confederates being beaten out, outflanked on both wings by General Joseph Hooker on the right and General Jesse Reno on the left. At the same time the Federal left wing attacked west through Crampton's Gap (qv). West of this, General Lafayette McLaws was supporting Jackson's offensive against Harper's Ferry. He turned to meet General William Franklin, who commanded the left wing (6 Corps) and was driven out of the valley. Here he deceived the Federals into hesitating and, while they delayed, Harper's Ferry fell to the Confederates, thus giving them a tactical advantage.

Lee now planned to withdraw south of the Potomac, having lost both passes, but when he heard that Jackson had taken Harper's Ferry and was on his way to join him at Sharpsburg, he took up a defensive position behind Antietam Creek.

McClellan continued to move slowly and spent all 16 September deploying for the attack, thus giving the Confederates another day to move up. Jackson arrived with 11,000 troops, 10,000 still on their way. The Federals attacked at dawn when 3 Corps attacked Lee's left, intending to roll it up while another corps crossed the creek to attack the centre and right. The piecemeal attack negated the Federal numerical superiority, but the Confederate left was driven back through Dunkard Church and West Woods until Hooker's advance was checked by the troops of Generals John Hood and J. E. B. Stuart. In the centre, Sumner's corps was committed precipitously and Sedgwick's division was thrown back with heavy casualties (2,200), though Generals William French and Israel Richardson took their divisions forward and drove Daniel Hill's men out of a sunken road known as Bloody Lane. Lee's centre was endangered and only the lethargy of the Federals prevented total rout. On the Confederate right General Ambrose Burnside launched his Federal troops in an attack at about midday and the attack drove the Confederates back to the south of Sharpsburg. The arrival of General Ambrose Hill reversed the situation, the flanking attack he launched on Burnside's 9 Corps driving it back to Antietam Creek. The halt of the Federal advance saved the Confederates from defeat. Confederate casualties were 13,724 (2,700 killed), and Federal casualties 12,140 (2,108 killed). It was the bloodiest single day's battle of the war.

Both armies bivouacked on the field that night, and battle was not resumed the following day. Lee withdrew across the Potomac on the night of 18 September unmolested, pursuit being negligible. The battle was a tactical victory for the Confederates, but a strategic one for the Federals, since the invasion was stopped. Lincoln used the opportunity to announce the Emancipation Proclamation, which changed the character of the war from the preservation of the Union to a crusade to free the slaves.

APPOMATTOX RIVER (Virginia)   American Civil War   9 April 1865
Fought between the Federals under General Ulysses Grant and the Confederates under General Robert E. Lee.
Strength: Federals 125,000; Confederates 30,000.
After the Confederate defeat of their right flank at Five Forks (qv) on 1 April, Lee decided to evacuate Richmond and Petersburg (qv). On the night of 2/3 April, the Confederates began to retreat westward below the Appomattox River. Lee's aim was to take his army around the Federal left flank and join up with General Joseph Johnston's army which was in N Carolina, falling back before General William Sherman's Federal advance. Grant sought to block Lee's escape and pursued vigorously. General Philip Sheridan with his cavalry corps cut the railroad south on 5 April, which forced Lee to move farther westward. At Sayler's Creek on the following day the Federal 2 Corps under General Andrew Humphreys attacked and defeated the Confederate rearguard, taking about 7,000 men prisoner, including six generals (Richard Ewell among them). Federal losses were 1,180 with 166 killed.

At Farmville Lee was forced to cross the Appomattox to the north because of the close pursuit on 7 April. Continuing westwards, he was followed by Humphreys and 6 Corps of General Horatio Wright while 5 Corps under General Charles Griffin and General Edward Ord with the Army of the James overtook Lee on his south flank and blocked his path at Appomattox Station. General John Gordon with his division of 1,600 infantry tried to break through the Federals early on 9 April, but he was beaten back. Lee was encircled and at 4 pm that day he surrendered his sword and army to Grant at Appomattox Court House.

Johnston surrendered in N Carolina on 18 April and General Edmund Kirby Smith surrendered at Shreveport on 26 May. This brought the Civil War to an end.

ARKANSAS POST (Arkansas)   American Civil War   11 January 1863
Fought between the Federals under General John McClernand and the Confederates under General Thomas Churchill.
Strength: Federals 29,000; Confederates 4,500.
Aim: When General William Sherman was attempting to take Vicksburg by way of Chickasaw Bluffs (qv) McClernand got permission from Washington to launch another attack on the town.
Battle: Arriving at Miliken's Bend, McClernand took over Sherman's command but, instead of attacking Vicksburg (qv), he moved 50 miles up the Arkansas River to attack Arkansas Post where Churchill was defending Fort Hindman. The Federals went up-river by transports, landing 3 miles below Arkansas Post. Supported by Admiral William Porter with 13 gunboats, the Federals marched to the fort the following day and, following a land action which drove the Confederates from their outlying earthworks, they launched a combined land and naval attack on the day after that. Porter's gunboats silenced the Confederate artillery and the fort then surrendered, along with the outlying defences. Federal casualties totalled 1,061. Confederate losses including prisoners were 4,500, of whom 791 were missing.
Result: The success was of no importance in the Vicksburg campaign. When General Ulysses Grant heard of it, he ordered McClernand back to Vicksburg to take part in the operations there.

ATLANTA (Georgia)   American Civil War   20 July-1 September 1864
Fought between the Federals under General William Sherman and the Confederates under General John Hood.
Strength: Federals 100,000; Confederates 50,000.
After the Federal repulse at Kenesaw Mountain (qv) Sherman began to manoeuvre against General Joseph Johnston, crossing the Chattenhoochee River above the Confederate position, whereupon Johnston fell back. Confederate President Jefferson Davis now replaced Johnston with Hood, while Sherman pressed on south towards Atlanta. This town was the chief centre of transportation, manufacturing and medical supply for the Confederates. The Federal objective was its fall.

At the same time as Sherman's advance took place and General George Thomas's

Army of the Cumberland began crossing Peach Tree Creek to the north of the city, General John Schofield's Army of the Ohio and General James McPherson's Army of the Tennessee drew in from the NE and east. The Confederate position was near Peach Tree Creek and Hood decided to attack the Federal army under Thomas while it was isolated from the other columns. The corps of General Alexander Stewart (W) and General William Hardee (E) were sent to attack the Federals.

The Confederates opened the attack at 3 pm along Peach Tree Creek. About 20,000 men were involved on each side. Though the Federals were surprised, they fought off the attack successfully with a loss of 1,600. Confederate losses totalled 2,500 killed or wounded, chiefly from Stewart's corps. Hood continued to withdraw into the defences of Atlanta and Sherman, thinking that he was going to evacuate the city, dispatched McPherson on a wide sweep to the SE in order to pursue and to cut the railway into the city. Hood, however, merely sent Hardee's corps in pursuit of the exposed left (S) flank of Sherman's army, which was attacked by the Confederates on 22 July. The Federals, though surprised, re-formed and beat off the assault, although Hardee (whose corps was the élite of the Confederate army) was later reinforced by General Benjamin Cheatham's corps. The Confederates lost 8,000. Federal losses totalled 3,700 including McPherson, who was killed. General Oliver Howard took over command of the Army of the Tennessee.

Sherman's strength was insufficient for a siege and he determined instead to move his army from the east to the west in order to continue operations against the railroads and cut the supply and communication lines. While Sherman sent cavalry raiding to the south, he began to move on 28 July. As the Federals (mainly Howard's Army of the Tennessee) moved in front of Ezra Church, SW of Atlanta, they were attacked by General Stephen Lee's corps (which was formerly Cheatham's command) and part of Stewart's corps. Once again, however, the Federals held their ground, with a loss of 632. Confederate losses totalled 4,300.

Sherman now renewed his attempts to turn Hood's left (SW) flank and cut the railroads running south from Atlanta. This was to be done chiefly by cavalry raids, whose other purpose was to free Federal prisoners at Andersonville. In none of these were the Federals successful. On 4 August General George Stoneman was captured with 2,000 men. Sherman was continuing to build his army on the west of Atlanta, and on 26 August he began the deep envelopment of Atlanta from the west, the armies of Schofield, Thomas and Howard stretching from north to south. The Montgomery railroad was cut on 27 August, the Macon railroad on 31 August. The only Confederate commander in the area was Hardee, and he fell back to Lovejoy's Station, 25 miles south, where he was pursued by the Federals who began to concentrate at Jonesboro. On 31 August and 1 September Hardee, endeavouring to hold the advancing Federals back, was beaten off at Jonesboro, where all but one of Sherman's army corps were now positioned. The railroads south of Atlanta were now in Federal hands and Hood's position was untenable. At 5 pm on 1 September Hood evacuated Atlanta to join Hardee. Confederate casualties were

27,565. Federal losses totalled 21,656.

On 2 September Sherman entered Atlanta. Hood moved west to threaten Sherman's line of communications in Tennessee. Thomas was sent to watch Hood, and on 15 November Atlanta was abandoned and the Federals marched for Savannah (qv), where they could be supplied by the Federal navy. Much of Atlanta was fired.

BALL'S BLUFF (Virginia)   American Civil War   21 October 1861
Fought between the Federals under Colonel Edward Baker and the Confederates under General Nathaniel Evans.
Aim: The main Federal army, in the hands of General George McClellan since the battle at Bull Run (qv), moved too slowly for public opinion and Baker was ordered to attack the Confederate position across the Potomac River at Ball's Bluff, 33 miles NW of Washington.
Battle: A column under Baker was ambushed by the Confederates. The Federals attacked piecemeal and were pushed back to the precipitous river-bank where they were pinned down and defeated. Baker was killed and other Federal losses were 48 killed, 158 wounded and 714 captured or missing as well as 3 guns. Confederate losses were 33 killed, 115 wounded and 1 missing.
Result: The battle was of no tactical importance, the ineptitude of Federal leadership being criticised in Washington.

BELLE GROVE   see CEDAR CREEK

BELMONT (Missouri)   American Civil War   7 November 1861
Fought between the Federals under General Ulysses Grant and the Confederates under General Leonidas Polk.
Strength: Federals 3,114; Confederates 4,000.
Aim: After the Battle of Wilson's Creek (qv) much of the state of Missouri fell into the hands of the Confederates who also held Columbus, Kentucky, across the Mississippi River. The Federals attacked the Confederate positions along the Mississippi in order to weaken their hold on the region.
Battle: Grant sailed down-river, to land 3 miles north of Belmont with the aim of attacking the Confederate camp held by men from General Sterling Price's command. Fighting their way through thick woodland, the Federals, with four and a half infantry regiments, two squadrons of cavalry and 6 guns, drove the Confederates down to the river where they came under the protection of Confederate guns. Polk sent a force of 10,000 to cut the Federals off from their boats, but Grant fought his way back to the transports with a loss of 607 casualties. Confederate losses were 642.
Result: The mission achieved its object in that pressure on Federal positions was relieved by the attack.

BENTONVILLE (N Carolina)   American Civil War   19 March 1865
Fought between the Federals under General William Sherman and the Confederates under General Joseph Johnston.
Strength: Federals (total forces) 60,000; Confederates 17,000.

After occupying Savannah, Georgia, at the end of 1864, Sherman moved north through the Carolinas from 1 February 1865. His army was divided into two wings: the Army of Georgia under General Henry Slocum on the left, and the Army of the Tennessee under General Oliver Howard on the right. Colombia, S Carolina, was reached on 16 February and was burnt the following day. As the Federals moved into N Carolina, Johnston collected his forces at Raleigh to stop Sherman's advance. When Sherman's left under Slocum reached Bentonville, the way was blocked by Johnston. The two sides clashed, but neither gained any advantage, as both held their ground throughout the day. On 21 March Sherman began to move up his right wing and the forces of Generals John Schofield and Alfred Terry which had moved inland from the coast to Toldsboro. Johnston withdrew because he was now severely outnumbered. Federal losses during the engagement were 1,646. Confederate casualties were 2,600.

Sherman now prepared to march into Virginia to link up with General Ulysses Grant, but when Johnston heard of General Robert E. Lee's surrender, he, too, capitulated.

BEVERLY FORD   see BRANDY STATION

BIG BETHEL (Virginia)   American Civil War   10 June 1861
Fought between the Federals under General Benjamin Butler and the Confederates under Colonel Daniel Hill.
Strength: Federals 4,400; Confederates 1,400.
Aim: The Federals under Butler held Fort Monroe at the entrance to Hampton Roads in SE Virginia. Butler ordered an attack on the Confederate outpost at Big Bethel, 10 miles NW of Fort Monroe.
Battle: Anticipating the assault, the Confederate commander on the peninsula between the York and James Rivers, Colonel John Magruder ('Prince John'), ordered a counter-attack. In an inexpertly handled action, Hill forced the Federals to fall back on Fort Monroe with losses of 76. Confederate casualties were 11.
Result: The Federal objective was not achieved, and the action was to be overshadowed by a major battle at Bull Run (qv).

This was the first land action of the war.

BRANDY STATION (Virginia)   American Civil War   9 June 1863
Fought between the Federals under General Alfred Pleasonton and the Confederates under General J. E. B. Stuart.
Strength: Federals 11,000; Confederates 10,000.

After the Battle of Chancellorsville (qv) Lee began to withdraw to the west. The cavalry corps of the Army of the Potomac under Pleasonton was sent by

Hooker to watch Lee and ascertain his movements.

Pleasanton's force included two infantry brigades and with these he crossed the Rappahannock towards Culpeper. Four miles beyond the river the Federals surprised a Confederate cavalry corps at Brandy Station. In the biggest cavalry battle in American history, the two sides charged and counter-charged for some hours until, in mid-afternoon, General Robert Rodes arrived with Confederate infantry to support Stuart. The Federals withdrew. Pleasonton's casualties totalled 936, including 486 prisoners, and Stuart's were 523.

Although Confederate casualties were lower, Pleasonton had made certain of the direction of General Robert E. Lee's withdrawal, a fact for which Stuart was much criticised in the South.

The action is known also as Fleetwood Hill or Beverly Ford.

BRICE'S CROSS ROADS (Mississippi)   American Civil War   10 June 1864
Fought between the Federals under General Samuel Sturgis and the Confederates under General Nathan Forrest.
Strength: Federals 4,800 infantry + 3,000 cavalry + 18 guns; Confederates 3,500 cavalry.
Aim: While General William Sherman was advancing on Atlanta, Confederate commander Nathan Forrest was menacing Federal lines of communication in Tennessee. An expedition was sent out from Memphis in order to destroy this force.
Battle: At Brice's Cross Roads in NE Mississippi Sturgis was attacked by Forrest before he had time to deploy his forces. With a force half the size of his own, Sturgis's cavalry was beaten back and, as the infantry came forward into position this, too, was attacked and beaten. By 5 pm, after four hours of fighting, the Federals were in full retreat to Stubb's plantation, 10 miles north. Federal losses were 223 killed, 394 wounded and 1,623 captured, along with 16 guns and 250 wagons. Confederate losses were 492.
Result: The Federal objective was not achieved. A Federal investigation ensued and, although Sturgis was not blamed for the defeat, he was never given another command.

BRIDGE   see NORTH ANNA RIVER

BRISTOE STATION (Virginia)   American Civil War   14 October 1863
Fought between the Federals under General Gouverneur Warren and the Confederates under General Ambrose Hill.
Aim: After Gettysburg (qv) the Federal army of the Potomac and the Confederate army of N Virginia manoeuvred constantly. General Robert E. Lee moved north against General George Meade's west flank, whereupon Meade withdrew 40 miles to Centreville. During this retreat, Hill overtook the Federal rearguard of 3 Corps under General William French. Hill planned to attack and destroy the corps.
Battle: The Confederates advanced on Bristoe Station, but met 2 Corps under

General Warren which, overlooked, was well entrenched behind a railroad embankment. Warren opened fire with infantry and artillery which caused heavy casualties. Two Confederate brigades from General Henry Heth's division charged the position and lost 700 and 602 men respectively. Hill withdrew, having suffered 1,900 casualties in all. Federal losses were 548.

Result: The Confederate objective was not achieved. Outnumbered, Lee returned to his position south of the Rapidan River, after which both armies retired into winter quarters.

BULL RUN I (Virginia)   American Civil War   21 July 1861
Fought between the Federals under General Irvin McDowell and the Confederates under General Pierre Beauregard.
Strength: Federals 35,000; Confederates 29,000.

The North believed that the Confederates could easily be crushed, and this idea led to a premature offensive, McDowell marching from Alexandria to Centreville, thence to the Bull Run stream where the Confederates were lying along a 14-mile front.

On 21 July the Federals attacked the Confederate left in a turning movement. Three divisions crossed the Bull Run at Sudley Springs and forced the Confederates back to Henry House Hill where several brigades held firm - notably that of General Thomas Jackson who earned the nickname 'Stonewall' as a result of his stand. Troops along the rest of the front which was largely quiet were transferred to the left (W) and by 4 pm the Confederates had checked the Federal advance and, counter-attacking, had enveloped them so that McDowell ordered the retreat of his exposed right wing. The retreat towards Centreville soon turned to flight, many of the men running straight to Washington DC. Federal losses were 2,896 killed, wounded or captured and 28 guns. Confederate losses were 1,982. Complete rout was only prevented by the rearguard action of Major George Sykes's infantry and Major Innis Palmer's cavalry. In this engagement General Robert Patterson brought in 9,000 Confederate troops by railway - the first time troops had been transported by rail for strategic purposes.

Confederate pursuit was desultory and President Jefferson Davis's decision to call off the pursuit was much criticised. General McClellan was summoned to rebuild the Federal army.

BULL RUN II (Virginia)   American Civil War   30 August 1862
Fought between the Federals under General John Pope and the Confederates under General Robert E. Lee.
Strength: Federals 75,000; Confederates 55,000.
Aim: Lee sought to attack Pope's army before it joined General George McClellan's larger force which was moving up the Potomac River.
Battle: Lee divided his army, sending General Thomas (Stonewall) Jackson upriver in order to encircle Pope's troops who were deployed along the Orange and Alexandria railroad, south of Manassas. Jackson marched to Manassas, thus

cutting off Pope's line of communication, where he seized what Federal stores he wanted and beat back a Federal attack led by General George Taylor who was guarding the Union Mills Railroad bridge. Jackson destroyed the bridge and moved up Bull Run to occupy a position near Sudley Springs (qv) at Stony Ridge. General James Longstreet, who had moved to Orleans, 30 miles to the west, was too far away to move quickly enough to help Jackson, so Pope advanced north to attack while he could. Jackson's diversionary manoeuvres confused Pope into scattering his units too widely. On 28 August, on the Warrenton pike, General Rufus King's division crossed the front of Jackson's corps. At Groveton (qv) Jackson's divisions under General Richard Ewell and General William Taliaferro attacked the Federals and both sides suffered heavy casualties before the Federals withdrew at midnight. On 29 August, Pope attacked Stony Ridge with three corps: 1 (General Franz Sigel), 9 (General Jesse Reno) and 3 (General Samuel Heintzelman). The frontal attacks were badly co-ordinated and were repulsed, and then Longstreet, who had had a clear passage through Bull Run Mountain which the Federals omitted to block, arrived with four divisions on Jackson's right. He was in a position to drive between General Fitz-John Porter's 5 Corps and Pope's main army but he did not avail himself of the opportunity to do so.

On 30 August the attack was renewed by the Federals because Pope had not realised that Longstreet was so near. The Confederates held their position and then counter-attacked. Longstreet attacked and drove in Pope's left flank and only the defence of Henry House Hill prevented the Federals from suffering a major defeat. Lee did not pursue, but sent Jackson north to move behind Centreville and make for Fairfax Court House. Pope sent two divisions - under Generals Isaac Stevens and Philip Kearny - to intercept Jackson. The forces met at Chantilly (qv) where Jackson failed to break through. Stevens and Kearny were among the dead. Pope retired to Fairfax and then to Washington DC on the approach of Longstreet. Federal casualties were 16,054 (21 per cent of their strength), Confederate losses 9,197 (19 per cent of their strength).
Result: The defeat demoralised Union troops and put them on the defensive while the Confederates assumed the offensive.

CEDAR CREEK (Virginia)   American Civil War   19 October 1864
Fought between the Federals under General Philip Sheridan and the Confederates under General Jubal Early.
Strength: Federals 31,000; Confederates 18,400.

The Federal army, under the temporary command of General Horatio Wright of 6 Corps while Sheridan was in Washington attending a conference, stood along Cedar Creek, near Middleton, Virginia. Sheridan, believing the Confederates in the Shenandoah valley to be defeated, was preparing to send reinforcements to General Ulysses Grant who was in front of Petersburg (qv). Early, however, had followed the Federal withdrawal to the north.

At dawn Early attacked the forward Federal position which was held by 19 Corps under General George Crook. Taken by surprise, the Federals fell back on

6 Corps, on the Federal right. These also broke when the Confederates continued to drive forward, supported by massed artillery and a rear attack on the left of the Federal position. 8 Corps broke and ran. With 19 and 6 Corps Wright retreated to fight in three successive positions, but by noon the Federal position seemed to be hopeless. The Confederates, having taken 1,300 men and 18 guns, fell to plundering the Federal camp without pressing the attack any further. Wright regrouped west of Middleton. Sheridan, however, riding from Winchester, arrived on the battle-field and immediately reorganised the army for a counter-attack, which was launched late in the afternoon. Taken by surprise, Early was swept from the field, losing all the plunder as well as most of his own supplies, artillery and baggage. Confederate losses were 2,000 killed or wounded and 1,000 missing. Federal losses were 5,665, including 1,591 missing.

The battle more or less ended the war in the Shenandoah valley. Early's corps gradually dwindled until General George Custer wiped out the few survivors the following year. Sheridan took most of his troops to Grant at Petersburg.

The battle is also know as Belle Grove or Middleton.

CEDAR MOUNTAIN (Virginia)   American Civil War   9 August 1862
Fought between the Federals under General Nathaniel Banks and the Confederates under General Thomas (Stonewall) Jackson.
Strength: Federals 8,000; Confederates 24,000.

When the Army of Virginia was created by President Abraham Lincoln under General John Pope, General George McClellan, who commanded the main Federal force, launched a drive on Richmond, the Confederate capital. On 26 June Pope ordered 2 Corps under General Banks to take Gordonsville, a key Confederate railroad junction. General Robert E. Lee ordered Stonewall Jackson to reach the position before the Federals, which he did, marching from a position NE of Richmond. Lee reinforced Jackson with General Ambrose Hill's division and Jackson marched north towards the Federals.

Banks attacked first and drove in the Confederate left. Among those killed was General Charles Winder who was commanding the Stonewall division. The arrival of Hill enabled Jackson to launch a counter-attack which checked the Federals who were now seriously outnumbered. By nightfall the Federals had been driven back with losses of 2,353. Jackson's casualties totalled 1,338. Banks withdrew and rejoined Pope's army. When Lee learned that McClellan aimed to attack Richmond, he marched his entire army north to strike Pope's army before it could join up with McClellan. Pope retired across the Rappahannock River.

CHANCELLORSVILLE (Virginia)   American Civil War   1-6 May 1863
Fought between the Federals under General Joseph Hooker ('Fighting Joe') and the Confederates under General Robert E. Lee.
Strength: Federals 75,000; Confederates 53,000.

After their defeat at Fredericksburg (qv), the Federals held the north bank of the Rappahannock while Lee guarded the south bank against any attempt by the

Federals to cross. Hooker sought to beat the Confederate army back from the river. On 27 April the Federals began to manoeuvre. The movement was designed to turn Lee's left, and General Henry Slocum was sent up-stream with three corps (5, 11 and 12) which crossed the Rappahannock at Kelly's Ford and Rapidan at Germania Ford. On 29 April Slocum reached Chancellorsville, behind Lee who was facing NE towards Fredericksburg. General Darius Couch then crossed the river to take up a position behind Slocum, and General John Sedgwick sent part of 1 and 6 Corps across the Rappahannock below Fredericksburg. The Confederates were caught between two Federal armies. Leaving General Jubal Early's division to hold off Sedgwick on the east, Lee turned his army to meet Hooker's main force to the west. The Federals did not begin to advance until 1 May, at noon.

The battlefield, known as 'the Wilderness', was made up of undergrowth and second-growth timber, and the action on it, despite Hooker's numerical superiority, was indecisive. The Federals called off the attack in order to withdraw to Chancellorsville, where they took up a fortified position. Lee sent Jackson on a 14-mile circuit with 2 Corps to attack the Federals from the west, since their right flank was exposed - a discovery made by General J. E. B. Stuart's cavalry. By 6 pm on 2 May Jackson was attacking the Federal position held by General Oliver Howard's 11 Corps and he had gained some ground by nightfall, having assaulted the Federals with his line perpendicular to the enemy entrenchments and rolled up the right flank. In order to complete the movement to cut Hooker from his Rappahannock communications, Jackson went out at dusk to reconnoitre and, being mistaken for a Federal general, was fired on by a S Carolina regiment and mortally wounded (he died on 10 May). The Confederate Second-in-Command, General Ambrose Hill, had also been wounded, so General Stuart took over, resuming the attack the following day.

Hooker continued to draw back, contracting his perimeter defences and thus allowing the Confederate line to contract and communications to be established between the wings of Lee's army. Stuart attacked the 3 Corps of General Daniel Sickles and the 12 Corps of Henry Slocum, but by noon Hooker, slightly wounded, drew the Federals back north into a position facing south in the junction of the Rapidan and Rappahannock Rivers. On the same day Sedgwick began to march towards Chancellorsville, assaulting Early's force on Marye's Heights which had seen heavy fighting at Fredericksburg. He made four attacks before gaining the heights, at which point Lee detached General Lafayette McLaws with 20,000 men to detain him, leaving only 25,000 men to contain Hooker who should at that point have been able to gain the advantage. Hooker, however, failed to push forward while McLaws, reaching Salem Church at 3 pm where he defeated Sedgwick, forcing him back across the Rappahannock, was able to return to the field while Early reoccupied Marye's Heights in the Federal rear. Lee turned back to Hooker who offered no battle, having been static throughout 4 May during the Salem Church engagement, and on the night of 5/6 May the Federals withdrew across the Rappahannock. Federal losses were 12,278 while Confederate casualties totalled 12,821.

The Confederate victory was marred by the irreplaceable loss of Jackson.

CHANTILLY (Virginia)   American Civil War   1 September 1862
Fought between the Federals under General John Pope and the Confederates under General Robert E. Lee.

The action formed part of the Battle of Bull Run II (qv), the Confederates pursuing the retreating Federals and attacking their rearguard. Jackson attempted to break through the Union reinforcements which were covering Pope's retreat. In a blinding rainstorm the Confederate advance was checked by General Philip Kearny, who was killed in hand-to-hand combat.

The Federals retired to Washington, Jackson making no further attempt to pursue in the direction of the heavily defended town.

CHARLESTON III (S Carolina)   American Civil War   7 April 1863-17 February 1865
Fought between the Federals under Admiral Samuel Du Pont, Admiral John Dahlgren and General Quincy Gillmore, and the Confederates under General William Taliaferro and General Pierre Beauregard.
Strength: Federals 9 warships (7 April) + 5,264 (11 and 18 July) + 400 (8 September); Confederates 1,200 (Fort Wagner only).
Aim: The Federals sought the fall of Charleston, S Carolina.
Battle: On 7 April Du Pont sent 9 ships against Fort Sumter in the mouth of the harbour. The attack was repulsed by the forts and shore batteries, one ship being sunk and several others crippled. Fort Wagner on Morris Island was then attacked by a joint naval and army expedition. A brigade under General George Strong was sent against the fort which was commanded by Taliaferro, but the assault was repulsed with a loss of 339 casualties. Confederate losses were 12. Siege artillery was then brought up and, under cover of its fire, General Truman Seymour took two brigades (those of Strong and General Putnam) to assault the fort again. After gaining a foothold in the fort's outer defences, the attackers were pushed back, both brigade commanders being killed. Seymour was wounded, among 1,515 casualties. Confederate losses were 174. Bombardment of the fort then began and, on the night of 6/7 September, Fort Wagner and all the Morris Island defences were evacuated by the Confederates. The loss of this fort diminished the town's importance as a blockade-runner's haven, but was otherwise of little note. An attempt to capture Fort Sumter on 8 September was repulsed, the Confederates inflicting 125 casualties on the force of 400.

Thereafter, the siege was no more than a naval blockade. On 5 October the Confederates made a submarine attack on the Federal ship the USS *New Ironsides* with the CSS *David,* a steam propelled, cigar-shaped vessel crewed by 4 men. The *David* exploded a 60-pound copper-cased torpedo which inflicted considerable damage on the *New Ironsides* and returned safely to port. Charleston itself, under the overall command of General Beauregard, held out until 17 February 1865 when the approach of Sherman's Federal army from the south forced the Confederates to evacuate the town. The garrison was by then 9,000 strong.

Result: The Federals did not achieve their objective until their victory over the south became a foregone conclusion.

CHATTANOOGA (Tennessee)   American Civil War   25-6 November 1863

Fought between the Federals under General Ulysses Grant and the Confederates under General Braxton Bragg.

Strength: Federals 56,000; Confederates 64,000.

After the Federal defeat at Chickamauga (qv), General William Rosecrans withdrew into Chattanooga while Bragg, declining likewise to take the offensive, settled down to besiege the Federals whose tenuous line of communication down the Tennessee from Bridgeport, Alabama, threatened starvation. Abraham Lincoln, in order to try and retrieve the situation, made Grant Supreme Commander of the Federal armies between the Alleghenies and Mississippi Rivers, while General George Thomas took over the Army of the Cumberland at Chattanooga and General William Sherman's Army of the Tennessee was moved from Corinth, Mississippi, to Thomas's left, up-river from Chattanooga. A third Federal force consisting of three divisions under General Joseph Hooker occupied Bridgeport.

Grant arrived at Chattanooga on 23 October to take command. His first offensive, during 26-8 October, successfully sent some of Thomas's troops over the river on pontoon boats, past the Confederates on Lookout Mountain and up the Tennessee River to Bridgeport, thus establishing a more secure supply line. Hooker guarded this line and a night attack at Wauhatchie on 28-9 October was repulsed. Grant now launched a small offensive. On 23 November Thomas moved east to take Orchard Knob and Indian Hill which were the main outposts of General John Breckinridge, who was forced to fall back to a defensive position on Missionary Ridge, Bragg's main position. The arrival of Sherman the following day enabled him to cross the river and move to Bragg's right flank, north of Missionary Ridge. After a forced march, Sherman's troops were allowed no rest before attacking and they were repulsed. Meanwhile, Hooker attacked Bragg's left between the Tennessee and Lookout Mountain. There was little resistance and Hooker's men went on to ascend the 1,100-foot mountain in thick fog, where again only weak defence was put up. The Federals swept the Confederates off the heights in what is known as the 'Battle above the Clouds'. On 25 November Grant ordered a double offensive, intending to roll up both flanks of Bragg's army, Sherman to attack the north, Hooker the south. Neither assault was successful, and in mid-afternoon Thomas was ordered to make a limited attack on the three-tiered Confederate defences in the centre on Missionary Ridge. The first charge carried the first line, but the Confederates continued their defence from the upper lines and the Federal troops, acting without orders, made a further assault on the remaining defences which drove the Confederates from their positions. Within an hour and a half the Confederates were routed, remaining actions being in the nature of rearguard clashes. Federal losses were 753 killed, 4,722 wounded and 349 missing. Confederates lost 361 killed, 2,160 wounded and

4,146 missing.

The Confederates withdrew to Dalton, Georgia, their lateral line of communication in the south having been cut, while the Federals were now free to push on to Atlanta.

CHEAT MOUNTAIN (W Virginia)   American Civil War   10 September 1861
Fought between the Federals under General Joseph Reynolds and the Confederates under General Robert E. Lee.
Aim: The Confederates sought to regain territory in W Virginia, which was conquered by the Federals during the summer.
Battle: Lee launched a two-pronged attack on the Federal positions on Cheat Mountain and in Elkwater, 7 miles west. Owing to rough terrain and bad brigade leadership, the Confederates made no progress and Lee was forced to withdraw. Few casualties were reported by the Confederates, but Federals claimed Lee's losses were 20 captured and 100 killed and wounded. Federal losses were 21 killed and wounded, and 60 prisoners.
Result: The Confederate objective was not achieved.

The action was the first in which Robert E. Lee played a part.

CHICKAMAUGA (Tennessee-Alabama-Georgia border)   American Civil War
19-20 September 1863
Fought between the Federals under General William Rosecrans and the Confederates under General Braxton Bragg.
Strength: Federals 58,000; Confederates 66,000.

After a long period of inactivity by both armies following the battle of Stones River (qv) Rosecrans moved from Murfreesboro to Tullahoma, forcing Bragg south of the Tennessee River to Chattanooga. Rosecrans moved across the Tennessee after a delay to a position SW of Chattanooga whence he moved east to get behind Chattanooga with three corps - General Thomas Crittenden, 21, General George Thomas, 14, and General Alexander McCook, 20, who were north, centre and south respectively - on a 40-mile front.

Bragg immediately evacuated Chattanooga, moving his army south towards Lafayette, Georgia, which was opposite the Federal centre. Because of the densely wooded and mountainous country, both sides manoeuvred for ten days before Bragg was able to concentrate three corps west of Chickamauga Creek, in a position to attack Crittenden who had in the intervening time occupied Chattanooga and returned to the main army. Thinking that Crittenden's corps was the left of Rosecrans's force, the leading corps of General James Longstreet's two divisions, those of Generals William Walker, John Hood and Simon Buckner, attacked Crittenden from the front. Instead of meeting Crittenden, however, they came up against Thomas who had moved his corps to the left rear of Crittenden. Although the Confederates had aimed to turn the Federal left and cut their line of communications, the Federals held firm throughout the day. The following day, after the Federals had been forced to bivouac in waterless country overnight, the Confederates renewed the attack with General Leonidas Polk in the right centre, where the assault began, extending to Longstreet, now commanding the south wing of the Confederates. Rosecrans, redeploying, left a gap in the Federal centre which Longstreet accidentally found. Advancing through it, he cut the Federal army in half and forced the Federal right, rolled up, on to its left. Rosecrans, believing the battle lost, began to withdraw to the NW, followed by Crittenden and McCook. Meanwhile, Polk's offensive did not break through Thomas's corps which held its ground although, in addition to Polk's attack from the east, it was now assailed by Longstreet. In the afternoon the reserve corps reinforced him from the north under General Gordon Granger. Thomas's stand earned him the nickname 'Rock of Chickamauga', and it limited the Federal defeat. At nightfall he withdrew to Rossville Gap, and thence, with the entire Federal army, to Chattanooga. Federal losses were 1,657 killed, 9,756 wounded and 4,757 missing. Confederate casualties were 2,312 killed, 14,677 wounded and 1,468 missing.

Bragg failed to pursue vigorously and this omission cost the Confederates a major win over the Federals. Rosecrans, McCook and Crittenden were all relieved after the battle, Thomas replacing Rosecrans. On the Confederate side, Generals Polk, Daniel Hill and Thomas Hindman were also relieved.

CHICKASAW BLUFFS (Mississippi)   American Civil War   29 December 1862
Fought between the Federals under General William Sherman and the Confederates under General John Pemberton.
Strength: Federals 32,000; Confederates 12,000.

When General Ulysses Grant began his march on the Confederate stronghold of Vicksburg (qv), General Earl Van Dorn destroyed his advance base at Holly Springs. This and other Confederate attacks on Federal communications forced Grant to withdraw. He sent Sherman down the Mississippi from Memphis towards Vicksburg.

Sherman landed on the banks of the Yazoo, above Vicksburg, and advanced through swampy terrain until he was in a position to attack Chickasaw Bluffs which overlooked the Mississippi. Pemberton had been reinforced and, when Sherman assaulted him on 29 December, the Federals were checked by heavy fire from the Confederate position. The Federals had no way of stopping this fire, since they could employ no artillery support because the bayous were impassable. After two days Sherman took his troops over the Mississippi to Louisiana, opposite Vicksburg. Federal casualties were 1,776 to Confederate losses of 207.

The Federals withdrew north. Vicksburg was to hold out for another six months.

COLD HARBOR (Virginia)   American Civil War   3-12 June 1864
Fought between the Federals under General Ulysses Grant and the Confederates under General Robert E. Lee.
Strength: Federals 108,000; Confederates 59,000.

Grant moved the Army of the Potomac by its left flank from the North Anna River (qv) towards the road junction of Cold Harbor, 10 miles NE of Richmond.

Lee moved his army to keep between Grant and the Confederate capital.

On 1 June Lee dispatched 1 Corps under General Richard Anderson to take Cold Harbor, which was only held by two cavalry divisions of General Philip Sheridan. The Federals were barely able to hold their ground until General Horatio Wright's 6 Corps reinforced Sheridan, repulsing the Confederate assault at 9 am. Both armies now moved into position, with a 7-mile front stretching north to south from the Chickahominy River to Totopotomoy Creek, the Confederates in a defensive position behind entrenchments. When Wright and General William Smith's 18 Corps counter-attacked at about 6 pm, they failed to break the strong Confederate line. Federal losses were 2,200.

Grant now decided to take advantage of his great numerical superiority to split Lee's army in two, believing that his line was over-extended. Lee, continuing to fortify his position and being reinforced by the arrival of troops from the Shenandoah and James valleys, remained static on 2 June. At 4.30 am on 3 June Grant ordered an attack on the Confederate centre and right (S) by three corps - those of Smith, Wright and General Winfield Hancock's 2 Corps. Their opponents were Anderson and General Ambrose Hill. The Federals charged the Confederate position, but were met by very heavy frontal and enfilade fire from the entrenchments. Within one hour the attack had been halted in its tracks and General George Meade, in command of the Army of the Potomac, ordered a withdrawal. Federal casualties in that assault alone were 7,000 killed and wounded.

The Federal troops dug in trenches 100 yards away from the Confederates and the two armies fought each other from these positions for the next eight days. Total casualties during the ten-day engagement were 13,078 Federals and 3,000 Confederates.

The repulse caused a change of tactics. On the night of 12/13 June Grant retired south to cross the James River, circle east of Richmond and threaten Petersburg (qv), which lay 23 miles south of Richmond.

CORINTH III (Mississippi)   American Civil War   3-4 October 1862
Fought between the Federals under General William Rosecrans and the Confederates under General Earl Van Dorn.
Strength: Federals 23,000; Confederates 22,000.
Aim: When General Sterling Price was defeated by the Federals at Iuka (qv), Van Dorn mustered all his forces at Ripley, whence he marched to Corinth, intending to strike at the Federal garrison there.
Battle: The Confederates assaulted the town and the first attack drove back the Federal exterior lines. Thereafter, however, the Federal defence was stubborn and, after the first day, Van Dorn decided to retire. The Federals pursued, reinforced by General Ulysses Grant with two brigades, who sought to effect a double envelopment of the Confederate army, as he had at Iuka. Rosecrans was dilatory, however, and though the Confederates had to fight a strong rearguard action all the way back to Ripley, the Federal objective was not achieved. Federal losses were 2,520. Confederate casualties were 2,470 killed or wounded and 1,763

missing, of whom at least 300 were captured.

Result: The Federals retained control of both Memphis and Corinth, important strategic outposts.

CRAMPTON'S GAP (Maryland)   American Civil War   14 September 1862

Fought between the Federals under General George McClellan and the Confederates under General Robert E. Lee.

This action formed part of the Battle of Antietam Creek (qv).

CRATER, BATTLE OF THE   see PETERSBURG

CROSSKEYS-PORT REPUBLIC (Virginia)   American Civil War   8-9 June 1862

Fought between the Federals under General John Fremont and General James Shields and the Confederates under General Richard Ewell and General Thomas (Stonewall) Jackson.

Strength: Federals 12,000 (Crosskeys), 5,000 (Port Republic); Confederates 6,500 (Crosskeys), 15,000 (Port Republic).

After Jackson escaped the Federal trap at Strasburg he withdrew up the Shenandoah valley. The Federals pursued, dividing the army into two, Fremont marching up the North Fork, with Shields taking the South Fork. Jackson turned to face the oncoming army at Port Republic which, because of Massanutten Mountain, was the only place he could unite his troops. Jackson sent Ewell 4 miles north to prevent the arrival of Fremont's column.

At Crosskeys, Ewell and Fremont met, the Federals launching a half-hearted attack to envelop the Confederate right, which was repulsed. Ewell burnt the only bridge which the Federals could have used to join Shields and, leaving a brigade under General Isaac Trimble to shadow Fremont, marched back to join Jackson at Fort Republic. On 9 June Jackson attacked Shields down the right bank of the South Fork with three assault brigades. The Federals held their ground for four hours until the arrival of Ewell's force, which had been delayed by the collapse of an improvised bridge, drove the Federals back a total of 20 miles north. At Crosskeys, Federal losses were 114 killed, 443 wounded and 127 missing. Confederate casualties were 41 killed, 232 wounded and 15 missing. At Port Republic, Federal losses were 1,018, including 450 prisoners, and Confederate losses were 800.

Jackson now occupied Brown's Gap, the east exit from the Blue Ridge, until ordered to Richmond by Lee. He had successfully tied a large Union force west of the gap.

DREWRY'S BLUFF (Virginia)   American Civil War   12-16 May 1864

Fought between the Federals under General Benjamin Butler and the Confederates under General Pierre Beauregard.

Strength: Federals 16,000; Confederates 18,000.

While General Ulysses Grant directed the offensive on Richmond from north of the Confederate capital, Butler, with the two-corps Army of the James, was ordered to approach Richmond from the SE. Butler moved up the James River to Bermuda Hundred at the junction of the Appomattox River, thence north to cut the Richmond-Petersburg railroad before retiring. Five miles below Richmond, on the right bank of the James, he deployed against Beauregard's men, though he was outnumbered, and attacked towards Drewry's Bluff with General Quincy Gillmore's 10 Corps on the left (W) and General William Smith's 18 Corps on the right. Before he could launch an assault, however, Beauregard attacked the Federal lines with ten brigades in heavy fog on 16 May, turning the right along the river. Butler was forced to retreat to Bermuda Hundred, where he remained practically useless until Grant moved round to the south of Richmond. Federal losses were 4,160 to the Confederate total of 2,506. Grant, on hearing of the defeat, ordered Smith to leave Bermuda Hundred and march north to him, thus leaving the garrison low in strength. Lee likewise took General Robert Hoke's division from Beauregard to join his own army.

FAIR OAKS (Virginia)   American Civil War   31 May-1 June 1862
Fought between the Federals under General George McClellan and the Confederates under General Joseph Johnston.
Strength: Federals 41,000; Confederates 41,000.
    When McClellan reached a point on the Chickahominy River 6 miles NE of Richmond, which was his objective, he sent 3 and 4 Corps across the river under Generals Erasmus Keyes and Samuel Heintzelman. These forces advanced to the east side of Richmond while McClellan remained stationary, awaiting reinforcements which were held by General Thomas (Stonewall) Jackson in the Shenandoah valley. Johnston built up the Confederate force to attack the exposed Federals on the east of Richmond. On 31 May he launched an attack there on 3 Corps, General James Longstreet advancing against Keyes with three columns while General Gustavus Smith diverted the Federals north of the river on the left. An enveloping manoeuvre was intended but Longstreet, instead of moving towards Fair Oaks with his left, attacked frontally, having delayed the advance from dawn to 1 pm. The piecemeal attack was backed up by General Daniel Hill, who struck the Federals at Seven Pines (by which the action is also known) and began to drive them back towards the Chickahominy. From north of the river, General Edwin Sumner saw the battle and sent General John Sedgwick's division across to anchor Keyes's right at Fair Oaks. Longstreet's progress was slowed and darkness ended the fighting. On 1 May Gustavus Smith took over from Johnston, who had been wounded twice, and the attack was renewed. The Federal line held, however, and when General Robert E. Lee arrived to take command of the Confederates he ordered a withdrawal to the position originally occupied, which they did unmolested. Federal losses were 5,031, Confederates 6,134.
    Neither side gained any ground.

FISHER'S HILL (Virginia)   American Civil War   22 September 1864
Fought between the Federals under General Philip Sheridan and the Confederates under General Jubal Early.
Strength: Federals 30,000; Confederates 8,000.

After being defeated at Winchester III (qv) Early retreated south to Fisher's Hill which overlooked Strasburg, deploying his infantry and dismounted cavalry in a 4-mile front. Sheridan, who was in close pursuit, came upon the Confederate position, and while two Federal corps (6 and 19) attacked frontally, General George Crook took his division to the west to attack Early's left late in the afternoon. The Confederate left, held by General Lunsford Lomax, further beset by a frontal attack up a wooded ridge, fell back in disorder, followed by the rest of Early's force. Confederate casualties (not counting Lomax, who was wounded) were 1,235 of whom 1,100 were captured. General Sheridan lost 528, including 52 killed.

Early withdrew to Harrisonburg while Sheridan retired to Winchester, devastating the country as he went.

FIVE FORKS (Virginia)   American Civil War   1 April 1865
Fought between the Federals under General Philip Sheridan and the Confederates under General George Pickett.
Strength: Federals 12,000 cavalry + 16,000 infantry; Confederates 19,000.
Aim: In order to stretch his siege lines SW of Petersburg (qv), General Ulysses Grant sent Sheridan to attack the Confederate right flank on 29 March.
Battle: Sheridan went NW from Dinwiddie Court House towards the crossroads at Five Forks which was held by Pickett, summoning reinforcements in the form of 5 Corps under General Gouverneur Warren, intending this force to attack Pickett's right. Sheridan attacked the entrenched position of the Confederates in the centre, but it was not until Warren attacked the right late in the afternoon that the Confederate line was rolled up. Of 5,200 prisoners taken, 3,200 were taken by Warren's corps. Despite Warren's success, he was relieved by Sheridan and replaced by General Charles Griffin.
Result: The Confederate defeat at Five Forks forced Lee to evacuate Richmond and Petersburg.

FLEETWOOD HILL   see BRANDY STATION

FORD   see NORTH ANNA RIVER

FORT DONELSON (Tennessee)   American Civil War   15 February 1862
Fought between the Federals under General Ulysses Grant and the Confederates under General John Floyd and General Gideon Pillow.
Strength: Federals 25,000; Confederates 12,000.
Aim: When the Federals captured Fort Henry (qv), Confederate General Albert Johnston was forced to alter his alignment, withdrawing his right (E) from Bowling Green, Kentucky, to Nashville, Tennessee, and reinforcing Fort Donelson on the

Cumberland River. The Federals advanced on the fort on 12 February, which they sought to capture.

Battle: Six Federal gunboats under Commodore Andrew Foote came up-river with the aim of subduing Fort Donelson by gunfire as they had done Fort Henry, but Confederate guns were well placed and on 14 February the Federal vessels were repulsed. Foote was severely wounded. On 15 February the Confederates attacked the Federal forces under Grant, attempting to break out of the fort to the south. The attack beat the Federals back, but the assailants under General Pillow were ordered back by Floyd who lost his nerve. By this time, some of the Confederate trenches were already occupied by Federal troops. Under cover of darkness Generals Floyd and Pillow escaped by river, leaving the garrison under the command of General Simon Buckner. The cavalry under Colonel Nathan Forrest also escaped through the Federal lines during that night. On the following day Buckner asked for terms and was given the ultimatum: 'No terms except an unconditional and immediate surrender'. Buckner surrendered and 11,000 men laid down their arms. Confederate losses were 2,000. Federal casualties were 500 killed, 2,108 wounded and 224 missing.

Result: The fall of the fort opened the way for Federal troops to advance into Confederate country up the Tennessee.

FORT FISHER (N Carolina)   American Civil War   13-15 January 1865
Fought between the Federals under General Alfred Terry and the Confederates under General William Whiting.

Strength: Federals 8,000; Confederates 8,000.

Aim: After the abortive attempt on Fort Fisher headed by General Benjamin Butler in December 1864 a new force was dispatched to take the fort, which was the last Confederate line to the sea. It guarded the entrance to the harbour of Wilmington, N Carolina.

Battle: The Federal force was landed on 13 January and siege artillery was brought ashore the following day. On 15 January a heavy bombardment was opened on the fort, and in the afternoon it was assaulted and taken. Confederate losses were 112 officers and 1,971 men captured, including Whiting, who was mortally wounded. Federal losses were 184 killed, 749 wounded and 22 missing. Federal naval casualties totalled 686. General Robert Hoke's division, which had also been part of the garrison, was driven off.

Result: The successful assault opened the port of Wilmington to the Federals. Terry then marched to Goldsboro with General John Schofield's army, joining General William Sherman on 23 March.

FORT HENRY (Tennessee)   American Civil War   6 February 1862
Fought between the Federals under General Ulysses Grant and Commodore Andrew Foote and the Confederates under General Lloyd Tilghman.

Strength: Federals 15,000 + 7 gunboats; Confederates 79 with 17 guns.

Because the State of Kentucky was neutral, the Confederates built its two forts on the Cumberland River in the State of Tennessee, just across the border. General Henry Halleck, Federal Commander of the Department of Missouri, authorised Grant to move up the Tennessee. The Federals moved to within 4 miles of Fort Henry while, on the river, the gunboats brought the fort under bombardment. Tilghman had realised that the fort was too weak to withold the Federals, being unfinished, and had evacuated most of the 2,500-man garrison to Fort Donelson (qv), 11 miles east. Little fire was returned before the garrison surrendered. Federal losses were 11 killed, 81 wounded and 5 missing. Confederate losses were 5 killed, 11 wounded and 63 missing.

Grant, moving overland, moved on to Fort Donelson as soon as he heard of the surrender.

FORT PILLOW (Tennessee)   American Civil War   12 April 1864
Fought between the Federals under Major Lionel Booth (later under Major William Bradford) and the Confederates under General James Chalmers (later under General Nathan Forrest).
Strength: Federals 262 (Negroes) + 295 (whites); Confederates 1,500 cavalry.

When the Mississippi fell into their control, the Federals guarded the waterway with a series of forts from Cairo, Illinois, to New Orleans, Louisiana. One of these was Fort Pillow, lying 40 miles north of Memphis. Forrest detached a division under Chalmers to attack the fort from Jackson. Investment was begun at dawn on 12 April. The commander was killed by a sniper and replaced by Bradford, who refused a surrender ultimatum from Forrest, who had arrived to take personal command, in mid-afternoon. The fort was then assaulted and captured with a loss of 14 killed and 86 wounded. Federal losses were high, 231 killed, 100 seriously wounded and 226 captured (including 58 Negroes). These figures are attributed to a stout defence by the Federals, though it is possible that many of the casualties were suffered after the surrender, giving rise to the name Fort Pillow Massacre.

Forrest continued his harassment of Federals in the area.

FORT SUMTER (S Carolina)   American Civil War   12-14 April 1861
Fought between the Federals under Major Robert Anderson and the Confederates under General Pierre Beauregard.
Strength: Federals 76 with 48 guns (92 guns of the fort were not in use); Confederates 600 with 30 guns and 17 mortars.

Anderson, who commanded the Federal forts in Charleston harbour, withdrew his men into Fort Sumter which was ringed by the Confederates who set up batteries which cut off the Federals from their source of supplies and reinforcements. Anderson therefore planned to evacuate the fort on 15 April.

On 12 April Beauregard opened fire on the fort, and during the next 34 hours fired 4,000+ shells into the fort, inflicting little damage and no casualties. The Federals returned the fire to equally little effect. Realising the hopelessness of his situation, Anderson agreed to evacuate the fort at noon on 14 April. The only casualties of the action came when 2 men were killed and 1 wounded in an accidental powder explosion during the final salute.

The success of the Confederate bombardment was one of the chief actions which provoked the Civil War.

FRANKLIN (Tennessee)   American Civil War   30 November 1864
Fought between the Federals under General John Schofield and the Confederates under General John Hood.
Strength: Federals 32,000; Confederates 38,000.

When Atlanta (qv) was lost to the Confederates, Hood resolved to hit at General William Sherman's communications which stretched from Atlanta to Chattanooga. Sherman, who had been following Hood, turned back to Atlanta at the end of October to organise the Federal move to Savannah (qv). He left General George Thomas to shadow Hood and ordered Schofield to fall back to Nashville (qv). Hood moved in order to intercept Schofield who withdrew across the Duck River in Columbia on 27 November while Hood crossed up-river.

The armies raced north on parallel courses and on 29 November the Confederates narrowly missed blocking off the Federal retreat. Schofield marched all night to avoid the Confederates and entrenched at Franklin in front of the Harpeth River. Hood came up on the afternoon of 30 November and assaulted the Federal centre. A gap was opened, but a counter-attack by General Emerson Opdycke blocked the hole in the defences and for the next five hours Hood's men attacked the Federal position without success. By 9 pm the fighting had almost ended. Confederate losses were 6,252, including 12 general officers. Federal losses were 2,326.

East of Franklin, General Nathan Forrest also suffered a defeat at the hands of Federal cavalry under General James Wilson. Schofield crossed the Harpeth to Nashville where Thomas assumed command. Hood followed, but was too weak to attack.

FREDERICKSBURG (Virginia)   American Civil War   13 December 1862
Fought between the Federals under General Ambrose Burnside and the Confederates under General Robert E. Lee.
Strength: Federals 120,000; Confederates 78,000.

After the Battle of Antietam Creek (qv) General George McClellan remained north of the Potomac until the end of October when he began to move south, crossing the river. In November President Abraham Lincoln replaced McClellan with General Burnside who planned to threaten Richmond by moving to Fredericksburg on the Rappahannock River. He arrived there on 17 November, but could not cross because of the lack of a pontoon train until 10 February when he began to cross the river to Fredericksburg on the south bank. Lee's army occupied the heights overlooking the city and the river. The Federals sought to beat the Confederates from their position.

General James Longstreet's 1 Corps was on Marye's Heights on the left (NW) and General Thomas (Stonewall) Jackson stood on the right down-stream with his 2 Corps. Burnside attacked on the morning of 13 December. To the SE, General William Franklin's Grand Division of 1 and 6 Corps assaulted Jackson and drove through the Confederate first and second lines. A strong counter-attack checked the Federal advance at 1.30 pm, but the Confederates were in turn stopped by a barrage of Federal artillery fire. At this point the fighting died down. On the Federal right up-stream, General Edwin Sumner's Grand Division of 2 and 9 Corps advanced on Longstreet across an open field through heavy artillery and rifle-fire but after two hours they withdrew, having suffered many casualties. The Centre Grand Division under General Joseph Hooker (3 and 5 Corps) was then sent against St Marye's Heights, but this was also repulsed with heavy loss. The Confederates held the strong natural position with a loss of 5,300 men, while Federal losses totalled 12,700 killed or wounded.

Burnside wanted to renew the offensive the following day, but his divisional commanders dissuaded him and the Federal army withdrew across the river on the night of 14-15 December. The Federals continued to try and turn Lee's left flank, but without success, and early the following year Burnside, Franklin and Sumner were all relieved and Hooker became the commander of the Army of the Potomac.

FRONT ROYAL (Virginia)   American Civil War   23 May 1862
Fought between the Federals under Colonel John Kenly and the Confederates under General Thomas (Stonewall) Jackson.
Strength: Federals 1,063; Confederates 16,000.

Returning to the Shenandoah valley, after winning the engagement at McDowell (qv), Jackson passed the main Federal army at Strasburg and crossed Massanutten Mountain to move down the east side of the valley, collecting General Richard Ewell's division at Luray on the way. His objective was the isolated Federal position at Front Royal.

Jackson knew the exact deployment of the Union troops from the reports of Belle Boyd, a Confederate spy. He attacked Front Royal on 23 May, killing, capturing or wounding 904 of the garrison strength. Kenly was wounded and captured. Confederate losses were less than 50.

The supplies which fell into the Confederates' hands were lost when a Federal force routed their rearguard at Front Royal on 30 May. Belle Boyd, a young Confederate spy, was captured.

GAINES'S MILL   see SEVEN DAYS' BATTLES

GARNETT'S and GOLDING'S FARMS   see SEVEN DAYS' BATTLES

GETTYSBURG (Maryland-Pennsylvania border)   American Civil War   1-4 July 1863

Fought between the Federals under General George Meade and the Confederates under General Robert E. Lee.

Strength: Federals 88,000; Confederates 75,000.

On 24 June, Lee's second invasion of the North began when the Confederate Army of N Virginia crossed the Potomac to close up behind 2 Corps of General Richard Ewell in the Cumberland valley, Pennsylvania. To protect Washington and Baltimore, the Federal army also moved north into Maryland under the command of General Joseph Hooker. Abraham Lincoln replaced Hooker with Meade on 28 June. Meanwhile, Lee began to concentrate his scattered forces at Cashtown.

Meade, who was trying to coax the Confederates into battle south of the Susquehanna, moved cautiously towards Emmitsburg and Hanover. The Federal cavalry under General John Buford which was reconnoitring the area, met the van of General Ambrose Hill's 2 Corps between Cashtown and Gettysburg. Both sides began immediately to build up strength. Hill pushed forward to Seminary Ridge, running north to south SW of Gettysburg, which they held, pushing back General Joseph Reynold's 1 Corps. Ewell advanced on Gettysburg itself from Heidlersburg to the north, driving out the 11 Corps of General Oliver Howard. Meade sent General Winfield Hancock to organise the Federal position south of Gettysburg. Hancock deployed the incoming troops on Culp's Hill and Cemetery Ridge in the 'fish-hook' shape, stretching as far south as the hills of Little Round Top and Big Round Top, which were not manned. The Confederates ended the first day with the upper hand, Howard's corps having lost over 4,000 men as prisoners and 1 Corps, now under the command of General Abner Doubleday after the death of Reynolds, also having suffered heavily. Ewell had not attempted to take Culp's Hill, which he had reached by nightfall.

Lee decided to envelop the Federal left the following day, using Longstreet's 1 Corps, which had not yet arrived on the field. The attack was not launched until 4 pm when Longstreet, Hill and Ewell delivered assaults all along the line. Longstreet's attack was made piecemeal against General Daniel Sickles's 3 Corps which was in an exposed position in a peach orchard. The Federals were forced back and the left almost turned, but General Gouverneur Warren, seeing that Little Round Top was unoccupied, swiftly deployed a brigade and artillery battery which successfully held the hill and saved the situation. Hill and Ewell made no headway to the left of Longstreet and on Culp's Hill respectively, and at the end of the day the line from Culp's Hill to Round Top was securely in Union hands.

Lee now resolved to launch an attack to break Meade's centre with a simultaneous attack by General J. E. B. Stuart's cavalry from the north. Stuart had only just arrived from carrying out a raid to the east. Under the direction of Longstreet the divisions of Generals George Pickett, James Pettigrew and Isaac Trimble assembled on Seminary Ridge to take part in what was to become known as 'Pickett's Charge'. First, 159 Confederate guns took part in a duel with the opposing artillery of General John Gibbon after which the Confederates marched across the intervening half mile of exposed country to the Federal position on Cemetery Hill. Continued Union gunfire blew great holes in the Confederate line which advanced up the hill to the Federal position. Some ground was gained before Meade threw his reserve in, beating back the Confederates with heavy losses. Ewell's last attempt on Culp's Hill also failed and Stuart's cavalry attack was beaten back, by General David Gregg. The Confederates withdrew, having lost half those engaged on the centre offensive, to await the Federal counter-attack.

Meade's troops were too exhausted, however, to take the offensive and on the night of 5/6 July Lee began his withdrawal. Federal losses were 3,155 killed, 14,529 wounded and 5,365 missing. Confederate losses were 3,903 killed, 18,735 wounded and 5,425 missing.

In driving rain the Confederates retreated towards the Potomac, which they crossed on 13 and 14 July. This defeat, coupled with that at Vicksburg (qv) on 4 July which split the Confederacy in two along the Mississippi, spelt the beginning of the end for the Confederate States.

Because of its ultimate result, the battle must be ranked as one of the decisive fights in history. During the three-day action, legend has it that more shells were fired than Napoleon used in all his battles, but, judging from the casualties, to considerably less effect than was achieved by French armies.

GROVETON (Virginia)   American Civil War   26 August 1862
Fought between the Federals under General Rufus King and the Confederates under General Thomas (Stonewall) Jackson.
Aim: To divert Federal attention from the approach of General James Longstreet's division at the opening of the Battle of Bull Run II (qv), Jackson attacked King's division.
Battle: The Confederates were repulsed as General John Pope concentrated his forces in this area, intending to destroy Jackson's force and unaware of the proximity of Longstreet. The Confederate General Richard Ewell lost a leg in this battle.
Result: Though the Confederates were pushed back their objective was achieved, in that Longstreet arrived on the scene unnoticed.

HAMPTON ROADS (Norfolk, Virginia)   American Civil War   8-9 March 1862
Fought between the Federals under Lieutenant John Lorimer Worden and the Confederates under Commodore Franklin Buchanan and Lieutenant Catesby ap Roger Jones.
Strength: Federals *Congress* (50 guns) + *Cumberland* (24 guns) + *Minnesota* (50 guns) + *Monitor* 2 11-inch guns, crew of 58); Confederates the *Virginia* 6 9-inch guns, 4 guns of smaller calibre, crew of 350).

The frigate *Merrimac* (originally *Merrimack),* sunk when the Confederates had captured the Norfolk navy yard, was raised by the Confederates and rebuilt as an ironclad ram, renamed the *Virginia.* Described as a 'floating barn roof' the vessel sailed into Hampton Roads to attack the wooden fleet of the Federals which blockaded her. The *Virginia*, whose hull was covered with an iron and oak carapace, rammed and sank the *Cumberland* while the *Congress* was forced aground, where she surrendered. The *Minnesota* also ran aground. Other ships were scattered, and at nightfall the *Virginia* retired to Norfolk to repair slight damage before returning the next day to finish off 3 remaining vessels. Overnight, however, the Federal *Monitor* arrived from New York. She was the first specially designed ironclad (by John Ericsson) and carried her guns mounted in a turret which revolved, covered in 11 inches of iron. She was known as a 'cheese box on a raft'. She took up a position between the *Virginia* and the rest of the crippled fleet and when the *Virginia* returned the two vessels engaged in an artillery duel which lasted two hours. Though the *Monitor* could inflict no real damage on the *Virginia,* she proved to be a more manoeuvrable vessel. At about midday, a shell struck the *Monitor*'s sight hole, partially blinding Worden and forcing the *Monitor* to retire. The *Virginia* withdrew to Norfolk. Federal losses were 409, and Confederate losses 21.

Hampton Roads remained in Federal hands and when a Federal attack on Norfolk forced the Confederates to evacuate the town, the *Virginia* was destroyed. The *Monitor* went down in a gale off the N Carolina coast at Cape Hatteras.

HANOVER JUNCTION   see NORTH ANNA RIVER

HARPER'S FERRY (Virginia)   American Civil War   14-15 September 1862
Fought between the Federals under Colonel D. S. Miles and the Confederates under General Thomas (Stonewall) Jackson.
Strength: Federals 12,000 with 73 guns; Confederates 1,300.
Aim: When General Robert E. Lee advanced into Maryland in September, he sent Jackson to capture the garrison of Harper's Ferry, the possession of which would give the Confederates a protected line of communications down the Shenandoah valley.
Battle: When Jackson moved on Harper's Ferry with the divisions of Generals Ambrose Hill and Alexander Lawton, the Federals withdrew into the angle made by the Potomac and Shenandoah Rivers. While Jackson approached from the west, General John Walker's division took up a position on Loudon Heights to the east, and another Confederate force, two brigades of General Richard Anderson's division under the command of General Lafayette McLaws, took up a position on the Maryland Heights, north of the Potomac. On 14 September Jackson's ring of artillery began to bombard Harper's Ferry, and that night Colonels Benjamin Davis and Amos Voss led 1,200 cavalry through McLaws's lines, but Miles did not take his infantry out. When the bombardment was renewed on 15 September Miles surrendered the garrison.

Leaving the division of General Ambrose Hill, Jackson immediately began a forced march north to where Lee was preparing for the Battle of Antietam Creek (qv). Hill secured the captured stores and 11,000 prisoners. Miles was accidentally killed during the capitulation.
Result: The Confederate objective was achieved.

ISLAND NO 10 (Mississippi River)   American Civil War   3-7 April 1862
Fought between the Federals under General John Pope and the Confederates under
General John McCown and General William Mackall.
Strength: Federals 7,000; Confederates 4,000 (of whom 1,500 were sick).
Aim: After the fall of Fort Donelson (qv) Confederate General Leonidas Polk was
forced to withdraw from W Kentucky and the Confederates resolved thereafter to
hold the Mississippi River farther down-stream at New Madrid, Missouri, and at
Island No 10, near the corner of the Tennessee. Pope was ordered to move against
New Madrid.
Battle: Pope arrived at New Madrid on 3 March and, ten days later, preparations
for a siege were complete. As soon as the Federals began bombardment of the
town the Confederates evacuated New Madrid and crossed the river into Upper
Tennessee. McCown was relieved of his command and replaced by Mackall. Pope
now cut a canal through the swamp, by which 2 gunboats were able to run past
the Confederate batteries on Island No 10 and the fire from the gunboats protected
the Federals when four regiments crossed the Mississippi to Tiptonville, Tennessee.
This move bottled the Confederates in a peninsula formed by the bend in the river
and Mackall promptly surrendered with 3,500 men, while 500 Confederates
escaped east.
Result: The Federal victory opened the Mississippi to them as far as Fort Pillow
(qv), Tennessee.

IUKA (Mississippi)   American Civil War   19 September 1862
Fought between the Federals under General William Rosecrans and the Confederates under General Henry Little.
Strength: Federals 9,000; Confederates 14,000.
    After the Federals won the Battle of Shiloh (qv), the Federal commander moved
south to Corinth, Mississippi, before dispersing his army between Memphis and
Chattanooga. General Henry Halleck, up to then the Federal commander, was
replaced by General Ulysses Grant in July. The Confederates moved from Tupelo
to Iuka on 13 September, placing themselves across the Federal line of communications, isolating General Don Carlos Buell in E Tennessee.
    Grant now attacked General Sterling Price, sending General Edward Ord with
8,000 men east along the railroad to Iuka while Rosecrans with 9,000 men .was
sent south to cut off the expected Confederate retreat. Rosecrans was within 2
miles of Iuka when Price's left (S) wing under General Little attacked. The attack
was checked in two hours of heavy fighting, during which Little was among 263
Confederates killed, the total casualties being 1,516. Federal losses were 782 men.
    When Price learnt of the proximity of Ord and that he intended to join the attack
the following day, he retreated under cover of darkness.

JERICHO MILLS   see NORTH ANNA RIVER

KENESAW (KINNESAW) MOUNTAIN (Georgia)   American Civil War   27 June 1864
Fought between the Federals under General William Sherman and the Confederates under General Joseph Johnston.
Strength: Federals 16,000; Confederates 17,700.
Aim: In Sherman's attack south, he endeavoured to force Johnston to retreat.
Battle: By 25 May the Confederates were at Dallas-New Hope Church. Sherman engaged in skirmishing for four days before changing his tactics. Refusing to be drawn into a frontal attack, he moved his three armies east to Kenesaw (Kinnesaw) Mountain which was held by General William Loring on the Confederate right. The attack was undertaken by the Army of the Tennessee under General James McPherson to the left (N), the Army of the Cumberland under General George Thomas in the centre and the Army of the Ohio under General John Schofield on the right. The Confederate corps under Generals William Hardee (facing Thomas) and John Hood (on the Confederate left) were barely engaged. The Federals stormed the heights for two hours with only 16,000 of their 100,000 men because of the cramped front, thus giving the Confederates local superiority of numbers. The Federals were unable to take the strong Confederate entrenchments and were beaten back with heavy losses of 2,000 killed and wounded, and 50 missing. Confederate losses were only 270 killed and wounded and 172 missing.
Result: The Federal defeat forced Sherman to change his tactics again, returning to a campaign of manoeuvre. McPherson was moved to the west flank, forcing Johnston to retreat south again.

KERNSTOWN I (Virginia)   American Civil War   23 March 1862
Fought between the Federals under General James Shields and the Confederates under General Thomas (Stonewall) Jackson.
Strength: Federals 9,000; Confederates 4,200.
Aim: When General George McClellan began amassing troops for his offensive against Richmond, Federals in the lower Shenandoah valley were called in to support the campaign. Jackson marched from Mount Jackson with the intention of keeping the command of General Nathaniel Banks within the valley.
Battle: At Kernstown, Jackson was involved in a small cavalry skirmish which encouraged him to believe that his only opposition was the Federal rearguard. This belief led him to storm Kernstown the following day, only to find it held by Shields's division. The Confederates were thrown back with a loss of 700 men. Federal losses were 590.
Result: The daring of the attack led Federal commanders to suspect that Confederate strength was greater than in fact it was and for this reason the movement eastwards was reversed.

KERNSTOWN II (Virginia)   American Civil War   24 July 1864
Fought between the Federals under General George Crook and the Confederates under General John Breckinridge.

After an unsuccessful raid to Washington DC, General Jubal Early returned to the Shenandoah valley at Berryville. Crook's Army of W Virginia was camped at Kernstown, south of Winchester, 10 miles west. Breckinridge was detached to attack the position. On 23 July cavalry skirmishes took place and a general assault was delivered the following day. The Federal army, consisting of two divisions, was routed and fled across the Potomac with a loss of 1,185 men, including 479 captured.

Grant now decided to launch an offensive to clear the Shenandoah valley of Confederates. Sheridan was assigned to the project.

KNOXVILLE (Tennessee)   American Civil War   29 November 1863
Fought between the Federals under General Ambrose Burnside and the Confederates under General James Longstreet.
Strength: Federals 6,000; Confederates 10,000 infantry + 5,000 cavalry.

While besieging Chattanooga, Confederate General Braxton Bragg was so sure of the impenetrability of his defences on Lookout Mountain and Missionary Ridge that he detached Longstreet with 15,000 men to besiege Burnside at Knoxville. Although unable to besiege the Federals completely, Burnside's men were soon on the verge of starvation. Longstreet decided to launch a dawn attack with General Lafayette McLaws's division. The objective of the Confederate assault was the salient of the defences called Fort Sanders (Loudon). The Confederate assault was repulsed with a loss of 813 men. Federal losses were 113.

Longstreet, discouraged by his failure and the news of Bragg's defeat at Chattanooga, and hearing of a Federal relief column (for which Abraham Lincoln and General Henry Halleck had been imploring by telegram since before Chattanooga) marching on Knoxville, withdrew NE to winter quarters at Greenville. Longstreet rejoined Lee's Army of Virginia in the following spring.

LEXINGTON II (Tennessee)   American Civil War   18 September 1861
Fought between the Confederates under General Sterling Price and the Federals under Colonel James Mulligan.
Strength: Confederates 8,000; Federals 3,000.
Aim: The Confederates sought to reduce the garrison held by the Federals.
Battle: After the Federal defeat at Wilson's Creek (qv) the Confederates moved north and besieged the garrison at Lexington. Having cut off the Federal supply line, the Confederates took the surrender of the town on 20 November, losing only 100 men during the siege.
Result: The Confederate objective was achieved.

LYNCHBURG (Virginia)   American Civil War   18 June 1864
Fought between the Federals under General David Hunter and the Confederates under General John Breckinridge.

Reaching Staunton, Virginia, on 6 June, Hunter went on SE towards Lynchburg, which was an important rail centre. Lee sought to block this advance by sending out

Breckinridge with two brigades followed by General Jubal Early's corps. Hunter attacked Lynchburg, but was repulsed by Breckinridge's main force as well as Early's advance guard. Hunter heard of the forces massing against him and retreated into W Virginia, moving thence north by rail and water.

Early was now free to march into the Shenandoah valley for his raid on Washington DC.

MALVERN HILL   see SEVEN DAYS' BATTLES

MCDOWELL (Virginia)   American Civil War   8 May 1862
Fought between the Federals under Generals Robert Schenk and Robert Milroy and the Confederates under General Thomas (Stonewall) Jackson.
Strength: Federals 3,000; Confederates 9,000.

After he was repulsed at Kernstown I (qv), Jackson withdrew up the Shenandoah valley to Swift Run Gap. General Nathaniel Banks pursued cautiously as far as New Market. Jackson heard of a plan to link Banks's army with that of General John Fremont in W Virginia and decided to prevent the conjunction of the two forces. Leaving a force in Swift Run Gap, he marched across the Shenandoah valley in front of Banks and, picking up General Edward Johnson's division at West View, reached McDowell on 8 May. Jackson was attacked here by Schenk and Milroy, but the latter were outnumbered and, being beaten back, were forced across Bull Pasture River with a loss of 256. Confederate casualties were 498.

Jackson pursued as far as Franklin, W Virginia, before returning to the Shenandoah to continue his campaign of tying Federal forces down there.

MECHANICSVILLE   see SEVEN DAYS' BATTLES

MEMPHIS III (Tennessee)   American Civil War   6 June 1862
Fought between the Federals under Commodore Charles Davis and the Confederates under Captain J. E. Montgomery.
Strength: Federals 10 gunboats; Confederates 8 armed vessels.
Aim: The Federals sought to destroy the Confederate gunboat flotilla and bring about the fall of Memphis.
Battle: Davis attacked the gunboats off Memphis and destroyed all but one of them. Memphis surrendered.
Result: The Federal objective was achieved and Davis's flotilla steamed down to the mouth of the Yazoo River, above Vicksburg (qv).

MIDDLETON   see CEDAR CREEK

MILL SPRINGS (Logan Cross Roads, Kentucky)   American Civil War
19 January 1862
Fought between the Federals under General George Thomas and the Confederates under General George Crittenden.

Strength: Federals 4,000; Confederates 4,500.

Both North and South vied for dominance in the border state of Kentucky which was neutral during the early part of the Civil War. A Confederate force under General Felix Zollicoffer moved west from Cumberland Gap to Mill Springs, thence to Beech Grove, north of the Cumberland River, where Crittenden took command. General Don Carlos Buell, based at Louisville, ordered a Federal force under Thomas to march south from Lebanon to attack the Confederates.

Crittenden moved north towards his assailants when he heard of their approach and the van of the two armies met early the following morning at Logan Cross Roads. In a fierce fight, during which Zollicoffer was killed, Thomas engaged enough men to break the Confederate left despite the arrival of Confederate reinforcements. Crittenden fell back, evacuating Beech Grove and crossing the Cumberland that night, losing most of his heavy equipment, including 12 guns. Federal losses were 39 killed and 207 wounded.

The defeat was the most serious suffered by the Confederates to that date and it caused many desertions. Action in Kentucky moved westwards to forts on the Tennessee and Cumberland Rivers.

MOBILE BAY (Alabama)   American Civil War   3-5 August 1864
Fought between the Federals under General Gordon Granger and Admiral David Farragut and the Confederates under Admiral Franklin Buchanan.
Strength: Federals 5,500 + 18 ships with 3,000; Confederates 1 ironclad + 3 gunboats with 470.
Aim: A joint Federal naval and land expedition was launched to reduce the important Confederate port of Mobile, Alabama.
Battle: Granger, with part of the 13 Corps, landed on the west of Dauphine Island in Mobile Bay, and during the next twenty days reduced the forts of Gaines, Powell and Morgan, each of which guarded the entrance to Mobile Bay. Little loss of life was sustained by either side, but the Federals took 1,464 prisoners and 104 guns. On 5 August Farragut ran his fleet into the bay to attack the ironclad, the *Tennessee.* The battle lasted less than two hours, during which time the *Tennessee* was crippled and Farragut's ship, the *Tecumseh,* was sunk by a mine (or torpedo) early in the action. Federal casualties totalled 319. Confederate losses were 312.
Result: Despite the success of this battle for the Federals, the town of Mobile did not fall until the following year when Lee surrendered at Appomattox (qv).

MONOCACY RIVER (Maryland)   American Civil War   9 July 1864
Fought between the Federals under General Lewis Wallace and the Confederates under General Jubal Early.
Strength: Federals 6,000; Confederates 10,000 infantry + 4,000 cavalry.
After repulsing Hunter at Lynchburg (qv), Early pressed on to the Shenandoah valley, up which he travelled, reaching Winchester on 2 July. He crossed the Potomac into Maryland and went east, but SE of Frederick, on the Monocacy River, he met Wallace with a blocking force.

Early sent a flanking force across the river, which attacked Wallace's left, over-powering the smaller force. The Federals fell back to Baltimore, having lost 1,880 men (of which 1,188 were missing). Early had less than 700 casualties.

Reaching Washington, Early found the defences too strong to attack and so withdrew on 12 July, crossing the Potomac at Leesburg and entering the Shenandoah valley at Snicker's Gap.

MURFREESBORO   see STONES RIVER

NASHVILLE (Tennessee)   American Civil War   15 December 1864
Fought between the Federals under General George Thomas and the Confederates under General John Hood.
Strength: Federals 49,000; Confederates 31,000.

After winning the action at Franklin (qv), General John Schofield retreated into Nashville, where Thomas took command. Hood pursued, but stopped short of the town without attacking and deployed his troops SE of the city, awaiting Thomas's arrival.

To the great annoyance of Washington, Thomas delayed for two weeks while he was training new recruits and he would not be hurried. On 15 December he launched a classic assault on Hood's troops. Early in the morning he delivered a secondary attack against Hood's right (E), held by General Benjamin Cheatham's corps. A main assault was then made on Hood's left which was held by General Alexander Stewart, the attack being made by the 16 Corps of General Andrew Smith who led the Federals, followed by 4 Corps of General Thomas Wood on Smith's left and 24 Corps of General John Schofield on Smith's right. Hood's left caved in and was only saved from complete destruction by nightfall when Cheatham was moved from the right to the left of General Stephen Lee's centre corps which had seen little action. The Federals held their positions overnight and moved up to the new Confederate positions the following day, launching a fierce attack at about 3.30 pm. The assault on the left under Thomas was stopped, but General James Wilson with dismounted cavalry attacked and penetrated the Confederate left rear (W), threatening the line of retreat. The entire defensive position was broken and Hood was driven from the field in disorder. Darkness and heavy rain enabled the Confederates to retreat south without being totally overwhelmed by the Federal pursuit. Confederate losses were 1,500 killed or wounded and 4,462 captured. Federal casualties were 387 killed, 2,562 wounded and 112 missing.

Hood retreated across the Tennessee River into Mississippi in December and was relieved of his command at his own request the following month. It was but an empty gesture, since the Army of Tennessee had more or less ceased to exist as a fighting force.

NEW HOPE CHURCH (Georgia)   American Civil War   25-8 May 1864
Fought between the Federals under General William Sherman and the Confederates under General Joseph Johnston.

Aim: The action was fought as part of Sherman's campaign to force the Confederates to retreat to the south.
Strength: Federals 98,000; Confederates 60,000.
Battle: The skirmish at Dallas, Georgia, lasted four days and led to Sherman changing his tactics, a move which culminated in the Battle of Kenesaw Mountain (qv).
Result: Neither side gained a positive advantage and casualties were about 3,000 on both sides.

NEW MARKET (Virginia)   American Civil War   15 May 1864
Fought between the Federals under General Franz Sigel and the Confederates under General John Breckinridge.
Strength: Federals 5,150; Confederates 3,500 (including 247 cadets from Virginia Military Institute).
   Sigel was engaged in a campaign of harassment of the Confederates in the Shenandoah valley. He had beaten the Confederate cavalry under General John Imboden back to New Market, where he was reinforced by two brigades under Breckinridge. From New Market, Breckinridge made a rapid flanking movement and fell on the Federals as they were marching from Cedar Creek. Sigel was forced to take refuge behind the artillery in a wood, but the guns were attacked by the cadets and, by 4 pm, the Federals had been forced back so far that Sigel ordered a retreat north towards Strasburg. Federal losses were 831 as well as 6 guns. Confederate losses were 577 (including 10 killed and 47 wounded among the cadets whose professor, Scott Shipp, was killed).
   General Ulysses Grant relieved Sigel and replaced him with General David Hunter, since he no longer brought any Federal pressure to bear in the valley.

NEW ORLEANS II (Louisiana)   American Civil War   18-25 April 1862
Fought between the Federals under Admiral David Farragut and Commodore David Porter and the Confederates under General Johnson Duncan and General Mansfield Lovell.
Strength: Federals 8 steam sloops and corvettes + 9 gunboats (mounting 200 guns between them) + 20 mortar vessels + 10,000 troops; Confederates 115 heavy guns + 11 gunboats + 4,000 militia.
   Federal naval supremacy enabled them to mount an attack against New Orleans although the Confederates still held Vicksburg and Port Hudson on the Mississippi River.
   The Federals moved to the mouth of the river, which was defended by two forts, Jackson and St Philip, on the west and east banks respectively. Porter began a bombardment with 13-inch mortars which inflicted little damage. The uncompleted Confederate ironclad, the *Louisiana,* which had no engines, was moored as a floating battery just above St Philip. A barrier of hulks and logs barred the way to river traffic. After six days of bombardment, which caused less than 50 casualties, Farragut began to run his fleet past the forts, which he achieved with

the loss of 3 small gunboats. Eleven Confederate gunboats attacked the Federals above the forts, 9 of which were sunk. At the approach of the fleet, Lovell, who commanded in New Orleans, evacuated the 4,000 militia without giving battle. The town was taken on 25 April. Federal losses were 36 killed and 135 wounded.

The forts still held out, but General Benjamin Butler had landed troops near Lake Pontchartrain on the Gulf Coast and with these men he surrounded the forts. The garrisons then mutinied and were forced to surrender. Butler marched on to occupy New Orleans while Porter, who had continued the mortar bombardment, took the forts' surrender.

The Federal fleet continued up-stream to Vicksburg (qv).

NORTH ANNA RIVER (Virginia)   American Civil War   20-6 May 1864
Fought between the Federals under General Ulysses Grant and the Confederates under General Robert E. Lee.
Strength: Federals 100,000; Confederates 50,000.

After the inconclusive action at Spotsylvania (qv), Grant moved his army SE to threaten Lee's right flank. Lee, seeing the danger, also shifted his force to a strong position on the North Anna River.

Deploying his three corps in a V-shape, Lee awaited Grant, whose four corps arrived on 23 May. On the left (W), General Horatio Wright's 6 Corps was crossing the river when it was attacked by 3 Corps of General Ambrose Hill. Wright forced his passage and Hill returned to his entrenchments, both sides having suffered about 600 casualties. On the right (E), General Winfield Hancock's 2 Corps was harassed by the Confederate 2 Corps under General Richard Ewell and did not manage to cross all his men that day. On the following day Hancock completed his crossing with the Federal 5 Corps under General Gouverneur Warren, who made up the right centre, taking up a position to the east of Wright. General Ambrose Burnside's 9 Corps was unable to cross the south side of the river because the Confederate opposition, the apex of the V-shape which was made up of General Richard Anderson's 1 Corps, was too strong to attack. Grant's army was thus in three widely split parts and vulnerable to attack. However both Lee and Hill were sick, Ewell was exhausted (he was fighting with only one leg) and Anderson, who was commanding vice General James Longstreet who was wounded, was inexperienced. Skirmishing took place for two days before Grant marched by his left flank towards Cold Harbor, 10 miles NE of Richmond. Lee moved with the Federals, keeping his own army between them and Richmond.

The action is also known as Hanover Junction, Jericho Mills, Ford or Bridge or Taylor's Bridge.

OAK GROVE   see SEVEN DAYS' BATTLES

OCEAN POND   see OLUSTEE

OLUSTEE (Florida)   American Civil War   20 February 1864
Fought between the Federals under General Truman Seymour and the Confederates under General Joseph Finegan.
Strength: Federals 5,100; Confederates 5,200.
Aim: The Federals sought to gain a foothold in N Florida.
Battle: Seymour landed at Jacksonville on 7 February and, meeting no opposition, marched inland to Olustee with three regiments. The Confederates, positioned strongly where they were protected by swamps and forests, attacked in mid-afternoon. Two Federal regiments were routed, but the third held its ground until nightfall, when Seymour withdrew. Federal losses were 203 killed, 1,152 wounded and 506 missing. They also lost 6 guns. Confederate losses were 934.
Result: Seymour fell back to Jacksonville.
   The battle is also known as Ocean Pond.

OPEQUON CREEK   see WINCHESTER III

PEA RIDGE (Arkansas)   American Civil War   7-8 March 1862
Fought between the Federals under General Samuel Curtis and the Confederates under General Earl Van Dorn.
Strength: Federals 11,000; Confederates 17,000 (including 3 regiments of Creek and Cherokee Indians).
   Curtis, Federal Commander of the Army of SW in Missouri, launched an offensive against Springfield, where General Sterling Price had quartered for the winter after his win at Wilson's Creek (qv). At Curtis's advance, Price retreated into the Boston Mountains of NW Arkansas and Curtis pursued. Price was reinforced by General Ben McCulloch's division and other units sent forward by Van Dorn, who himself came up to meet Curtis. The Federals took up a position near Pea Ridge, overlooking Little Sugar Creek to the south.
   Van Dorn launched a diversionary attack to the west, while concentrating his main effort against the Federal left at Elkhorn Tavern. Both Confederate attacks gained ground but, at the end of the day, neither had succeeded in breaking through the Federal defences. McCulloch was killed during the fighting.
   The Federals launched a counter-attack early the following morning, two divisions under General Franz Sigel attacking the east wing of the Confederates to drive them back from the Elkhorn Tavern-Pea Ridge area. This assault, along with another on the west flank, broke the tired Confederate lines and Van Dorn retreated south to the Arkansas River. Confederate losses were 800 to the Federals' 1,384. Van Dorn was then ordered east to help with the defence of the Mississippi River.
   The victory was one of the most important for the Union in the Mississippi area.

PERRYVILLE (Kentucky)   American Civil War   8 October 1862
Fought between the Federals under General Don Carlos Buell and the Confederates under General Braxton Bragg.
Strength: Federals 39,000; Confederates 16,000.

When Buell was ordered east from Shiloh to Chattanooga, Bragg moved north through E Tennessee into central Kentucky, forcing Buell back almost as far as the Ohio River. At the same time, Confederate General Edmund Kirby Smith occupied Lexington, having won a battle at Richmond. Bragg seized Munfordsville on 17 September and Buell retreated to Louisville, where he was reinforced. He then began to march SE against Bragg's force, then at Bardstown. The Confederates fell back to Perryville.

Bragg sent a corps east to aid Kirby Smith and, when a battle suddenly developed, only part of his army under Generals Leonidas Polk and William Hardee was engaged, opposing the corps of Generals Charles Gilbert and Alexander McCook. General Thomas Crittenden was in supporting distance for the Federals, but he was not involved in the battle. The action was confused as both forces were scattered, but the Confederates withstood the attack and retreated at nightfall through Cumberland Gap. Federal losses were 845 killed, 2,851 wounded and 515 missing. Confederate losses were 510 killed, 2,635 wounded and 251 missing.

When Buell failed to Pursue Bragg towards Murfreesboro, he was replaced by General William Rosecrans.

PETERSBURG (Virginia)   American Civil War   15 June 1864-3 April 1865
Fought between the Federals under General Ulysses Grant and the Confederates under General Robert E. Lee.
Strength: Federals 95,000 (rising to 125,000); Confederates 57,000.

In order to threaten the Confederate capital of Richmond, Grant marched south from Cold Harbor (qv) to the rail centre of Petersburg, 23 miles south of the capital.

The Federal 18 Corps of General William Smith arrived in front of the town on 15 June and attacked from the east with 13,700 infantry and 2,400 cavalry that afternoon. His deployment was so cautious, however, that although a portion of the first line was carried, General Pierre Beauregard prevented a breakthrough into the city itself. 2 Corps under General Winfield Hancock (who was later succeeded by General David Birney) and 9 Corps under General Ambrose Burnside arrived the following day. Federal strength was now 48,000. Beauregard, who had the defence of Bermuda Hundred as well as Petersburg under his charge, brought the force screening Bermuda Hundred to Petersburg the same day, reinforcing his troops from 3,000 to 14,000. Neither side attacked that day or the next and by 18 June the Federals had a strength of 95,000 to the Confederates' 20,000. Grant launched a major assault in the morning, but the Confederates, knowing that Lee was on his way, held on to their position. Lee had 38,000 men deployed by the end of the day; the Federals had lost their chance of a quick capture. Their losses during that day were 1,688 killed, 8,513 wounded and 1,185 missing. Confederate losses were unreported. The Confederates had withdrawn to the second line of defences, stronger than the outer line which had been evacuated after an abortive attack on it by the Federals on 16 June.

The town now prepared for trench warfare, which was combined with sorties as Grant extended his encirclement of Petersburg. A group of Federal coalminers under Lt-Colonel Henry Pleasants dug a tunnel 511 feet under Confederate entrenchments and planted a mine made of 8,000 pounds of gunpowder in the section commanded by Ambrose Burnside. At 4.40 am on 30 July the mine was exploded, making a crater 60-80 feet wide and 30 feet deep, killing 278 Confederates and blowing a gap of 500 yards in the Petersburg defences. The action which followed is known as the Battle of the Crater.

Burnside sent in General James Ledlie's division to follow up the advantage, but the attack was badly co-ordinated and was made worse by the fact that Ledlie remained in his dugout, drunk. Twenty thousand Federals took part in the eventual assault, but Beauregard, who took personal command of the Confederates, poured fire into the crater, causing heavy casualties among the Federals. The break was sealed and no ground was gained by the exploit. Burnside resigned as a result of the affair. Federal losses were 3,798 to Confederate losses of 1,500.

Although Grant probed at Lee's defences round Petersburg and Richmond north of the James and extended the siege of Petersburg to the south and SW, every attempt to break through was repulsed. Operations here were affected by the war elsewhere, and although General Jubal Early had threatened Washington, Sheridan had gained the Shenandoah valley for the Federals and the Confederates suffered as a result of General William Sherman's campaign, which ended by crushing Hood's army at Nashville (qv).

The winter of 1864-5 was mild and wet and curtailed operations on both sides, but on 25 March Lee launched his last offensive. General John Gordon took his division into action against Fort Stedman which was the north end of the Federal line, but General John Parke with 9 Corps repulsed the attack with a loss of 2,000. Confederate losses were 4,400. Grant now took the initiative. South of Petersburg he drove the siege lines so far west that the defences could not be adequately manned by the remaining 57,000 Confederates. The Confederates were defeated at Five Forks (qv) on 1 April. The win by the Federals 11 miles SW of Petersburg convinced Lee that Richmond and Petersburg had to be evacuated. On 2 April General Horatio Wright with 6 Corps broke through the Confederate position between Richmond and Five Forks, in which action the Confederate commander General Ambrose Hill was killed. On the night of 2/3 April the Confederates, now 30,000 strong, began retreating westward along the Appomattox River (qv). Both Petersburg and Richmond were occupied on 3 April. Federal casualties were 42,000. Confederate losses were 28,000. Lee surrendered his army on 9 April.

PHILIPPI (W Virginia)   American Civil War   3 June 1861
Fought between the Federals under General George McClellan and the Confederates under General Robert Garnett.
Strength: Federals 20,000; Confederates 5,000.

After the outbreak of hostilities at Fort Sumter (qv), both sides hastily fielded armies in NW Virginia. McClellan pushed east towards Cumberland, Maryland, and the Confederates moved north from Beverly. The van of the Confederate force reached Philippi on 3 June and that night was surrounded by the Federals whose enveloping attack routed the Confederates, inflicting 15 casualties. Two Federals were wounded.

The action, the first land 'battle' of the war, gave the Federals the advantage. It is also known as the Philippi Races.

PIEDMONT (Virginia)   American Civil War   5 June 1864
Fought between the Federals under General David Hunter and the Confederates under General William (Grumble) Jones.
Strength: Federals 11,000 + 5,000 cavalry; Confederates 3,500 + 5,000 cavalry.

When Hunter was put in charge of Federal forces in the Shenandoah valley, he marched south from Strasburg for Staunton, ordering General George Crook to meet him there, taking a more westerly route. At Harrisonburg Hunter circled east to avoid Confederate defences which had been thrown up by Jones. The Confederates came out of Harrisonburg to intercept the Federals at Piedmont, 7 miles SW of Port Republic. Hunter, who outnumbered Jones, attacked on 5 June and by mid-afternoon had beaten the Confederates, whose defence collapsed. Jones was killed. Confederate losses were 600 killed and wounded and 1,000 men captured. Federal losses were 780.

Hunter occupied Staunton the following day, and Crook arrived on 8 June.

PORT HUDSON (Louisiana)   American Civil War   26 May-9 July 1863
Fought between the Federals under General Nathaniel Banks and the Confederates under General Franklin Gardner.
Strength: Federals 20,000; Confederates 16,000.
Aim: As part of the Federal campaign to clear the Mississippi, the port was besieged.
Battle: Banks's 14 Corps closed in on Port Hudson, 25 miles north of Baton Rouge, on 26 May. On 27 May the Federals attacked the port, but were repulsed, after which Banks laid siege to the place. On 11 and 14 June two more unsuccessful assaults were delivered. Despite privation, the garrison held out until 9 July when, hearing of the fall of Vicksburg (qv) which made Port Hudson untenable, Gardner surrendered. Federal losses were 3,000 killed, wounded and missing. Confederate losses were 7,200, including the 5,500 who surrendered, as well as 2 steamers, 60 guns, 5,000 small arms, 150,000 rounds of ammunition and 45,000 pounds of gunpowder.
Result: The Mississippi was now in the complete control of the Federals.

PRAIRIE GROVE (Arkansas)   American Civil War   7 December 1862
Fought between the Federals under General Francis Herron and the Confederates under General Thomas Hindman.
Strength: Federals 3,000; Confederates 11,000.
Aim: The Federals, having won the battle at Pea Ridge (qv), kept a grip on NE Arkansas, and General James Blunt, with 7,000 men, held Prairie Grove, 15 miles south of Fayetteville. Hindman sought to destroy this isolated force.

Battle: Leaving Van Buren, Hindman made for Prairie Grove and was ready to attack Blunt when he heard that a Federal force was approaching from Missouri. Hindman left a cavalry screen to divert Blunt and circled to come between the two Federal armies. On 7 December the Confederates attacked the van of Herron's advancing force and drove it back, but instead of pursuing this advantage, Hindman took up a defensive position. Herron, who had just completed a 125-mile march, made three unsuccessful attacks against the entrenched Confederate position. Blunt had heard the sounds of battle and had turned his back on the cavalry screen and now fell on Hindman's left. Only a fierce defence by the Confederate cavalry prevented them from breaking. Nightfall ended the fight. Federal losses were 1,251 and Confederate losses 1,317. Hindman had had difficulty in making the Arkansas troops attack, and one entire regiment deserted. Federal burial parties found that the Confederate conscripts had fired blanks, having removed the bullets from their cartridges.

Result: Hindman withdrew south, his objective not achieved; N Arkansas was still in Union hands.

RESACA (Georgia)   American Civil War   14 May 1864
Fought between the Federals under General William Sherman and the Confederates under General Joseph Johnston.

Strength: Federals 98,000; Confederates 60,000.

Sherman, who had replaced General Ulysses Grant, built up the Federal forces after the fall of Chattanooga (qv) and divided it into three armies: the Tennessee (General James McPherson), the Cumberland (General George Thomas) and the Ohio (General John Schofield). The Confederates under Johnston, who had replaced General Braxton Bragg, occupied a strong position on Rocky Face Ridge, overlooking Dalton, Georgia.

Sherman began to advance on Atlanta and, turning his SW line, forced Johnston from his position. The Confederates retired south and took up another position at Resaca, where Sherman attacked on a broad front north and west of the town with Schofield to the left, Thomas in the centre and McPherson to the right. The Confederates beat off the Federal attack, but Sherman threatened to move west to encircle his flank and attack the rear. Johnston retreated to the south on the night of 15 May.

Sherman continued his drive on Atlanta.

RICHMOND (Kentucky)   American Civil War   30 August 1862
Fought between the Federals under General George Morgan and the Confederates under General Edmund Kirby Smith.

Strength: Federals 8,000; Confederates 9,000.

Both western armies moved into E Tennessee and Kentucky to widen the front. The Confederates moved north towards the Federal position at Cumberland Gap, but instead of engaging the Federals, they marched round them into E Kentucky, forcing Morgan to evacuate the position. Kirby Smith continued northwards and reached Richmond, which was held by 6,500 inexperienced Federals sent from Louisville under Generals Mahlon Manson and Charles Cruft. On 29 August the Federals attacked the Confederates and checked their advance; but during the night the Confederates closed up and on 30 August they launched a vigorous assault on the Federals, driving them back into Richmond where General William (Bull) Nelson failed to rally them. Manson was wounded and captured in the retreat towards Louisville. Federal losses were 206 killed, 844 wounded, 4,303 missing (mostly captured), 9 guns and 1,000 stand of arms. Confederate losses were 78 killed and 372 wounded.

Kirby Smith moved on to Lexington, then turned SW to join with General Braxton Bragg's army at Perryville (qv).

RICH MOUNTAIN (W Virginia)   American Civil War   11 July 1861
Fought between the Federals under General William Rosecrans and the Confederates under Lt-Colonel John Pegram.
Strength: Federals 15,000; Confederates 6,000.

At the outbreak of hostilities, both armies tried to gain a foothold in Virginia, a state whose sympathies were largely with the Union. Confederate General Robert Garnett posted two regiments under Pegram at Rich Mountain in Randolph County. General George McClellan sent Rosecrans with four regiments to attack the position. The Federals circled the south flank of Pegram's force and cut off his line of retreat. The Confederates gave battle, but the action was short and Pegram surrendered with 553 officers and men on 12 July. Federal losses totalled 46. Pegram was among those captured. He was later exchanged, and in 1865 he was killed.

Garnett began a withdrawal of Confederate troops when he learned of the defeat at Rich Mountain. He was killed during the retreat. The victory by the Federals enhanced McClellan's reputation greatly.

ROANOKE ISLAND (N Carolina)   American Civil War   7-8 February 1862
Fought between the Federals under General Ambrose Burnside and Captain Louis Goldsborough, and the Confederates under General Henry Wise.
Strength: Federals 3 regiments + 20 gunboats; Confederates 1,800 + 7 gunboats.
Aim: The island, garrisoned by the Confederates, commanded the entrance to Albemarle Sound and the Federals sought to capture it.
Battle: Three Federal brigades embarked from Annapolis, Maryland, in 65 vessels. The force landed under covering fire from the gunboats. On the following day the garrison was overpowered and the island taken by the Federals who lost 235 killed and wounded and suffered 14 naval casualties. Confederate losses were 2,500 captured and 5 out of 7 gunboats.
Result: The Federals left a garrison on Roanoke and went on to occupy New Bern and Beaufort.

SABINE CROSSROADS-PLEASANT HILL (Louisiana)   American Civil War 8-9 April 1864

Fought between the Federals under General Nathaniel Banks and the Confederates under General Richard Taylor.

Strength: Federals 12,000 (9 April); Confederates 5,300 infantry + 3,000 cavalry + 500 artillerymen (all on 8 April).

Banks was ordered by General Henry Halleck to undertake an overland invasion of Texas via Red River, one objective of the expedition being to discourage the French from intervening in the war from Mexico. Admiral William Porter took 12 of his gunboats above the rapids at Alexandria, Louisiana, and continued up-stream while Banks took his men along the riverside. Their objective was Shreveport, Louisiana, which Banks left the river to make for at Grand Encore. Confederate Generals Richard Taylor and Edmund Kirby Smith, retreating before the advance, decided to make a stand at the road junction of Mansfield and sent a force to the Sabine Crossroads, a few miles forward, to defend the position which the Federals were approaching.

The van of Banks's army met the Confederate van at Sabine Crossroads, and though neither commander had intended it, both armies were drawn into battle. In a fiercely contested struggle, Banks was driven back in disorder. That night, Banks withdrew south to Pleasant Hill, where he left a force to detain the pursuing Confederates while he went on to Alexandria. On the afternoon of 9 April Taylor attacked, but, despite his slight numerical superiority, he was beaten. In the two-day fight he had lost 2,500 men. Federal losses were 3,500 men, 22 guns and 220 wagons of stores and ammunition.

Kirby Smith, Confederate commander west of the Mississippi, ordered Taylor to withdraw to Mansfield, but on hearing of Banks's retreat, sent Taylor to harass the Federals, who abandoned their plan to take Shreveport. Banks fell back to Red River where Porter's gunboats were stuck above the rapids because of the falling river. The Federals constructed a flume and dam to extricate the boats and fought skirmishes to free themselves on 8 May. Banks was relieved during that month and Taylor was also relieved by Kirby Smith.

This action ended the fighting west of the Mississippi.

SAVAGE'S STATION and ALLEN'S FARM   see SEVEN DAYS' BATTLES

SAVANNAH III (Georgia)   American Civil War   10-21 December 1864

Fought between the Federals under General William Sherman and the Confederates under General William Hardee.

After the fall of Atlanta Sherman made sure that no Confederate threat existed before rendering the town indefensible and marching SE. He took with him 62,000 men and rations for twenty days (55,000 infantry, 5,000 cavalry, 2,000 artillerymen, 64 guns). The Federals moved in two wings, the right being composed of 15 and 17 Corps under General Oliver Howard (Army of the Tennessee), the left of 14 and 20 Corps under General Henry Slocum (Army of Georgia), the whole screened by General Hugh Kilpatrick's cavalry. The army destroyed all railroads and other possible strategic positions on a front 50-60 miles wide, their only opposition being cavalry attacks on the flanks and rear by General Joseph Wheeler. The Federals reached Savannah, 225 miles from Atlanta, on 10 December and opened up communications with the Federal fleet which stood off-shore. Savannah itself, commanded by Hardee, refused to surrender, but siege guns from the fleet were set up and the town was evacuated on 21 December when Hardee retreated north.

Sherman's 'march to the sea' had succeeded.

SECESSIONVILLE (S Carolina)   American Civil War   15 June 1862
Fought between the Federals under General Henry Benham and the Confederates under General Nathan Evans.
Strength: Federals 6,000; Confederates 2,000.
Aim: The Federals sought to drive the Confederates from their position.
Battle: Against orders, Benham attacked the strong position held by the Confederates at Secessionville and was repulsed with a loss of 600 men. Confederate losses were 200.
Result: The Federal objective was not achieved. Benham was relieved of his command.

SEVEN DAYS' BATTLES (Virginia)   American Civil War   25 June-1 July 1863
Fought between the Federals under General George McClellan and the Confederates under General Robert E. Lee.
Strength: Federals 90,000; Confederates 108,000.
Aim: The Federals were deploying to besiege Richmond, the Confederate capital. The Confederates sought to remove the threat.
Battle: McClellan moved the bulk of his army south of the Chickahominy River, leaving only the 30,000 men of General Fitz-John Porter's 5 Corps behind. Lee then moved 65,000 men to attack Porter, leaving only 25,000 to protect the east side of the city. On 25 June a division of the Federal 4 Corps of General Samuel Heintzelman under General Joseph Hooker attacked Oak Grove in the Fair Oaks-Seven Pines area south of the river. It was a probing attack, losses being 626 Federals and 441 Confederates, and a minor action, but it opened hostilities in the Seven Days' Battle. It is known also as Henrico, King's School House and The Orchards.

On 26 June Lee was in a position to envelop the separated wing of Porter's division. General Thomas (Stonewall) Jackson, coming up from the Shenandoah valley with 18,000 men, was to attack from the north, while three other divisions attacked from the west. Jackson failed to arrive and Porter repulsed piecemeal attacks on his position. At 3 pm General Ambrose Hill attacked alone from Mechanicsville, but, trying to cross Beaver Dam Creek which was strongly held by the Federals, his assault was repulsed with heavy loss. Confederate losses were 1,400 to Federal 361. The action is also known as Ellison's Mills and Beaver Dam Creek.

McClellan ordered the corps to fall back to Gaines's Mill, anticipating a fresh attack by Lee the next day. On 27 June the divisions of Generals Daniel Hill, Jackson, Ambrose Hill and James Longstreet deployed in a semicircle from NE to SW, but Jackson again delayed the assault until the afternoon. The Federals were not enveloped in the rear as Lee intended, but though they were reinforced by men from other Union divisions, sheer weight of numbers broke Porter's lines SE of Gaines's Mill and the Federals retreated across the Chickahominy River with a loss of 6,837 and 20 guns. Confederate losses totalled 8,751. The engagement is also known as First Cold Harbor and Chickahominy.

McClellan decided to withdraw, changing his base from White House on the Pamunkey, a tributary of the York, to Harrison's Landing on the James. 28 June was spent chiefly in marching to the base. When Lee was certain of the Federal destination, he ordered pursuit. General John Magruder, who had been fighting diversionary actions for the past three days (at Garnett's and Golding's Farms) now attacked the Federal rearguard from the west at Savage's Station and Allen's Farm, on the Richmond-York River railroad. The rearguard, under General Edwin Sumner, consisted of 2 Corps and was meant to be attacked by Magruder and Jackson from the north. Again Jackson hesitated, and though Magruder was aided by an armoured train, Sumner held off the Confederate attack until the entire army had retreated through White Oak Swamp, leaving many supplies. Federal losses were 1,590 men and Confederate casualties were 625. This battle is also known as Peach Orchard.

On 30 June three divisions overtook the Federal rearguard at White Oak Swamp and, during an artillery duel, the Federals lost some guns. The co-ordinated attack by six divisions planned by Lee did not take place, and only two divisions attacked, being those of Longstreet and Ambrose Hill, both of which assaulted General George McCall's division of 5 Corps at Frayser's Farm, south of Glendale and White Oak Swamp. The Federals were overwhelmed and McCall was captured. However, neighbouring Union troops prevented further penetration by the Confederates under cover of darkness. Federal losses were 2,853. Confederate losses were 3,615. This battle is known also as Glendale, Charles City, New Market Cross Roads, Nelson's Farm, Frayser's Farm and Turkey Bend.

McClellan, who had gone on ahead to inspect the new base, now deployed his troops on top of Malvern Hill, overlooking the James River. It was a strong position, but Lee attacked it on 1 July. Federal superiority in artillery (250 guns strongly positioned) caused Lee to call off the attack, which was renewed late in the afternoon. Piecemeal attacks by Generals Daniel Hill, Jackson and Benjamin Huger were beaten off and darkness ended the fight. Federal losses were 3,214 and Confederates were 5,355. The engagement is also known as Crew's Farm.

McClellan continued his retreat to Harrison's landing and Lee returned to Richmond. Total casualties were 36,000, of whom 20,000 were Confederate.
Result: The Federal army was recalled to Washington in August. Lee's objective in relieving Richmond was achieved.

SEVEN PINES   see FAIR OAKS

SHILOH (Tennessee)   American Civil War   6-7 April 1862
Fought between the Federals under General Ulysses Grant and the Confederates under General Albert Johnston.
Strength: Federals 42,000; Confederates 62,700.

President Abraham Lincoln put General Henry Halleck in overall command of the western offensive. Grant was ordered to the Pittsburg Landing on the west of the Tennessee River, while General Don Carlos Buell was to move up from Nashville to link up with Grant. Johnston, seizing the initiative, marched north from Corinth to Pittsburg Landing.

Confederate divisions under Generals Leonidas Polk, Braxton Bragg and William Hardee attacked the divisions of Generals William Sherman and Benjamin Prentiss, driving them back 2 miles, engulfing the divisions of Generals John McClernand, Stephen Hurlburt and William Wallace. These outposts had been caught unprepared and Grant came up from Savannah, Tennessee, to supervise the defence of the landing area. The Confederates continued to make ground in action so concentrated that corps commanders took charge of whatever units were available, regardless of deployment and structure. When Johnston was killed at about 2.30 pm General Pierre Beauregard took over command. William Wallace was killed and Prentiss surrendered 2,200 Federal troops after failing to hold a patch of woodland called the Hornet's Nest.

At 6 pm Beauregard halted the attack, expecting to finish off the Federals the following day, but overnight General Lewis Wallace's division arrived, as did three divisions of Buell's army which came up on the left of the river, some troops being shipped across. At dawn a counter-offensive was launched and the Confederates, now outnumbered, steadily gave ground, fighting particularly strongly around Shiloh Church. At 2.30 pm Beauregard ordered a retreat and the Confederates marched back to Corinth, while the Federals occupied the camps they had held before the battle. Two Federal gunboats had added flanking fire which had also weakened the Confederate attack. Federal pursuit of the retreating army on 8 April was halted by General Nathan Forrest's cavalry. Federal casualties were 1,854 killed, 8,408 wounded and 2,885 missing. Confederate losses were 1,723 killed, 8,012 wounded and 959 missing.

The narrow Federal victory opened the way to the conquest of the entire Mississippi.

SOUTH MOUNTAIN (Maryland)   American Civil War   14 September 1862
Fought between the Federals under General Ambrose Burnside and the Confederates under General Daniel Hill and General James Longstreet.

After winning the Battle of Bull Run II (qv) Lee moved north to threaten Maryland. The Federal commander, General George McClellan, moved slowly to meet him but sent Burnside, commander of the Federal right wing, with two corps to guard Turner's Gap and Crampton Gap in South Mountain to ensure the

Federal advance.

Burnside arrived at the position to find it already occupied by the Confederates of Hill's division, later supported by Longstreet's division. The Federals attacked, and the battle lasted until after nightfall. The Confederates held their ground until they were outflanked to the right (N) by General Joseph Hooker's 1 Corps and on the left by General Jesse Reno's 9 Corps, whereupon they retreated to the upper slopes, withdrawing the following day. Federal casualties were 1,813, including Reno, who was mortally wounded. Confederate losses were 2,685.

Although the Federals won the encounter, the action had given Robert E. Lee another day in which to assemble his widely scattered army and to delay the Federal advance and ensure the fall of Harper's Ferry (qv). Lee massed his troops at Sharpsburg.

SPOTSYLVANIA (Virginia)   American Civil War   10-12 May 1864
Fought between the Federals under General Ulysses Grant and the Confederates under General Robert E. Lee.
Strength: Federals 101,000; Confederates 56,000.

After the Battle of the Wilderness (qv), which ended in deadlock, Grant moved SE on the night of 7 May, beginning with General George Meade's Army of the Potomac whose objective was New Spotsylvania Court House which was a key road junction on the Richmond road. Only a fast march by Lee's 1 Corps under General Richard Anderson blocked the Federal advance, following which Lee brought up the rest of his Army of N Virginia. Both sides now concentrated for a battle while Grant sent General Philip Sheridan on a raid to Richmond - which was dashing if inconclusive (YELLOW TAVERN). The Confederates entrenched in their position and, as Grant closed up, the left (W) of Lee's army under Anderson was threatened by General Winfield Hancock's 2 Corps. Hancock was recalled, however, to take part in a frontal assault on the Confederate centre which was held by General Richard Ewell's 2 Corps. On 10 May 5 and 6 Corps under Generals Gouverneur Warren and Horatio Sedgwick attacked the left of Lee's line. The assaults were beaten off, but 1,000 Confederates were captured.

On 11 May Grant massed for an attack against the centre of Lee's line. Ewell's corps was deployed in a horseshoe-shaped salient known as the 'bloody angle' or 'mule shoe'. At 4 am on 12 May General Ambrose Burnside's 9 Corps attacked the east of the position, while Hancock followed up on the centre and Wright on the west. The battle lasted all day and the Federals took 2,000 men and 20 guns. They also gained ground where Hancock had forced the surrender of General Edward Johnson's division. The ground lost amounted to about a mile. Elsewhere, Confederate defences stood firm.

During the next six days Grant continued to probe the Confederate flanks but, owing to Lee's skilful manoeuvring of reserves, these were always strongly held. On the night of 20 May Grant began shifting towards Richmond, to the SE. Ewell, anticipating this possibility, had attacked on 19 May to the north, but had found the Federals entrenched strongly. Federal losses during the battle were 17,000.

Because the Confederates were well entrenched, their losses were less, amounting to between 9,000 and 10,000.

Federal offensives SE of Richmond and in the Shenandoah valley had been checked.

STONES RIVER (or MURFREESBORO) (Tennessee)   American Civil War
30 December 1862-3 January 1863

Fought between the Federals under General William S. Rosecrans and the Confederates under General Braxton Bragg.

Strength: Federals 45,000; Confederates 38,000.

After the indecisive battle at Perryville (qv) the Confederates withdrew to concentrate at Murfreesboro, Tennessee, while the Federals moved to Nashville. On 26 December Rosecrans moved towards Murfreesboro, but was stopped by the corps of Generals William Hardee and Leonidas Polk which were posted on the west side of Stones River.

On 31 December each side attacked the other's right. Hardee moved first and drove the Federals' line back 3 miles before Rosecrans managed to stabilise it in a position almost 90 degrees from his original front. The Federal attack on the Confederate right wing was recalled to strengthen both this position and the centre, which Polk had assaulted with less success, the Federal divisions of Generals Philip Sheridan and George Thomas holding fast. Confederate General John Breckinridge kept 8,000 men on the east side of the river, in order to prevent the Federals from renewing the attack, and this weakened the Confederates who were engaged on the left and centre. Bragg finally ordered Breckinridge to bolster the Confederate left, whose offensive was now waning. Moving up, Polk sent Breckinridge's men in piecemeal, each assault being repulsed by the Federals with heavy loss. Nightfall stopped the fighting, with the Federals in a semicircular position, their back to the river. On 1 January both armies held their position without fighting. On 2 January Rosecrans sent a detachment from General Thomas Crittenden's corps east of the river. Breckinridge was also sent over and late in the afternoon the Confederates attacked the Federal bridgehead, but were repulsed with 1,700 casualties. Rosecrans held the position on 3 January and Bragg decided to withdraw towards Tullahoma, 36 miles S. Federal losses were 12,906, Confederates 11,739.

The Federals occupied Murfreesboro but went no farther. The battle was a tactical victory for the North.

SUDLEY SPRINGS (Virginia)   American Civil War   29 August 1862

Fought between the Federals under General John Pope and the Confederates under General Thomas (Stonewall) Jackson.

Aim: After a forced march the Confederates, under Jackson, sought to surprise the Federals.

Battle: While awaiting the arrival of Generals Robert E. Lee and James Longstreet, Jackson took up a strong position in the rear of the Federal army. Pope's repeated

assaults on the Confederates were repulsed with a loss of more than 5,000 men.
Result: The Confederates under Jackson remained where they were and the Federals were attacked on the flank by Longstreet the following day (BULL RUN II).

TAYLOR'S BRIDGE   see NORTH ANNA RIVER

TREVILIAN STATION (Virginia)   American Civil War   11-12 June 1864
Fought between the Federals under General Philip Sheridan and General George Custer and the Confederates under General Wade Hampton.

When Grant launched his offensive against Petersburg (qv) he sent Generals Sheridan and David Hunter raiding west, ordering them to unite and push SE to meet the main Federal army. Lee retaliated by sending Hampton with two cavalry divisions after Sheridan and transferring General Jubal Early's corps to the Shenandoah valley to check Hunter.

Sheridan rode to 60 miles NW of Louisa Court House, and Hampton with his own and General Fitzhugh Lee's divisions pursued to Trevilian Station. The Confederates prepared to move farther north towards Sheridan when, on 11 June, Custer's brigade came between the two Confederate divisions. In a confused action Custer was checked and Hampton then dismounted and entrenched to withstand Sheridan's expected attack. On 12 June Sheridan assaulted the Confederate position, but was repulsed with a total loss in the two days of 735. Confederate casualties suffered were 612 by Hampton, and about half that by Lee.

Sheridan turned back to rejoin Grant on 28 June.

TUPELO (Mississippi)   American Civil War   14-15 July 1864
Fought between the Federals under General Andrew Smith and the Confederates under General Stephen Lee.
Strength: Federals 11,000 infantry + 3,000 cavalry + 20 guns; Confederates 6,600.
Aim: After the Federal defeat at Brice's Cross Roads (qv) the Federals decided to launch another expedition against the Confederate cavalry leader, General Nathan Forrest.
Battle: At Columbus, Mississippi, Lee assembled a Confederate force, which consisted chiefly of Forrest's troopers, to combat the Federal force. Smith reached Tupelo on 13 July and began deploying in a strong position. At 7 am the next morning Lee attacked the Federals, but this and other assaults were all repulsed by heavy and accurate Federal fire. That night Forrest sought to envelop Smith's rear, but was again repulsed. A further attack on 15 July was also beaten off, after which Smith began a cautious withdrawal to Memphis. Federal losses were 77 killed, 559 wounded and 38 missing. Confederate losses were 210 killed and 1,116 wounded - including Forrest himself.
Result: The Federal attack dealt the most severe blow to Forrest that had yet been achieved.

VICKSBURG (Mississippi)   American Civil War   24 June 1862-4 July 1863
Fought between the Federals under General Ulysses Grant and the Confederates
under General John Pemberton.
Strength: Federals 41,000 (rising to 71,000); Confederates 30,000 (Vicksburg
garrison only).
Aim: The Federals sought the surrender of the Confederate town of Vicksburg
which blocked Union control of the Mississippi River.
Battle: The city was invested in June 1862 by a fleet of 13 gunboats under Admiral
David Farragut and a land force of 4,000 under General Alpheus Williams. The
Federals bombarded the town with no success, and during this siege, the Confederate armour-plated river steamer the *Arkansas,* mounting 8 guns and commanded by Captain Jonas Brown, attacked the Federal ships, mounting 200 guns,
and ran the gauntlet successfully, losing 14 killed and wounded to Federal losses
of 82. The Federals re-embarked the land force and withdrew on 24 July.

On 9 January 1863 the Federals reinvested the city with two corps under
General John McClernand and a flotilla of gunboats under Admiral William Porter.
The garrison, under General Thomas Churchill, totalled 3,000. On 11 January the
Federals took the garrison of the fort, but the town defences held out and the
siege was not pressed. Grant moved south to take over personal command and the
army continued to probe the town defences, gaining little as Grant was waiting
for the end of the rains and for the rivers to subside. Porter also sent 2 gunboats,
the *Queen of the West* and the *Indianola*, to engage the Vicksburg batteries and
interrupt river traffic. In this they succeeded, but the *Queen of the West* was
eventually captured and the *Indianola* was destroyed. Land forces attempted to
capture the city four times during the first three months of 1863: by the Lake
Providence route; by a canal to bypass the city; by Steele's Bayou route and the
Yazoo route, all of which were unsuccessful. Grant then planned an envelopment
from the south and east and sought to divert the attention of the Confederates
by sending Colonel Benjamin Grierson with 1,200 cavalry on a raid. From La
Grange, Tennessee, Grierson moved south through Mississippi and N Louisiana to
Baton Rouge, while Grant moved the army down the west side of the Mississippi
to Hard Times, Louisiana, below Vicksburg. Protected by Porter's gunboats, Grant
sent 13 Corps of General John McClernand and 17 Corps of General James
McPherson across the river to Bruinsburg, encountering no Confederate opposition,
since Pemberton, who now commanded the forces at Vicksburg, had been distracted
by Grierson's raid and his only forces in the area were posted at Grand Gulf and
Port Gibson, both to the north of Bruinsburg. At Port Gibson, General John Bowen
tried to block the Federal advance, but on 1 May McClernand attacked. Supported
by McPherson, the Federal commander outnumbered the Confederates considerably and succeeded in turning Bowen's right (N) flank, forcing his withdrawal. Grand
Gulf was evacuated by the Confederates the following day.

Hearing that a Confederate army lay at Jackson, 45 miles east of Vicksburg,
Grant moved to interpose himself between the two towns and thus divide the
Confederate forces. He was joined by General William Sherman's 15 Corps on 7

May. The Federals moved three corps abreast, and at Raymond the right flank
brushed the Confederate brigade of General John Gregg. McClernand was left to
hold the Raymond-Clinton line against the advancing Confederate army under
Pemberton. McPherson and Sherman turned towards Jackson where General
Joseph Johnston, in nominal command of the Confederate forces in the west, had
the brigades of Gregg and General William Walker - 6,000 men. On 14 May Grant
attacked Jackson. Sherman advanced from the SW and overwhelmed Gregg, and
McPherson, from the west, routed Walker's men. The Federals entered Jackson at
4 pm while Johnston's army fled north. Sherman was left in Jackson to destroy
war supplies and Grant moved west with two corps on 15 May. Pemberton,
probing for a non-existent Federal line of communication, had been advancing on
Jackson and now stood on Grant's route to Vicksburg. On 16 May the two forces
met at Champion's Hill (Baker's Creek), 20 miles east of Vicksburg. McPherson
attacked fiercely on Pemberton's right (N) flank, but McClernand moved more
slowly on the left so as to negate the advantage of Grant's numerical superiority
(29,000-22,000).

Champion's Hill changed hands several times during a fierce battle. McClernand's
laxity forced Grant to take personal command of the Federal army which drove
the Confederates from the field. General William Loring was in charge of the
covering of the retreat, but his division was cut off from the main Confederate
army and was forced to escape SE. Confederate losses were 3,851, including 381
killed. Federal casualties were 2,441, with 410 killed. Sherman arrived after the
battle. Pemberton fell back towards Vicksburg, leaving a force of 5,000 to hold a
bridgehead east of the Big Black River which was outflanked by Sherman to the
north. On 17 May the main Federal army under Grant overwhelmed this rearguard
in one hour and captured 1,700 men and 18 guns. The Confederates did, however,
destroy the bridges, slowing pursuit. Grant now advanced to Vicksburg whence
Pemberton had withdrawn, although Johnston had ordered him to avoid being
trapped there.

On 19 May a Federal attack on the town was repulsed by the strong defences
which had been thrown up and, on the same day, Grant opened a line of communication up the Mississippi. On 22 May another, better-organised assault was made
on the city, but after a day's fighting, during which the Federals suffered 3,200
casualties, the garrison was still intact. Grant then laid siege to the town, completely investing it. He dug approaches, mined and countermined and built up his
army to 71,000, half of whom were to the north and east of the town as protection
against a relief army which was being organised by Johnston at Jackson. Sherman's
corps was to the north, McPherson's was to the east and McClernand's was to the
SE. (McClernand was relieved by General Edward Ord on 18 June.) Vicksburg's
9-mile line of defences was manned from north to south by divisions under Generals
Martin Smith, John Forney and Carter Stevenson. The reserves were made up of
General John Bowen's division. No further Federal assaults took place after 22
May, but bombardment was continual and this, coupled with the shortage of
rations and the growing incidence of disease, forced the Confederates to surrender

on 4 July, by which time half of Pemberton's men were dead, wounded or sick. Johnston, who had begun his relief march, heard of the surrender of Vicksburg at Big Black River. He returned to Jackson. Federal casualties totalled 9,362.
Result: Grant's success split the Confederacy in two. This action, coupled with that at Gettysburg (qv), ended all hopes of an ultimate Confederate victory.

WHITE OAK SWAMP   see SEVEN DAYS' BATTLES

WILDERNESS (Virginia)   American Civil War   5-6 May 1864
Fought between the Federals under General Ulysses Grant and the Confederates under General Robert E. Lee.
Strength: Federals 119,000 with 316 guns; Confederates 64,000 with 274 guns.

When Grant took command of all the Federal armies, he himself took the field with General George Meade's Army of the Potomac against the Confederate Army of N Virginia under Robert E. Lee, while General William Sherman advanced against the Army of Georgia under General Joseph Johnston.

On 4 May the Federals began crossing the Lower Rapidan River before dawn, aiming to turn Lee's right (E) flank. The Federals found themselves in terrain known as the Wilderness, aptly enough since it consisted of rough tangled woodland. Lee moved east to attack the Federals, sending 2 Corps under General Richard Ewell along the Orange-Fredericksburg Turnpike and 3 Corps under General Ambrose Hill along the Orange Plank Road, while General James Longstreet's 1 Corps closed in from the south. On 5 May Ewell met the Federal 5 Corps under General Gouverneur Warren, the Federals turning (westward) to meet the enemy. South of this encounter, Hill bumped into General George Getty's division of General John Sedgwick's 6 Corps. General Winfield Hancock's 2 Corps, by now the farthest into the Wilderness, counter-marched to come to Getty's aid. Late in the day a clash took place on this front, but the action was confused and neither side gained any advantage. On 6 May the Federals attacked early, but the right flank, made up of Sedgwick's and Warren's corps, was checked by Ewell, sustaining heavy losses. To the south, Hancock broke through Hill's corps, but the Federals ran into Longstreet's corps on the Orange Plank Road as they pursued the routed Confederates. Longstreet attacked Hancock, but did not succeed in breaking through. Fighting continued until 11 am when the whole front quietened down owing to exhaustion on the part of the combatants. During the lull, Longstreet dispatched four brigades under Generals William Mahone and Gilbert Sorrel to encircle the south flank of Hancock's position which was exposed. In this they succeeded, but when Longstreet sought to back it up by a renewed frontal assault, he was seriously wounded as a result of being accidentally fired upon by his own men. Although it had nearly broken, Hancock's line now held firm. Fighting had broken out again to the north, but by the end of the day the two sides had exhausted themselves without having gained any advantage. On 7 May both sides sought to improve their defensive positions, and that night Grant began to move his army towards New Spotsylvania Court House, which battle ended the confused action at Wilderness. Federal losses were 2,246 killed and 12,073 wounded, the balance of 17,666 casualties being listed as missing. These losses included two generals killed, two wounded and two captured. Confederate losses were estimated at 7,750 including 3 generals killed and 4 wounded.

The battle formed a prelude to Spotsylvania (qv).

WILLIAMSBURG (Virginia)   American Civil War   5 May 1862
Fought between the Federals under General George McClellan and the Confederates under General John Magruder.
Strength: Federals 40,700; Confederates 31,800.

The Federals pursued the Confederates as they retreated up the peninsula from Yorktown (qv) to Richmond.

The Federal 2 Corps under General Edwin Sumner found the Confederates holding a strong line 2 miles east of Williamsburg where Generals James Longstreet and Daniel Hill had deployed their men to delay the Union advance. The Federal divisions under Generals Joseph Hooker and Philip Kearny attacked the Confederate centre, which held firm. An attack by General Winfield Hancock late in the afternoon turned the Confederate left (NE) and, with his line of retreat endangered, Longstreet retreated farther up the peninsula during the night. Confederate casualties were 1,603. Federal losses were 2,239.

The Confederates had fought a successful delaying action, but McClellan continued to advance on Richmond.

WILSON'S CREEK (Missouri)   American Civil War   10 August 1861
Fought between the Federals under General Nathaniel Lyon and the Confederates under General Sterling Price and General Ben McCulloch.
Strength: Federals 5,400; Confederates 11,600.

The border state of Missouri was a target of much fighting at the beginning of the war. Nathaniel Lyon took charge of Federal military operations in the state, which was part of the Union, and took up a position at Springfield, in SW Missouri. The Confederates moved against him from Arkansas.

Lyon marched on the Confederate encampment at Wilson's Creek and launched a two-pronged attack on the position. An attack on Oak Hill, held by the Missouri State Guard under Sterling Price, was successful, the position being carried; but at the same time, the supporting attack east of the creek was routed as was the southern assault, an encircling manoeuvre led by General Franz Sigel. McCulloch now gathered his troops together for a counter-attack on Oak Hill. Three assaults on the position were beaten back, and during this action Lyon was killed. His successor, Major Samuel Sturgis, ordered a withdrawal to Rolla, NE of the position. Federal losses were 223 killed, 721 wounded and 291 missing. Confederate losses were 257 killed, 900 wounded and 27 missing.

The retreat enabled the Confederates to occupy Springfield and to press on north. They took the surrender of a Federal brigade at Lexington, moving east towards Belmont. Sturgis's decision to withdraw was the subject of controversy at the time.

WINCHESTER I (Virginia)   American Civil War   25 May 1862

Fought between the Federals under General Nathaniel Banks and the Confederates under General Thomas (Stonewall) Jackson.

Strength: Federals 8,500; Confederates 17,500.

At Strasburg Banks learnt that Fort Royal, on his east flank, had been attacked and he began to withdraw down the Shenandoah valley. Jackson pursued.

The Federals arrived at Winchester, but had no time to fortify the heights SW of the town before the Confederates arrived. The Confederates rested until dawn the day after their arrival and attacked on three sides, west, south and east, supported by heavy artillery fire. The assault caused the Federal lines to collapse and Banks retreated farther north, crossing the Potomac the following day. His losses were 2,000 men and Confederate casualties were about 350.

Jackson pursued until he heard of a Federal design to envelop his force, whereupon he retreated south, thus escaping the trap. The manoeuvre caused the Federals to suspend 40,000 of their troops' operations in the Peninsular Campaign, SE of Richmond.

WINCHESTER II (Virginia)   American Civil War   14 June 1863

Fought between the Federals under General Robert Milroy and the Confederates under General Richard Ewell.

When General Robert E. Lee moved towards the Shenandoah valley in preparation for his second invasion of the North, his van beat a Federal brigade at Berryville, thus endangering Milroy's position at Winchester. Milroy was ordered to withdraw, but it was too late. Ewell, closing in on Winchester on 14 June, moved round to the west, which made Milroy's position untenable. Milroy began retreating towards Harper's Ferry that night, but was cut off and attacked by the Confederates who had pursued. Milroy lost a third of his command, 4,443 men, of whom 3,358 were captured, as well as all guns and supplies. Confederate losses were only 269.

The Confederates now pressed on north towards the Shenandoah and Cumberland valleys, thence to the vital Battle of Gettysburg (qv).

WINCHESTER III (Virginia)   American Civil War   19 September 1864

Fought between the Federals under General Philip Sheridan and the Confederates under General Jubal Early.

Strength: Federals 40,000 (33,600 infantry + 6,400 cavalry); Confederates 11,400 (8,500 infantry + 2,900 cavalry).

Aim: In order to eliminate the Shenandoah valley as a supply route for the Confederates, Sheridan was given the task of flushing out the Confederates in the area.

Battle: In mid-September Sheridan attacked up the valley at Early's base in Winchester, Virginia. The Confederates came out to meet the Federals and, although they were at first successful, a charge by General George Custer broke their left wing and pushed them back into Winchester. By nightfall the Confederates had evacuated the town and were falling back through Strasburg to Fisher's Hill (qv). Federal losses were 697 killed, 3,983 wounded and 330 missing. Confederates losses were 276 killed, 1,827 wounded and 1,818 missing.

Result: The Federal objective was achieved, and Sheridan pursued the retreating Confederates to Fisher's Hill.

This action is also known as the Battle of Opequon Creek.

YELLOW TAVERN (Virginia)   American Civil War   11 May 1864
Fought between the Federals under General Philip Sheridan and the Confederates under General J. E. B. Stuart.
Strength: Federals 10,000; Confederates 4,500.
Aim: While Federal troops were moving from Wilderness to Spotsylvania (qv), General Ulysses Grant ordered Sheridan to raid against Richmond.
Battle: On 9 May Sheridan circled west and south of Lee's army while Stuart divided his force into two, one part under General James Gordon following Sheridan while the other part went east to block the Federals' road. On 11 May Sheridan attacked the blocking force at Yellow Tavern 6 miles north of Richmond, on the outskirts of the city's fortifications. The Confederates were driven off and Stuart was mortally wounded by a pistol-shot. Sheridan's rearguard routed the force under Gordon at the same time. Federal losses were 625.
Result: The raid achieved little except the death of Stuart.

Sheridan continued on his way, passing north of Richmond and turning south to the James River where he got supplies from General Benjamin Butler's army at Haxall's Landing. Going north three days later, Sheridan rejoined Grant's army along the North Anna River (qv).

YORKTOWN II (Virginia)   American Civil War   4 April-4 May 1862
Fought between the Federals under General George McClellan and the Confederates under General John Magruder.
Strength: Federals 60,000 with 103 siege guns; Confederates 13,000.
Aim: Put in charge of the Army of the Potomac, McClellan resolved to strike at the Confederate capital Richmond from the SE, up the peninsula between the York and James Rivers. Magruder sought to block the advance.
Battle: From Fort Monroe McClellan launched his offensive, but found his way blocked at Yorktown. Although the Federals had superior numbers, McClellan was deceived into conducting a regular siege of the town. An attack on 16 April was beaten off and siege batteries were erected. By this time, however, Confederate General Joseph Johnston had moved the main army from Culpeper to Richmond. McClellan had opened his heavy Parrott guns on Yorktown on 1 May, but Magruder withdrew towards Richmond on 3 May, covered by the cavalry of General J. E. B. Stuart, his mission accomplished.
Result: General Edwin Sumner's 2 Corps occupied Richmond on 4 May, but Magruder's objective had been achieved and Richmond was now safe.

SECTION SIX

NORTH AMERICA AND MEXICO

See Map Section, nos 12, 17 and 18

ACAPULCO (Mexico)   Mexican Liberal Rising (War of Reform)   9 August 1855
The troops of the Mexican government under General Antonio López de Santa
Anna were totally defeated by the Liberals under Benito Pablo Juárez, and General
Santa Anna was forced to flee the country.

ACULTZINGO (Mexico)   Franco-Mexican War   28 April 1862
Fought between the French under General le Comte de Lorencez and the Mexicans
under General Igancio Zaragoza.
Strength: French 7,500; Mexicans 10,000.
Aim: The French sought to drive the Mexicans from their position.
Battle: The Mexicans held the Cumbres Pass where the French attacked them,
forcing them to retire upon Puebla.
Result: The French objective was achieved.

ALAMO (Texas)   Texan War of Independence   23 February-6 March 1836
Fought between the Texan defenders of the fort and the Mexicans under General
Antonio López de Santa Anna.
Strength: Texans 188; Mexicans 3,000.
Aim: Americans settled in the Mexican state of Texas north of the Rio Grande
wanted independence from Mexico. In order to quell the unrest, Santa Anna
marched into the state with an army. At the Alamo, a Spanish Franciscan mission
converted into a fort, 188 American soldiers and frontiersmen took refuge.
Battle: They were besieged on 23 February. Several Mexican assaults were beaten
off by American sharpshooters who inflicted many casualties. On 6 March the fort
was stormed with no quarter given and everyone within was massacred except 30
women and children. Mexican losses in the final assault were 1,600.
Result: The Mexicans went on to fight seven more battles with American soldiers.
Texan independence was proclaimed in Washington on 2 March.

The Siege gave rise to the war-cry 'Remember the Alamo!'. Among the defenders
were American frontier heroes William B. Travis, Davy Crockett, James Bowie and
James Bonham.

AROOSTOOK 'WAR' (Maine)   12 February-May 1838
In this conflict between the Canadians of New Brunswick and the Americans of
Maine there was no bloodshed. Violations of lumbering territory in the USA
threatened to bring war. At the insistence of Maine congressmen, the Federal
Government voted a force of 50,000 men and $10 million in the event of war. But
General Winfield Scott was sent to prevent a clash and settled the dispute diplo-
matically. The border disputes were finally resolved by the Webster-Ashburton
Treaty of 1842 which agreed to the findings of an Anglo-American boundary
commission.

ASH HOLLOW (Mississippi)   Sioux Wars   3 September 1855
Fought between the Sioux Indians under Little Thunder and the Americans under

General W. S. Harney.
Strength: Indians 200; Americans 1,200.
Aim: West of the Mississippi River, Sioux and Cheyenne Indians attacked emigrants to California. When 18 men under Lieutenant Grattan were killed near Fort Laramie, a punitive expedition was sent out.
Battle: Harney encountered the Brule Sioux at Ash Hollow, west of Fort Kearny and, attacking the Indians, virtually destroyed the force, killing 136 braves.
Result: The American objective was achieved.

BAD AXE (Wisconsin)   Black Hawk War   2 August 1832
Fought between the Sauk and Fox Indians under Black Hawk and the Americans under Colonel Zachary Taylor.
Strength: Indians 500 braves; Americans 400 regulars + 900 militia.
Aim: The Sauk and Fox tribes sought to regain their lands on the east of the Mississippi. Throughout the summer of 1832 they terrorised the area of W Illinois and Wisconsin without inflicting much damage. The Americans sought to crush the uprising.
Battle: In SW Wisconsin, at the mouth of the Bad Axe River, the Americans trapped the Indians against the Mississippi and beat them decisively.
Result: The war was ended and the Sauk and Fox tribes were resettled in W Iowa.

BATOCHE (S central Saskatchewan)   Canadian Rebellion   12 May 1885
Fought between the Canadians under General Frederick Dobson Middleton and the Métis rebels under Louis Riel and Gabriel Dumont.
Strength: Canadian militia 750; Métis 300.
    Following the incorporation of Northwest Territories into the Dominion of Canada, Riel organised a rebellion of Métis (French half-breeds). In September 1870 the force had captured Fort Garry (Winnipeg) but had disbanded on the approach of a force led by a British officer, Colonel Garnet Wolseley. Riel staged a second revolt in Manitoba and Saskatchewan in 1885.
    Middleton gradually drove the rebels west until on 9 May they reached Batoche, where they made a stand. Batoche fell on 12 May with a loss of 224 Métis. The Canadians suffered 54 casualties. On 15 May Riel was captured by a scout and, after being convicted of treason, was hanged on 16 November, despite the fact that his counsel had rested the defence mainly on the plea of insanity.

BEAR PAW MOUNTAINS (Oregon)   Nez Percé War   30 September 1877
Fought between the Americans under General Nelson Miles and the Nez Percé Indians under Chief Joseph.
Strength: Americans 2,000; Indians 300.
    The Americans attempted to move the Nez Percé from their reservation in NE Oregon, whereupon Joseph took his tribe into the mountains of N Idaho. General Oliver Howard sent troops to round up the Indians, who embarked on a long delaying action under their chief. On 17 June 40 casualties were inflicted on a

100-man force led by Captain David Perry at White Bird Canyon, and on 11 and 12 July an attack by Howard on the Clearwater River was beaten back. The Indians crossed the Bitter Root Mountains into E Montana, and on 9 August Colonel John Gibbon surprised them at Big Hole River, at a cost to his force of 31 killed and 28 wounded. Gibbon's force killed 89, but the Indians escaped again. Joseph moved south into Wyoming, but suddenly swung north again into Montana, his objective being the Canadian border. On 13 September he repulsed an attack at Canyon Creek led by Colonel Samuel Sturgis. A force from Fort Keogh in Wyoming now took the field against the Indians.

General Miles marched to intercept the Indians, reaching them on 30 September, 30 miles from the Canadian border. Surrounded, Joseph held out for five days before surrendering to General Howard. He had lost a total of 239 men, women and children. American losses were 266.

The capitulation of the Nez Percé ended the war.

BEECHER ISLAND (Colorado)   Cheyenne and Arapahoe War   17 September 1868
Fought between the Americans under Colonel George Forsyth and the Indians under Roman Nose.
Strength: Americans 50; Indians 750 (Cheyenne, Arapahoe and Sioux).
Aim: During the fighting between the Plains Indians and the Americans Forsyth marched from Fort Wallace, Kansas, with a hand-picked force into Colorado with the aim of crushing the Indian uprising.
Battle: On the night of 16 September the Americans camped at the Arickaree Fork of the Republican River where, at dawn the following morning, they were attacked by Indians. The frontiersmen withdrew to a small island in the dry river-bed (later named Beecher Island after Lieutenant Frederick Beecher who was killed during the fight). The Indians attacked in waves, backed by steady fire, but the marksmanship of the Americans caused each attack to be repulsed. The use of repeating rifles also increased their fire-power. Roman Nose was killed, the fight ending at nightfall after Forsyth had sustained casualties of 7 killed and 17 wounded.
Result: The Indians laid siege to the island, but Forsyth sent 2 men back to Fort Wallace and the siege was relieved nine days later. By this time the survivors were nearly dead from starvation and exposure.

BUENA VISTA (Mexico)   US-Mexican War   22-3 February 1847
Fought between the Americans under General Zachary Taylor and the Mexicans under General Antonio López de Santa Anna.
Strength: Americans 4,500; Mexicans 22,000.
Aim: An amphibious expedition was launched against Veracruz early in 1847, for which Zachary Taylor had some of his troops taken from him. Taylor was ordered to remain on the defensive along the Monterrey-Saltillo line, but he took the offensive, marching SW beyond Saltillo in February. Santa Anna mustered his men at

San Luis Potosí and marched north towards the Americans.
Battle: Leaving his rearguard at Saltillo, Taylor took up a defensive position commanding the Angostura Pass. Santa Anna, on arrival, demanded the Americans' surrender. This Taylor refused. Santa Anna sent a brigade of cavalry to the NE to cut off Taylor's line of communication and, on the first day, he drove in American outposts. On 23 February the Mexicans launched a complicated and disjointed attack on the Americans with their main body. They captured 2 guns during their initial success, but when American volunteer infantry fell back, the US regular artillery put up a stubborn defence over open sights. The Mexican infantry almost reached the American guns before breaking under the fire. An attack on the American left flank was checked by Mississippi volunteers under Colonel Jefferson Davis. The Americans then counter-attacked and drove the Mexicans from the field. The cavalry sent to cut off the American communications collapsed after a short encounter with the American rearguard at Saltillo. Mexican losses were 500 dead and 1,000 wounded. American losses were 267 killed, 456 wounded and 23 missing.
Result: The battle ended the war in N Mexico, and operations now shifted to the east coast of the country. Taylor was relieved from command at his own request in November of that year and Santa Anna retired to Mexico City, where he became President.

CALPULALPAM (Mexico)   Mexican Liberal Rising (War of Reform)
20 December 1860
The Liberals under Benito Pablo Juárez defeated the government forces, opening the way to Mexico City, and forcing the demise of Miguel Miramón's administration. Juárez assumed executive powers in 1860 and became President in 1861.

CARRIZAL (Mexico)   US Expedition against Villa   21 June 1916
The Mexican guerillas under the leadership of General Francisco (Pancho) Villa raided Columbus, New Mexico, and General John Pershing was sent south with a provisional cavalry division to capture him. Although Villa was also fighting the Mexican government of Venustiano Carranza, many Mexicans regarded the US force not as a punitive expedition but as an invading army which was interfering in internal politics. Local hostility hampered Pershing's advance. At Carrizal, 85 miles south of Ciudad Juárez, a force of Mexican regulars barred the way but was routed after a short skirmish. Pershing went on to advance 400 miles into Mexico, and Villa's forces temporarily dispersed into smaller bands in true guerilla fashion.
   Pershing's force was withdrawn on 5 February 1917 at the insistence of the Mexican President, having achieved very little from a military point of view but increased anti-American feeling in Mexico.

CERRO GORDO (Mexico)   US-Mexican War   17-18 April 1847
Fought between the Americans under General Winfield Scott and the Mexicans under General Antonio López de Santa Anna.

Strength: Americans 8,500; Mexicans 12,000.

Aim: The Mexicans held the fortified defile at Cerro Gordo. The Americans sought to break through the Mexican defences.

Battle: The American column halted while engineers (including Captains Robert E. Lee, George McClellan, Lieutenants Joseph Johnston and Pierre Beauregard) reconnoitred the Mexican position, the flanks of which seemed to be impregnable. A mountain trail outflanking the Mexicans was found and the main American army began to deploy so as to envelop both flanks of the Mexican force. A premature assault on the Mexican left by General David Twiggs opened the battle on 17 April. On 18 April the main attack was launched and, after severe hand-to-hand fighting, the Mexicans were defeated, the Americans taking the pass. The Mexicans fell back having lost 1,000 killed and wounded, 204 officers and 2,837 men, 43 guns and 4,000 small arms captured. American losses were 63 killed and 337 wounded.

Result: Winfield Scott pressed on to occupy Jalapa and Puebla, where he was joined by reinforcements under General Franklin Pierce which enabled him to continue his march on Mexico City, 65 miles away.

CHAPULTEPEC (Mexico)   US-Mexican War   13 September 1847

Fought between the Americans under General Winfield Scott and the Mexicans under General Antonio López de Santa Anna.

Strength: Americans 7,200; Mexicans 15,000.

Aim: The capture of Mexico City.

Battle: The hill of Chapultepec was the last obstacle between the Americans and Mexico City. Santa Anna had deployed 1,000 men on it, with 4,000 men manning the secondary defences. Bombardment was opened on 12 September and continued until 8 am the following day, when the divisions of Generals John Quitman and Gideon Pillow launched an assault on the hill. Under heavy fire, Pillow's men scaled the hill using ladders and pickaxes and by 9.30 am they had cleared the summit, despite stiff resistance from Los Ninos, the cadets of the Mexican military academy who defended the academy itself. The capture of Chapultepec enabled the Americans to attack the *garitas,* police-customs stations at the edge of the city, two of which had fallen to Worth's and Quitman's divisions by evening. American losses were 130 killed, 703 wounded and 29 missing. Mexican losses were estimated at 1,800.

Result: The capture of Chapultepec opened the way to the capture of Mexico City. American troops cut their way into the city through the walls with picks and crowbars, preparing for a final assault, but the following day Santa Anna surrendered, having withdrawn the army under cover of darkness. The Americans immediately occupied Mexico City. This action finished the US-Mexican War. A peace was signed whereby Mexico ceded New Mexico and California to the US in exchange for a cash payment.

CHIHUAHUA (Mexico)   US-Mexican War   1 March 1847

Fought between the Americans under Colonel Alexander Doniphan and the

Mexicans.

Aim: Colonel Stephen Kearny, in command of the US Army of the West, decided to send an expedition into Mexico from Santa Fé. Accordingly, Doniphan left with the 1st Regiment of Missouri Mounted Volunteers and marched south.

Battle: Encountering feeble opposition, Doniphan reached El Paso on 27 December, having left Santa Fé on 23 September, and, crossing the Rio Grande, continued south. Resistance here was slight as well, and on 1 March Doniphan entered Chihuahua, having fought an engagement at Sacramento River the previous day where he had beaten a much larger Mexican force. From Chihuahua, he marched SE to Saltillo, thence back to the Rio Grande and American transports. In a 3,500-mile march he had lost 7 killed and wounded, having inflicted on the Mexicans a loss of 600, half of whom were killed.

Result: The punitive expedition was entirely successful from a military point of view.

CINCO DE MAYO, LA   see PUEBLA II

COLUMBUS (New Mexico)   Raid by Villa   8-9 March 1916
Fought between the Mexicans under Francisco (Pancho) Villa and the Americans.
Strength: Mexicans 500+; Americans 350.

After 1914 Mexico was largely in a state of anarchy. Several revolutionary leaders set up their own governments, and in the north Pancho Villa was dictator.

On the night of 8 March Villa took 500 men across the border to Columbus. The Mexicans burnt part of the town before being beaten off by men of the 13th US Cavalry on 9 March. 190 Mexicans were killed or wounded. American losses were 7 soldiers and 8 civilians killed, 5 soldiers and 2 civilians wounded.

Subsequently a punitive expedition was sent into Mexico in pursuit of Villa (CARRIZAL).

CONTRERAS-CHURUBUSCO (Mexico)   US-Mexican War   19-20 August 1847
Fought between the Americans under General Winfield Scott and the Mexicans under General Antonio López de Santa Anna.
Strength: Americans 10,000; Mexicans 20,000.

Aim: The Mexicans sought to block the American advance on their capital, Mexico City.

Battle: Scott left Puebla for Mexico City, having been reinforced by General Franklin Pierce's troops. In the valley of Mexico Santa Anna had concentrated his troops in two villages, Contreras and Churubusco, which guarded the southern approaches to Mexico City. On 19 August a detachment of 3,300 men under General Gideon Pillow attacked Contreras which was held by General Gabriel Valencia with 5,000 men. The attack was repulsed, but on the following day the Americans, led chiefly by General Persifor Smith, made another attack which routed the Mexicans with a loss of 700 killed and 800 captured. The Americans recaptured 2 guns taken by the Mexicans at Buena Vista (qv).

Pressing on to the next village, Churubusco, where the Mexicans had converted a church and convent into a fortress, the Americans stormed and took the position after a hard fight which cost them 133 killed and 900 wounded with 40 missing after both battles. This total meant a loss to the Americans of one-seventh of their effectives. Mexican losses were greater, totalling one-third of their fighting force: 4,297 killed and wounded, 2,637 prisoners and 3,000 missing.
Result: Santa Anna retired into Mexico City, 5 miles away, and requested an armistice. Fighting resumed on 7 September when negotiations broke down.

EL CANEY (Cuba)   Spanish-American War   1 July 1898
Fought between the Americans under General William Shafter and the Spanish under General Joaquín Vara del Rey.
Strength: Americans 12,000; Spanish 520.
Aim: A twin offensive aimed at Santiago de Cuba (qv) was prepared by the Americans, the main effort to be against San Juan Hill (qv), launched by 5 Corps, with a secondary attack against El Caney which would precede the main assault.
Battle: El Caney was NE of San Juan Hill and the overall commander sent General Henry Lawton's division to take the village early on 1 July. The Spanish defenders fought hard against the charges of the Americans but were finally driven back towards Santiago late in the day, having suffered 235 killed (including del Rey) and wounded, with 120 captured. American losses were 81 killed and 360 wounded.
Result: Lawton had planned to rejoin the main assault, but the attack on El Caney had taken much longer than anticipated and he was unable to do so.

FENIAN UPRISING (Canada)   1866
A number of American-Irish who had learnt the business of fighting during the American Civil War decided to attempt to overthrow British rule in Canada in 1866. They were members of the Irish Revolutionary Brotherhood, formed early in the nineteenth century, whose object originally was to overthrow British government in Ireland, and establish a government there. Later they named themselves the Fenians after the legendary warrior bands (Fianna) of early Irish history.

About 400 Fenians marched over the border into Canada where, having been tipped off, the authorities quickly rounded them up. Although disowned by the USA, they were pushed back over the border, as Canada wished to avoid the embarrassment of having to imprison them.

FISH CREEK (Saskatchewan)   Canadian Rebellion   24 April 1885
Fought between the Canadians under General Frederick Middleton and the Métis rebels under Louis Riel.
Strength: Canadians 400; Métis 280.

The rebels, under Louis Riel, held a strong position near Fish Creek from whence the Canadians tried to drive them. Having lost 50 men, Middleton withdrew. Rebel losses were 29 killed and wounded.

FORT PHIL KEARNY (Nebraska)   Sioux, or Red Cloud War   2 August 1867
Fought between the Americans under Captain James Powell and the Sioux and Cheyenne Indians under Red Cloud whose Indian name was Mahkpiya-Luta.
Strength: Americans 32 (soldiers and workmen); Indians 1,500 (Sioux and Cheyenne).

Because of aggression by Indians, Fort Phil Kearny (nicknamed Fort Perilous) was built on the Bozeman Trail (which ran from South Platte near Julesburg, via the Yellowstone River to the goldfields at Virginia City) to protect emigrants.

Captain William Fetterman and 80 men were killed on 21 December 1866 while constructing the fort. Again, on 2 August 1867 a party of the garrison under Captain Powell which was cutting wood was surrounded by Indians. Powell beat off six successive attacks before relief arrived from the fort. Indian losses were 180, American losses 7. The success of the defence was largely due to the use of breech-loading rifles and the marksmanship of the 18th Infantry Regiment. The following year, by the Treaty of Fort Laramie, the US government ordered the evacuation of Fort Kearny, which was then destroyed by Indians. The Bozeman Trail was also abandoned, but was reopened in 1877, after the suppression of the Sioux, for cattle moving north from Texas to Wyoming.

The action by Powell is also known as the Wagon Box Fight.

FORT TEXAS (Texas)   US-Mexican War   3-9 May 1846
Fought between the Mexicans under General Mariano Arista and the Americans under Major Jacob Brown.
Aim: The state of Texas was admitted into the United States in 1845 and, when both Mexico and America claimed a 150-mile strip of territory between the Nueces River and the Rio Grande, the strained situation was aggravated. General Zachary Taylor was sent into the area to build Fort Texas on the Rio Grande opposite the Mexican position at Matamoros on the right bank. Following a cavalry clash on the north bank of the river, Arista crossed the Rio Grande in strength and besieged Fort Texas, in an attempt to capture it.
Battle: The garrison put up strong resistance and Zachary Taylor marched his main army to the relief of the fort. This he succeeded in doing on 9 May, forcing Arista back across the river to Matamoros.
Result: The Mexican objective of the capture of the Fort was not achieved.

The fort was renamed Brown in honour of its defender.

INDIAN WARS I   1850-65
There were at least thirty separate conflicts during this period. In the ten years before the American Civil War, 90 per cent of the 16,000-17,000 troops of the US army were in the million square miles area west of the Mississippi patrolling or fighting. Small detachments of the army were also in Florida fighting the Seminoles. Other tribes involved in these operations were Apaches, Sioux, Cheyennes, Navajos, Mojaves, Arapahoes, Kiowas and Comanches, as well as various tribes of the NW Pacific area. Thirty-seven combat operations were under-

taken in 1857 alone, as well as many others that did not involve fighting. The Civil War drew attention away from the west where, however, hostilities continued. Atrocities were as yet rare, particularly on the American side, the worst being the Sand Creek (qv) massacre which helped to inflame the Plains Indians over the next two decades.

INDIAN WARS II   1865-98
As the United States expanded west, there were continual clashes with Indians. It is estimated that 943 actions were fought in twelve campaigns, the warfare being mainly of a guerilla type, fast moving and fought against the Plains Indians - Sioux, Cheyennes and Comanches - who, though incapable of fighting in close order, were respectable light cavalry. The Apache tended to fight on foot, using his horse as transport - like a dragoon! The main campaigns were:
1865-8: S Oregon, Idaho, N California and Nevada.
1867-75: Kansas, Wyoming (Fort Phil Kearny [qv]), Colorado, Texas, New Mexico and Indian Territory.
1872-3: The Modoc Rebellion.
1873: Apaches in Arizona.
1876-7: N Cheyennes and Sioux (Little Big Horn [qv]).
1877: Nez Percé.
1878: Bannock War.
1878-9: N Cheyennes.
1879: Sheep-eaters, Piutes and Bannocks.
1885-6: Apaches in Arizona and New Mexico under Geronimo and Naishe, against General George Crook and General Nelson Miles.
1890-1: Sioux in S Dakota.
   Miles and Crook were probably the best, most sympathetic and most constructive of the counter-insurgent commanders who undertook the taming of the Indian tribes who naturally were opposed to becoming engulfed by Western civilisation.

KANSAS, CIVIL WAR   21 May-15 September 1856
Fought between the Free Staters under John Brown and the pro-slavery faction.
   Lawrence was   sacked on 21 May by a pro-slavery mob, following which Brown, a fanatical abolitionist, raided Potawotomi on 24-5 May. Free Staters took Franklin on 13 August and Brown was driven out of Osawatomie by pro-slavery guerillas who sacked the settlement on 30 August. Twenty people were killed and $2 million of damage was caused before Federal troops arrived in the state to take control on 16 September, restoring temporary calm.

KILLDEER MOUNTAIN (N Dakota)   Sioux Wars   28 July 1864
Fought between the Americans under General Alfred Sully and the Sioux Indians.
Strength: Americans 2,200; Indians 5,000.
Aim: During the Civil War Sully had responsibility for the protection of settlers and emigrants west of the Missouri River in the Dakotas. He sought to disperse an

Indian concentration on the Knife River, a west tributary of the Missouri.
Battle: Sully came upon the Indians on Killdeer Mountain (Tahkahokuty) in the Badlands and, using cavalry charges and artillery to good effect, drove them off the heights with a loss of 100. American losses were 15 killed and wounded.
Result: The American objective was achieved.

LAS GUASIMAS (Cuba)   Spanish-American War   24 June 1898
Fought between the Spanish under General Arsenio Linares and the Americans under General Joseph Wheeler, with some Cuban support.
Strength: Spanish 1,500; Americans 1,000 + Cubans 800.

When the US and Spain declared war, the US assembled troops in Tampa, Florida, whence they embarked for Cuba. The US 5 Corps arrived off Santiago de Cuba (qv) on 20 June, and on 22 June they began disembarking at Daiquiri, 14 miles east of Santiago, and at Siboney, farther west.

The Spanish offered little resistance on the beaches but chose instead to defend Las Guasimas, a gap through the hills leading to Santiago. The senior commander ashore, General Wheeler, led an attack west along a ridge 250 feet high. Cuban support under General Calixto García was slight. In a fierce fight, the Spanish were driven back with a loss of 10 killed and 25 wounded. American losses were 16 killed and 52 wounded.

General William Shafter held up the advance in order to prepare a major offensive against Santiago.

LAVA BEDS (California)   Modoc Rebellion   14 April-1 June 1873
Fought between the Modocs under their chief, Kintpuash (Captain Jack), and the Americans under General Jefferson Davis.
Strength: Modocs 75 warriors; Americans 1,000+.

The Indians of the Great Plains continued to fight the white men, and the Modocs in the far west also took the warpath in an effort to avoid being moved on to a reservation. Having gone on a rampage of murdering and pillaging, the Modocs retired to the natural defences of the Lava Beds near Tule Lake in N California. The warriors, accompanied by 150 women and children, held the so-called Modoc Line here.

In January 1873 General Edward Canby sent 400 men, including elements of the 1st Cavalry and 21st Infantry Regiments, to dislodge the Indians. The Americans attacked in two columns, but were repulsed with the loss of 16 men killed and 53 wounded. Canby withdrew and built his force up to 1,000 men. During peace talks on 11 April Canby and a preacher, Eleazer Thomas, were killed by the Indians.

Jefferson Davis, with a fresh force under Colonel A. C. Gillem, fought his way into the Lava Beds three days later under cover of mortar fire. After six weeks of fierce fighting, the Modocs were finally overpowered. The Americans lost 82 men. Captain Jack and three others were captured, tried and executed, thanks to the evidence of Hooker Jim, a Modoc who turned state's evidence.

Surviving Modocs were moved east to Indian Territory, now Oklahoma.

LITTLE BIG HORN (Montana)   Sioux Wars   26-7 June 1876
Fought between the Americans under Major Marcus Reno, Captain Frederick
Benteen and Colonel George Custer and the Indians under Sitting Bull, Crazy
Horse and Gall.
Strength: Americans 600; Indians 3,000-3,500 (Sioux and Cheyenne).

Americans continued to march into Sioux country after their check at Rosebud
River (qv), General Alfred Terry and Colonel John Gibbon planning to link up at
Little Big Horn River.

Custer was detached with 600 men from Terry's force to reconnoitre the area
and reached the river on 25 June. Here he divided his force into three, unaware
that an Indian village stood just across the river. Reno took three troops of cavalry
up-stream to attack from the south, with Benteen on his left, also with three
troops. Custer took five troops down-stream, leaving one troop to guard the train.
On the west of Little Big Horn Reno met a superior force of Indians and was
driven back across the river, where he took up a defensive position on high bluffs
which he held with Benteen, who joined him during the day. They maintained
their ground on 26 June also, at a cost of 53 killed and 52 wounded. Custer,
meanwhile, was assaulted from north and south when opposite the rear and flank
of the village. In one hour Custer and all his men (211) were killed in what is known
as 'Custer's last stand'. On 27 June Terry and Gibbon arrived to relieve Reno and
Benteen.

The defeat was the worst suffered by the Americans throughout their warfare
with the Indians. Seven of Custer's men were British citizens.

MANILA II (Philippine Islands)   Spanish-American War   1 May-14 August 1898
Fought between the Americans under General Wesley Merritt with the Filipino
guerillas under General Emilio Aguinaldo y Famy, and the Spanish under General
Fermin Jaudenes.
Strength: Americans 10,700 + Filipinos 10,000; Spanish 13,000.

After the destruction of the Spanish fleet in Manila Bay (qv) the Americans
awaited reinforcements and blockaded Manila with a fleet under Commodore
George Dewey.

Merritt had deployed his men south of Manila by 25 July and Filipino guerillas
under Aguinaldo were ready to aid the Americans, having proclaimed their
independence on 1 July. Aguinaldo had been sent into the Philippines by Dewey
before hostilities broke out in order to stir up trouble against the Spanish. A
demand for the Spanish to surrender made by Dewey and Merritt on 9 August was
refused, and on 13 August the city was assaulted and taken, little resistance being
met from the Spanish garrison. The Spanish capitulated the following day, after an
almost bloodless battle.

Spain and America had signed an armistice two days before the action and the
Americans continued to occupy Manila. This enraged the Filipino guerillas who

had been frustrated in their ambition to take Manila and had failed in their aim of securing their immediate independence as promised them by Dewey. An insurrection against the Americans was therefore launched led by Aguinaldo y Famy. This was to keep up to 50,000 American soldiers busy for the next few years.

MANILA BAY (Philippine Islands)   Spanish-American War   1 May 1898
Fought between the Americans under Commodore George Dewey and the Spanish under Admiral Patricio Montojo.
Strength: Americans 4 modern cruisers + 2 gunboats; Spanish 4 old cruisers + 3 gunboats + 3 auxiliaries.
Aim: The Americans sought the destruction of the Spanish fleet as a prelude to landing in the Philippines.
Battle: At dawn on 1 May Dewey steamed directly at the Spanish fleet anchored off Cavite Point, 7 miles from Manila. In a battle lasting seven hours every Spanish vessel was crippled or destroyed with a loss of 381 Spaniards. The Americans suffered only 8 casualties, all wounded.
Result: With no land force to support him, Dewey blockaded Manila and awaited reinforcements.

MASSACRE HILL (Wyoming)   Sioux Wars   21 December 1866
Fought between the Sioux Indians under Crazy Horse and Red Cloud, and the Americans under Captain William Fetterman.
Strength: Indians 2,000; Americans 82.

Fort Phil Kearny (qv) was constructed along the Upper Powder River in order to protect the Bozeman Trail leading from Wyoming into Montana Territory. Nicknamed Fort Perilous, it was garrisoned by the 18th Infantry Regiment of Colonel Henry Carrington.

On 21 December a wood train of wagons was attacked by Sioux about 5 miles from the fort. Fetterman led a counter-attack with 2 other officers and 79 men. He underestimated the Indians' strength, however, and the men were surrounded beyond Lodge Trail Ridge on what is now known as Massacre Hill. The troops fought fiercely, but every one of them was killed. About 60 Indians were killed.

The fort was then besieged by the Sioux, but a frontiersman, John (Portugee) Philips got through the Indian lines and rode to Fort Laramie, 263 miles away, to bring reinforcements which broke the siege.

MEXICO CIVIL WAR   April-July 1920
The followers of President Venustiano Carranza were defeated by those of Generals Alvaro Obregón, Adolfo de la Huerta and Plutarco Elías Calles.

On 21 May, Carranza was overthrown and killed while Francisco (Pancho) Villa, the bandit-revolutionary who had raided into the United States, surrendered to the victorious generals on 27 July. Obregón was elected President on 5 September and the US recognised him on 31 August 1923.

Mexico now began to stabilise itself as a nation, Obregón remaining in office until 1924 when Calles succeeded him. In 1928 Obregón was again chosen to be President, but, on 17 July 1928, before he could assume office he was murdered.

MOLINO DEL REY   US-Mexican War   8 September 1847
Fought between the Mexicans and the Americans under General William Worth.
Strength: Mexicans 12,000; Americans 3,450.
Aim: Before attacking Mexico City itself and the hill which was its chief defence, General Winfield Scott decided to attack Molino del Rey as a diversion. The position was believed to hold a gun foundry.
Battle: Worth attacked the position, SW of Chapultepec (qv), and found the complex of buildings heavily guarded. After a fight lasting all day the Americans overran the position, having inflicted 2,700 casualties, of whom 700 were captured. American losses were high, being 117 killed, 653 wounded and 18 missing.
Result: American losses were so heavy that Worth withdrew south to the suburb of Tacubaya after gaining the position.
   Scott now prepared a full-scale offensive against the city.

MONTERREY (Mexico)   US-Mexican War   20-5 September 1846
Fought between the Americans under General Zachary Taylor and the Mexicans under General Pedro de Ampudia.
Strength: Americans 6,000; Mexicans 7,000 regulars + 3,000 militia.
Aim: After crossing the Rio Grande into Mexico, Taylor marched on Monterrey. His objective was to capture the city.
Battle: On 20 September General William Worth was detached with a force to make an assault from the west. On 21 September Worth captured the key position of Federation Hill and on 22 September he took Independence Hill. On 21 September Taylor entered the city after hard fighting and drove the garrison into the citadel (Black Fort). Ampudia was now blockaded on all sides and three days later he capitulated. The garrison marched out with the honours of war, having lost 367 casualties. American losses were 488 men, including 120 killed.
Result: Taylor granted the Mexicans an armistice, of which the US President disapproved. Informing the Mexicans of this, Taylor began once more to advance into Mexico.

PALO ALTO (Texas)   US-Mexican War   8 May 1846
Fought between the Americans under General Zachary Taylor and the Mexicans under General Mariano Arista.
Strength: Americans 2,300; Mexicans 6,000.
Aim: Taylor sought to relieve Fort Texas which was besieged by the Mexicans.
Battle: At Palo Alto, 10 miles NE of Point Isabel, Taylor's relieving force was met by Mexican troops, who attacked at 2 pm. Better American fire-power in rifles and artillery broke up the Mexican cavalry attack and prevented them from using their superior numbers to any advantage. After five hours' fighting Arista fell back, having suffered the loss of between 300 and 400 casualties. American losses

were 9 killed and 45 wounded.
Result: Taylor went on to relieve Fort Texas, later renamed Brownsville after its defender who died during the siege.

PLATTE BRIDGE (Wyoming)   Sioux Wars   25 July 1865
Fought between the Cheyenne, Sioux and Arapahoe Indians under Roman Nose, and the Americans under Lieutenant Casper Collins.
Strength: Indians 3,000; Americans 25 (cavalry).

   After the massacre of Indians at Sand Creek (qv) the tribes were provoked   into retaliation.

   During the summer of 1865 warriors converged on the Platte Bridge Station of the Oregon Trail. On 25 July the Indians ambushed a supply wagon train bound for the station. Collins rode out to protect the train, but as the party he brought with him crossed the bridge, they were surrounded by the Indians and 11 Americans were killed before they were able to cut their way out and get back to the fort. The battle lasted four hours. The wagon train guard was annihilated.

   Casper, Wyoming, founded on the spot where the battle took place, was named after Collins.

PUEBLA I (Mexico)   US-Mexican War   14 September-12 October 1847
Fought between the Americans under Colonel Thomas Childs and the Mexicans under General Joaquín Rea.
Strength: Americans 2,300 (mainly wounded and convalescents); Mexicans 8,000 (plus those under Rea).
Aim: The reduction of the garrison of Puebla held by the Americans.
Battle: While General Winfield Scott was taking control of Mexico City the Mexicans made a bid to cut the American line of communication to Veracruz (qv). Rea surrounded Puebla, where most of the garrison was made up of convalescents. The Commander, Colonel Childs, refused to surrender and the American position deteriorated when General Antonio López de Santa Anna, who had fled from Mexico City and renounced the presidency, arrived to join the besiegers with 8,000 more men. Santa Anna left Puebla on 1 October, however, an action which weakened the will of the troops he left behind. When an expedition from Veracruz headed by General Joseph Lane arrived at Puebla, Rea was forced to raise the siege.
Result: This was the last conflict of the war and on 2 February 1848 the Treaty of Guadelupe Hidalgo was signed.

PUEBLA II (Mexico)   Franco-Mexican War   5 May 1862
Fought between the French under General le Comte de Lorencez and the Mexicans under General Igancio Zaragoza.
Strength: French 7,500; Mexicans 1,200.
Aim: The Mexican government suspended the repayment of foreign debts at the start of the American Civil War and, as a result, French, Spanish and British troops occupied Veracruz in 1861. In 1862 the Spanish and British withdrew, but Napoleon

III sought to establish a Mexican government under French domination and sent an army inland.

Battle: On the route to Mexico City the French troops came to Puebla which they attacked, endeavouring to take the ridge of the Cerro de Guadalupe which commanded the town. They were repulsed by a Mexican contingent of 1,200 men under General Negreti. French losses were 456 killed and wounded. Mexican losses were 215.

Result: The French objective was not achieved.

The action is also known as the Battle of La Cinco de Mayo.

PUEBLA III (Mexico)   Franco-Mexican War   4 May 1863

Fought between the French under General Elie Forey and the Mexicans under General Jesus Gonzales Ortega.

Strength: French 25,000; Mexicans 20,000.

Aim: The French sought the reduction of the garrison of Puebla.

Battle: The French force was too small for a complete investment so Forey sought to gain a foothold in the town. On 29 March, the fort of San Xavier was stormed and carried, French losses being 230, Mexican losses 600. From this point, the French advanced into the town by capturing one house at a time; but resistance was so strong that little progress was made and by 7 April they had lost another 600 men with almost no ground gained. An attack on the convent of Santa Cruz was repulsed with a loss of 480. On 4 May a Mexican relieving force under General Ignacio Comonfort was ambushed by a French detachment under General Achille Bazaine. Comonfort was killed and the French took 1,000 prisoners and 8 guns. Ortega then surrendered Puebla with 1,455 officers and 11,000 men.

Result: The French went on to Mexico City which they reached on 7 June. There the Archduke Maximilian of Austria was proclaimed Emperor.

QUERÉTARO (Mexico)   Franco-Mexican War   14 May 1867

Fought between the Mexicans under General Mariano Escobedo and the Franco-Mexican forces under Miguel Miramón.

France had control of Mexico through the puppet Emperor, Maximilian of Austria, and this forced the Mexican government of Benito Pablo Juárez to flee across the border to the United States. Escobedo here raised a new Mexican army with which he entered his country in 1865.

The Mexicans fought their way south opposed by Miramón, but in 1867 Napoleon III withdrew the French army from Mexico under pressure from the USA. Escobedo trapped Maximilian and Miramón in Querétaro, 160 miles NW of Mexico City. On 14 May the Mexicans stormed the town and took it, capturing Maximilian and Miramón, both of whom were executed.

On 19 December Juárez was elected President of Mexico.

ROSEBUD RIVER (Montana)   Sioux Wars   17 June 1876

Fought between the Americans under General George Crook and the Sioux and

Cheyenne Indians under Crazy Horse.
Strength: Americans 1,200; Indians 1,500.

The goldrush of 1874-5 angered the Sioux in the Dakota confederacy, the largest group of Plains Indians. Crook marched from Fort Laramie in an effort to put down the uprising.

In SE Montana the Americans met the Cheyennes and Sioux who held their ground and inflicted 34 casualties. Crook was forced to fall back for supplies while the Indians escaped.

Two more forces now took the field against the Indians.

SAINT-CHARLES (Quebec)   French-Canadian Rising   23 October-25 November 1837
Fought between the Loyalists under Lt-Colonel Charles Wetherall and the Canadian rebels under Thomas Storrow Brown.

On 23 October 1837 delegates of the *patriotes* of six counties held a mass meeting in which they passed a declaration of independence based on that of the US. Led by Louis Joseph Papineau, Dr Wolfred Nelson and their military commander, Thomas Storrow Brown, the *patriotes* came out in revolt but were decisively defeated by a Canadian Loyalist force under Lt-Colonel Charles Wetherall on 25 November 1837.

SAINT-DENIS (Quebec)   French-Canadian Rising 1837
The Canadian rebels under Dr Wolfred Nelson beat the British and Canadian loyalists under Colonel Charles Gore, but dispersed when other *patriotes* were defeated at Saint-Charles (qv) on 25 November. The British troops promptly sacked the township of Saint-Denis on 1 December as a reprisal for the shooting of one of their officers who had been taken prisoner.

SAINT-EUSTACHE (Quebec)   French-Canadian Rising   14 December 1837
Fought between the rebels under Jean-Olivier Chénier and the government troops under the Lieutenant-Governor, Sir John Colborne. The rebels took refuge in a stone church which was shelled and set alight. The *patriotes* were defeated and the rebellion was finally quelled by this action.

SALT RIVER (Arizona)   Apache Wars   26 December 1872
Fought between the Americans under General George Crook and the Apaches under Cochise and Geronimo.

Arizona Apaches went on the warpath and were pursued by Crook in a winter campaign. The Americans marched from Camp Date Creek through the Tonto Basin and, in a canyon along Salt River, a party of cavalry and infantry met the outlawed Indians. Both here and farther down the river at Turret Butte, the Apache forces were destroyed.

The Apaches returned to their reservations until 1885, when they went on the warpath again.

SAND CREEK (Colorado)   Cheyenne and Arapahoe War   29 November 1864
Fought between the Americans under Colonel John Chivington of the militia and
the Cheyenne and Arapahoe Indians under Black Kettle.
Strength: Americans 900; Indians 200.
Aim: When Indians killed an emigrant party near Denver, hostility between the
settlers and the Indians increased. Retaliation was demanded and the fanatical
Chivington marched against the Indians.
Battle: Although many of the warriors were attending peace negotiations elsewhere, Chivington attacked a camp on Sand Creek in Kiowa County killing 300, of
whom 225 were women and children. American losses were 10.
Result: The battle came to be known as the Sand Creek massacre and was largely
responsible for the hostility which ensued between the Plains Indians and the
white settlers and US army in the west.

SAN JACINTO II (Texas)   Franco-Mexican War   12 February 1867
Fought between the French-Mexican force under Miguel Miramón and the
Mexicans under General Mariano Escobedo.
Aim: The Mexicans sought to drive the French-backed Emperor, Maximilian of
Austria, out of their country.
Battle: In the engagement the French were defeated and the army surrendered.
Miramón escaped from the battlefield with difficulty.
Result: Miramón was eventually captured with Maximilian at Querétaro (qv) and
both were executed.

SAN JACINTO RIVER (Texas)   Texan War of Independence   21 April 1836
Fought between the Texans under General Sam Houston and the Mexicans under
General Antonio López de Santa Anna.
Strength: Texans 600; Mexicans 1,200.
Aim: The Mexicans marched east towards Calveston Bay after the storming of
the Alamo, where 147 Texans fought it out and were killed to a man. Houston
sought to prevent their advance.
Battle: On the west bank of the San Jacinto River, 18 miles from Houston, General
Houston met Santa Anna. The Texans, though outnumbered, defeated the
Mexicans, and Santa Anna was captured. About 500 Mexicans were killed or
wounded. The Texans lost 16 killed, 24 wounded including General Houston.
Result: Mexico agreed to recognise the independence of Texas, though it later
repudiated this. Sam Houston became the first President of the Republic of Texas,
which was refused admittance to the United States in 1837, but Texas remained a
republic for nine years and 301 days during which time the republic asked to join
the British Empire. The British government, not wishing to upset Anglo-American
relations, refused this request.

SAN JUAN HILL (Cuba)   Spanish-American War   1 July 1898
Fought between the Americans under General William Shafter and the Spanish

under General Arsenio Linares.
Strength: Americans 8,400; Spanish 10,400.

When the Americans landed on Cuba and captured Las Guasimas (qv), a two-column attack was organised westwards against Santiago de Cuba (qv). The right column under General Henry Lawton attacked El Caney (qv) and was to join the main attack against San Juan Hill when that operation was completed.

The attack on San Juan Hill and Kettle Hill to the NE was launched on the morning of 1 July. The right flank, made up of part of the dismounted 1st US Volunteer Cavalry Regiment (under Colonel Leonard Wood and Lt-Colonel Theodore Roosevelt) was commanded by General Samuel Sumner (the actual commander, General Joseph Wheeler, was ill). The left flank was commanded by General Jacob Kent. The advance was slow because the Americans used black-powder ammunition as opposed to the Spaniards' smokeless powder and this gave their position away. An assault was finally ordered by subordinate commanders and both San Juan and Kettle Hills were taken while the Spanish fell back to the outskirts of Santiago. American losses were 1,572.

Lawton, who had taken much longer than anticipated to capture El Caney, rejoined the main body after an all-night march. The precarious American position was strengthened by the arrival of Admiral William Sampson's fleet which destroyed the Spanish fleet outside Santiago harbour.

SAN PASQUAL (Mexico)   US-Mexican War   6 December 1846
Fought between the Americans under Colonel Stephen Watts Kearny and the Mexicans.
Strength: Americans 100 dragoons; Mexicans 80.
Aim: The Americans sought to open the roadblock which stood on their road to San Diego.
Battle: Meeting with a Mexican roadblock, Kearny charged the defenders and finally routed them. American losses were 18 killed and 13 wounded. Mexican losses were probably less.
Result: Kearny reached San Diego six days later. This was the only pitched battle of the war in this area.

SANTIAGO DE CUBA (Cuba)   Spanish-American War   3 July 1898
Fought between the Americans under Admiral William Sampson and Commodore Winfield Scott Schley, and the Spanish under Admiral Pascual Cervera.
Strength: Americans 5 battleships + 2 cruisers; Spanish 4 cruisers + 3 destroyers.

Cervera steamed for the Caribbean Sea from the Cape Verde Islands at the out-break of the Spanish-American War while the American Atlantic fleet under Sampson did likewise in order to hunt for the Spanish fleet. The Flying Squadron under Schley located the Spanish first in the harbour of Santiago de Cuba on the SE coast of the island. Sampson arrived to take command of a blockade but, despite the fact that an American collier, the *Merrimac* (originally *Merrimack*), was scuttled at the harbour mouth in an effort to keep the Spanish bottled up, there was no way to keep the Spaniards in except by a blockade, which Sampson held in a tight semicircle 6 miles off-shore (3 miles at night). With the land forces advancing on Santiago from the east, Cervera attempted to run the blockade. As the Spaniards emerged from the harbour, they turned west along the coast and came under heavy fire from the Americans. In a four-hour mêlée every Spanish ship was sunk or run ashore in flames. Spanish losses were 323 killed, 151 wounded and 1,813 captured, including Cervera. Owing to inefficient Spanish gunnery, American casualties were only 1 killed and 2 wounded.

The advancing land troops and the destruction of the Spanish fleet forced the Commander of Santiago, General Arsenio Linares, to surrender the garrison of 12,000 as well as 12,000 troops in outlying areas on 17 July. The war in the Caribbean was now over except for the almost bloodless occupation of Puerto Rico by General Nelson Miles.

SEMINOLE WAR, FIRST (Florida)   1818

During the War of 1812 the Seminole Indians - an eastern branch of the Creek Indians - had sided with the British. After the conclusion of the war, the Seminoles continued to make raids. Negro Fort, on the Appalachicola River, one of the Seminole strongholds, so called because it was manned largely by escaped slaves, was destroyed by American regulars in November and December 1817. Thereafter the Seminoles carried out their raids from Spanish Florida, massacring and pillaging American border towns.

Ordered to take punitive action, General Andrew Jackson moved from Nashville with 1,800 regulars and 6,000 volunteers. The besieged garrison of Fort Scott on the Georgia-Florida border was relieved and Jackson then went on to destroy the Seminole sources of supply and shelter. On 7 April 1818 Jackson occupied the Spanish post of St Marks with 1,200 regulars, and on 24 May the Spanish capital of Pensacola was occupied. When the Governor fled to Fort Barrancas, Jackson shelled the post and captured it. At the same time, American militia columns destroyed Seminole villages and broke their power. Two British traders caught aiding the Indians were court-martialled and executed. America now virtually occupied Spanish Florida and came close to war with Britain. The Seminoles had ceased their raids and Jackson's actions were upheld by the American government and, though the posts captured from the Spaniards were returned, negotiations to gain Florida were begun.

On 22 February 1819 the Adams-Onis Treaty was signed, whereby Spain surrendered all claim to W Florida and ceded E Florida to America. Spanish claims to the Pacific NW were also rescinded. To the SW, the treaty laid down the boundary line of Spanish Mexico from the mouth of the Sabine River in the Gulf of Mexico NW to the Pacific Ocean.

SEMINOLE WAR, SECOND (Florida)   1835-42

Fought between the Seminoles and Creeks under Osceola and the Americans.

Indians of Alabama, Georgia and Florida objected to being moved west and resisted attempts to compel them to do so. The Indians attacked frontier settlements in Florida, where the army garrisons were too small to protect them.

On 28 December 1835 a detachment of 150 regulars under Brevet-Major Francis L. Dade was ambushed in the Wahoo Swamp of the Withlacoochie River. Only 3 men escaped from what became known as the Dade massacre. Colonel Zachary Taylor was ordered to lead a punitive expedition.

On 25 December 1837 1,000 men, half regulars, half volunteers, under Taylor attacked the Seminole position at Lake Okeechobee. Taylor deployed his force in two lines, volunteers leading, and advanced. The volunteers broke, as expected, and the Seminoles were then confronted with the regulars who defeated them. American losses were 26 killed and 112 wounded. The organised resistance of the Seminoles was broken by the battle, but the war continued for four more years, consisting of guerilla activity.

Osceola, whose pseudonym was Billy Powell after his half-breed Scottish grandfather, was lured out of the Everglades in October 1837 ostensibly to attend a conference with General T. S. Jesup. After emerging under a white flag he was seized and imprisoned, an act which enraged the American people. He died in prison at Fort Moultrie, S Carolina, on 30 January 1838 of chronic malaria.

TACUBAYA (Mexico)   Mexican Liberal Rising   11 April 1859
Fought between Mexican government troops under General Leonardo Márquez and the Liberals under General Santos Degollado.

Degollado, instead of attacking Mexico City which was held by a weak Conservative president, marched his 4,000 men first to Chapultec and then to Tacubaya where he waited for a few days, expecting the population to welcome him in without much fighting. Instead, the fierce government general, Márquez, who with 4,000 men had quietly followed Degollado, fell on the Liberal army and, in a bloody four-hour battle, totally routed it, capturing all the artillery and the baggage train. The remnants of the army fled to the hills. Márquez slaughtered all the Liberal wounded and prisoners and earned himself the sobriquet of the Tiger of Tacubaya.

TORONTO (Ontario)   Canadian Rebellion   5 December 1837
Fought between the British under the Lieutenant-Governor Sir John Colborne and the insurgents under William Mackenzie.
Strength: British 2,500; Insurgents 800.

Differences between the British-appointed governors and the elected assemblies flared into open rebellion in 1837. In Lower Canada the risings were confined to the Montreal area where they were quickly put down, their leaders fleeing to the United States. In Upper Canada, Mackenzie attacked Toronto with an army of insurgents, his aim being to set up a provisional government there. Colborne beat off the attack and Mackenzie fled to Buffalo, NY, where his activities strained relations between the United States and Canada.

Despite the fact that Mackenzie's mission failed, the action highlighted problems in the British administration of Canada and was instrumental in the satisfactory achievement of dominion status by Canada thirty years later.

VERACRUZ (Mexico)   US-Mexican War   29 March 1847
Fought between the Americans under General Winfield Scott and the Mexicans under General Morales.
Strength: Americans 13,000; Mexicans 5,000.
Aim: Scott aimed to take Veracruz, a seaport in the Gulf of Mexico, as the base for his advance on Mexico City.
Battle: The US President, James Polk, thought that General Zachary Taylor could not win a final victory in N Mexico, so he ordered a new offensive on the east coast. Commodore David Connor's squadron landed Scott's men almost unopposed south of Veracruz, then the strongest fortress in the western hemisphere. The landing was the first large-scale amphibious operation in American history. For two weeks the Americans secured their beachhead after which they invested the town of Veracruz. A six-day bombardment by artillery and naval guns brought the surrender of both the town and its celebrated fort of San Juan de Ulúa, on one of the reefs in front of the city. Mexican losses were 80 military and 100 civilians. American casualties were 82, including 19 killed.
Result: The Americans prepared to march inland swiftly so as to get away from the yellow fever area.

It should be noted that Veracruz was captured by the French in 1838, and again in 1861.

WAGON BOX FIGHT   see FORT PHIL KEARNY

WASHITA RIVER (Oklahoma)   Cheyenne and Arapahoe War   27 November 1868
Fought between the Americans under Colonel George Custer and the Indians under Black Kettle.
Aim: A winter campaign was launched in order to crush the Indian uprisings on the Great Plains.
Battle: Custer took the 7th Cavalry from Camp Supply in Indian Territory (now Oklahoma) towards the Washita River. Along that river, the Americans surprised an encampment consisting of Cheyenne, Arapahoe, Kiowa, Comanche and Apache Indians, killing over 100 warriors, including the chief, Black Kettle. When the Indians rallied for a counter-attack, the cavalry fell back to Camp Supply, having lost 2 officers and 14 men killed.
Result: The immediate American objective was achieved.

WOLF MOUNTAIN (Montana)   Sioux Wars   7 January 1877
Fought between the Americans under General Nelson Miles and the Indians under Crazy Horse.

Strength: Americans 436; Indians 1,000.

After their victory at Little Big Horn (qv) the Indians split up into small parties which were defeated piecemeal by Generals Alfred Terry and George Crook at Slim Buttes, NW Dakota, on 9 September, and Crazy Woman Creek on the Powder River, Montana, on 25 November. Sitting Bull escaped to Canada.

The last of the large Sioux forces was trapped by Miles at Wolf Mountain along the Tongue River in Montana. With 2 field guns, the American force routed the last of the warriors that had taken part in the battle at Little Big Horn River. Crazy Horse surrendered later that year, was betrayed by Red Cloud, and was killed by a guard while trying to escape. Crazy Horse was not originally an Indian chief but rose through the ranks to become the Sioux Indians' greatest leader.

WOUNDED KNEE CREEK (Dakota)   Ghost Dance War   28 December 1890
Fought between the Sioux Indians under Big Foot and the Americans under Colonel James Forsyth.
Strength: Indians 120; Americans 470.

After the Sioux Chief, Sitting Bull, was killed by Indian police while he was being arrested, a Sioux tribe under Big Foot fled in a panic into the Badlands of S Dakota. The American 7th Cavalry pursued.

The Indians were surrounded at Wounded Knee Creek on 28 December, and when the Americans started to disarm them the following day, they opened fire. A six-hour massacre followed in which 145 men, women and children died, including Big Foot. Of the 33 who were wounded, some froze to death. American losses were 30 killed and 34 wounded, many of whom were hit by their own comrades' bullets.

This was the last major Indian uprising in the west, and its conclusion gave the 7th Cavalry revenge for the massacre at Little Big Horn (qv).

SECTION SEVEN

SOUTH AMERICA

See Map Section, no 19

ALTO DE LA ALIANZA   see TACNA

ANDES, ARMY   Argentine War of Independence   1817
Formed by General José de San Martín at Mendoza, Argentina.
Strength: 5,000-6,000 (including a Chilean contingent, miners and other auxiliaries).
Aim: To cross the Andes and drive the Spanish out of Chile.

In January 1817 San Martín sent the smaller part of his army south to cross the Cordillera by the Uspallata Pass and took his main force by the difficult Los Patos Trail to fall on the Spanish at Chacabuco (qv). He lost many horses and pack mules, but few men, from cold and exhaustion. By striking at the Spanish forces in central Chile he secured the independence of that country, which then became the base for his thrust northwards against Lima, the heart of viceregal power. A great feat of planning and organisation, the crossing of the Andes was the outstanding achievement of a career which included the victory of Maypo (qv), the dispatch of a Chilean-Argentine expeditionary army to Peru (1820), and a period as Protector of Peru before resigning his claims to the leadership of the South American War of Independence (qv) in favour of Simón Bolívar. Neither San Martin nor Bolivar - two great liberators - ever divulged what they said to each other when they met, and it remains one of the great question marks in history.

ANGOSTURA   see LOMAS VALENTINAS

AQUIDABAN RIVER (CERRO CORÁ) (Paraguay)   Paraguayan War   1 March 1870
Fought between the Paraguayans under General Francisco Solano López and the Allied forces of Argentina and Brazil under General Câmara.
Strength: Paraguayans 400; Allies 8,000 (main force, not fully engaged).
Aim: To complete the destruction of the remnants of López's army.
Battle: After his defeat at Lomas Valentinas (qv) López and his few remaining men were pursued by the Allies. By mid-February he had reached the hills of Cerro Corá, in the extreme NE of Paraguay. He was overtaken and killed, with most of his men, two weeks later on the banks of the Aquidaban River. His Irish mistress, Eliza Lynch, escaped to Europe with her jewels.
Result: The battle ended the Paraguayan War.

ARROYO GRANDE (Uruguay)   Uruguayan Civil War   1842
Fought between the Argentinians under Manuel Oribe and the Uruguayans under José Fructuoso Ribera.
Aim: The Argentinian Dictator, Juan Manuel de Rosas, took advantage of the Uruguayan Civil War in order to try and annex that country. He supported the Blancos as opposed to the Colorados (Liberals), who were represented by Ribera.
Battle: The Colorados under Ribera were totally defeated and retreated to Montevideo, which the Argentinians then besieged.

Result: The Argentinians now held the upper hand, but their intervention in Uruguay embroiled Rosas with France and England.

AVAY (Paraguay)   Paraguayan War   December 1868
Fought between the Paraguayans under General Bernardino Caballero and the Brazilians under General Manael Osório.
Aim: The Brazilians sought to pursue and annihilate the Paraguayan army.
Battle: After the Battle of Ytororó (qv) the Paraguayans, numbering about 4,000, turned to face the Brazilians. They were cut to pieces by the enemy cavalry. Most of the few prisoners taken later escaped, including Caballero. Brazilian casualties were about 4,000.
Result: The survivors joined the rest of the Paraguayan army to fight the Battle of Lomas Valentinas (qv).

AYACUCHO (Peru)   Peruvian War of Independence   9 December 1824
Fought between the Spanish Royalists under General José de La Serna and José Canterac and the Patriots under General Antonio José de Sucre.
Strength: Spanish 9,310; Patriots 5,780.
Aim: The expulsion by the Patriots of the Spaniards.
Battle: Following the pursuit of the defeated Royalists after the Battle of Junín (qv), Sucre caught up with the Spaniards 200 miles SE of Lima at Ayacucho and attacked them. A Spanish offensive was contained by Sucre's left and centre while his right, which consisted chiefly of cavalry, turned the Spanish left. When Sucre threw in his reserve, the Spanish army collapsed and fled. Spanish casualties were 1,400 killed, 700 wounded, 3,500 prisoners (including La Serna) and 15 guns, while the Patriots lost 300 killed and suffered 600 wounded.
Result: La Serna's successor, Canterac, capitulated the next day. The victory assured Peruvian independence.

BAY OF PIGS (COCHINOS or PLAYA GIRÓN) (Cuba)   Invasion Attempt
17-19 April 1961
Fought between the Cuban army under Fidel Castro and expeditionary force of anti-Castro exiles led by Manuel Artime.
Strength: Castro forces (when fully mobilised) 20,000 with tanks, artillery and aircraft; Exiles 1,300.
Aim: The overthrow of the Castro régime.
Battle: The operation had been planned and equipped with undercover US support, but President John F. Kennedy's new administration proved unwilling to commit the logistic backing essential to its success. The expeditionaries established a bridgehead but failed to make headway against difficult swampy terrain, the opposition of the militia, and the failure of the local population to rally to them. Castro was able to bring up regular units, tanks, artillery and air power and overwhelm them. The exiles' casualties were 120 killed and missing, and 1,180 prisoners. Castro forces lost 87 (official figure), though the unofficial estimate was 1,650

killed and 2,000 wounded.
Result: Total military and political failure of the invasion. The US paid S53 million in compensation.

BOGOTAZO (Colombia)   Colombian Riot   April 1948
Jorge Eliécer Gaitán, a popular radical politician, was murdered in the streets of Bogotá on 9 April 1948. This sparked off riots - the worst ever seen in Latin America - lasting several days. They took place during a meeting of the Inter-American Conference when anti-US feeling was stirred up. Large areas of the capital were burned down and 4,000 lives were lost.

BOLIVIA   Guerilla Rising   1966-7
Fought between the rebel guerillas and Bolivian government forces.
Strength: 50 guerillas; 650 American-trained Bolivian rangers and some conscripts.
Aim: First to overthrow the Bolivian government; and second to establish a base from which revolutionary action could be conducted against other strategic targets in Latin America.

The success of his Sierra Maestra guerilla campaign (qv) in Cuba encouraged Fidel Castro to promote guerilla movements elsewhere in Latin America. At the end of 1966 his chief lieutenant, 'Che' Guevara and other Cuban veterans established a base at Ñancahuazú, near Camiri in E Bolivia. Their presence was discovered in March 1967 before preparations were complete. Though they defeated the first government units encountered, they failed to gain local support and were annihilated by the Bolivians' American-taught counter-insurgency tactics, Guevara himself being killed at Villagrande..An attempt to restart guerilla activity in.the Teoponte area (July 1970) was also crushed. The guerillas lost 35 killed, and the government troops lost 40.
Result: The immediate objective of overthrowing the Bolivian government failed, and Cuban hopes of promoting revolution through guerilla warfare suffered a sharp setback.

BOYACÁ (Colombia)   Colombian War of Independence   7 August 1819
Fought between the Colombian and Venezuelan Patriots under Simón Bolívar and the Spanish Royalists under Colonel Barreiro.
Strength: Patriots 2,000; Spanish 3,000.
Aim: The Patriots sought to free their country from Spanish rule and the Spaniards, in order to prevent this, came out to block the Patriots' road to Bogotá.
Battle: From his base at Angostura, Bolívar led his forces across the Venezuelan plains and over the Andes, arriving in New Granada (modern Colombia) with a third of his original army. Reinforced, he marched round the Spanish Royalists and took up a position between Barreiro and Bogotá, cutting the Spaniards off from their line of communications. The Spanish attacked, but the Colombians drove back the Spanish left and Bolívar's British Legion assaulted the Spanish frontally, defeating their cavalry. The Spanish were routed, losing 1,600 men,

most of whom were taken prisoner, and all their equipment.

Result: Bolívar entered Bogotá three days later and established the republic of Gran Colombia. At a later date (CARABOBO) Bolívar stated that the English, Irish and Scottish 'brigades' of the British Legion, many of them veterans of the Peninsular War, were his best troops.

CALLAO I (Peru)   Peruvian War of Independence   5 November 1820
Fought between the Spanish and the Chileans under Admiral Lord Cochrane.
Aim: The Patriots sought to expel the Spanish from S America.
Battle: Cochrane, who was blockading the Spanish in Callao with 3 Chilean frigates, took a party of men in a rowing boat into the harbour and cut out the *Esmeralda.* a 44-gun Spanish frigate, under the 300 guns of the shore batteries. The entire crew of the *Esmeralda,* including the Spanish Admiral, were captured or killed. Cochrane lost 41 killed and wounded.
Result: The immediate objective of the Patriots was achieved. Lord Cochrane was given the command of the newly formed Chilean navy. He later performed similar services in the Brazilian and Greek independence movements.

CALLAO II (Peru)   Peruvian-Spanish War   2 May 1866
Fought between the Spanish and the Peruvians.
Strength: Spanish 11 warships; Peruvian coastal batteries.
Aim: Spain attempted to re-establish her influence over the west coast of S America.
Battle: Spain picked a quarrel with Peru over the issue of the latter's debts and alleged ill-treatment of Spanish subjects. A Spanish squadron entered the Pacific and seized Peru's profitable guano-producing Chincha Islands. Peru, in alliance with Chile, Bolivia and Ecuador, declared war on Spain. The Spanish bombarded the Chilean port of Valparaiso and then sailed north to bombard Callao. Peruvian shore batteries drove off the attackers. Peruvian casualties were 1,000 killed and wounded, and Spanish 300.
Result: The Spanish squadron sailed away without achieving any lasting gains.

CANCHA RAYADA (Chile)   Chilean War of Independence   16 March 1818
Fought between the Chilean and Argentine Patriots under José de San Martín and the Spanish Royalists under General Mariano Osorio.
Strength: Patriots 6,600; Spanish 5,000.
Aim: The Spanish Royalists sought to restore their authority in Chile.
Battle: The Patriots were defeated and forced back towards Santiago. They lost 120 killed and 22 guns, while 200 Spaniards were killed.
Result: Although the Patriots lost this battle, they were able to retrieve their fortunes at Maypo (qv).

CARABOBO (Venezuela)   Venezuelan War of Independence   24 June 1821
Fought between Colombian and Venezuelan Patriots under Simón Bolívar and the

Spanish Royalists under General Miguel de la Torre.
Strength: Patriots 6,500; Spanish 4,000.
Aim: The liberation of Venezuela from Spanish rule.
Battle: Bolívar, President of Colombia, moved into Venezuela and united his force with that of José Antonio Páez. De la Torre held the valley of the Carabobo at the southern foot of the pass and Bolívar, pushing aside Spanish outposts, found a route through the mountains which was taken by his cavalry and the British Legion. These fell on the Spanish flank and de la Torre counter-attacked with a detachment of his army. The British Legion held its ground and the cavalry broke up the Spanish attack. The division of de la Torre's force rendered it vulnerable and once the right flank had broken the rout became complete. Barely 400 Royalists reached Puerto Cabello.
Result: Bolívar entered Caracas, 100 miles east of the battlefield, and Venezuelan independence was assured.

CASEROS   see MONTE CASEROS

CEPEDA I (Argentina)   Argentine Civil War   1 February 1820
Fought between the Unitarians under General José Rondeau and the Federalists.
   Rondeau was defeated, and the provinces were able to increase their influence over the capital, Buenos Aires.

CEPEDA II (Argentina)   Argentine Civil War   23 October 1859
Fought between the troops of the Argentine Confederation under Justo José de Urquiza and the force of the State of Buenos Aires under Bartolomé Mitre.
Aim: The Confederation sought to quell the uprising in Buenos Aires.
Battle: The troops of Buenos Aires were defeated.
Result: Buenos Aires was incorporated in the Confederation.

CERRO CORÁ   see AQUIDABAN RIVER

CHACABUCO (Chile)   Chilean War of Independence   12 February 1817
Fought between the Argentine and Chilean Patriots under José de San Martín and Bernardo O'Higgins, and the Spanish Royalists under General Maroto.
Aim: The Patriots sought to drive the Spanish out of Chile.
Battle: San Martín led his Army of the Andes (qv) across the Cordillera and engaged a force of 1,350 Spanish Royalists who attempted to bar his way to Santiago at the Chacabuco Ridge. An assault led by the Chilean leader Bernardo O'Higgins carried the day. The Spanish were routed and the Army of the Andes entered the Chilean capital. The Patriots lost 100 killed, and Spanish losses were 500 killed and 600 prisoners.
Result: O'Higgins became Supreme Director and Chilean independence was proclaimed.
   O'Higgins, son of an Irishman, Ambrosio O'Higgins, who became Marquis of

Orsono and Viceroy of Peru, had many British volunteers serving in his army and navy.

CHACO WAR   1932-5
Fought between Bolivia and Paraguay.

The aim of both countries was to secure possession of the N Chaco wilderness, which was thought to contain oil. Disputes over possession of the region in 1928 had ripened into war by 1932. Other S American states and the League of Nations endeavoured to mediate, but neither met with any success and the war went on, although both sides were under considerable economic strain.

The Paraguayans, though inferior in numbers and equipment, gained initial control over the area, but the Bolivians then employed the German, General Hans von Kundt, to train and command their army. The Bolivians also intended to establish military posts in the area claimed by Paraguay. Fort López (Pitiantuta) was taken by the Bolivians on 15 June 1932, temporarily achieving one object, which was to control the Upper Paraguay River. The Paraguayans now began to expand their army from 3,000 to 60,000 men. They retook Pitiantuta in mid-July and set up a supply line from there through Puerto Casado in preparation for a major offensive which was headed by Colonel José Felix Estigarribia. Employing their favourite *corralito,* or encirclement, tactics, the Paraguayans advanced steadily through the jungle and, during the next eighteen months, conquered most of the Chaco region, taking the Bolivian headquarters and more than 30,000 prisoners.

A truce was signed on 12 June 1935, which brought outright hostilities to an end. In the Treaty of Buenos Aires, signed on 21 July 1938, Paraguay was given three-quarters of the Chaco region, while Bolivia was granted an outlet to the S Atlantic via the Paraguay River.

CHALCHUAPA (El Salvador)   Central American War   2 April 1885
Fought between the Guatemalans under Justo Rufino Barrios and the Salvadorians.

Since their liberation from Spain, the states of central America tried periodically to form a union. In 1885, Barrios, President of Guatemala, decided to form such a union. He won the support of Honduras, but was opposed by Costa Rica, Nicaragua and El Salvador. Barrios formed an army of unification and invaded El Salvador.

At Chalchuapa the invaders were defeated by the Salvadorians. Barrios was killed and the effort to form a union collapsed.

CHILOÉ (S Chile)   Chilean War of Independence   19 January 1826
Fought between the Spanish Royalists under Quintanilla and the Chilean Patriots under Ramón Freire.
Strength: Spanish 2,000; Patriots 4,000 + a small squadron of warships.
Aim: The reduction of the garrison holding this island in southern Chile for Spain.
Battle: The island surrendered to the Chilean Patriots.
Result: The Spanish lost their last foothold in Chile.

CHORRILLOS (Peru)   Peruvian-Chilean War   13 January 1881
Fought between the Chileans under General Manuel Baquedano and the Peruvians under General Andrés Avelino Cáceres.
The Peruvians attempted to bar the way to Lima but were defeated. Peruvian casualties were 9,000 killed and wounded, and 2,000 captured. Chilean casualties were 800 killed and 2,500 wounded.
   The battle opened the way to the Chileans' occupation of Lima and their final victory in the War of the Pacific (qv).

COCHINOS   see BAY OF PIGS

CONCÓN (Chile)   Chilean Civil War   21 August 1891
Fought between the Congressists under General del Canto and the Balmacedists under General Barbosa.
Strength: Congressists 10,000 + 3 warships; Balmacedists 11,000.
   Congress opposed the reforms and authoritarian rule of President José Manuel Balmaceda. Setting up their headquarters in N Chile, they then sailed south and landed unopposed at Concón on 20 August. Aided by the fire from 3 warships, they stormed the entrenchments of the Balmacedists, who were driven out with a loss of 1,646 killed and wounded and 1,500 prisoners. The Congressists lost 869.
   The Congressists' objective was achieved. After their further victory at Placilla (qv) Balmaceda was forced to resign, and committed suicide.

CUASPUD (Ecuador)   Ecuador-Colombia War   6 December 1862
Fought between the Ecuadorians under Juan José Flores and the Colombians under Tomás Cipriano de Mosquera.
Strength: Ecuadorians 6,000; Colombians 4,000.
   The Ecuadorians were completely routed and lost 1,500 killed and wounded, as well as 2,000 men and all their guns captured.

CUBA   War of Independence   1895-8
The Cubans strove to gain independence from Spain.
   From the mid-nineteenth century Cuban opposition to Spanish rule had increased. Fighting continued throughout the Ten Years' War (qv) of 1868-78, despite the rebels' defeat at Jimaguayú. War was resumed in 1895 by Máximo Gómez and the national hero José Martí, who was killed almost immediately.
   Following the sinking of the battleship *Maine* in Havana harbour on 15 January 1898, the US declared war, defeated the Spanish fleet and landed an expeditionary force. Finally Spain was forced to renounce sovereignty over Cuba.

CURUPAÍTY (Paraguay)   Paraguayan War   22 September 1866
Fought between the Argentinians, Brazilians and Uruguayans under General Venancio Flores, and the Paraguayans under General Francisco Solano López.
Aim: The Allies invaded Paraguay in order to destroy the régime of General López.

Battle: The Paraguayans established a strong position in a bend of the Paraguay River. The Allies attempted to shell it from 8 ironclads, and then sent in a force of 11,000 Brazilians and 7,000 Argentinians to storm it. They were caught in a devastating enfilading fire and repulsed with very heavy losses, suffering 9,000 killed and wounded. Paraguayan casualties were less than 100.

Result: The Argentine army was temporarily knocked out of the war.

DOMINICAN REPUBLIC   Civil War and US Intervention   April 1965

A rising was led by Colonel Francisco Caamaño in order to overthrow the governing junta and secure the recall of the left-wing ex-President Juan Bosch, leader of the Democratic Revolutionary Party.

Units of the Dominican armed forces, joined by left-wing sympathisers, attempted to seize power in Santo Domingo. General Wessin, from an air base outside the capital, counter-attacked with tanks. The rebels (Constitutionalists) held the city centre and civil war developed. On 28 April the US, fearing another Cuban-style take-over, began to send in the marines 'to protect lives and property'; some 20,000 men were committed. A truce was imposed, ostensibly by the Organisation of American States forces, and Caamaño and Wessin were forced into exile. In all, about 3,000 casualties were suffered.

On the failure of the rising, a provisional President was installed and the Constitutionalists were offered reintegration into the armed forces.

ECUADOR-PERU WAR   July 1941

Peru had long claimed part of Ecuador's huge, sparsely populated Amazonian territory. In July 1941 her troops attacked and occupied Machala, the provincial capital, and Puerto Bolivar, easily crushing Ecuadorian resistance. International pressure imposed a cease-fire.

Peru gained some 70,000 square miles of Ecuadorian territory.

EL SALVADOR-HONDURAS ('THE FOOTBALL') WAR   July 1969

Conflict between El Salvador and Honduras, which came to a head when the former country determined to stop the expulsion of Salvadorian settlers from Honduras.

El Salvador is small, densely populated and relatively industrialised, and linked to her larger, more sparsely populated and backward neighbour Honduras in the Central American Common Market. The advantage allegedly given by the latter to El Salvador fanned Honduran resentment, whilst the Salvadorians were angered by the expulsion of many of their people who had settled without authorisation in Honduras. Mutual resentment boiled over during incidents at a football match in which the two countries competed for the representation of central America in the World Cup.

Hostilities (the 'Football War') broke out soon afterwards and lasted five days. The Salvadorian army crossed the border, most of the Honduran air force was destroyed on the ground, and the roads linking Honduras with Guatemala and

Nicaragua were cut. Further advance was checked by the intervention of the Organisation of American States and by US pressure. El Salvador casualties were between 700 and 800, while Honduran losses were between 1,200 and 1,300.

El Salvador had demonstrated her military superiority but had to evacuate Honduran territory and absorb the settlers already expelled. The war was a setback for central American integration.

ESTERO BELLACO (Paraguay)   Paraguayan War   2 May 1866
Fought between Paraguayans under Díaz, and Argentinians and Brazilians under General Venancio Flores.
Strength: Paraguayans 5,000; Allies 45,000.
Aim: The Paraguayans attempted to surprise the numerically superior enemy before they could advance into Paraguay.
Battle: The Paraguayans attacked the Allies on marshy ground, routed their advance guard and overran their artillery. Instead of withdrawing after this success, they pushed on against the main body of the enemy and were outflanked and outnumbered, and lost much of the captured material. Allied losses totalled about 1,600.
Result: The battle was inconclusive, but the Allies were able to advance and fight at Tuyutí (qv).

HONDURAS, CIVIL WAR   1909-11
Fought between the followers of former President Manuel Bonilla and President Miguel Dávila.

This civil war was the outcome of the defeat of Honduras by Nicaragua in 1907 when Tegucigalpa, the capital of Honduras, was occupied. Resentment grew against the President, Miguel Dávila, who had signed the peace treaty, and dissidents, under Manuel Bonilla, attempted a *coup d'état.*

Stalemate resulted from the conflict and an armistice came into effect on 8 February 1911. On 29 October Bonilla was elected President but unrest and disorder continued until in January 1912 US marines landed, ostensibly to protect US property. Order was rapidly restored.

HUMAITÁ (SW Paraguay)   Paraguayan War   16 July 1868
Fought between Paraguayans under Colonel Paulino Alén and the allied forces of Argentina, Brazil and Uruguay under General Manoel Louis Osório.
Strength: Paraguayan garrison 3,000; Allies 12,000.
Aim: The Allies aimed to capture the fortress of Humaitá, key to the Paraguayan defensive system known as the *Quadrilátero.*
Battle: General Francisco Solano López had evacuated most of his army from the Humaitá defensive system and withdrawn them across the Paraguay into the Chaco. After three months, when supplies had grown low, and the Allies saw no sign of life from the fortress, they thought it must have been completely abandoned. But as they were about to enter it, the Paraguayans ambushed them and forced them

to retreat, inflicting over 2,000 casualties.
Result: Despite the success of this stratagem, the Paraguayans were obliged to evacuate this key fortress a few days later.

INGAVI (Bolivia)   Bolivian-Peruvian War   18 November 1841
Fought between the Peruvians under their President, Agustín Gamarra, and the Bolivians under their President, José Ballivián.
Strength: Peruvians 5,200; Bolivians 3,800.
Aim: Gamarra, who had served in the Chilean army during the war of the Bolivian and Peruvian confederacy, now marched his army south into Bolivia. The Bolivians sought to block the invaders' advance.
Battle: South of La Paz, at the mountain of Ingavi, the armies fought a pitched battle wherein the Peruvians were routed. Gamarra was among those killed.
Result: The battle ended the invasion and the war.

ITUZAINGÓ (Uruguay)   Uruguayan War of Independence   20 February 1827
Fought between the Argentinians and Uruguayans under Carlos de Alvear and the Brazilians under the Marques de Barbacena.
Aim: When Argentina and Brazil both gained their independence, the territory between the two countries was incorporated into Brazil as the Cispalatine Province. The people of this area sought Argentina's help in gaining their independence and a revolt ensued.
Battle: In NE Argentina the two armies met and the Brazilians were decisively beaten.
Result: Great Britain intervened on behalf of Uruguay, which was set up as an independent nation the following year.

JUNÍN (Junín Province, Peru)   Peruvian War of Independence   6 August 1824
Fought between the Patriots under Simón Bolívar and General Antonio José de Sucre, and the Spanish Royalists under General José Canterac.
Strength: Patriots 900; Spanish 1,300.
Aim: When Peruvian independence was proclaimed, the Royalists carried on the war in the highlands, where Sucre and Simón Bolívar pursued and endeavoured to destroy them.
Battle: The engagement was fought entirely between cavalry. The Patriots were victorious and their losses were 150. The Spanish lost 250 men.
Result: The Royalists retreated farther into the highlands, where they were finally defeated at Ayacucho (qv).

LA PAZ (Bolivia)   Bolivian Civil War   January 1865
Fought between the followers of General Manuel Isodoro Belzú and those of Colonel Mariano Melgarejo. Both commanders sought to substantiate their claims as provisional President of Bolivia.
    The forces of Belzú were totally routed and he himself was killed. Melgarejo

became Dictator.

LIRCAY (Chile)   Chilean Civil War   April 1830
Fought between the Federalists under General Zastera and the Pelucones under General Joaquín Prieto.

The Federalists, or Government Party, were defeated by the Pelucones, or Unitarians, and forced out of office. The Pelucones then abrogated the Constitution of 1828 and embarked on thirty years of Conservative rule.

LOMAS VALENTINAS (ANGOSTURA) (Paraguay)   Paraguayan War   21 November-7 December 1868
Fought between the Brazilians and Argentinians under Field-Marshal Luíz Aldes de Lima e Silva, Marquis of Caxias and the Paraguayans under General Francisco Solano López.
Strength: Allies 25,000-30,000; Paraguayans 2,000-2,500.
Aim: The Allies sought to annihilate the Paraguayan army and end the war.
Battle: The remnants of the Paraguayan army established their positions behind a semicircular line in the region of Angostura. As the main allied force advanced from Villeta, a column was detached to attack the rear of the enemy positions which were held by some 1,500 defenders, mostly boys and invalids, 700 of whom were killed and 200 taken prisoner. A general attack was then ordered against the Paraguayan centre but was repulsed. After two days' comparative lull, a bombardment and general assault, headed by Argentine contingents, was undertaken and the Paraguayan army overwhelmed. Allied casualties were 4,000. Paraguayan losses were over 2,000 killed, wounded or made prisoner.
Result: The battle proved the Waterloo of the Paraguayan War. López himself escaped, with less than 100 men, but, after a period of fierce guerilla resistance, was killed at the Aquidaban River (qv) two years later.

MAYPO (MAIPÚ) RIVER   Chilean War of Independence   5 April 1818
Fought between the Chilean Patriots under José de San Martín and the Spanish Royalists under General Mariano Osorio.
Strength: Patriots 9,000; Spanish 6,000.
Aim: After being defeated at Cancha Rayada (qv) San Martín regrouped his army to defend the approaches to Santiago.
Battle: The Chileans took up their position on the banks of the Maypo (Maipú) River. After foiling an attempt by Osorio to cut the road to Santiago, San Martin concentrated his attack on the Spanish left, which he turned. The Spanish army collapsed and was routed, losing 1,000 killed and wounded, 2,350 men and 12 guns captured. Chilean losses were 1,000 killed and wounded.
Result: The battle virtually assured the independence of Chile.

MIRAFLORES (Colombia)   Peruvian-Chilean War   15 January 1881
Fought between the Chileans under General Manuel Baquedano and the Peruvians

under General Andrés Avelino Cáceres.

The Peruvians sought to halt the advance of the Chileans against the Peruvian capital. In the action the Peruvians were completely defeated with a loss of 3,000 killed and wounded. The Chileans lost 500 killed and 1,625 wounded.

Lima was occupied by the Chileans on 17 January and the war with Peru was ended.

MONCADA (Cuba)   Cuban Revolt   26 July 1953
Fought between the rebels under Fidel Castro and the government forces of President Batista (Fulgencio Batista y Zaldívar).
Strength: Rebels 160; Garrison 1,000.
Aim: The Castro supporters set out to storm the barracks in Santiago.
Battle: The radical leader Fidel Castro hoped to overthrow the government of President Batista by first seizing Santiago, capital of Oriente Province. Though some key points were taken, his attack on the Moncada Barracks failed. Castro was imprisoned and later took refuge in Mexico, whence he returned with his guerillas to the Sierra Maestra (qv). The rebels lost 90, mostly captured and executed. The government forces lost 19 killed.
Result: Though unsuccessful, Moncada was the prelude to the armed struggle which was to bring Castro, and the first Communist government in Latin America, to power.

MONTE CASEROS (Argentina)   Argentine Civil War   3 February 1852
Fought between the government (gaucho) troops under the Dictator, Juan Manuel de Rosas, and the insurgents under Justo José de Urquiza.
Strength: Gauchos 25,000; Insurgents 20,000.
Aim: The insurgents sought the overthrow of the gaucho party and the end of the Rosas dictatorship.
Battle: Supported by Uruguay, which Rosas had repeatedly tried to annex, and Brazil, Urquiza defeated Rosas at Monte Caseros, 300 miles up the Uruguay River.
Result: Rosas was forced to take ship for England. Urquiza became Chief Executive of Argentina, at times ruling from outside the country.

MONTEVIDEO II (Uruguay)   Uruguayan Civil War   16 February 1843-8 October 1851
Fought between the Blancos under Manuel Oribe and the Colorados under José Fructuoso Ribera.
Aim: The Blancos sought the reduction of Montevideo, which was held by the Colorados.
Battle: The Argentinian Dictator, Juan Manuel de Rosas, supported the Blanco party when it marched on Montevideo. An assault on the city failed and the town was invested. The siege was a loose one and an Argentinian revolt under Justo José de Urquiza weakened the besiegers. On 8 October 1851 Urquiza led a combined force of Colorados, Brazilians and Paraguayans on Montevideo. Oribe

was defeated and the siege, which had lasted for eight years, was lifted.
Result: The Colorados did not achieve their objective.
  One of the chief defenders of Montevideo was Giuseppe Garibaldi.

MONTEVIDEO III (Uruguay)   Uruguayan Civil War   August 1863
Fought between the Colorados, or Liberals, under General Venancio Flores and
the Blancos under General Medina.
Aim: The Blancos sought to quell the Colorados' uprising.
Battle: In the action the Blancos were victorious.
Result: The Blancos' objective was achieved. President Francisco Solano López of
Paraguay had supported the Blancos, and his intervention was one of the causes
of the alliance between Uruguay, Brazil and Argentina in the Paraguayan War.
When López was eventually defeated and killed in 1870 at Aquidaban River (qv)
the Colorado party unseated the Blancos and took control of Uruguay for nearly
nine decades.

MONTONEROS, ARGENTINA   1961-
The Montoneros were originally gauchos or mounted guerillas who were active in
Argentina's nineteenth-century civil wars. In the 1960s a left wing Peronista
guerilla group became active under this name. In 1970 they kidnapped and
assassinated ex-President General Pedro Eugenio Aramburu who had ousted
President Juan Domingo Peron. From 1971-4 they carried out more kidnappings
and, on 11 March 1974, obtained US $14 million for the release of Victor
Samuelson, the Esso executive.
  In October 1973 the Montoneros, now led by Mario Firmenich, joined with the
Fuerzas Armadas Revolucionarias (FAR) under Roberto Quieto to form a left
wing Peronist challenge to orthodox Peronism. They stepped up armed insurgency
in 1975.
  The Montoneros is not the only active revolutionary party in Argentina but it is
the most internationally well-known.
  With the advent to power of General Jorge Rafael Videla on 24 March 1976,
the outlook for the continued operations of the Montoneros and similar revolutionary groups became bleak.

NICARAGUA, CIVIL WAR   July 1912
Fought between rival political parties.
  US marines were landed to restore order and ensure that free elections were
held. This was in accordance with the 'Roosevelt Corollary' enunciated in a message
from President Theodore Roosevelt to Congress in 1904 wherein he stated that
the Monroe Doctrine (after President James Monroe) meant that the US would take
police action against any trouble in the western hemisphere. After restoring order
the US marines trained the *guarda nacional* to take their place and maintain order.

NICARAGUA-HONDURAS WAR   February-December 1907
Fought over a frontier dispute between Nicaragua and Honduras.

The Hondurans were defeated and their capital, Tegucigalpa, occupied by the Nicaraguans (HONDURAS, CIVIL WAR). Civil War, due to dissatisfaction with the peace treaty imposed by the US, subsequently broke out in both Nicaragua and Honduras, resulting in US marines being required to restore order.

OBLIGADA (Uruguay)   Uruguayan Civil War   November 1845
Fought between the Argentine fleet under Manuel Oribe, and French and British squadrons.
Aim: The Allies sought to force Oribe to raise the siege of Montevideo (qv).
Battle: The Allies engaged the Argentinian fleet and defeated it, forcing Oribe to raise the siege.
Result: The Allied objective was achieved.

ORURO (Bolivia)   Bolivian Civil War   1862
Fought between government troops under the President, General José Maria de Achá, and the rebels under General Pérez.
Aim: The rebel General Pérez had proclaimed himself President and endeavoured to implement the claim by force.
Battle: Pérez and his followers were utterly routed.
Result: The rebel objective was not achieved.

PACIFIC, WAR OF THE   1878-83
Fought between Chile and Peru.
Strength: 22,000 on each side (in final campaign).
Aim: To decide possession of coastal areas containing nitrate deposits.

The Pacific coastal desert had been of little value until the discovery there of nitrate deposits. These were in territory belonging to Bolivia and Peru (which were allied by a secret treaty of 1873) but were developed largely by Chilean interests. A naval engagement off Iquique gave the Peruvians initial command of the sea, which they lost after the capture of their ironclad *Huascar* at Cape Angamos on 8 October 1879.

On land the Chileans occupied the Peruvian desert province of Tarapacá. A second expeditionary force under General Manuel Baquedano defeated the Allies outside Tacna (qv) and forced Bolivia out of the war. The capture of the Morro fortress commanding Arica enabled the Chileans to move on Lima, which they occupied after the Battles of Chorrillos and Miraflores (qqv). Mopping-up operations continued for two more years. Chilean losses were 5,500 and Peruvian losses 9,000.
Result: Chile achieved her main objective. She gained Tarapacá and Arica, though Tacna later reverted to Peru. Bolivia was left, a resentful, land-locked state.

PANAMA CANAL ZONE RIOTS 1964
Since 1903 the US has controlled a 10-mile-wide zone on either side of the canal

which runs through Panamanian territory. Panama's demands for recognition of her sovereignty over the zone and renegotiation of US treaty rights have led to repeated tension and disturbances. In 1964 the hoisting of the Stars and Stripes by students in the zone provoked Panamanian threats to invade it and caused serious riots in Panama City and several casualties.

The Americans remained in control of the canal zone and diplomatic relations between Panama and the US were broken off. In 1974 the US and the Republic of Panama signed a protocol for a new treaty which would restore the canal to Panamanian control. Treaty negotiations have continued off and on since that date and a new US approach was made on 23 April 1976.

PARAGUAYAN CIVIL WAR   30 March-20 August 1947
Fought between the followers of ex-President Rafael Franco and President Higinio Morinigo, who retained control of the country.

PARAGUAYAN WAR (WAR OF THE TRIPLE ALLIANCE)   1864-70
Fought between Paraguay and the Allied states of Argentina, Brazil and Uruguay.

The war was caused largely by the military ambitions of Paraguay's President, Francisco Solano Lopez, and his resolve to resist Brazilian interference in the internal affairs of Uruguay. Argentina came into the war through the refusal of her government to allow the passage of Paraguayan forces to attack Brazil. The war was characterised by its great ferocity and the disparity in numbers and resources between land-locked Paraguay and her three neighbours. López took the initiative by sending his forces into the Brazilian province of Matto Grosso, and also across the Argentine province of Corrientes into Brazil's Rio Grande do Sul. The Paraguayans were forced back; their attempts to gain command of the all-important river communications were frustrated at Riachuelo (qv). The Allies' advance into Paraguay was hampered by marshy terrain and a strong defensive position centring round Humaitá (qv). After the Paraguayan victory at Curapaíty (qv), the Argentinians let the Brazilians bear the brunt of the fighting. Superior numbers at length wore the Paraguayans down, and López was obliged to abandon his defences and retreat into the Chaco to the north where he continued to wage a fierce guerilla campaign until his forces were decimated and he himself was killed at the Aquidaban River (qv).

Paraguay was devastated by the war and her population of 1,500,000 was reduced to about 28,000 men and 200,000 women and children. She also lost about 55,000 square miles of territory. The principal battles were fought in the junction of the Paraguay and Paraná Rivers and the capital, Asunción.

PICHINCHA   Ecuadorian War of Independence   24 May 1822
Fought between the Spanish Royalists under the Spanish Governor of Quito, Melchoir Aymerich, and a rebel force of Patriots under Simón Bolívar's famous lieutenant, Antonio Jose de Sucre.
Strength: Spanish 2,500; Patriots 2,000.

Bolívar had sent an invading force into Ecuador at the same time as he advanced on Venezuela. Bolívar's own advance was brought up short by the Spanish at Bombino, and Aymerich then turned his attantion to Sucre who was encamped near a Spanish fortress on the slopes of a volcano at Pichincha. The Spanish attacked the rebels and were at first successful, but Sucre launched a flank attack which drove the Spaniards down the mountain into Quito. Spanish casualties were 400 killed and 190 wounded, with 14 guns lost. The Patriots' casualties were 200 killed and 140 wounded.

Aymerich surrendered Quito the following day, and Bolívar was accepted as President.

The name of Bolívar has always tended to overshadow that of his great military commander Antonio de Sucre, who is without doubt South America's greatest and most accomplished general.

PLACILLA (Chile)   Chilean Civil War   28 August 1891
Fought between the Congressists under General del Canto and the Balmacedists under General Barbosa.
Strength: Congressists 10,000; Balmacedists 14,000.
Aim: The Congressists sought to occupy Valparaiso.
Battle: Following their successful landing at Concón (qv) the Congressists routed the Balmacedists, with a loss of 3,363 killed and wounded. Thousands laid down their arms on the battlefield. Congressist losses were 1,609.
Result: The victors immediately occupied Valparaiso.

José Manuel Balmaceda committed suicide some days later.

PLAYA GIRON   see BAY OF PIGS

PRESTES' COLUMN   'Lieutenants' Revolt', Brazilian Rising   1922-4
Former army Captain Luiz Carlos Prestes organised a rebel force, led by radical junior officers, through Brazil's backlands in an attempt to mobilise peasant discontent.
Strength: Rebels 2,000 (dwindling to 620).
Aim: The rebels sought to seize power by a combination of military revolt and the exploitation of rural unrest.

Avoiding major clashes, Prestes' Column ranged south to the Paraná, north to the São Francisco, and west to the Bolivian lowlands. After two years, it was broken up by government troops and its leaders escaped into exile.
Result: The Prestes Column achieved little in practical terms but became a symbol of revolutionary protest. The failure of the 1935 rising proved a setback for Comintern strategy in Latin America and left strong anti-Communist resentment in the Brazilian armed forces.

Prestes went to Russia where he was made leader of the clandestine Brazilian Communist Party. He returned secretly to organise an army revolt in Natal, Recife and Rio (November 1935).

RIACHUELO (Brazil)   Paraguayan War   June 1865
Fought between the river fleets of Paraguay and Brazil.
Strength: Paraguay 1 war steamer + 8 unarmoured converted merchant and passenger vessels + 30 guns (mostly 14-pounders), supported by gun-carrying rafts and units on land; Brazil 9 large armoured war steamers with 59 guns (including 120- and 150-pounders).
Aim: The Paraguayans sought to surprise and capture the Brazilian fleet.
Battle: The Brazilian fleet, under Admiral Barroso, was moored in the Riachuelo, a tributary of the Paraná. The plan of the Paraguayan President Francisco Solano López was to board and capture as many enemy vessels as possible. Though the Brazilian fleet suffered heavy damage, the Paraguayan plan miscarried, and only 4 of their ships returned to base.
Result: The Brazilians retained command of the waterways.

SIERRA MAESTRA GUERILLA CAMPAIGN   Cuban Civil War   1956-9
Fought between guerillas led by Fidel Castro and President Batista's (Fulgencio Batista y Zaldívar) government forces.
Strength: Guerillas nucleus of 82 expeditionaries, rising to about 2,000 fully armed guerillas; government forces about 40,000.
Aim: Castro sought to overthrow the Batista régime.
   Following the abortive attack on Moncada (qv) Castro trained his followers in Mexico and at the end of 1956 returned to Cuba with a small expeditionary force. His guerillas established themselves in the Sierra Maestra, where they won the support of the peasants and gradually wore down the government forces. Other guerillas started operations (the 'Second Front') in the Escambray hills between the Sierra Maestra and the capital. Both were linked with underground organisations (the '26th July Movement') in the towns. After sending his brother Raul and 'Che' Guevara to co-ordinate operations in the Escambray, Castro occupied all Oriente Province and closed in on Havana, which he entered on 8 January 1959. Batista's forces disintegrated, surrendered or joined the guerillas. Batista fled abroad and Castro took power.
Result: The campaign demonstrated the ability of a small group of determined guerillas to overthrow an unpopular and demoralised régime. It led to the establishment of the first Communist state in the western hemisphere and provided a model imitated (so far unsuccessfully) by revolutionaries elsewhere in Latin America.

SOUTH AMERICAN WAR OF INDEPENDENCE   1806-24
By the beginning of the nineteenth century political and economic discontent had become widespread in Spain's overseas possessions. In 1806 Francisco Miranda led a short-lived rebellion in Venezuela. The Napoleonic Wars opened up new prospects. In 1808, after the French had invaded Spain and Portugal, Ferdinand VII was forced to surrender his throne to Napoleon Bonaparte's brother. The Spanish people revolted. The S American colonies turned against their Spanish masters,

ostensibly in loyalty to Ferdinand, but in reality to gain national independence.

Their greatest leader was the Venezuelan, Simón Bolívar. In 1813 he entered Venezuela with an army from Colombia (then New Granada) and liberated it. Forced into exile, he returned in 1817, reorganised his forces at Angostura and led them in a vast outflanking movement across the plains and over the Andes to defeat the Spaniards at Boyacá (qv). Returning to Venezuela, he proclaimed its union with New Granada and Ecuador in the Republic of Gran Colombia, and sealed its independence by the victory of Carabobo (qv). Bolívar then joined forces with San Martín, who had led his Army of the Andes (qv) from Argentina into Chile before striking at Peru. After the victories of Junín (qv) and Ayacucho (qv), Bolívar returned to Gran Colombia. Despite the leading part he had played in bringing about the independence of S America, political difficulties there caused his downfall and death in 1830.

British volunteers, including General Daniel O'Leary, Bolívar's trusted aide-de-camp, Admiral Lord Cochrane, Commander of the Chilean navy, and William Miller, who became a Marshal of Peru, played a prominent part in the War of Independence.

TACNA (ALTO DE LA ALIANZA) (Peru)   Peruvian-Chilean War   26 May 1880
Fought between the Peruvian army and a 10,000-strong Chilean expeditionary force under General Manuel Baquedano (PACIFIC, WAR OF THE).

After landing at Ilo the Chileans marched across the desert and engaged the enemy at Alto de la Alianza, outside Tacna. Baquedano at first committed his troops piecemeal but then concentrated them against the Peruvian left and drove the enemy from the field. Peruvian losses were 3,000, including 197 officers, and Chilean losses 2,000.

The Chileans were enabled to advance on Arica and Lima.

TARQUI (JIRÓN)   Peruvian-Colombian War   28 February 1829
Fought between the Peruvians under José de la Mar and the Colombians under Antonio José de Sucre.
Aim: De la Mar, President of Peru, had launched an expansionist policy which had forced Sucre to withdraw from Bolivia when de la Mar invaded it in 1827. Sucre raised an army in Ecuador and marched back into Bolivia.
Battle: The action was indecisive, both sides claiming victory, but the advantage rested with Sucre.
Result: The Peruvian navy lost Guayaquil which they had captured, and de la Mar's expansionist policy collapsed. Peace was signed on 23 September.

TEN YEARS' WAR   Cuba   1868-78
During the period 1868-78 there was a succession of small peasant uprisings in Cuba, mainly directed against the Spanish landowners. These uprisings were put down by police action supported by the Spanish garrisons.

The best known folk heroes were António Maceo and Calixto García who kept the flames of rebellion fanned after a negotiated peace had been signed at El Zanjon in 1878.

These Cuban revolts naturally attracted American sympathisers who tried to run the Spanish naval blockade of the Cuban guerillas. One blockade runner, a former Confederate vessel *Virginius,* which some Americans sold to the Cubans for gold, was captured by the Spanish warship *Tornado* on 1 October 1873 off Morant Bay, Jamaica.

The so-called 'Ten Years' War' was an unsuccessful prelude to Cuba's War of Independence (CUBA).

TRIPLE ALLIANCE, WAR OF THE   see PARAGUAYAN WAR

TUMUSLA (Bolivia)   Bolivian War of Independence   1 April 1825
Fought between the Bolivians under Antonio José de Sucre and the Spanish Royalists under Antonio Pedro Olañeta.

Sucre engaged the Spanish Royalists outside Potosí. The Spanish were totally defeated and their commander mortally wounded.

This was the last battle fought in the South American War of Independence (qv).

TUPAMAROS, URUGUAY   1962-76
Left-wing urban guerilla organisation in Montevideo named after the Peruvian Inca resistance leader Tupac Amaru. Starting by cultivating a 'Robin Hood' image through kidnapping rich bankers, exacting 'donations' for the poor etc, it passed on to large-scale terrorist activity and achieved international notoriety by kidnapping the British Ambassador in 1971. The President Juan Maria Bordaberry suspended civil rights throughout the country and a new State Security Law became effective on 12 July 1971, which extended the period of martial law. At its maximum the strength of Tupamaros was about 3,000. The mastermind of the movement, Amílcar Manera Lluveras, was captured on 22 June, followed by the wounding and capture of the founder of the movement, Raúl Sendic, in September. Other prominent leaders, Julio Marenales Sáenz and Eleuterio Fernández Huidobro, were also apprehended. By the end of November 1973 2,600 people had been gaoled and 42 killed.

The effect of the Tupamaros rebellion was to cause a reaction and usher in a period of right-wing government in Uruguay. A 'Raul Sendic' International Brigade tried in 1974 and 1975 to continue resistance from outside the country but President Juan Maria Bordaberry, who had been primarily responsible for the destruction of this movement, saw to it that the Tupamaros were reduced to comparative impotence by strict laws which were supported by the vast majority of the population.

TUYUTÍ I (S Paraguay)   Paraguayan War   24 May 1866
Fought between Paraguayans under Francisco Solano López, and Argentinians, Brazilians and Uruguayans under General Venancio Flores.

Strength: Paraguayans 25,000; Allies 45,000.

Aim: The Argentinians, Brazilians and Uruguayans were attempting to advance into Paraguay and subjugate it.

Battle: After the Battle of Estero Bellaco (qv) the Allies advanced, while the Paraguayans prepared defensive positions at Tuyutí. On the eve of the battle López changed his plans in favour of a surprise attack. In a four-hour engagement of exceptional ferocity the Paraguayans just failed to break through the enemy lines. Paraguayan casualties were 6,000 killed and 7,000 wounded, and 350 prisoners. Casualties suffered by the Allies were 8,000 killed and wounded.

Result: The Allies gained a victory, though not a decisive one, and they were too exhausted to attempt an immediate attack on the main Paraguayan defences at Humaitá (qv).

TUYUTÍ II (Paraguay)   Paraguayan War   3 November 1867

Fought between the Paraguayans under Francisco Solano Lopez and the Argentinians and Brazilians.

Strength: Paraguayans 8,000; Allies 16,000.

Aim: The Paraguayans attempted to inflict severe damage on the enemy investing their positions and to capture their heavy guns.

Battle: After two years of fighting the Allies had hemmed in the Paraguayan defensive positions. López planned a surprise attack to relieve the pressure, demonstrate his fighting spirit and capture war material. Four brigades of infantry were sent against the enemy trenches, and two cavalry brigades against the redoubts on their right flank. The surprise succeeded brilliantly. The cavalry returned to base after performing their task. The infantry overran the trenches but broke formation in order to sack the camp, without securing the inner fortress. The Allies counter-attacked and forced them to retreat in disorder with their booty. Each side lost about 2,400 killed and wounded.

Result: The battle was inconclusive. The Allies' stranglehold was loosened but not broken, and they were later able to tighten it and capture the key fortress of Humaitá (qv).

YTORORÓ (Paraguay)   Paraguayan War   December 1868

Fought between the Paraguayans under General Bernardino Caballero and the Brazilians under Field-Marshal Luíz Aldes de Lima e Silva, Marquis of Caxias.

Aim: The Brazilians sought to pursue and annihilate the Paraguayan army.

Battle: A Paraguayan force of 5,000 and 12 guns attempted to hold a bridge over the Ytororó River. In ferocious hand-to-hand fighting the bridge changed hands three times, until Caxias arrived with reinforcements and dislodged the Paraguayans who were heavily outnumbered. The Paraguayans lost 1,200, the Brazilians 3,000.

Result: The Brazilians were delayed by this action, but regrouped to overtake the Paraguayans at Avay (qv).

YUNGAY (Chile)   War of the Peruvian-Bolivian Confederation   20 January 1839

Fought between the Army of the Confederation under Andréas Santa Cruz and the Chileans under General Manuel Bulnes.

Aim: The President of Bolivia, Santa Cruz, formed a Confederation of his country and Peru which was virtually a union of the two countries. Chile sought to destroy the threat of domination which the Confederation presented.

Battle: SE of Concepción the two armies met at Yungay for a decisive action, in which Santa Cruz was beaten.

Result: Santa Cruz was overthrown and the Confederation ended.

SECTION EIGHT

FIRST WORLD WAR: WESTERN FRONT

See Map Section, no 20

AISNE I (France)   First World War   13-28 September 1914
Fought between the British and French under Field-Marshal Joseph Joffre and the Germans under General Erich von Falkenhayn.

After the Battle of the Marne (qv), an Allied strategic victory, the Germans withdrew to the heights north of the Aisne, a tributary of the Oise.

The German armies - from west to east, 1st (General Alexander von Kluck), 7th (General Josias von Heeringen), 2nd (General Karl von Bülow), 3rd, 4th, 5th and 6th - were deployed from the Aisne to the Swiss frontier. The French, seeking in a counter-attack to envelop the German right, attacked across the river using the Allied left (W) wing which consisted of the 6th (General Michel Joseph Maunoury), the British Expeditionary Force (Field-Marshal Sir John French) and the 5th (General Louis Franchet d'Esperey). The 9th, 4th, 3rd, 2nd and 1st Armies stood to the east. On the first day, the French and British crossed the Aisne on pontoon bridges and on the following day assaulted the German positions on the plateau. They made considerable gains, but German counter-attacks drove Maunoury's army back almost to its start line on the Aisne. The counter-attacks of the Allies again took them forward, but the battle soon deteriorated into an artillery duel. On 28 September when the Allies were under pressure at Rheims, Joffre called off the attack.

The Allies began to suspect after this battle that, in trench warfare, a frontal assault was useless without strong artillery support. Their attempt to outflank their opponents' right at Noyon had been marked by the Germans who also moved troops to the area to outflank them in turn. Both armies continued to try and outflank each other until the Allies reached the sea at Nieuwpoort, Belgium, in October. The manoeuvre is known as the Race to the Sea.

AISNE II (France)   First World War   16 April-15 May 1917
Fought between the French under General Robert Nivelle and General Henri Pétain and the Germans under General Paul von Hindenburg and General Erich Ludendorff.
Strength: French 800,000; Germans about 650,000.
Aim: After the British attack at Arras Nivelle launched a French offensive along the Aisne River on a 50-mile front between Soissons and Rheims on the River Suippes.
Battle: On 16 April the two armies, the 6th under General Charles Mangin and the 5th under General Olivier Mazel on the left and right respectively, began the attack. They were under the overall command of Army Group Commander General Joseph Alfred Micheler. After a long artillery bombardment the French advanced towards Laon and the strong entrenchments of the Germans on the north slopes of the Aisne. Heavy machine-gun fire from General Max von Boehn's 7th Army in the Chemin des Dames area and General Otto von Below's 1st Army to the east checked the French advance. About 150 French tanks were rendered useless before they could come to the aid of the infantry. Nivelle pressed the attack and the Germans abandoned Fort Malmaison and most of the Chemin des Dames

ridge. On 20 April the French 10th Army under General Denis Duchêne moved into position between the 6th and 5th Armies, but the Germans knew what the French planned to do and had concentrated troops behind their lines. As the French continued to attack, their assaults became more and more costly and the offensive finally came to a standstill on 9th May. French casualties amounted to about 130,000 men, and German losses were about 163,000, including 30,000 prisoners and 227 guns.

Result: The failure of the attack caused widespread mutiny in the French ranks. Pétain, who succeeded Nivelle as Commander on the Western Front on 15 May, quelled the mutiny without the Germans ever knowing about it. Of 23,385 men convicted of mutiny, only 55 were shot.

AISNE III (France)   First World War   27 May-2 June 1918
Fought between the Germans under Ludendorff and the Allies under Pétain, Field-Marshal Lord Haig and General John Pershing.

Aim: The third offensive by the Germans in 1918 was planned as a diversionary attack before a further major attack against the British in Flanders.

Battle: Ludendorff, with forty-one divisions which made up the 1st (General Bruno von Mudra) and 7th (von Boehn) Armies, attacked the strong position held by the French 6th Army (Duchêne) in the Chemin des Dames area which included four French and four battered British divisions. As the position was naturally strong, this 'quiet sector' was not heavily manned. Just after midnight on 27 May an artillery bombardment was opened along the 9-mile front by 4,600 guns in one of the heaviest bombardments of the war. The first wave of seventeen German divisions attacked before dawn and the French were pushed back so fast that bridges over the Aisne were captured intact. Although the British held their line, by nightfall the Germans had penetrated 13 miles into the French lines between Rheims and Soissons, the greatest advance made in one day since the stabilisation of the Western Front in 1914. Because of the success of the attack, Ludendorff chose to concentrate his reserves here, instead of north against the British. Soissons fell on 28 May and, by 30 May, the Germans had reached Château-Thierry on the river Marne, 37 miles from Paris. In three days the Germans advancing 10 miles a day had taken 40,000 prisoners.

Pershing's 3rd American Division (under Major-General Joseph Dickman) reached Château-Thierry on 1 June and fought for three days, to hold the Marne crossings. The Americans recaptured Bligny, SW of Rheims, and drove the Germans back SW of Château-Thierry. On 28 May the Americans captured Cantigny (qv), a critical point in the line. To the west the US 2nd Division under Major-General Omar Bundy counter-attacked the van of the German force under Ludendorff which was greatly superior in numbers. The mile-square Belleau Wood (qv) was finally cleared by the marines after three weeks of fighting, but the advance had been stopped by 6 June. American losses in this, their first encounter with the Germans, were 1,811 killed and about 8,000 wounded. In June alone they took 1,687 Germans prisoner.

Result: The offensive ended with Ludendorff holding a salient 35 miles deep pointing at Paris.

AMIENS (France)   First World War   8 August-3 September 1918
Fought between the Allies under Marshal Ferdinand Foch and the Germans under General Erich Ludendorff.
Aim: The German salient on the Marne was eliminated and Foch now launched his second offensive of 1918 which was designed to force back the German salient at Amiens. This would clear the Paris-Amiens railway from German artillery fire and open the northern coalfields to the Allies.
Battle: General Sir Henry Rawlinson's 4th Army, consisting of three Canadian, two Australian, one American and two British divisions with four in support, as well as 400 tanks and three British cavalry divisions, and the left wing of General Marie Eugène Debeney's 1st French Army to the south, attacked the twenty divisions of General Georg von der Marwitz's 2nd and General Oskar von Hutier's 18th Armies. A short artillery bombardment and a tank assault preceded the attack, which was made on a 14-mile front. In two hours 6,000 prisoners were taken as well as 100 guns, and by nightfall the Allies were 10 miles inside the German lines. For the first time, entire units had collapsed under the onslaught in what Ludendorff called ' the Black Day of the German Army'. On the following day the offensive continued with the capture of 24,000 prisoners and 200 guns. On 10 August the French 3rd Army under General Georges Humbert beat the Germans out of Montdidier on the south of the salient, freeing the Paris-Amiens railway. By 15 August the massif of Lassigny was in Rawlinson's hands and he was able to observe the Germans' communications all along their south front and over the north plain. The British 3rd Army under General Sir Julian Byng joined in the offensive on 21 August, followed by the British 1st Army under General H. Horne, north of Byng (who was north of Rawlinson). Ludendorff then ordered a withdrawal east along a 30-mile front.

The Allies pursued the retreating Germans closely, forcing them back to the Siegfried Line on 3 September. The Amiens salient, created by the Germans five months earlier, had been eliminated. German losses during the battle were 50,000 killed and wounded, 33,000 prisoners, a total of 83,000. British and Commonwealth losses were 22,000 and French losses 24,000.
Result: This battle was the turning point for the Allies on the Western Front.

ANTWERP III (Belgium)   First World War   6-10 October 1914
Fought between the Germans under General Erich von Falkenhayn and the Belgians under King Albert I and the British under Lt-General Sir Henry Rawlinson.
Strength: Germans 120,000 rising to 200,000; Allies 233,000 (Belgians 150,000, British 30,000) + 2 battleships, 3 monitors and numerous lighter vessels.
Aim: After the Germans occupied Brussels on 20 August the great port of Antwerp was the only real stronghold of the Belgian army, and, potentially, an anchor

for the Allies' left flank.

Battle: The Belgian army withdrew from Brussels when the Germans advanced through Liège (qv) and Namur and fell back on a second line based on Antwerp. In successive sorties the Belgians than recaptured Malines and Alost (NW of Brussels) and attacked Cortenberg. The Germans besieged Antwerp, General Hans von Beseler using siege guns on the town and forts, which were destroyed one by one. On 6 October the Belgian army drew out of the town SW along the Flemish coast. They met a British force under Rawlinson marching from Ostend to relieve them, but the combined armies continued to retreat and on 10 October the Germans entered Antwerp. Winston Churchill, First Lord of the Admiralty, lent his enthusiastic support to the defence of Antwerp, but in vain.

Result: The Belgian army took up a position on the Allied line between the North Sea and Dixmude. Establishing themselves on the River Yser they clung to a fragment of their national territory.

The loss of Antwerp, which could have been prevented had the British reinforced the city in time, was a heavy blow to the Allies.

ARRAS II (France) First World War 9 April-16 May 1917
Fought between the British under Field-Marshal Sir Douglas Haig and the Germans under General Paul von Hindenburg.

Aim: The French aimed their principal offensive for 1917 at the Aisne section (see AISNE II). To draw the German reserves north, the British planned a diversionary attack at Arras to take place a week earlier.

Battle: From 23 Febuary to 5 April the Germans undertook a voluntary withdrawal to the Hindenburg Line, a strongly defended front east of the original line occupied by the Germans. On 9 April after five days of bombardment by 2,800 guns and gas, the British attack was launched and, to the left, north of Arras, the Canadian Corps of the 1st Army stormed up Vimy Ridge the first day under General H. Horne. South of them, the 3rd Army under General Sir Edmund Allenby moved 3½ miles into the German lines. The British now prepared to thrust deeper into enemy-held territory, but the German 6th Army under General Baron Ludwig von Falkenhausen had reserves 15 miles east and these were rushed up to the front to block the advance. The south end of the attack, undertaken by the 5th Army under General Sir Hubert Gough, was blocked by the Germans who held fast. By 11 April General Sir Julian Byng's Canadian Corps had taken part of Vimy Ridge, Lt-General Ferguson's 17 Corps was advancing on Thelus, Lt-General Haldane's 6 Corps overran Blangy in front of Arras and 7 Corps took a fortress known as the Harp. Twelve thousand prisoners and 150 guns had been taken. Thereafter, however, little ground was captured, though counterattacks were mostly repulsed. The offensive was pressed while the French launched their main attack on the south pivot of the Siegfried Line and while Haig prepared the British offensive at Ypres (qv). Along a 20-mile front the British had taken 20,000 prisoners by the end of May as well as 257 guns, 227 mortars, 470 machine-guns and the northern 6 miles of the Siegfried Line.

German casualties were 75,000. British losses were 84,000.
Result: The immediate British objective was achieved, though at considerable cost.

ARTOIS II (France)   First World War   9 May-18 June 1915
Fought between the Allies under Field-Marshal Joseph Joffre and the Germans under General Erich von Falkenhayn.

During the second action at Ypres (qv) Joffre built up Allied forces in Artois and on 9 May, after a massive artillery bombardment, launched his offensive on a 6-mile front north of Arras. During the first days of the attack the Germans were pushed back 3 miles and the Allies siezed part of Vimy Ridge. The Germans counter-attacked and drove the Allies back and thereafter the battle became one of attrition, ending on 18 June. French losses were 100,000 and German casualties totalled 75,000.

ARTOIS-LOOS (France)   First World War   25 September-15 October 1915
Fought between the Allies under General Sir Douglas Haig and General Auguste Dubail and the Germans under General Erich von Falkenhayn.
Aim: Field-Marshal Joseph Joffre planned an offensive in Champagne (qv) which was to be accompanied by co-ordinated assaults on German positions in Artois. Joffre's aim was to break German communications from east to west along the Aisne and force their retreat from their front along the Oise and Somme.
Battle: On 25 September, Dubail led the French 10th Army against German positions on Vimy Ridge and Haig led the British 1st Army against the village of Loos, to the north. The British used poison gas for the first time. The French attack carried much of the German first line and some of the second line of defences. From La Bassée Canal to Lens and in front of Loos, the British reached as far as the German rear lines before energetic counter-attacks directed by Falkenhayn pushed back both Allied attacks. The British assault failed largely owing to the lack of reserves at hand. French casualties were 120,000, British were 50,000 and German 165,000.
Result: The line was back to what it had been the previous year. Two months later, Haig replaced General Sir John French as the British Commander in France.

During the first two days of this battle the British lost twice as many dead as all three armies (British, American and German) lost on D-day in the Second World War, yet the British effort at Loos was still comparatively minor compared with the French and German.

BELLEAU WOOD (Vaux, France)   First World War   6 June-1 July 1918
Fought between the Americans under General John Pershing and the Germans under General Erich Ludendorff.

The German offensive across the Aisne (AISNE III) had penetrated as far as Vaux on the Paris-Metz road and Belleau Wood, just to the NW. Major-General Omar Bundy's 2nd American Division was sent forward by Pershing in a counter-attack on 6 June. The marine brigade of General James Harbord and the 3rd Infantry

Brigade of Brigadier-General Lewis bore the brunt of the attack. The wood, which was a mile square, was full of four German divisions and was not cleared until 1 July when Vaux was also retaken. Casualties suffered by the Americans totalled 9,777, and they took 1,600 Germans prisoner.

CAMBRAI I (France)   First World War   20 November-7 December 1917
Fought between the British 3rd Army under General Sir Julian Byng and the German 2nd Army under General Georg von der Marwitz.
Aim: An impeding armistice between the Russians and Germans threatened to release German troops from the Eastern Front and augment their numbers on the Western Front. Field-Marshal Sir Douglas Haig decided to launch an attack on the north of the line before these troops could be brought up. This offensive was also designed to relieve the pressure on the Italians.
Battle: In order to effect complete surprise, the attack was not preceded by an artillery bombardment, but was instead spearheaded by 324 tanks in the first massed assault of tanks in history. Von der Marwitz's 2nd Army was taken by surprise and a hole 6 miles wide was made in the German front. The British poured through this gap and penetrated 3 miles into enemy territory, but by nightfall German counter-attacks coupled with mechanical failures in the tanks had caused the assault to bog down on the St Quentin canal. Fierce fighting, especially round Bourlon Wood, produced no further penetration of the Siegfried Line and on 30 November the Germans, who had been reinforced on both flanks of the salient, launched a massive counter-attack which drove forward south of the salient. The British lines were shelled with gas. Haig now ordered the front of the salient to be shortened, and this was done between 4 and 7 December. British losses were 44,000 killed and wounded, 6,000 prisoners, who were taken on the first day of the counter-offensive, and 160 guns. German losses were 50,000 killed or wounded, 11,000 prisoners and 136 guns.
Result: Little was gained by the offensive except proving the great importance of tanks in the offensive against dug-in positions. One reason for the failure of the tank attack was the lack of close supporting infantry, whose necessary use with armour was not yet known.

CAMBRAI II-ST QUENTIN (France)   First World War   27 September-
11 November 1918
Fought between the Allies under Marshal Ferdinand Foch and the Germans under General Erich Ludendorff and, later, General Wilhelm Groener.
Aim: The day after the American-French attack was launched, Foch set off the west half of the offensive on the Western Front, the second half of the pincer movement designed to trap the German army.
Battle: From Cambrai south to St Quentin, four Allied armies under the immediate control of Haig stood ready to attack. The British 1st (General H. Horne) and 3rd (Byng), the two north armies, attacked on 27 September and the British 4th (General Henry Rawlinson) and the French 1st (General Marie

Eugene Debeney) followed on 29 September. The British 4th was aided by several American divisions. In this drive 26,500 prisoners and 340 guns were taken and the German armies of General Max von Boehn, suffering under heavy artillery fire, yielded the line of the St Quentin Canal. The Siegfried (Hindenburg) Line fell under Allied pressure. On 30 September, the 3rd Army were in the western suburbs of Cambrai while the Canadians threatened to outflank it from the north. The Germans surrendered St Quentin to the French on 1 October. By 4 October, the Allies held the entire defensive position. Ludendorff withdrew to the line of the Selle, a tributary of the Scheldt. On 17 October the Allied advance resumed and on 19 October the German line on the Selle was forced back south. Ludendorff resigned a week later and was replaced by Groener.

By the end of the month the German armies in the north had been driven back to a 20-mile front behind the Scheldt. Field-Marshal Lord Haig's armies closed up on the Germans and were joined by three armies to their left (N) under King Albert I of Belgium, the Belgian, the French 6th and the British 2nd which had moved up from Flanders. To the right (S), the French 5th and 10th Armies prevented the Germans either from moving reserves north against Haig or south against the American offensive of General John Pershing. On 1 November the Allied offensive was resumed along a 30-mile front and the line of the Scheldt was turned. By 11 November, when the armistice came into effect, a Canadian division held Mons and Albert's troops to the north held Ghent. A pincer movement to the south had made equal progress, but the two forces never actually joined up.

Result: The German armies on the Western Front were now defeated.

CANTIGNY (France)   First World War   28 May 1918
Fought between the Americans under General John Pershing and the Germans under General Oskar von Hutier. Pershing insisted that American units coming into the Western Front be committed only under his direct command. General Ferdinand Foch agreed to this.

The American 1st Division under General Robert Bullard took over the part of the front occupied by the French 1st Army under General Marie Eugene Debeney. To the east of this sector stood the village of Cantigny which was held by the German 18th Army under von Hutier. On 28 May the second day of the huge German offensive on the Aisne River (AISNE III), the Americans assaulted and took Cantigny as well as 200 prisoners. The Germans counter-attacked, but the Americans held the village although the German assaults were ferocious. The Americans suffered 1,607 casualties, including 100 killed.

The tactical advantage of the victory was small, but the American presence brought great psychological gain to the Allies. The American 2nd and 3rd Divisions went into action on the Marne front four days later.

CHAMPAGNE I (France) First World War   20 December 1914-17 March 1915
Fought between the Allies under Field-Marshal Joseph Joffre and the Germans

under General Erich von Falkenhayn.

Despite the fact that it was becoming evident that the Western Front was deadlocked, both sides continued to fight from trenches during the winter. Joffre concentrated most of his effort in Champagne, but the German defences proved impenetrable and the French assault was called off in March.

The difference in tactics - Germans fighting from trenches with machine-guns as opposed to the French who employed bayonet charges principally - showed the superiority of the former method of warfare.

CHAMPAGNE II (France)   First World War   25 September-6 November 1915
Fought between the Allies under General Fernande de Langle de Cary and General Henri Pétain and the Germans under General Baron Ludwig von Falkanhayn.
Aim: The French sought to break the Germans' line of communication from east to west along the Aisne.
Battle: After a quiet summer on the Western Front the French launched a major offensive when the French 2nd Army under Pétain and 4th Army under de Langle de Cary attacked westward from Rheims towards the Argonne Forest. The French gained some ground and took thousands of prisoners and some guns before 30 October, when in counter-attacks the Germans retook most of the ground they had held and recaptured the lost rail communications in the area. The battle ended on 6 November with the French back where they had started, except in a few places where gains of 2½ miles had been made, a useless addition along a 15-mile front. Joffre had captured 25,000 men and 160 guns, but his own casualties were 145,000 killed or wounded. A complementary attack to the north was equally unsuccessful.
Result: The Allies' objective was not achieved.

FRONTIERS OF FRANCE, BATTLE OF THE   First World War   20-4 August 1914
Fought between the Germans under General Count Helmuth von Moltke and the Allies under Field-Marshal Joseph Joffre.

At the outbreak of the First World War both sides planned offensives - the Germans with the Schlieffen Plan and the French with Plan 17 - and in August the two armies met on a front which stretched from Mons in Belgium down to the Swiss frontier. Four separate actions, interrelated, took place: Lorraine, Ardennes, Charleroi (known also as Sambre) and Mons.
Lorraine: On the Eastern Front the French 1st (General Auguste Dubail) and 2nd (General Noël de Castelnau) Armies advanced into Lorraine, crossing the border into Germany on 14 August. The French marched on Sarrebourg and Morhange while von Moltke forbade the Germans to counter-attack, wanting the French to commit themselves by marching so deep into Germany that they would be unable to pull out to support the French to the north, where the Schlieffen Plan was being implemented. When the French began to disengage on 20 August the German 7th (General Josias von Heeringen) and 6th (Prince Rupert of Bavaria) Armies, both under Rupert, counter-attacked and defeated the French at Sarrebourg with

heavy losses. A German counter-offensive then got under way on 23 August, when the French 15 and 16 Corps were beaten back though the 20 Corps held its ground at the Battle of Morhange. The French line stabilised at the line of the Moselle, their front being along the line of Épinal, Charmes, Nancy and Toul. This line was held until the Battle of the Marne (qv) which began on 5 September.

Ardennes: In the centre of the front Joffre sent the 3rd (General Pierre de Ruffey) and the 4th (General Fernande de Langle de Cary) into the Ardennes with the aim of smashing the German centre and thus outflanking their turning movement in Belgium. The French advanced in wooded country and dense fog, meeting the Germans advancing towards them. This was the pivot of von Moltke's right in S Ardennes and was composed of the 5th Army (Prince Frederick William). Prince Frederick William also directed the 4 (Duke of Württemberg) in N Ardennes. The two armies clashed for two days of fierce fighting after which the French retreated - the 3rd Army to Verdun, the 4th to Stenay and Sedan. Frederick William pressed on to Longwy on 23 August and advanced still farther, leaving the fortress there to be taken by siege troops. Joffre replaced Ruffey with General Maurice Sarrail a week later. On 26-8 August the French 4th Army checked the German 4th, but the action opened a gap of 50 miles between it and the 5th Army. Joffre filled this with three corps under General Ferdinand Foch which, on the eve of the Battle of the Marne, became the 9th Army.

Charleroi: On the Western Front the French 5th Army of General Charles Lanrezac faced the German 3rd Army under General Max von Hausen to the NE, and the approach of the 2nd under General Karl von Bülow, leaving troops to besiege Namur (qv), had forced two crossings of the Sambre between Namur and Charleroi. On 21 August von Bülow took Charleroi. The French fought fiercely to try and halt the German advance, but were compelled to fall back south, which left a 10-mile gap between the French left and the BEF (British Expeditionary Force) which was still deploying at Mons. On the night of 22/3 August von Hausen crossed the Meuse and struck west towards the French right, left vulnerable by the withdrawal of the French 4th Army. Lanrezac began a withdrawal on the night of 23 August to escape the trap, losing 5,000 men on the Sambre in the action. The French retreated south for six days before turning on von Bülow on 29 August and counter-attacking towards Guise. Von Bülow's advance was checked for thirty-six hours but the BEF, withdrawing on the left, and the defeat of the French 4th Army forced the 5th Army to continue its retreat on 30 August.

Mons: The BEF, on the extreme left (W) of the Allied line, 35 miles beyond Charleroi, crossed the border into Belgium to take up a position at Mons. The four divisions (70,000 men + 300 guns) were still deploying behind the 60-foot wide Mons Canal on 23 August when the German 1st Army under General Alexander von Kluck attacked with 160,00 men and 600 guns. Von Kluck was carrying out that part of the Schlieffen Plan which called for a wide turning movement in Belgium in order to move south into France. The BEF held its ground for nine hours, despite numerical inferiority, but withdrew at nightfall.

The two divisions of 2 Corps under General Sir Horace Smith-Dorrien bore the brunt of the attack. The British lost 4,244 men in the fighting, but only held von Kluck's advance up by one day. The steadiness and rapid fire of the BEF had disconcerted von Kluck's troops but made little difference to the outcome.

The Allied defeat at all points ensured that the war would be fought on French soil. Of 1,250,000 French soldiers engaged, about 300,000 were casualties and German losses were comparable. For the number of men engaged on both sides and for the rate and number of losses sustained by both sides in the battle, this was the largest action of the war.

HAELEN Belgium)   First World War   12 August 1914
Fought between the Germans under General Georg von der Marwitz and the Belgians under General de Witte.

The opening battle of the war was fought at Liège (qv), but while this town was under bombardment, a cavalry corps under Marwitz was sent across the Meuse River to the north and, riding through Limburg Province, made for Louvain. At Haelen, the Belgian cavalry were defending a bridge and, when the Germans came up, the Belgians dismounted and fought as riflemen, beating off repeated German attacks from 8 am to 6 pm. Marwitz withdrew, having suffered heavy losses.

Although the action was hailed as a great victory for the Allies, it actually represented only a small check to the Germans who continued their sweep through Belgium when the Liège forts fell four days later.

LE CATEAU (France)   First World War   26 August 1914
Fought between the British under General Sir Horace Smith-Dorrien and the Germans under General Alexander von Kluck.

After being defeated at Mons Field-Marshal Sir John French led the BEF (British Expeditionary Force) in a southerly retreat, along with the French army. The German right (W) moved into France on a 75-mile front and threatened the left of Field-Marshal Joseph Joffre's army which was held by French and five and a half British divisions. The wide-sweeping German 1st Army caught up with 2 Corps on French's left flank at Le Cateau, 18 miles north of St Quentin. The Forest of Mormal separated 2 Corps from 1 Corps under General Sir Douglas Haig. Smith-Dorrien was compelled to give battle, as his troops could march no more.

The engagement lasted eleven hours, during which the three and a half divisions fought against ceaseless onslaughts from the Germans who outnumbered them. After dark the British disengaged and fell back towards St Quentin on the Somme. British losses in the action were 8,077 men and 36 guns (15,000 men had been lost during the first five days of the war). German losses were much heavier.

The delaying action enabled the BEF to escape the Germans' sweeping movement as they marched into France. The Allied left was so weak that Joffre now moved the Army of the Lorraine under General Michel Joseph Maunoury west towards Amiens, naming it the French 6th Army. The battle was the biggest in which British troops had been involved since Waterloo, about a century previously.

LIÈGE (Belgium)   First World War   4-16 August 1914
Fought between the Belgians under General Gérard Leman and the Germans under General Otto von Emmich.
Strength: Belgians 70,000; Germans 320,000.
Aim: The Germans invaded neutral Belgium in order to march on France. The Belgians, who had not armed themselves as the other great European powers had done in preparation for the war, now resisted the German advance against great odds.
Battle: The Germans struck Liège, the gateway to Belgium, on the left bank of the Meuse on 4 August. By 6 August the Germans had penetrated the system of twelve protective underground forts east of the river and the city was entered on 7 August when the citadel surrendered to General Erich Ludendorff in person. Leman, commanding the forts ringing the city, had retreated across the Gette River, where he skirmished with units of the German army and awaited the advance of the Allies. Eleven of the twelve forts held out under Leman until German 420mm and 305mm guns blasted them into submission. Leman was captured unconscious, the resistance he had put up for eleven days (the forts fell on 16 August) having enabled the Allies to deploy before the German advance which was held up at Liège.
Result: Having captured Liège, the Germans began to implement the Schlieffen Plan (FRONTIERS OF FRANCE), moving in a wide turning movement, forcing the Belgians to fall back to Antwerp (qv). Brussels was occupied on 20 August without resistance by General Alexander von Kluck's 1st Army.

LYS (Belgium)   First World War   9-29 April 1918.
Fought between the Allies under Field-Marshal Sir Douglas Haig and the Germans under General Erich Ludendorff.

With the first major German offensive of the year completed, Ludendorff decided to attack the thinly held British front in Flanders and to roll up the British line from the north. The river Lys, about 100 feet wide, formed the boundary between the British 1st and 2nd Armies. After an artillery bombardment which lasted from 7 pm on 7 April until 4 am on 9 April General Ferdinand von Quast's 6th Army attacked west from Armentières, south of the river. They struck the centre of the British 1st Army under General H.S.Horne which was held by a Portuguese division. This section collapsed and retreated 5 miles, forcing the rest of the 1st Army to follow suit.

On 10 April Friedrich Sixt von Arnim's 4th Army joined the attack and threw back General Herbert Plumer's 2nd Army, whose reserves had been called south to the Lys River (Plumer stood north of Armentieres), regaining Messines Ridge. By 11 April the two German armies had joined up and Ludendorff decided to turn what had been a secondary offensive into a major attack, his objective being the ports of Calais, Dunkirk and Boulogne. Haig rushed as many troops as he could into the area and, though heavily outnumbered, five British and one Australian divisions managed to contain the German advance. The situation was still very dangerous when, on 21 April, General Ferdinand Foch also sent French troops to reinforce the Allies. Meanwhile, on 17 April, the Belgians had beaten back an attack near the Ypres salient and a force of British and Canadians defeated an attack on La Bassée Canal, the former attack inflicting very severe casualties on the enemy. In the north, the Germans made their final assaults on the Allies with their eleven divisions in mass formation, but they were repulsed. By 29 April the battle was over. British losses were nine-tenths of the total Allied loss of 305,000. Germany had lost 350,000 for a territorial gain of 10 miles in an awkward salient south of Ypres.

MARNE I (France)   First World War   3-9 September 1914
Fought between the Germans under General Helmuth von Moltke and the Allies under Field-Marshal Joseph Joffre.
Strength: Germans 900,000 (44 infantry divisions + 7 cavalry divisions comprising 5 armies); Allies 1,082,000 (56 infantry divisions + 9 cavalry divisions comprising 6 armies).

The Battle of the Frontiers of France (qv) ended in Allied defeats all along the line. This enabled the German armies to enter France on the centre and right of the line, from Verdun west to Amiens.

The German 1st Army under General Alexander von Kluck proved the greatest danger to the Allied line north of Paris where the French 6th Army, unable to check the German advance, fell back until 30 August when it was within 30 miles of Paris. At this point it came under the control of the Military Governor of the capital, General Joseph-Simon Galliéni. To the right of the 6th under General Michel Joseph Maunoury was the British Expeditionary Force under Field-Marshal Sir John French which, after its defeats at Le Cateau and Mons, was withdrawing rapidly through Compiègne, leaving French flanks exposed on either side of it. The BEF recrossed the Marne on 3 September, turning east, and the other French armies facing north, the 5th (General Charles Lanrezac, who was replaced by General Louis Franchet d'Esperey on 3 September), the 4th (General Fernand de Langle de Cary) and the 3rd (General Maurice Sarrail) yielded ground steadily to the four other German armies, though they fought hard. On 31 August, Kluck altered the course of his offensive from south to SE, thus departing from the Schlieffen Plan which had called for Kluck's force to encircle the French armies west and south of Paris. Believing the Allies to be beaten, Kluck formed an inner wheel to the north of Paris in order to roll up the Allied left (a plan which was approved by von Moltke). The French and British, who had been ordered to go on retreating in a line south of the Seine while the French 6th Army went to reinforce the Paris garrison, now learnt of the German change in plan from aviation reports. Instead of swinging west of the city as had been planned, the Germans now came east and thus moved across the Allied front and exposed their right flank. Reaching the Marne on 3 September the Germans crossed it only a day behind the BEF and French 5th Army, and by 5 September the Germans stood midway between the Marne and the Seine, directly east of Paris. On 6 September the German 1st Army began to withdraw north on the orders of von Moltke who was concerned about the exposure of the right flank. Galliéni had, however, urged Joffre to launch a counter-attack upon this wing which, though he was reluctant to, he eventually agreed to do. Maunoury's army was ordered forward at 08.30 on 4 September but the orders did not reach the other generals until 5 September by which time both French and d'Esperey felt it was too late to counter-attack and continued retreating.

On 6 September Maunoury and Galliéni launched the counter-offensive against the 4 Reserve Corps of General Hans von Gronau along the Ourcq River. On the left, Maunoury's troops (150,000 strong) hit hard at the exposed German flank and d'Esperey, who had now turned back to fight his pursuers, moved into the 30-mile gap, created by the attack on the German 1st Army, between that and the German 2nd Army (General Karl von Bülow). The BEF, who had also returned to the front under French's reluctant orders, followed d'Esperey into the gap. To the right of this counter-offensive, General Ferdinand Foch's 9th Army, newly created, struck at the weak junction between the German 2nd and 3rd (General Max von Hausen) Armies and then held their ground during furious counter-attacks below the St Grond marshes. Along a 100-mile front, the battle continued for three days, Allied reinforcements coming from Paris in commandeered taxi-cabs (6,000 of 4 Corps). Von Kluck's army swung round to meet the Allied flanking attack. On the night of 8 September d'Esperey launched a night attack on the German 2nd Army (von Bülow) and drove back their right flank, forcing von Kluck to withdraw north to protect his left rear from the BEF who were now advancing once again across the Marne.

On 9 September the Germans began a withdrawal, fighting as they went, for 40 miles to the Aisne River (AISNE I). The retreat became disorderly owing to untrue rumours that British and Russian troops had landed on the Belgian coast, to the German rear. The front stretched from Verdun west to Noyon. On the east of the French line, the 1st (General Auguste Dubail) and 2nd (General Nöel de Castelnau) French Armies held the fortress cities along the Marne of Epinal, Charmes, Nancy and Toul despite the fact that two of their corps were transferred to the Marne front. For eighteen days these armies were constantly assaulted by two armies under Prince Rupert of Bavaria, his own 6th Army and General Josias von Heeringen's 7th. Between these two fronts Crown Prince Frederick William directed his 5th and the Duke of Württemberg's 4th armies in an unsuccessful attempt to penetrate the French line held by the 3rd and 4th Armies, this line lying between Verdun and the Upper Marne. About 25 per cent of men engaged were casualties on both sides.

On 14 September von Moltke was replaced by General Erich von Falkenhayn.

The French did not achieve a major triumph in that they did not pierce the German line, but their counter-attack ensured that the war would be a long one, and both offensive plans which had been designed to bring the war to a quick close had now failed. The battle can thus be said to be one of the decisive conflicts of history as it prevented a quick German win over France as in 1870, before France's allies and potential allies could bring their strength to bear.

MARNE II (France)   First World War   15 July-5 August 1918
Fought between the Allies under Foch and the Germans under Ludendorff.
Strength: Allies (15-17 July) 36 divisions (French 23, American 9, British 2, Italian 2), (18 July-6 August) 37 divisions (French 23, American 8, British 4, Italian 2) + 350 tanks; Germans 52 divisions.
Aim: The fifth German assault on the Western Front was aimed at the Marne River, east of Paris. Two armies attacking either side of Rheims were to converge after beating the French armies that stood between them.
Battle: To the east, the German 1st (General Bruno von Mudra) and 3rd (General Karl von Einem) made small gains before being stopped by 11 am under the fire of General Henri Gouraud's 1st Army all along their 26-mile front. To the SW of the town, above Château-Thierry, and below Epernay, General Max von Boehn's 7th Army smashed through General Jean Degoutte's 6th Army on a 22-mile front and had made a bridgehead 9 miles long and 4 miles deep before being checked by the French 9th Army under General Marie Mitry and the American 3rd Division with the British and Italian divisions in support. This marked the end of the so-called Champagne-Marne offensive which was the last major German offensive on the Western Front. It had cost Ludendorff 800,000 casualties and had so weakened his armies that the initiative now passed to the Allies.

On 18 July Foch ordered a counter-offensive against the Marne salient, the main attack being carried out by the 6th and 10th (General Charles Mangin) Armies with fourteen Allied divisions in support, while secondary attacks on the east and south were made by the 5th (General Henri Berthelot) and 9th respectively. The main attack in the west began with Mangin early in the morning. He was followed by the other armies, which came in a clockwise direction. With 350 tanks, the Allies advanced between 2 and 5 miles the first day. As they continued to advance into the salient, they threatened to cut the German communications link between Château-Thierry and Soissons. Ludendorff began to withdraw from the Marne and Soissons was liberated on 2 August. By 3 August the Germans occupied a line along the Vesle and Aisne Rivers at the base of the former salient. When the Americans attacked on 6 August they found the Germans solidly entrenched and the action ended the battle.
Result: What had begun with a German offensive ended up as an Allied victory.

MESSINES (Belgium)   First World War   7-14 June 1917
Fought between the British 2nd Army under General Herbert Plumer and the German 4th Army under General Friedrich Sixt von Arnim.
Aim: The British wanted to break out of the salient at Ypres which they had held for over two and a half years. In order to undertake a major offensive, Field-

Marshal Sir Douglas Haig had first to force the Germans out of their positions commanding the Messines Ridge to the south. The importance of this attack was heightened in the spring of 1917 since it became imperative to keep the Germans occupied while General Henri Pétain restored confidence in the French army which had mutinied after the 1917 Battle of the Aisne (AISNE II). Plumer had in all twelve divisions and von Arnim fifteen.

Battle: Nineteen mines, containing almost 500 tons of high explosive, were planted by the British under the Messines Ridge and, after a ten-day preliminary bombardment, the mines were detonated at dawn on 7 June. Nine divisions of Plumer's 2nd Army (including an Australian and a New Zealand division)went in to clear the ridge. The ruined German lines were cleared by 7 am and General Sir Hubert Gough's 5th Army went in to exploit the opening along with General François Anthoine's 1st French Army. After a few days all German positions on the salient had been taken; but to the east, German resistance stiffened as Prince Rupert of Bavaria ordered von Arnim's 4th Army to fall back and counter-attack. The British advance was therefore limited to this point and the tactical advantage gained was also lessened. However, the ridge was held until 12 April 1918. The British losses were 25,000; but the German losses, which included 7,200 prisoners, were much greater.

Result: The British objective was partly achieved.

MEUSE RIVER-ARGONNE FOREST (France)   First World War   26 September-11 November 1918

Fought between the Allies under Marshal Ferdinand Foch and the Germans under General Erich Ludendorff and General Wilhelm Groener.

Aim: Four Allied thrusts were planned by Marshal Foch and Field-Marshal Lord Haig in order to force the Germans out of the Hindenburg Line and into surrender. The Belgians were to attack at Ypres, the British at Cambrai and St Quentin (qv) and the French and Americans were to undertake an associated operation designed to trap the Germans in a pincer movement. The French were to attack from the south, the Americans from the west.

Battle: The Americans under General John Pershing held a 17-mile front from Forges on the Meuse to the centre of the Argonne Forest whence General Henri Gouraud's 4th Army ran to Auberive on the Suippe. Pershing's three corps, 3, 5 and 1, advanced on 26 September with Gouraud on his left. Pershing faced the defensive position of the German army of General Max von Gallwitz, Gouraud that of Crown Prince Frederick William. The Allied advance was restricted to 9 miles during the first five days of the assault, as the hilly, tangled terrain was to the Germans' advantage. The Americans took 5 miles of the Meuse heights, but only 2 miles of the difficult Argonne Forest sector. On 1 October the attack was stopped by the Americans who rested for three days before resuming the offensive once more. From that time until 31 October the Americans pushed on in a series of tough frontal attacks which gradually forced the Germans back. (It was during this fighting that Whittlesey's Lost Battalion was produced and

Sergeant Alvin York took 132 prisoners.) On 12 October Pershing divided his command, giving the 1st Army to General Hunter Liggett and the 2nd, which was engaged in a diversionary attack to the east of the Meuse, to General Robert Bullard. By 31 October the Argonne Forest was cleared and the Americans had advanced 10 miles. By this time Gouraud's 4th Army had reached the Aisne River, 20 miles from the jumping-off point. On 1 November both armies advanced once more against the Germans, who were now under Groener, and by 11 November when the armistice was declared, the French and Americans had moved another 21 miles forward to reach Sedan on the east and within 6 miles of Montmédy to the west. The Belgians had forced the Germans out of Ostend, Zeebrugge and Bruges and the Germans were already behind the Scheldt. German casualties were 100,000, American losses were 117,000.

Result: The Allied objective was achieved and the war was now over.

MULHOUSE (France)   First World War   9 August 1914

Fought between the French under General Bonneau and the Germans under General Josias von Heeringen.

While the Germans launched an offensive on France through Belgium, Field-Marshal Joseph Joffre attacked over the Vosges Mountains into Alsace, which had been in German hands since 1871. The French 7 Corps under General Bonneau fought its way into Altkirch, losing 100 men, and the following day entered Mulhouse without firing a shot.

The French proceeded with their liberation, but the German 7th Army under von Heeringen came up from Strasbourg and, early on 9 August, they counter-attacked. The French remained in Mulhouse for twenty-four hours, but, fearing envelopment, they withdrew SW until they were within 10 miles of Belfort.

Bonneau was relieved of command by Joffre, charged with lack of aggressiveness. General Paul Pan was given command of a new three-corps Army of Alsace.

NAMUR II (Belgium)   First World War   20-5 August 1914

Fought between the Belgians under General Gérard M. Leman and the Germans under General Alexander von Kluck.

Strength: Belgians 37,000; Germans 100,000 + 450 guns.

In the third week of the war 25 divisions of infantry and some cavalry, with about 500 Skoda 420mm mortars and howitzers, made their way up the Meuse into S Belgium. At the confluence of the Meuse and the Sambre lay Namur, the last fortress between the Germans and France. General Charles Lanrezac's 5th French Army and the British Expeditionary Force were still deploying and General Karl von Bülow took most of the German 2nd Army on to cross the Sambre above Namur, dropping troops off to besiege the fortress. The garrison of Namur consisted of the Belgian 14th Division, and the defence rested chiefly on ten supposedly impregnable forts, such as were round the city of Liège (qv), as well as minefields, electrified barbed wire and trenches. Many of the 420mm and 305mm guns which had been used to bombard Liège were now brought up, and on 20 August the Germans opened fire. Two-ton shells as well as other heavy missiles fell on the trenches and forts at the rate of twenty a minute. The entrenched infantry suffered heavily, whole regiments being decimated. Five forts had fallen by the end of the first day, and the Belgian infantry had been forced back in a fierce battle. By 25 August the last forts surrendered and the city capitulated, the Germans taking 50,000 prisoners.

The two offensives (the Germans' Schlieffen Plan and the French Plan 17) now got under way (FRONTIERS OF FRANCE).

NEUVE-CHAPELLE (Belgium)   First World War   10-13 March 1915
Fought between the British and French under Field-Marshal Sir John French, and the Germans under General Erich von Falkenhayn.

At the beginning of 1915 the French held the salient at Ypres with two corps. Field-Marshal Joseph Joffre asked Sir John French to relieve these troops with British.

French decided to make a strong attack on the German-held village of Neuve-Chapelle before releasing the French troops. Accordingly, on 10 March, he began one of the war's first great artillery barrages against the village and followed this with an assault by the British 1st Army under General Sir Douglas Haig. The village was captured that day, but Falkenhayn immediately rushed 16,000 reinforcements into the area and these slowed the British advance the second day. By 13 March the British attack had been contained, short of a high ridge to the east of Neuve-Chapelle. French now released the men Joffre had requested for his projected offensive at Artois (qv). Casualties amounted to 13,000.

Joffre's offensive in Artois was pre-empted by Falkenhayn's attack against Ypres (YPRES II).

NOYON-MONTDIDIER (France)   First World War   9-13 June 1918
Fought between the French under General Ferdinand Foch and the Germans under General Erich Ludendorff.
Aim: In order to maintain the German offensive, Ludendorff decided to launch another attack, aiming to threaten Paris by joining the Amiens salient with that on the Aisne-Marne to the south.
Battle: On 9 June the German 18th Army under General Oskar von Hutier advanced south from the Noyon-Montdidier sector, forcing the French 3rd Army under General Georges Humbert to fall back. On 10 June General Max von Boehn's 7th Army moved west from Soissons against the French 10th Army under General Charles Mangin. He was not able to move far in his drive, being held back by Mangin after making only small gains. Hutier advanced 6 miles towards Compiègne where the two German forces were scheduled to link up. By 13 June the offensive had been stopped, the Germans having suffered heavy losses.
Result: As well as halting the German advance, French deep-zone defences had reduced their own casualties.

SOMME I (France)   First World War   1 July-18 November 1916
Fought between the Allies under General Ferdinand Foch and the Germans under General Erich von Falkenhayn.

The second of two offensives launched by the Allies in 1916, this offensive was originally intended as a heavy attack south of the Somme by the French, with the British making a diversionary attack to the north. The Battle of Verdun (qv) had used up so many French divisions, however, that when the attack was launched in June, it was the British with eighteen divisions who undertook the major assault. The British were, at last, beginning to take some appreciable burden off the French army which had borne the main brunt of the land war in the west.

Haig's objective was Bapaume, towards which he attacked on a 15-mile front. The French assault, along a 10-mile front by sixteen divisions, was towards Péronne.

The artillery bombardment commenced on 24 June, but the infantry attack was delayed until 1 July because of bad weather. The French 6th Army on the right (S), which was astride the Somme, quickly broke through the German lines, the French being commanded by General Marie Emile Fayolle and the Germans by General Otto von Below. In the north Rawlinson's attack ran into heavy fire from prepared German positions which took the heaviest toll of the British army that they have ever suffered in a single day's fighting (57,450). The attack was pressed, despite the opposition, which was greatest in the sector which ran north of Fricourt. To bolster the assault, General Sir Douglas Haig sent General Sir Hubert Gough's newly formed 5th Army in on the right to hold gains made by 13 Corps (the southernmost British corps) and the French. Falkenhayn now turned over command south of the river to General Max von Gallwitz and concentrated on the German position to the north.

For the next ten weeks the Allies settled for a battle of attrition. The British had made gains of only 1,000 yards during the first battle, which had been designed chiefly to push the Germans out of the entrenchments where they had dug in among the low hills between Arras and St Quentin after the Battle of the Marne (qv) in 1914. The British shelled the Germans constantly and made small but costly gains while the French did likewise. On 29 August Falkenhayn was replaced by General Paul von Hindenburg and General Erich Ludendorff.

On 15 September Haig renewed the offensive by trying to force a breakthrough opposite the centre of the British line. The use of tanks by the British - for the first time ever in battle - helped, mainly owing to shock tactics, to deepen the Allied penetration to 7 miles, but the Germans were not routed. Eighteen out of 36 tanks took no part in the action because of mechanical trouble.

The battle then resumed its former pattern and finally ended with bad weather on 18 November, only 125 square miles having been gained. Total casualties were 1,265,000 - 650,000 German, 420,000 British and 195,000 French.

Foch and Joffre were retired the following month, and on 12 December General Robert Nivelle took command of the French armies on the Western Front.

SOMME II (France)   First World War   21 March-5 April 1918

Fought between the French and British under Field-Marshal Lord Haig and General Foch, and the Germans under General Ludendorff.

Strength: Allies 29(+) divisions: Gough 15 (5th Army), Byng 14 (3rd Army); Germans 71 divisions.

Ludendorff wanted to gain a decisive victory in the west before the Americans could come up in enough strength to negate the Germans' numerical advantage gained from the collapse of the Russian front. This was the biggest offensive undertaken by Ludendorff, and it was aimed at the two British armies, the 5th under Gough in the left (N) and the 3rd under General Sir Julian Byng in the south, which held a 50-mile front south of Arras.

After a bombardment of 6,000 guns and a heavy gas attack, the Germans advanced on 21 March, thirty-seven divisions coming in first, followed swiftly by another twenty-four. Ludendorff aimed to split and defeat the Allies by breaking the British right centre. The German attackers from north to south were: the 17th (von Below), 2nd (General Georg von der Marwitz) and 18th (General Oskar von Hutier). Under cover of heavy artillery fire, the Germans advanced only 3 miles during the first three days, but then Gough's 5th Army, weakened by heavy losses, gave way on the south and fell back behind the Somme. This move exposed Byng's left flank, which forced the 3rd Army to retire to Le Sars, almost half-way to Albert. In the first four days the Germans had advanced 14 miles, but the 5th Army (which was later to be commanded by Rawlinson when Gough was replaced) was reduced to only two corps.

Ludendorff then moved the weight of his attack south of the Somme to where Hutier was making the largest gains. Here the British and French armies linked at Roye, 35 miles SE of Amiens. Fayolle commanded the mixed forces, but divided command weakened the Allies and Foch was made chief co-ordinator of troops on the Western Front in an effort to unify the Allied armies. Albert fell on 26 March and Montdidier, an important railway junction 28 miles SE of Amiens, fell on 27 March. Hutier's army slowed down now, owing to exhaustion and lack of supplies which were slow in reaching the front. The Germans were also ahead of their heavy guns; they were 40 miles from their starting point. Ludendorff now tried to capture Amiens and cut the Calais-Paris railway. The French 3rd Army repulsed the Germans when they launched an attack at Arras, but in the south the French were driven back and, on 3 April, Hanguard was captured as well as the railway station at Moreuil, 12 miles from Amiens. On 4 April the Germans made a last effort to break the Allied link near Hanguard and take the Calais-Paris railway, but though the French were pushed back to within 2 miles of the railway, the line held and the Germans did not get through.

Exhaustion stopped the German offensive at this point. It was the first of five that Ludendorff would undertake during 1918. German losses in killed and wounded almost equalled Allied casualties, which amounted to 160,000 in addition to 70,000 prisoners and 1,100 guns.

ST MIHIEL (France)   First World War   12 September 1918

Fought between the Germans under General Erich Ludendorff and the Americans under General John Pershing.

On 30 August Pershing formally took over the St Mihiel sector, a salient reaching to the Meuse River SE of Verdun which the Germans had taken in 1914. When the Germans were beaten back by the two Allied assaults on the Marne and east of Amiens, they began to retreat from the St Mihiel salient. Their withdrawal came too late, however, for, early on 12 September, the day after the Germans had begun to retreat, sixteen American divisions, supported by a French colonial division, French tanks and artillery and an air force made up of several units under US Colonel William Mitchell, attacked. The American 1 and 4 Corps attacked on the west. The Germans, taken by surprise, were driven from the salient within thirty-six hours, losing 15,000 prisoners and 250 guns. Americans suffered 7,000 casualties.

Although the American offensive could have penetrated deeper, it was deliberately cut short by Marshal Ferdinand Foch who now moved the Americans west for a major offensive in the Argonne Forest.

VERDUN (France)   First World War   21 February-18 December 1916
Fought between the Germans under General Erich von Falkenhayn and the Allies under Field-Marshal Joseph Joffre, General Henri Pétain and General Robert Nivelle.

The Germans resolved to attack the French position at Verdun which Falkenhayn believed they would hold until the last for reasons of patriotism. The region was held by the French 2nd Army, and the German 5th Army under Crown Prince Frederick William, consisting of 1 million men, was to launch the attack on the salient.

On 21 February, following a twenty-one-hour artillery bombardment with 1,400 guns, the Germans advanced along an 8-mile front east of the Meuse. The outer ring of French defences had been destroyed by the bombardment and these were taken with little opposition by the Germans. Several French-held forts in the area were left deliberately unmanned and the Germans, moving south, captured the partially dismantled Fort Douamont on 25 February. Joffre put Pétain in charge of the Verdun defences the same day, being himself preoccupied with the Somme (qv) offensive. Resistance now stiffened and, south of Fort Douamont, French counter-attacks and accurate artillery fire checked the German advance. On 6 March Prince Frederick William moved the weight of his attacks to the west bank of the Meuse. The French held Hill 295 (Le Mort Homme), 6 miles NW of Verdun, and Hill 304, 2 miles farther west, against all German attacks until, in the end, Frederick William transferred his attention back to the right bank (E) of the river. Hill 295 fell on 29 May, but Hill 304 was never completely taken, even at the limit of German penetration on this flank on 8 August. Once more on the left flank, the Germans captured Vaux on 29 March (3 miles from Verdun), but were unable to take Fort de Vaux until 6 June.

The German advance was now very slow, but they continued to move forward, and on 23 June an attack was made on the heights east of the river which commanded the Verdun and Meuse bridges. Repeated assaults were narrowly repulsed, the last of them, on 11 July, being only just beaten back. French losses on the heights were 315,000 to German losses of 280,000. At this point, exhaustion stopped the German advance. During six months the Germans had failed to take Verdun while the French had held many vital points with only one line of communication open to them. This was the by-road to Bar-le-Duc, 40 miles south, known as La Voie Sacrée, because along it reinforcements and supplies were sent despite constant harassment from enemy artillery.

For the next three months the front remained quiet, but Pétain had been replaced by Nivelle, and on 24 October he launched a counter-attack. The German 5th Army, exhausted by their struggle and severely handicapped by casualties, began to withdraw before the French attack. On 2 November the French recovered Forts de Vaux and Douamont. A further French assault on 15 December won back more ground and by 18 December fighting had ceased.

In the bloodiest engagement in history and the longest battle of the war France lost 542,000 casualties and Germany 434,000. In the final assault, the leadership of General Charles Mangin, first as a division and later as a corps commander stood out.

YPRES (IEPER) I (Belgium)   First World War   19 October-21 November 1914
Fought between the Allies under Field-Marshal Sir John French and General Ferdinand Foch, and the Germans under General Erich von Falkenhayn.

After the Race to the Sea (AISNE I), the line of the Western Front stabilised with the Belgians, driven out of Antwerp (qv), occupying the left of the line from the Sea to Ypres (Ieper) and the British taking over the line from Ypres to La Bassée, south of the Belgians. The French armies held the remaining nine-tenths of the Allied line as far as the Swiss border. The Germans sought to effect a penetration of the Allied line at Ypres and sent the German 4th and 6th Armies against the British Expeditionary Force and Belgians. The Germans advanced several miles before the Belgians flooded their front by opening sluice gates at Dixmude to the sea. During this offensive 35 per cent of the Belgian force was lost. Foch, in command of the Allies on the north line, launched a counter-attack on 20 October, but since this gained as little ground as the German advance had done, on 28 October it was called off. Falkenhayn renewed the German attack on 29 October, but no ground was gained though both sides suffered heavily. Rain and snow finally brought the battle to an end.

Both sides now entrenched deeper for the winter, but the British held a salient that jutted 6 miles east into the German lines. Ypres was at the base of the salient, and the ruins of this town were grimly defended by the BEF. At the last major battle of the Western Front in 1914, the BEF lost 80 per cent of its force - 2,638 officers and 55,787 men. French casualties were about 50,000 and German losses 130,000. In the first months of the war the total Allied casualties were 380,000 killed, 600,000 wounded and missing. German casualties were marginally less.

YPRES (IEPER) II (Belgium)   First World War   22 April-24 May 1915
Fought between the British under General Sir Horace Smith-Dorrien and the Germans under General Erich von Falkenhayn.

The German offensive of 1915 began against the salient held by the British at Ypres. Before it was launched, the first use of chlorine gas was made in an attack which created a 4-mile gap in the Allied lines. The Germans began to exploit the opportunity, but the hole was filled by Canadian troops who held the line on 24 April through a second gas attack, against which they had no adequate protection. On 27 April Smith-Dorrien ordered a 'voluntary' withdrawal to the edge of Ypres, whereupon he was relieved of his command and replaced by General Herbert Plumer. Plumer, however, did what Smith-Dorrien had planned to do, beginning on 1 May.

The Germans continued to attack the British position, which was held at great cost, until 25 May, when the battle ended. The poor defensive position is shown by the casualty rate which reverses the normal ratio of offensive-defensive figures, the Germans losing only 35,000 to British losses of 60,000. The high rate was also the result of the use of chlorine gas by the Germans.

YPRES (IEPER) III (PASSCHENDAELE) (Belgium)   First World War   31 July-6 November 1917
Fought between the British under Field-Marshal Sir Douglas Haig and the Germans under General Friedrich Sixt von Arnim.

After capturing the heights of Messines Ridge, the British were able to launch their major offensive into Flanders in order to try and break out of the Ypres salient and to relieve pressure on the French to the south who were still recovering from the effects of the mutiny the previous year.

After a ten-day bombardment, which shattered the drainage system of the reclaimed swampy ground, the British 5th Army under General Sir Hubert Gough led the attack NE from the Ypres salient. The British advanced 2 miles on the first day, but then heavy rain flooded the craters which had been created by the preliminary bombardment and the advance stopped. Most of Gough's tanks were ditched. The weight of the attack shifted south to Plumer's 2nd Army, but here too the momentum was slowed by the soggy ground and the stiff resistance put up by von Arnim's 4th Army. Plumer persisted, however, and Langemarck, 5 miles north of Ypres, was taken on 16 August, and Meenen Road Ridge and Polygon Wood to the east between 20 September and 3 October. The Germans attacked with mustard gas, but even this did not stop the British advance. Then, on 30 October, the Canadian 3rd and 4th Divisions and the British 58th and 63rd moved off at dawn to attack the main ridge of W Flanders which was held by the Bavarian 5th and 11th Divisions. The terrible conditions and enemy resistance first contained and then stopped the attack until 6 November when the Canadians moved on and carried the entire objective, including the village of Passchendaele from which the Germans had commanded the British salient at Ypres for three years. The village, 7 miles from Ypres, was now in Allied hands. Here the battle ended at a cost to the British of nearly 400,000 casualties, including 17,000 officers. German losses were less than 300,000, including 37,000 prisoners.

Haig was criticised for the heavy losses sustained by the British, for this was the costliest advance ever made by them. He had, however, succeeded in taking the pressure off the French armies. But his advance, only a sixth of his stated objective, was of little use. In his defence, the argument has been brought forward that his offensive had been weakened by the removal of five divisions to the Italian front after the Austrian victory at Caporetto. They were fortunate, as their lives were probably saved.

But the damage to the morale of the British army as a result of Passchendaele was serious and there was considerable loss of confidence in British army leadership both by the British and Dominion troops. The British Chief of the Imperial Guard Staff, General Sir William Robertson, must take some responsibility for this costly and largely futile battle as he overruled Gough who wanted to abandon the battle in August, and supported Haig who curiously kept himself out of touch with the battle and the casualties involved, on the grounds that, by seeing the ghastly results of his calculated decisions, his resolution might be lessened. The memory of this battle affected British leadership in the Second World War, causing many commanders to go to extremes to try and avoid casualties. This often caused them not to press home an advantage, and thus many chances of bringing a battle or campaign to a successful conclusion were lost through lack of determination.

SECTION NINE

FIRST WORLD WAR: NON-WESTERN FRONT AND THE ARAB REVOLT

See Map Section, nos 7, 21–4

ASIAGO (Italy)   First World War   15 May-25 June 1916
Fought between the Italians under General Count Cadorna and the Austrians under Field-Marshal Count Conrad von Hötzendorf.
Aim: While the Italians continued to launch futile assaults on the Isonzo front, Hötzendorf decided to take the offensive in the Trentino. The capture of Padua, 22 miles west of Venice, would isolate Italian troops in the Carnic Alps and on the Isonzo. Hötzendorf took fifteen divisions from other fronts and placed them, with much heavy artillery, on a line south of the Trentino. His objective was a drive into the N Italian plain.
Battle: Hötzendorf's force was organised into the 11th Army, and on 15 May it attacked south from the Trentino bulge. The Italian 1st Army was caught by surprise, although it was known that an Austrian offensive had been in preparation. Asiago fell on 31 May, opening the gap at the foot of the Dolomite Alps, and Arsiero was taken the same day. Cadorna now moved troops by rail from the Isonzo front to contain the Austrians and by 3 June had checked their advance. By 13 June, however, the Austrian offensive had halted because of the difficult terrain and the need to move troops to the Russian front. The Italians now launched a counter-attack and pursued the Austrians back to their starting point. On 25 June Cadorna attacked the Austrians with his 5th Army, but they were too well entrenched and the Italians were unable to move them. The action ended the battle. Both sides suffered casualties amounting to about 100,000.
Result: The Italians retired to the Isonzo.

ATLANTIC OCEAN I   First World War   18 February 1915-1 October 1917
Fought between the British and the Germans under Admiral Alfred von Tirpitz.

   The fleets of Britain and Germany fought few pitched naval battles during the war, serving more as blockading forces. After 18 February 1915, when Britain was blockaded by von Tirpitz, Allied shipping in the Atlantic was open to submarine attack and Allied ships were henceforth torpedoed without warning.

   In the *Lusitania,* sunk on 7 May 1915, 139 American as well as 1,059 British lives were lost. The United States came near to declaring war on Germany that summer, but on 1 September received an undertaking from Germany that no ship would be attacked without warning and that the safety of non-combatants on liners which offered no resistance and did not try to escape would be provided for. Merchant vessels continued to be the target for German submarines, however, and the amount of shipping tonnage sunk gradually increased throughout the year. On 1 March 1916 Admiral Eduard von Capelle, now in charge of German submarines, widened the campaign to take in all shipping in the Atlantic. Once again American pressure forced German submarines to restrict their targets. German light cruisers escaping from the British blockade added to the toll of shipping until, by the latter part of 1916, over 100 submarines were sinking 300,000 tons of shipping a month. By April 1917 this toll reached a peak when 875,000 tons were sunk in one month, more than half of which was British. This total was much more than could be built in a month even in British shipyards and Britain was in danger of being completely isolated. Under pressure from the British Prime Minister, David Lloyd George, the Allies began to move ships in convoys, and after this move was implemented, on 10 May, shipping losses fell dramatically. The aid of American ships, and the more frequent use of destroyers and submarine chasers using depth charges, helped to turn the tide.

Although by 1 October 1917 more than 8 million tons of shipping had been destroyed, 50 German submarines had been lost and the 134 still in service were becoming less and less effective with the new Allied tactics. By the end of the year more shipping was being constructed than was being destroyed. The battle was won by the Allies. This victory ensured that American contingents, once America had joined the war, could be carried across the Atlantic to France in comparative safety. In fact no American soldier's life was lost in these convoys as a consequence of action by German submarine or surface vessels.

BAGHDAD IV (Iraq)   First World War   17 February-11 March 1917
Fought between the British under Lt-General Sir Stanley Maude and the Turks under Kara Bekr Bey and Halil Pasha.
Strength: British 50,000; Turks 12,000 (Kut-al-Amara) + 11,000 (Baghdad).

In December 1916 Maude left Basra with an Anglo-Indian force for an offensive up the Tigris River to Baghdad. The British force spent two months wiping out Turkish detachments south of the river on their way up to Kut-al-Amara. On 17 February Maude started a series of manoeuvres against the fortress which forced the Turks under Kara Bekr Bey to evacuate Kut on 25 February. On 4 March Maude reached the Turkish defences on the Diyala River, 10 miles south of Baghdad. Here he deployed his men so skilfully that the Turks were forced to abandon their lines without a major fight, whereupon they withdrew to the north of Baghdad. On 11 March the British marched into the city, taking 9,000 prisoners.

BEERSHEBA (Israel)   First World War   31 October 1917
Fought between British, Australian and New Zealand forces under General Sir Edmund Allenby, and Turkish and Arab forces under General Erich von Falkenhayn.
Strength: British 2 mounted divisions + 8 infantry divisions + raiding party of Hejaz Arabs (Lt-Colonel Newcombe, RE) Camel Corps etc. Total 75,000 infantry, 17,000 cavalry and 475 guns; Turks 1 depleted cavalry division + 9 infantry divisions. Total 40,000 infantry, 1,500 cavalry, 300 guns.

The British front-line strength was about 40,000. The Turks were well dug in around the town of Beersheba but lacked depth. The British plan was to attack on the night 30/1 October with the 60th (London) and 74th (Yeomanry) Divisions, with the 53rd Division and Camel Brigade covering the northern flank. By 7 pm the infantry had achieved their objectives by overrunning the Turkish defenders, sustaining 1,200 casualties. The Anzac Desert Mounted Corps under General H.G. Chauvel followed through and, after a brisk series of actions including a cavalry charge by the New Zealanders at Telas Saba, captured the town of Beersheba,

1,400 Turks and 14 guns. The Turks counter-attacked strongly with 10,000 troops against the north flank of the British forces at Sheria, but after heavy fighting were routed.

The actions of Lt-Colonel S.F. Newcombe's Hejaz Arabs on the Hebron road deflected some of von Falkenhayn's reserves from the battle and helped cause his counter-stroke to fizzle out. Unfortunately, after a spirited resistance in positions across the road, Newcombe's small force, attacked by six battalions, was destroyed and Newcombe captured.

The British cavalry, supported by the Royal Flying Corps, now advanced rapidly towards Jerusalem (qv), pursuing the Turks until, after being driven out of Huj (qv), they made a stand at El Mughar (qv).

CAPORETTO (Italy)   First World War   24 October-12 November 1917
Fought between the Italians under General Count Cadorna and the Germans and Austrians under General Otto von Below.

After eleven fruitless assaults on the Austrian lines on the Isonzo, Cadorna went on the defensive with his 2nd and 3rd Armies. Germany had meanwhile undertaken to help Austria knock Italy out of the war and seven German divisions united with eight Austrian divisions to form the German 14th Army. This force was commanded by von Below. The army moved to Caporetto, on the north of the Isonzo lines opposite the Italian 2nd Army under General Luigi Capello. On von Below's left and right the Austrian 5th and 10th Armies prepared offensives against the Italian 3rd and 4th Armies respectively.

At dawn on 24 October, after a massive five-hour artillery bombardment planned by General Oskar von Hutier, the German 14th Army attacked the Italian 2nd Army in heavy snow, and, because Capello had neglected his front-line defences, the Germans broke the Italian line between Zaga and Auzza almost at once. Shortly after dawn the Germans had crossed the river and the Italian border and taken 100,000 prisoners and 700 guns. The Germans advanced 10 miles the first day and the advance of the Austrians on the flanks of the 14th Army forced the withdrawal of the Italian 4th and 3rd Armies. Cadorna planned to make a stand on the Tagliamento River, but von Below's advanced guard forced a crossing farther up-stream on the night of 2 November, near Cornino, and the Italians were forced back to the Piave River (qv). The Austrians seized the heights commanding the area between the Piave and Brenta Rivers and a bridgehead across the Piave at Zenson. Here, 70 miles inside Italy, the advance was halted by five British and six French divisions which had been rapidly sent from France. After a four-day battle in the Brenta valley (11-15 December), these experienced divisions stopped the Austro-German advance. Italian losses were 305,000: 275,000 prisoners, 45,000 killed or wounded, and 3,000 guns. Cadorna was replaced by General Armando Diaz and the Italian line was stabilised along the wide and torrential Piave.

CORONEL (SE Pacific)   First World War   1 November 1914
Fought between the British under Rear-Admiral Sir Christopher Cradock and the

Germans under Rear-Admiral Graf Maximilian von Spee.
Strength: British 2 cruisers (*Good Hope, Monmouth*) + 1 light cruiser (*Glasgow*) + 1 armed merchantman (*Otranto*); German 2 heavy cruisers (*Scharnhorst, Gneisenau* [11,400 tons]) + 3 light cruisers (*Leipzig, Nürnberg, Dresden*).

At the outbreak of the war 5 of Germany's 8 cruisers which were at sea or were stationed abroad in the Far East made for S America. Off Coronel, Chile, on 1 November 1914, the Germans encountered an inferior British squadron and, finding their artillery range first, sank the two British heavy cruisers, the *Good Hope* and the *Monmouth.* The light cruiser *Glasgow* and the merchantman, the *Otranto,* escaped. Cradock went down with the *Good Hope.*

British naval reinforcements, taken from the Grand Fleet, were immediately sent to the S Atlantic.

CTESIPHON III (Iraq)   First World War   22 November 1915
Fought between an Anglo-Indian army under General Sir Charles Townshend and the Turks under General Nur-ud-din.
Strength: British 14,000; Turks about 30,000.
Aim: After capturing Kut-al-Amara Townshend sought to take Baghdad.
Battle: Marching from Kut-al-Amara, Townshend moved up the river Tigris towards his objective. At Ctesiphon, on the east bank of the river, a Turkish force was strongly entrenched and Townshend, though outnumbered, ordered an attack. The British drove the Turks from their forward entrenchments and prepared for an assault on their main position. But the Turks brought up strong reinforcements and Townshend was forced to withdraw to Lejj, with a loss of 4,500 casualties.
Result: The British objective was not achieved. Townshend evacuated his sick and wounded back to Kut-al-Amara and withdrew there himself on 3 December.

DAMASCUS (Syria)   First World War   1 October 1918
Fought between the Egyptian Expeditionary Force under General Sir Edmund Allenby, supported by Arabs under Prince Feisal and Colonel T.E. Lawrence, and the rearguards of three Turkish Armies (4th, 7th and 8th) under General Liman von Sanders.

General Sir Edmund Allenby's aim was to exploit his great victory in the battles of Megiddo (qv) by a pursuit to Damascus and Aleppo. Von Sanders hoped to delay the British on the line from Lake Huleh-Sea of Galilee-Yarmuk Valley, so as to gain time to prepare the defences of Damascus. But his orders never even reached the 7th or 8th Armies. After minor victories at Samakh (25 September) and Jisr Benat Yakub (qv) (27 September) the Allies approached Damascus without major opposition. On the 30th Arab flags were openly hoisted in Damascus, and the roads to Homs and Beirut were choked with retreating Turks.

The 3rd Australian Light Horse were the first British troops to enter Damascus. They hurried through in pursuit of the Turks retreating towards Homs. Soon afterwards Lawrence and his Arabs arrived, closely followed by the leading troops of the 5th Cavalry Division.

The Australians rounded up some 12,000 Turks in the city.

Allenby handed over the administration of the city to the Arabs, a generous act which had unfortunate repercussions since, by the Sykes-Picot Agreement, France was to have a mandate over Syria when the Turkish Empire should collapse.

Lawrence claimed that the Arabs took Damascus, but Wavell's evidence (*The Palestine Campaigns*, p 229, Constable, 1928) is not to be dismissed. The point is a political rather than a military one, since there was no serious fighting in the city itself.

An armistice was concluded between the Allies and Turkey on 31 October.

DARDANELLES (Turkey)   First World War   19 February-18 March 1915
Fought between the British under Vice-Admiral Sackville Carden and Vice-Admiral John de Robeck, and the Turks.

On 3 November 1914 the outer forts at the Dardanelles were bombarded by 4 battleships (2 British, 2 French) under Admiral Carden, without effect. On 13 December the British submarine *B11* passed through the Narrows and sank the Turkish battleship *Messudiya,* but on 15 January 1915 the French submarine *Saphir,* attempting the passage, was sunk. It was then decided, as there was deadlock on the Western Front, to open a new front against Turkey. A passage was to be forced through the Dardanelles so that an attack on Constantinople could take place. A supply route could also then be established to Russia via the Black Sea when, as was planned, the Bosporus was cleared. The advantages of such a success would be incalculable.

Carden, with 12 aged British and French ships, opened the attack on 19 February. The forts at Cape Helles and Kum Kale were reduced during the next four weeks and minesweepers cleared the Narrows of 11 belts of mines which guarded the entrance to the Sea of Marmara. When Carden's health broke down he was replaced by de Robeck who decided to make an all-out assault on 18 March with minesweepers preceding the battleships. However, unknown to the Allies, General Liman von Sanders had strengthened the Turkish defences. Turkish artillery on either side of the waterway took a heavy toll of the minesweepers before, four hours after the attack was begun, the warships reached the Narrows. The French battleship *Bouvet* was sunk by an unswept mine. The British battleships *Irresistible* and *Ocean* were sunk. Other ships were damaged by gunfire or mines. Winston Churchill, First Lord of the Admiralty, had ordered replacements for the lost ships to steam to the Dardanelles. Casualties had been light, but de Robeck got cold feet and asked that the naval operation be called off and a landing made in a month's time. Churchill ordered the attack to be resumed, but encountered 'insuperable resistance' from the British Admiralty, though not from the French navy which had suffered more severely. The Turks considered themselves defeated and, if another naval thrust had been made, the Dardanelles might have fallen had an adequate land force been available. A Royal Marine reconnaissance force had already landed and found many deserted gun positions. But de Robeck withdrew.

This naval failure led to a land operation being mounted, but after the Turks had been put thoroughly upon the alert. Winston Churchill, having failed to carry the Admiralty with him in his plans, was dismissed and removed from the Cabinet.

DOGGER BANK II (North Sea)   First World War   24 January 1915
Fought between the British under Admiral Sir David Beatty and the Germans under Admiral Franz von Hipper.
Strength: British 5 battle-cruisers (*Lion, Princess Royal, Tiger, New Zealand, Indomitable*) + 1 light cruiser squadron + 8 light cruisers + 26 destroyers; Germans 3 battle-cruisers (*Seydlitz, Moltke, Derfflinger*) + 1 armoured cruiser (*Blücher*) + 4 light cruisers (*Graudenz, Stralsand, Kolberg, Rostok*) + 22 destroyers.

The Germans, attempting to make a surprise sweep of the North Sea, found the British, who had been alerted as the result of a captured code, awaiting them on the Dogger Bank, 60 miles off the English coast. The Germans turned at once to head back to the Heligoland base, wishing to draw the British into the minefields and within reach of a waiting submarine flotilla. The British pursued the Germans, overhauling them before they reached home. The British flagship *Lion* hit the slow-moving *Blücher* at a range of 10 miles, the *Tiger* attacked the *Seydlitz* and the *Princess Royal* took on the *Derfflinger.* The *Seydlitz* and the *Derfflinger* were both on fire by 11 am when the *Blücher* was sinking, but the *Lion* was then hit by a shell which damaged her fuel system and forced her to retire. Moore, in the *New Zealand,* took over; but he did not press the attack for fear of German minefields. As it was, he broke off the action while still 40 miles (1¼ hours' sailing time) from the minefields, at a point when he could have sunk the burning cruisers, both of which escaped. British casualties were only 14 killed and 6 wounded. German losses, including 123 saved from the *Blücher*'s crew of 885, were 1,313.

The Royal Navy's failure to press home their advantage was a deep disappointment to the British public.

EAST AFRICAN CAMPAIGN (Tanzania)   First World War   4 August 1914-25 November 1918
This remarkable campaign was fought between a small German/African force under Colonel (later General) Paul von Lettow-Vorbeck and a very large Allied force of British, Indian, S African, Rhodesian, African, Belgian and Portuguese troops under a succession of commanders including Brigadier-General J.M. Stewart, Major-Generals Aitken, Wapshire, Northey and Tighe, General Sir Horace Smith-Dorrien, Lt-General (later Field-Marshal) Jan Christiaan Smuts, Major-General Jacob Louis van Deventer and Lt-General A.R. Hoskins.
Strength: Germans/Africans initially 261 Europeans + 2,540 Askari (African soldiers) + 2,154 African police: maximum 3,000 Europeans (including crews of *Königsberg,* her 4.1-inch guns, Tanganyika lake fleet, *Hedwig von Wissman, Graf von Gotson* and *Kingani*) + 11,000 Askaris supported by African porters: at armistice 155 Europeans + 1,168 Askaris + 3,000 porters; Allies maximum 139 generals + 350,000 (including 200,000 carriers [porters], and including in July

1918 the King's African Rifles (KAR) - 1,193 officers + 1,497 British NCOs + 30,658 Askaris who, with the S African, Portuguese and Belgian troops, continued the war after all the Indian troops had been sent home).

Aim: Von Lettow-Vorbeck decided in July 1914 that his rôle was to occupy the attention of as many British forces as possible to keep them away from the main front in Europe. In this he was successful. The British aim was initially entirely defensive, but Vorbeck's tactics of raids on the Mombasa-Kisumi railway eventually impelled the British to take offensive action which, including the building up of lines of communication in a vast undeveloped area, tied up an ever-increasing number of troops and their necessary carriers, and camp followers.

On arrival a few months before the outbreak of the 1914-18 war Vorbeck undertook an extensive but detailed reconnaissance of his territory. He decided that his rôle was to fight a guerilla-type war, in order to tie up as many Allied forces as possible. On the outbreak of war his civil governor Dr Heinrich Schnee did not want to fight, so Vorbeck had the doctors declare him mentally deficient, deprived him of all powers and kept him locked up until the armistice, thus providing an interesting example to other officers faced with a similar situation.

BATTLE OF TANGA

Strength: British 8,000 with 1 mountain battery + HMS *Fox*'s 6-inch guns; German 1,000.

An Indian expeditionary force, consisting of a brigade group, started to arrive on 1 September 1914. A further 8,000 men (including a British battalion) under Major-General Aitken, were gathered from all over India and landed in October. Aitken, against advice, decided to capture Tanga. Some of the badly trained Indian battalions proved unreliable. Two Indian brigades were landed, but the surprise element had already been discarded when the Royal Navy had decided that it was necessary for HMS *Fox* to steam in ahead into Tanga to notify the Germans of the abrogation of a truce which the navy had illegally arranged! German machine-guns and well-organised fire-power put the expedition, especially the Indian force, to flight, in the course of which all their guns, machine-guns, equipment and even some personal weapons were left behind. British casualties were 800, in contrast to German losses which were negligible.

As a result of the Tanga disaster control of operations in East Africa was taken away from the Indian army and given to the War Office, London. Aitken was sent home and Wapshire took over.

Vorbeck countered by attacking Rhodesia to the south, British E Africa to the north, and Belgian Congo to the west. On 17 January 1915 Vorbeck attacked the E African border town of Yasini and captured it on 19 January. Wapshire was again ordered by Field-Marshal Lord Kitchener to go on the defensive. He organised a native carrier corps, eventually rising to a total of 200,000, which proved invaluable. Vorbeck continued his depredations throughout the rainy season, and increased his strength to 2,998 Europeans and 11,300 Askaris. Tighe captured the Lake Victoria town of Buboka on 22 June 1915 at a cost of 7 British killed and 27 wounded. In November 1915 General Sir Horace Smith-Dorrien took overall command of the campaign and the KAR was expanded. By December Smith-Dorrien had 27,350 effectives with 71 guns and 123 machine-guns. But he disagreed with the way the campaign should be run and Jan Christiaan Smuts, aged twenty-eight, who had been a successful Boer guerilla in 1899-1902 and who had completed a successful campaign in SW Africa, was promoted to Lieutenant-General and took over command on 22 February 1916. He decided on offensive operations but without risking casualties. In this he failed and the campaign became a vast drain on Allied resources much needed elsewhere.

NAVAL OPERATIONS

In 1914 the German cruiser *Königsberg* was stationed at Dar-es-Salaam, and immediately sailed out as a raider and sank British shipping in the Indian Ocean, including the *City of Westminster* off Aden on 6 August, and the cruiser *Pegasus* on 20 September. The *Königsberg* retired to the Rufiji delta to refit and was eventually sunk by the monitors *Severn* and *Medway*, sent out from Britain especially for the purpose. But the *Königsberg*'s 4.1-inch guns were salvaged to give von Lettow-Vorbeck his only artillery of the four-year campaign.

The Germans formed a Lake Tanganyika fleet consisting of the river boats *Hedwig von Wissman, Graf von Gotson* and *Kingani*, all armed with 3.5-inch guns. The British transported 2 40-ft-long gunboats, *Mimi* and *Toutou*, by rail and road from Cape Town to Lukaga on Lake Tanganyika. The British fleet, under Lt-Commander G. Spicer-Simson succeeded in sinking or capturing the 3 German ships within a few weeks of launching at Lukaga on 28 October 1915.

SMUTS'S OPERATIONS

Smuts was not keen on his S African whites suffering too many casualties, so he tried to manoeuvre von Lettow-Vorbeck into surrender. He brought the S African 1st, 2nd and 3rd Divisions into the campaign as well as Belgian forces from the Congo and Rhodesian troops. After an enormous amount of organisation and expense, during which thousands of Allies lost their lives by disease, Smuts handed over to General Hoskins in January 1917, having failed in eleven months' campaigning to inflict one single tactical defeat on the Germans. Large parts of German E Africa had been occupied and the central railway from Dar-es-Salaam to Lake Tanganyika was in British hands, but von Lettow-Vorbeck's force remained in being and full of fight. Smuts told Hoskins that all the Germans had been defeated and all that remained was mopping up. Hoskins soon learnt that Smuts had talked himself and others into believing this, but that it was not true. Smuts was a better politician than a general.

After two years of further fighting, during which the Germans operated in Portuguese Mozambique and eventually in Rhodesia, where they captured vast supplies of Allied quinine, vital for the prevention of malaria, the German nation was defeated on the Western Front of Europe. Von Lettow-Vorbeck, undefeated, agreed to an honourable surrender of his remaining force of 155 Europeans (who were allowed to retain their arms), 1,168 Askaris and 3,000 carriers (having previously released for employment over 5,000 of them), on 25 November 1918. He and his German survivors were given a heroes' reception through E Africa and on the journey home until they reached Germany, where this great German guerilla general was not surprised to find that the Germans knew little or nothing of his campaign.

Total casualties (killed or died from disease) suffered by the British, S Africans, Rhodesians and Indians were 20,000, by African soldiers and porters 60,000, as well as 140,000 horses and mules. Losses of the other Allies are unknown. On the German side, European losses were 2,500 killed, died or wounded as well as 8,000 Askaris and porters. The incidence of disease (mainly malaria) casualties to battle casualties was 31 to 1.

Result: German E Africa became a League of Nations trust territory under a British mandate.

EL MUGHAR (Israel)   First World War   13 November 1917
Fought between the 6th Mounted Brigade under Brigadier-General Godwin and a Turkish force dug in on the El Mughar Ridge.

General Sir Edmund Allenby had ordered 21 Corps (75th and 52nd Divisions) to attack, in order to clear the way for his continued advance on Jerusalem (qv). The Yeomanry Division was to attack on the left of 21 Corps. When the infantry attack was held up it was agreed that the 6th Mounted Brigade (Dorset, Buckinghamshire and Berkshire Yeomanry supported by Berkshire Battery RHA and 6 machine-guns of the MG Squadron) should make a mounted attack on the El Mughar Ridge. The distance to be covered was 3,000 yards uphill, exposed to view and fire all the way. With the Bucks and Dorset Yeomanry leading, the regiments advanced at the trot but galloped the last 1,000 yards and gained their objectives on the crest of the ridge. The Turkish position was strong and well sited, but there was no barbed wire. The reserve regiment (the Berkshires), fighting on foot, passed through and, with the aid of the support squadrons of machine-guns and Royal Horse Artillery, captured the village of El Mughar. Casualties of the Turks were 400 dead, as well as 1,100 prisoners and the capture of 2 field guns and 14 machine-guns. British losses were 16 killed, 113 wounded and 265 horses (16 per cent of personnel, 33 per cent of the horses).

21 Corps, with the Australian Mounted Division and New Zealand Mounted Brigade, cleared further opposition and entered Jaffa on 16 November 1917. In ten days since breaking the Gaza-Beersheba line British forces had advanced 50 miles, in which they took 10,000 Turkish prisoners and captured 100 guns. British losses in the pursuit, caused by stubborn rearguard action, were 6,000.

ERZURUM-ERZINCAN (Turkey)   First World War   17 January-14 August 1916
Fought between the Russians under General Nikolai Yudenich and the Turks under General Abdul Kerim Pasha.

After the failure of the Allied expedition to Gallipoli (qv), Turkish forces moved to the Lake Van-Black Sea front to launch an offensive against the Russians now under Yudenich, with Grand Duke Nicholas in immediate control. The Russians attacked before the Turks were in position.

Moving west, the Russians took Köprukoy on 17 January, forcing the Turks to fall back. The Russians moved with them and, 40 miles farther west, they stormed and captured Erzurum from 12 to 16 February. Trabzon (Trebizond) was captured by another Russian column on the Black Sea on 18 April. The Turks brought in reinforcements from Europe, but the Russians continued their offensive. On 2 July Yudenich split the Turkish front at Bayburt, 60 miles NW of Erzurum. Moving west once more, the Russians took Erzincan, 96 miles west of Erzurum, on 25 July. By now the Turkish 3rd Army had lost more than 17,000 killed and about the same number captured. Those who remained were constantly pursued by the Cossack cavalry. Only on the Russians' left (E) front did the Turks hold off the advance. A corps under Mustafa Kemal (Kemal Atäturk) attacked eastward and took Mus, 45 miles from Lake Van, and Bitlis, 15 miles from the lake, on 15 August. Here, however, the Turkish 2nd Army also was beaten by Yudenich, and the villages were both recaptured by 24 August.

Formal fighting on the Caucasus front now ended. When the Russian revolution broke out in 1917, Czarist troops disappeared from the front and the Turks began to advance, retaking all their lost territory, and were marching through the Caucasus when the armistice took effect on 31 October 1918.

FALKLAND ISLANDS (S Atlantic)   First World War   8 December 1914
Fought between the British under Vice-Admiral Doveton Sturdee and the Germans under Vice-Admiral Graf Maximilian von Spee.
Strength: British 2 battle-cruisers (*Invincible, Inflexible*) + 3 armoured cruisers (*Carnarvon, Cornwall, Kent*) + 2 light cruisers (*Glasgow, Bristol*); Germans 5 cruisers (*Scharnhorst* (flagship), *Gneisenau, Nürnberg, Leipzig, Dresden*) + 3 supply ships.

After the British defeat at Coronel (qv) the Admiralty quickly sent a squadron into the S Atlantic, and this reached the Falkland Islands (off the coast of Patagonia) one day before von Spee arrived there. Sturdee's flotilla was coaling when the Germans were sighted. Von Spee turned to flee, but Sturdee gave chase and, in a running battle on 8 December, sank 4 German cruisers - the *Scharnhorst, Gneisenau, Nürnberg* and *Leipzig.* Von Spee and his two sons were among the 1,800 Germans killed or drowned. The cruiser *Dresden* escaped with a supply ship, but was hunted down and destroyed off the Juan Fernandez Islands in the S Pacific.

The British, having for the present removed the threat of German ships on the high seas, were able to concentrate on defence of the waters nearer home.

GALICIA (Poland)   First World War   23 August-26 September 1914
Fought between the Austro-Hungarians under Field-Marshal Count Conrad von Hötzendorf and the Russians under General Nikolai Ivanov.

Austria and Hungary, a dual monarchy, acted together and opened their war with an offensive on two fronts. A secondary attack was made against Serbia, and repulsed, but the main effort was concentrated against Russia and was launched from Austria's easternmost province, Galicia.

Under General Viktor von Dankl, the Austrian 1st Army crossed the border into Poland and clashed with the Russian 4th at Krasnik. Von Hötzendorf had concentrated three armies (later augmented to four) NE of the Carpathian Mountains; misjudging the Russian offensive, he had sent his 1st and 4th Armies north along the railway through Lublin, and it was one of these forces that collided with the Russians SW of Lublin at Krasnik. The Russians were pushed back in three days of fighting both here and at Komarow, where the Austrian 4th met the Russian 5th Army.

Meanwhile the Russian 3rd Army under General Nikolai Russky had crossed the Galician border near Brody, threatening the Austrians to the east, and the Russian 8th Army under General Alexei Brusilov advanced from Odessa to menace the Austrians from the south, the intention being to converge on the 3rd Army for the main Russian offensive. The Austrian army had advanced to the Gnila (Gnilaya) Lipa River, a tributary of the Dniester, and it was here that the two Russian armies, which had joined on 27 August, met and defeated the Austrians on a 200-mile front in an advance on Lemberg (L'vov). On 27 August Brusilov captured Tarnopol and occupied Halicz. The Russians, with a numerical superiority of 3 to 1, turned north on Lemberg which was captured after fierce fighting on 3 September. They took 100,000 prisoners.

The Austrian 2nd Army now arrived from Serbia and came into line on the Austrian right (S) flank. The Russians pushed them back as they did the Austrian 3rd and 4th (Auffenberg) Armies to the north. The Austrians' counter-attack failed and the Russians, launching an offensive from the Vistula to the Upper Dniester, penetrated the Austrian right. This defeat opened a 40-mile gap in the Austrian line at Rava Russkaya, 32 miles NW of Lemberg. On 9 September the Russian 5th Army began to advance through the gap, isolating the Austrian 1st Army to the NW. The Austrians now began to retreat in disorder and continued to do so until they reached the Carpathian Mountains, 100 miles away, on 26 September.

Austrian losses in this campaign were 350,000 men (about two-thirds of the force), of whom 120,000 were captured. The total includes 100,000 men who were besieged in Przemysl from 24 September until 11 October when it was relieved. The city was again besieged from 6 November until 22 March 1915, when it was forced to capitulate and 100,000 men and 1,000 guns were captured. Przemysl was the only town to undergo a prolonged siege during the war on this front.

The heavy losses sustained by Austria crippled them for the rest of the war. Ivanov's victory in Galicia opened the way for Russia to launch an offensive towards Cracow and Silesia. The German 9th Army was sent to the area to try to prevent this.

GALLIPOLI (Turkey)   First World War   25 April 1915-9 January 1916
Fought between the British under General Sir Ian Hamilton and, later, General Sir Charles Monro, and the Turks under General Otto Liman von Sanders.
Strength: British 469,000 total (80,000 initial landing) + French 80,000 (15,000

initial landing); Turks 400,000 (60,000 initially).

After the failure of the seaborne offensive against the Dardanelles (qv) a land force was sent to the ill-mapped Gallipoli peninsula with the eventual objective of capturing Constantinople. That achieved, the Turks would be unable to prevent the Allies joining the Russians in the war against Austria, Hungary and Turkey herself. The German General Liman von Sanders was in charge of Turkish defences and he deployed the 5th Army around the entrances to the Dardanelles. The British expedition moved from Alexandria to Lemnos Island on 21 April. On 25 April two opposed landings were made on the Gallipoli Aylmer peninsula, the main force under Lt-General Hunter-Weston of 35,000 men landing at Cape Helles. Owing largely to bad co-ordination, this force proceeded no farther in face of stubborn resistance from the Turks. A smaller Anzac corps of 17,000 men landed at Ari Birun, a mile north of their objective, under General Sir William Birdwood. This force was checked before it had gone far by a force of Turks under Mustafa Kemal (Kemal Atatürk) and it too ended the day back on the beaches. Little progress had been made.

For two weeks the Allies remained on the beaches unable to drive the Turks from the heights above them, but the Turks, for their part, were not able to drive the invaders into the sea. Hamilton attempted to command the operation from aboard ship: a fundamental error. Stalemate had been established by 8 May and Hamilton had lost a third of his force at Cape Helles and Ari Birun (now called Anzac Cove). After much controversy at home, it was decided to strengthen the force at Gallipoli to four British, two French and three Anzac divisions, and another 25,000 men (two divisions) were landed north of Anzac Bay on 6 August. While these new forces were being landed, a secondary attack was made at Helles to front of the Turks while Birdwood, his force increased to 37,000, made an eastward thrust in the primary offensive. Both strikes met with no success as the Turks held firm everywhere. The new force under Lt-General the Hon Sir Frederick Stopford landed without serious opposition, however, but Stopford himself was lethargic and slept on board ship when he should have been moving inland. As it was, by the time he launched his offensive inland, the Turks had had time to deploy against him and his attack was stopped cold, on 9 August. Stalemate persisted until 22 November when Hamilton was relieved by Monro who was also directing the Salonika campaign and he put Birdwood in charge of the Gallipoli operations. In the end, the offensive was called off. The Suvla Bay and Anzac Cove troops were evacuated on 20 December and those at Cape Helles were out by 9 January. The evacuation was completed without loss of life. British casualties were 41,000 killed and missing, 78,500 wounded; French losses 9,000 killed and missing, 13,000 wounded. In addition, a total of 100,000 British and French were sick. The Turks suffered 66,000 killed and missing, and 152,000 wounded.

The direct results of this campaign were that pressure was taken off the Russian front on the Caucasus where the Russians gained a great victory; on the other hand the eventual Allied failure encouraged Bulgaria to join the central powers.

On 8 November 1918, under the conditions of the armistice with Turkey,

British troops occupied Gallipoli and the Royal Navy steamed up the Narrows to Constantinople.

GAZA III (Egypt)   First World War   26 March-19 April 1917
Fought between the British under General Sir Archibald Murray and the Turks under Colonel Kress von Kressenstein.
Strength: British 80,000 (3 infantry and 2 cavalry divisions); Turks 16,000 (plus considerable reinforcements after first attack).

As soon as the British occupied El 'Arish in December 1916, they were ordered to invade Palestine. In order to clear the way for the British advance, Murray attacked two Turkish outposts at Magdhaba and Rafa which stood *en route* to the frontier of Palestine. These two actions, undertaken on 23 December and 9 January, cost the British 550 casualties for a gain of 2,900 prisoners. The road to the frontier, 27 miles NE of the British position, was now open. Early in 1917 the British advanced slowly, extending their water-line and railway as they went. This network stretched as far as the Suez Canal.

The British objective was Gaza, which was strongly defended by the Turks under Kress von Kressenstein. The attack on the Turks was commanded by General Sir Charles Dobell who sent two cavalry divisions under General Sir Philip Chetwode to the east and north to cut off possible Turkish reinforcements while the 53rd Infantry Division attacked the Ali Muntar Ridge which overlooked Gaza. The assault was successful at first, but when victory seemed certain, Chetwode withdrew his cavalry from the east, thus exposing the right flank of the infantry which was also forced to withdraw although it had reached the northern outskirts of the city. The attack was resumed the next day, but the Turks had been reinforced and they drove the British back with a loss of 4,000. Turkish losses were 2,400. The Turks now extended their line from Gaza SE to Beersheba, and the British, who had been reinforced with one infantry division, made a frontal assault on their position, beginning on 17 April. Three divisions abreast, the British were able to make only small gains at great cost against their numerically inferior opponents. On 19 April, after a further assault, the attack was called off. The British had lost 6,444 men to the Turks 2,000. Murray now relieved Dobell, but on 28 June he was replaced by General Sir Edmund Allenby.

GAZA IV (Egypt)   First World War   31 October-9 December 1917
Fought between the British under General Sir Edmund Allenby and the Turks, who were commanded by Field-Marshal Erich von Falkenhayn.
Strength: British 88,000 (including Anzacs and Indian divisions, comprising 7 infantry divisions + 3 cavalry divisions + Camel Corps) + 8 tanks; Turks 35,000.

The British assaulted the 30-mile Turkish Gaza-Beersheba line at Beersheba from west and east with five divisions. Allenby had previously deceived the Turks of the direction of the attack by a ruse, whereby his attaché case with false plans in it was allowed to fall into their hands. The Turkish 7th Army in the foothills to the west of the Judaean Hills was rolled up and forced to retire west to Tel el Sheria. The line, which was heavily defended, was reduced after a week of fighting, the British operation on the coast being aided by naval gunfire. Allenby struck east again on 6 November, forcing the Turks out of Tel el Sheria and pushing his cavalry towards the coast behind the Turkish 8th Army. Gaza was evacuated on 6-7 November to avoid being cut off, and Askalon fell on 9 November. Allenby pursued vigorously and took Junction Station on 14 November, then Jaffa (Haifa), 35 miles NW of Jerusalem, on 16 November. Swinging east, Allenby outflanked Jerusalem from the NW and Turkish resistance on the Nebi-Samwil Ridge, the key to the city, was overcome by 9 December. Jerusalem now surrendered, and Allenby entered the city on 11 December, to read a proclamation guaranteeing religious toleration to all.

Jerusalem had been under Ottoman domination for four centuries. Its fall to the Christians contributed to the downfall of the Turkish Empire.

GORLICE-TARNOW (Poland)   First World War   2 May-September 1915
Fought between the Germans under General Paul von Hindenburg and the Russians under Grand Duke Nicholas.

Hindenburg determined to crush the Russian army in order to knock that country out of the war. The German 11th Army was moved from the Western Front to the Gorlice-Tarnow sector, SE of Cracow, in complete secrecy. The Austrian 4th Army was united with the German force and both were placed under the command of General August von Mackensen. The Russian 3rd Army, one of ten armies deployed between the Baltic Sea and Romania along the frontier, was opposite this force.

On 2 May the Germans opened a bombardment between Gorlice and Tarnow after a tactical move on Gorlice on 1 May. The Germans unleashed 700,000 shells on the sector and, when they charged, the surprised Russians found their line was shattered. The 3rd Army was almost obliterated by the end of the second day, 120,000 prisoners having been taken. Gorlice and Ciezkowice (SE of Cracow) fell on 3 May and, in order to keep their line intact, the Russians evacuated Przemysl on 1 June. General Alexei Brusilov attempted to make a stand along a 40-mile front on the Dniester and did prevent the Germans from crossing the river, claiming he had inflicted 150,000 casualties on them. The setback was only temporary, however, for Lemberg (L'vov) fell on 22 June. Mackensen, reinforced by the Austrian 3rd Army and the newly formed Bug (River) Army, turned north towards Brest-Litovsk, 120 miles east of Warsaw. The Russians continued to retreat all along the front and the Polish capital became increasingly isolated. The German 12th Army under General Max von Gallwitz marched north under the orders of General Erich von Falkenhayn who had taken command of this operation and on 4-5 August Warsaw fell. Brest-Litovsk fell on 25 August.

The Russians had no means to combat the German heavy artillery and by mid-September the Russian front was a 600-mile line stretching from Lithuania on the Baltic Sea to the Pripet Marshes and down to the Romanian border. The German line ran from Vilna in the north, Pinsk and Luminetz in the centre, east of the Pripet Marshes to Dubno on the Romanian frontier in the south. The battle cost the Russians about 1 million men killed or wounded and another million captured, though large forces had escaped the German net. Czar Nicholas II now took personal command of the troops on the Eastern Front, but thousands of square miles of food-producing land had been lost as a result of inadequate military equipment. The catastrophe lengthened the war and contributed to the Bolshevik Revolution.

GUMBINNEN (GUSEV) (USSR)   First World War   17-20 August 1914
Fought between the Russians under General Pavel Rennenkampf and the Germans under General Max von Prittwitz und Gaffron.
Strength: Russians 200,000; Germans 150,000.

Russia opened the war on the Eastern Front by invading E Prussia with their 1st Army. The Russians advanced on a 35-mile front and encountered the van of the German 8th Army under Prittwitz at Stallupönen, 5 miles inside Prussia. The Prussian 1 Corps under General Hermann von François made a spoiling attack which checked the Russian advance, but that night (17 August), the Germans had to fall back 10 miles west to Gumbinnen (Gusev, now in USSR), 68 miles east of Königsberg (Kaliningrad). The Russians moved slowly west and Prittwitz deployed the Germans in front of Gumbinnen for a counter-attack. Under a heavy bombardment von François launched this attack at dawn on 20 August from the German left (N). The Germans charged the Russian ranks on this wing until Rennenkampf's ammunition was exhausted and his men were decimated by German infantry and cavalry. In the centre, General August von Mackensen's 17 Corps launched his attack at 8 am, four hours later than von François.

The Russians, forewarned by the attack on their right, opened an artillery bombardment which at first checked the German advance and then drove them back 15 miles in a disorderly retreat. To the south, General Otto von Below attacked the Russian left four hours after 17 Corps had gone into battle; but, before the attack could get under way, the rout of Mackensen's corps forced von Below to withdraw. The departure of both the centre and right exposed the German left and von François was therefore also forced to withdraw that night. Rennenkampf did not pursue, but Prittwitz wished to abandon E Prussia and retire behind the Vistula River (qv), a decision he pressed when he heard that the Russian 2nd Army under General Alexander Samsonov was advancing on the German rear from the south on a 50-mile front.

General Helmuth von Moltke relieved Prittwitz of his command and called Hindenburg out of retirement to take command of the 8th Army with General Erich Ludendorff as his Chief of Staff. Thus was born the formidable Hindenburg-Ludendorff combination.

HAIFA (Israel)   First World War   23 September 1918
By 20 September 1918 British forces had cleared the coastal plain of Palestine, the greater part of the Turkish 8th Army being taken prisoner and the 7th Army

having ended all resistance. The British 5th Cavalry Division under Major-General H.J.M. MacAndrew was ordered to take Acre and Haifa. Acre was occupied on 22 September, its garrison of 200 men and 2 guns being quickly overcome. The 15th Brigade (Mysore and Jodhpur Lancers), after capturing Mount Carmel, and supported by machine-guns and the Essex battery of the Royal Horse Artillery, galloped into the town of Haifa, swiftly overcoming all opposition and capturing the garrison of 1,250 and 17 guns.

Haifa, from where a good railway line ran east to Deraa and north to Damascus (qv) could now be used as a sea base for General Sir Edmund Allenby's continued advance north. This eased his supply problem considerably. The destruction of the Turkish 4th Army was his next aim.

HEJAZ (Saudi Arabia)   Arab Revolt   5 June 1916-1918
Sherif Hussein of Mecca, urged on by British diplomacy, revolted against the Turks on 5 June 1916 when Bedouins overran the Turkish garrisons in their summer quarters around Taif, SE of Mecca. Hussein had conceived the idea of a revival of the Arab Empire to include Arabia, Iraq, Palestine and Syria. The seaport of Jeddah was captured on 12 June and Taif was taken on 21 September, but in Medina Fakhreddon Pasha held out stubbornly. At this resistance the Arab tribesmen lost heart and started to melt away.

The control of the Hejaz operations was under the Sirdar and Governor-General of the Sudan, Sir Reginald Wingate, whose headquarters were in Cairo. Captain (later Colonel) T.E. Lawrence served on this staff. Lawrence was sent to see Feisal, Hussein's third son and Commander of the Arab forces in the Hejaz. He informed the Arab Bureau, the intelligence wing of Wingate's staff in Cairo, that it would be much better and more suited to the Arab capabilities and temperament, not to attempt to capture Medina but to leave it as a 'running sore' of the Turkish army, while the Arabs would march north on Wejh and threaten the Turkish communications. Lawrence was then confirmed as the British representative at Hussein's headquarters and thenceforward practically led the Arab rising while directing its strategy as Chief of Staff to Feisal.

The Arab move to Wejh on the coast in January 1917 had immediate results. The Turkish advance to recapture Mecca was stopped short and the Turks were compelled wastefully to scatter forces along the Hejaz Railway for protection. The C-in-C Egypt was thus relieved of all worry and responsibility for the defence of the Hejaz. It was decided to train a force of regulars for Feisal at Wejh mainly from Arab prisoners of war held in Egypt.

In order to make the Arab revolt a worthwhile military asset it was essential that it should be capable of exerting influence on the Turkish left (desert) flank. For this to be successful it was necessary to capture the port of Akaba, to shorten the lines of communication. A naval attack being ruled out, Lawrence decided to take Akaba by land by surprise. In April 1917 with a handful of men, and without the support of General Sir Archibald Murray, C-in-C British army in Egypt, Lawrence rode by camel almost up to Damascus and succeeded in enlisting a force of tribesmen. Early in July, after destroying a Turkish force at Aba-el-Lissan, he stormed and captured Akaba. Feisal's forces were moved round by the Royal Navy, under Admiral Sir Rosslyn Wemyss, C-in-C India and Egypt and a good friend of the Arabs, and established their base at Akaba. When General Sir Edmund Allenby succeeded Murray as Commander of the Egyptian Expeditionary Force on 28 June 1917, Lawrence and Feisal gained much greater administrative and tactical support for their plans, including, eventually, armoured cars, air support and, what was more important to them, appreciation of the value of their operations. Colonel A.P. Lord Wavell wrote in his *Campaigns in Palestine* (Constable, 1928): 'The value of the Arab movement to the British commander was great, since it diverted considerable Turkish reinforcements and supplies to the Hejaz, and protected the right flank of the British armies in their advance through Palestine. Further it put an end to German propaganda in SW Arabia and removed any danger of the establishment of a German submarine base on the Red Sea. These were important services and well worth the subsidies in gold and munitions expended on the Arab forces.'

By a right flank movement, the Arab forces under Lawrence eventually reached and occupied Damascus (qv) before Allenby's forces, which caused some international political complications. They were unaware that the British had previously agreed that the French should have a mandate over Syria.

HELIGOLAND BIGHT (North Sea)   First World War   27-8 August 1914
Fought between the British under Commodore Reginald Tyrwhitt and Vice-Admiral Sir David Beatty and the Germans under the overall command of Admiral Alfred von Tirpitz.
Strength: British 8 submarines + 2 flotillas of destroyers + 2 light cruisers (*Arethusa* and *Fearless*) + 5 battle-cruisers (*Lion, Queen Mary, Princess Royal, Invincible, New Zealand*); Germans 2 light cruisers + 9 destroyers + 4 heavy cruisers (*Mainz, Köln, Yorck, Ariadne*).

The first naval battle of the war was provoked by the British. Tyrwhitt took a flotilla of submarines followed by two flotillas of destroyers and 2 light cruisers from Harwich to the Bight and attacked 9 German destroyers with the light cruisers *Arethusa* and *Fearless*, sinking one. A German squadron came out and attacked, but was driven off, mainly by the *Arethusa*, which was damaged. The Germans, unaware that a heavy cruiser force under Beatty had moved down from Scapa Flow, now brought their heavy cruisers *Mainz, Köln* and *Yorck* into action. They shelled the light cruisers, which avoided engaging seriously while the main British fleet came up, negotiating the German minefield successfully. The *Lion,* which led the British fleet, sank the *Mainz* and *Köln* with her 13.5-inch guns, as well as another heavy cruiser, the *Ariadne.* Three other German cruisers were crippled and a destroyer sunk. Nearly 1,000 Germans were drowned and 379 were captured, while 31 British died and 52 were wounded.

This raid 'right up to the enemy's gate', in which Beatty lost not a single ship, had a profound moral effect. Kaiser William II ordered Tirpitz henceforth to 'avoid any action which might lead to heavy losses'.

HUJ (Israel) First World War 8 November 1917

Fought between the British under Major-General J.S.M. Shea and the Turks, with German and Austrian support.

The advance of the 60th Division was held up by a Turkish rearguard, well dug in on a ridge south of the village of Huj, east of Gaza. The assistance of the Desert Mounted Corps was requested, as a move by infantry across 1,000 yards of open ground would be slow and costly. All the cavalry that was immediately available was one and a half squadrons of the Worcestershire Yeomanry and one and a half squadrons of the Warwickshire Yeomanry, ten troops in all, comprising 12 officers and 158 troopers from 5th Mounted Brigade. One charge by the yeomanry dispersed the infantry, they then turned on the guns from the flank. In a second charge they rode straight at the guns, while in a third charge they dispersed some reinforcements. All the charges went right home. The gunners, who included Germans and Austrians as well as Turks, stood to their guns to the last and were killed with the sword. Eleven guns, 4 machine-guns and 70 prisoners were taken, but at a cost. The 3 British squadron commanders were killed and 6 officers were wounded. In addition British casualties were 26 men killed and 40 wounded, and 100 horses out of 170 killed

ISONZO RIVER I-XI (Italy) First World War 23 June 1915-12 September 1917

Fought between the Italians under General Count Cadorna and the Austrians under Archduke Eugene and General Svetozar Borojevic von Bojna.

Although Italy remained neutral at the outbreak of the war, she was a member of the Triple Alliance. When the Allies promised her gains in Austrian territory, she renounced the alliance with the Austro-Hungarian Empire and declared war on the Dual Monarchy on 23 May 1915. (War was not declared on Germany until 28 August 1916.) The Austrian border with Italy generally followed the line of the Alps, allowing little ground suitable for the Italians to launch an offensive. The only area where it was possible for the Italians to attack was in the east, along the Isonzo River at the head of the Adriatic Sea. Here the Italians' main objective was Trieste. On a 60-mile front Cadorna amassed thirty-five divisions. Field-Marshal Count Conrad von Hötzendorf, the Austrian Chief of Staff, assembled a force of fourteen Austrian divisions under Eugene and Borojevic von Bojna. (This force was later increased to twenty-two divisions.)

Throughout the next twenty-seven months the Austrians successfully defended this defence line despite the fact that they were always outnumbered. At the end of that time, after enormous losses on both sides, Cadorna had gained 11 or 12 miles of ground. The Austrians had the advantage of terrain consisting of mountains and foothills which overlooked the Isonzo valley, and superior artillery, but the dogged persistence of the Italian 2nd Army (on the left), and the 3rd (S) won the regard of the world.

Isonzo I: 23 June-7 July 1915.
Isonzo II: 18 July-3 August 1915.
Isonzo III: 18 October-3 November 1915.
Isonzo IV: 10 November-2 December 1915.

These actions cost the Italians 66,000 killed, 190,000 wounded and 22,500 captured. Austrian losses were 165,000.

Isonzo V: 9-17 March 1916. In snow, rain and fog Cadorna once again attacked the Austrian defences at the request of the Allies who wanted a diversionary offensive. The assault achieved nothing and had to be called off because the Austrian thrust in the Trentino, aimed at Asiago and Padua, had to be met.

Isonzo VI: 6-17 August 1916. The Austrian advance in the Trentino was blocked by troops from the Isonzo Line. Having achieved this, Cadorna moved his men back to the main front. The Austrian position was now weakened as a result of the Trentino offensive and Cadorna assaulted it, capturing Gorizia on 9 August. A bridgehead was also gained across the Isonzo, but the lack of reserves and stiffening Austrian resistance prevented any further advance. It was the first Italian success.

Isonzo VII: 14-17 September 1916.

Isonzo VIII: 10-12 October 1916.

Isonzo IX: 1-4 November 1916. In an attempt to lower the casualty rate, Cadorna changed his tactics from all-out offensive to making several sudden stabs at the Austrian line. The casualty rate was lowered, but no gain was made.

Isonzo X: 12 May-8 June 1917. Reinforced over the winter by fresh troops and more armament, the Italians launched a new offensive. They gained a few yards of ground before an Austrian counter-attack on 4-8 June beat them back to their starting place.

Isonzo XI: 19 August-12 September 1917. Now fifty-one divisions strong, with 5,200 guns, the Italians launched another offensive. The 2nd (General Luigi Capello) and 3rd (Duke of Aosta) Armies assaulted Austrian lines in a massive attack which pushed the Austrian line back, but the Italian infantry outran artillery support and supplies and the advantage thus gained by the Italians could not be capitalised.

No more fighting took place on this front between the Italians and the Austrians alone. The Germans, at the behest of the Austrians, sent troops in, which led to the battle of Caporetto (qv).

JADAR RIVER (Yugoslavia)   First World War   16-21 August 1914
Fought between the Serbs under General Radomir Putnik and the Austrians under Major-General Oskar Potiorek.

Austria launched two offensives at the start of the war. One, the main attack, was against Russia. The secondary assault was on Serbia, the crushing of which would open the Berlin-Baghdad railway.

A two-pronged invasion was launched across the northern frontier of Serbia on 12 August, the 2nd Army striking from the north and the 5th and 6th Armies crossing the Drina River from the west. The chief danger to the Serbs came from the Austrian 5th Army, and Putnik moved the Serbian 2nd and 3rd Armies to block the advance of that force. Along a 30-mile front on the Jadar River the Serbs attacked the pivot between the Austrian 8 and 13 Corps and drove them back. 4 Corps of the weakened Austrian 2nd Army was also beaten back, and in the SW the Austrian 6th Army did not gain any ground. The Austrian armies, poorly co-ordinated and now exhausted, were recalled by Potiorek on 21 August. Austrian casualties numbered 40,000, and by the end of August the survivors were back on their own soil.

The invasion of Serbia had resulted in defeat on all fronts. Serbian losses were relatively light. Putnik's conduct of his defensive campaign is considered a classic. He kept his three armies under his hand in a central position from which he manoeuvred so as to defeat the Austrians in detail.

JERUSALEM (Israel)   First World War   18 November-11 December 1917
Fought between the British, Australian, New Zealand and Indian forces under General Sir Edmund Allenby, and the Turks under General Erich von Falkenhayn. *Strength:* Allies 88,000 (21 Corps, 52nd, 54th, 75th Infantry Divisions, Yeomanry Mounted Division, Australian Mounted Division); Turks 16,000 (7th Army).

After the Battle of Junction Station (13-14 November) the Turks were reinforced and von Falkenhayn, taking over command from General Kress von Kressenstein, re-established a front from Jerusalem to the sea, with his 8th Army on the plains and the 7th Army in the Judaean Hills around Jerusalem. Allenby decided to follow up his success with a rapid thrust at Jerusalem, while establishing a defensive line on the plains to cover his communications. But bad weather, lack of reconnaissance and naturally strong defensive positions made a swift capture out of the question. On 24 November Allenby ordered that all further attacks be discontinued.

During the next fortnight Allenby reshuffled his forces in order to bring in fresh troops. The capture of Jerusalem was entrusted to 20 Corps, under General Sir Philip Chetwode. During this period the Turks counter-attacked with a series of 'stormtroop' actions which caused them heavy casualties and no gains and so weakened the defence. The deliberate prepared attack started on 8 December on a two-divisional (60th and 74th) front, with 53rd Division in reserve. The Turkish defences had been hewn out of the hillside with great labour the year before and should have been impregnable, but their best troops had been wasted in futile counter-attacking and the morale of the defenders was low. By dawn on 9 December the last Turkish soldiers had left the city and the Mayor of Jerusalem surrendered the keys to Major-General J.S.M. Shea as the 60th Division marched in. British casualties had been 1,667.

After a brief resistance on the Mount of Olives, the Turks withdrew altogether and General Allenby made his formal entry into Jerusalem on 11 December 1917. On 26 December a Turkish counter-attack was repulsed for a loss of 1,000 killed and 750 prisoners.

During the campaign from the Third Battle of Gaza (qv) to the capture of Jerusalem British casualties were 18,000 men, and 10,000 horses, camels, mules and donkeys (11.5 per cent of the total). Turkish losses were 25,000, including 12,000 prisoners and 100 guns.

Heavy rains had set in and as the line from Jerusalem to the sea was now secure, the British army settled down for the winter.

JISR BENAT YAKUB (Syria)   First World War   27 September 1918
Fought between the Australian Mounted Division under Major-General H. W. Hodgson and a Turkish and German rearguard.

At midday on 27 September leading troops of the Australian Mounted Division starting on their march to Damascus (qv) were fired on as they reached Jisr Benat Yakub (Bridge of the Daughters of Jacob). The Turks had destroyed the stone bridge and numerous German machine-gunners covered the approaches from positions on the north bank of the Jordan.

The French Spahi Regiment of the 5th Australian Light Horse (ALH) Brigade worked down towards the bridge while the 5th ALH sought a ford to the south. The 3rd ALH went north. After a difficult advance in rocky country both approached the bridge as darkness fell. Attacked on each flank the Turko-German rearguard withdrew hastily at nightfall, losing a number of prisoners.

JUTLAND (North Sea)   First World War   31 May 1916
Fought between the Germans under Admiral Franz von Hipper and Admiral Reinhard Scheer and the British under Admiral John Jellicoe and Admiral Sir David Beatty.
Strength: Germans (von Hipper) 5 battle-cruisers + (Scheer, High Seas Fleet) 8 old battleships + 16 new battleships + (in addition) 11 light cruisers + 63 destroyers; British (Beatty, southern fleet) 6 battle-cruisers + 4 battleships + (Jellico, main fleet) 3 battle-cruisers + 24 battleships + (in addition) 34 light cruisers + 80 destroyers.

The British blockade of the German ports was so strong that Scheer decided to take the offensive in an attempt to force the British Grand Fleet in the North Sea to relax its hold on enemy shipping.

On 31 May Scheer sent von Hipper north along the coast of Jutland while he followed 50 miles behind with the main fleet. Jellicoe knew of the sortie because German radio messages had been decoded, and the British fleet put to sea in two divisions, Beatty to the south and Jellicoe, with the main fleet, 70 miles north. Von Hipper and Beatty sighted each other at 3.25 pm. The Germans had seen the British first and were already steaming back to join the main fleet. Beatty's force was divided into two parts, steaming east in line-ahead with the battle-cruisers to the right and the dreadnoughts under Rear-Admiral Sir Hugh Evan-Thomas to the left. Beatty turned on a parallel course to the retreating Germans and signalled Evan-Thomas, whom von Hipper had not yet sighted, to follow. At a range of 16,500 yards (9+ miles) the two fleets opened fire and the Germans, with more accurate gunnery, sank 2 British battle-cruisers. The *Von der Tann* hit and sank the *Indefatigable* while the *Derfflinger* sank the *Queen Mary*. Beatty's flagship,

Lion, was hit several times, but still engaged the Germans. Evan-Thomas was still out of range and Beatty now signalled to his 4 remaining ships to engage von Hipper closer, although he was now outnumbered by one. At 4.42 Beatty sighted the main German fleet and immediately turned back to lure the enemy towards Jellicoe's fleet. At 6 pm Beatty sighted Jellicoe, whose force was divided into six divisions, steaming SE in parallel columns, preceded by Rear-Admiral Horace Hood's battle squadron. Beatty, still engaging the Germans, turned east in order to be in line with Jellicoe, whom the Germans had not yet sighted. The main fleet aligned itself with Beatty, both British commanders having the aim of swinging round Scheer and cutting him off from his base. The British dreadnoughts opened fire on the German ships just as Scheer sighted Hood's squadron to his starboard bow. At about 6.30 pm the entire fleets of both sides became engaged in a furious battle. Von Hipper's flagship, the *Lützow,* was crippled and put out of action while Hood's flagship, the *Invincible,* was sunk at 6.34 pm with all hands. The British cruisers *Defence* and *Warrior* also went down. The British fleet, in line, crossed the German 'T' (sailed across the van of the German fleet) during the engagement and the German fleet was gradually surrounded by the British. Scheer, realising this, set up a destroyer attack and a smoke-screen, under cover of which his fleet executed a 180-degrees turn and began steaming west, by which manoeuvre he was able to sail out of range of British guns. The British, knowing they were still between the Germans and their base, continued to move south.

At 6.55 pm Scheer, apparently thinking that Jellicoe had divided his fleet, made another 180-degrees turn and sailed back into the range of British guns. Scheer once again veered off, but the *Derfflinger* stayed to screen the German withdrawal with the *Von der Tann,* whose guns were out of action, but which remained to spread the British fire. The *Seydlitz* and *Derfflinger* both caught fire while the main German fleet carried out the turning manoeuvre at close range to the British. German destroyers moved in to launch a torpedo attack and to make a smoke-screen and Jellicoe turned away to avoid the torpedoes, thus allowing Scheer through. By the time the British re-formed the Germans were out of range but once again steaming west away from the German coast which the British still blocked. After dark, at about 10 pm, Scheer, knowing that his ships could not survive another battle, turned SE and sailed straight at the tail of the British fleet which consisted of light cruisers. In a confused night battle, in which the German battleship *Pommern* was cut in two and the British cruiser *Black Prince* was sunk with all hands, the Germans fought their way through the line and into anchorage at Jade. The British fleet returned to its bases. The British lost 3 battle-cruisers, 3 light cruisers and 8 destroyers, a total of 117,025 tons and almost double the German losses which were 4 cruisers, 5 destroyers, 1 old battleship and 1 battle-cruiser (about 61,180 tons). British losses were 6,784 men: German casualties were 3,029.

Although the Germans claimed the battle as a victory, they now knew that they could not beat the British Grand Fleet and the morale of German sailors suffered, so that eventually they mutinied rather than risk another such battle.

This was the last great naval engagement fought solely with surface ships. The action is also called the Battle of the Skaggerak.

KOVEL-STANISLAV (USSR)   First World War   4 June-20 September 1916
Fought between the Russians under General Alexei Brusilov, and the Germans and Austrians under General Paul von Hindenburg and Field-Marshal Count Conrad von Hötzendorf with some support from the Turks.

The Russians amassed a force consisting of four armies (8th, 11th, 7th and 9th) along a line stretching 300 miles from the Pripet Marshes in the north to the Romanian border in the south. After an artillery bombardment the Southwest Army Group launched its offensive on 4 June. Hötzendorf, who commanded the Austrian armies in the Ukraine, was caught unawares and forced to fall back before the Russian advance. Lutsk fell on 6 June, and by 10 June the Russians had advanced as far as Kovel, a vital transport centre on the north end of Brusilov's line. To the south, Czernowitz (Chernovtsy) in Bucovina fell on 17 June. Russia had inflicted more than 700,000 casualties on the Austrians and Germans by the end of the month.

Both sides now reinforced, but the central powers, owing to superior rail communications, were able to move faster than the Russians. Hindenburg moved sixteen German divisions from the Western Front and the Austrians brought seven divisions up mainly from the Trentino offensive (Asiago [qv]), and the Turks two. General Alexander von Linsingen took command of the defences at Kovel and after fierce fighting checked and stopped the Russian offensive here in July. To the south, Brusilov moved as far west as Stanislav before the stabilised Austrian-German line halted the Russians here as well. By 20 September the advance had been contained on all fronts and Russia had exhausted her supplies of manpower, arms and ammunition. Both sides lost over 1 million men, about half being prisoners or deserters.

This was the last major battle on the Russian front. It had so weakened Austria that from then on she was forced to take orders directly from Germany. Romania entered the war on the Allied side, but was soon beaten, and internal unrest in Russia led to the revolution the following year.

KUT-AL-AMARA (Iraq)   First World War   28 September 1915-29 April 1916
Fought between the Anglo-Indian army under General Sir Charles Townshend and the Turks under General Nur-ud-din.
Strength: British 11,000; Turks 10,500.

The campaign by Britain against Turkey began in Mesopotamia when an Anglo-Indian force occupied Basra, which lay at the confluence of the Tigris and Euphrates. The force under General Sir John Nixon then moved north to take Amara on the Tigris on 3 June and Nasiriya, also north, on the Euphrates on 25 July. Because Turkish opposition was slight, Nixon decided to send a division north to Baghdad. This force under Townshend met the Turks at Kut-al-Amara, where they occupied a strong position. Townshend manoeuvred so that he could attack the Turks from the north, and on 28 September he routed them. However, owing to the confusion engendered by the attack, most of the Turkish force managed to escape to Ctesiphon (qv). Townshend, having reorganised and re-supplied his army, moved on to attack the Turks there.

The failure of his assault forced Townshend to move back down the Tigris to Kut-al-Amara, which he reached on 3 December. Deciding to risk a Turkish siege, he shut himself up in the town with a force of 12,000 Anglo-Indian troops. Nur-ud-din and Marshal Kolmar von der Göltz with two Turkish divisions closed in on the British, who fortified the piece of land round the village, a U-shape formed by a meander in the Tigris, and awaited relief. The Turks assaulted the defences, but failed to penetrate them, whereupon they set up a blockade. Nixon sent a column out from Basra under General Sir Fenton Aylmer but the two new Indian divisions were repulsed between 18 and 21 January 1916, Turkish resistance being too strong. Floods finally forced Aylmer to retire with a loss of 6,000 men.

On 1 April General Lake, who had succeeded Nixon, sent General Sir George Gorringe with another relief force. Gorringe attempted a surprise attack on the Turks from the south bank of the Tigris, but was repulsed by von der Göltz commanding the Turkish 6th Army. In repeated attacks most of the Turkish defences were taken, but the British were beaten back by a Turkish counter-attack on 22 April.

The garrison in Kut ran out of food and was by now weakened by sickness and starvation. On 29 April Townshend surrendered the garrison in order to save the surviving 10,000 men (including 2,000 British). Of these, 8,000 were taken prisoner, more than half of the British among them dying in captivity, as was the case with at least a third of the Indians. Von der Göltz died of cholera just before Townshend's surrender.

General Sir Stanley Maude now arrived in Mesopotamia to take charge of operations.

LEMBERG (L'VOV) (USSR)   First World War   1-19 July 1917
Fought between the Russians under General Alexei Brusilov and the Germans under Field-Marshal Paul von Hindenburg.

After the March Revolution of 1917 and the forced abdication of Czar Nicholas II, Alexander Kerensky became Prime Minister of Russia (on 25 July) and tried to mount a formidable offensive against the Germans. But this ran counter to the wishes of the Russian people who were eager for peace, resulting in the disintegration of the Russian forces on the Eastern Front. The Germans watched the process and themselves made no aggressive move that would have served to unify the armies, apart from dispatching the revolutionary, Vladimir Lenin, into Russia to hasten the disintegration. The Allies pressed Kerensky to take the offensive and Brusilov was finally ordered to attack west towards Lemberg (L'vov).

The Russian army, now consisting chiefly of Finns, Poles and Siberians, advanced 30 miles before the Germans launched a counter-attack on their right (N) flank on 19 July. The Russian force promptly fell to pieces and began a disorderly retreat, which lasted for two weeks until the army was at the Galician frontier in hopeless confusion.

Called the Kerensky Offensive, this was the last Russian effort of the war. Kerensky was pushed out of office by the Bolshevik *coup d'état* on 7 November 1917, and there followed six years of internecine war throughout Russia, during which millions were killed or died of disease and starvation.

LODZ (Poland)   First World War   11 November-6 December 1914
Fought between the Germans under Field-Marshal Paul von Hindenburg and the Russians under General Pavel Rennenkampf.

Hindenburg moved the German 9th Army north by rail to Posen-Thorn (Poznan-Torun) and the surrounding region. The move followed the collapse of the German offensive on Warsaw and sought to block an anticipated Russian attack into Silesia.

On 11 November the Germans under General August von Mackensen attacked SE towards Warsaw. South of the Vistula River (qv), the Germans attacked the Russian 1st Army under Rennenkampf and beat it back, going on to advance 50 miles in four days. By 16 November the Germans had driven deeply into the Russian line between the 1st and 2nd Armies. Meanwhile, on 14 November, the Russians had launched an offensive into Silesia as the Germans had foreseen, but it was recalled on 16 November and the Russian 5th Army moved swiftly north to aid the Russian 2nd Army, now threatened with encirclement in front of Lodz, whither they had retreated after the initial German advance. On 19 November the 5th Army, having marched 70 miles in forty-eight hours, attacked Mackensen's right flank at Lodz. The German 25 R Corps, east of the town, was surrounded by the Russians and only just managed to fight its way out on 24-6 November. On 6 December the Russians withdrew from Lodz in order to straighten their line and protect Warsaw.

The Germans had not crushed the Russian army, but they had saved Silesia from invasion.

L'VOV   see LEMBERG

MASURIAN LAKES I (Poland)   First World War   5-13 September 1914
Fought between the Russians under General Pavel Rennenkampf and the Germans under General Paul von Hindenburg.

The Russians had sought to envelop the German army in E Prussia in a pincer movement. The Russian force at Tannenberg (qv) was decisively defeated by the Germans under Hindenberg and General Erich Ludendorff who then turned the German 8th Army to face the other arm of the pincer - the Russian 1st Army under Rennenkampf.

Hindenburg was reinforced by two corps sent from the French front by General Helmuth von Moltke which arrived too late to take part in the battle of Tannenberg. The Russian army, which had not taken part in the battle which destroyed the 2nd Army, had been to the NE of Tannenberg, moving slowly through the

Insterburg Gap between Königsberg (Kaliningrad) and the Masurian Lakes. Hearing of the defeat of General Alexander Samsonov, Rennenkampf pulled back to anchor his left (S) at the Masurian Lakes and to strengthen his line north to the Baltic Sea with cordon defences. On 5 September the German 8th Army began to attack the Russian line, concentrating their attention on the south. The offensive threatened to outflank the Russians, and on 9 September Rennenkampf ordered a general withdrawal. On 10 September the Russians made a counter-attack to protect their left from General Hermann von François's 1 Corps which had arrived to reinforce the German right. The attack, made on the German centre, delayed Ludendorff's advance for forty-eight hours and enabled many Russian troops to escape encirclement. The Germans pursued the retreating Russians, but by 13 September, when the Russians were out of E Prussia, the pursuit slackened. The invasion had been stopped at a cost of only 10,000 casualties. Russian losses were 125,000.

General Yakov Grigorievich Jilinsky, who had misdirected the offensive in E Prussia, was replaced by General Nikolai Russky.

MASURIAN LAKES II (Poland)   First World War   7-21 February 1915
Fought between the Germans under Field-Marshal Paul von Hindenburg and the Russians.

The Germans planned to knock Russia out of the war, the chief attack coming through E Prussia against the Russian 10th Army under General Sievers which stood north of the Masurian Lakes.

On 7 February the German 8th Army under General Otto von Below attacked the Russian south flank from the west in a heavy snowstorm. The Russians were taken by surprise and began to fall back. The following day they were assaulted from the north by the German 10th Army under General Hermann von Eichhorn. The four Russian corps which formed the 10th Army seemed to be in danger of total destruction, but the resistance of 20 Corps in the Forest of Augustow enabled the other three corps to escape. 20 Corps surrendered on 21 February. Russian casualties during this battle were 200,000. German battle losses were light, but the army suffered severely from exposure.

The action is sometimes called the Winter Battle of Masuria.

MEGIDDO III (Israel)   First World War   19 September-30 October 1918
Fought between the British, French, Indians and Arabs under General Sir Edmund Allenby, and the Turks under General Otto Liman von Sanders.
Strength: Allies 57,000 infantry + 12,000 cavalry + 540 guns; Turks 40,000 infantry + 4,000 cavalry + 430 guns.

The pressure of German attacks on the Western Front meant that the British had to recall many of the troops serving in Palestine after Jerusalem (qv) fell in 1917. Allenby spent the summer of 1918 training new recruits from India in order to rebuild his army. At the same time he raided east of the Jordan River several times, aided in these thrusts by the Arab force of Colonel T.E. Lawrence which struck continually at Turkish communication lines. The activity on the Turkish left made von Sanders concentrate his troops (the 4th Army) east of the Jordan when Allenby was actually aiming at the Turkish right flank (on the coast). A third of von Sanders's men were so deployed when Allenby, who had massed most of his infantry north of Jaffa, attacked along a 65-mile front which was thinly held by eleven Turkish divisions from Jaffa to the Jordan. The line collapsed within three hours and the cavalry corps went through the gap created towards Megiddo, wheeling right to block the northern retreat of the 7th and 8th Armies, forcing the Turks to retreat east across the Jordan. They left 25,000 prisoners. The Turkish 4th Army on the east flank also drew back. As the Turks made for Damascus (qv) they were harried by British cavalry and aircraft, being given no opportunity to make a stand. The Arabs also raided them as they withdrew. The German Asienkorps also joined in the retreat which went on through Damascus, which the British reached on 2 October, after it had been taken by the Arab army under Lawrence. Beirut fell on 8 October, Baalbeck on 11 October, Tripoli on 18 October and Aleppo on 25 October. On 30 October the Turks asked for and were granted an armistice. In the Battle of Megiddo they had lost 75,000 prisoners (of whom 200 officers and 3,500 other ranks were German) 430 guns and an enormous amount of stores. The Turkish armies in Syria had been destroyed while in six weeks the British had advanced 350 miles. Allied casualties were 5,600. The 5th Cavalry Division covered over 500 miles in thirty-eight days of operations, losing only 21 per cent of its horses. The action is also known as the Battle of Damascus.

The Palestine campaign in its entirety cost the Allies (the Indians and Anzac troops outnumbering the British) 550,000 casualties, of which 90 per cent were stricken by disease.

The Turkish Empire was to have been Germany's stepping-stone to the Persian Gulf and central Asia.

NAROCH LAKE (USSR)   First World War   18-26 March 1916
Fought between the Russians under Czar Nicholas II and the Germans under Field-Marshal Paul von Hindenburg.
Aim: The Czar, who assumed personal command of his armies in September 1915, responded to appeals from the French for a diversionary attack by preparing an offensive against the German lines at Naroch Lake in White Russia (Byelorussia), north of the Pripet Marshes.
Battle: On 18 March the Russian 10th Army attacked the German lines after a short artillery bombardment. The infantry carried the first and second German lines, but the Russian gunners then left the field with their weapons. The Germans, hearing of this, shelled the Russian trenches heavily and their accurate fire decimated the attackers. The spring thaw turned the battlefield into a sea of mud, bogging the Russian army down so that the offensive ground to a halt. Russian losses were over 80,000.
Result: No advantage was gained by the badly organised offensive.

PIAVE RIVER (Italy)   First World War   15-22 June 1918
Fought between the Italians under General Armando Diaz and the Austrians under General Svetozar Borojevic von Bojna and Field-Marshal Count Conrad von Hötzendorf.
Strength: Italians 57 divisions (including 5 Anglo-French divisions from the Western Front); Austrians 58 divisions.

After their defeat at Caporetto (qv) the Italians retreated behind the Piave River, to which line they clung grimly, particularly around Monte Grappa, near the western end of the line which became known as the 'Sacred Mountain'. German troops were also recalled to the Western Front, as some Anglo-French and Italian divisions had been, weakening the Austrian line north of the Piave. The Austrians launched one more offensive in an effort to knock Italy out of the war. The Austrian command was divided into two with Borojevic von Bojna on the left (E) and Hötzendorf, demoted from his position as Austrian Chief of Staff, on the right, in the Trentino.

After diversionary attacks, the main Austrian assault began on 15 June, when both armies advanced. On the right, Hötzendorf met a swift counter-attack by the 4th and 6th Armies, which included the Anglo-French contingent, on the day after the attack was launched. The small advance which the Austrian 10th and 11th Armies had made on the first day was maintained, but no further advance was made. Lower down the river, however, Borojevic von Bojna forced a crossing with the 6th and 5th Armies (100,000 men) and advanced 3 miles before being counter-attacked by the Italian 8th and 3rd Armies. For the next eight days a fierce struggle took place while the Austrians fought to enlarge their bridgehead, and the Italians fought to beat them back. The Austrians advanced 6 miles before heavy rain swept away ten of the fourteen bridges they had constructed across the Piave, slowing the movement of supplies. Reinforcements could not be brought up from Hötzendorf's hard-pressed armies, and on 18 June the Italians counter-attacked strongly. By 21 June they had turned the Austrian left flank, forcing their withdrawal across the Piave, in which manoeuvre they sustained heavy losses. In this, the last offensive undertaken by the Dual Monarchy of Austria and Hungary, 24,000 Austrians were captured out of a total of 150,000 casualties.

Diaz did not pursue the Austrians beyond the Piave.

RAFA (Egypt)   First World War   8 January 1917
Fought between the British, Australians and New Zealanders under Lt-General Sir Philip Chetwode, and some 2 battalions of 31st Turkish Regiment with a battery of mountain guns under the overall command of the German Colonel Kress von Kressenstein.

Following the Battle of Romani (qv) the British pushed their coastal railway forward to El Arish, which was occupied on 21 December. The Royal Navy brought in supplies at El Arish on 23 December. The only Turkish force remaining in Egypt was the detachment at Rafa, 25 miles east of El Arish. The railway reached El Arish on 4 January 1917.

On the evening of 8 January Chetwode rode out with the Anzac Mounted Division (less one brigade), the 5th Mounted Brigade (yeomanry), the Imperial Camel Corps and No 7 Light Car Patrol. The Camel Corps consisted of eighteen companies (ten Australian, six British and two New Zealand) with an Indian mountain battery and a machine-gun squadron. Each man could operate for five days of desert warfare.

After a skilful night march the strong Turkish position at El Magruntein, SW of Rafa, was surrounded by dawn on 9 January. Chetwode attacked but made little headway against well-dug emplacements, with bare fields of fire of some 2,000 yards. In the afternoon Turkish reinforcements were reported and at 4.30 pm Chetwode ordered a withdrawal. But before orders arrived the New Zealand Mounted Brigade cleared the central keep of the defences by a bayonet charge and the Camel Corps assaulted another work. By nightfall the Turkish garrison had been wiped out. A battery of guns and 1,635 prisoners were taken and about 200 Turks killed. British casualties were 71 killed and 415 wounded.

RAMADI (Iraq)   First World War   28-9 September 1917
Fought between the British under General Sir Stanley Maude and the Turks.

After capturing Baghdad in 1916, Maude consolidated his position during the summer and moved against the Turks in Mesopotamia when the cooler weather came. The Anglo-Indian Army marched 60 miles west to Ramadi, where the Turks had a strong garrison on the right bank of the Euphrates. In an attack which began on 28 September the British overwhelmed the Turks, taking most of them prisoner. Maude returned to Baghdad, where he died of cholera on 18 November. He was replaced by General Sir William Marshal who was ordered to send two divisions to General Sir Edmund Allenby in Palestine. This reduction in his own strength limited his future operations, though he continued to keep up the pressure on the Turks.

RIGA II (USSR)   First World War   1-3 September 1917
Fought between the Russians under General Lavrenti Kornilov and the Germans under Field-Marshal Paul von Hindenburg.

The speed with which the Russian attack on Lemberg (L'vov) collapsed, convinced Hindenburg that one more offensive would cause the fall of Alexander Kerensky's government and force Russia out of the war.

On 1 September the German 8th Army under General Oskar von Hutier stormed over the Dvina River into Riga. Russian resistance was slight and at the end of two days was completely crushed. The German victory was due to concentrated fire support. Hutier's brilliant gunner, Colonel Georg von Brüchmuller, had massed one gun per 8 yards on a 4,600 yard front. The Germans now threatened to march on Petrograd (Leningrad), but this proved to be unnecessary as the fall of Riga produced the desired consequences. The beaten Russian commander, Kornilov, led a counter-revolutionary movement in the period 8-14 September and Kerensky was deposed during the October Revolution, which brought Lenin and Trotsky to power. By 2 December hostilities on the Eastern Front had ceased. Russian negotiators stalled for better terms in the new year, and on 18 February the Germans once again resumed the offensive on the Eastern Front, thereby forcing the Russians to capitulate formally on the treaty terms. These were signed at Brest-Litovsk on 3 March.

The end of the war on the Russian front meant that an enormous number of German troops were released for action on the Western Front.

ROMANI (Egypt)   First World War   3-9 August 1916
Fought between the British (Egyptian Expeditionary Force) under General Sir Archibald Murray and Lt-General the Hon H.A. Lawrence, and the Turks and Germans under Colonel Kress von Kressenstein.
Strength: British 25,000; Turks 3rd (Anatolian) Division and Germans 16,000 with 30 guns and 38 machine-guns.

In May the 52nd (Lowland) Division had occupied a position at Romani. They built 18 redoubts, each holding about 100 men and 2 machine-guns. A railway-line to Kantara on the Suez Canal ensured their supplies.

Von Kressenstein's aim was to establish a position within artillery range of the Canal and so interrupt traffic. On 9 July he marched from Shellal, NW of Beersheba, and reached Bir el Abd and Oghratina on 19 July. As soon as his presence was reported the British reinforced No 3 Section of the Canal Defences. The Turks came forward to within 10 miles of the Romani position and there halted for 10 days.

The Turks, predictably, tried to turn the British right since their left was unapproachable. They were compelled to advance through the soft sand of a waterless desert, making about one mile an hour. They advanced on the night of 3rd August and in the teeth of strong resistance from the 1st Australian Light Horse fought their way forward to Wellington Ridge, where they were held up, spent and discouraged. The British, however, were slow to counter-attack, and on 5 August von Kressenstein managed to withdraw most of his men. On the next two days he fought skilful rearguard actions against the mounted troops and on the 9th repulsed the Anzac Mounted Division at Bir el Abd. He then fell back on El Arish. His men had fought with determination and had outmarched the British.
Casualties: The Turks lost some 8,000 men, including 3,000 prisoners, and 4 guns besides a number of machine-guns. The British lost 1,100, mostly in the Anzac Mounted Division.

Romani was a decided success for the British. But, with their HQ back at Kantara, they were too slow to go over to the counter-attack. Had General Lawrence given command of the Romani position to one of his two divisional commanders the victory might have been exploited more effectively.

ROMANIA   First World War   28 August 1916-6 December 1917
Fought between the Germans and Austrians under General Erich von Falkenhayn and the Romanians under General Alexandru Averescu.

The Romanian government of King Ferdinand I declared war against the central powers on 27 August and, the following day, the Romanian 1st, 2nd and 4th Armies attacked NW through the Transylvanian Alps while the 3rd Army remained in the south to defend the line of the Danube against Bulgaria. Because other fronts were at this time quiet, Germany and Austria were free to concentrate on the Romanian offensive.

In the first two weeks of the war the Romanians advanced 40 miles through the mountains to the NW, driving the Austrian 1st Army under General Baron Artur Arz von Straussenburg back before it. Their front, however, was 200 miles long, and poor communications and strong Austrian resistance halted the advance by 18 September. In the SE, General August von Mackensen marched into the Dobruja with the Army of the Danube, which consisted of Germans, Bulgars and Turks. Moving north between the Danube and the Black Sea, this army took Turtucaia on 6 September and Silistra on 9 September. At Constanta, Romania's only Black Sea port, he was checked by an Allied force under Zaionchovsky which was made up of the remnants of Averescu's 3rd Romanian Army, a Russian corps and a division of Serbian volunteers. Three Romanian divisions were moved from the Transylvania front to strengthen this line. On 20 October von Mackensen, who had been reinforced with two more Turkish divisions, renewed his attack. Zaionchovsky's line broke and the Army of the Danube pushed through to take Constanta on 23 October. All hope of Allied aid was now gone. Von Mackensen left a small holding force in the port and moved west to take part in a combined attack on Bucharest.

Meanwhile, in the west, another threat developed with the arrival of von Falkenhayn, who took command of the German 9th Army which opposed the Romanian left flank in the Transylvanian advance. On 18 September von Falkenhayn counter-attacked the Romanians in a series of engagements which drove back the 1st, 2nd and 4th Armies in turn. Aided by the Austrian 1st Army to the north and other reinforcements, von Falkenhayn increased pressure on 10 November. The Romanians fell back everywhere. The German 9th Army was now advancing on Bucharest from the west and von Mackensen, crossing the Danube on 23 November, moved on the capital from the south. On 1 December Averescu made one last attempt to avoid defeat. Collecting all the troops in the area, he attacked hard through the gap between Falkenhayn and Mackensen. He took 3,000 prisoners from the Danube army, but was obliged to retreat hurriedly when the 9th Army advanced on his right and rear. On 6 December the Romanians evacuated Bucharest and fled north to escape the German net which was closing in on the capital. By 7 January the Romanian army, now only about 150,000 men strong, with King Ferdinand, had retreated behind the Seret (Sereth) and Pruth Rivers into Moldavia. Russia aided them here and they held out while Germany, at a cost of 60,000 casualties, took advantage of all the vital granaries and oil fields they had captured. Romanian losses amounted to about 400,000.

A truce was signed on 6 December 1917 and a peace treaty on 7 May 1918. The Romanians fought with great gallantry under generals who were willing to sacrifice them. Total Romanian soldiers killed in the war amounted to 336,000, which was 50 per cent of the mobilised forces and represented a higher proportion per head of population than any other combatant nation. In addition, there were 170,000 civilian casualties.

RUDNIK RIDGES (Yugoslavia)   First World War   3 December 1914
Fought between the Serbs under General Radomir Putnik and the Austrians under Major-General Oskar Potiorek.

After the first Austrian offensive into Serbia had failed, Potiorek launched a second invasion a fortnight later. The Austrian 5th Army attacked from the north and the 6th from the west. The three Serbian armies were deployed behind the Save and Drina Rivers for the purpose of checking the invaders. On 17 September, two weeks after the invasion had been launched, Potiorek halted the advance in order to regroup his forces at the Austrian bridgeheads in Serbia. At the same time Putnik made a general withdrawal east to a more defensible line. On 5 November the Austrians began to advance once more, driving the Serbs before them. Valjevo fell on 15 November and the Austrians then moved the weight of their attack to the north, threatening Belgrade, the Serbian capital. Putnik evacuated the city in order to safeguard his right flank and the Austrians occupied the capital on 2 December. Further south, they now held a position beyond the Kolubra River, whence a thin supply line stretched back through mountainous terrain. The Serbians had taken up a position in a north-south line along the Rudnik Ridges, the armies being in this order: 2nd, 3rd, 1st. On 3 December the Serbians launched a furious frontal counter-attack. Inspired by the presence of their King, Peter I, at the front, the Serbs fought fiercely and, after five days, the Austrians were forced to withdraw, the 5th Army through Belgrade, the 6th through Sabac.

On 15 December the Serbs reoccupied Belgrade. Once again the Austrian objective was not achieved.

SALONIKA II (Greece)   First World War   3 October 1915-30 September 1918
Fought between the Germans and Bulgarians under General Jekov and the Allies under General Maurice Sarrail, General Marie Louis Guillaumat and finally General Louis Frachet d'Esperey.
Strength: Germans/Bulgarians 500,000; Allies 350,000.

Bulgaria mobilised in September 1915 to act with the Austro-Hungarians and Germans against Serbia. On 3 October a British and French division under Sarrail was rushed to Salonika, and on 12 October it began its march to the aid of Serbia. The relief was, however, too little and too late. The Bulgarians cut the railway from Salonika on 23 October to screen the Allied advance, and they pressed on into Serbia. Two more French divisions joined Sarrail, who fell back to Lake Dojran on the Greek border; but when Serbia was finally defeated, on 3 December, the Allies were forced to fall back to Salonika. The uncertain attitude of King Constantine I of Greece contributed to the necessity to withdraw. Despite the fact that Salonika (known as the Bird Cage) had only limited port facilities and that the climate was malarial, the Allies decided to hold it. By mid-1916 the Armée d'Orient was 250,000 strong, including the Serbian army which had been reconstituted in Corfu. In the summer Sarrail began to advance north towards the Macedonian frontier of Greece. At the same time, however, the German 11th Army and the Bulgarian 1st, 2nd and 4th Armies attacked eastward and limited the Allied advance. A new front was stabilised on 27 August.

When Romania entered the war with the Allies, Sarrail launched an offensive to help her. Bitolj (Monastir) was taken on 19 November, but enemy resistance checked any advance by French, British, Russian, Italian and Serbian troops. The central powers suffered 60,000 to the Allies 50,000 casualties. Romania was knocked out of the war and the front once again quietened down.

In March 1917 Sarrail launched another offensive, which had inconclusive results. King Constantine I, the pro-German monarch of Greece, was forced to abdicate under Allied pressure and his son, Alexander, came to the throne. Greece entered the war on the Allied side at the end of June. Sarrail, however, remained in command and little was achieved because of his quarrelsome disposition. He was relieved on 22 December 1917 and replaced by Guillaumat, who reorganised the Salonika army, which now numbered 350,000. In July 1918 Guillaumat was recalled to the Western Front and Franchet d'Esperey took over this army. Two months later Germany had almost withdrawn completely from the Salonika-Bulgaria front. The Bulgarian army was poorly supplied and suffered from low morale. When, on 14 September, d'Esperey launched an offensive against the Bulgarians, resistance quickly collapsed. The Allied advance, well organised, was undertaken by the French on the left (W), the Serbians, the remainder of the French, the British and the Greek armies on the right. By 17 September the Allies had advanced 20 miles in the centre, with the Bulgarians driven before them in full retreat from Albania to the Struma (Strymon) River. The French cavalry overtook the infantry and entered Skoplje on 29 September, whereupon the German 11th Army, which had no German personnel except the staffs, surrendered. The road to Sofia was now opened, and on 30 September Bulgaria signed an armistice. King Ferdinand I abdicated four days later. The central powers were beginning to collapse.

The campaign used up men and supplies which might have been employed on the Western Front. The British army, who felt that they did nothing but dig in during the campaign, called themselves the 'Gardeners of Salonika'. Casualties in the Allied ranks were more numerous from malaria (481,000 during the campaign) than they were from battle (18,000). The French had 35,122 hospital cases during the summer of 1916, of whom only 672 were battle casualties.

SARIKAMIS (Turkey)   First World War   29 December 1914-3 January 1915
Fought between the Russians under General Myshlayevsky and the Turks under Ahmet Izzet Pasha.
Strength: Russians 60,000; Turks 95,000.
On 29 October Turkish warships and the 2 ex-German cruisers, the *Goeben*

and the *Breslau,* began bombarding the Russian Black Sea ports of Odessa and Sebastopol. On 2 November Russia declared war. Land fighting was limited, being mainly on the isolated Caucasian front. The Turks sought to draw the Russians from their bases at Kars and Ardahan and destroy them. In December the Russians left Kars and marched into Asia Minor, reaching Sarikamis on 29 December. Here, 30 miles inside Turkey, they met the Turks, and for five days the two armies battled in bitterly cold weather. At the end of that time, the Turks, who had fallen to a mere 18,000, were routed and began a disorderly retreat to Lake Van.

In 1915 the two armies - now under General Nikolai Yudenich and General Abdul Kerim Pasha - fought indecisive engagements around Lake Van until the Russians were repulsed at Manzikert. The Turks then tried to press their advantage home, but, moving forward, they were outflanked and defeated at Karakilisse.

SERBIA   First World War   6 October-November 1915
Fought between the Serbians under General Radomir Putnik and the central powers under General August von Mackensen.
Strength: Serbians 200,000; central powers 300,000.

Austria had failed three times to crush Serbia in 1914, but, being preoccupied with the Russian front, had made no new attempt to conquer her for almost a year. With the entrance of Bulgaria into the war in the autumn of 1915, a three-nation offensive was planned against Serbia from the north and east. Three invading armies were commanded by von Mackensen.

To the north, the Austrian 3rd Army and three German divisions stood west of Belgrade with the German 11th Army to the east of the capital. To the NE was the Bulgarian 1st Army; and to the SE the Bulgarian 2nd Army stood ready to cut the Salonika-Belgrade railway. Putnik, with four armies, deployed his 1st and 3rd on the northern frontier and his 2nd (Timok) and Macedonian Armies faced east. On 6 October the Austrians crossed the Save River and the Germans bridged the Danube. Belgrade was thus caught between these two forces and on 9 October it surrendered. The two Serbian armies on the northern front fell back, still fighting, as the Bulgarian 1st Army advanced from the east across the frontier on 11 October. Within a week the armies of the central powers were advancing in line, pushing the Serbs back from both north and east, although they retreated grudgingly and in good order, despite the fact that they were badly armed. On 23 October the Bulgarian 2nd Army reached Kumanovo and cut the railway from Salonika. The Allies were now blocked.

The Serbians now had a choice as to whether to surrender or to withdraw through the mountains into Albania, which was neutral. Despite the fact that it was by now mid-November, the Serbians chose to withdraw through the Albanian mountains, and 100,000 of them reached the Adriatic Sea. In January 1916 the French navy transported the troops to Corfu. The advance of the central powers had stopped at the Albanian-Greek border on 4 December. More than 100,000 Serbians were killed, wounded or imprisoned in the offensive.

Serbia was knocked out of the war and the road from Berlin to Constantinople was opened. King Nicholas I of Montenegro, who had supported Serbia, fled to Italy when the Austrians occupied his country. The Serbians who had escaped through Albania were reorganised in Corfu and later joined the Allies in their Salonika (qv) campaign.

SHARQAT (Iraq)   First World War   29 October 1918
Fought between the British under Lt-General A.S. Cobbe and the Turks under General Ismael Hakki.

The British command under Lt-General W.R. Marshall in Mesopotamia resolved to resume the offensive late in the war in order to secure British possession of the Mosul (Iraqi) oilfields.

On 23 October an Anglo-Indian mounted corps left Baghdad under Cobbe and marched north up the Tigris River. In thirty-nine hours the force covered 77 miles to reach the Little Zab River. Here the Turkish Commander, Hakki, resolved to make a stand with his 6th Army. Cobbe, however, manoeuvred so that the Turkish rear was threatened, and the Turks retreated to Sharqat, 60 miles from Mosul. The British pursued and attacked on 29 October with cavalry and horse-drawn artillery. The British took 11,300 prisoners and 51 guns and, although his lines were still intact, Hakki surrendered with a further 7,000 men the following day. British losses were 1,886. An Indian cavalry division occupied Mosul on 14 November.

The action at Sharqat ended the fighting in Mesopotamia. Total Allied casualties throughout the campaign amounted to 92,000 (British and Indian), of whom 28,621 were killed or died of disease. The success of the British campaign in Palestine contributed largely to this final British victory in Mesopotamia.

SKAGGERAK   see JUTLAND

SUEZ CANAL (Egypt)   First World War   26 January-4 February 1916
Fought between the 10th Indian Division under Major-General A. Wilson and the Turks under Djemal Pasha, but guided by Colonel Kress von Kressenstein, a Bavarian officer.

Immediately on declaration of war with Turkey the British in Egypt withdrew their forces in Sinai and the Turks followed up and occupied El Arish and Nekhl, assembling 20,000 men and 10 batteries at their rear base, Beersheba. They had no aircraft. The British had 70,000 troops in Egypt in January 1915 but only about 30,000, mostly Indian Army, were available for the defence of the Suez Canal. However, these were supported by Allied navies and a small but pugnacious Royal Flying Corps.

On 26-7 January the Turks made some probing attacks at El Kantara and Kubri. On 1 February 1916 15,000 Turks were concentrated between Serapeum and Ferđan, 7 miles north of Ismailia. The Turks attacked at 3 am on 3 February but failed to cross the Canal. Renewed attacks next day met no better success. The enemy withdrew unpursued, as British policy was still to let the Canal defend the army rather than to make the army defend the Canal. By 5 February normal ship traffic was passing along the Canal. British casualties were 150, in contrast to those of the Turks, which amounted to about 1,320.

Criticism of the timid policy followed in the defence of Egypt forced the British command to pursue a more forward policy and when, in August 1916, the Turks made a second attempt on the Canal, they were met at Romani (qv) on 8 August and decisively defeated, losing 10,000 men.

TAFILEH (Jordan)   Arab Revolt   16-26 January 1918

Since the capture of Akaba (HEJAZ) the Arabs under Emir Feisal and Major T.E. Lawrence had gradually spread their influence northwards with continuous raids on Turkish trains and posts along the Hejaz railway. Their mobility and independence of communications ensured these raiding parties complete surprise. Only at Tafileh did Lawrence deliberately allow his Arabs to become committed to a pitched battle.

On 16 January 1918 the Arabs under Lawrence seized Tafileh, 15 miles SE of the Dead Sea, which acted as a bait. On 26 January a Turkish force of brigade strength complete with artillery and machine-guns advanced against the Arabs and was almost completely annihilated. In March a Turkish column, stiffened by a German battalion, reoccupied the place.

TANNENBERG II (Poland)   First World War   26-30 August 1914

Fought between the Russians under General Alexander Samsonov and the Germans under General Paul von Hindenburg.

Strength: Russians 300,000 with 600 guns; Germans 300,000.

The Russians failed to follow up their victory at Gumbinnen (qv) on 20 August, which gave the German 8th Army time to reorganise under the new leadership of Hindenburg and General Erich Ludendorff and to march against the Russian 2nd Army which was moving up from the south under Samsonov. The Russian force, five corps strong, attacked the German 20 Corps of General Friedrich von Scholtz on 22 August and drove it back to Tannenberg, by which time the German 8th Army had already turned away from the dormant General Pavel Rennenkampf to concentrate on Samsonov. In a plan worked out by Colonel Max Hoffmann, General August von Mackensen's 17 Corps and General Otto von Below's 1 Reserve Corps were to march against the Russian right flank, while General Hermann von François's 1 Corps was sent by rail to close on the Russian left. The plan was implemented on 26 August and on the same day Samsonov, unaware of the German manoeuvre (which had been helped by the interception of Russian wireless messages) resumed his offensive on a 70-mile front. To the NE, the Russian 7 Corps, which had been detached from the main body, met Mackensen's 17 Corps. Fighting was confused and when, towards the end of the day, von Below's corps came up to support Mackensen, the Russians fell back, having suffered heavy losses.

The move exposed Samsonov's centre where the Russians had made little headway. Samsonov ordered a fresh attack the next day, but von François had now come up on the west and he assaulted the Russian left early the following morning (27 August), driving it back with heavy artillery bombardment. The armies continued to engage along a 40-mile front throughout the day, but on 29 August von François pushed east again and turned the Russian left under a barrage of artillery fire. The exposed Russian east flank was meanwhile attacked by von Below at Allenstein (Olsztyn) while Mackensen pursued the broken right wing of 6 Corps. From his headquarters at Neidenburg, Samsonov rode to the front in an attempt to rally the Russian troops under his personal command. But the situation was hopeless and that night he ordered a general retreat of the 2nd Army. During 29 ard 30 August the Russians retreated east through marshes and dense woods. The two centre corps under Generals Martos and Kliouev which had penetrated farthest into Germany, had the farthest to go to extricate themselves from the German trap. Both commanders were captured and both corps fell apart. Samsonov disappeared on the night of 29 August and presumably committed suicide. He was never seen again. The Russian 2nd Army was totally destroyed: 92,000 were taken prisoner, 30,000 were killed or missing and 400 out of 600 guns were taken. German casualties were 13,000 killed, wounded or missing.

Rennenkampf, who had been ordered by General Yakov Grigorievich Jilinsky to move to the assistance of Samsonov, had done almost nothing to implement his orders and was moving slowly through the Insterburg Gap. The German 8th Army now moved against him.

The victory did much for the morale of Germany. The significance of the Battle of the Marne (pp 332-4) which was going on at the same time was overlooked as a result of the resounding defeat of the Russians. The Allied confidence in the Russians was shattered.

TSINGTAO (Shantung Province, N China)   First World War   18 September-6 November 1914
Fought between the Japanese and British, and the Germans.
Strength: Allies 24,500 (Japanese 23,000, British 1,500); Germans 4,000.
Aim: The only battle of the war to be fought in the Far East was against Japan's major objective, the colony and fortress of Tsingtao on the Chinese Shantung peninsula. Japan had joined the Allies early in the war, chiefly in order to make territorial gains from the Germans in the Far East.
Battle: Landing above the city, the Japanese were joined on 23 September by a small British force of military and naval units. Britain feared Japanese aggrandisement in the Far East and sought to mitigate such an influence. Tsingtao was then invested and, while land artillery bombarded it, Japanese and British warships also pounded it from the sea. By 6 November siege parallels had been constructed close enough to launch a general assault. On 7 November, however, the Germans surrendered, having suffered 700 casualties. Allied losses were 1,800 Japanese and 70 British.
Result: The Japanese gained their objective.

VISTULA RIVER-WARSAW (Poland)   First World War   28 September-17 October 1914

Fought between the Germans and Austrians under General Paul von Hindenburg and the Russians under General Nikolai Ivanov.

Aim: The Germans, in order to aid their hard-pressed allies the Austrians, moved the 9th Army from E Prussia into S Poland, aiming at Warsaw which was then under Russian rule.

Battle: General August von Mackensen took up a position on the left of the Austrians whose 1st, 4th, 3rd and 2nd Armies were all south of the Germans. Von Mackensen, advancing more quickly than the Austrians, moved towards the Upper Vistula, reaching it on 9 October. The German thrust on Warsaw was defended all along the Vistula by Siberian and Caucasian troops. A concentration of Russians under General Nikolai Russky, combined with the slowness of the Austrians, forced von Mackensen back and, on 17 October, Hindenburg ordered a general retreat. The Germans were at Radom on 25 October and at Kielce by 3 November, continuing their withdrawal under cover of rearguard actions, for the Russians pursued closely. German casualties were 40,000 throughout the operation.

Result: The failure of the German attack left Silesia vulnerable to Russian attack. Hindenburg now ordered an attack from the Posen-Thorn (Poznan-Torun) region.

VITTORIO VENETO (Italy)   First World War   24 October-3 November 1918

Fought between the Allies under General Armando Diaz and the Austrians under Archduke Joseph and Field-Marshal Artur Arz von Straussenburg.

Strength: Allies 57 divisions (including 3 British, 2 French, 1 Czechoslovak and an American regiment) with 7,700 guns; Austrians 52 divisions in 2 Army Groups with 6,030 guns.

As the strength of the central powers gradually dwindled in the autumn of 1918, Diaz prepared one last offensive to drive Austria out of the war, by dividing the Austrians on the Trentino front from those on the Piave. To the left (W), the Italian 5th and 6th Armies were opposing the Archduke Joseph's Austrian Group (18 divisions) in the Trentino, and on the right the remaining five Italian armies, which included the Allied formations, faced Field-Marshal Borojevic von Bojna (34 divisions). This latter force was to carry out the main attack which began on 24 October when 4th Army made a fierce attack on the link between the two Austrian army groups in the region around Monte Grappa. The Austrians held their ground for three days and drew reserves in from the Lower Piave where the primary attack was intended. During those three days three Allied armies - the 12th, the 8th and on the right the 10th under General Lord Cavan - had forced three small bridgeheads across the Piave. The 23rd (British) Division had surprised Papadopoli Island on the night of 23 October, and Cavan had pushed ahead, outstripping the armies on his flanks. By 28 October the diversionary attack north had drawn enough enemy troops away from the main theatre for the bridgeheads to join, enabling a further advance to be made. The 8th Army took Vittorio Veneto on 30 October and, to its right, the 10th and 3rd Armies reached the Livenza

River the same day. Here the Italians were checked for two days until troops under Diaz forced a crossing at Sacile on 1 November.

From the Trentino to the Adriatic Sea, Austrian resistance crumbled and many units deserted as a body. Fleeing in confusion, the Austrians were caught in their droves by Italian cavalry and armoured cars. Late on 3 November the Austrians signed a truce at Villa Giusti, near Padua. Fighting ended the following day. The Austrians had about 200,000 men taken prisoner with 5,000 guns and their armies had ceased to exist. Italian casualties in the final campaign were 38,000.

Total Italian losses throughout the war were 650,000 killed, almost 1 million wounded, and great numbers of prisoners.

WINDHOEK (SW Africa)   First World War   12 May 1915
Fought between the S Africans under General Louis Botha and the Germans.
Strength: S Africans 20,000; Germans 6,000 (including administrative cadres).

The German colony of SW Africa produced a fighting force at the outbreak of the war which occupied the British outpost of Walvis (Walfish) Bay on the Atlantic Coast, 710 miles north of Cape Town. Anti-British activity in S Africa prevented any action being taken until the end of 1914.

Botha halted the rebellion later in the year and reoccupied the settlement at Walvis on 25 December. Windhoek, the capital of the German colony, stood 170 miles inland. Botha marched there and captured it on 12 May 1915. The German survivors fled to Grootfontein, 220 miles NE of Windhoek.

At Otavi, west of Windhoek, 3,500 Germans surrendered on 9 July. No further resistance was encountered in the area. German SW Africa became a mandate of the Union (later the Republic) of S Africa.

WINTER BATTLE OF MASURIA   see MASURIAN LAKES II

SECTION TEN

FIRST WORLD WAR: THE AIR WAR

THE AIR WAR   First World War   1914-18
The war in the air from 1914 to 1918 was concentrated for the most part on the Western Front. While valuable work was done in Mesopotamia, Palestine, Bulgaria and at sea, this can in no way overshadow the fact that the development of aircraft, of their armament, of reconnaissance, radio communications, and the origin of strategic bombing sprang from the conflict which raged between the Channel ports and the Swiss border.

At the outbreak of war each of the major powers involved possessed what could loosely be described as an air force. To the Italians must go the dubious honour of being the first to use air power as an offensive weapon, which they did in their war against Turkey of 1911. The United States had started with promise, only to fall back into military stagnation: while it is avowed that aircraft were used for reconnaissance purposes in the US government's perennial wars with Mexico, by 1914 the United States Army Air Arm had only some 20 aircraft and 35 pilots.

If Italy was the first to make use of the possibilities of air power, France was the first nation to realise its full potential. Following the widespread interest in the internal combustion engine, the French were by 1900 supplying engines and other parts for many of the cars and motorcycles of Europe. This complex of experienced manufacturers was to be of great value, when, in 1910, the first military aviation unit was formed. By 1911 regional flying schools had been set up all over France; by 1912 an Aviation Corps was formed in three groups, and the manufacture and purchase of aircraft had become the responsibility of the Service des Fabrications de l'Aéronautique (SFA), the equivalent of the Royal Aircraft Factory at Farnborough. By August 1914 France had twenty-one squadrons of 6 aircraft each for army co-operation, and a further four units of 3 aircraft each for liaison with cavalry.

In 1910 the German army possessed no aircraft. From 1900 German aerial development had been confined almost entirely to airships - the rigid Zeppelin L71 making the world's first practical controlled flight of a power-driven aircraft on 2 July of that year. By 1912, however, the Imperial Military Air Service had a number of pilots in training under contract to schools run by aircraft manufacturers, and by 1913 it was equipped with 120 monoplanes and 120 biplanes. At the outbreak of war the Military Air Service had 246 aircraft and 7 Zeppelins, while the Imperial German Naval Air Service had 36 seaplanes and 2 Zeppelins. By contrast, Germany's chief ally, Austro-Hungary, had 36 aircraft and 1 airship. Russia had as yet no aircraft industry, though by 1913 Igor Sikorsky had built the first four-engined passenger aircraft, forerunner of the Ilya Mourometz bomber which was later to do good service as a bomber.

Britain was another late developer. The year 1911 had seen the formation of the Air Battalion of the Royal Engineers, equipped with one company of aeroplanes, one of balloons, and one of man-lifting kites and small airships. The Royal Flying Corps was formed in 1912 and drew as its first pilots officers of the army and

Royal Navy who had learnt to fly at their own expense. What had previously been a balloon factory became by 1912 the Royal Aircraft Factory, Farnborough, responsible for designing one of the best fighters of the war, and many of the worst. Despite these good beginnings the RFC remained small and its trained pilots few. In 1913 an irate Member of Parliament demanded of the War Secretary in the House of Commons the number of aircraft possessed by the army, to be told 'something more than one hundred'. On this being challenged a count was made, which revealed a total of 13 serviceable aeroplanes. From that point the British government purchased aircraft until, by August 1914, the Royal Flying Corps and Royal Naval Air Service (formed from the Naval Wing, RFC, on 1 July 1914) possessed 113 aeroplanes and 6 airships, of which 63 aeroplanes flew to France with the British Expeditionary Force.

It is difficult at this remove to view dispassionately the short-sightedness of the prevailing official attitudes - in all countries - towards the new weapon. Aircraft were widely regarded as having only one use, reconnaissance, though it was thought that the cavalry were more suited to this purpose. Against these mists of officialdom, however, some visionaries vainly struggled. In 1911 Major (Air Marshal, 1941) H.R.M. Brooke-Popham of the British Air Battalion was rebuked by his Commanding Officer for attempting to fit a machine-gun on his Blériot. In 1912 the American Colonel Isaac Newton Lewis fitted his famous air-cooled machine-gun to a Wright Biplane. Official reaction was tepid, though the weapon was to do valuable service on the Allied side both in the trenches and in the air. More remarkable, by 1914 both Raymond Saulnier of the French aircraft company Morane-Saulnier and Franz Schneider of the German Luft Verkehrs Gesellschaft (LVG) had successfully fitted gun-synchronising gear to aircraft, permitting forward firing through the airscrew arc, and others in other countries had similar devices. While Saulnier's device was of little practical value (requiring a single fixed engine-speed for operation) Schneider installed his in 1915 in an LVG E IV - the first German aircraft to have a synchronised gun. Yet, despite the spirit of individuals, the air forces of 1914 went to war unarmed, ill-trained, ill-equipped and largely unsupported by any manufacturing capability. It was a situation soon to be rapidly reversed.

THE AIR FORCES

There were no fighter aircraft in 1914, no bombers - the distinctions were of monoplane, biplane or triplane, single-seater, single engine, and so on. When war came the predominating British types were the Royal Aircraft Factory-designed BE2As and BE2Bs, though a number of squadrons were still equipped with French Blériots (almost identical to the aircraft in which Louis Blériot flew the Channel in 1909) and Farmans. The French Aviation Militaire was equipped mostly with the same single-seater Blériots, with a smattering of Breguets, Farmans, Morane-Saulniers, Caudrons, Nieuports and Voisins. It had 160 aircraft and 15 airships at the beginning of the war. The prevailing German type was the Austrian-designed Taube, a two-seater monoplane which quite remarkably resembled the dove from which its name was taken. By this time, however, the great German names were beginning to appear, Albatros, Halberstadt, Pfalz and Fokker. The Italian air force (though Italy did not join the war until 1915) was equipped with a number of French aircraft and also with some native products - Ansaldos, Capronis, Macchis and SVAs. Little is known of the Russian air force (then the Imperial Flying Service) at this date, or indeed at any date since. Certainly Sikorsky had designed two fighters as well as the giant bomber. But the Russians, like so many others, relied heavily on French equipment, although Lebedoff and Anatra aircraft were in use by 1914, as were numbers of Russian-built Voisins. The air forces of Bulgaria, Turkey and Austro-Hungary were equipped almost exclusively with German types, although the latter had some native industry, notably Phönix. The air forces of Romania, Serbia and Greece used French aircraft, as did that of Belgium, although Belgium was later to produce one of the most successful small fighter of the mid-war period, the French-designed Hanriot HD1. Portugal's air operations were confined to anti-German submarine patrols from the Azores, in which a number of British and French flying-boat types were used. Japanese air operations were restricted to artillery and gunnery spotting at the siege of Tsingtao in 1914, for which aircraft of French design were employed. A number of home-designed Japanese types appeared during the course of the war and by 1918 several British types were in service. Despite being an ally, China's tiny air force undertook no war operations - such aircraft as they had were mainly French. When America joined the war in 1917 her air force was equipped with French Spads and British DH4s and SE5As and a small number of American types, notably the Thomas Morse Scout.

1914

While the German air force was numerically superior, it was the French who took the initiative in the embryo air war. On 14 August French Voisin aircraft attacked and bombed the Zeppelin sheds at Metz. On 3 September 1914 French reconnaissance aircraft spotted the increasing gap between the German 1st and 2nd Armies approaching the Marne, information that led to the Allied victory which halted the Germans. General von Kluck's change of direction was reported by British aircraft. And on 5 October another Voisin, armed with a Hotchkiss machine-gun used by its observer, destroyed a German Aviatik two-seater - the first truly air-to-air victory.

The RFC had not been slow: on 22 August, during the Battle of Mons, British aircraft spotted and successfully reported not only the German outflanking movement, but also the unexpected French withdrawal. In mid-September, during the Battle of the Aisne (p 321), RFC aircraft brought about the first successful instance of artillery co-operation, and in October 1914 Flight Sub-Lieutenant Marix, flying a Sopwith Tabloid biplane from the RNAS Squadron at Antwerp, succeeded in bombing and destroying the Zeppelin Z1X in its shed at Düsseldorf.

The Germans were the first to make a bombing attack, however. On 13 August a German Taube attacked Paris with a few grenades - the first instance of bombs being dropped on a city. For some weeks this lonely aircraft was to be a feature of the Parisian evening: regularly, at 6 o'clock, it would turn up to drop its handful of grenades.

In the face of some odds the air services had quickly proved their worth. As a result, it was soon appreciated that some means of defending the reconnaissance and bombing forces must be developed. Two-seaters, even when armed, were at best slow and cumbersome, and it was thus that the purpose-built, single-seat fighter was born. Previously shot-guns, rifles or pistols had been fired from the cockpits of ordinary aircraft, but the difficulties of aiming an unfixed gun, coupled with the instability of the machines, paved the way for an altogether different design philosophy. The aerial fighter was hampered (as indeed were two-seaters) by the airscrew - official lack of interest had been the death of a device such as Schneider's. Two courses were left open to designers: either a two-seater with a gun on a mobile mounting positioned in the observer's cockpit; or a single-seater with a 'pusher' engine (i.e. with the engine set behind the pilot and with the propellor pushing, rather than pulling), carrying a machine-gun firing forward from a fixed or mobile mounting. In the days before practical syn- chronising gear the pusher aircraft was not as ridiculous as it now looks, for it permitted the whole aircraft to be aimed at a target, a relatively simple operation for the pilot, whereas other types might require his flying in one direction and either he or the observer firing in another. Thus it was that the first fighter was a design of this type, the Vickers FB5 'Gunbus', a two-seater pusher biplane with the observer in the forward cockpit armed with a single air-cooled Lewis machine-gun. The FB5 arrived too late, however, to be anything but imperilled by the design limitations - notably of performance - of the pusher layout. What outclassed it was the world's first single-seater fighter, the Fokker E1 monoplane, armed with a Parabellum machine-gun firing through the airscrew. The interrupter gear had at long last arrived.

The two-seaters in 1914 were the most important type of aircraft. Their work of reconnaissance, observation, contact patrol and bombing involved low flying at steady speeds, and for their defence the fighter was born.

1915

Perhaps the most far-reaching event of 1915 was the forced landing of the French pilot Lieutenant Roland Garros, a pre-war aerial stuntman of some fame. A single rifle-bullet from the ground had fractured a petrol pipe in his Morane- Saulnier monoplane and it was thus that his secret weapon fell into German hands. Annoyed by the difficulties of 'aiming off', Garros had fitted to his propeller two triangular steel deflectors which permitted him to fire a fixed automatic rifle through the propeller arc. It was a crude, not to say dangerous, device, in that ricocheting bullets could have damaged either pilot or aircraft. But for all that it was very effective - Garros had downed 5 German aircraft in a few weeks, at a time when even pusher aircraft with forward-firing guns were scarce. The immediate result of Garros's capture was that the German High Command summoned the brilliant young Dutch designer, Anthony Fokker, and commanded him to perfect and fit a similar device to as many German aircraft as possible. Fokker did better than that. Within forty-eight hours he had designed and tested a simple mechanical interrupter which prevented the gun from firing when aimed at either propeller blade, and had fitted this device to one of his E1 monoplanes. The German thinking that, had all Allied aircraft been fitted with a Garros deflector, then no German aircraft would have been left in the sky, was substantially correct, but Fokker had turned the tables. Within three days Oswald Boelcke had downed an Allied aircraft using the E1 and on the following day Lieutenant Max Immelman did the same. Fokker returned to produce the interrupter gear in as great a quantity as possible, and in weeks many German squadrons had received numbers of the 'Eindekkers', all fitted with the Fokker interrupter gear.

It was now that the greater manufacturing ability of Germany began to tell. In a very short space of time the Germans had designed and built a range of fighters and two-seaters which were superior both in performance and fire-power to those of the Allies. From July 1915 to the end of the year the 'Fokker Scourge' was to take a heavy toll of Allied men and machines. Revised German air tactics were to contribute to this - in the late summer of 1915 the Bavarian Air Force, a small independent force, formed three *Kampfeinsitzerkommando* (single-seat fighter units) designed specifically for an offensive rôle rather than their former escort duties. Two members of one of these units were Immelman and Boelcke. Although he died after achieving only 15 victories, Immelman was the first air ace, and is famous as well for the 'Immelman turn', a manoeuvre whereby an aircraft, by means of a half loop and half roll off the top, could either evade attack from behind or, either by climbing and changing direction, or by diving and changing direction, attack an enemy from the blind spot in the rear. Oswald Boelcke went on to achieve 40 victories before his death in a flying accident but, more than that, he was to become the father of the German Air Service by his initiative in the organisation and tactics of the *Jastas* - the German fighter squadrons. One of the pilots recruited by Boelcke was the Rittmeister (Cavalry Captain) Freiherr Manfred von Richthofen, the highest scoring pilot of the war with 80 victories confirmed at the time of his death in 1918.

It is a measure of the inferiority of British and French aircraft types of that date that so mediocre an aircraft as the Eindekker Fokker could gain control of the skies by dint simply of superior fire-power. The Vickers 'Gunbus', specifically designed as a fighter, was to suffer the same fate as the many unwieldy two-seater types then in use with the Allies. To some extent, however, the losses suffered by the RFC at least were the result of the offensive policies of the Air Commander, Major-General H.M. Trenchard, the father of the Royal Air Force and indeed of strategic bombing. Trenchard insisted that the air war in the British sector north of Verdun, where a vast infantry and artillery battle was being waged, should be carried to the Germans at all times. The inferior British BE2s, FB5s and FE2Bs (the two latter were pusher types and all were two-seaters, largely flown by inexperienced pilots straight from flying school) were destroyed in large numbers, the direct consequence of an offensive policy for which the aircraft were unsuitable and the men untrained. Allied to this, the prevailing wind over this sector was such as to carry any RFC aircraft deep into German-occupied territory in the course of a dogfight, making it doubly difficult for it to return in the teeth of a high wind which had so obligingly carried it over the German lines.

The year ended with the Allied air forces fighting a losing battle against the greater numbers and better equipment of the German Air Service. Despite this, Trenchard's policy, though wasteful, was effective, and the important and unsung activities of the reconnaissance and observation two-seaters continued with notable success.

1916

If there are heroes other than the aces in the First Air War, it is the aircraft themselves. Many times the delicate structure of air power on the Western Front was to crumble in the face of some technical innovation. Thus it was that by the spring of 1916 the 'Fokker Scourge' had become a broken reed, brought about by the introduction of two Allied types - the French Nieuport 11 and the de Havilland-designed DH2. The former was a light and manoeuvrable biplane with a good rate of climb armed with a single Lewis gun mounted on the top plane and fixed to fire outside the propeller arc. Surprisingly the latter was a pusher type, the first of Britain's single-seater fighters. While in the hands of inexperienced pilots the DH2 was difficult to handle, earning the unlovely sobriquet 'Spinning Incinerator', it was nevertheless sufficiently fast and sufficiently manoeuvrable as to be more than a match for the Eindekkers. Nieuports had begun arriving with French squadrons in late 1915 and the first DH2 squadron, No 24 RFC, reached France in February of the new year.

In preparation for the coming offensive against Verdun in February 1916 the German Air Service built up a great numerical superiority of machines of all types. Much artillery spotting, both by aircraft and balloons, was to account for the great accuracy of the German bombardment, and indeed numbers of forward Allied aerodromes were shelled. Bombing raids were made against headquarters, railway lines, supply depots and other targets, adding to the demoralisation of the Allied air forces. General Henri Petain issued an Order of the Day calling for the restoration of Allied air supremacy and to this the response was effective. The French formed the first large-scale fighter unit, *Les Cigognes*, equipped with new Nieuport 11s, arguably the first modern fighter aircraft; while the RFC developed new offensive tactics in which, instead of waiting for enemy aircraft to attack the two-seaters and their escorts, the fighters ranged ahead and above to find the enemy first. When the French counter-attacked at Verdun in May 1916 German air supremacy had been broken and the Germans lost large numbers of aircraft and pilots to the vengeful Allied fighters.

The Nieuport 11s had been joined by a new machine, the Spad V11, a robust and fast biplane armed with a single Vickers synchronised gun. Anthony Fokker's invention had been so highly considered by the German High Command that they had forbidden aircraft fitted with the interrupter device to fly over Allied lines. Four months after Boelcke had made the first kill with it a German aircraft was captured intact when it force-landed behind the French lines. As a result British and French engineers discovered the secret and rapidly combined the best features of Fokker's gear with those of a hydraulic synchronising gear invented by a Romanian. Georges Constantinesco, before the war, though not then put to practical effect. This gun-synchronising gear was used in a number of Allied fighters following this date, and proved to be both reliable and efficient.

Trenchard's policy of offence coupled with the new aircraft was beginning to pay off. The RFC took delivery of the Sopwith 1½ Strutter (so called from the position of the centre-section struts) a two-seater reconnaissance bombing aircraft, which could also serve as a day or night fighter, and armed with a single synchronised Vickers gun and a Lewis gun in the rear cockpit. Some 1½ strutters had another Lewis gun mounted on the centre section of the top mainplane. By May 1916 French squadrons were being equipped with the Nieuport 17, a faster and better armed development of the Nieuport 11 and which proved to be one of the best-loved aircraft of the war. It was in such aircraft that many of the Allied aces like Albert Ball, William (Billy) Bishop, Georges Guynemer and Charles Nungesser enjoyed many of their successes.

The Allies had succeeded in gaining control of the air in time for 1 July 1916, the beginning of the Battle of the Somme (see p 338). The freedom granted to Allied aircraft permitted great success that was in no way equalled by the gains on the ground. Not for the first time the aircraft fought a war on their own, unhampered by the conditions which restricted the infantry. Major successes of observation, notably by balloons, accounted for the destruction of numbers of German guns and other tactical targets, while even the fighter aircraft would at times come down to attack German supply and relief columns, giving rise to the supposed German infantryman's motto: *'Gott strafe England und unsere Flieger'* (God blast England and our flyers).

While Allied air supremacy continued long after the Somme battles had ground to their inevitable halt, the Germans had not been idle. New fighters and better armed reconnaissance aircraft and light bombers particularly - in the former category the Fokker, Albatros and Halberstadt 'D' series, and in the latter the Albatros, DFW, Rumpler and AEG 'C' series - were beginning to show the promise which in 1917 their descendants would fulfil.

1917

While at the beginning of 1917 the Allies were developing yet another generation of fighters, the Germans put into service the Albatros DI and DII fighters, which wrought havoc among the Allied two-seater types, the BE2s and RE8s, and yet older aircraft. While in terms of performance the 'Albatri', as the RFC pilots nicknamed them, were little better than the best Allied fighters, their fire-power was considerably greater as they were equipped with 2 belt-fed synchronised machine-guns, while their reliability was greatly enhanced by their water-cooled Mercedes engines.

German tactics in the air remained largely defensive, while the Allies continued to carry the war to them. In April 1917 preparations began for the major Allied offensive against Arras (see p 324), combined with a French offensive farther to the south. The French army was badly defeated, resulting in demoralisation and at times mutiny, and for nearly a year it lost most of its attacking capability. While the British land offensive at Arras enjoyed some success, that in the air was a complete disaster. The RFC's casualties amounted to nearly one-third of its total strength. Perhaps the greatest loss to the RFC (and a direct result of Trenchard's continuing aggressive policies) was that of experienced pilots and observers who were by now schooled in the new aerial warfare that had developed since 1916. New pilots were arriving from England often with only four hours' total training (solo and under instruction in the air) and it was naturally these who suffered the most. There are instances recorded of officers arriving at aerodromes and being forced to take to the air before even placing their kit in their billets, only to be killed or captured on their first sortie. It is worth noting that parachutes, invented before the war, were not issued to pilots for 'morale reasons' (though balloon observers had them); thus a pilot was as likely to be lost to the ever common failure of aircraft or engine as to enemy action. The average life-expectancy of an RFC subaltern at this time - 'Bloody April' - was from eleven to twenty-one days. The Germans, elated at their successes in the air, grouped their *Jastas* into *Jagdgeschwader,* a fixed unit of four *Jastas* which could muster at any given time some 50 aircraft. It was thus that the 'flying circus' was born, so called from the sight of 50 brilliantly coloured and widely differing aircraft milling about at one time.

Desperately pressed, the RFC called for help from the RNAS, which responded with eight squadrons of Sopwith Triplanes. While it could not greatly affect the decimation of British and French squadrons, it remains one of the great unsung fighter aircraft, being fast, very manoeuvrable and with an outstanding rate of climb. A number of these 'Tripehounds', known as the 'Black Flight' of No 10 Naval Squadron from their black-painted engine cowlings, fuselage panels and wheel covers, were to achieve outstanding successes in the hands of 5 Canadian pilots, chiefly Flight Sub-Lieutenant Raymond Collishaw, the top-scoring naval pilot of the war with 63 enemy aircraft to his credit. So devastating was the triplane that no fewer than 14 German and Austrian manufacturers produced aircraft conforming to that type, though only one, the famous Fokker DR1, was to prove of any service. While it is claimed that Fokker's design was developed from the Sopwith, its designer, Reinhold Platz, had never seen the British machine and was indeed sceptical of the value of triplanes. The Sopwith Triplane was phased out by the summer of 1917 (perhaps the only aircraft of the war to be taken out of service before it became obsolescent, some months before the Fokker Triplane first appeared.

It is worth mentioning one other British design of this period which had to face the Albatroses, Rolands and Pfalzes. This was the Sopwith Pup, which looked like a smaller version of the 1½ Strutter, from which it derived. The Pup gained its name because pilots, on first seeing it, believed that the 1½ Strutter had pupped. Incensed officialdom insisted that this nickname should be dropped; it was natural enough, therefore, that the name 'Pup' should stick for good. It was an extraordinarily light and easy-handling aircraft which achieved miracles of speed and climb on a very small engine. While outclassed by the Albatros DIIIs now being introduced, the Pup's lighter wing loading permitted it to operate at a height above its enemies, a great advantage in light of the maxim 'whoever gains height gains victory'.

It was during the battles of spring and summer 1917 that the German aces like von Richthofen, Kurt Wolff, Werner Voss, Hermann Göring and Ernst Udet - the last two figure prominently in a later war - began their climb to the top.

But the German success in destroying countless Allied observation and fighter aircraft was not to last long. By the end of April the SE5, the forerunner of the Royal Aircraft Factory's most successful fighter, arrived; in late May the French Spad XIII appeared; and in July came the most famous and, in terms of aircraft shot down, the most successful fighter of the war - the Sopwith Camel. These three aircraft, or rather the two latter and the SE5A, an improved version of the SE5, were to bear the brunt of Allied air fighting until the end of the war; the Sopwith Camel alone was to account for 1,294 enemy aircraft. One other British fighter is worth mentioning, the Bristol F2B, a two-seater which because of great speed and good armament was a match for any German aircraft. Despite early heavy losses, owing to its being used in conventional two-seater tactics, it became, once pilots realised that it was a true fighter, widely respected for its versatility in bombing, night fighting, observation, ground attack or virtually any other use to which it was put, and remained in service with the RAF until 1932. The Germans also developed two-seater fighters, especially the Halberstadt CLII and Hannoveraner CLIII which were used, like the Bristol, for ground attack, an increasing duty of the air forces. German aircraft used in this rôle had greatly contributed to the British halt at Cambrai (p 326).

The British counterpart in air tactics to the *Jagdgeschwader* was the Wing, comprising anything up to five squadrons, which could be moved rapidly to any point of emergency. The French, however, tended to retain the small *Escadrilles*, interspersing them with élite units, though these, too, could be combined in the case of emergency. The Germans had hurridly produced the Albatros DV, an uprated DIII, though little better, and not even the introduction of the Fokker Triplane could sway the balance, despite the fact that it was only issued to the best pilots.

The American declaration of war on Germany on 6 April, coupled with the increasing Allied air strength, caused senior German air officers to formulate a plan for early 1918, to merge with the High Command's plan for a major Western Front offensive. The air plan provided for the formation or enlargement of training schools, the increase of machine-gun production, additional fuel, engine and aircraft production and the reallocation of skilled workers from other services. The end of 1917 saw the Germans, while increasingly worried by the potential of America and barely holding their own in the sky, poised for a single all-out blow in the spring of 1918.

1918

As it happened, the US Army Air Service was in no position materially to aid the Allies. It was estimated that the Americans would need 7,500 officers, 54,000 men and 5,400 aircraft to be an effective force. In the event they had 35 officers who could fly, none with combat experience, and 55 training aircraft, of which 4 were obsolescent and the remainder obsolete. But other Americans, by attaching themselves to the Allied air forces, had been at war in the air for some time, the most notable being the members of the *Escadrille Américaine* of the French air force. The *Escadrille Lafayette,* as it became known, produced aces of its own, like Rickenbacker and Lufbery, and was known as much for its independent character on the ground as its exploits in the air, It was absorbed into the United States Army Air Service in February 1918, becoming the 103rd Aero Squadron.

The German plan for air power had been remarkably successful. By March 1918 they could field eighty-one fighter *Jastas,* thirty-eight ground attack units, 153 observation and reconnaissance units and seven bomber squadrons, making some 3,700 aircraft. When the German attack on the Somme began on 20 March 1918 they achieved surprise both on land and in the air, and for a time it seemed that the gap driven between the British and French armies would permit the Germans to drive through to the sea and thus end the war. But the line was held by the French and successive German attacks failed to make any headway. By 29 March the steam had run out of the attack and the Germans were exhausted. Allied aircraft were desperately pressed throughout this period, both in air duties and ground strafing, and had the Germans not committed two-thirds of their air strength to reserve, it is possible that aircraft alone could have decisively influenced the outcome on the ground. As it was, the delicate balance was maintained and when the Allied offensive at Amiens (p 323) began on 8 August the Americans, French and RAF (formed 1 April 1918, an amalgamation of the RFC and RNAS) enjoyed complete mastery of the air. By then the US Army Air Service under General William Mitchell had achieved a typical American miracle of supply and equipment. When the armistice was signed total strength of the American combat squadrons at the front was 740 aircraft, while the total strength of their entire air force was some 14,000 aircraft.

For the Germans their losses between the beginning of the Second Battle of the Somme and at the end of the Battle of the Lys (pp 331-2) had been 659 aircraft; but losses of men, particularly leaders like von Richthofen, were the hardest blow. By August the German Air Service was outnumbered and desperately short of fuel, ammunition and equipment. Not even the adoption of the magnificent Fokker D7 biplane, Germany's finest fighter and arguably the best of the war, could stem the increasing tide of Allied two-seaters and fighters. In an atmosphere of defeat, the German air force was strangled by failures of supply, and could do little for its collapsing army. By the time of the armistice on 11 November 1918, Allied aircraft ruled the air.

THE BOMBING CAMPAIGNS

What small glamour there was in the air war of 1914-18 attached itself to the fighter arms. Press and propaganda uninhibitedly praised the fighter pilots, lauding their exploits to nations which could no longer grasp the magnitude of daily casualties. The idea of aces quickly gained favour with war-weary and often hungry civilians, and they too joined in the adulation of these pilots. It was a harmless enough indulgence, though it sometimes placed enormous burdens upon the ace himself: it also caused the world to forget the prime purpose of fighter aircraft - the defence and escort of the two-seaters.

THE TWO-SEATERS

Tactically, two-seater reconnaissance and bombing aircraft proved the most valuable and, even when the 'reconnaissance only' myth had been exploded, such aircraft continued to make the largest contribution to the development of air warfare and technology. Artillery observation, reconnaissance, photo-reconnaissance and tactical bombing occupied the greater part of any major air force's operations, and it was in this field that Germany excelled.

By 1915 Germany had a large and experienced domestic aircraft industry, and competition between manufacturers was to bring about many of the finest two-seater designs of the war. In the spring of that year the C-type two-seater aircraft began to appear, most readily notable for the fact that the observer occupied the rear cockpit, permitting far better defence and allowing the pilot greater ease of flying. German two-seaters were regarded with circumspection by Allied fighters, and in the hands of an experienced crew were capable of beating off all but the most determined attack. They were relatively fast, manoeuvrable, well built and well armed, and some of the later types, particularly those used for photo-reconnaissance, could climb far above the maximum ceilings of Allied fighters.

The British continued with the Royal Aircraft Factory-designed BE2 series, and lost them in their hundreds. Slow, stable, badly armed and with a poor rate of climb, they fell easy prey to the Fokker Eindekkers and later biplanes. Furthermore, they continued the practice of having the observer in the front cockpit, where struts, flying wires and the propeller itself greatly limited his field of fire. With some exceptions - notably the Sopwith 1½ Strutter, the Armstrong-Whitworth FK8 of 1917-18, and the DH4, the first British aircraft to be designed specifically for high-speed day bombing - British two-seaters for the rest of the war were little better, though this was often owing to non-availability of engines, causing less powerful or less reliable units to be fitted.

Until early 1918 France's reconnaissance and tactical bombing forces did much good work with pre-war designs like Voisins, Bréguets, Caudrons and Farmans, and other more modern, though unexceptional, types. In the last year of the war, however, a new line of French two-seaters arrived - sturdy, reliable, fast, and well armed - perhaps the best being the Salmson 2.

Italy, whose contribution to both the theory and practice of bombing was enormous, produced what was probably the finest two-seater of the war, the Ansaldo SVA5. Originally designed as a fighter, it was hampered by lack of manoeuvrability, and was thus relegated to reconnaissance and light bombing duties. There, however, its incredible top speed of 143 mph (some 20 mph faster than an SE5A), good armament and great range soon proved it most effective in the campaign against Austro-Hungary. Other Italian two-seaters, though not so remarkable, earned great respect from their opponents, chiefly the SAML S types of 1916-18 and the ubiquitous Pomilio P types.

The only Russian-designed and -built two-seaters, the Anatra D and DS types, were unexceptional designs made worse by poor production methods and non-availability of engines and raw materials: as a result these aircraft had an enormously high crash record. Other two-seaters, generally French designs built under licence in Russia, suffered the same difficulties; many of them were worse than the luckless Anatras.

Throughout the war, on all land fronts and at sea, these aircraft continued their appointed duties. The French formed a tactical bombing force in 1915 and carried out raids behind the German lines for the duration of hostilities. Germany, pinning her faith first on the Zeppelins and then on the giant bombers, did little tactical bombing. Both the RNAS and RFC made repeated raids behind German lines throughout the conflict. The former, committed to a policy of tactical and strategic bombing, made numerous raids with seaplanes and other aircraft against German naval bases, submarine pens and airship sheds. Badly defeated from the outset, torn by revolution, Russia's bombing campaigns were small and largely ineffective, and the Russian air force was further hampered by poor aircraft, appalling maintenance and difficult conditions.

Italy's policy was vastly successful, and on numerous occasions helped sway the balance of land actions. While it has become fashionable to deride that country's showing in the Great War on the strength of Second World War evidence, it is a grave mistake to do so. Italian pilots and aircraft of 1914-18 were among the finest in the world, and it was they who laid down many of the guidelines for later bombing offensives.

STRATEGIC BOMBING

Strategic bombing falls into two broad spheres: raids against military or military-supply targets, and raids against civilian targets as a means of breaking morale. In this latter field, the French Aviation Militaire early took the lead. By 1915 the French bomber force, equipped with squadrons of 20 aircraft each, began raids against Germany, hitting Karlsruhe on 13 June and Munich on 17 November 1915. By 1916 French bombing policy definitely embraced the idea of retaliation - in that year they made another attack on Karlsruhe in direct reprisal for German raids on French towns.

But there was another reason for bombing large towns. Equipped only with primitive bomb-sights, attacking aircraft were forced higher by rapidly improving defences, making it many times more difficult to hit specific targets. Blanket bombing was as much a necessity as it was a deliberate policy.

In the early stages of the war the German and Austro-Hungarian air forces relied solely upon airships for bombing attacks. As a result, much of the Allies' bombing was directed against hangars, moorings and manufacturing plants for the Zeppelins, and in this the RNAS excelled. The Royal Navy was in charge not only of Home Defence but also of defending the fleet bases, and to this end the RNAS rapidly formulated both offensive and defensive policies.

The Zeppelins had a major psychological advantage as a 'terror' weapon, and, in addition, could bomb with great accuracy owing to their ability to hover. Their raids against Britain began on 19 January 1915, when 2 Zeppelins bombed Yarmouth and King's Lynn. Damage was minor, but the public and political outcry was considerable. Ground defences were sparse, however, and suitable fighter aircraft few and far between, and it was not until 2 September 1916 that a Zeppelin was destroyed over Britain. On that night Lieutenant William Leefe Robinson of 39 Squadron RFC shot down the SL11, one of 16 airships sent to bomb London, for which exploit he was awarded the Victoria Cross. (It will be appreciated that at this date night flying was an extremely hazardous operation, and the difficulty of finding a marauding aircraft at night was enormous.) Some days later 2 more Zeppelins, the L32 and L33, were brought down by a combination of ground and aircraft fire, and from this point the Zeppelin declined as an effective weapon. In 1917 only seven airship raids were made against Britain, and in 1918 a mere four. Psychologically, perhaps, the greatest 'terror' weapon since the submarine, the airships were doomed by low speed, poor manoeuvrability and, worst of all, inflammability. Furthermore, they were susceptible to poor weather conditions and difficult to control in a wind, and many were lost through accidents and on landing. In fifty-one raids on Britain they dropped 196½ tons of bombs, killing 557 people, injuring 1,358, and causing some £1½ million worth of damage. Their strategic value in many ways exceeded that of merely striking an enemy, in that trained squadrons and front-line aircraft had to be brought back from France to deal with the menace, and the cost of the installation of ground defences was high - way out of proportion to the damage done.

But the airships paid a heavy price. Better searchlights, increased-range anti-aircraft guns using phosphorus shells, and incendiary ammunition for aircraft were a combination too strong for the hydrogen-filled dirigibles. The first Zeppelin to be destroyed in aerial combat, LZ37, was set alight by Flight Sub-Lieutenant R.A.J. Warneford by the simple expedient of dropping 6 20-pound bombs along the length of the airship from his Morane Parasol Type L monoplane, on 7 June 1915, over Ghent. From that point the myth of invincibility was shattered, and out of 88 airships built by Germany during the war some 60 were destroyed, 34 by accidents and forced landings, and the rest by Allied aircraft and ground defences.

The German bombing of Britain, by both airships and conventional bombers, took in both cases the same form - daylight raids meeting with little opposition, followed by night bombing as resistance stiffened, followed in turn by the cessation of attacks as the cost in men and aircraft became too high. The Zeppelin raids were carried out mostly by the Imperial German Naval Air Service, as the military arm turned increasingly to long-range bombers - the next stage in the strategic bombing of Britain. Daylight raids by the vast twin-engined AEG and Gotha biplane bombers began properly towards the end of 1917, though the first daylight raid by an aeroplane was made on 28 November 1916. Once the raids were switched to night-time (in September 1917) it became increasingly difficult to destroy the bombers, as they were manoeuvrable for their size, heavily armed (Gotha GIV and GV types had up to 4 free-firing machine-guns), and difficult to find in the days before radar and radio direction-finding. More fell to anti-aircraft defences than to the night-fighters, but more still were lost in accidents or on landing.

Their effectiveness as bombers was not great. On the night of 31 October 1917 22 Gothas dropped 85 bombs on London and a number on Kent and Essex, but damage was on the whole light. While none was brought down by the defences, 5 were damaged or destroyed on landing. On the night of 6 December 19 aircraft bombed London, Dover, Ramsgate, Sheerness and Margate, starting a number of fires. Two Gothas, damaged by anti-aircraft fire, crash-landed in England; 2 more, similarly damaged, crashed outside their Belgian base; a fifth went missing at sea; and a sixth was destroyed on landing. In the next raid, on the night of 18 December, 15 aircraft did more severe damage to London, but Captain G.W. Murlis-Green in a Sopwith Camel destroyed one Gotha, which fell into the sea, and other aircraft were damaged or destroyed on landing.

The pattern was set. The raids by Gotha, AEG and Friedrichshaven multi-engined bombers became less and less frequent as defences improved, finally stopping in May 1918, and nothing seemed to alleviate the major problem of these types, that of safe return to base. Even the introduction of the 'Giants' - the Zeppelin Staaken R types - four-engined biplane bombers with an increased bomb load did little to improve the effectiveness of the raids.

Like the airship raids, the Gotha bombing campaign did not significantly damage Britain's war effort. But, also like that of the Zeppelins, it did succeed in tying up much-needed aircraft and pilots for the defence of Britain; in denying vitally needed aircraft for the Middle East campaigns; and, owing to persistent air-raid warnings, in disrupting production, and that is the greatest measure of their success. In all, German bombers made 52 raids against England, killing 856 people and injuring a further 2,050.

By 1918, the requirements of the German offensives tied the bombers to military targets and raids against French cities, but even despite this, the high loss rate had made the raids on Britain uneconomical, and by August 1918 the German High Command had decided that bombing attacks on London and Paris were, politically speaking, a disaster. The giant bombers ceased to be a threat.

Italy joined the war on the Allied side on 24 May 1915. While her air force was small and mostly equipped with French types, it did have a number of Caproni CA2 triple-engined bombers, an aircraft with sufficient range and reliability to bomb targets in Austro-Hungary. Italian bombing policy was aggressive, forward-looking and imaginative, and as far as that theatre of war was concerned the Corpo Aeronautica Militare maintained mastery of the air, despite the calibre of enemy pilots and equipment.

Much of the credit for Italy's long-range bombing philosophy goes to Gabriele D'Annunzio, the Italian soldier-poet (later famous for his capture of Fiume in 1919) who, by June 1915, was flying over those Italian towns under Austro-Hungarian rule - Trieste, Trento, Pola, Zara - dropping propaganda leaflets. It was but a short step to bombing raids and, urged on by the vociferous D'Annunzio, a squadron of Capronis made their first raid, on 20 August 1915, against the Austrian airfield at Asiovizza. As the Capronis were updated and their range increased, raids were made against Ljubljana, Trieste, Fiume and Pola, almost always against military targets. The Caproni squadrons flew in fixed formation with escorts of Italian-built Nieuport fighters, and as a result of these tactics Italian daylight raids had a high record of success for a relatively small loss of men and aircraft.

Besides long-range disruptive bombing, the Italians learnt early the value of bombing and fighter aircraft used in conjunction with attacking ground forces. At the Eleventh Battle of Isonzo (pp. 364-5) in August 1916, 85 Capronis bombed the Austrian supply and relief columns, as well as ammunition dumps and head-quarters in the rear areas. With the disaster at Caporetto (p. 349) in October 1917 the Caproni squadrons were pressed still further into tactical support of the armies on their retreat to the Piave, and few long-range raids were made. On the night of 4 October 1917, however, 12 Caproni CA3s bombed the Austrian naval base at Cattaro with great success, damaging the torpedo store, seaplane hangars, the submarine base and a petrol dump at Kumbor.

Long-range bombing continued, though often disrupted by the Caproni squad-rons' continued tactical support. Throughout 1918 they bombed railway lines and stations, major roads, airfields, artillery and troop concentrations, and thus greatly contributed to the final Italian victory at Vittorio Veneto (p. 384) in October-November 1918. Furthermore, the introduction in February 1918 of the Ansaldo SVA5 two-seater, with its great speed and enormous range, permitted much long-range reconnaissance and photo-reconnaissance work - one of the reasons for the Italians' seemingly miraculous intelligence of enemy movements and dispositions. On 9 August 1918 one of these aircraft, with an escort of 7 single-seaters, flew to Vienna and dropped propaganda leaflets over the city - a round trip of over 600 miles. One may imagine the surprise and consternation of the Austrians on realising, in the face of tangible evidence, that their capital was within range of so energetic an enemy. In the observer's cockpit of the SVA5 sat Gabriele D'Annunzio, no doubt delighted to be meting out punishment to an enemy he so ardently loathed.

In many ways the Italian bombing campaigns were a model of both the tactical and strategic use of aircraft. While material damage to Austro-Hungarian cities was small, the psychological effect of the long-range raids was enormous, particularly on a population which considered itself beyond the reach of bombs. Moreover, the determination and accuracy of Italian attacks on military targets were such as to prove thoroughly the value of bombing aircraft as weapons.

The British bombing offensive against Germany, first by the RFC and RNAS and later by the RAF, began in direct reprisal for the Gotha raids on England. By October 1917 General Trenchard had ordered the 41st Wing, comprising one RNAS and two RFC squadrons, to commence bombing German cities, chiefly Mannheim, Coblenz, Stuttgart, Mainz, Cologne and Frankfurt. Daylight raids were undertaken by the fast two-seater DH4s of No 55 Squadron RFC, and night raids by the elderly two-seat pusher FE2Bs of No 100 Squadron RFC, and the large twin-engined Handley Page 0/100s of Naval 'A' Squadron. The Handley Page, the first of Britain's long-range heavy bombers, had been ordered in 1914 to meet the Royal Navy's request for a 'bloody paralyser of an aeroplane', though it did not enter service until 1916. Its early history was unfortunate, in that the second production 0/100 was mistakenly landed behind German lines in France, but, with its much more numerous successor, the uprated 0/400, it bore the brunt of Britain's heavy bombing campaigns. By early 1918 a number of RFC and RNAS squadrons were bombing German cities as well as airfields, manufacturing plants and military targets.

Meanwhile, the German bombing offensive against Britain had led indirectly, by dint of vociferous complaints about poor defences, to the formation of the RAF by amalgamation of the RFC and RNAS. Following German bombing raids in July 1917, the S African Field-Marshal Jan Christian Smuts - who had fought against the British in the Second Boer War - was called in to resolve the perennial but vituperative argument that raged between the RFC and RNAS and their supporters, and which greatly hindered Britain's air policy. The argument, centred upon supply, equipment, training and allocation of duties, drew political support-ers to both sides, and Lord Curzon's Air Board, lacking executive powers, had been unable to resolve it. The RNAS was in many ways the more technologically advanced service, for it had established early links with private manufacturers and, moreover, was not fighting a full-scale air war on the Western Front. As a result, the RFC had great difficulty in obtaining the aircraft and engines it required, and was more or less committed to the products of the Royal Aircraft Factory at Farnborough (indeed, the Sopwith Triplanes which performed such fine service for the RFC in April 1917 were only loaned from the RNAS). As a direct result of Smuts's report of September 1917, the two forces were joined into the Royal Air Force in March-April 1918, with Trenchard as Chief of Air Staff, and much of the difficulty was resolved. In January the Air Ministry, a central controlling body, had been created, with responsibility for all air operations, and out of these two new institutions emerged, on 6 June 1918, the Independent Bombing Force. This force, specifically designed to bomb strategic targets, absorbed Trenchard's strategic bombing squadrons already operating from around Nancy.

Trenchard's policy for bombers favoured day bombing (as was to be expected from his aggressive fighter policy) for its greater accuracy and supposed value as a destroyer of morale. Needless to say, it put a great strain on pilots and maintenance services, though German home defence squadrons were fortunately not of the high order of the Western Front *Jastas*. German cities were bombed by day and night, causing some material damage, but it was already becoming clear that bombing civilian targets, far from breaking morale, merely stiffened resistance. The forma-tion of the RAF and the arrival of the American squadrons called for an increase in strategic bombing, but French army opposition to the Independent Bombing Force, as it became, failure of aircraft and engine supplies, and Field-Marshal

Lord Haig's insistence on retaining bombers for tactical support, put a severe damper on such an increase, and by the armistice Trenchard's long-range bombing squadrons were only nine in number.

During September 1918 the Independent Bombing Force was used in support of the American offensive at St Mihiel (pp. 339-40) and, while attacks on major German cities continued into October, they were hampered by conflicting orders and high losses of aircraft, especially the notoriously underpowered two-seater DH9 day bomber. Given better aircraft and a freer hand, the Independent Bombing Force would without doubt have become a major factor in Germany's defeat, particularly had it received the new giant bombers designed to attack Berlin, the Handley Page V/1500s. As it was, in just over a year the Independent Bombing Force and its forerunners dropped 665 tons of bombs on German targets for the loss of some 304 day and 148 night bombers. The day-bombing squadrons lost 203 men killed or missing, and 58 wounded, while the night bombers lost 87 killed or missing and 11 wounded.

Material damage caused by bombing during the First World War was light compared to damage by other means. (One slightly ridiculous statistic is that the German bombing of Britain by airships and aeroplanes did damage to the extent of £3 million: on the other hand it has been calculated that damage to material caused by rats amounted to £70 million per year.) But it had a pronounced effect on the formulation of inter-war air policy, and gave rise to the mistaken belief, propagated mainly by Trenchard and the Italian General Giulio Donhet, and later upheld by Göring, that air power alone could win wars. The bombing offensives of 1914-18 did prove, however, that by tying up an enemy's resources in costly defence of his homeland, it was possible to maintain a fluid and fast-moving war relying on smaller units of highly trained troops. To that end, aside from all physical or psychological effects they may have, bombers are the decoy *par excellence.*

One other aspect emerged - that of disrupted production, a field which, in a later war, was greatly to influence the outcome. But it was some time before it was realised that a single aircraft could cause thousands of workers to cease production of vital war material.

OTHER THEATRES

Air operations in theatres other than the Western Front were largely overshadowed by the extent and complexity of European campaigns. Only one - General Sir Edmund Allenby's campaign in Palestine - demonstrated the use of aircraft as a definitive weapon, though other theatres were, on all sides, greatly affected by the lack of men and material, most of which were swallowed by the increasing demands of the war in France and Flanders.

Italy's air operations have been dealt with in some detail elsewhere and, while a number of squadrons of seaplanes and other aircraft were employed in anti-submarine duties in the Adriatic and Mediterranean, other Italian air operations were restricted to the provision of a squadron of Capronis in France in early 1918.

Never large to start with, Russia's air force, the Imperial Russian Flying Service, was hamstrung by conditions on the Eastern Front, by poor maintenance and material, by difficulties of supply, poor aircraft design or manufacture, and by the eventual total breakdown of the armed forces which preceded the revolution of October-November 1917. From that date the Bolsheviks commenced negotiating a peace treaty with Germany, effectively halting all operations on the Eastern Front and releasing large numbers of men and much material for Germany's offensive in the west.

One Russian squadron is worth mentioning: Czar Nicholas II's 'Squadron of Flying Ships' (the EVK), equipped with the world's first four-engined bomber, the Sikorsky-designed Ilya Mourometz. This was a by no means ineffective aircraft, being capable of lifting 1,500 pounds of bombs and armed with 4 or 5 machine-guns, though up to 7 could be carried. It was a well-built machine fitted with a remarkably accurate bomb-sight of Russian design and manufacture, which enabled the squadron to score hits on over 60 per cent of its targets. The *Eskadra Vozdushnykh Korablei* was an interesting formation: more than a bomber squadron, it was completely self-contained, carrying out its own maintenance, training, testing and supply. The EVK made its first raid from its base at Jablonna in Poland on 15 February 1915, and until the revolution made a total of some 400 bombing raids on German and Lithuanian territory. In all that time only 1 aircraft was lost to enemy action (2 others were damaged in landing crashes), on 12 September 1916, though not before the Ilya Mourometz's gunners had accounted for 3 of the attacking fighters, which speaks highly for the training and discipline of the EVK, at least. Mourometzes were also used for long-range and photographic reconnaissance, apparently with a high degree of success. But, on the whole, little is known of Russia's air operations in this war. It is certain that raids were carried out by Russian aircraft against German bases in the Baltic, but there is a dearth of information from Russian sources about the success of these missions.

In the Dardanelles campaign British aircraft operated from a base on the island of Tenedos, a Turkish counter-attack having recaptured the sole Allied airfield on the Gallipoli (pp. 357-9) peninsula. There was little the aircraft could do to help the embattled troops on the peninsula, and that little was made less by the motley array of outdated or ill-designed aircraft employed. Better aircraft would have permitted greater tactical support of troops (the Turkish air force was little better equipped, having mainly German or Austro-Hungarian cast-offs) and strategic bombing of Turkish cities. One notable event occurred, however, when a British aircraft sank an enemy ship with a torpedo - the first successful instance of such an attack.

In Macedonia the three squadrons supporting the British attack of September 1918 succeeded in catching the Bulgarians in a narrow pass, demoralising them with successive bombing and strafing runs. It was proof that, given intelligent command and the ability to use terrain in their favour, aircraft could do great material and psychological damage to a stubborn enemy. Further proof was provided by General Sir Edmund Allenby's handling of his air squadrons during the Palestine campaign of the last months of the war. This was a highly mobile war in which aircraft, both as offensive weapons and in their reconnaissance rôle, played a valuable part. Allenby's use of cavalry, armoured cars and aircraft, in a classic pattern of tactical feints followed by swift advances, permitted him to gain some 300 miles in six weeks. By September 1918 Allenby's five squadrons had succeeded in depriving the Turks of virtually all air reconnaissance or defence. British aircraft bombed the Turkish army headquarters and its attendant telephone system, while RAF fighters continually bombed and strafed the main Turkish airfield. Supporting RAF aircraft laid smoke-screens along the line of advance, and provided the troops with intelligence and, on 19 September, two Turkish divisions were trapped in a defile and severely mauled by fighters and bombers. Allenby, thanks to much early photo-reconnaissance, had correctly predicted the Turkish lines of retreat, laying ambushes of cavalry and armoured cars along these paths. The appearance of these units along their route of retreat caused the Turkish soldiers to panic and, under harassing attacks from RAF aircraft, the retreat quickly became a rout.

With limited resources, but with great imagination, General Allenby used all his units, on land and in the air, as an extension of a single principle: mobility. His use of aircraft showed an intelligent grasp of the tactics of long-range reconnaissance and sudden attack. Furthermore, the maps of Palestine were limited in detail, unlike those of the Western Front, and commanders were therefore forced to rely far more on aircraft for accurate information, not only concerning enemy dispositions, but also about the very terrain itself.

Two other examples of the usefulness of the developing weapon are provided by the campaign in East Africa (pp. 352-5). In 1917 the German High Command sent the Zeppelin L59 in an attempt to take supplies and ammunition to Colonel Paul von Lettow-Vorbeck, the German Commander in E Africa. L59 was forced to return to its Balkan base after reaching Khartoum, but its abortive flight nevertheless sowed the seeds of a new usefulness for aircraft - air supply and transport.

The other example is provided by the sinking of the German raider *Königsberg*. A cruiser, the *Königsberg*'s usefulness had been that of threatening shipping in the Indian Ocean approaches to the Suez Canal. Her victories numbered only a single merchant ship and the British light cruiser *Pegasus,* sunk off Zanzibar on 20 September 1914. Plagued by lack of supply and maintenance and worried by the British fleet's persistent hunt for her, her captain sailed her into the mouth of the Rufiji River in German E Africa, where the British promptly bottled her up by sinking an old ship across the navigable stream. She was still a nuisance, however, providing food, supplies, medical aid and trained men for the brilliant von Lettow-Vorbeck in his remarkable (and undefeated) campaign, and there was still a chance that she might escape to harass shipping further. Several attempts were made to sink her by naval gunfire, but she was well camouflaged and protected by thick jungle, and remained largely unscathed. In July 1915, however, two naval aircraft were sent up to 'spot' her, reporting her position and plotting shell-falls for two monitors. The bombardment was successful and *Königsberg* was sunk, though von Lettow-Vorbeck managed to remove two of her guns and later used them as part of his artillery.

NAVAL FLYING

In 1914 the Royal Navy was the largest in the world and, as a direct result of its technical competence, and the vision of men like Admiral Lord Fisher and Winston Churchill, very soon possessed the most efficient and modern air service, the RNAS. Squadrons of the RNAS, better trained and better equipped than their RFC counterparts, and not engaged in a costly battle, tended to be more highly qualified than those of the army service. True, the bulk of naval flying was connected with the fleet and its defence, and impact on the Great War as a whole was small: nevertheless, the RNAS was responsible for a number of significant advances.

The Imperial German Naval Air Service, engrossed in its Zeppelins, made little impact on flying in general, aircraft operations being restricted to defence against British ships, and accompanying the German fleet on its few sorties. French and Italian naval air operations were mainly in the field of anti-submarine warfare, while America, starting late, followed the RNAS's lead.

From the beginning, the RNAS attacked German U-boat bases on the Belgian coast with seaplane raids, though often with little effect. In view of this failure, the Admiralty introduced new techniques to combat the 'U-boat menace', using submarine-searching airships and long-range aircraft. The former 'blimps' were quite capable of keeping up with ships and were generally disliked by enemy submarines, not because of their rather ineffective bombs, but because they carried a wireless set, and could thus call up destroyers. For that reason, shipping escorted by blimps went largely unmolested. While blimps made a reasonable short-term deterrent, their susceptibility to bad weather soon made the Admiralty consider the other solution.

The RNAS turned to seaplanes and flying-boats and produced, in Squadron Commander John Porte's Felixstowe series, a reliable and efficient long-range anti-submarine weapon which was to influence flying-boat development for the next twenty years. Developed by Porte from the inefficient American Curtiss H series, the Felixstowe flying-boats were powerful twin-engined aircraft having a six-hour range, and armed with from 4 to 7 Lewis guns and 2 230-pound bombs. Operating on patrol in the North Sea they accounted for numbers of German submarines, the first being *UC-36*, sunk by a bomb from a Felixstowe on 20 May 1917. Further successes were against marauding airships and, because of their armament and manoeuvrability, the Felixstowes were treated with caution by enemy fighters.

The potential of the torpedo bomber had been understood by the Admiralty some time before the outbreak of war. By October 1916, Captain Murray F. Sueter, an ardent advocate of this method of attacking enemy ships, had approached Sopwith with specifications for a land-based, long-range single-seat aircraft of this type. Torpedoes had formerly been carried by seaplanes specially adapted for the purpose, but they were at best a compromise, and at worst downright dangerous.

The aircraft which appeared, the Sopwith Cuckoo, was the first purpose-built torpedo bomber and, while it was delivered too late to see action in the Great War, numbers were embarked upon the aircraft-carriers HMSS *Argus* and *Furious* before the war ended.

But if Porte and Sueter were harbingers of things to come, Squadron Commander E.H. Dunning's impact was even greater. On 2 August 1917 Dunning landed a Sopwith Pup on the forward deck of the aircraft carrier HMS *Furious*, the first such landing on a ship under way. Tragically, Dunning was killed five days later making the third of such landings, but the feat was proved and aircraft carriers became a reality. Squadron Commander H.R. Busteed continued experiments with arrestor gear, using skid-equipped Sopwith Pups at the Royal Navy's Isle of Grain testing airfield, eventually producing the system of tensioned wires which remains largely unchanged today.

Admiral Sir John Jellicoe was cast in the same mould. Alarmed by the twin threats of submarines and Zeppelins, it was he who instigated, with Fisher's and Churchill's backing, the policy of aircraft at sea. From this thinking sprang first seaplane tenders and then platforms on gun turrets from which aircraft could take off, with platforms overhanging the stern for landing (though, until Dunning's feat, pilots preferred to ditch in the sea). It was but a short step to the removal of the funnel and the decking-over of the superstructure, and the aircraft carrier was born. Furthermore, by 1918 the Grand Fleet carried with it some 150 aircraft, capable of rapid take-off for defence or reconnaissance.

Still worried by the Zeppelin threat, the RNAS carried out a number of strategic strikes against their bases. On 19 July 1918 HMS *Furious*, now in service, launched her aircraft against the airship sheds at Tondern. Complete surprise was achieved, and the Zeppelins L54 and L60 were destroyed by bombs.

To the Royal Navy must also go the credit for the long-range Handley Page bombers. Four RNAS squadrons of these aircraft served in France, one of them with Trenchard's Independent Bombing Force, and were used repeatedly in night attacks behind the German lines.

In a sense, the air war at sea, specifically that of the RNAS, was a sideshow. But, in the birth of anti-submarine techniques, aircraft carriers, torpedo bombing, fleet reconnaissance, air-sea rescue, and contributions to radio telegraphy and strategic bombing, it did more than any other service to develop the theory of air power.

CONCLUSION

The air forces of the Great War won no major battle, nor did they decisively influence the outcome. The prevailing static military thinking which laid the foundations of a vast stagnant struggle nearly killed the new weapon at birth. To most soldiers, aircraft were remote and seemingly fragile objects which rarely served a purpose, unless it were to draw further artillery upon their entrenched positions. Pilots seemed overpaid and overfed, and lived in comfortable billets well beyond the range of guns. But if the infantryman saw air power as a meaningless waste of time, the airmen viewed the land war with confusion. The nature of their struggle could take them rapidly deep into enemy territory; their height gave them the power to see for scores of miles; their armament the ability to destroy trained men and what was, even then, thousands of pounds' worth of equipment, with a single light weapon. Thus the airman saw the failure to exploit gaps he had reported in the enemy lines, saw supplies he had destroyed replaced through inability to follow up the advantage, and was often issued with meaningless orders by a High Command whose concept of air power was limited to the merest grasp of cavalry patrols.

The Great War was, in a sense, the last of the 'medieval' wars, but concealed within its static strategy lay the beginnings of a new and infinitely powerful weapon. Few outside the air forces realised it, while civilian grasp of this concept was limited to rage at bombing raids and adulation of a handful of heroes. If the legacy of the development of air fighting during the Great War was the destruction of Dresden and Hamburg, Hiroshima and Nagasaki, it is also the creation of a whole new technology—radio telegraphy, air-sea rescue, aircraft carriers, navigation, metallurgy, engine design, armaments and, of course, civil flying. But perhaps the greatest bequest of the air forces of 1914-18 is that the continued existence of air power prevented for all time a repetition of the stagnant butcher's shop on the Western Front.

SECTION ELEVEN

SECOND WORLD WAR

See Map Section, nos 25–34

ALAMEIN   see EL ALAMEIN

ALAM EL HALFA (Egypt)   Second World War   31 August 1942
Fought between the British under General Bernard Montgomery and the Germans under Field-Marshal Erwin Rommel.

Rommel had driven across Cyrenaica and W Egypt only to be stopped by the British at the First Battle of El Alamein (qv). A month after his arrival there and seventeen days after Montgomery took command of the British 8th Army, Rommel launched an attack on the British position at Alam el Halfa with three veteran armoured divisions. This was to be his last attempt to break through the British and head for the Nile and Cairo. The drive on the centre right of the British position turned the south flank, but reconnaissance planes observed the action and the British organised a defence which stopped the Germans cold. Minefields were laid, strong artillery posts set up and bombing raids instigated. On 4 September Rommel acknowledged defeat and pulled back the armour from its salient to a defensive line which ran north to south. British losses were 1,750, but German losses were considerably heavier.

The British continued their build-up along this front for the Second Battle of El Alamein (qv).

ALEUTIAN ISLANDS (North Pacific)   Second World War   3 June 1942 – 30 May 1943.
Fought between the Americans and the Japanese.

When the Japanese were planning their attack on Midway Island (qv) they launched a diversionary attack on the Aleutian Islands to the north in an effort to draw the US Pacific Fleet away from Midway. It was intended to destroy the fleet on its return to harbour. The Americans, however, knew of the Japanese intention and remained where they were.

Meanwhile, a small Japanese force under Admiral Moshiro Hosogaya moved towards the Aleutians and, on 3 and 4 June, carrier-based bombers attacked the US air and naval bases at Dutch Harbour on the Aleutian Island of Unalaska. On 7 June Japanese troops made two landings on the islands of Kiska and Attu, 150 miles west. The Japanese were now at the end of a long supply line and they made no attempt to move any farther east along the Aleutian islands, giving General Simon Buckner, Commander of the Aleutian-Alaska region, time to set up American bases on the islands of Adak and Amchitka. At the same time, Butler's 11th Air Force and Admiral Thomas Kinkaid's naval force subjected Kiska and Attu to incessant attack. On 11 May 1943 three landings were made on Attu by the US 7th Infantry Division, at Holtz Bay and Chichagof Harbour in the north and Massacre Bay in the south. General A. E. Brown's troops forced the Japanese defenders back into the mountains of the interior. Fighting in heavy fog and bitter cold, the two-pronged attack finally drove the Japanese into an untenable position. On 29 May they launched a furious counter-attack, which was beaten back. Resistance then collapsed altogether on 30 May, but only 28 men were captured while a total of 2,350 Japanese were killed or committed suicide. American losses were 552 killed and 1,140 wounded.

Kiska became the next target and naval and air attacks on the island were increased. On 15 August a force of 29,000 Americans and 5,300 Canadians were landed, only to find the island deserted. Under cover of heavy fog, the Japanese had evacuated the place some days earlier.

The conquest of the Aleutians safeguarded the American north flank in the Pacific and freed troops for fighting in the central and SW Pacific areas.

ANZIO (Italy)   Second World War   22 January – 24 May 1944
Fought between the Allies under General John Lucas and the Germans under Field-Marshal Albert Kesselring.
Strength: Allies 50,000; Germans 4 divisions with 450 guns.

When the Allied drive on Rome was blocked by the Gustav-Cassino Line (qv), General Sir Harold Alexander who commanded all the Allied ground forces, launched an amphibious attack known as Operation Shingle. An Allied force was sent to Anzio, 70 miles behind the German lines and 30 miles south of Rome.

Early on 22 January Lucas's 6 Corps landed on the beach at Anzio, the British 1st Infantry to the left (N) and the US 3rd Infantry to the right. Although little opposition was encountered, the Allies moved inland slowly and, before they could cut Highway 7, the German line of communication with Rome, Kesselring brought up General Ebehard von Mackensen's 14th Army to block the Allied advance. Lucas then dug in his beachhead which was 15 miles long by 7 miles deep. The 5th and 56th British and US 1st Armoured and 45th Infantry Divisions were brought up as reinforcements against an expected counter-attack. During this phase 6 Corps lost 6,923 men killed, wounded or missing. On 16 February the Germans attacked with four divisions and 450 guns which bombarded the Allied position (within which were 18,000 vehicles, landed at the start of the invasion). The German attack was slowed after two days of heavy fighting and the next German thrust, at the end of February, was beaten back so that by 1 March the beachhead was secure.

The Anzio landing did not achieve its objective in that the quick conquest of Rome did not come about; but when Cassino fell on 17 May (GASTAV-CASSINO LINE), 6 Corps, reorganised and now under the command of Major-General Lucius Truscott, was able to break out of the beachhead and link up with 2 Corps of the 5th Army. During the four months' fighting 9,200 British and 29,000 American casualties were evacuated from the beachhead.

Because of his lack of thrust after landing Lucas was relieved of his command in the middle of the battle on 23 February to be succeeded by General Truscott.

ARDENNES II (Belgium/N France)   Second World War   1944 – 5
Fought between the Allies and the Germans.

The German defence of the Siegfried Line (qv) enabled the top command to reorganise their forces. Field-Marshal Walther Model's Army Group 'B', consisting of the reserve armies of 250,000 men and 1,100 tanks, launched a winter offensive aimed at the recapture of Liège and Antwerp, both Allied supply bases, and cutting the Allied forces under General Dwight D. Eisenhower into two halves. The objective which followed this design was the destruction of the Allied army lying north of the Bastogne – Brussels – Antwerp line. This force consisted of the Canadian 1st, British 2nd, US 9th and most of the US 1st Armies. The Ardennes was chosen as the line of attack where General Troy Middleton's US 8 Corps was widely deployed along a 75-mile front stretching from Monschau south to Echternach.

The German offensive began on 16 December. Known as Operation Watch on the Rhine, the advance commenced in dense fog when General Sepp Dietrich's 6th Panzer Army headed the drive forward, supported by the 5th Panzer of General Hasso von Manteuffel on the left and the 7th Army of General Ernst Brandenburger on the right. The twenty-division onslaught drove the US 28th and 106th Infantry and 9th Armoured back in disorder. Meanwhile, a German Commando unit under Captain Otto Skorzeny had penetrated the American rear disguised as US troops, disrupting communications and transport. In addition, 1,000 Germans were parachuted into the area near Malmedy under Colonel Friedrich von der Heydte; their function was to prevent Allied reinforcements from coming into the Ardennes from the north. The sudden attack drove a bulge into the line of General Courtney Hodges's 1st Army; but to the north near Malmedy, General Leonard Gerow's 5 Corps recovered to halt the German advance on Liège, deflecting the 6th Panzer's southern drive. From 17 to 23 December the Germans were halted by a roadblock set up by the US 7th Armoured Division at St Vith. In this area 125 American prisioners were shot by the SS on 23 December. This check in the north caused Model to switch his offensive south to the 5th Panzer Army of Manteuffel, which shattered the remains of Middleton's 8 Corps and reached Houffalize and Bastogne on 20 December. The vital road junction here was rapidly surrounded by German infantry and the US 101st Airborne Division was sent to join the 10th Armoured and elements of other divisions under General Anthony McAuliffe to help hold it. German Panzers meanwhile moved west and NW towards the Meuse.

The Allies threw up a strong defensive perimeter and repulsed all German attacks on Bastogne. Near Echternach, Brandenburger's 7th Army made some progress before being halted by the US 4th Infantry and 9th Armoured Divisions. The German advance had isolated the American 1st and 9th Armies from their 12th Army Group HQ, and on 20 December Eisenhower placed all American forces north of the salient under the command of Field-Marshal Sir Bernard Montgomery in order to avoid problems of communication. General George Patton's US 3rd Army was at the same time ordered to attack the German salient from the south, having as an additional purpose the objective of relieving the pressure on Bastogne. Although bad weather had grounded Allied aircraft at the start of the battle, an improvement in conditions on 23 December enabled the Allies to attack by air. The advancing Germans had their convoys badly damaged by 5,000 Allied aircraft and the beleaguered troops at Bastogne were supplied by airlift. The destruction of the German convoys meant that front-line troops were isolated and short of supplies. By 24 December Manteuffel's thrust had reached farthest west, but here General Ernest Harmon's US 2nd Armoured Division and the 29th British Armoured Brigade clashed with the Panzers and in a decisive two-day action forced them to halt their advance only 4 miles from the Meuse. They had moved forward 60 miles from their starting point. Thirty-five miles SE, Patton's 4th Armoured Division created a narrow corridor through to Bastogne on 26 December. A German demand for the surrender of Bastogne earlier had received the laconic response of 'Nuts' from McAuliffe.

The German advance had now been stopped on all fronts, but the deep bend in the Allied line needed to be eliminated. The Germans continued to make attempts to cut the corridor to Bastogne, but three corps from the 3rd Army prevented them from doing so. Montgomery stabilised his front to the north and began to counter-attack on 3 January, first with the US 7 Corps and then, on the following day, with the British 30 Corps under Lt-General Brian Horrocks. On 8 January Model began to pull the German forces back. Fighting all the way, he successfully extricated all major units. On 13 January the British 6th Airborne Division patrols met up with those of the US 3rd Army at St Hubert, and on 16 January the US 2nd Armoured (from the north) and 11th Armoured (from the south) made contact at Houffalize, joining the Allied line once more and enabling the 1st Army, though not the 9th, to come once more under the command of General Omar Bradley from 12th Army HQ. By 25 January the bulge which had remained was eliminated and the original front was restored.

A secondary action took place to the south in the region of Alsace-Lorraine. Here the German 1st Army under General Obstfelder had attacked on 1 January towards the Laverne Gap, where General Jacob Devers's 6th Army Group was covering the gap left by troops of the 3rd Army who had moved north to the Ardennes. The Germans were successful at first, but General Alexander Patch's US 7th Army held its position behind the Moder River on 20 January. South of this, General Jean Lattre de Tassigny's 1st French Army with four American divisions moved on the Colmar pocket and, between 20 January and 9 February, squeezed it out. This closed the fighting with a loss to the Allies of 76,900 killed, wounded or missing. The Germans lost 70,000 killed and wounded, 50,000 captured along with 600 tanks and 1,600 planes destroyed.

The Allied offensive into the Rhineland had been delayed by only six weeks and nearly all the German reserves had been committed to this costly stalling action, seriously weakening their position and helping to ensure their ultimate defeat.

The operation is also known as the Battle of the Bulge.

ATLANTIC, BATTLE OF THE   Second World War   1940–4
Fought between the Allies and the Germans.

A total blockade on Britain was announced by Adolf Hitler on 17 August 1940, a campaign intensified by the fall of France. The Royal Navy and Royal Air Force began a four-year battle against U-boats, surface ships, aircraft and every kind of mine (acoustic, magnetic and contact) to break the enemy's challenge to Britain's command of the sea. Neutral ships sailing to Britain were to be sunk on sight and the entire Atlantic Ocean now became a battlefield. Lone merchantmen (often American, as US shipping was not yet geared to convoy sailing) were particularly vulnerable. From 1 June 1940 to 1 July 1941 899 British ships were sunk (4 million gross tons) and 471 Allied and neutral vessels (1,800,000 gross tons), three times the joint annual production of Britain and the USA. Imports into the British Isles fell from 1,200,000 tons per week in June to 800,000 tons in December (excluding oil). Crippled vessels also filled Allied ports. Half the total shipping sunk had fallen prey to U-boats which hunted in wolf-packs, guided by reconnaissance aircraft to their victims.

By the end of 1940, the RN and RAF had destroyed 31 U-boats, leaving only 22 in service; but in 1941 German shipyards were producing 18 boats a month, so that by August over 100 were constantly at sea. The danger from the air was nearly as great. German Fokke-Wulfs accounted for a quarter of all Allied and neutral shipping.

Surface ships were a menace as well, hunting alone for merchant vessels, troopships and small warships. The *Scharnhorst* and *Gneisenau* sank or captured 22 vessels (115,600 tons) in February and March 1941, and the *Scheer* accounted for 16 ships (93,000 tons) in five months up to April 1941. But in May the *Bismarck* (qv) was sunk in the N Atlantic.

The Allies now instituted a convoy system whereby the maximum number of Allied capital ships available sailed with the merchantmen. These included destroyers, corvettes, aircraft carriers whose planes provided air cover, though this was also given by bases in Iceland, Greenland and Britain.

In September 1941 the first escort carrier, the *Audacity*, with 6 aircraft on board, came into operation. In the first six months of 1942 the Germans sank 900 ships, totalling over 4 million tons, and the total for the year was 1,664 vessels (7,790,697 tons), of which 1,660 were the victims of U-boats. Broken down, the figures for the separate months in the first half of the year show how swiftly the tally rose. In January 31 ships (200,000 tons) were sunk in the W Atlantic and Caribbean, but by May in the same sector 91 ships (452,000 tons) were sunk. In June 80 ships (416,000 tons) went down.

During the year, however, the convoys were improved by closer co-operation between air and sea forces, and weapons and tactics were also improved. Asdic underwater radar and seagoing radar was fitted to ships and some merchantmen were equipped to catapult planes into the air to fight German aircraft. Long-range aircraft were put into Coastal Command, and on 1 April 1942 the Americans instituted coastal convoys. In the first six months of the year 14 submarines were sunk, and 14 more were destroyed in July alone. The number reached 16 in October, but despite this the German U-boat fleet had doubled to 200 by the end of the year.

The battlefield was extended by the sending of convoys to Murmansk and Archangel with basic supplies for Russia. British and US vessels took vehicles, tanks, aircraft ammunition and fuel into these ports, and during 1941 and 1942 102 British ships and 117 US vessels arrived safely, although 22 British and 42 US ships were lost to German air and sea attacks. Convoy PQ 17 (qv) was hardest hit, losing 23 of 34 cargo ships in June and July of 1942. Forty convoys went to Russia, taking 3,700,000 tons of goods. They lost 91 merchantmen and 300,000 tons of supplies.

On 30 January 1943 Hitler forced Admiral Erich Raeder to resign, being unsatisfied with this heavy toll of shipping. Admiral Karl Dönitz replaced him and began to strengthen the U-boat fleet on which he placed the emphasis of his strategy. By the spring of 1943 235 U-boats were in action in the Atlantic and over 500,000 tons of shipping were sunk each month; but at the same time, more U-boats than ever were being destroyed – 12 were sunk in March, 15 in April and 40 in May. The tonnage of shipping being sunk began to fall. In April the losses were down to 253,000 tons and in May they were 206,000. Dönitz recalled the U-boat fleet for a rest and refit, to go out again in less hazardous waters. In June only 28,000 tons of shipping were sunk, and during the last three months of 1943 more U-boats were sunk than merchantmen – 53 to 47. The battle against the U-boats had been won.

New construction of Allied shipping also outweighed that sunk. Eleven million tons were the net gain over a year in which 14,600,000 tons were built. The growing potency of Allied air strength also helped to cut losses. Long-range fighters accounted for many Nazi bombers.

On 26 December 1943 the *Scharnhorst*, sister ship to the *Gneisenau* which had been crippled by a mine between Brest and Kiel on 11 February 1942, was involved in an attack on an Arctic convoy off Spitsbergen. She was engaged by a British squadron headed by the 35,000-ton *Duke of York* under Admiral Sir Bruce Fraser, C-in-C Home Fleet, and sunk with the loss of all her 1,970 crew except for 36 men. The *Tirpitz*, the only remaining heavy German warship, had been immobilised by air attacks on European ports. She was tracked down to Tromsö Fjord, Norway, where 29 RAF Lancasters bombed her to destruction. The attack, which took place on 12 November 1944, caused the death of more than half the crew of 1,900 at a cost of one bomber.

Throughout the rest of the war the U-boats continued to fight doggedly. They sank 52,000 tons of shipping during the last five weeks of the war, but lost 23 boats with valuable crews in the process. When Germany surrendered, Dönitz ordered the U-boats to surrender too. While 156 did so, 221 were scuttled.

British and US shipyards built 45,600,000 gross tons of shipping during the war. Their total losses were 23,500,000, of which 14 million tons were sunk by U-boats. The Germans lost 781 U-boats, 415 of which were destroyed by aircraft. During the Battle of the Atlantic 30,248 British merchant seamen were lost, RN casualties being 51,578 killed or missing.

AUSTRIA   Second World War   March – April 1945
Fought between the Allies and the Germans.

When the Russians captured Budapest on 18 February 1945 Austria was doomed to fall under the continuing sweep of the Red armies. In March General Rodion Malinovsky's 2nd Ukrainian Army drove into Austria from the SE with a two-pronged attack. To the right, one force marched up the Danube and captured Vienna between 8 and 13 April before moving west towards the US 7th Army near Linz. General Alexander Patch's 7th Army had invaded Austria from Bavaria late in April. The left wing moved west into Upper Austria before turning south to link up with the British 8th Army which was moving up through the Alps from Italy. Before any junction was made between the Allies, however, Germany surrendered unconditionally on 8 May.

BALKANS   Second World War   20 August – 20 October 1944
Fought between the Russians and the Axis.

After the Russian sweep through the Ukraine (qv) two drives moved west, crushing all the German defences before them until they arrived in the Balkans. To the north General Georgi Zhukov crossed the Upper Prut and drove along the N Romanian border, while south of him General Ivan Konev moved through Moldavia and crossed the Prut and Jassy (Iasi). The Russian offensive then halted for five months to reorganise and resupply.

On 20 August the Russians renewed their attack on Romania, their main attack being directed against the German salient between the Dniester and Prut Rivers. General Rodion Malinovsky and General Fedor Tolbukhin attacked SW and, crossing the Lower Prut, moved towards the Lower Danube. On 23 August the Romanian government under King Michael capitulated, whereupon many Romanian troops changed sides to fight against the Germans. As a result of this occurrence sixteen German divisions of General Johannes Friessner's Army Group South were destroyed in this sector. On 17 August Galati, at the mouth of the Danube, fell; and on 30 August Bucharest was occupied, as were the Ploesti oilfields. On 8 September Tolbukhin entered Bulgaria by crossing the Danube, and that country immediately changed sides and began to fight for the Russians. Germans in Bulgaria were disarmed and imprisoned. On 6 September the Russian left wing reached the Yugoslav frontier at Turnu Severin, having marched up the Danube valley. General Maxiimilian von Weichs's SE Army Group 'F' was driven back by Tolbukhin, aided by Partisan forces. Belgrade fell on 20 October.

During this drive Malinovsky moved into Hungary (qv).

BARDIA (Libya)   Second World War   3 January 1941
Fought between the British under Lt-General Richard O'Connor and the Italians under Marshal Rodolpho Graziani.
Strength: British 32,000; Italian 45,000.

After defeating the Italian 10th Army at Sidi Barrani (qv) the British 7th Armoured Division followed it across the Libyan border to the port of Bardia, where it surrounded the Italian force. Under heavy fire the 6th Australian Division bridged an anti-tank ditch, across which the armour was able to move. The Italian defences were then penetrated, and in two days of fighting the Italians suffered 40,000 casualties, most of whom were prisoners. British losses were light.

Leaving the infantry to cope with the aftermath, the armour moved along the coast west towards Tobruk (qv).

BATAAN–CORREGIDOR (Philippine Islands)   Second World War   1 January–7 May 1942
Fought between the Americans and Filipinos under General Douglas MacArthur and the Japanese under General Masahura Homma.
Strength: Americans 15,000 + Filipinos 65,000 (10,000 only being well trained); Japanese 50,000.

The Japanese invasion of Luzon from north and south closed in on Manila late in December 1941. MacArthur withdrew his command to the Bataan peninsula on the west coast of the island. By New Year's Day 1942 a total of 80,000 men were assembled on the peninsula and a line of defence stretching 15 miles from Subic Bay on the west in the S China Sea to Manila Bay on the right. General Jonathan Wainwright commanded the western half with 1 Corps and General George Parker the eastern half with 2 Corps. Just off the coast, MacArthur and Philippines President Manuel Quezon (Manuel Luis Quezon y Molina) established headquarters on Corregidor Island, a fortified rock at the mouth of Manila Bay.

It was envisaged that US naval, air and ground reinforcements would soon relieve the Bataan force whose position was somewhat precarious, but Japanese supremacy in the W Pacific grew and the Filipino position became ever more isolated. MacArthur had few fighter aircraft left to dispute the Japanese superiority of the air and he possessed no naval vessels other than small craft. Because of the difficulties, troops received only half rations from the beginning, and medical supplies, weapons and ammunition were severely rationed.

Homma, with the Japanese 14th Army, launched an offensive on the night of 10 January, concentrating his attack on the east (Abucay) half of the line. Parker repulsed the attack (during the action, Lieutenant Alexander Nininger Jr became the first man to win the Medal of Honour–posthumously–during the Second World War).

The Japanese continued to pressurise both ends of the line, and on 22 January MacArthur ordered a retreat to the east–west Pilar–Bagac road which ran across the middle of Bataan. The eastern sector was further forced back four days later to Orion, but here the new line stabilised. There was, however, a chronic shortage of medical supplies and almost 1,000 men a day were entering the two small hospitals on the tip of the Bataan peninsula, suffering from malaria. On the night of 11 March President Franklin D. Roosevelt ordered MacArthur and his staff to leave Corregidor by patrol torpedo (PT) boat. They went to Mindanao, whence a B-17 flew MacArthur to Australia where he took up his position as Supreme Commander of Allied forces in the SW Pacific. Wainwright became Commander of all forces in the Philippines, General Albert Jones took over as Commander of 1 Corps and General Edward King assumed command of the Bataan troops.

On 3 April Homma launched a heavy attack against the Allied line, incendiaries burning many men out of their positions. On 5 April the Japanese broke through the eastern defences and took Mount Samat, which gave them a good view of the Allied defences that were now crumbling. In the following two days the Japanese attacked the 2 Corps front until, by 8 April, they were completely defeated. That night 2,000 nurses and others escaped to Corregidor in small boats, and on the following day King surrendered 76,000 men, including 12,000 Americans.

After this, the worst capitulation in US history, the Japanese marched the prisoners 55 miles up the Bataan peninsula where, from San Fernando, the survivors were taken in freight wagons to Camp O'Donnell, beyond Clark Field. The captives were deprived of food, water and rest. Beaten and murdered on the way, it is estimated that between 7,000 and 10,000 men died during what is known as the Death March. Of those victims, 2,330 were Americans. (After the war General Homma and General Tomoyuki Yamashita – who had taken the surrender of Singapore (qv) and who took over command in the Philippines late in the campaign – were both tried and executed as war criminals.)

On Corregidor Wainwright had 13,000 men who were subjected to an ever-increasing artillery barrage – 16,000 shells landed on the island from Homma's siege guns on Bataan. Of the 4,000 men defending the beaches, 1,000 became casualties, the rest being in the Malinta Tunnel. On the night of 5 May two Japanese battalions of infantry landed on the NE of Corregidor and under cover of artillery and mortar fire moved towards the east end of the Malinta Tunnel. By mid-morning on 6 May tanks had joined the attack and Wainwright signalled that he surrendered the island. Homma, holding the helpless men on Corregidor as hostages, refused to accept the surrender until a general cease-fire was called by the Americans. At midnight on 6/7 May Wainwright agreed to the cease-fire which was to take effect over all American troops still resisting in the Philippines. Pockets of guerilla activity continued, however, throughout the war in the Pacific.

Although the Allies had suffered a severe defeat, the Japanese advance had been slower than planned and it was the last major victory they would gain in the Pacific.

BEDA FOMM (Libya)   Second World War   5 – 7 February 1941
Fought between the British under Lt-General Richard O'Connor and the Italians under Marshal Rodolpho Graziani.
Strength: British 12,000; Italians 20,000.

After taking Tobruk (qv) the British moved towards Benghazi, 240 miles west, the 6th Australian Infantry Division moving along the coast road while the 7th Armoured Division moved SW through the desert to rejoin the coast road at Beda Fomm on 5 February. The town lay beyond Benghazi and thus cut off the Italian retreat. Graziani tried for two days to break through the British defences, but was unable to do so and finally surrendered his entire army and 84 tanks. British losses here were 9 killed and 15 wounded. The rest of 13 Corps had taken Benghazi at equally small cost. This force halted when it reached El Agheila.

The British army had, in its sixty-two-day campaign, destroyed ten divisions of the Italian army, taking 130,000 prisoners, 380 tanks and 850 guns at a cost to themselves of 500 killed, 1,380 wounded and 55 missing. At this point, however, 13 Corps was reduced drastically to send aid to Greece while the Axis sent General Erwin Rommel into the desert. This altered the course of events, as the Afrika Korps recaptured most of Cyrenaica, with the exception of Tobruk, with little difficulty.

BERLIN (Germany)   Second World War   16 April – 2 May 1945
Fought between the Russians and the Germans.
Strength: Russians 1,593,000 with 20,000 guns; Germans 744 guns + 600 AA guns used as field guns + 700 tanks.

By the spring of 1945 the Russian offensive had reached the line of the Oder and Neisse Rivers. The Russians were commanded by Marshal Georgi Zhukov, whose group was in the centre, with General Ivan Konev to the south and General Konstantin Rokossovsky to the north. The greatest threat to Berlin was at Küstrin (Kostrzyn) where, in March, the 1st White Russian Army Group under General Vasily Sokolovsky had created a bridgehead 30 miles long by 10 miles wide across the Oder. The German forces in the area were severely depleted because Adolf Hitler had sent five Panzer divisions south to Prague where he believed the main Russian attack would be made.

On 16 April 20,000 guns opened an artillery barrage and, covered by an escort of 6,500 fighters and bombers, the Russian tanks, spearheaded by the Russian 8th Guards Army, broke out of the bridgehead and made for Berlin. Simultaneous attacks by Rokossovsky, Zhukov and Konev protected the flanks of the Russian assault. The German line along the Oder, commanded by General Gotthard Heinrici, was broken and the Germans withdrew to their second line of defences in the Seelow Heights where General Kurt Weidling's 56th Panzers fought to contain Zhukov's attack. North of Zhukov's drive, Rokossovsky with the 2nd White Russian Army Group moved west towards the Lower Elbe. To the south Konev's 1st Ukrainian Army Group launched a more effective artillery attack and forced a crossing of the Neisse along an 18-mile front and pushed their way through 10 miles of German defences before turning north towards the German High Command Headquarters at Zossen and Berlin itself.

Meanwhile, on 20 April, one of Sokolovsky's tank columns met General Hasso von Manteuffel's 3rd Panzer Army north of the city, and on 25 April these two pincers met west of the capital. The first shells fell into the city itself on 21 April. General Theodor Busse's small force was encircled to the east on 22 April and that day Zossen fell to General Pavel Rybalko's 3rd Guards Tank Army. Zhukov and Konev, shelling the city from east and south, fought their way in, driving the Germans back before them in a series of fierce street battles which laid the city waste. On 26 April Tempelhof airfield was taken and the Russians proceeded into the centre of the city to Unter den Linden and the Tiergarten. On 1 May Zhukov's forces planted the Red Flag on the Reichstag building, Hitler having committed suicide the previous day. On 2 May Weidling, to whom Hitler had entrusted the city before his death, surrendered to the Russians with 140,000 men.

It must be said that the decisions, made by President Franklin D. Roosevelt against Winston Churchill's advice, and also General Dwight D. Eisenhower's, led to changes in Allied policy which enabled the Russians to enter Berlin first and so take their greatest prize of the war, causing infinite trouble to the Western Allies for the next thirty years.

BERLIN, AERIAL BOMBARDMENT (Germany) Second World War 1943–4
Fought between the Allies and the Germans.

The Allied Bomber Command's offensive during the winter of 1943–4 was against Berlin. The major offensive began on the night of 18 November 1943 when 444 bombers attacked the city, losing only 9 aircraft. In all, sixteen raids were made, in which about 14,000 people were killed, 3 million homes destroyed and 5,000 acres of the city devastated. As time went on, however, German night fighters began to gain superiority and 300 RÀF aircraft were lost. The US 8th Air Force obtained the necessary fighter cover to resume daylight raids early in 1944, and on 8 March 590 bombers attacked the Erkner ball-bearing factory in Berlin, inflicting damage which caused considerable production delay. US losses were 37 aircraft.

BISMARCK (N Atlantic)   Second World War   27 May 1941
Fought between the British under Admiral Sir John Tovey and the Germans under Vice-Admiral Günther Lütjens.
Strength: British 2 battleships (*King George V* and *Rodney*) + 2 cruisers (*Norfolk* and *Dorsetshire*) + torpedo bombers from *Ark Royal*; Germans *Bismarck*.

The 45,000-ton battleship *Bismarck* joined German ships in the Battle of the Atlantic (qv) in 1941. Believed to be the most powerful battleship afloat, she was the first ship to have radar-controlled guns for use at night. The British found her with reconnaissance planes off the coast of Greenland and on 24 May attacked her with a squadron which included 4 capital ships. The *Hood* went down within minutes, sunk by a single shell from one of the 8 15-inch guns of the *Bismarck*, which exploded the magazine and blew up the entire ship. Only 3 of her 1,500-man crew survived. The *Prince of Wales* was also severely damaged. Thereafter the *Bismarck* was kept under surveillance during a 2,500-mile chase SE.

Tovey now concentrated all the naval strength he could afford in the N Atlantic, and on 27 May the *Bismarck* was cornered 400 miles from Brest by the *King George V*, *Rodney*, *Norfolk* and *Dorsetshire*. The *Ark Royal* sent in torpedo bombers and the *Rodney* opened the attack by torpedoing the *Bismarck,* the first battleship ever to torpedo another. Heavy shelling and torpedoing silenced the guns of the German ship, and at 10.40 am the *Dorsetshire* made a torpedo attack that finally sank her. The *Bismarck* went down with all her crew, her colours flying, at 10.56 am. 2,000 lives were lost, including that of Lütjens.

BISMARCK SEA (S Pacific)   Second World War   2 – 5 March 1943
Fought between the Allies and the Japanese.
Strength: Allies 86 aircraft + patrol torpedo (PT) boats; Japanese 8 transports + 8 destroyers.

When the Allies beat the Japanese out of Papua in E New Guinea the Japanese tried to reinforce their garrisons at Lae and Salamaua on the Huon Gulf. A convoy from Rabaul, New Britain, moved west into the Bismarck Sea, where it was located by the US 5th Air Force under General George Kenney and the Royal Australian Air Force. Aided by American PT boats on the surface, the planes subjected the convoy to a four-day bombardment, sinking all 8 transports and 4 destroyers. Of 7,000 reinforcements, only 1,000 reached their destination. The remaining 4 destroyers, badly damaged, limped into Rabaul Harbour. Japanese traffic in the Bismarck Sea was thereafter confined to small operations carried out under cover of darkness.

During this air/sea battle, which again illustrated the superiority of the air in such a situation, many ships were sunk by the 'skip' bombing technique – bouncing bombs along the surface of the water towards the target.

BRITAIN, BATTLE OF   Second World War   10 July 1940 – 10 May 1941
Fought between the British under Air Marshal Sir Hugh (later Lord) Dowding and Lt-General Sir Fredrick Pile (GOC-in-C, Anti-Aircraft Command), and the Germans under Field-Marshal Hermann Göring, and Albert Kesselring and Hugo Sperrle.
Strength: British 600 fighters (Hurricanes, Spitfires and Defiants) + AA support; Germans 1,015 bombers (Junkers 87 and 88, Dorniers 17 and 215, Heinkels 111K) + 350 dive bombers (Stukas + Junkers 87) + 930 fighters (Fokke-Wulfs and Messerschmitts) + 375 heavy fighters (Fokke-Wulfs and Messerschmitts).

The first battle in history to be fought entirely in the air.

After the fall of France Britain was the only country to withstand the German onslaught. Adolf Hitler planned to subdue the island by aerial bombardment or, if that failed, to destroy all naval and air defences as a prelude to invasion (Operation Sealion). The Luftwaffe, based mainly in French and Belgian airfields, undertook the operation in three overlapping phases.
Phase I: Beginning on 10 July Nazi bombers began to attack southern coastal ports from Dover to Plymouth. This area was good territory for an invasion and the destruction of all shipping and port installations was necessary. Bombers, escorted by fighters, flew across the Channel in waves, blasting all harbours and port facilities. The peak of the operation came on 15 August when 940 German planes attacked both north and south England. German losses were always heavy, but on this occasion 76 planes were shot down with a loss to the RAF of 34 fighters, as well as 21 bombers which were destroyed on the ground. The pilots of the fifty operational RAF squadrons, since known as 'The Few', were responsible for this total which was so high that the German High Command decided to change tactics. Many of the RAF pilots were originally from the British dominions,

as well as from Poland, Czechoslovakia, France and some from the USA, but the majority were British.

Phase II: Airfields, aircraft factories, radar stations and gun sites now became the prime target in an effort to break Britain's air power. The height of the phase came between 24 August and 6 September when 466 Hurricanes and Spitfires were destroyed or crippled and a quarter of the pilot strength became casualties (103 killed, 128 wounded). Although these losses were high, German casualties were even higher. They lost twice the number of aircraft and more than double the number of pilots.

Phase III: Having failed to cripple Britain's military strength, Göring now decided to bomb London into submission and instigated daylight raids on the capital. On 7 September between 5 and 6 pm, 320 Heinkels, escorted by 600 fighters, launched the first attack. This was followed at 8.10 pm with another wave of 250 bombers, which raided until 4.30 am. The following day 200 bombers, escorted by fighters, made another attack. On 15 September the raids reached their height when 400 bombers attacked London. The destruction of 95 of these aircraft by fighters and anti-aircraft artillery caused Göring to change tactics once again. This time, he switched to night raids. An average of 200 planes attacked the capital every night for the following fifty nights, the worst time being 15 October when 480 planes dropped 380 tons of HE bombs and 70,000 incendiaries. Radar-guided night-fighters and 2,000 AA guns fought off the attackers.

Operation Sealion was called off by Hitler on 12 October and, although the night attacks continued, it was now clear that British fighter pilots had broken the back of the Luftwaffe in forcing them to change to night-time bombing. The four-month battle cost the RAF 915 fighters, 481 men killed or missing and 422 wounded. German losses were 1,733 aircraft (British pilots claimed 2,698).

On 4 November the night raids were widened to include industrial centres. On 14 November Coventry was bombed with 600 tons of HE by 500 aircraft. Between 19 and 22 November Birmingham was severely hit, and London once again became the target on 29 December when about 1,500 fires were started. Bombing went on throughout the winter, ports being a chief target as part of the policy of blockading Britain. Over the winter period 15 to 20 German aircraft were destroyed each month, but in 1941 better AA guns, better radar and rocket batteries helped to push the total up so that, by May, 70 Luftwaffe aircraft were shot down in a month. The last incendiary attack on London took place on 10 May and was the most damaging of any single raid. More than 2,000 fires were started and 3,000 people were killed or wounded. Of the raiders 16 aircraft were destroyed, the most shot down during a single night attack throughout the 'Blitz'.

During the official period of the battle German aircraft killed 1,700 and seriously wounded 3,360 people during daylight hours, and killed 12,581 and wounded 16,965 persons, mostly civilians, by night.

Some of the less obvious reasons for the RAF victory were that their pilots had undergone a longer and more sophisticated training period and so were more highly trained; the interchange of knowledge with battle-experienced Polish,

French and Czechoslovak pilots made for less stereotyped tactics; the British aircraft were better armoured with bullet-proof armour in front and behind the cockpit, and mounted 8 machine-guns able to fire 9,600 rounds per minute; and RAF pilots shot down over England could parachute to safety and live to fight again. On both sides the supply of pilots was a deciding factor, and the advent of an increasing number of pilots coming from British communities all over the world was of growing importance. The effect of the searchlights, anti-aircraft guns, balloon barrages, the Royal Observer Corps and other civil defence organisations manned by regulars, the Territorial Army and various volunteer units also played a vital part in the defeat of the Luftwaffe and must not be forgotten when assessing the reasons for victory.

The British had now inflicted on Germany her first major defeat. This was unquestionably one of the decisive battles of history. Five weeks later, all the Nazi military resources were thrown into the invasion of Russia.

BULGE, BATTLE OF THE   see ARDENNES II

BURMA I   Second World War   16 January – 17 May 1942
Fought between the British, Indians and Chinese under Lt-General Thomas Hutton, Lt-General Harold Alexander and Lt-General Joseph Stilwell, US army, and the Japanese under Lt-General Shojiro Iida.
Strength: British 165,000: Burma Corps (Lt-General Sir William Slim) + 17th Indian Division (Major-General John Smyth, Major-General Cowan) + 1st Burma Division (Major-General Bruce Scott) 47,000 + Chinese 5th and 6th Armies (Stilwell) 95,000 + 2 squadrons RAF + American Volunteer Group (Flying Tigers) + area administrative troops, police and paramilitary forces 23,000; Japanese 85,000: 15th Army (Iida) + initially 33 (Lt-General Sharo Sakurai) and 55 (Lt-General Yiroshi Takeuchi) Divisions 35,000, reinforced by 18 and 56 Divisions with extra tanks and artillery 40,000 + 5th Air Division 10,000.
Aim: Britain was still allowing supplies to China to pass along the Burma Road (which had reopened on 18 October 1940) from Rangoon to Lashio and on to Kunming in order to help support China in her war against Japan. The main purposes of the Japanese invasion of Burma were to cut this lifeline through Burma to China and round off her invasion of SE Asia by establishing a western bulwark against any counter-attacks from the west.

When the Japanese seized Thailand in December 1941 it gave them a base from which they could consolidate their thrust south down the Malay peninsula and threaten Burma to the west. At the same time that Lt-General Tomoyuki Yamashita was invading Singapore (qv) the Japanese 15th Army attacked Burma on 16 January 1942. The scratch Anglo-Indian 17th Division opposed the attack but was driven back to the Bilin River with their backs to the Sittang River. On 23 January the Japanese captured the only bridge in the British rear over the mile-wide Sittang and completely routed the British, only 80 officers and 3,404 other ranks getting away over the river on improvised rafts, with 1,420 rifles. Their other arms and equipment were all lost. Hutton ordered the abandonment of Rangoon, but not before a battle-experienced British 7th Armoured Brigade from the Middle East was landed. This gave the British superiority in tanks by numbers, fire-power and armour which was to save the army in Burma.

By this time the Chinese 6th Army (which General Chiang Kai-shek had offered two months earlier but which had been refused by the C-in-C, General Sir Archibald Wavell, for political reasons) entered Burma. The 1st Burma Division was switched from Toungoo, north of Rangoon, to Prome where, with a reconstituted 17th Division and the redoubtable 7th Armoured Brigade, the 1st Burma Corps was formed under General Slim. An attempt by Slim to counter-attack was forestalled by the more aggressive Iida who now had two more divisions, and thus the Burma Corps had repeatedly to withdraw, losing men by battle casualties and disease, as the Japanese, carrying out encircling movements and establishing blocks which only British armour could remove, again and again cut their precarious communications overland to India.

Meanwhile Alexander had been sent out by Winston Churchill, who believed in personalities, to take over the campaign and try to salvage the situation. Hutton was appointed Alexander's Chief of Staff. Alexander had no reserves with which he could influence the battles and his main contribution was to lend an air of calm, composure and common sense to the situation, which prevented the long 1,000 mile retreat from deteriorating into a rout. At the same time Hutton attended to the multifarious administrative problems endemic in such a situation, having to improvise all the time, as no new supplies could now reach the Burma Army.

The Chinese 5th and 6th Armies, whom the Japanese feared most and con-centrated their main strength against, under Chiang Kai-shek's US Chief of Staff General Stilwell (Vinegar Joe), tried to hold the Japanese NE thrust successively at Toungoo, Mandalay and Taunggyi but, lacking tanks, had to retreat rapidly along their long lines of communication to Yunnan in China. They lacked sufficient transport and were unable to live adequately off the land as they were used to do in China, as the British administration tried to prevent their doing so. If they had been allowed in two months earlier it might have been a different picture, but political considerations militated against the idea of Burma being saved by the Chinese. Unfortunately this experience embittered Chiang Kai-shek and soured relations with the British army from 1943 to 1945.

The newly arrived Japanese 18th Division – under Lt-General Renya Mutaguchi, who had captured Singapore – rushed north to take Mandalay, Mogaung and Myitkyina, while the Japanese 56th Division captured the vital town of Lashio on the Burma Road near the Chinese frontier. The last overland supply route to China was now severed. The majority of Chinese divisions filtered back to China, having lost most of their guns and vehicles; but one, encouraged by Stilwell, took the route to Assam. This, the 38th Division under Lt-General Sun Li-jen, was to form the nucleus of an American-trained Chinese force which was later to invade Burma down the Ledo road.

Meanwhile the remnants of Alexander's army, after a last battle at Shwegyn on the Upper Chindwin where a bridgehead against an attack by a Japanese regiment could not be held, resulted in the loss of all except one of the British tanks and most of the remaining artillery. The Burma Corps, wracked by disease and vitamin deficiency if not actual hunger, plodded slowly back in their rags in the drenching rain of the monsoon over the border to India where they expected relief and some praise, only to be told that they must hold the frontier during the monsoon (which was India's most effective defence at that time) as there were no other troops available. Over 400,000 refugees, mostly Indians employed by the British in Burma, fled back along the same route as the Army causing chaos and a virtual breakdown in supply and administration in spite of Herculean efforts by civilian forestry, tea and other firms and the RAF to dump supplies along their line of retreat. Indian-based RAF and USAAF aircraft had evacuated 8,600 wounded and essential staff and technical personnel from inside Burma.

The casualties suffered by the British, Indian and Burmese were 13,000 killed, wounded or missing, 20,000 eventually evacuated sick + 115 aircraft. Over and above these, were 10,000 Burmese who returned to their homes. Chinese casualties were 40,000 killed, wounded, missing or deserted, and 100,000 Indian refugees died as well. Japanese losses were 6,500 killed and wounded. Very many suffered sickness, and the Japanese considered Burma the worst of their fronts for casualties from disease, especially malaria.

The Japanese had now cut off China from her Allies. From this time onwards the Allies' main aim in this theatre was to help keep China in the war, while the Japanese aim was to eliminate her. All other operations such as the military and subversive attacks on India, and naval operations in the Bay of Bengal, were ancillary to this main purpose.

BURMA II   Second World War   1942–5

Fought between the Allies under General Sir Archibald Wavell, Lt-General Joseph (Vinegar Joe) Stilwell, Admiral Lord Louis Mountbatten, General Sir George Giffard, Air Marshal Sir Richard Pierse, Air Marshal Sir John Baldwin, Lt-General Sir Oliver Leese, Lt-General Sir William Slim and General Sun Li-Jen; and the Japanese under Field-Marshal Count Terauchi, Lt-General Shojiro Iida, Lt-General Shozo Kawabe, General Hyotaro Kimura, Lt-General Renya Mutaguchi, Lt-General Masaki Honda and Indian National Army under Subhas Chandra Bhose.

Strength 1943–5: Allies equivalent 27 divisions (British/Indian/African armies): 2 British divisions + 8 Indian divisions + 2 West African divisions + 1 East African division + 2 Indian tank brigades + 2 independent brigades (Parachute and Commandos) + Special Force (Chindits 20,000), equal to 2 light divisions + 1 Lushai brigade – equivalent 17 divisions + reserves and reinforcements in India (Note: each Indian division was composed of about one-third British and two-thirds Indian personnel in which British officers predominated. About half the Indian Battalions were Gurkhas from independent Nepal.) + (Chinese/American): 3 new Divisions (Stilwell on the Ledo road) + 2 new 'armies' in Yunnan

+ Allied air forces 1,000 aircraft with reserves: 3rd Tactical Air Force (TAF under Baldwin) 23 to 30 squadrons + USAAF (not including aircraft used for transport of stores over the 'hump' and in supporting China); Japanese equivalent 13 divisions: 10 divisions (including 49 and 53) + 2 Independent Mixed Brigades (IMB) + 1 Indian National Army (INA) division + 1 Air division (maximum 80 aircraft) (Note: from August 1944, after the arrival of 49th and 53rd Divisions, no further reinforcement reached the Japanese in Burma).

Although the Allies had numerical and material superiority in this theatre their weakness was the majority of their forces were made up of colonial troops of many differing nationalities. Moreover, Britain, the USA and China had differing political aims. And owing to lack of communications, apart from air, it was difficult to apply the Allied strength against the Japanese whose forces were operating ideally on interior lines, while their opponents had to cross mountains or seas from widely and geographically separated places. The Japanese also had the advantage that they were homogeneous, better trained, were more idealogically motivated, were generally in a less disease-ridden area and had a better and more straightforward command set-up. But once the US navy started operating in the S China Seas and the Formosa Straits, the Japanese could not afford to reinforce this front without serious risk. The orders for their forces in Burma were then to tie down as many Allied forces for as long as possible.

The aim of the Allies, as laid down in the Quebec Conference, was not necessarily to drive the Japanese out of Burma but to open up land communication to China through N Burma and Yunnan, with sufficient space south of this road and pipeline to protect it, in order to keep China in the war. The Japanese aim in 1944, after having seen the significance of Major-General Orde Wingate's first Chindit long-range penetration operation into N Burma, was to carry out an active defence of Burma by cutting the communications and destroying the main Allied threat from the 4 Corps area around Imphal. A raid on the Arakan front was to take place as a diversion to draw off reserves to that front prior to the attack on Imphal.

CAMPAIGN 1942–3

Before any overall Allied plans had been made General Wavell was unwilling, when Burma fell, to adopt a purely defensive posture. But a land attack early in 1943 on the port of Akyab, after a seaborne operation had been ruled out for lack of landing craft, proved not only a disaster but that the Indian units taking part, although outnumbering the enemy by 6 to 1, were insufficiently trained and motivated to face the Japanese. At that time there was flood and famine in Bengal which cost the lives of 4 million civilians. Also, on 14 July 1942, the Indian Congress Party under the leadership of Mahatma Gandhi and Pandit Nehru had demanded the immediate total relinquishment of British rule in India, saying that they would prefer to be ruled by the Japanese if they could not be free.

In spite of the imprisonment of Gandhi and other prominent subversive leaders, E India erupted into unprecedented scenes of riot, rebellion and sabotage which required over sixty British and Indian battalions and a total of 100,000 troops to suppress and restore order. At one time all communications to the army facing the Japanese in Burma were cut by Congress civilian saboteurs. So, when first a total of twelve British/Indian battalions supported by six batteries of artillery were held for a period of thirteen weeks from 23 October 1942 to 22 January 1943 by only two Japanese battalions and then nine British/Indian brigades (twenty-seven battalions), initially under Major-General Lloyd and then under General Slim, were defeated, with a loss of 5,000 battle casualties, by eight battalions under Lt-General Takishi Koga and driven right back on to Cox's Bazaar (21 February– 11 May), Wavell became all too aware that his forces were not yet ready to take on the Japanese. As the official British history states: 'The morale of the troops was generally poor and in some units very low.' There was consequently a sorting out of senior officers and Wavell, at the instigation of a very angry Prime Minister, Winston Churchill, appointed a special committee to 'enquire into and report on the readiness for war of British and Indian infantry battalions in India, and to make recommendations for improvement'.

Later Wavell was appointed Viceroy of India to stiffen civilian morale. General Sir Claude Auchinlech was appointed Commander-in-Chief to improve India as a base and training area and to raise a new model Indian army; and Admiral Lord Louis Mountbatten was appointed Supreme Commander of all forces (British, Chinese and US).

However, there was a ray of hope for the ill-trained army in India. In early 1942, as the British were retreating the 1,000 miles from Moulmein to India, Wavell, who as C-in-C Middle East had sent Wingate into Abyssinia (EAST AFRICA) knew his worth and fully appreciated what he had achieved against odds, dis-patched him into Burma to carry out a reconnaissance to report on the possibility of organising guerilla activity against the Japanese. Wingate travelled extensively throughout Burma and visited China, following which he wrote in his report to Wavell that the time was not yet ripe for guerilla warfare against the Japanese as there was neither the will amongst the people of Burma who were apathetic, nor any willingness or resolution amongst the civil and military authorities en-gaged in the retreat and evacuation of that country, to adopt such a course. So Wavell called Wingate back and ordered him to train a brigade of sufficient strength to carry out long-range penetration raids into territory where it was not possible to rely on the local inhabitants for support. Such a force would be supplied by air. The far-seeing and offensive-minded C-in-C anticipated that, with communications so bad throughout the area of his command, the extensive use of air supply and air support would be the only means whereby the war could be waged on land in other than a defensive way. Wavell's military and civilian advisers in India were constantly advocating that only a defensive rôle was possible, whereas Churchill was urging him to fight back against the Japanese.

So when news of the repeated failure of British/Indian forces in the Arakan became known, Wavell felt it necessary to try and retrieve the situation and raise morale by dispatching Wingate's 77th Indian Infantry Brigade (17th Kings [Liverpool] Regiment, 3/2nd Gurkha Rifles and a detachment of Burma Rifles, 142 Commando Company and RAF) to raid into N Burma, cutting Japanese lines of communication wherever possible. A further reason for Wavell's decision was that he considered it essential to mask from the Japanese in Burma the great weakness in morale of his forces in India caused by Congress subversion, interruptions in training while units were employed on a counter-insurgency rôle and the breakdown in internal communication. Wingate's troops were neither volunteers nor high grade and consisted of a British second-line battalion from Liverpool and a very young and inexperienced Gurkha battalion reinforced by hurriedly trained Gurkha muleteers. 142 Commando, recruited mostly from officers and men who had seen active service either during the retreat from Burma or the Middle East, were the only experienced troops in the brigade, but they numbered only 100 out of the total brigade strength of about 3,000.

In the middle of February 1943 the brigade advanced on a wide front over the Chindwin in seven columns (3 British, 4 Gurkha), each about 400 strong including 100 mules and 18 horses per column. Although one Gurkha column suffered a disaster early on and was dispersed, the remainder successfully attacked the main Burma railway from Mandalay to the north, blowing bridges across a length of 100 miles of rail and attacking garrison troops. Wingate who, with a tactical headquarters, took part in the raid, found it difficult to maintain control of the columns. After the attacks on the railway, six of the columns crossed the 1,000-yard-wide Irrawaddy River and reached an area within attacking distance of the Burma Road before General Mutaguchi, who had been put in charge of the counter-penetration operation, organised sufficient units to pen the Chindit columns in between the Shweli and Irrawaddy Rivers. General Wingate ordered a dispersal and a return to India. Most of the columns successfully carried out deliberate dispersal drill as taught in training and escaped through the net in small parties, which included crossing the Irrawaddy. One column made its way to Yunnan in China. A number of widely dispersed small actions took place throughout N Burma as these forces made their way back the 200 miles to the river Chindwin where they expected help from 4th Indian Corps as was planned. Unaccountably, 4th Indian Corps had retreated and the line of the Chindwin was held by the Japanese. Of the 818 Chindits who were killed, wounded, captured or failed to return (some of the Burma Rifles returned to their homes) half were caught while crossing the Chindwin where they thought they were safe under the surveillance of the Indian army. The average distance that they had marched through enemy territory was 1,500 miles.

Just when, owing to the failure in Arakan, morale was at its lowest in India and British, American and Chinese relations were most strained, news of this raid was published. The main results of this were a rise in the morale of the British/Indian troops who felt that they too could emulate the actions of this not very special brigade. It was proved that air supply could be trusted as a means of complete subsistence without any ground communications being necessary. Many commanders who had doubted Wingate's tactical and strategical views were now converted and desired to emulate his offensive example. But the greatest effect was on General Renya Mutaguchi who admired Wingate and his exploits. He successfully persuaded General Iida, at that time Commander of Burma Area, that he should carry out a similar operation against the three divisions of 4 Corps dependent on the vulnerable Imphal–Dinapur road. When Kawabe replaced Iida, Mutaguchi succeeded, against the advice of the Japanese air force, in persuading him that such an operation against the Allied communications running parallel to the Burma frontier was possible.

The result was that in March 1944 while Wingate, having landed most of his twenty battalions by air, operated against the spokes of the Japanese communications spreading out from Mandalay to three of the four Japanese fronts, Mutaguchi also crossed the Chindwin with three divisions to cut 4th Indian Corps communications. Meanwhile, in the north, General Stilwell had retrained and re-equipped three Chinese divisions with which he advanced slowly down the Ledo valley from Assam while his chief engineer built an all-weather road behind him. The destination of that road was China.

1944 CAMPAIGN IN BURMA – AIR WARFARE

It is a matter for consideration as to whether the 1944 campaign in Burma should not come under the category of air warfare, since without the operation of the 3rd Tactical Air Force, under Air Marshal Sir John Baldwin who commanded all aircraft including fighters, bombers and transports supporting Slim's 14th Army, the Allies could scarcely have operated at all and would certainly never have won a battle. These air forces, besides the overwhelming RAF component, included the American Colonel Philip Cochrane's No 1 Air Commando (Mustangs, B25s, Mitchells, DC3 transports, Waco gliders, L1 and L3 liaison and ambulance light aircraft), some Dutch units, the embryo Royal Indian Air Force and units of the USAAF. These latter were mainly concerned with the resupply of China over the 'hump' and supporting Stilwell's Chinese forces. This air force rescued Allied ground forces when cut off in the Arakan by transporting 5th Division reinforcements and air supply to the area; flew in the 77th Brigade into Burma by glider; flew in 18,000 Chindits and 3,000 mules, guns and stores to create defended bases behind the Japanese lines from which they could attack communications; flew divisions from Arakan into the Imphal plain and flew out over 50,000 civilians and other useless mouths from Imphal; supplied nearly all these forces by air; kept the air clear of Japanese intruders; evacuated thousands of sick and wounded who would otherwise have undoubtedly died; and carried out very many air strikes against the enemy and their material. Certain Japanese consider that the air force caused as many casualties against their ground troops as the Allied infantry divisions themselves inflicted. Undoubtedly the Allied army could not have operated without the 3rd TAF despite the fact the Japanese air threat by early 1944 was negligible, consisting of less than 80 aircraft.

1944 LAND BATTLES – ARAKAN

In the Arakan, 15 Corps under Lt-General Sir Philip Christison was deployed with the 15th Indian Division on the coastal strip and the 7th Indian Division (Messervy) further west as far as the Mayu River. The 81st W African Division had been sent on a rather vague flanking movement down the Kaladan valley farther to the east. On 26 January 1944 5th Division attacked Rabazil and Christison moved his heavy artillery over the main range to support 7th Division which, supported by tanks, was due to attack Buthidaung. Christison's opponent was Lt-General Hanaya commanding 55th Division. He had been given the task of carrying out the 'Ha-Go' plan whose object was to draw the Allied reserves to the Arakan front before the 'U-Go' offensive against 4 Corps on the Imphal plain was set in motion. Hanaya's immediate plan was to penetrate behind the 7th Division, cut its communications, destroy it and then do the same to the 5th Division. He sent one company to keep 81st W African Division occupied.

Hanaya had no armour, medium artillery or air supply and his artillery was on a pack basis. He started his attack on 3 February 1944 when Major-General Sakurai with 5,000 men advanced through the 114th Indian Brigade, turned left and cut all the communications of 7th Division. In five days Sakurai had also cut 5th Division communications but failed to capture the 'Administrative Box' from which Hanaya hoped to replenish his supplies. The two Indian divisions were placed on air supply while the reserve 26th Division was ordered to move forward. At this juncture Slim, who was now commanding the newly formed 14th Army (which included Stilwell and Wingate's forces besides those at Imphal and the Arakan), took a hand. He ordered 5th and 7th Divisions to stay where they were and then launched as many troops as possible to their aid. Besides 26th Division the British 36th Division and the Indian 25th Division were brought in, supported by a Commando brigade and a Parachute brigade. Hanaya's one division was now faced with six divisions (5th, 7th, 25th, 26th, 36th and 81st) plus two brigades and tanks. Hanaya, having achieved his object of attracting the 14th Army's reserves to the Arakan, with the approval of the army headquarters, started to withdraw to Akyab on 24 February, after inflicting on 15 Corps 3,506 casualties compared to less than 1,000 of his own. The RAF delivered 2,710 tons of supplies to the beleaguered divisions and carried out 714 close air-support sorties.

1944 CHINDIT AIRBORNE LONG-RANGE PENETRATION OPERATIONS

The Allies were not deterred by the Japanese Arakan offensive from carrying out their own offensive on the lines laid down at the Quebec Conference. As Stilwell advanced down the Ledo road with three Chinese divisions assisted by his own short-range penetration brigade, the Merrill's Marauders, it was planned that Wingate's brigades would fly in by glider and transport aircraft, form bases, and cut all the lines of communication to the Japanese facing Stilwell. Originally the plan was to use only two brigades at a time (Wingate had trained six of these large four-battalion brigades totalling seventeen British, four Gurkha and three W African battalions plus artillery and support troops) and for an Indian division to be flown in to hold an air base at Indaw from which two brigades would permanently operate for two months at a time.

The first two brigades, 77th (Brigadier Michael Calvert) and 111th (Brigadier Joe Lentaigne) were flown in successfully after losing some casualties on the first day owing to changes of plan because one of the dropping zones was blocked. Meanwhile 16th Brigade (Brigadier Bernard Fergusson) marched in on a route parallel to the Ledo road and seized Lonkin in order to protect Stilwell's flanks, and then marched south towards Indaw. Calvert, having first installed an air base in a fairly remote area which he named Broadway, as soon as the remainder of his brigade arrived, formed a block named White City, at Mawlu on the railway, overcoming all Japanese opposition after a brisk fight which included a bayonet charge. Lentaigne's force landing in another area were inadvertently split and those east of the Irrawaddy reinforced Calvert's other commitment, to block the Bhamo–Myitkyina road 100 miles farther east. With the forces that he had managed to get over the Irrawaddy, Lentaigne's job was to cut the railway south of Indaw airfield to hold up Japanese reinforcements coming from the south while 16th Brigade attacked Indaw. However, Lentaigne's brigade had had a setback in crossing the Irrawaddy and was unable to carry out this task. The result was the Japanese quickly gathered six battalions, which formed the 24th Independent Mixed Brigade (IMB) for the defence of Indaw and the railway. Lt-General Masakuzu Kawabe, Commander Burma Area Army, also took three battalions from each of three divisions (one from the U-Go offensive against Imphal which was just about to start) to attempt to drive out the airborne raiders. Although the airborne operation began on the night 5/6 March, it was only a fortnight later that Kawabe had realised the full extent of it. So by 4 April Kawabe sent the 24th IMB (six battalions) and the 4th Infantry Regiment (four battalions) under Major-General Hyashi to the Indaw area to defeat the Chindits and to clear 18th Division's communications to Mogaung and Myitkyina. He also dispatched a further two battalions to eradicate the air base of Broadway and the Chindit guerillas operating on the Bhamo road. In a series of battles between 4 April and 1 May all these Japanese forces were decisively defeated and virtually destroyed by the Chindits. In the greatest of these engagements in which altogether ten British, Gurkha and W African battalions from different brigades engaged and which took place in and around the well dug-in and wired White City railway block which was supported with artillery, mortars and machine-guns and unlimited quantities of ammunition, as they were supplied by air, Hyashi's forces attacked every night for ten days. But in each case his attacks were repulsed. On the single occasion that he did penetrate the wire, he was driven out by a counter-attack. After ten days Calvert was ordered to form a four-battalion counter-attack force and assault the enemy in the rear. He formed a temporary base across Hyashi's communications and drove at Hyashi's rear, pinning his battalions against the wire of White City. Then, in a soldiers' battle, but with great support from No 1 Air Commando, the Chindits virtually destroyed the Independent Mixed Brigade as a fighting force. Their remnants retired to Indaw and beyond.

Japanese losses over the whole Chindit area amounted to over 8,000, including Hyashi who was killed in a last fanatical charge against White City's barbed wire. The Chindits lost 1,100 men who were not replaced. Their greatest loss was that of their leader, Wingate himself, who was killed on 24 March in an air crash on a fine night in India after he had been visiting Air Marshal Baldwin at Imphal to co-ordinate air and ground operations against Japanese communications. Sabotage was suspected but never proved.

However, the Chindits fought on. After an initial repulse 16th Brigade walked over the undefended Indaw air-strip, but by now the Japanese U-Go operation was fully extending Slim's forces in the Imphal area and there were no troops available to fly in to hold Indaw except some reserve Chindit brigades which were originally intended to relieve the first brigades. 14th Brigade and the W African Brigade were flown in and Fergusson's tired 16th Brigade flown out. 14th Brigade was directed to operate against the communications of the Japanese divisions attacking Imphal and Kohima, as was the reconstituted 111th Infantry Brigade. These two brigades were so successful in cutting communications to 31st Division operating against Kohima that its Commander, Lt-General Saito, asked Mutaguchi whether he could call off the offensive altogether as his communications were cut and his men were so short of both food and ammunition that they were starting to eat their supply mules. On receiving this request Mutaguchi promptly fired Saito.

At this time Mutaguchi's offensive was still in full swing, but he had relied on 53rd Division, due into Burma in April, as a reinforcement to keep up the momentum of his attack. But Kawabe was more concerned with what the airborne forces were doing close to his headquarters in Burma. So, after Hyashi's failure and death at Mawlu, Kawabe ordered 53rd Division (Lt-General K. Takeda) north to clear the railway as far as Mogaung and to assist 18th Division to resist Stilwell's advance. The remnants of the 24th IMB were put under his command, but he used them to protect his rear as he advanced. So Mutaguchi went without his reinforcements and faced defeat at Imphal. By this time Major-General Lentaigne, Wingate's successor, had decided that the Chindits' gains could not be held during the approaching monsoon, so Slim placed the Chindits directly under Stilwell's command to assist him to capture his two objectives, Mogaung and Myitkyina. Therefore, when Takeda mounted attacks on White City and Broadway, he found that they were booby-trapped and deserted as Calvert had moved his forces north. A reconstituted 111th Brigade (Brigadier John Masters) installed a new block (Blackpool) in the railway valley near Hopin, south of Mogaung. But before Masters had time to get settled Takeda launched the full strength of his 53rd Division at Blackpool and, after five days of heavy fighting, chased the Chindits out of the valley. Calvert was then ordered to capture Mogaung, which was now held by a regiment of 53rd Division, but, owing to casualties and disease and having sent reinforcements to other brigades, his strength was now only 2,000. Following three weeks' methodical attack in monsoon conditions, and after suffering another 1,000 battle casualties and many more from disease, though supported by lavish aid from the USAAF, 77th Brigade captured Stilwell's objective, Mogaung, on 26 June with the last-minute help of a Chinese regiment. Other Chindit brigades moved into the railway valley south of Mogaung and exploited the success.

Meanwhile Brigadier Morris's Chindit forces east of Myitkyina had ambushed many Japanese columns on the Bhamo road and finally closed it, thus materially assisting in the final capture of Myitkyina in August. By August all the Chindit forces had been withdrawn, having captured one of Stilwell's objectives, helped in the capture of Myitkyina and, for a long while, put out of action all communications to 31st Division at Kohima. Their operations had drawn off over twenty battalions (including 53rd Division) and half the Japanese air force from the main fronts on the Ledo road and at Imphal, besides cutting the Japanese communications to these fronts. This was all at a cost of about 5,000 killed, wounded and missing, 3,800 of which occurred after Wingate's death when Lentaigne was forced by Stilwell to use the lightly armed Chindits as assault troops against Japanese defended positions.

THE N BURMA FRONT

Stilwell, who after long years of experience in China thoroughly believed in the fighting capabilities of the Chinese troops, had in E Assam organised and trained three European-sized Chinese divisions which were superbly equipped, with the object of their opening a road and pipeline to their compatriots in Yunnan. Against all criticism and opposition Stilwell slowly forced his way down the Ledo valley towards Kamaing, using Brigadier-General Frank Merrill's all-American regiment of Marauders, who had trained with the Chindits, to carry out short-range hooks behind the regiments of the Japanese 18th Division confronting him. When Mutaguchi advanced on Kohima and the American lines of communication in the Brahmaputra valley were threatened, Stilwell ceased to advance and offered to assist Slim. But by this time the Chindit closure of the 18th Division's communication and consequent weakening of their opposition encouraged Stilwell to continue his advance.

After the capture of Kamaing Stilwell, using his Marauders, seized Myitkyina airfield on 17 May 1944 and flew in his 30th Chinese (New) Division, but was unable to capture Myitkyina town which was defended by 3,000 resolute Japanese. In spite of repeated attacks by 30,000 Chinese they held out until 3 August, causing the Allies 5,383 casualties. But by December 1944 Stilwell, who had received the British 36th Division in exchange for the exhausted and depleted Chindits who had been flown out, had achieved his objective and the road from India to China was open with the construction of an oil pipeline alongside being hurried on. This was more of a morale-booster than of material benefit to the Chinese, and it kept them in the war which they had threatened to leave to the Allies. Total Chinese–American losses in the northern front were 14,945 of which 1,327 were American.

THE IMPHAL–KOHIMA BATTLE – 5 MARCH–30 JUNE 1944

As the first glider of Calvert's 77th Brigade crossed the Chindwin River on the night of 5/6 March 1944 the advance guards of the Japanese 33rd, 15th and 31st Divisions were crossing the same river in boats, only in the opposite direction. General Mutaguchi's great gamble to destroy the three divisions of the 4th Indian Corps before the reinforcements, which had been deflected to the Arakan, could relieve them, had started.

Mutaguchi's plan was for 33rd Division to cross at Kalemyo and to cut off the 17th Indian Division (Major-General Cowan) in the hills around Tiddim, while his tanks would advance north on a fair-weather road to Tamu to assist 15th Division to capture Imphal. The 15th Division was ordered to cross the Chindwin in the Sittaung–Thaungdut area and advance direct on Imphal. Saito's 31st Division was given the hardest task of all and so was on an all-pack basis. Its job was to advance from Homalin–Tamanthi on the Chindwin, across the roadless 7,000-feet mountain ranges and cut the Dinapore–Imphal road at Kohima. Mutaguchi's 15th Army totalled 84,280 Japanese and 7,000 Indians. He also received 4,000 reinforcements during the campaign.

The whole operation was a gamble, as only three weeks' supply of food was dumped forward, and this invasion into India relied on the Allied rations dumps falling into Japanese hands. If the Japanese failed to capture these supplies within three weeks and the British/Indian units could hold out, the operation was doomed to failure. Mutaguchi, having defeated the British in Malaya, Singapore (qqv) and Burma several times, underestimated the British capacity for renewal and British tenacity. Owing to air superiority and air supply the Allied forces could hold out so long as their nerve lasted, and his gamble was bound to fail.

The Japanese 33rd Division failed to destroy 17th Division which, after giving the Japanese a hard knock, escaped adroitly to the Imphal plain ready to fight again. 15th Division forced back 23rd Infantry Division but received as many casualties as they inflicted and achieved no lasting result. The 31st Division reached Kohima and cut the road but was unable to capture the village because of the courageous resistance of a scratch British force which held out until Lt-General Stopford's 33 Corps relieved it. By early April 4 Corps under Lt-General Geoffrey Scoones, with its road communications to India cut, was defending the Imphal plain. Lord Louis Mountbatten took some US aircraft off the 'hump' route to China and flew in 5th Division from the Arakan to reinforce Scoones. So by mid-April Slim, commanding the 14th Army, who had underestimated the strength and momentum of the Japanese attack, had four divisions and two tank brigades (155,000 troops) under Scoones in the Imphal plain and the newly formed 33 Corps under Stopford starting its advance from Dinapore, with parts of Wingate's airborne force cutting Mutaguchi's communications in the hills east of the Chindwin. He also had twenty-three invaluable squadrons of Baldwin's 3rd TAF supporting him. He was faced with Mutaguchi's three divisions, an INA brigade and a few tanks.

During the next few weeks Scoone's division which, with their preponderance of tanks and artillery, were much stronger than the Japanese when the battle reached the plains, fought off the attacks by 33rd and 15th Divisions and prevented them getting any supplies, while Stopford's 33 Corps, headed by the well-trained British 2nd Division (Major-General J. M. L. Glover) forced its way slowly up and down the 140 miles of road, over passes up to 5,000 feet to the relief of Imphal. A Chindit brigade under Brigadier Lancelot Perowne was sent out on the east flank further to threaten the 31st Division's communications back to the Chindwin and to try and capture Ukhrul. By this time the Japanese were suffering severely from lack of food and ammunition and all three divisional commanders had been dismissed by Mutaguchi for complaining. On 22 June Stopford's 33 Corps joined up with Scoones's 4 Corps at Milestone 109, just north of the Imphal plain. The Japanese thrust had been defeated. The monsoon having broken, disease, lack of supplies and a continued onslaught by the RAF were to complete the defeat.

Mutaguchi's 15th Army lost 30,502 men killed, died of wounds, sickness or starvation. Most of the remaining 60,000 were wounded or suffering from disease and malnutrition and many died later. British and Indian casualties totalled 16,700 (a few more than Stilwell on the northern front), of which about a quarter had been lost in the Kohima battle. At the same time the Chindits at the hub of the Japanese communications had lost 5,100.

The part the air forces played in this victory was invaluable. Between 18 April and 30 June 18,824 tons of stores and 25,000 men were flown to Imphal and 13,000 casualties and 43,000 non-combatants were evacuated. In addition 1,540 transport sorties were flown to resupply units in the field by parachute. Between 10 March and 30 July the RAF fighter bombers of Baldwin's 3rd TAF flew 18,860 sorties in support of the troops on the ground and the USAAF flew 10,800, at a loss of 130 RAF and 40 USAAF aircraft. During the same period the JAAF flew only 1,750 sorties on this front. In no land battle to date had the air forces played a greater part in a victory. Air Marshal Sir John Baldwin, who commanded all the aircraft taking part in the Imphal operations, was originally an 8th Hussar before joining the Royal Flying Corps in the First World War. Later he became Colonel Commandant of the Hussars. He had previously bombed Cologne in 1918 and led the 1,000-bomber raid on Cologne in 1942, the most senior RAF officer to go on a bombing raid. His services to the nation went largely unrecognised and unrewarded, as he had a cavalryman's habit of expressing his opinions forthrightly.

ADVANCE INTO BURMA – DECEMBER 1944

After Stilwell's capture of Mogaung and Myitkyina and Slim's defeat of the Japanese 15th Army at Imphal, Chiang Kai-shek allowed his 1st and 6th New Armies on the Salween to advance under Stilwell's command into Burma. Facing Stilwell was the Japanese 33rd Army consisting of the 18th and 56th Divisions, the newly arrived 49th Division and the 24th IMB, of which only the 49th had not been depleted by casualties. In fact the 33rd Army's total strength was only 25,400. Stilwell had six Chinese divisions, the British 36th Division and Mar's Task Force (475th Infantry and 124th US Cavalry Regiments), totalling about 150,000. Supplied by the USAAF, this Allied force pushed back the Japanese 33rd Army, 36th Division going down the railway from Mogaung as far as Wuntho and the Chinese/Americans capturing Bhamo to open a direct route to China.

Owing to weather conditions and a rather ponderous reorganisation procedure in order to relieve divisions in the line, Slim's 14th Army was slow to follow up the Japanese 15th Army and, by the time Slim had reached the Chindwin River on 1 December, the Japanese flanks of their new position on the Zibyutaung-dan range, between the railway and the Chindwin, were threatened by the British 36th Division advancing from the north. Slim had worked out a plan called 'Capital' to capture Mandalay from the north, but this was now outdated. So he put into action a turning movement called 'Extended Capital', whose main purpose was to seize the road/rail junction of Meiktila in central Burma and south of Mandalay while 19th Division attacked Mandalay from the north.

At this juncture the British forces were irretrievably weakened by a decision in London to repatriate all soldiers who had been over three years and eight months overseas. This meant the virtual destruction of the British 2nd and 36th Divisions and of the Chindits. Before dissolution the 2nd Division was, however, to cross the Chindwin SW of Mandalay and materially to assist in its capture, while 4 Corps (Lt-General Frank Messervy) and 17th and 7th Divisions, with tanks, completed the bold turning and capture of Meiktila. Messervy, after a good fight and making·the maximum use of his overwhelming superiority of tanks in good tank country, captured Meiktila and quickly swept the area south of Mandalay. Mandalay fell a few days later.

The Japanese opposition had not been strong before the attack on Mandalay and Meiktila, the total strength of the divisions forming 15th Army being respectively: 53rd Division, 4,500; 31st Division, 7,000; 33rd Division, 5,400; and 15th Division, 4,500. This made a total of 21,400. Moreover they had only about one-third of establishment strength of artillery and were short of ammunition. For the attack on Mandalay and Meiktila Slim's 14th Army of six divisions and two tank brigades with ancillary troops east of the Chindwin numbered 260,000. But in this difficult country the skill lay in being able to apply strength at the right place at the right time. Air supply made this possible.

OPERATIONS ON THE ARAKAN COAST OF BURMA

The Japanese, owing more to being unable to switch their forces elsewhere rather than for strategic reasons, had a still unbeaten 28th Army between Akyab and Rangoon, consisting of 54th and 55th Divisions and the 72nd IMB. Christison's 15 Corps, comprising 25th and 26th Indian Divisions, 81st and 82nd W African Divisions, 3rd Commando Brigade (1, 5, 42, and 44 Commandos) and one E African brigade, totalling 130,000 men, faced these depleted Japanese forces. The landings at Akyab, Myebon and Kangaw, supported by powerful air and naval support, prevented the Japanese 28th Army from disengaging, crossing into the Irrawaddy plain, and assisting in the defence of Rangoon. The British Commandos under Brigadier Campbell Hardy, were at the forefront of the landings and had an especially severe engagement at Kangaw, where Lieutenant George Knowland was posthumously awarded the Victoria Cross. During all these operations 15 Corps lost 1,150 killed, 3,500 wounded.

FALL OF RANGOON – 3 MAY 1945

After the capture of Mandalay and Meiktila by the 14th Army and after Stilwell's forces had cleared the Burma road from Mandalay to the Chinese border, all that remained was for the 14th Army to divide into two (4 and 33 Corps) and to follow the two main routes south to Rangoon, clearing away opposition as they went. For this purpose the force was reduced in strength, put on wheels and on an air-supply basis. In the meantime, after the Gurkha Parachute Brigade had landed at Elephant Point to clear the way for a seaborne attack, 26th Division sailed up the Irrawaddy delta and occupied Rangoon unopposed on 3 May 1945. Advancing north from Rangoon, elements of 26th Division met the vanguard of Messervy's 4 Corps at the end of its 350-mile journey south at Hlegu on 4 May 1945.

All that was left was to mop up the Japanese forces in Burma. Only a small proportion of the original eleven Japanese divisions escaped over the Sittang River. This was the greatest land defeat the Japanese had suffered during this war. A naval force consisting of the battleships *Queen Elizabeth* and *Richelieu*, escort carriers *Empress* and *Shah*, cruisers *Cumberland*, *Suffolk* and *Ceylon* and 6 destroyers supported the seaborne landing on Rangoon.

The British Commonwealth portion of the Allied Land Forces at the beginning of 1945, after many of the British and African troops had been sent home, consisted of 127,139 British, 581,548 Indians (including Gurkhas), 44,988 E Africans, 59,878 W Africans and 158,275 civilian labourers, totalling 971,828.

Statistics of Indian army troops in 1944 as calculated for the government of India budget:

Troops allotted to SE Asia	1,050,000
Defence of India	300,000
Training formation and establishments	520,000
Staffs of arsenals, depots etc	480,000
Indian state forces	100,000
TOTAL	2,450,000
Troops in European theatres	200,000
GRAND TOTAL	2,650,000

CASUALTIES IN BURMA 1942–5

At the beginning of the campaign casualties from disease, mainly malaria, outnumbered battle casualties by more than 100 to 1. At no time, even during the Imphal battles, were they less than 20 to 1. The Japanese suffered as badly from disease.

Total British Commomwealth battle casualties in the army in the campaign in Burma 1942–5:

	Killed	Wounded	Missing	Total
Officers	947	1,837	307	3,091
British other ranks*	5,037	10,687	2,507	18,231
Indian other ranks	8,235	28,873	8,786	45,894
African other ranks	858	3,208	200	4,266
Burmese other ranks	249	126	3,052†	3,427
TOTAL	15,326	44,731	14,852	74,909

* Figures do not include Royal Marine Commandos.
† Many Burmese soldiers on the retreat simply returned to their homes in Burma.

Casualties among Indian and Africans were comparatively small, as the British dared not ask too much of them in case India (or the Colonies) might want to opt out of the war. This affected all strategic as well as tactical decisions and slowed down the campaign. Without appreciating this factor and the political situation in India, coupled with problems of geography, weather, lack of landing craft and disease, it is not possible fully to understand the British difficulty in fighting the campaign in Burma.

Although the Indian soldiers were as brave as any they were subject to subversive propaganda not only directed against the British but to spare themselves for a possible communal war after the Japanese war had ceased. The problem the Allies had in Asia was to keep not only China in the war but also India.

Comparison of total British casualties:
These figures, which include Rhodesia and Newfoundland, cover the 1939–45 war and casualties in the war against Japan. They are taken from the *Statistical Digest of the War* prepared by the Central Statistical Office in 1947. The average total British manpower in army, navy and air force in 1944 = 4½ million males.

	Killed, and missing believed killed		
	Throughout whole war	Against Japan	Percentage of total of those killed against Japan
Royal Navy	46,911	3,847	8.2%
Army	121,484	22,595	18.7%
Royal Air Force	66,080	3,526	5.3%
TOTAL	234,475	29,968	12.8%
Merchant Navy	28,748	1,500	5.3%
GRAND TOTAL	263,223	31,468	12.4%

CAUCASUS (USSR)   Second World War   12 May 1942 – 15 March 1943
Fought between the Russians and the Germans.

After the initial German offensive into Russia, they held a front 1,500 miles long deep inside Russian territory, their only withdrawals being minor movements to the west. The Russian winter and counter-attacks had caused so many casualties by the following spring, however, that a further German advance all along their front, as had been undertaken the previous year, was unattractive. The Germans therefore decided to concentrate their efforts in the south on Stalingrad (Volgograd) (qv) and the Russian oilfields in the Caucasus. German armies stood along the Donetz and Mius Rivers in this sector, the Mius line being the most advanced into Russian territory, 50 miles from Rostov, the gateway to the Caucasus. Army Group 'A' was specially formed for the attack into the Caucasus. It was commanded by General Siegmund List – who was soon to be relieved. A new Army Group 'B' stood to the north, forming a guard on the left flank. It was commanded by General Maximilian von Weichs, who replaced General Fedor von Bock on 13 July.

The Germans were pre-empted in their attack, however, by Marshal Semyon Timoshenko, who assaulted Kharkov on 12 May. The Russian advance was slow, however, and the German 17th Army counter-attacked five days later, regaining all lost ground and taking 80,000 prisoners by 31 May. This Russian attack, because it had committed too many troops too early, opened the way for the Germans to attack eastwards.

On 22 June the German left wing advanced from Kursk towards Voronezh on the Don River. To the south, General Hermann Hoth's 4th Panzer Army reached the bend in the Don 100 miles from the starting point at the beginning of July. This force then turned SE, moving down the corridor formed by the Don and Donetz Rivers, spearheading General Friedrich von Paulus's 6th Army which was making for Stalingrad. The 4th Panzer Army screened General Paul von Kleist's 1st Panzers which enabled him to launch the principal German thrust. From near Kharkov the fifteen divisions of the army moved SE to cross the Lower Don above Rostov on 22 July. South and west of the Donetz, the German 17th Army moved east to come up on Kleist's right and support his advance. On 27 July Rostov fell to the Germans. The Russians blew up a dam on the Manych River, east of the Don, but the Panzers crossed the flooded river nonetheless, after which Kleist's Panzers moved south in three columns between the Black and Caspian Seas.

The most westerly oilfields at Maikop were reached by the right (W) column on 9 August, 200 miles from Rostov. The other two columns moved on to the Caucasus foothills, 150 miles SE of Maikop. Just beyond that point lay an opening to the whole of the Middle East. At this juncture the advance slowed, first because fuel for the tanks became increasingly difficult to get hold of, and second because the fierce fighting around Stalingrad drew in some of Kleist's strength, some motorised troops, the Flak Corps and nearly all of his air force.

The Germans also had an exposed flank between Stalingrad and the Caspian which had to be protected. General Ivan Iyulenev, directing Russian resistance, increased the pressure and 800 bombers started to attack the Panzer divisions. Kleist failed to cross the Terek River and was compelled to force a passage further down-stream (E) at Mozdok. By 18 November the front was stabilised and the Panzers had ceased to be of such tactical importance. Novorossisk, to the west, was taken on 11 September but 90 miles farther on into the Caucasus the seaward flank of the 17th Army came to a halt at Tuapse. Kleist assumed command of the Army Group 'A' on 22 November and this force remained exposed in the Caucasus throughout December; but in January the Russians launched a counter-attack down the Don River which threatened to cut off the Germans' retreat. The Germans began to retreat. The Russians arrived at Rostov when the Germans were still 390 miles SE under heavy pressure from General Ivan Maslennikov's pursuit.

General Erich von Manstein's Army Group Don (later called Army Group South), with the aid of Kleist, managed to hold Rostov open until 14 February by which time Kleist had withdrawn across the Lower Don, for which success he was promoted Field-Marshal. A small German force, the only one left in the Caucasus, held a bridgehead at Novorossisk. West of the Don, the Germans still found themselves endangered by General Georgi Zhukov's advance. South from Stalingrad, where a pincer movement had taken place, came General Nikolai Vatutin's armies which had crossed the Donetz at Izyum on 5 February.

From the Upper Don General Filip Golikov had moved west to Kursk on 7 February and the two forces combined to take the town on 16 February. An early thaw slowed the Russians down and gave Manstein time to regroup the 9th Panzer and 12th Infantry Divisions in the Stalingrad sector and launch a counter-attack. General Gunther von Kluge's Army Group Central helped in this design and the armies fought their way north to retake Kharkov once more on 15 March. At this time the Germans also became prey to the thaw on the steppes and the offensive collapsed. Except for continued guerilla activity the entire front now quietened down until midsummer.

The Caucasus was the one front where the Russians had had time to prepare 'stay behind' guerilla activity in a well-organised manner. About 200,000 irregular Partisans operated against the German communications on this front from sanctuaries which the Germans could not penetrate. For instance, a total area of 1 million square kilometres was devoid of German presence. The operation of these well-armed guerillas was an essential part of the Russian planned withdrawal. The Germans formed a special infantry corps, armoured division, police regiments and security divisions to compete with these guerilla forces which, although losing heavily, reduced the efficiency of German communications by about 75 per cent and caused a high proportion of men to be used up every night on static defence. More than on any other front the Partisans of the Kuban, with their tradition of irregular warfare fully exploited, played a decisive part in the defeat of the Germans and their Allies.

CEYLON   Second World War   5–6 April 1942
Fought between the Allies under Admiral Sir James Somerville and the Japanese under Admiral Chuichi Nagumo.

Because of Japanese successes in the S China and Java Seas, the British were forced to build up their Eastern Fleet. On 24 March, Somerville arrived at Colombo, Ceylon. The former Commander of Force H at Gibraltar was to direct defensive operations in the Indian Ocean.

On 5 April the Japanese took a strong force, including 5 aircraft carriers and 4 battleships, into the Bay of Bengal and attacked Colombo with 80 dive-bombers. Nagumo, who had led the attack on Pearl Harbor (qv), was in command and the port was damaged while a destroyer and an armed merchant cruiser were both sunk. In this engagement 21 Japanese aircraft were lost and 19 British fighters and 6 naval aircraft were shot down. The attack widened later in the day when the British cruisers *Dorsetshire* and *Cornwall*, lying south of Ceylon, were attacked by waves of bombers. Both ships went down within fifteen minutes with a loss of 29 officers and 395 men. The rest of the fleet was fortunately at sea between Ceylon and Port T, Addu Atoll, 600 miles SW of the island. The Japanese attack was renewed on 6 April when Trincomalee's dock and airfield were bombed. A small carrier and destroyer were sunk off-shore with the loss of more than 300 British lives. Of the 54 Japanese aircraft which took part in the attack, 15 were shot down by Ceylon-based fighters; while 11 British aircraft were lost. In the following few days 93,000 tons of shipping were sunk in the Bay of Bengal, thus demonstrating Japan's domination of the E Indian Ocean.

The British Eastern Fleet was forced to withdraw to Bombay, on the west coast of India, and to Kilindini on the east coast of Africa. The Japanese withdrew their fleet at the same time in order to concentrate their strength on an offensive towards Australia in the south and Midway Island (qv) in the east.

CHINA II   Second World War   1941–5
Fought between the Allies and the Japanese.

The day after the Japanese attacked Pearl Harbour (qv) China declared war on Japan, thus escalating the hostility which had existed between the two nations since Japanese aggression had begun in 1931 (CHINA I, pp. 163–5), General Chiang Kai-shek became Supreme Commander of Allied Forces on the China front and he sent the three best Chinese armies (5th, 6th and 66th) to the Burma (qv) front where General Joseph (Vinegar Joe) Stilwel took command of them. On no front did the Allies have adequate time to prepare defences, however, and the Japanese forced the capitulation of Thailand on 9 December. By 16 January 1942 the Japanese had reached the Burmese border and began a relentless advance into the country despite fierce resistance. Lashio, the end of the road to Kunming, fell on 29 April and the Japanese force then split, one portion wheeling north to menace W Yunnan Province, the main army continuing its advance through Burma. By 15 May Burma had been overrun and the Chinese forces decimated. Stilwell retreated west to Ledo on the Indian border with some of the remaining troops, while the rest returned to China to bolster the defence of Yunnan Province. The Allies gave their most effective aid in the air, particularly after the Japanese had cut the Burma Road by taking Lashio. US Air Transport Command flew supplies to Kunming from India, across the Himalayas. Fighters had been aiding the Allies since 1941 when the American Volunteer Group, known as the Flying Tigers, had set themselves up under General Claire Chennault at Kunming. The group had 50 aircraft, and with these they shot down 284 Japanese aircraft and destroyed 100 more on the ground. When US military aid increased in 1942, on 4 July they became part of an enlarged group. In 1943, when they had won superiority of the air locally, they became the US 14th Air Force.

The Japanese objective now lay on the ground, where they sought to destroy the Chinese–American bases and to cut a north–south corridor through Canton–Hankow–Peking. In late 1941 the first attack took place at Changsha in south central Hunan Province. By 15 January the attack had been repulsed with heavy loss. During the summer east central China was attacked along the Chekiang–Kiangsi border, the objective being the neutralisation of the Chuhsien airfield. To the NW, the Japanese reached the Upper Yellow (Hwang Ho) River, but did not attempt to cross it; the sector was defended by Mao Tse-tung and the Communist forces who did not always co-operate with Chiang's. The Japanese feared that a major offensive in the area would unify the Chinese troops.

In 1943 the Japanese drove west in Hupeh Province and threatened the town of Chungking which had been the capital of China after the fall of Peking. By 31 May the Chinese had repulsed the enemy who launched a second drive, beginning on 2 November, when 100,000 troops attacked south in Hunan Province through the centre of Changteh, the main rice-producing area. Both sides suffered heavy losses in the engagement which lasted until the Japanese were finally thrown back in late December. The 280 bombers provided by the US were largely responsible for the Chinese victory, more because they boosted the morale of the Chinese troops than for any significant destruction they achieved. For it was the first time that substantial air support had been given to Chinese ground forces.

In April 1944 the Japanese launched Operation Ichi-Go in an intensification of their aggression. The attacks were aimed particularly at air bases in south central China and fighting was heavy around Kiangsi and Kwangsi. Seven airfields were taken. The Japanese also concentrated on gaining control of the Peking–Canton railway. In April the Chinese were forced out of Chengchow in Honan, an important strategic point on the Peking–Hankow line. By 17 June the entire railway line north of the Yangtze was in Japanese hands. On 19 June, 10 Japanese divisions south of the river moved into Changsha and drove down the Hankow–Canton railway to Hengyang in S Hunan where they met the Chinese 10th Army under General Hsueh-yueh. This force fought until it was defeated and dispersed on 8 August. Although the rest of the railway fell into Japanese hands six months later, it was in such bad repair that they were never able to use it along its entire length.

The year 1944 was a successful one for the Japanese only in the east. In SW China the Allies began to attack Burma from across the Indian border. These troops included American-trained Chinese, as well as the first US ground troops to go into action in this theatre, the brigade-strength 'Merrill's Marauders'. These 3,000 men were the only US soldiers who fought on the continent of Asia, and they fought very well indeed.

The Chinese section of the attack was under the immediate command of Stilwell who was directed by Lord Louis Mountbatten, Commander in SE Asia. The Allied force moved towards Yunan Province while Marshal Wei Li-huang launched a drive down the Burma Road from Kunming with twelve Chinese divisions. The Burma Road was to unite with the Stilwell road which was being built as the Allies advanced from Ledo, 300 miles west. General Albert Wedemeyer took over from Stilwell in October 1944 and the India–Burma forces were put under the command of General Daniel Sultan.

On 28 January 1945, 75 miles north of Lashio, the two forces met, and on 7 March Lashio itself was taken. This enabled the Allies to move road convoys along the Ledo–Burma road to Kunming. From air bases in the heart of China, B-29 bombers (Superfortresses) were attacking Japanese ports.

The Chinese army now began to take the initiative. The Japanese attacked the Chinese in W Hunan, but they were decisively beaten. In Kwangsi, Nanning, Liuchow and Kweilin were all liberated. Guerilla warfare increased, but the Japanese were suffering reversals elsewhere and on 14 August 1945, General Yasutsuga Okamura, Commander of the Japanese Expeditionary Force in China, accepted unconditional surrender terms, thus ending the hostilities which had continued between the two countries for eight years. The Japanese Kwantung Army in Manchuria surrendered to the USSR. Total Chinese losses during the war were 3,200,000 officers and men, of which 1,319,000 were killed. Civilian casualties were probably higher.

COMMANDO RAIDS, EUROPE AND MADAGASCAR Second World War 1941–2

Fought between the British, and the Germans and the Vichy French.

After the fall of France in 1940 it became obvious that major military action on the continent would be impossible for some time and Commando units were set up to undertake forays on to the continent against German installations. Not only would these small forces gain experience in combined operations and help to raise British morale, but they would also hold down German troops who might be needed elsewhere. The British army was in need of modern battle experience and this could be gained by using men from all units in the Commandos, as prototypes to test out new tactical methods.

The first big raid was carried out by 500 men from Nos 3 and 4 Commandos against the fish-oil factories in the Lofoten Islands, off the NW coast of Norway. The force, under Brigadier J. C. Haydon, left Scapa Flow in converted cross-Channel steamers on 1 March, escorted by 5 destroyers under Captain C. Caslon.

On 4 March the Commandos landed, meeting no opposition until they had disembarked, when they destroyed all the fish-oil plants, took 200 Germans prisoner as well as 300 Norwegian volunteers. A fish factory ship, the *Hamburg*, was sunk by the Royal Navy as well as several cargo ships. On 19 August a mainly Canadian force under Rear-Admiral Philip Vian succeeded in destroying 450,000 tons of coal in the installations at Spitzbergen and capturing 3 colliers. The Norwegian inhabitants were evacuated. On 3 September the German training ship *Bremse* was encountered and sunk.

In December another raid was made on the Lofoten Islands. It was not very successful as one of the transports broke down and, after some minor landings and the capture of some small coasters, the force was back in Scapa Flow by 1 January 1942.

The other raid was on Vaagso, SW of Trondheim, and was extremely successful. The force commanders were Brigadier J. C. Haydon and Rear-Admiral Harold Burrough. Thanks to the fire support of the 6-inch guns of HMS *Kenya*, men of No 3 Commando wiped out the German coast defence battery on Maaloy Island, and destroyed most of the garrison of the little port of Vaagso. Fish-oil factories were burnt, and 16,000 tons of shipping sunk. The casualties of the force which landed were 20 killed and 57 wounded.

Adolf Hitler was sensitive to any threat to Norway and as a direct result of the Vaagso raid doubled the garrison of that country, so that by June 1944 it numbered 372,000 men. It was as well that they were not sent to Russia or Normandy!

The German radar station at Bruneval, Normandy, was the subject of a successful attack on 27 February when parachutists landed and captured the station from the landward side, destroying it and taking parts for British scientists to examine. The Royal Navy evacuated the force, which lost 3 killed and 7 wounded.

In May 1942 it was decided to overrun Diego Suarez in Madagascar (Malagasy), which was held by the Vichy French, to prevent it from falling into Japanese hands and being used as an air base for attacks on Suez and the Far East shipping routes or as a base for German or Japanese submarine or surface raiders. A force under Rear-Admiral E. N. Syfret attacked Diego Suarez on 5–7 May, but when a Japanese aircraft was seen over the harbour on 29 May and the battleship *Ramillies* was damaged by a midget submarine on 30 May, it was decided to capture the rest of the island and eliminate what was believed to be a secret base (in fact both aircraft and midget submarine had come from a Japanese submarine in the area). The conquest of the island was complete by 5 November when the Governor capitulated to Lt-General Sir William Platt (MADAGASCAR). Temporary British military occupation of the island followed, the Free French being given possession in January 1943.

CONVOY JW51A and B (Barents Sea, Arctic Ocean)   Second World War
30–31 December 1942
Fought between the British under Captain R. Sherbrook and Rear-Admiral R. L.

Burnett, and the Germans under Vice-Admiral Oskar Kummetz.

Strength: British 6 destroyers + 2 cruisers (*Sheffield* and *Jamaica*) + (covering force under Vice-Admiral Sir Bruce Fraser) 1 battleship + 1 cruiser + 3 destroyers; Germans 1 heavy cruiser (*Hipper*) + 1 pocket battleship (*Lützow*) + 6 destroyers.

Following the destruction of Convoy PQ–17 (qv) the system of Arctic convoys was changed, the ships being divided into two small sections which were easier to defend. JW51A reached Murmansk without loss, and its escort of 2 cruisers under Burnett turned back to JW51B which was covered by 6 destroyers under Sherbrook. When a U-boat reported sighting this half of the convoy. Admiral Wrich Raeder, Commander-in-Chief of the German navy, resolved to send the pocket battleship *Lützow* out in the hope that, if she were to prove successful on this raid, she could be sent into the Atlantic.

Adolph Hitler's standing orders imposed tactical restrictions on the force, however, but it was decided that the main force under Kummetz would attack the escort while the *Lützow*, under Captain Stänge, would take on the convoy. The Germans were unaware of the presence of the forces under Burnett and Fraser when they set sail on 30 December. They approached the convoy on the morning of the 31st. Kummetz turned south to meet it, but was sighted by the destroyer escort. As one vessel laid a smoke-screen, another made dummy attacks on the *Hipper* which, though veering away, then decided to return to the attack.

Meanwhile, Sherbrook had sent 2 of his destroyers to the convoy to deal with the 6 enemy destroyers and was thus unprepared for the return of the *Hipper* which inflicted severe damage on the *Onslow*. As the *Hipper* withdrew again, Burnett began to close in from the south and the *Lützow* appeared from the same direction, moving in on the convoy and trapping it on one side with the *Hipper* on the other. Instead of engaging, however, she drew off, as she was uncertain of the identity of the ships she had sighted.

The *Hipper* went in to attack, sank the destroyer *Achates* and withdrew before the threat of a torpedo attack. As she drew back, she moved into a trap between Sherbrook and Burnett. The *Hipper* was hit three times before 2 of her 3 destroyer escorts were engaged. One of them was sunk. When the *Lützow* finally opened fire on the convoy she was unable to inflict any damage because of a smoke-screen laid by the escort destroyers. Kummetz then disengaged and ordered the Germans to retire south.

Despite superior fire-power and their tactical advantages, the Germans had failed in their design. Hitler ordered all major surface units to be scrapped. Raeder dissuaded him from this plan but himself resigned. He was succeeded by Admiral Karl Dönitz.

CONVOY PQ–17 (Barents Sea, Arctic Ocean)   Second World War   27 June – 8 July 1942
Fought between the Allies and the Germans.
Strength: Allies 36 merchantmen + (close cover to Bear Island) 4 cruisers +

3 destroyers + (long-range cover to Bear Island) 2 battleships + 1 aircraft carrier + 2 cruisers + 14 destroyers + (close cover from 30 June) 3 mine-sweepers + 4 trawlers + (long-range cover from 30 June) 6 destroyers + 4 corvettes + 2 submarines; Germans 1 battleship + 1 pocket battleship + 6 destroyers + 6 submarines + land based aircraft.

Convoys to Russia were begun after the invasion of the country by the Germans in August 1941 and ceased in September 1943. The journey to Murmansk and Archangel was circumscribed by the Arctic ice-floes which, in winter, advanced south forcing the convoys closer to the Scandinavian coast which was occupied by or allied with Germany. In the summer, the long days created danger from U-boats which were able to travel farther afield. Allied air cover could not be kept up throughout the journey and the convoys were vulnerable as they moved over the top of Norway, within the ranges of German air bases in the Norwegian and Barents Seas.

When convoy PQ–17 began its journey, the threat from German units in the area was so great that it was given considerable escort cover. On the day after the convoy had reached Bear Island (Björnöya Island, Norway) and its escort had been changed, U-boats and aircraft sighted and attacked it. The Germans retired without inflicting any damage. On 2 July Convoy PQ–13, on its way back to Britain, was passed. An air attack that evening was repulsed, but the close escort was 40 miles north of the convoy by then and, when fog closed in, the air cover lost contact with the ships as they swung north to go round Bear Island. At the same time, the German battleships *Tirpitz*, *Scheer* and *Hipper* left their bases in S Germany. They arrived at Altenfjord on the north coast of Norway on 4 July, but could not intercept the convoy because Adolf Hitler had issued standing orders forbidding it. On the same day an air attack on the convoy cost it 2 merchantmen. A third ship, though damaged, continued on its way. The First Sea Lord, Admiral Sir Dudley Pound, anticipating the probable interception by the German surface ships, ordered the distant escort to return to the convoy – it had been withdrawn earlier. Meanwhile, as the convoy was still in danger, it was ordered to scatter on 4 July, so that it might be better able to evade the Germans. The long-range cover, under Commander J. E. Broome, reaching the convoy, went on to rendezvous with the close cover. This force, under Rear-Admiral L. H. K. Hamilton, was under the mistaken impression that it was returning to Home Fleet and Hamilton refused Broome permission to rejoin the convoy which, now scattered, was therefore also defenceless. On 5 July the *Tirpitz*, *Scheer* and *Hipper*, plus 6 destroyers, left Altenfjord to intercept the convoy, as anticipated; but that evening the operation was abandoned, since the submarines and aircraft were adequate to the task. Between 5 and 10 July 22 ships were sunk or run aground. Of the 11 ships which arrived at Archangel 3, the *Silver Sword, Troubadour* and *Ironclad*, had been escorted by the trawler *Ayrshire* into the ice, where they had been painted white, thus passing unnoticed until it became safe to proceed. Allied losses were 3,350 vehicles, 430 tanks and 210 aircraft as well as 99,316 tons of other cargo.

CORAL SEA (S Pacific)   Second World War   7-8 May 1942
Fought between the Americans under Admiral Frank Fletcher and the Japanese under Admiral Shigeyosu Inouye.

At the end of April 1942 the Japanese renewed their offensive in the Pacific. Their ultimate objective was Australia, and on 4 May Inouye left Rabaul, New Britain, for Moresby in the south of New Guinea. Meanwhile, another strong Japanese force headed by 2 aircraft carriers, the *Shokaku* and *Zuikaku*, moved into the Coral Sea, NE of Australia. An American task force was swiftly formed in the Coral Sea.

On 7 May US aircraft located and attacked Inouye's invasion fleet north of the Louisiade archipelago. The bombers, from the carriers *Yorktown* and *Lexington*, sank the Japanese carrier *Shoho*, and the transports, now without air cover, were forced to turn back. On the following day the other Japanese force in the Coral Sea came into contact with the American force. Throughout the ensuing battle neither side saw the other's ships. It was the first naval battle in history during which no ships fired on one another. The entire action took place from the air. Of 82 attacking US aircraft, 33 were lost in a foray which damaged the carrier *Shokaku*. The Japanese sank the *Lexington*, a destroyer and a tanker, but lost 43 out of 69 aircraft in the process. American casualties totalled 543, but, despite their heavier losses, they had inflicted the first check on Japanese forces in the Pacific.

Port Moresby was now safe and the Japanese withdrew from the Coral Sea.

CRETE (E Mediterranean)   Second World War   20-7 May 1941
Fought between the Allies under General Sir Bernard Freyberg and the Germans under General Kurt Student.
Strength: Allies 41,500 (British, Australians and New Zealanders 27,500, Greeks 14,000) + 9 tanks + 35 aircraft + 45 field guns; Germans 22,000.

After the conquest of Greece (qv) by the German 12th Army, Allied troops were evacuated to Crete to reinforce the garrison of three infantry battalions (composed largely of Australians and New Zealanders). The Germans maintained superiority of the air and these troops, plus two Greek brigades, were poorly equipped and short of supplies and ammunition. On 19 May the Germans bombed the airfields on Crete and the few RAF planes which remained serviceable after the attack were flown out, leaving the Nazis in complete control of the air. The following day, German parachutists and glider-borne troops landed at the airfields of Maleme and Rethymnon and at the port of Heraklion (Candia), all of which lay on the north of the island. Despite fierce opposition, these points were taken by the end of the week in the first entirely airborne assault in history. The German 11 Air Corps continued to attack from the air and the defenders took a heavy toll of the Germans, but they were finally overwhelmed by the relentless pressure. On the nights of 27 and 28 May 16,500 British troops were evacuated to Egypt, while most of the 13,000 Allied casualties became prisoner, the last surrendering on 31 May. Naval losses were high, 3 cruisers and 6 destroyers being sunk with a loss of 2,000 men. German losses were 5,600 killed, a high proportion of them being parachutists. German Crete-bound convoys were attacked and sunk by the British E Mediterranean fleet under Admiral Sir Andrew Cunningham and the Germans lost 5,000 in the action.

The German campaign in SE Europe ended with the Battle of Crete. The Nazis' next target would be the USSR. It was known later that, owing to the heavy casualties suffered by his paratroops, Student was considering withdrawing his forces, so that if Freyberg had hung on, Crete might not have been lost at that time.

CRIMEA (KRYM) (USSR)   Second World War   1941–4
Fought between the Russians and the Germans.

The South Army Group under General Gerd von Rundstedt invaded the USSR east of the Crimean peninsula, after sweeping through the Ukraine. In October of 1942 the German 11th Army of General Erich von Manstein attacked the peninsula itself. On 8 November the Germans broke through the isthmus of Perekop, which was heavily fortified, and overran all of Crimea (Krym) very quickly. The only town which did not fall to the German drive was Sebastopol, which was fiercely defended by the Russians. The Kerch peninsula, to the east, was also taken by the Germans, but in December the Russians in a counter-offensive retook it. Both Sebastopol and the Kerch were then put under heavy siege until the spring of 1942 when, on 7 May, fifteen divisions (including two Panzers and five Romanian) launched a massive assault against the Kerch which was overrun in six days. Some of the Russian force of three divisions crossed the Kerch Strait to the Taman peninsula in the Caucasus, while the rest became prisoners along with the Russian casualties, which totalled 150,000. On 3 June Manstein attacked Sebastopol and began an assault which lasted a month until, on 1 July, the defenders surrendered, 90,000 prisoners being taken. Sebastopol had been the Russians' main Black Sea base and it was lost at a time when the German offensive in the Caucasus was preparing to attack down the eastern shore of the sea. At this juncture Manstein, with five divisions, was transferred to the Leningrad (qv) front, but he was unable to force the capitulation of that city as he had done Sebastopol.

In November 1943 a Russian offensive under General Fedor Tolbukhin pushed along the northern shore of the Sea of Azov and the Black Sea and cornered the Germans in the Crimea. In the spring of 1944 Petrov launched a drive in the Caucasus which drove the German forces in the Taman peninsula across the strait to the Kerch, pursuing them at the same time as Tolbukhin attacked the defences of the Perekop isthmus in the north on 8 April. On 11 April the Perekop defences were penetrated and the Germans were forced to retreat to Sebastopol. The garrison surrendered on 9 May and the last Germans in the Crimean peninsula capitulated on 12 May.

The Russian drive cleared the fourth (S) Ukrainian front.

CZECHOSLOVAKIA   Second World War   1945
Fought between the Allies and the Germans.

In their winter offensive of 1944–5 the Russians surrounded Czechoslovakia on three sides and drove into the German-occupied country, General Ivan Konev's 1st Ukrainian Army from Saxony to the north, General Andrei Yeremenko's 4th Ukrainian Army from the east and General Tolbukhin's 3rd Ukrainian Army from the south, the latter marching into the centre of the country. While Czech Patriots led an uprising in Prague, General George Patton's 3rd Army crossed the border from Germany to Pilsen in April. Before the four converging forces could link up, however, Germany surrendered unconditionally on 8 May.

DAKAR (Senegal, W Africa)   Second World War   23–5 September 1940
Fought between the Allies under Admiral Cunningham and the Free French forces under General Charles de Gaulle, and the French Pétainists (loyal to the Vichy government) under General Pierre Boisson.

After the fall of France, an Allied force sought to seize the important strategic port and air base of Dakar in French W Africa (now Senegal). Forces loyal to the French government at Vichy under the governor, Boisson, fought off the attack by sea. Owing to lack of security amongst the Free French, Boisson had been forewarned of the invasion and so was prepared.

When the British and Americans invaded French N Africa on 8 November 1942, Dakar came under Allied control without a fight.

DARWIN (Northern Territory, Australia)   Second World War   19 February 1942
Fought between the Australians and the Japanese under Admiral Chuichi Nagumo.

During the early part of the year Japanese forces overran all opposition on the islands (except Timor [qv], where Australian independent companies operated for twelve months), which stretched in a 4,000-mile chain from the Malay peninsula to Australia. One of their objectives was Australia itself.

Supplemented by bombers from Celebes, 80 Japanese carrier-based aircraft were sent to attack Darwin on 19 February. Docks, warehouses and the airport were destroyed and all the 17 ships in the harbour were sunk, including the US destroyer *Peary*. The Allies lost 22 aircraft, but only shot down 5 Japanese bombers. The Japanese advance continued inexorably.

This attack on the continent of Australia had the desired effect as the Australian Prime Minister, John Curtin, insisted that all Australian forces in the Middle East should be brought home, and refused to allow one division to reinforce Burma (qv). This insistence caused some tension between the British and Australian governments. At the time of Dunkirk Australia had denuded herself of nearly all her weapons which she had sent to Britain, so that in early 1941 there were only 36 Bren guns (one damaged) left in all Australia. Many Australians felt that Britain was unable to see Australia's point of view, and so Curtin turned to the Americans for succour.

D-DAY   see NORMANDY

DIEPPE (France) Second World War   19 August 1942
Fought between the Allies under Major-General John Roberts and the Germans.
Strength: Allies 7,000 (British 2,000 [Nos 3 and 4 Commandos and No 40 (RM)], Canadians 5,000 [2nd Canadian Division]); Germans 10,000 (in the immediate vicinity).

From the time of the fall of France (qv) in June 1940 until the invasion of Normandy in June 1944 the Germans held the entire European coastline from the Arctic to the Mediterranean. Allied raids were continuously carried out on the Nazi coastal positions, mainly at night, as much to keep up morale in Britain as to damage the enemy. The largest such raid took place by day, when a 'reconnaissance in force' was carried out by 7,000 Allied troops aided by a force of tanks. Their objective was German strongpoints and buildings held in and around Dieppe.

The beach at Dieppe was strongly defended by the Germans, and Canadian tanks were unable to move across the shingle, holding up the troops, many of whom were killed there. The force fought for nine hours, during which the only troops to gain their objective were Lt-Colonel Lord Lovat's No 4 Commando unit which took a battery at Varengeville. The Allies re-embarked as planned, having sustained heavy losses, including 3,670 men killed, wounded or taken prisoner (of whom 900 Canadians were killed and nearly 2,000 taken prisoner), 27 tanks, several landing craft and 106 aircraft. German losses were 46 aircraft and about 500 men.

The raid provided valuable experience in daylight landing operations which was put to some use in the planning of Operation Overlord, the Allied invasion of Normandy (qv).

DODECANESE ISLANDS (E Mediterranean) Second World War September – November 1943
Fought between the British and the Germans.

After the surrender of the Italian government on 9 September 1943, Winston Churchill ordered the seizure of the Dodecanese Islands in the Lower Aegean Sea. The islands would make air and naval bases close to the Balkans and it was hoped that this might persuade Turkey to enter the war on the Allied side. General Sir Henry Maitland-Wilson, British Commander in the Mediterranean, put a battalion on each of the islands of Cos, Leros and Samos. The largest island in the group, Rhodes, was strongly held by the Germans.

On 3 October the Germans counter-attacked by dropping parachutists on Cos and recapturing it. Two more battalions were put on to Leros and the British garrison from Samos was later also transferred to that island. On 12 November the Germans made landings on the north and south of Leros and 600 parachutists were dropped in the centre of the island later in the day. The island was overrun by the Germans within four days and 3,000 prisoners were taken. As a result of this action 1,200 British and Greek troops were evacuated by sea, which resulted in the sinking of 6 Allied destroyers and 2 submarines.

This defeat ended the Allies' hopes of gaining a swift hold in the Aegean.

DRESDEN, AERIAL BOMBARDMENT (Germany)   Second World War 13/14 April 1945

Fought between the Allies and the Germans.

Strength: Allies 1173 bombers.

Operation Thunderclap took place on the night of 13 April and morning of 14 April 1945. Two raids in February had previously wrought considerable damage on the city itself. But a further large-scale operation, on 13/14 April, the last great raid by Bomber Command, by 723 Lancasters, followed by a US B–17 daylight raid by 450 bombers, inflicted between 50,000 and 100,000 casualties on a population swollen to 830,000 by the influx of 200,000 refugees. Such an attack was justified as being against the important industrial complex as well as the hub of communications for the southern sector of the Eastern Front, and was made at the request of Russia.

DUNKIRK see FLANDERS

EAST AFRICA   Second World War   10 February – 17 May 1941

Fought between the Allies under General Sir Alan Cunningham and General Sir William Platt, and the Italians under the Duke of Aosta.

The Italians entered the war on 10 June 1940 and surrounded British Somaliland on three sides. On 15 August seventeen battalions of Italian infantry moved on the port of Berbera and forced the weak British garrison under General A. R. Godwin-Austen to evacuate via the Gulf of Aden. This was the only victory which the Italians achieved over the British during the war, and their dominance was brief.

On 10 February 1941 Cunningham marched NE from Kenya into Somaliland with the 11th African and 1st S African Brigades. On 22 February a force of 30,000 Italians was routed by the Allies at Jelib after crossing the Juba River at Kismayu. They then went on to take Mogadishu, the capital and chief port of Italian Somaliland, three days later, and to travel up the Gerrer River valley, 550 miles north to take Jijiga in east central Ethiopia. Turning west up the Madar Pass, Harrar was taken on 26 March, Diredawa on 29 March and Addis Ababa on 6 April. The Italians abandoned the city two days later. Berbera had been re-occupied by the British on 16 March.

Meanwhile, as part of a two-pronged drive directed by General Sir Archibald Wavell, Platt, with the 4th and 5th Indian Armies, had moved east from Kassala in the Sudan and had beaten a force of 30,000 Italians at Agordat on 31 January. A crack force of Italian infantry took up a defensive position in the fortress of Keren in Eritrea, which the British took on 27 March with the loss of 4,000 killed. The Italians lost 3,000 killed. Platt went on to take Asmara on 1 April and Massawa on 4 April. Platt and Cunningham now linked up to launch an attack against the 200,000-strong Italian army under the Duke of Aosta.

Meanwhile, a number of guerilla groups had been raised by special missions sent out by the War Office. The most successful of these was commanded by Colonel Orde Wingate who, with 400 Sudanese and Abyssinian guerillas, harassed the Italian army communications. At one time, by use of deception, 14,000 Italians surrendered to Wingate's 400 men. At the same time Platt's more orthodox offensive continued. Wingate, whose orders were to place Emperor Haile Selassie back on his throne before any usurper could claim it, rode into Addis Ababa with Haile Selassie on 5 May 1941. He also had to get rid of some other groups who were trying to place Ras Tafari or other claimants on the throne. The Duke of Aosta surrendered to General Platt at Amba Alagi on 17 May and the Allied Armies formally took possession of the capital. Having been the first monarch to be driven from his country by the Axis, Haile Selassie was the first to be restored.

Wingate's plan for organising an Abyssinian army to fight alongside the Allies in N Africa was turned down at the insistence of the Colonial Office and General Jan Christiaan Smuts of S Africa. In a fit of depression at this news, and from the rigours that he had experienced as a guerilla leader, Wingate had a nervous breakdown and attempted suicide while in Cairo. He recovered and later raised, trained and operated the Chindits (Special Force) in Burma (qv) in 1943–4 until his death in a flying accident.

EAST INDIES   Second World War   1941 – 2
Fought between the Allies under General Sir Archibald Wavell and the Japanese.

In order to try and block the all-victorious Japanese advance, the Allies formed a command known as ABDA (Australian, British, Dutch, American) which was headed by General Wavell.

On 10 January Wavell arrived to take up his appointment at Bandoeng, near Batavia (now Djakarta) on Java, and discovered that most of the area to be defended was already under heavy attack. The E Indies, mainly Dutch-held, were almost ready to fall. Sarawak and Brunei in N Borneo had fallen between 16 and 23 December 1941. Tarakan, on the NE coast of Borneo, had fallen on 10 January; Celebes, an island to the east, was invaded the following day. The Japanese advance went on through the islands until, on 23 January, the Japanese bypassed Dutch New Guinea to take Rabaul on New Britain and Kavieng on New Ireland in the Bismarck Islands. They turned back on themselves at this point and took Ceram in the Moluccas, to the west of New Guinea, on 31 January. It was decided that ABDA should hold Java, the vital central island, but the Japanese began closing on it on three sides. On 14 February Palembang was taken by Japanese paratroops and a base was swiftly established to the west on Sumatra. S Borneo was invaded on 16 February and the Java Sea (qv) became the only obstacle which stood in the way of a Japanese invasion from the north. To the east, Bali was occupied on 19 February and parts of Timor (qv) between 20 and 24 February. Japanese superiority at sea and in the air was now so complete that ABDA's efforts to defend Java were hopeless. Wavell dissolved the command on 25 February and flew out to resume command over India.

The Dutch Admiral Conrad Helfrich refused to accept defeat, however, and sent Dutch, British and American ships into the Java Sea to stop the Japanese invasion convoys, of which two were heading for Java. The force was defeated (JAVA SEA) while the US aircraft tender *Langley*, which had 32 P–40s in a state of readiness as well as 32 pilots on board as reinforcements, was sunk south of Java on 27 February. On 1 March the Japanese landed on the east and west of Java and were in control of the island by 9 March, when General Heinter Poorten surrendered the remaining Allied troops: 11,300 Dutch, 5,600 British, 2,800 Australians and 800 Americans. A number of specialist personnel from the British forces in Malaya and Singapore (qqv), who had been sent out before Singapore fell, were picked up from the south coast of Java and Sumatra by British and Australian warships.

Only Port Moresby in the south of New Guinea and the Allied domination of the Coral Sea stood between the Japanese and Australia.

EL ALAMEIN I (Egypt)   Second World War   1–27 July 1942
Fought between the British under General Sir Claude Auchinleck and the Germans and Italians under General Erwin Rommel.
Strength: British 25,000; Germans 8,000 + 12,000 Italians + 55 tanks.
After their defeat at Mersa Matruh (qv) the British withdrew to a line which stretched 40 miles from the coastal village of El Alamein to the impassable salt marshes of the Qattara Depression which anchored their left (S) flank. The Afrika Korps pursued closely. The British line, hastily thrown up, was manned by Lt-General Willoughby Norrie's 30 Corps on the right at El Alemein and Lt-General W. H. E. Gott's 13 Corps on the left.

On 1 July the Germans attacked the right centre of the British position with 6,500 infantry and 90 tanks – of which only 55 were in full working order. The 90th German Light Division and the 15th and 21st Panzers, both weakened by the Battles of Gazala (qv) and Mersa Matruh, gained some ground before intense artillery fire from the British 4th and 22nd Armoured Brigades drove them back, this counter-attack being directed at the south flank of the German salient. In the north the Italians made no impression on the British line when Rommel switched the main force of his attack to the coastal position and he consequently turned his attention back to the desert. Auchinleck tried to cut the German line of retreat, but did not succeed, managing only to force Rommel back with a loss of 12 tanks. Having lost 18 tanks during the first assault, the Germans were left with only 26 fit tanks against the British total of 119. Despite the inferiority of numbers, the Germans contrived to extricate themselves and the battle then petered out, both sides exhausted by the intense heat. British and German troops then retired behind barbed wire. The British lost 13,000 men in the battle, while the Germans and Italians lost 1,000 and 6,000 prisoners respectively. Axis casualties were about equal to British losses.

Auchinleck was now relieved of his command and on 15 August General Sir Harold Alexander became Commander of the Middle East and Lt-General Bernard Montgomery took command of the 8th Army. Auchinleck had in fact won a battle which was as decisive as the second, better recognised action, since it stopped Rommel's sweeping advance through N Africa and robbed him of his last chance to take Cairo. The victory forced on Rommel the action at Alam el Halfa (qv), and gave the British the opportunity to rebuild the 8th Army.

EL ALAMEIN II (Egypt)   Second World War   23 October–4 November 1942
Fought between the British under Lt-General Bernard Montgomery and the Germans and Italians under General Rommel.
Strength: British 200,000 + 1,100 tanks; Germans 53,000 + 200 tanks + Italians 43,000 + 300 tanks.

After Rommel's final attempt to reach the Nile valley and Cairo, 60 miles east, had been blocked at Alam el Halfa (qv) two months earlier, the initiative passed to the British. Both forces spent the intervening weeks reinforcing and rebuilding their armies and both were at peak strength. The British had overwhelming superiority in both artillery and air.

On the night of 23 October the British launched an artillery barrage of 800 guns under cover of which Lt-General Oliver Leese's 30 Corps (51st Highland, 1st S African and 4th Indian Divisions), spearheaded by the 9th Australian Division, moved west from El Alamein. Both infantry and armour took a heavy toll from the Axis artillery when extensive minefields held up their advance. Rommel's Afrika Korps was strongly positioned for defence. The following morning, Major-General Herbert Lumsden's 10 Corps followed Leese from the same point (1st and 10th Armoured, 2nd New Zealand). A secondary attack was also launched to the south by Lt-General Brian Horrocks with 13 Corps (7th Armoured, 44th and 50th British Divisions). The defences were manned chiefly by the 15th and 21st Panzers and the 90th Light (motorised) Divisions, the veteran Afrika Korps, and none of the British attacks initially made any impression on the German position. 10 Corps was ordered to fight its way out, but this was impossible. On 27 and 28 October the Germans counter-attacked fiercely, but were beaten back by the ground forces, aided by the RAF. The British had lost 10,000 men without penetrating the German defences.

Montgomery, authorised to continue the attack without counting the cost, now launched Operation Supercharge on the night of 30 October. This attack, followed by two more attacks on 2 and 4 November, was strongly backed up by the RAF which succeeded in getting through the enemy's defended zone and, as the ground forces followed, attacking their flanks. The great holes punched in the German line allowed the British to pour through into the open desert, thus squeezing Rommel out of his defences. Although the Germans began to disengage on 3 November, they were ordered by Adolf Hitler to stand fast. On the night of 4 November, however, the withdrawal started again, and this time it continued without stopping for 1,500 miles, the British in close pursuit. The threat to the Nile valley was removed and wider victory was assured when, on 8 November, the Anglo-American invasion in the west of Africa took place.

Axis casualties were 59,000 killed, wounded and captured, which included 34,000 Germans, plus 500 tanks and 400 guns. Allied losses were 13,000 killed or wounded and 432 tanks. The Allied victory was one of the decisive battles in history.

Montgomery retook Tobruk on 13 November, Benghazi a week later, El Agheila on 23 November, Tripoli on 23 January 1943 and finally both armies crossed into Tunisia on 13 February, where Rommel also met defeat. The Germans lost another 20,000 men during the retreat, mainly prisoners. British losses were small.

The Royal Navy's and RAF's contributions – often neglected by military historians – in preventing supplies reaching Rommel, must always be taken into account as an important factor helping the British victory at El Alamein.

FALAISE-ARGENTAN POCKET (France)   Second World War   8–12 August 1944

Fought between the Germans and the Allies under General Sir Bernard Montgomery.

When the Americans broke through at St Lô (qv), General George Patton's 3rd Army was free to move east towards Le Mans on 8 August. Thence 15 Corps turned north towards Argentan, cutting off the rear of the Germans who faced the British 2nd Army and the Canadian 1st Army which both stood to the north. Reaching Argentan on 13 August, Patton halted on the orders of the 12th Army commander, General Omar Bradley, before moving east in the direction of the Seine. The American 5 Corps took Argentan and moved north and the Canadian 1st Army under General Henry Crerar moved south to Falaise. Three German armies in the area were now threatened with encirclement and General Gunther von Kluge began to withdraw them; he was relieved by Field-Marshal Walther Model on 18 August. The Germans managed to hold a gap 10 miles wide for five days and many of the forces were able to escape east despite the fact that they were heavily bombarded from the air and hard pressed on the ground. On 19 August the ring was closed at Chambois, and by 22 August the Falaise–Argentan pocket had been wiped out. German losses were 10,000 killed and 50,000 captured, as well as much of their heavy equipment. The Germans retreated to the Seine, closely pursued by Allied armour.

Montgomery has been criticised, especially by Patton, for not encircling Kluge earlier in the battle. But this is to overlook the tiredness of units which had been operating with little respite since 6 June. Patton's army did not go into action until 1 August.

FINLAND   Second World War   30 November 1939 – 19 September 1944

Fought between the Finns under Field-Marshal Baron Carl von Mannerheim and the Russians under General Kirill Meretskov.
Strength: Finns 130,000; Russians 465,000.

The City of Leningrad stood only 16 miles from the Finnish border. The Russians sought to strengthen the frontier in the NW of their country. Behind the border with Finland stood the Mannerheim Line (qv) across the Karelian isthmus. The Russians invaded Finland on a trifling pretext on 30 November 1939, while the air force bombed Helsinki (Hensingfors). Twenty-six divisions advanced on six fronts, though the main body was concentrated between Lake Ladoga and the Gulf of Finland. Though badly outnumbered, the Finns fought fiercely and repulsed attacks by the Russian 7th and 13th Armies along the Mannerheim Line. Between 8 December and 11 January the 163rd and 44th Russian Divisions were annihilated by the Finns in the Suomussalmi region. Finnish losses were 900 killed and 1,770 wounded.

A new offensive was now organised by Meretskov and the vastly superior numbers of Russian men, arms and aircraft was utilised in a massive attack on the Mannerheim Line, directed by Marshal Semyon Timoshenko. The assault began on 1 February 1940 and Viipuri (Vyborg) was captured on 11 March. The Finns surrendered on 12 March, having lost 25,000 killed and 44,000 wounded. Russian losses were over 200,000 killed alone. Leningrad was now more deeply surrounded by defensive territory. Its position was further strengthened when Lithuania, Latvia and Estonia were taken over three months later.

On 26 June 1941 Finland allied itself with Germany when the latter invaded the USSR. The lost Finnish territory was quickly retaken by Mannerheim, and the Finns then aided the Germans in their blockade of Leningrad (qv). The Russians, however, counter-attacked in 1944 and in June they broke the Mannerheim Line again and the Finns sued for peace on 19 September.

On 3 March 1945 Finland declared war on Germany, but no military action resulted.

FLANDERS (Belgium)   Second World War   10 May – 4 June 1940
Fought between the Germans and the Allies.

The German attack on the rest of W Europe began at 4 am on 10 May when General Fedor von Bock's Army Group 'B' began a right-wing sweep through the Netherlands and Belgium. Five hundred German parachutists captured two bridges over the Albert Canal and airfields in both countries, as well as neutralising the important strongpoint of Fort Eben Emael. General Walther von Reichenau's 6th Army of twenty-three divisions advanced through the S Netherlands to cross the Meuse and Maastricht. Holland's army, consisting of ten divisions, lost 100,000 men before surrendering on 14 May.

In Belgium, the German Panzer army outflanked Liège to take it from the rear (W). The seventeen divisions of the Belgian army began to fall back to the line of the Dyle River where they were joined on 13 May by the thirteen divisions of the British Expeditionary Force (BEF) under General Lord Gort and the French 1st Army under General Georges Blanchard. The Nazis pursued, however, and the Panzers forced the Allies beyond the Scheldt River on 19 May. This line collapsed on 20 May, the 1st Army Group of the Allies, under General Pierre Billotte, being outmanoeuvred and outfought as a result of their belief in static warfare as opposed to Blitzkrieg. This western movement of Bock, however, was only a screen for the main German effort which was thrusting south through the Ardennes, terrain which the Allies considered impassable. General Gerd von Rundstedt commanded the Army Group 'A' in this area and his forty-four divisions moved forward on 10 May, meeting only token opposition. By 12 May they had moved 70 miles to reach the French frontier, and on 13 May they established bridgeheads by the Meuse River at Sedan. The three corps of General Paul von Kleist's Panzer group broke through on a 50-mile front between Sedan and Namur into good tank country. This force was backed up by General Gunther von Kluge's 4th Army and General Wilhelm List's 12th Army. The French 9th Army under General André-Georges Corap tried to block the German advance, but it was smashed and the Second in Command, General Henri Giraud, was taken prisoner.

On 19 May General Maxime Weygand replaced General Maurice Gamelin as Commander-in-Chief of the French armies, but by this time the Germans had already won the battle. The whole Panzer army under General Heinz Guderian broke through along their 50-mile front and advanced 220 miles in seven days to reach the Normandy coast at Abbeville on 20–1 May, leaving behind them a 60-mile belt to the rear of the Allied left wing in Belgium and cutting British communications. On 17–19 May, Brigadier-General Charles de Gaulle's 4th Armoured Division attacked the German thrust from the south at Montcornet, while to the north Gort's BEF made an attack towards Arras. Both assaults were repulsed. Boulogne fell to Kleist on 23 May, and Calais on 27 May. On 28 May King Leopold III surrendered the Belgian army to the German 6th Army and went into internment.

The Admiralty now ordered the BEF and the remnants of the French 1st Army to evacuate the north coast, and Operation Dynamo was begun. The Allies retreated to Dunkirk where the British had obtained temporary superiority of the air, and the French 16 Corps and the BEF held a 45-mile front surrounding the town which was being bombarded. The evacuation was begun at 6.57 pm on 26 May and lasted nine days. During this time 338,226 men, including 120,000 French, were transported to Britain in a fleet comprised largely of every sort of small craft, which had sailed across the Channel from England. Altogether 861 vessels took part, of which 243 were sunk. British warships were also involved, 6 destroyers being sunk and 19 badly damaged. Besides the final 50,000 Frenchmen who held the line while the evacuation took place, 30,000 British soldiers were left on the beaches – dead, wounded or taken prisoner. During the battle more than 1 million of the Allies were taken prisoner alone, while the Germans only lost 60,000. The French lost thirty divisions (including most of their armour); the BEF nine divisions and a group of Free Poles.

The Germans were now free to penetrate deep into France.

FRANCE   Second World War   5 – 22 June 1940
Fought between the French under General Maxime Weygand and the Germans under General Gerd von Rundstedt, General Wilhelm von Leeb and General Fedor von Bock.

The German triumph in Flanders (qv) wiped out a third of the fighting strength of France and weakened her ability to defend her frontiers, along which the Germans were aligning themselves. The Nazi army groups 'B', 'A' and 'C' commanded by Bock, Rundstedt and Leeb respectively, were positioned from the north coast, east to the front of the Maginot Line and then south to Switzerland. The French took up an improvised defensive position which ran east along the Somme and Aisne Rivers and then along the Maginot fortifications; but with only sixty-five divisions left, this line, which was longer than the original French frontier, was only thinly held.

On 5 June 140 German divisions, led by the Panzer groups, began to advance along a 100-mile front. In the west Bock's 4th Army under General Gunther von Kluge reached the Seine River at Rouen on 9 June and Bock's 6th under General Walther von Reichenau moved down the Oise valley north of Paris. When the French 10th Army in this sector collapsed, the Royal Navy evacuated 136,000 British and 20,000 Polish soldiers to England. Rundstedt began to move forward on 9 June. His three armies, the 9th (General Maximilian von Weichs), 2nd (General Adolf Strauss) and 12th (General Wilhelm List) were halted on and below the Aisne, but General Heinz Guderian's Panzers broke through to cross the Marne at Chalons on 12 June, and General Paul von Kleist crossed the Marne at Château-Thierry at the same time. The advance of the Panzers broke the French armies up until they were useless as fighting units. Bock's armour took Cherbourg on 18 June, Brest and Nantes a day later. Kleist occupied the Loire at Nevers, Dijon on 16 June and then Lyons down the Rhône valley. East of Kleist, Guderian moved round the end of the Maginot Line to the Swiss border, forcing the French out of their fortified positions on the night of 14 June. Leeb's 1st and 7th Armies moved into NE France.

On 11 June Paris had been declared an open city and the French government had moved to Tours, later fleeing to Bordeaux. The 18th Army of General Georg von Küchler occupied Paris on 14 June, and on 17 June Marshal Henri Pétain sued for peace, the formal surrender taking place on 22 June at Compiègne. Meanwhile, Mussolini had declared war on France on 10 June and had sent troops towards the Riviera. Allied with German ground attacks there had been thorough air attacks by Stuka dive bombers which had devastated the fighting area, while Field-Marshal Hermann Göring's tactical fighters had been equally successful. The Germans lost 27,000 killed, 111,000 wounded and 18,000 missing during their conquest. French casualties were not reported, but the Germans claimed to have taken 1,900,000 prisoners.

After the collapse of France only Britain stood unconquered in W Europe, and the Wehrmacht now laid plans for the invasion of the island in Operation Sealion (see BRITAIN, BATTLE OF).

FRANCE, NORTHERN   Second World War   August – September 1944
Fought between the Allies under General Dwight D. Eisenhower and the Germans under Field-Marshal Walther Model and General Gerd von Rundstedt.

Following the Allied victory in the Falaise–Argentan Pocket (qv), combined with the successes of General George Patton's armoured columns farther east, the battle for N France became nothing more than the pursuit of Model's retreating

Germans. The Allies sought to trap and wipe out as many German forces as possible south of the Seine. Withdrawal across this river presented problems to the Nazis, as the Allied air force destroyed all the bridges over it.

Patton's right wing, based on the Loire, formed the hinge of the 3rd Army which passed through Le Mans on 14 August. Three corps then moved NE towards the Seine north and south of Paris. Dreux and Orléans were both liberated on 16 August and Chartres was retaken on 18 August. West of Paris, 15 Corps took a bridge over the Seine at Mantes on 19 August. Between then and 25 August the 15 and 12 Corps crossed the Seine SE of Paris in force. Meanwhile, on 23 August, the Free French within the capital began an uprising. The 2nd French Armoured Division under General Jacques Leclerc (part of the US 5 Corps) went to their aid and entered Paris on 24 August. On 25 August, the Germans were driven out of the capital and General Charles de Gaulle set his headquarters up there the same day. On the Allied left, three armies had swung NE to move on the Seine. The 1st Canadian under General Henry Crerar was on the coast, next to it was the 2nd British under General Sir Miles Dempsey and inland was the American 1st under General Courtney Hodges. The Germans crumbled before the advance; only 120 Nazi tanks recrossed the Seine.

On the left of the Allied line Field-Marshal Sir Bernard Montgomery's 21st Army Group moved into the Low Countries, the Canadian 1st Army bypassing the Channel ports, which were mopped up after them between 1 and 30 September, to reach Bruges on 9 September. On their right, the British 1st Army took Amiens on 31 August and captured the German commander General Hans Eberbach in the process. They took Antwerp on 3 September and Brussels itself the next day. The Germans, however, did not relinquish their hold on the Scheldt estuary, thereby preventing the Allies from using the port of Antwerp. On the right of the Allied line, General Omar Bradley's 12th Army Group moved forward with equal success. On 3 September 25,000 prisoners were taken at Mons, and from 5 to 10 September Namur, Liège and Luxembourg were all liberated.

To the right, the US 3rd Army passed through Rheims and Chalons and took Verdun on 1 September. They crossed the Moselle west of Nancy on 7 September. The US 7th Army under General Alexander Patch, moving up the Rhône valley, linked with Patton's forces on 11 September and joined the Allied line north of the Swiss border.

Behind this spectacular advance the newly created US 9th Army under Lt-General W. H. Simpson began to reduce the German-held ports in Brittany. The Allied advance was now slowed by the ever-increasing length of supply lines and stiffened resistance of the Germans as they reached the Siegfried Line (qv). The battle on this front was preceded by a change in the German High Command, Model being replaced by Rundstedt. On 5 September, four days before this change occurred, Eisenhower had moved SHAEF (Supreme Headquarters, Allied Expeditionary Forces) to the continent in order to be in direct contact with the front.

FRANCE, SOUTHERN Second World War   15 August – 11 September 1944
Fought between the Allies and the Germans.

Following the Allied invasion of N France (NORMANDY), a secondary landing called Operation Dragoon (originally Anvil) was made along the Mediterranean coast. Its object was to open the port of Marseilles, after which the forces, consisting of experienced US troops and French troops from the Italian front, would move up the Rhône valley to threaten the flank and rear of the German forces menacing General Dwight D. Eisenhower's northern forces.

Eight thousand American and British soldiers were dropped by parachute before the main invasion, which took place on 15 August when General Alexander Patch's 7th Army landed between Cannes and Toulon. The US 6 Corps, composed of the 36th, 45th and 3rd Infantry under General Lucius Truscott, established a firm beachhead, meeting little opposition from the Germans, and proceeded to move NW towards the Rhône valley. Landing behind them were the French 2 Corps, which moved west towards Toulon and Marseilles, both of which were liberated by 28 August. When the French 1 Corps joined the attack a new force was created – the French 1st Army, commanded by General Jean de Lattre de Tassigny. 7 Corps, moving up the Rhône valley, isolated large segments of the German 19th Army under General W. Weise. Grenoble fell on 24 August, Lyons on 3 September. The corps linked with the right flank of Patton's 3rd Army on 11 September at Sombernon, NW of Dijon. In thirty-one days 270 miles had been covered and 57,000 prisoners taken. Twenty thousand troops of the German 1st Army in SW France surrendered without a fight.

The US 7th Army and the French 1st Army now came under Eisenhower's jurisdiction and became known as the 6th Army Group, under the command of General Jacob Devers.

GAZALA (Libya)   Second World War   26 May – 25 June 1942
Fought between the Allies under General Sir Neil Ritchie and the Germans and Italians under General Erwin Rommel.
Strength: British 849 tanks + 320 aircraft; Germans 332 tanks + Italians 228 tanks + Axis 704 aircraft.

After the British had forced Rommel to retreat back to El Agheila, Libya, following the first German offensive in N Africa, the Germans waited only four days before launching a counter-attack in W Cyrenaica. The 1st Armoured Division, which had only just arrived, was overrun or forced to retreat, along with the rest of Ritchie's troops. On 29 January Benghazi, which was full of supplies for the planned invasion of Tripolitania, fell. A defensive line was established at Gazala six days later. It shielded Tobruk (qv) and held for nearly four months with General W. H. E. Gott's 13 Corps of infantry along the coast on the right(N) and Lt-General Willoughby Norrie's armoured 30 Corps on the left, stretching south as far as Bir Hacheim.

The Gazala line consisted of a system of minefields and boxes 40 miles long and 10 miles deep, each box being garrisoned by a brigade group which held its own supplies for a week. On 26 May Rommel moved three armoured divisions around Bir Hacheim and attacked the British left flank and rear, heading for Tobruk, El Adem and Akroma to the NE. Having refuelled early on 27 May, Rommel advanced. Ritchie's development was at fault, however, for three armoured brigades from 30 Corps were widely separated and the 7th Armoured Division was altogether out of the battle. The situation was rectified after some piecemeal fighting, by which time Rommel's tanks were very short of fuel. After two weeks of fighting, the Germans broke through the British infantry in the centre and their supplies were brought safely through the Trigh Capuzzo. During this action, Lt-General Frank Messervy of the 7th Armoured Division was twice captured, and he twice escaped. The British counter-attacked the German bridgehead, but failed to take it and the Free French Brigade under General Pierre Koenig which bravely held Bir Hacheim was eventually forced to retreat. Ritchie, hoping that one more armoured clash might exhaust Rommel, attacked near the Knights-bridge crossing on 12 and 13 June. As a result, British armour suffered the worst defeat of its history, losing 250 out of 300 tanks, while the Germans were left with only 100 and the Italians with 60. The 'Gazala Gallop' followed when the remnants of the 8th Army raced for the Egyptian border. The 2nd S African Division was left to hold Tobruk, a major tactical error as the town fell two days later. It had withstood a siege of seven months a year earlier, but the defences were no longer in good order.

The British made a stand on 25 June at their Mersa Matruh (qv) base, which ended the fighting begun at Gazala and also the pursuit. General Sir Claude Auchinleck flew to the base from Cairo and relieved Ritchie, taking personal command of the 8th Army. The British lost 45,000 men during the battle and retreat and 33,000 men at the fall of Tobruk. Axis losses in killed and wounded were much the same.

GERMAN RAIDER SHIPS   Second World War   1940–1
Fought between the Allies and the Germans.

Following the exploits of the *Deutschland* and the *Graf Spee* at the outset of the war, Germany realised that an effective way of dislocating Allied shipping was to send out raider ships, forcing the Allies to alter their conventional naval dispositions. A further refinement was added whereby some German raiders were to be disguised as merchantmen, which would give them a greater chance of approaching and destroying Allied ships. Armed with 6–8 5.9-inch guns, torpedoes, mines and spotter aircraft, the vessels were capable of remaining at sea for a year. Seven merchantmen were converted to perform this task:

Atlantis (known as Ship 16 to the Germans and Raider C to the British): She sailed on 31 March 1940 and sank or captured 22 ships totalling 145,697 tons before the British cruiser *Devonshire* sank her on 22 November 1941.

Orion (Ship 36, Raider A): She set sail on 6 April 1940 and sank 9 ships totalling 57,744 tons, returning to port on 21 August 1941.

Widder (Ship 21, Raider D): She left port on 6 May 1940 to sink or capture 10 ships totalling 58,645 tons before returning on 31 October 1940.

Thor (Ship 10, Raider E): She sailed on 6 June 1940 and sank 11 ships totalling 83,000 tons, and was also involved with 3 British armed merchant cruisers, the *Alcantara, Caernarvon Castle* and *Voltaire* – the latter was sunk – before returning to port.

Pinguin (Ship 33, Raider F): She left port on 22 June 1940 and sank or captured 28 ships (of which 11 were whalers) totalling 136,551 tons. She was sunk by the British cruiser *Cornwall* on 8 May 1941.

Komet (Ship 45, Raider B): She left Germany on 9 July 1940 and, bound for the Pacific, sailed round the north of Russia using Russian ice breakers. She sank 6 ships totalling 42,959 tons before returning home.

Kormoran (Ship 42, Raider G): She sailed on 3 December 1940 and sank or captured 11 vessels totalling 68,174 tons before the Australian cruiser *Sydney* sank her on 19 November 1941.

As well as these armed merchantmen, Germany also sent out warships as raiders. Because of their limited range, they had to remain in the chief shipping lanes and ran much more serious risks of interception by large Allied forces. Moreover, they were ordered to avoid provoking battle. The *Admiral Scheer*, however, made a successful cruise in which she sank 16 ships totalling 99,059 tons between 23 October 1940 and 1 April 1941. On 5 November 1940 she had sunk the British armed merchant cruiser *Jervis Bay*. The *Scharnhorst* and *Gneisenau* made a punishing raid, leaving Germany on 21 January 1941 and returning to Brest on 22 March. In the interim they sank 22 ships totalling 115,622 tons. The *Admiral Hipper* made two forays (30 November – 27 December 1940 and 1 – 13 February 1941), during which she sank 9 ships totalling 40,078 tons.

GERMAN VENGEANCE-WEAPON BOMBARDMENT   Second World War
8 September 1944 – 29 March 1945
Fought between the Allies and the Germans.

After the D-Day invasion of France by the Allies (NORMANDY; also FRANCE, SOUTHERN), the Germans began launching what they called V-weapons against England ('V' standing for *Vergeltung*, or vengeance) from bases on the Atlantic coast. The first of these weapons was the V-1 or 'buzz bomb', a pilotless aircraft carrying a ton of explosives. The V-2, which was first launched on 8 September, was a rocket with the same amount of explosive packed into its warhead. The rocket was, however, still in an experimental stage and its average accuracy error was 10 miles. Altogether, 8,000 V-1 bombs were launched against England and about 10,000 against cities on the continent, mainly Antwerp. Of V-2s, 1,200 were launched against England and 1,750 against Antwerp, Liège and Brussels. In these attacks 24,000 British were killed or wounded by the V-1 and 9,100 by the V-2. Continental casualties were about the same.

Many V-1s were shot down by fighter aircraft and anti-aircraft guns, but a more effective defence was constant harassment of the launching sites. The attacks were stopped on 29 March 1945 when the last of these bases fell into Allied hands.

GERMANY, AERIAL BOMBARDMENT   Second World War   1942-5
Fought between the Allies and the Germans.

It was the Germans who fostered the idea of knocking out enemy cities and strategic sites by aerial bombardment and, although it was at first a successful policy, it failed in the Battle of Britain (qv) largely because no land invasion followed up the air attacks. When, in 1942, the Allies took the offensive against the Germans, they used strategic bombing only as a preliminary to invasion by ground forces which would in turn be supported by tactical bombing and strafing attacks.

The chief air offensive against Germany began on the night of 30 May 1942 when the first of three 1,000-plane raids, under the personal command of Air Marshal John Baldwin, hit Cologne with 2,000 tons of bombs in ninety minutes. (Baldwin had bombed Cologne in the First World War and was the most senior RAF officer to take part in an air bombardment of Germany. He was originally in the 8th Hussars.) Essen was similarly treated the following night and Bremen on 25 June. During June the US 8th Air Force was setting up bases in England, and the first American raid took place on 18 August when B–17 Flying Fortress bombers were sent on a daylight raid on strategic Nazi points around Rouen.

Henceforth the pattern of Allied bombing was to be thus: the Halifaxes and Lancasters of RAF Bomber Command carried out night raids of saturation strikes and the American B–17s concentrated on daylight raids to wipe out specific targets. Night raids were at first the more effective, but the armament of the B–17s was improved, long-range fighter escort developed and the Americans gradually took over more of the bombing. Airfields, transport and communications centres, aircraft factories and fuel refineries were among the targets that both offensives struck, both having the same objectives. Necessity forced the swift development of both aircraft and bombs; in 1942 the largest bombs were 4,000 pounds, but by 1944 12,000- and 22,000-pound bombs were being used against targets all over Europe. By the same token bombs loads also increased, the average load in 1942 being 2,800 pounds while in 1943 it was 7,500 pounds. Three major attacks against Germany were launched by Air Chief Marshal Sir Arthur Harris in 1943. The first of these, from March to July, was concentrated on the Ruhr. Then, between 24 July and 3 August, Hamburg became the target. The third and final onslaught was against Berlin, sixteen large-scale attacks being undertaken in four months beginning in November.

The switches in target occurred chiefly because it was necessary to be one step ahead of the Luftwaffe night fighters all the time and also because it was then possible to outwit the anti-aircraft crews. When the British undertook an attack on Nuremberg (Nürnberg) on the night of 30 March 1944, 94 out of their 795 aircraft were shot down, making the raid the most costly of the war.

Under General Ira Eaker and then General Carl Spaatz, the US 8th Air Force continued to increase their daylight attacks, their main targets being German fighter squadrons and the aircraft industry. There was no long-range fighter cover for these bombers throughout 1943 and the operations became increasingly costly. On 14 October 291 B–17s attacked the Schweinfurt ball-bearing factories and 65 bombers were shot down during the raid, chiefly by ME–109s and FW–190s – the date is known as 'Black Thursday'.

Earlier in the Year, on 1 August, B–24s (Liberators) based in N Africa had attacked Ploesti, Romania, at low level. This was the main petroleum base in Nazi-held Europe. Out of 178 aircraft, 53 were shot down and 310 crewmen killed, while 108 were captured in Romania and 79 interned in Turkey. American long-range fighters were now being produced in great quantity, their limit of activity being increased from 475 miles to 850 miles. Thunderbolts (P–47s), Lightnings (P–38s) and Mustangs (P–51s) were all ready to be committed to the air offensive by 23 February 1944. General James Doolittle sent them with the B–17s and, after a week of heavy precision bombing, the Allies had gained control of the air over Germany.

From then on Allied air superiority continued to increase. From March 1944 the Allies moved the main effort of their bombing to railways in France, Belgium and W Germany as a prelude to the D-Day invasion (NORMANDY). In three months 66,000 tons of bombs were dropped, and this onslaught had the effect of more or less isolating German troops in Normandy. Just before 6 June, bridges and rolling stock became the targets, and during the invasion on the ground the US 9th Air Force under General Hoyt Vandenberg and the 2nd British Tactical Air Force under Air Marshal Sir Arthur Coningham gave close support to the ground forces. Nine thousand aircraft attacked targets on the front line and hit communications and transport farther back, out of the range of troops on the ground. During the main Allied crossing of the Rhine, between 21 and 24 March, 42,000 raids were flown against the Germans. The worst air attack in history was made against Dresden (qv) on the night of 13 April 1945 when 723 Lancasters attacked the city, followed the next day by 450 B–17s. It is estimated that between 50,000 and 100,000 people were killed during the two raids, leaving too few able-bodied people to bury the victims.

The Allies dropped a total of 2,700,000 tons of bombs on Europe, of which over two-thirds fell after the D-Day invasion. During the Battle of the Bulge at Ardennes (qv) in 1945, the Luftwaffe made their final major counter-attack, destroying 156 Allied aircraft on 1 January. German losses were so high, however, that the attacks were not maintained and Adolf Hitler's last hope of regaining air superiority, the piloted jet-propelled aircraft, was never exploited owing to constant harassment by the Allies. Undoubtedly the massive air bombardment contributed to the Allied victory; but the cost was high, since each American heavy bomber carried 10 men, and each British bomber 7. The total cost of establishing Allied air superiority over Europe was 140,000 men (including over 70,000 crew of Bomber Command), ten times as many casualties as were caused by the D-Day invasion itself. The RAF effort also included supplies and support to the French

Partisans (the Maquis), whose efforts General Dwight D. Eisenhower considered were worth twelve divisions to him at the time of the invasion of Normandy.

GERMANY, EAST   Second World War   January–May 1945
Fought between the Russians and the Germans.

Three Russian army groups had thrust their way through Poland during the winter offensive of 1944–5 to cross the German border at Pomerania, Brandenburg and Silesia. On 31 January Marshal Georgi Zhukov's armoured van from the 1st White Russian Army Group reached the Oder River at Küstrin (Kostrzyn), 45 miles from Berlin. At this point the Russians paused to extend their flanks, clear up behind them and regroup themselves before continuing their drive deeper into Germany.

In the north, Zhukov moved down the east bank of the Oder to reach the Baltic opposite Stettin (Szczecin) on 4 March. Joined by General Konstantin Rokossovsky's 2nd White Russian Group, Zhukov cleared the Baltic coast and Rokossovsky then moved west to form the right flank of the final offensive. General Vasily Sokolovsky moved up on his left to take command of the 1st White Russians at Küstrin. Zhukov assumed command of the whole front which now lay along the Oder and Neisse Rivers. To the south, General Ivan Konev's 1st Ukrainian Army Group had moved through Silesia, leaving Breslau (Wroclaw) encircled–it did not fall until 7 May. Moving west, Konev outflanked the Oder to come up on the Neisse, so that the Russians stood on a more or less straight line stretching from the Baltic to the Czechoslovakian border. Colonel-General Ferdinand Schörner was given command of the defences of the line in March, when he was promoted to Field-Marshal and given command of all German armies in the east. General Gotthard Heinrici replaced General Heinrich Himmler as Commander of the German forces on the Oder east of Berlin. While, on this front, the two armies faced each other for ten weeks remaining nearly inactive, Allied heavy bombers struck at targets just behind the front, and on 7 March, Allied armies crossed the Rhine and began moving east. By 14 April only 75 miles separated the two fronts. On that day Konev moved across the Neisse, following a heavy artillery bombardment, to drive towards Dresden. His force averaged an advance of 18 miles per day.

On the north of the Russian front, the 1st White Russians burst out of the Küstrin bridgehead supported by most of the Soviet tactical air force. A force of 4,000 tanks moved on Berlin while Rokossovsky crossed the Oder north of Küstrin. Konev, moving north up the Spree River, changed the axis of his march and routed a large German force which threatened Sokolovsky's left flank. By 18 April the line of the German defences had broken, and on 20 April Russian armour reached Berlin (qv), which was encircled by 25 April and fell on 2 May. In the north, Russian armies had passed through Rostock on 27 April on their way west to link up with Field-Marshal Sir Bernard Montgomery's 21st Army Group. To the south Konev moved towards the Elbe, and on 25 April at Torgau, 60 miles south of Berlin, a Russian patrol met a patrol from the 69th Division of the 1st Army, part of General Omar Bradley's 12th Army Group.

The country was now split in two. Adolf Hitler committed suicide six days later and the German government sought surrender terms. On 4 May all German armies in the north, including those in Denmark and the Netherlands, capitulated. All German forces surrendered unconditionally on 8 May.

GERMANY, WEST   Second World War   March–May 1945
Fought between the Allies and the Germans.

Following the Allied victory in the Rhineland (qv), General Dwight D. Eisenhower regrouped his forces before continuing his offensive deeper into Germany. Eighty-five divisions were divided into seven armies and three army groups. To the north, Field-Marshal Sir Bernard Montgomery had under his command General Henry Crerar's Canadian 1st, General Sir Miles Dempsey's British 2nd and Lt-General W. H. Simpson's US 9th. In the centre, General Omar Bradley had General Courtney Hodges's US 1st, General George Patton's US 3rd, and in the south General Jacob Devers commanded General Alexander Patch's US 7th and General Jean de Lattre de Tassigny's French 1st. The Allies also had almost total control of the air both tactically and strategically. The German forces were so depleted that though Field-Marshal Albert Kesselring mustered sixty divisions to face the Allies, they were so under-strength that only about twenty-six full-strength divisions could be made up of the decimated forces. The Allied superiority in the air made distribution of ammunition, fuel and other supplies difficult; the only German advantage lay in the fanaticism of some units, notably the SS, and the knowledge of the territory which the Germans had, fighting on their own ground. Any errors by German commanders meant that they would be relieved by Adolf Hitler.

On 23 March the British 2nd Army crossed the Rhine at Wesel. The US 9th, to the right, began to cross the following day. An airdrop of the US 17th and British 6th Airborne Divisions aided the Allies in their thrust east. On 28 March the Allies reached the N German Plain near Haltern and Simpson's 9th moved along the north edge of the Ruhr towards Lippstadt. The US 1st and 3rd Armies both moved across the river from their bridgeheads on the east on 25 March. Hodges then moved east to take Marburg on 28 March before turning north towards Lippstadt. To the right, Patton moved through Frankfurt NE towards Kassel. South of this drive, Patch's 7th forced a passage of the Rhine at Worms on 26 March and took Mannheim on 29 March. The French 1st crossed the Rhine at Philippsburg on 1 April. On 28 March Eisenhower ordered Bradley to make the main attack along a front stretching from Kassel through Mühlhausen to Leipzig. Three armies were to be used and the 9th came under his control on 1 April. Montgomery was ordered to cover the left flank by attacking through the Netherlands and N Germany. Devers was to perform the same task on the south flank. The 1st and 3rd Armies moved east at an average of 30 miles a day, and on 1 April Hodges's left wing linked with Simpson's 9th Army near Lippstadt, thus surrounding the Ruhr valley. Troops from the 9th Army were ordered to hold the north side of the encirclement while the rest of the force moved east. Simpson took Hanover on 9 April and reached the Elbe on 11 April after a fierce fight at Magdeburg. On his right, Hodges wiped out an SS unit at Paderborn, took Kassel on 2 April and Leipzig on 19 April. On 25 April a Russian patrol met an American one from the 69th Infantry, 5 Corps, near Torgau. Kesselring's defences were shattered and Germany was cut in two. The left wing of the US 3rd took Mühlhausen on 4 April and crossed the border into Czechoslovakia on 17 April.

The advance was halted by Allied directive at Pilsen, and Patton's right wing turned south, crossed the Danube at Ingolstadt on 25 April and moved into Austria at Linz on 4 May. On the SW, Nürnberg was taken by Patch's 7th Army on 20 April, Stuttgart fell on 23 April and Munich on 30 April following the crossing of the Danube. Berchtesgaden and Salzburg fell on 4 May, on which day Patch's right wing moved through the Brenner Pass to meet up with the US 5th Army coming up from Italy. The south of the Allied line, held by de Lattre de Tassigny's French 1st, moved to take Karlsruhe on 4 April and, having cleared the Black Forest, moved SE along the Swiss border. It had feared that German guerillas (Nazi Werewolves) would continue the fight from a strong redoubt in Bavaria, but on 5 May all German forces on the south front capitulated. On the north end of the Allied line, Montgomery advanced quickly. Crerar's Canadian 1st moved north towards Emden and Wilhelmshaven and so cut off General Johannes von Blaskowitz's German troops in the Netherlands. To the right, Dempsey with the British 2nd thrust towards the Elbe, beating back rearguard actions which were occasionally encountered, fought by Field-Marshal Ernst Busch. The left bank of the river was clear by 26 April and Lübeck and Wismar were taken on 2 May. Hamburg fell on 3 May and all German troops in the north surrendered to Montgomery on 4 May. Hitler was by now dead and Admiral Karl Dönitz was in command of Germany. Pressed on both sides by the Allies and Russia, he sued for peace and Germany surrendered unconditionally on 8 May.

Since D-Day (NORMANDY), eleven months earlier, the Allies had lost 187,000 killed, 546,000 wounded and 110,000 missing. German losses were 80,000 killed, 265,000 wounded and 500,000 missing.

GOTHIC LINE (central Italy)   Second World War   4 June 1944–2 April 1945
Fought between the Allies and the Germans.

After the Allies broke through the Gustav–Cassino line (qv) and took Rome on 4 June the 15th Army Group, commanded by General Sir Harold Alexander, pressed north. During this drive seven Allied divisions (the US 6 Corps and a French corps) were taken out of the line to take part in the projected invasion of France, while the Germans on the other hand were reinforced by eight new divisions which were fed into the 10th and 14th Armies. The Allied 5th Army (General Mark Clark) and 8th Army (General Sir Oliver Leese) encountered heavy opposition as a result. A strong German defence held the road and rail junction of Arezzo for a week before a strong British assault on 16 July forced them to withdraw. To the right, the Polish 2 Corps moved up the Adriatic coast to take Ancona, and to the left the 5th Army approached the Arno River, taking Leghorn on 19 July and threatening Pisa and Florence.

Having moved 250 miles in just over two months, the Allies were checked in early August by the outposts of the Gothic Line, a prepared defence to which the Germans now fell back. The weight of the Allied attack now shifted to the 8th Army on the right. On 26 August ten divisions of the 8th Army attacked along a 20-mile front on the Adriatic flank. Although progress was slow, it was steady. Rimini, the eastern anchor of the Gothic Line, fell on 20 September. On the left, the eight divisions of the 5th Army took up the attack and captured Pisa on 2 September. In the centre, the Allies moved on Bologna, but a German counter-attack on 20 October halted the advance. Field-Marshal Albert Kesselring had now blocked the holes made by the Allied advances along the Gothic Line, and with the approach of winter the Allies were unable to make an end to the Italian campaign. From the end of October until 2 April the following year only Ravenna was taken in the 8th Army's push to the south side of Lake Comacchio. It was the longest period of inaction during the Italian campaign.

During the winter, Alexander replaced General Sir Henry Maitland-Wilson as Supreme Commander in the Mediterranean and Clark took command of the 15th Army Group. General Lucius Truscott took command of the 5th Army and General Sir Richard McCreery of the 8th. General Heinrich von Vietinghoff-Scheel took command of the German forces in Italy, replacing Kesselring. In April the offensive was renewed and carried to the Po valley (qv).

GRAF SPEE (S Atlantic)   Second World War   12–17 December 1939
Fought between the Germans under Captain Hans Langsdorff and the British under Commodore Henry Harwood.

In this first naval battle of the war a weak British squadron consisting of a heavy cruiser, the *Exeter*, and 2 light cruisers, the *Ajax* and *Achilles*, met the German pocket battleship *Graf Spee* in the S Atlantic. In a running battle on 12 December the *Exeter* was crippled by the heavy guns of *Graf Spee*, which was also faster. *Ajax*, too, was hard hit, but the fire of the two light cruisers distracted the German captain. The German ship was, however, badly damaged – some 70 hits – and Langsdorff put into Montevideo for repairs. On the following day the Uruguayan government gave the Germans the legal seventy-two hours in port. Langsdorff left almost immediately, but scuttled the *Graf Spee* outside the harbour and then committed suicide.

Allied shipping lanes in the area were made safer by the destruction of the German ship.

GREECE   Second World War   28 October 1940–24 April 1941
Fought between the Italians under Benito Mussolini and the Allies.

The Italians sought conquests in the Balkans commensurate with German victories in the north, and the occupation of Albania in April 1939 served as the jumping-off point for the invasion of Greece the following year.

On 28 October six Italian divisions under General Visconti Prasca crossed the border in NW Greece on four fronts. Three divisions which guarded the border were driven back for the first two weeks, but when these were reinforced, the invasion faltered and, by 8 November, the difficult terrain and stiffened resistance halted the attack. General Alexandros Papagos began a counter-attack on 14 November with a force which was soon sixteen divisions strong. The Greeks moved 40 miles into Albania, but were not able to win a decisive victory over the Italian army which now totalled twenty-six divisions. Marshal Pietro Badoglio, the Italian Chief of Staff, was replaced by General Count Ugo Cavallero on 6 December, but no offensive was undertaken. Heavy fighting took place throughout the winter, the Greeks being aided by five squadrons of British aircraft (this was later increased to seven). In February Greece accepted the help of a small British and Commonwealth force from N Africa, amounting to about five divisions. In March the 2nd New Zealand, 6th Australian Divisions and the 1st Armoured Brigade took up positions west of Salonika from the Vardar valley NW along the line of the Aliakmon River–Vermion Range. On 6 April the Germans entered the scene by invading S Yugoslavia and Greece simultaneously. During the first four days of fighting, four Greek divisions were isolated and destroyed in E Macedonia when the Germans attacked from Bulgaria through the Metaxes Line. West of this, a German corps advanced down the Vardar valley to the Salonika region where it met the British line on 9 April. Meanwhile, three German divisions reached Bitolj (Monastir) in SW Yugoslavia and prevented any link-up between the forces of the two invaded countries. The advance of this force threatened to cut off the fifteen Greek divisions in Albania and to envelop the left of the British line which was commanded by General Sir Henry Maitland-Wilson. The Allied forces began to fall back to a line running west from Mount Olympus on 12–13 April, but continued German pursuit and air attacks from 800 aircraft forced the forces to withdraw on 20 April to a position west of Thermopylae.

Belgrade had meanwhile surrendered on 13 April, and on 17 April King Peter II capitulated. On 20 April 300,000 Greek troops on the Albanian border surrendered and the British began to evacuate those that remained of the 56,657 troops who had landed only a month earlier. By the night of 28 April 41,000 men had been embarked, 26,000 of whom went to Crete, the rest to Egypt. Twenty-six ships involved were sunk by air attacks. King George II surrendered Greece on 24 April. British and Imperial troops suffered 13,000 casualties, of whom 8,000 were taken prisoner. The Italians lost 125,000, the Germans 5,500. Although Greek losses were not reported, the Germans claimed to have taken 270,000 prisoners.

Although Germany had won the battle in Greece, the concentration of troops needed there is said to have delayed the invasion of Russia for five weeks. The engagement marked the third time that British troops had been beaten on the continent, the other two being in Flanders and Norway (qqv). The follow-up to this battle was taking shape in Crete. However, Britain gained from Greece over 2 million tons of merchant shipping and some naval ships, all with their crews, which, at this time, was worth more to her war effort than her military losses. Enver Hodja, in neighbouring Albania, continued to resist the Germans from his mountain sanctuaries until near to the end of the war. In 1945 he became Prime Minister.

GUADALCANAL (S Pacific)   Second World War   7 August 1942–9 February 1943

Fought between the Americans under General Alexander Vandegrift and the Japanese under General Haruyoshi Hyakutake.

Strength: Americans 3 aircraft carriers (*Saratoga, Enterprise, Wasp*) + 1 battleship (*North Carolina*) + 6 cruisers + 15 destroyers + (initially) 19,000 marines, (later) 50,000 marines and US army; Japanese 8th Fleet (Vice-Admiral Gunichi Mikawa) + (initially) 6,000, (later) 25,000.

Throughout 1942 the Japanese moved south through the Solomon Islands until in July they reached the island of Guadalcanal, 1,000 miles off the NE coast of Queensland, Australia. The Japanese began at once to construct an airfield on the island which, if completed, would introduce a serious threat to Allied communications in the SW Pacific, particularly the supply line in that area. The 1st US Marine Division and two Raider battalions under Vandegrift landed on the north side of Guadalcanal on 7 August in order to prevent this from happening. The force landed on Tulagi and two smaller islands near by. In the first Allied counter-offensive against Japan, called Operation Cactus, the marines secured all their objectives, including the incomplete airfield near Lunga Point, within forty-eight hours of their arrival. The Japanese reacted strongly, however, pouring reinforcements into Guadalcanal and sending naval units south to bombard both US shore positions and the US fleet which was in the vicinity endeavouring to protect the American garrison. There ensued one of the longest and bloodiest battles of the war in the Pacific.

On the island, the Americans constructed a defensive line of 7 miles by 4 miles around the airfield–called Henderson Field, after a marine major killed in the Battle of Midway Island (qv). To the east, the Japanese massed at the Tenaru River for a counter-attack; this force was to become the Japanese 17th Army, commanded by Hyakutake. The attack was beaten back on 20 and 21 August at the Ilu River. US aircraft had begun to use the airfield on 20 August and troop landings increased American strength on the island to about 6,000. The Japanese, also reinforced, concentrated their efforts against the east and south between 12 and 14 September, attacking the perimeter defences in the Lunga River–Bloody Ridge area and, although the marines held their ground, their bridgehead was threatened by Japanese warships which bombarded the position from off-shore and by bombers which attacked it from the air. The equatorial climate and malarial jungle took a heavy toll on both sides, but both knew that whatever the outcome of the combat on land, the battle would be won by the force which won supremacy of sea and air, enabling reinforcements to be brought in to the island.

On 18 September the 2nd Marine Division and the Army Americal Division began to land, but the Japanese strength was increasing so much faster that they soon outnumbered the Americans, having built their strength up to 25,000. On 27 September at Matanikau River the marines launched an attack, which was beaten back with a loss of 60 killed and 100 wounded. The Japanese continued relentlessly to try and recapture Henderson Field and their attacks were most dangerous at night. Throughout October and November ground forces tried to infiltrate the position every night. The Americans held their ground, however, and inflicted high casualties at a ratio of about 10 to 1. Admiral William Halsey, now in command in the S Pacific, had energetically counter-attacked on sea and in the air and, after the naval actions at Guadalcanal (qv) on 15 November, he forced the Japanese to the defensive, so that no further landings were made on the island, enabling the Americans to take the initiative on land.

In close-range, fierce fighting the Japanese were steadily forced to give ground. On 9 December General Alexander Patch took command on the island for the army, relieving the marines (1st Division). The 25th Infantry Division arrived on the island on 2 January 1943 and the 14 Corps was formed. Nearly 50,000 US troops were now on the island and victory was ensured. By 6 February Japanese destroyers had skilfully evacuated 12,000 men from Cape Esperance, on the NW tip of Guadalcanal: a fact that was not realised by the Americans until 9 February! Still 14,000 Japanese were left behind, killed or missing, of whom 9,000 died from disease or starvation, and 1,000 Japanese were captured. American losses were 1,600 killed and 4,200 wounded. There were many casualties from disease; in November 3,200 were incapacitated by malaria alone.

The American victory in Guadalcanal opened the way for further advantages to be gained over the Japanese in the Solomon Islands (qv). It was the first time that the Japanese sweep south had been checked. Five men of the United States Marine Corps won the Medal of Honor, including Captain Joe Foss, a Wildcat ace who shot down 26 Japanese aircraft.

GUADALCANAL NAVAL ACTION (S Pacific)   Second World War   7 August – 30 November 1942

Fought between the Allies and the Japanese.

The actions connected with the landing on and reinforcing of Guadalcanal fall into six separate battles. At the start of the operation the Americans landed a force of marines on the island of Guadalcanal and captured a half-completed airfield which the Japanese had begun to build when they had occupied the island as a stepping-stone on their sweep south down the Solomon Islands (qv). The American action roused them to strong retaliation. The Japanese navy dominated the central and N Solomon Islands and the channel which ran between two parallel chains of islands, known as the Slot. Nipponese traffic on this waterway was so heavy that it was nicknamed the Tokyo Express. Japanese naval units moved down this channel to attack the Allied fleet which protected the Americans on shore and the focus of the action took place in Sealark Channel, north of Guadalcanal, and facing the beachhead behind which lay the airfield called Henderson Field. So many ships were sunk here that it became known as Iron Bottom Bay.

The Allied Commander in the S Pacific, US Admiral Robert Lee Ghormley, ordered the US landing on the island and the 1st Marines were put ashore by Admiral Richmond Turner's amphibious force, which was protected by a group of aircraft carriers under Admiral Frank Fletcher. It was then that the Japanese moved reinforcements down the Tokyo Express, their transports protected by cruisers, destroyers and submarines. The Allied fleet was forced to try and defend in two opposing directions at once; they had to keep the US bridgehead on the island open and they wished to try and stem the incessant flow of Japanese reinforcements emerging from the Tokyo Express. Whichever side gained superiority both at sea and in the air would win the battle on land, since the land forces were dependent on receiving reinforcements and supplies from their respective navies.

7 August, Savo Island: Admiral Gunichi Mikawa's Japanese force entered Iron Bottom Bay before dawn and sank four heavy cruisers – the Australian *Canberra*, and the US *Chicago*, *Quincy* and *Vincennes* – with the loss of 1,000 seamen. Admiral Frank Fletcher's carriers, which had stood off while the marines were put ashore, had left the area, so the Japanese were able to pull back up the Slot, suffering only minor damage. Turner's amphibious force also pulled out later that day, leaving the marines unsupported on Guadalcanal.

24–5 August, E Solomon Islands: Admiral Nobutake Kondo attacked the Allied fleet with carriers and badly damaged the US carrier *Enterprise*. This time, however, the Japanese light carrier *Ryujo* was sunk and 90 Japanese aircraft were shot down. Both sides lost a destroyer and the Japanese withdrew. From that time on, the Japanese sent in their reinforcements under cover of darkness, their warships having as complete control of the Solomon Islands waters at night as the US planes had by day. On 15 September the US carrier *Wasp* was sunk by submarines in these waters, as were several destroyers.

11–12 October, Cape Esperance: Yet another Japanese attacking force disgorged from the Slot after dark to attack Henderson Field, and although Admiral Norman Scott's cruisers and destroyers beat back a strong thrust, on following nights the field was heavily bombarded and damaged by naval gunfire. At the same time, Japanese reinforcements were being landed at night. On 18 October Ghormley was replaced by Admiral William Halsey as the Allied Commander in the S Pacific.

26 October, Santa Cruz Islands: Halsey took the initiative in the first of his Guadalcanal actions, sending his carriers out against the Japanese fleet, which lay in the waters to the east of the Solomons. Although 2 Japanese carriers and a cruiser were bombed and 100 planes shot down, 74 US aircraft were lost and the *Hornet* – which had seen action at 'Shangri-La' and Midway (qqv) – was sunk. The *Enterprise* was once again badly damaged, and now there was no operational US aircraft carrier in the Pacific.

13–15 November, Guadalcanal: The battle for naval supremacy reached a climax in November when both sides were putting reinforcements ashore at the same time. Turner, having put a further 6,000 marines ashore with his amphibious force, withdrew SE. He detached Admiral Daniel Callaghan with 5 cruisers and 8 destroyers. At the same time Admiral Raizo Tanaka was moving down the Slot with 11,000 troops in 11 transports and 12 destroyers. He was preceded by a force which included 2 battleships, the *Hiei* and *Kirishima*, under Kondo. This force met Callaghan's in Iron Bottom Bay during the night of 12 November.

In half an hour Callaghan was killed, 3 US destroyers and 2 cruisers – the *Atlantic* and *Juneau* (700 men with them) – were sunk, and the cruiser *Portland* was crippled. The Japanese renewed the attack the next night, bombarding Henderson Field with about 1,000 shells. At dawn, however, planes from the *Enterprise*, now operational again, and bombers from Henderson Field itself and Espiritu Santo, a base in the New Hebrides, attacked the Japanese. A cruiser was sunk and 3 others were damaged, and in addition 6 transports were sunk and 1 was crippled. On the night of 14 November Tanaka pushed on with his remaining 4 transports to Guadalcanal and disembarked the troops behind a screen of the *Kirishima*, 4 cruisers and 9 destroyers. The *Kirishima* and a destroyer were sunk by the battleship *Washington*, commanded by Admiral Willis Lee. Allied losses were 4 destroyers sent to the bottom, and the battleship *South Dakota*, which was crippled.

30 November, Tassafaronga: This was the last attempt to land troops on Guadalcanal by the Japanese. It was a feeble effort, in which 8 destroyers, serving as transports, were turned back after 1 had been sunk and another badly damaged. The Americans lost the cruiser *Northampton*.

After this, the Guadalcanal garrison was no longer reinforced by the Japanese, although destroyers brought supplies in to the troops under cover of darkness. After the land battle was won by the Allies, the Japanese took 12,000 surviving troops off in destroyers. The battle for naval supremacy was dearly won, but the Americans now had a foothold in the Solomons. Total Allied losses were 2 heavy carriers, 8 cruisers and 14 destroyers. Japanese losses were 1 light carrier, 2 battleships, 4 cruisers, 11 destroyers and 6 submarines.

GUAM (Central Pacific)   Second World War   10 December 1941
Fought between the Americans and the Japanese.
Strength: Americans 430 of the United States Marine Corps + 180 Chamorro guards; Japanese 5,400.

The Japanese invaded Guam in the Mariana Islands (qv) as part of their opening attack on American bases in the Pacific. McMillin, Governor of Guam, had only a few troops to defend the island against a strong amphibious landing, against which they fought for three hours before being overwhelmed and surrendering the island. The Americans and Guamanians lost 17 men killed, the Japanese losing only a single invader.

The Japanese went on to conquer all the Pacific.

GUSTAV–CASSINO LINE (Italy)   Second World War   November 1943–August 1944
Fought between the Allies and the Axis.

The Allies overran the south of Italy during the autumn of 1943. After taking Naples on 1 October the 5th Army under General Mark Clark moved north across the Volturno River on 12–15 October. By mid-November, however, as the force approached the Garigliano, mud and the increasingly strong German defences halted the advance.

To the right (Adriatic), the British 8th Army under General Sir Bernard Montgomery crossed the Trigno and Sangro (qv) rivers before being blocked on 28 December at Ortona. Across a natural line of defence, Field-Marshal Albert Kesselring had constructed fortifications known as the Gustav Line, held by a German army of eighteen divisions under General Heinrich von Vietinghoff-Scheel. The line stretched from the mouth of the Garigliano River on the west across the Apennines to a site north of Ortona on the Adriatic Sea. The two main roads to Rome were Highway 7, running near the Tyrrhenian coast, and Highway 6, which ran through the Liri valley (a tributary of the Garigliano), entering it at Cassino. The eleven divisions of General Sir Harold Alexander's 15th Army Group had to break through the Gustav Line (known as Winterstellung, the winter line) in order to reach Rome, the main objective in the Italian offensive. Although the Allies had superiority of the air, the German positions in the mountains were strongly entrenched so that this advantage was offset. Seven Allied divisions were taken from the front to prepare for the cross-Channel offensive the following year and this weakened their position. On 10 December General Dwight D. Eisenhower also went to England, to be replaced by General Sir Henry Maitland-Wilson and Montgomery, whose command of the 8th Army was given to General Sir Oliver Leese. In January 1944 the Allies had deployed from left to right the six divisions of the 5th army consisting of the British 10 Corps (General Sir Richard McCreery), the US 2 Corps (General Geoffrey Keyes) and the Free French Corps (General Alphonse Juin), the five divisions of the 8th Army comprising the British 5 and 13 Corps. The US 6 Corps was withdrawn from the line. It was to make the Anzio landing in order to try and outflank the Gustav Line.

Although the winter weather was bad, the Allies continued to attack the line, particularly at the point where Monte Cassino dominated it. On 17 January the British 10 Corps forced a crossing of the Lower Garigliano on the left, but no further progress was made. On 20 January the US 36th Infantry was thrown back at the Rapido. The 34th Infantry, the other division of 2 Corps, tried but failed to take Cassino early in February. This sector of the Gustav Line was dominated by Hill 516, 1,100 feet high with a Benedictine monastery on its summit. To the right of the 5th Army, the French made small gains but were unable to move far. On 16 February, after the monastery had been heavily bombed, the New Zealand 2 Corps under General Sir Bernard Freyberg, taken from the British 8th Army, tried to take the hill. It, too, failed.

On 15 March another attack was made. This, the third assault, was undertaken by Freyberg's 2nd New Zealand, 4th Indian and 78th British Divisions, but although they reached the town of Cassino, they were unable to ascend the hill being blocked by the German 1st Parachute Division. The attack was at a standstill by 23 March and 2,400 casualties had been sustained. Most of the 8th Army was then moved from the Adriatic to the Cassino area and the 5th Army massed on the Lower Garigliano. A 2,000-gun bombàrdment on 11 May preceded a surge forward by the Allies, four corps abreast. Along a 20-mile front stretching from Cassino to the sea, the Germans were gradually pushed back, and on 17 May, General Wladislaw Anders's Polish 2 Corps finally took Cassino.

On the left, the US 2 Corps moved up the coast and joined with 6 Corps, which had broken out of its beachhead at Anzio two days previously. The 5th and 8th Armies had meanwhile broken through both the Gustav Line and the Adolf Hitler Line, a secondary defence behind the front. The Germans stood SE of Rome, but they were beaten back and the US 2 Corps, led by the 88th Infantry, entered the city on 4 June. The Allies pursued the retreating German 14th (General Hans Georg Mackensen) and 10th Armies, and by 4 August they had moved 250 miles north to a line stretching from Pisa and Florence to Ancona. Here the Germans had built further defences, the Gothic Line (qv).

HABBANIYA (Iraq)   Second World War   18 April–14 July 1941
Fought between the Allies and the Iraqis under Rashid Ali.

At the beginning of the war the Axis was so successful in the Middle East that a pro-German government under Rashid Ali was established in Iraq. The rightful regent of that country, Emir Abdul-Ilah, fled to a British warship at Basra on the Persian Gulf and on 18 April the British, in order to protect their treaty rights, landed a brigade from India. On 2 May the Iraqis laid siege to the British air base at Habbaniya, 40 miles west of Bagdad, with 9,000 troops and 50 guns. Air Vice-Marshal Smart had 250 British infantry, 1,000 RAF personnel and 1,000 native troops with which to defend the base, plus 9,000 civilians. Hampered by the absence of any artillery, the decisive factor in the battle was the continual attacks by aircraft which finally silenced Iraqi artillery altogether, so that after four days Rashid Ali's troops began to withdraw. The British promptly counter-attacked and on 7 May drove the Iraqis back across the River Euphrates taking 400 prisoners. With the base at Habbaniya relieved by a motorised unit from Haifa the British pursued on 19 May and captured Al Falluja, pressing on to take Baghdad on 30 May. Rashid Ali left the country and Emir Abdul-Ilah resumed government on 31 May.

Allied dominance was now won over the Middle East. On 14 July a force of British and Free French removed the pro-Vichy government of Syria to the west with a loss of 4,600 British and 6,500 French. Iran, to the east, was occupied by British and Russian troops on 25 August in order to forestall a possible *coup* by pro-Axis forces in that country. British casualties were 22 killed and 42 wounded. General Sir Archibald Wavell, Commander in the Middle East, directed the operations in Iraq. He and his successor, General Sir Claude Auchinleck, directed the Syrian campaign, and Auchinleck was responsible for the *coup* in Iran.

HOLLAND, AIRBORNE OPERATION AMHERST Second World War 7 – 16 April 1945

Fought between the Allies and the Germans.

Lt-General G. G. Simonds, in command of the Canadian 2 Corps anticipated difficulty in continuing the momentum of his advance towards Emden because of having to cross the river Ijssel and the canal country east of the Zuider Zee (Ijsselmeer). It was also feared that the German forces in the Amsterdam area might stream across the Zuider Zee viaduct (which could not be bombed) back to Emden. Therefore it was decided to use the Special Air Service Brigade (Brigadier Michael Calvert) to land in the Groningen–Coevorden–Zwolle area to neutralise German forces in the area, and to seize certain bridges and the airfield at Steenwijk for the Canadian army.

Calvert's plan was to drop the 2nd and 3rd Battalion Chasseurs Alpins Parachutistes (Colonel Paris de Bollardière) on fifty-five dropping zones from 1,500 feet on the night of 7/8 April to carpet the area with troops and, assisted by deceptive parachutes with battle-noise containers, to deceive the German parachute division resting in the area as to the direction and strength of the attack. It was decided not to alert the Dutch Resistance in this area, as previous experiences (at Arnhem and elsewhere) showed that they had been penetrated by German intelligence and were unable to ensure security. Calvert decided to take over a follow-up force of his Belgian SAS battalion in armoured jeeps. A Polish SP battery was in support.

The landing was successfully carried out by about 800 French SAS in fifty-five sticks on the night 7/8 April, and most of the objectives were seized. Some sticks were dropped off target, as the drop was through cloud at 1,400. feet at night. The German reaction was intense but, being roadbound on vehicles, they found it difficult to attack the French over the innumerable small canals.

It was planned that the Canadians would overrun the French within seventy-two hours of landing, but they were held up mainly by administrative difficulties at the Ijssel. So Calvert launched his Belgian SAS which, helped by the Polish artillery and close support from the RCAF, overran the French positions, followed up by Canadian reconnaisance units. The Belgians under Colonel Blondeel had a stiff fight at Assen but overcame all opposition. Groningen was captured. Casualties among the French were initially thought to be high, but many of the French soldiers, eager for action, carried on fighting alongside the Canadians in captured German armoured vehicles, and did not return to their rendezvous for some days. The French captured and held fifteen out of eighteen small bridges and the airfields at Steenwijk, Helve and Leeduwarden. Throughout the rest of the operation, which was considered completed by 16 April 1945, supplies were brought in by 38 Group RAF.

German casualties inflicted by the French were estimated at over 500, while the final French casualties numbered less than 100. Lt-General Sir Richard Gale (Allied Airborne Army), Lt-General Simonds, and the AOC 38 Group (who had been concerned with all airborne operations in Europe to date) considered this was the most successful airborne operation of the war. The whole operation was mounted in five days of planning. However, because Winston Churchill was having some difference of opinion with General Charles de Gaulle at the time, a security clamp was put on the news of the operation so that it obtained no publicity. Also the Dutch felt that they should have been consulted before being 'liberated' by French, Belgians and Poles. This viewpoint was reinforced by the Dutch Resistance movement who resented not being informed. There is no doubt that this operation was brilliantly carried out by French parachute troops, ably supported by the staunch Belgian SAS, Polish artillery and RCAF.

HONG KONG   Second World War   8 – 25 December 1941

Fought between the British/Canadian garrison under Major-General C. M. Maltby and one reinforced Japanese division, the 38th, under Lt-General Tadayoshi Sato of 23rd Army, commanded by Lt-General Takashi Sakai.

On the same day as Japanese forces attacked Pearl Harbour (qv) and Manila, 8 December 1941, one specially trained Japanese division (Sato), with strong artillery and air support, crossed the boundary between Hong Kong and China and attacked the British/Canadian garrison of 12,000 troops. Two British and two Indian battalions, supported by the Hong Kong and Singapore Royal Artillery (HKSRA), defended the Gindrinkers' Line on the mainland, while Victoria Island was defended by a weak, and only partially trained, Canadian brigade of two battalions, and an efficient volunteer force of British, Portuguese and Anglo-Chinese and Portuguese-Chinese units, and the HKSRA.

After five days of heavy fighting the Japanese overcame the Royal Scots who manned the Shingmun redoubt, which was the key to the whole defence line on the mainland, and the defence folded. The British forces retired across the water to the island. During this evacuation a ferry carrying over 500 tons of ammunition and explosives from Stonecutters Island was hit and exploded as it was nearing the wharf on the island. This explosion destroyed many of the defences and helped demoralise some of the garrison. A demand for surrender on 13 December was refused by Maltby. On 18 December the Japanese, after an intense bombardment, carried out an amphibious assault on the island. The Canadian counter-attack failed, and the Japanese continued to enlarge their bridgehead and advance into the heights above. In spite of counter-attacks by the Canadians, the Japanese captured the reservoir and the water mains were destroyed. Fierce fighting continued over the island until on 25 December the Governor, Sir Mark Young, surrendered the island, although many units, especially the volunteers, outnumbered 5 to 1, were continuing to resist. One small unit of elderly businessmen held out at the Repulse Bay Hotel until all of them were killed. The Chinese Royal Engineers, one of the few all-Chinese units in the garrison, especially distinguished themselves, and many of them, after surrender, escaped overland to

India and continued to fight against the Japanese with Major-General Orde Wingate's Chindits in Burma (qv).

British losses were severe, totalling 4,400, the remainder of the garrison being taken prisoner. Canadian losses were especially severe, over 45 per cent of them being killed or wounded. The Japanese lost 2,745 in the assault. The one-armed Chinese Admiral Chan-chak, who had been operating with the Royal Navy in motor torpedo boats, organised the escape of his men and over 100 RN personnel who reached Burma through Yunnan. One-third of the British prisoners taken in Hong Kong died subsequently in captivity.

The British Pacific Fleet under Admiral Sir Henry Harwood steamed back into Hong Kong harbour on 15 August 1945 and reoccupied the colony. It was necessary to do this quickly and decisively as President Franklin D. Roosevelt had promised in 1944 to give Hong Kong to Generalissimo Chiang Kai-shek as an incentive to get him to continue to fight the Japanese. Except for a sharp clash with Japanese 'suicide' troops in the dockyard area, the reoccupation was orderly.

Hong Kong became a haven of refuge for Chinese escaping from the trouble on the mainland and soon again became the fourth greatest port in terms of import and export trade in the world. The defence of its isolated garrison by a heterogeneous force for eighteen days against a specially trained and experienced Japanese division, with overwhelming air superiority and complete control over the sea, deserved more praise than has been registered, especially by comparison with the behaviour of other more experienced Allied armies at this time.

HUNGARY   Second World War   October 1944 – 18 February 1945
Fought between the Germans and the Russians.

While General Fedor Tolbukhin's left (S) flank of the Russian sweep moved up the Danube River to Belgrade, which was reached on 20 October, the Ukrainian 2nd Army under General Rodion Malinovsky moved into Hungary from the south. Army Group 'S', the German force under General Johannes Friessner (later, General Woehler) defending this area, fought fiercely to hold the region of Budapest and the Lake Balaton oilfields which lay to the SW. Another Russian force had meanwhile moved through a pass in the Carpathian Mountains to come up on the rear of Budapest. Although the capital was surrounded by 24 December, it continued to hold out. Much of the Wehrmacht reserve had been wasted in a futile counter-attack against the Russians, but Adolf Hitler now ordered it to relieve the city. Pest fell to the Russians on 18 January, and Buda, on the west bank, on 18 February. The route into Austria was now cleared for Malinovsky.

In the fighting around Budapest, the Russians reported the deaths of 49,000 Germans and the capture of 110,000.

ITALY, SOUTHERN   Second World War   3 September – October 1943
Fought between the Allies and the Axis.

Three weeks after the invasion of Sicily, the Allies made their first landing on the continent of Europe by invading Italy. On 3 September two divisions of General Sir Bernard Montgomery's 8th Army crossed the Strait of Messina and landed at Reggio Calabria, in Operation Baytown. The Italian army, which was trying to surrender to the Allies anyway, offered little resistance and 13 Corps moved through Calabria, the British 5th Division along the west coast and the 1st Canadian Division along the east coast. Although the terrain was rugged and hilly, the offensive made good progress and helped convince Marshal Pietro Badoglio to surrender the Italian government. This he did on 8 September. On the morning of 9 September the 5th Army landed at Salerno (qv), 150 miles north. 13 Corps continued to push north, driving back the retreating Germans under General Traugott Herr. A week later, the British force met the right flank of the 5th Army near Vallo, thus uniting the Allied forces on the west coast. On 9 September Admiral Sir Andrew Cunningham's fleet had landed the British 5 Corps at Taranto, inside the heel of Italy. The 1st Airborne Division captured the naval base there and moved across the heel towards Foggia, 110 miles north, where there was an important complex of airfields. On 22 September the British 78th Division landed at Bari, and five days later Foggia was taken. On 3 October a Commando attack at Termoli, 50 miles north of the base, ensured that Foggia would be safe for use by securing the line of the river Biferno.

The 8th Army on the Adriatic coast and in the interior now linked with the drive of the 5th Army and the Allied force pressed north towards the Gustav Line, protecting Rome (GUSTAV–CASSINO LINE).

IWO JIMA (West Pacific)   Second World War   19 February–26 March 1945
Fought between the Americans and the Japanese.
Strength: Americans 45,000; Japanese 22,000.

Seven hundred miles south of Tokyo lay the tiny island of Iwo Jima, $4\frac{1}{2}$ miles by $2\frac{1}{2}$ miles, whence Japanese fighters issued to intercept and harass US B–29 Superfortress bombers on their way to Japan from the Marianas. The Americans sought to capture the island, not only to eliminate the Japanese base there, but also to provide an emergency landing base for crippled or fuelless B–29s on their way back to Saipan and Tinian 1,500 miles away. The Japanese also realised the importance of the base and packed a great number of troops on it as well as the heaviest fire-power and strongest defences of the Pacific War: 1,500 fortified caves, many ferro-concrete pillboxes, blockhouses and trenches with miles of interconnecting tunnels.

From General Harry Schmidt's 5 Amphibious Corps, the US 4th and 5th Marine Divisions undertook the assault. After weeks of heavy aerial bombardment and three days of naval shelling, the troops landed on 19 February. On the left (S), General Keller Rockey's 5th Marine Division fought its way across the narrow isthmus at one end of the island, isolating Mount Suribachi's defences on the south tip of the island. To their right, General Clifton Gates's 4th Marine Division gained ground as far as Airfield No 1, securing the north flank of the landing beach. However, the Japanese defence of intense arillery and small-arms fire took a heavy toll of the Americans on the first day: 2,400 marines were lost, including 600 killed. On 20 February the 5th Marines turned south and attacked towards Suribachi, and although the division met heavy resistance, it carried on until by 23 February it carried the whole mountain. At 10.30 am Lieutenant Harold Schrier's patrol raised a small flag on a pipe at the top of the 550-feet peak, and at 2.30 pm, when the slopes had been cleared, a larger flag was hoisted – the photograph which Joe Rosenthal took of the incident was to become one of the most dramatic battle pictures in American history.

In the north, the 4th Marines took Airfield No 1 and turned right to march up the east coast while the 5th Marines began to march up the west coast. General Graves Erskine's 3rd Marines occupied the centre between these two advances, and this reserve division marched through Airfield No 2 on 24 February. The Japanese defence of the northern half of the island was fanatical. They clung fiercely to the cross-island defences which had as their key position the Motoyama plateau. On 9 March the 3rd Division reached the sea in the NE, and a week later the 4th Division on the right (E) flank had crushed all resistance; but the 5th Division took until 26 March to crush all the fighting in their sector (the left). The fighting on Iwo Jima cost the marines 6,821 dead and more than 18,000 wounded – twenty-six Medals of Honor were awarded, half of which were posthumous. Nearly all the Japanese defenders were killed.

The first fuelless B–29 landed in the island on 4 March. Afterwards, 2,251 aircraft and 24,761 crewmen were to make use of this invaluable conquest.

JAPAN, AERIAL BOMBARDMENT   Second World War   24 November 1944 – 15 August 1945
Fought between the Allies and the Japanese.

The ultimate objective of the Allied offensive in the Pacific was Japan itself. Carrier-based bombers attacked the islands in April 1942 and B–29.Superfortresses also struck from China, but it was not until air bases at Saipan and other Mariana Islands (qv) were established that the Japanese began to suffer heavily from bombing.

The B–29s of 21 Bomber Command – under General Haywood Hansell, and later General Curtis LeMay – of the 20th Air Force, commanded by General Henry Arnold in Washington DC, carried out these raids. For over three months high-level raids (from 25,000 feet) continued, but on 9 March 1945 234 B–29s flew over Tokyo at an altitude of 7,000 feet to drop 1,667 tons of incendiaries on the heart of the city. As a result 16 square miles of land were devastated, 250,000 homes lost and 83,793 people killed. The attack was more lethal, certainly in its immediate effect, than both the atomic bombs which fell on Hiroshima and Nagasaki and was second only to the double raid on Dresden (qv), which was the most devastating air attack in history. Nagoya, Osaka, Kobe and Yokohama were also struck by these low-level raids, so that by mid-June a total of 100 square miles had been laid waste and the centres of all five cities were in ruins. When, on 8 May 1945, Germany surrendered, the air attacks on Japan were increased.

The 8th Air Force was moved from Europe to Okinawa and, under General Carl Spaatz, carried out strategic bombing along with the 20th Air Force in the Marianas, now under General Nathan Twining. In July 1,200 sorties a week were made against Japan. Long-range strategic bombing caused the death of 260,000 Japanese and rendered over 9 million homeless. Allied losses were 343 planes and 243 crewmen.

In February 1945 land-based bombers were supplemented by carrier planes from the US fleet, later reinforced by a British task force. From 10 July onwards Halsey's 3rd Fleet moved into Japanese coastal waters and fired its naval guns on targets ashore.

Meanwhile, the Americans had developed the atomic bomb. On 27 July the Allies demanded Japan's immediate surrender as an alternative to use of the bomb. When Japan rejected the ultimatum, on 6 August a B–29, the *Enola Gay* from Tinian, piloted by Colonel Paul W. Tibbets, dropped one bomb on Hiroshima. Three-fifths of the city was destroyed and approximately 78,000 people were killed out of a total population of about 300,000. In addition 10,000 were missing and 37,000 injured. The bomb which, three days later, was exploded over Nagasaki, caused only slightly less destruction and casualties.

While air and sea attacks were being made against Japan itself, Allied submarines were conducting an equally successful campaign against Japanese merchant shipping. At a cost of 45 American submarines, 5 million tons of shipping (1,113 ships) were sunk out of a total of $8\frac{1}{2}$ million tons.

Russia had declared war on Japan on 8 August but, although she invaded Manchuria, no decisive action was fought. Halsey made another strike at Honshu with the 3rd Fleet on 9 August, and on 14 August 800 B–29s raided the island. On 15 August Japan accepted unconditional surrender, which brought all hostilities in the Second World War to an end.

JAVA SEA   Second World War   27 February–1 March 1942
Fought between the Allies under Admiral Karel Doorman and the Japanese under Admiral Sokichi Takagi.
Strength: Allies 5 cruisers + 9 destroyers; Japanese 14 destroyers + 4 cruisers.

By the end of February 1942 Japan had overrun most of the W Pacific south to Java, and ABDA (Australian, British, Dutch and American) attempts to stem the advance were pushed aside. The Allied organisation was dissolved. The only obstacle now lying between the Japanese and Java, which was garrisoned by 120,000 European and Indonesian troops, was a small Allied squadron. The Allies lacked any air cover at all.

North of Sourabaya, the Allied fleet under the Dutch Admiral Doorman intercepted the Japanese squadron. In a battle lasting seven hours Doorman was killed, while his flagship, *De Ruyter*, was sunk along with the Dutch light cruiser *Java*. Three destroyers, 2 British (*Electra* and *Jupiter*) and 1 Dutch (*Kortenaer*), were sunk and the British heavy cruiser *Exeter* was crippled. One Japanese destroyer was crippled. Those Allied vessels which survived tried to make for Australia. On the following day the American cruiser *Houston* and the Australian light cruiser *Perth* made for the Sunda Strait, at the west end of Java, but they were met by a Japanese force of warships which sank them both on the night of 28 February. Over half the *Houston*'s 1,000-men crew and the *Perth*'s complement of 680 were killed or drowned. Before they went down, however, they themselves sank 2 Japanese transports.

The *Exeter*, badly damaged, was being escorted by the British destroyer *Encounter* and the American destroyer *Pope* when they were intercepted at the Sunda Strait on 1 March and sunk, 800 survivors being captured by the Japanese. Only 4 American destroyers escaped the Japanese and reached Australia via the Bali Strait on the east end of Java.

There was now no Allied fleet in the Java Sea, and by 9 March Java was secured by Japan. Meanwhile, south of the island, the US oiler *Pecos* was lost as were 2 destroyers, the *Pillsbury* and *Edsall*. Other ships were also lost as the Japanese increased their hold on the W Pacific area.

KIEV (USSR)   Second World War   9–17 September 1941
Fought between the Germans under General Heinz Guderian and General Paul von Kleist and the Russians under Marshal Joseph Stalin.

By 9 September 1941 the German advance was approaching Kiev, Guderian's Panzers were 100 miles NE of Kiev at Nezhin, and Kleist's Panzers were 60 miles SE of the city across the Dnieper at Pereyaslav. To avoid encirclement, General Semyon Budënny and Nikita Khrushchev ordered withdrawal from the city, an order which Stalin is said to have countermanded, at the same time replacing Budënny with Marshal Semyon Timoshenko.

Timoshenko arrived at Kiev on 13 September when the bottleneck was still loose enough to enable the four Russian armies inside to get out through the 20-mile gap. Stalin, however, was still adamant, and by 16 September Guderian and Kleist had tightened the net. Late on 17 September Stalin ordered withdrawal in response to repeated requests, but made no mention about breaking out across the river Pysol where German defences were not yet consolidated. The result was that several units tried to break out across the river while the majority of the Russian troops stayed to fight. About 150,000 men contrived to escape, while 526,000 officers and men defended the city, suffering heavy loss or being taken prisoner.

Although the encirclement of Kiev was tactically well executed, it delayed the German advance on Moscow at a vital time.

KWAJALEIN–ENIWETOK (central Pacific)   Second World War   1–22 February 1944
Fought between the Americans and the Japanese.

Following the US conquest of the Gilbert Islands in 1943, the Americans' next objective was the Marshall Islands, 2,200 miles north of Australia and 600 miles NW of the Gilberts.

Four US carrier task groups approached the islands, and by 1 February General Holland Smith's 5 Amphibious Corps was ready to attack the Kwajalein atoll in the centre of the archipelago. Heavy air and naval bombardment preceded the attack, and then General Charles Corlett's 7th Infantry Division landed on the islet of Kwajalein, defended by Rear-Admiral Yakiyama and 5,000 Japanese, while General Harry Schmidt's 4th Marine Division landed on Roi–Namur, 45 miles north. On the first day, Roi was taken by a marine regiment; the islet of Namur was overrun by noon of the next day. In these attacks 3,500 Japanese were killed and 264 captured. American losses were 190 dead and 547 wounded. Kwajalein was taken by the 7th Infantry in three days, in the course of which 3,800 Japanese were killed with a loss to the Americans of 177 killed and 1,000 wounded. The island was secure by 4 February.

This swift success persuaded Admiral Chester Nimitz to press on to Eniwetok, 400 miles NW, two months ahead of schedule. On 18th February the independent 22nd Marine Regiment under General John Walker landed on Engebi. The 106th Regiment of the 27th Infantry under General Thomas Walker struck Eniwetok itself the following day. By 22 February it had been cleared. The remaining islands in the Marshalls were occupied soon after. In a futile defence of the island, Admiral Masashi Kobayashi lost 9,000 Japanese. Total American casualties were 640 killed and 1,885 wounded.

The Mariana Islands (qv) became the next American target for attack.

LENINGRAD (USSR)   Second World War   1941–4
Fought between the Russians and the Germans.

Russia was invaded on three fronts by the Germans in the summer of 1941, from the north, centre and south. Leningrad, Russia's main Baltic port, was the chief objective on the northern front. It was the second largest city in the USSR.

General Wilhelm von Leeb amassed two German armies, the 16th and 18th, in E Prussia to attack the objective, and he was joined by the 3rd Panzer Group of General Erich Hoeppner. On 22 June the force moved NE into Lithuania. Crossing the Niemen River, the capital, Vilnius (Vilna), was captured four days later on 26 June. General Erich von Manstein, with his Panzer Corps, moved on north to capture bridges over the Dvina River 200 miles away in Latvia. Riga, the capital of Latvia, fell on 1 July. Tanks moved to Lake Ilmen while the German infantry marched into Estonia. The left wing of Leeb's army completed the conquest of the Baltic states, reaching to Narva on the border between Russia and Estonia. Tallin, the capital of Estonia, fell on 30 August, while the right wing moved through Pskov, Staraya Russia and Novgorod. Hoeppner moved north to Luga, which lay only 90 miles from Leningrad.

On 26 June Finland had declared war on Russia and, in collaboration with the Germans, the twelve-division force of the Finnish army under Field-Marshal Baron Carl von Mannerheim moved on Leningrad from the north via the Karelian isthmus. The advance was slow, however, and Vyborg (Viipuri) was not taken until 30 August. The pincer movement from north and south forced the Russian forces under General Kliment Voroshilov, which amounted to about 200,000 men, to withdraw inside the city while the population was set to work building defences. General Mikhail Khozin took over as commandant of Leningrad and by 4 September the town was under fire. The defences held, but Leningrad was subjected to a long siege, during which the inhabitants suffered terrible privation. Thousands were killed and wounded by artillery shells, while many more died of starvation and cold. Supplies of food, fuel and military goods were slipped through the German blockade across Lake Ladoga, which was frozen. The German 16th Army lay at Lake Ilmen and the Russians attempted a counter-attack here in February 1942. The assault was repulsed.

During the summer, Manstein, who had been in the south conquering the Crimea (Krym) (qv), was ordered north to repeat his successful assault on Sebastopol. The Leningrad defences proved impenetrable, though another counter-attack by the Russians under General Leonid Govorov and General Kirill Meretsov in January 1943 was beaten back. The failure of the Germans to take Leningrad and the relentless pressure to which they were subjected by the Russian counter-attacks resulted in frequent changes in German command. Leeb was replaced by Field-Marshal Ernst Busch who, the summer after his appointment in early 1942, was in turn replaced by General Georg von Küchler.

Four Russian armies launched a drive to relieve the siege of Lenengrad in mid-January 1944. The four armies were Govorov's Leningrad Army, Meretsov's Volkhov Army, General Markian Popov's 2nd Baltic Army and General Ivan Bagramian's 1st Baltic Army. They attacked along a front which stretched 120 miles from Lake Ilmen north to Leningrad. Meretsov reached Novgorod on 15 January and on 25 January, aided by Govorov, cleared the east bank of the Volkhov River. The action opened the Moscow–Leningrad road and ended the thirty-one-month siege of Leningrad.

The Russians pursued the Germans west, taking Luga on 14 February and Staraya Russia on 18 February. Field-Marshal Walther Model, who now commanded the Army Group of the North, checked the Russian advance along the Estonian border on the Narva–Lake Peipus–Pskov line in March. The Finnish army was now isolated in the north and the Finns requested an armistice in February. Govorov, promoted to Marshal, was put in command of the drive to knock Finland out of the war.

Meanwhile, negotiations for an armistice proceeded. On 10 June the Russians attacked up the Karelian isthmus as they had done five years earlier. The Mannerheim Line (qv) was broken as far as Vyborg (Viipuri) by 20 June, while Meretsov's renamed army (the Karelian) moved up the railway towards Murmansk, taking Petrozavodsk on 29 June. An armistice was finally agreed on 19 September.

SE of Leningrad, General Gerhard Lindemann had taken over command of the German Army Group North in a four-month period of deceptive quiet. Govorov withdrew his army from the Karelian isthmus during this time and moved west to attack the German left flank north of Lake Peipus. Narva was captured on 26 July, and the Russians moved into Estonia. At the same time, General Ivan Maslennikov's 3rd Baltic Army attacked south of Lake Peipus. Pskov fell on 24

July, the last major Russian city to be liberated before the Red Army was able to thrust into S Estonia.

South of this action, the Russians were performing an even wider sweep. Generals Bagramian and Ivan Yeremenko moved north from Vilnius, which they had taken on 13 July, towards the Gulf of Riga. They reached Jelgava (Mitau) on 1 August, menacing the German 18th and 16th Armies, now under the command of General Ferdinand Schörner. Govorov continued his advance in the north and captured Tallin on 23 September. The Russians had cleared the state by the end of the month, but the Germans at the Gulf of Riga counter-attacked in an attempt to open a channel to the west. The Russians took Riga on 14 October, but Schörner had withdrawn his twelve divisions (all under-strength) to the Kurland (Courland) peninsula on the Baltic Sea. Three Russian armies closed in on them and besieged them throughout the winter. Although the Germans could only be supplied by sea, they held out until the spring when the Russians wiped out the German forces there as part of their great April offensive in central Europe.

LEYTE (Philippine Islands)   Second World War   20 October–26 December 1944
Fought between the Allies and the Japanese.

In September 1944 General Douglas MacArthur began to move north towards the Philippines, taking Morotai between New Guinea and Mindanao while Admiral Chester Nimitz's 2 Marine Corps overran the islands of Peleliu and Angaur (qv) to the east. The US fleet under Admiral William Halsey found little opposition on Mindanao when that island was reached on 9–10 September and it was therefore decided to bypass the S Philippine Islands and to attack Leyte, which lay in the centre of the group.

The 6th Army was to undertake the invasion under the command of General Walter Krueger. The force consisted of two corps, 24 (7th, 77th and 96th Infantry Divisions) under General John Hodge, transferred from Nimitz to MacArthur to support 10 Corps, newly created, which was composed of the 1st Cavalry and 24th Infantry Divisions and commanded by General Franklin Sibert. The Japanese 35th Army under General Sosaku Suzuki was responsible for the defence of Mindanao and the Visayan Islands in the central Philippines. Under air cover provided by General George Kenney's SW Pacific Air Forces, Admiral Thomas Kinkaid's 7th Fleet took the force to Leyte. On 17 and 18 October the small islands defending the eastern entrance to Leyte Gulf were taken by US Rangers. After a two-hour naval bombardment on 20 October four infantry divisions landed on the east coast of the island between Tacloban and Dulag, 17 miles south. On the right, the two divisions of 10 Corps and the 96th and 7th Divisions of 24 Corps on the left fought their way inland during the first four days and created a beachhead big enough to take new airfields. By 2 November the Americans controlled Leyte valley from Carigara on the north coast to Abuyog on the SE. On the left, the 7th Infantry crossed the island to Baybay on the west coast. Progress was then halted by heavy rain and Japanese resistance from the mountains of the interior. The overall Japanese commander in the Philippines, General Tomoyuki Yamashita, was also pouring reinforcements on to Leyte from neighbouring islands. About 45,000 Japanese soldiers landed at Ormoc on the west coast between 23 October and 11 December, even though the Japanese were defeated in the naval battle of Leyte Gulf (qv).

A two-pronged offensive was launched against the Ormoc valley by Krueger in November in order to prevent the Japanese build-up. On the right (N) 10 Corps, which was reinforced by 32nd Infantry, assaulted Limon, the northern entrance to the valley. The village fell on 10 December after stiff fighting. On the left, the 11th Airborne Division joined 24 Corps, while the 7th Infantry made another crossing of the island to reach Balogo on 22 November. At the beginning of December the 77th Infantry landed at Ipil, 3 miles south of Ormoc, which fell on 10 December. The 77th then made contact with the 7th which had in turn linked up with the 11th Airborne Division. The two corps met at Libungao on 20 December, having driven up from both ends of the Ormoc valley. Palompon, the last Japanese port on Leyte, lying on the NW coast, was taken on 25 December. On 26 December General Robert Eichelberger's 8th Army took command of the island, and 24 Corps was assigned to the Okinawa invasion. It was, however, four months before all resistance on Leyte and on the coast of Samar, to the NE, was wiped out.

Japanese determination to hold Leyte had cost them the loss of much irreplaceable shipping and aircraft: 70,000 Japanese men were lost, a total of six divisions. Of the 15,584 American casualties, 3,584 were killed.

LEYTE GULF (Philippine Islands)   Second World War   23–5 October 1944
Fought between the Americans and the Japanese.
Strength: Americans 15 carriers + 7 battleships + 21 cruisers + 58 destroyers (Admiral William Halsey) + 16 escort carriers + 6 battleships + 11 cruisers + 86 destroyers (Admiral Thomas Kinkaid); Japanese Northern Force 4 carriers + 2 battleships + 3 cruisers + 8 destroyers (Admiral Jisaburo Ozawa). Japanese Central Force (in two halves) 5 battleships + 12 cruisers + 15 destroyers (Admiral Shoji Nishimura) + 2 battleships + 4 cruisers + 8 destroyers (Admiral Kiyohide Shima) all under the command of Admiral Takeo Kurita.

When the Americans invaded Leyte, they threatened to cut Japan's vital oil supply line from the E Indies. It was necessary that the Japanese should hold the Philippines, therefore, and to this end Admiral Socmu Toyoda ordered the Japanese fleet to take the offensive. The result was one of the biggest and most complex battles in naval history.

On 22 October Admiral Ozawa left Japanese waters for the Philippines with the Northern Force, a bait designed to draw Admiral Halsey's fleet away from Leyte Gulf. In case this entire fleet should be lost, Toyoda had retained his 6 largest carriers in Japan. Two Japanese task forces were converging on the Philippines from the west, their intention being to drive Admiral Kinkaid's fleet away and to annihilate the American invasion force in the Leyte Gulf. The left hook of this Japanese attack, the Southern Force, was directed by Admiral Takeo Kurita who headed for the Sibuyan Sea and San Bernardino Strait, intending to enter Leyte Gulf from the north. The right hook of this attack, in two halves under Admirals Shoji Nishimura and Kiyohide Shima, formed the Southern Force which moved up from the Sulu and Mindanao Seas to the south. The American naval force had one weakness: its command structure. Halsey's 3rd Fleet was under the control of Admiral Chester Nimitz in the Pacific Fleet, while Kinkaid's 7th Fleet was directed by General Douglas MacArthur as part of the SW Pacific Command. The battle, which was in fact three separate actions, began on 23 October, two days before the Japanese had planned.

Kurita's Central Force was attacked by 2 American submarines, the *Darter* and *Dace*, off Palawan in the S China Sea. Two cruisers, including the flagship, *Atago*, were sunk and a third was crippled. Carrier aircraft from Halsey's fleet made five air attacks on Kurita's force in the Sibuyan Sea the following day. Five warships were damaged and the super-battleship *Musashi* capsized with the loss of 1,100 men, half its complement. Kurita complained to the High Command over the radio about the lack of air cover and turned back west. At the same time, east of the Philippines, 76 aircraft from Ozawa's Northern Force attacked Halsey's fleet and destroyed the carrier *Princeton*. In this attack, 56 Japanese aircraft were lost. Halsey then moved north and exposed the beachhead on Leyte as the Japanese had desired. On 25 October the three engagements took place.

Surigao Strait: Admiral Jesse Oldendorf, given command of the fighting ships of the 7th Fleet, was ordered by Kinkaid to block the southern entrance into Leyte Gulf. Before dawn, the Japanese Southern Force was ambushed as it came out of Surigao Strait. Patrol torpedo boats, destroyers and capital ships decimated Nishimura's fleet in under two hours, destroying 6 out of 7 ships. Shima, steaming up 40 miles behind, reversed his course and withdrew with his 7 ships. This was probably the last line battle fought. In it, the Americans only suffered 1 damaged destroyer.

Cape Engano: After the victory of the 7th Fleet in Surigao Strait, Halsey found the Japanese Northern Force off Cape Engano on NE Luzon at dawn. The 3rd Fleet launched five air strikes and sank all 4 of Ozawa's carriers as well as a destroyer. The Americans were on the point of completing the destruction of the Japanese force when they received calls from Leyte Gulf which said that Kurita's Central Force had turned back and was steaming through the San Bernardino Strait, threatening to annihilate the exposed invasion force in the gulf. Halsey disengaged at once and turned south towards Leyte, 300 miles away.

Samar: Having come through the San Bernardino Strait on the morning of 25 October, Kurita encountered a 7th Fleet of 6 escort carriers, 7 destroyers and destroyer escort half-way down the east coast of Samar Island. The American force was commanded by Admiral Clifton Sprague and at once turned back from the stronger and faster Japanese force. Although the American screening ships fought desperately and fierce carrier–aircraft attacks were launched, the US fleet seemed to be in imminent danger of annihilation. After two hours of heavy shelling, however, Kurita called off the attack and turned north towards the San Bernardino Strait. The carrier *Gambier Bay* had been sunk as well as 3 escorting ships. The Japanese had lost 3 cruisers. The 7th Fleet, designed for assault rather than combat, would probably have taken a severe beating had it not been for Kurita's inexplicable withdrawal. The Battle of Leyte Gulf ended the following day when American carrier aircraft attacked Kurita's retreating force and sank another cruiser in the Sulu Sea.

The main Japanese objective – the destruction of the amphibious shipping in Leyte Gulf – had not even been approached. As it was, 300,000 tons of their shipping – 3 battleships, 4 carriers, 10 cruisers and 9 destroyers – had been lost and consequently they were unable to fight another naval battle. The Americans lost 37,000 tons of shipping, including 1 light and 2 escort carriers. The *St Lo*, one of the escort carriers, was, along with 3 damaged carriers, one of the first victims of Japanese *kamikaze* pilots who dive-bombed their aircraft into their targets, committing suicide in the process. (*Kamikaze* means divine wind.)

This victory meant that the way was clear for the Americans to extend their Philippine conquests and to move farther north, closer to Japan itself.

LUZON (Philippine Islands)   Second World War   9 January–1 July 1945
Fought between the Americans and Filipinos, and the Japanese.
Strength: Americans 200,000 (including reinforcements) + 850 combat, transport and support ships + 1,000 aircraft; Japanese 250,000 + 150 aircraft.

Following the US victory on Leyte and in Leyte Gulf (qv) General Douglas MacArthur was able to organise the liberation of the Philippines through Luzon, the chief island of the group. Before the main invasion took place, however, the island of Mindoro, to the south, was invaded on 15 December 1944 by General Robert Eichelberger's 8th Army. A beachhead large enough to accommodate two airfields was quickly established at San Jose and General George Kenney's aircraft began to strike at Japanese installations on Luzon.

On the island, General Tomoyuki Yamashita had grouped his 14th Army into three defensive sections: Shobu (140,000 men) in the north, Kembu (30,000) in the centre and Shimbu (80,000) in the south. Carrier aircraft from Admiral William Halsey's 3rd Fleet attacked Japanese air bases in the area while Admiral Thomas Kinkaid's 7th Fleet transported General Walter Krueger's 6th Army to the island. During this period, 20 Allied ships were sunk and 24 severely damaged by *kamikaze* attacks. On 9 January Krueger's army landed in the Lingayen Gulf on the NW of the island, two corps abreast. The Japanese had landed in the same place when they had invaded three years earlier. General Innis Swift landed on the left (E) with 1 Corps, comprising 43rd and 6th Infantry Divisions, and General Oscar Griswold landed on the right with 14 Corps, made up of the 37th and 40th Infantry Divisions. On the first day 68,000 men landed and the attacking force moved rapidly inland. By 20 January they were 40 miles inland. 1 Corps drove eastward, meeting bitter opposition from the Shobu group which slowed them up despite their reinforcement by the 158th Regiment on 11 January, the

25th Infantry Division on 17 January and the 32nd Infantry Division before the end of the month. During the fighting in this sector US Rangers carried out a raid behind the Japanese lines and released several hundred Allied prisoners at Cabanatuan. To the right, 14 Corps moved south quickly across the Central Plain to reach Clark Field on 23 January. A week later the base was secured and a further advance of 25 miles had been made to Calumpit. On 29 January General Charles Hall's 11 Corps had landed to the right of 14 Corps on the west coast, coming up against the Kembu group. With the aid of Filipino guerillas, the 38th and 24th Infantry sealed off the Bataan peninsula, which was cleared by 21 February, while Corregidor at the mouth of Manila Bay had fallen to a combined amphibious and airborne assault five days earlier.

Before his drive on Manila, Krueger reorganised 14 Corps. The 1st Cavalry Division reached the outskirts of the city on the night of 3 February and liberated 3,500 Allied internees in Santo Tomas University. The 37th Infantry reached the NW edge of Manila the next night and another 1,300 Allied prisoners were freed from Bilibid Prison. Falling back behind the Pasig River, the Japanese began a fanatical resistance that in one month destroyed much of the city and caused the death of 16,000 Japanese. Manila fell on 4 March, the forces surrounding it having been augmented by the arrival of the 11th Airborne from the 8th Army which had been dropped SW of the city on 31 January. Having taken the southern suburb of Paranaque on 4 February, they were stopped short by strong Japanese defences. Later in the month, however, civilian internees at Los Banas were rescued.

Meanwhile, 1 Corps in the north was moving northward and eastward against strong resistance by the Shobu group in mountainous terrain. When, on 14 February, the 6th Infantry passed through Bongabon to reach the east coast, it was transferred to the Manila front. Left of them, the 25th, 32nd, 33rd and, later, the 37th Infantry Divisions, as well as Filipino army units, fought against savage resistance and achieved only small gains. Baguio, the summer capital, fell on 27 April and Santa Fé, the key communications centre, on 27 May.

The 37th Infantry then began to move down Cagayan valley, and on 26 June they met a force attacking southwards from Aparri which had been taken five days previously. The Shobu group was thus split into two and rendered incapable of undertaking a major counter-attack. On 15 March, in the south and east of the Manila front 11 Corps had taken charge. The 6th and 43rd Infantry and 1st Cavalry were unable to make any major gain because of the strength with which the Shimbu line was held in the Sierra Madre Mountains. The American advance was slow but sure and by 1 July only the 38th Infantry remained in the interior of Luzon to continue pushing against the ever-decreasing enemy pocket. In S Luzon the 1st Cavalry, which had been transferred from the Manila front, and the 11th Airborne of 14 Corps moved SE down the Bicol peninsula where, on 1 April, the 158th Regimental Combat Team had taken Legaspi. In May the two forces met near Naga, and by 1 June all resistance in this area had been mopped up. On 1 July the 8th Army assumed control of Luzon, freeing the 6th Army which was to take part in the planned invasion of Japan in the autumn. On 4 July Luzon was declared secure by MacArthur. However, when the war ended on 15 August, the 6th, 32nd, 37th and 38th Divisions of 14 Corps were still containing over 50,000 Japanese soldiers in a pocket in N and E Luzon which Yamashita surrendered.

MADAGASCAR (MALAGASY) (Indian Ocean)   Second World War   5 May–5 November 1942

Fought between the British under Rear-Admiral E. N. Syfret and Major-General Robert Sturges, and the Vichy French under Armand Annet.

Aim: Japan's conquest of Malaya and Singapore (qqv) in 1942 endangered Britain's position in the Indian Ocean. The most important port in the west of the ocean was Diego Suarez, a valuable harbour on Madagascar (Malagasy), which was ruled by the Vichy French under Annet, the Governor-General. In order to prevent the possible seizure of the island by the Japanese, a British force under Rear-Admiral Syfret and Major-General Sturges was sent out to capture the port.

Battle: On 5 May two brigades and No 5 Commando landed on the NW coast of the island and fought their way across the narrow northern part, taking Diego Suarez on 7 May (the port is also known as Antsirane). This success was greatly helped by a *coup de main* by a small force of Royal Marines who landed from a destroyer. Negotiations for the administration of the island were opened with the French, but the British battleship *Ramillies* was torpedoed in the harbour and negotiations broke down. Lt-General Sir William Platt, Commander in E Africa, was then ordered to occupy the rest of the island, and on 10 September, by means of an amphibious assault on the west coast, he took Majunga. Tamatave, on the east coast, was taken on 18 September, and Inland, the capital of Tananarive, fell on 23 September. The Vichy French retreated south, but on 5 November Annet surrendered and was interned in Durban.

Result: Britain now had a valuable naval base in the Indian Ocean and Allied communications with the Near and Far East were ensured.

On 8 January 1943 General Charles de Gaulle's Free French took control of the island.

MALAYA (MALAYSIA)   Second World War   8 December 1941 – 27 January 1942

Fought between the Allies under Lt-General A. E. Percival and the Japanese under General Tomoyuki Yamashita.

Strength: Allies 138,000 (including 15,000 non-combatants); Japanese 100,000.

The day after the Japanese attack on Pearl Harbour (qv) the Upper Malaya (Kra) peninsula was invaded by the largest concentration of Japanese troops anywhere within their widespread field of attack. Five landings were made by seaborne forces at Singora and Patani in S Thailand, Kota Bharu on the west coast of Malaya (Malaysia) and Alor Star and Penang Island on the east coast.

The British, under Percival, whose force consisted of the 9th and 11th Indian

Divisions, were swiftly beaten back as the Japanese advanced. Airfields were rapidly overrun, giving the Japanese complete superiority of the air while the British, who were able to fight no more than delaying actions, had been pushed 150 miles south by the end of December, by which time the Japanese reached the region around Ipoh, 200 miles north of Singapore (qv). In January the Japanese 25th Army, now four divisions strong, continued south, increasing their attacks by making amphibious landings behind the British lines. The British, though reinforced by the 8th Australian and 18th Indian Divisions, were unable to counter the expert jungle warfare fought by the Japanese. By 27 January the Japanese were putting pressure on the ever-decreasing bridgehead on the tip of the Malay peninsula, and on 31 January Percival ordered a withdrawal across the Johore Strait (1,100 yards wide) to Singapore (qv). The retreat was made over a causeway which the British only succeeded in partially destroying after their evacuation of the mainland.

MALTA III   Second World War   November 1940–May 1943
Fought between the Allies and the Axis.

Malta was strategically placed not only as a naval but as an air base for the Allies, enabling them to give air cover to convoys moving through the Mediterranean and to attack Axis ships plying between Italy, Sicily (qv) and Tripoli. The Axis forces therefore attacked it constantly and heavily for over twenty months. From Cyrenaica, Libya, the Germans and Italians bombed the island from April to November 1941 and February to November 1942, paralysing the island with as many as 300 bombers attacking in a day, all directed by Field-Marshal Albert Kesselring. The RAF was crippled, the naval bases dispersed and the inhabitants forced to take refuge underground. By May 1942 2,470 air attacks had been made on the island, making it one of the most bombed areas in the world. Supply convoys were also attacked and the blockade was so effective that very little food, fuel or ammunition reached the island, which seemed to be in imminent danger of capitulating.

In March 1942 a convoy of 4 ships carrying 26,000 tons of supplies left Alexandria. All 4 were sunk before reaching their destination, despite strong cover by the Royal Navy. In the spring of that year the British aircraft carrier Eagle, and the American carrier Wasp, brought 126 Spitfires into the island and these quickly stopped the daylight raids, 37 Axis aircraft being shot down on the first day, with a loss of 3 Spitfires. In June, however, 15 out of 17 merchantmen bringing supplies to the island were sunk and the resolute Governor, General Sir William Dobbie, was replaced by General Lord Gort. Because of the gravity of the situation, in August Operation Pedestal was launched, in a major effort to get supplies through to the island before it collapsed altogether. Fourteen merchantmen steamed into the Mediterranean, the convoy being guarded by a task force of 4 carriers, 14 battleships and cruisers and 40 destroyers commanded by Vice-Admiral E. N. Syfret. The Axis brought in 21 U-boats, 23 E-boats and 540 aircraft. The Eagle and 2 cruisers, the Manchester and Cairo, were sunk in the engagement which followed and several other battleships were damaged. Nine supply ships did not get through, but 5 others did, the only tanker in the survivors being the USS *Ohio*, which was crippled. The supplies were not generous, but they were sufficient and when, three months later, the Axis forces in N Africa were defeated, most of the air attacks against Malta ceased and the island became secure.

For its part in the battle, Malta was awarded the George Cross—an honour bestowed on the whole island.

MANNERHEIM LINE (Finland)   Russo-Finnish War/Second World War
30 November 1939–21 February 1940
Fought between the Finns and the Russians under Marshal Semyon Timoshenko.

After invading Poland (qv) in 1939 the Russians turned to Finland (qv). With a force estimated at 1 million men, they took Petsamo in the north, but were unable to penetrate the Mannerheim Line, a system of concrete and steel fortifications which ran from the Gulf of Finland to the inland lakes.

When the Russians attempted an outflanking movement through E Finland, Finnish ski troops, using guerilla tactics, harassed the communications of the Russian 163rd Division. They were supported by the infantry of the Finnish 9th Division. The 163rd Division was enveloped and cut off, and attempts by the Russian 44th Motorised Division to assist failed. The 163rd Division was annihilated, and the 44th Division cut to pieces. The Russians lost 27,500 killed or frozen to death and 1,300 captured. This was the Battle of Suomussalmo, fought between 11 December 1940 and 8 January 1941. All the Russian tanks and artillery were captured. Finnish losses were 900 killed and 1,770 wounded.

France and Britain prepared a strong force to assist Finland, hoping to enter via the ice-free port of Narvik in Norway, but the Swedes did not venture to give permission for their territory to be crossed to help their small neighbour, and so the project was dropped, though not until after the force had been assembled.

The Russians began an artillery bombardment of the Mannerheim Line on 1 February, and on 11 February attacked with twenty-seven divisions and tank support. The line was broken along an 8-mile front on 21 February. The Finns fought fiercely, but their army was only one-tenth of the Russian strength and they were forced to surrender, ceding the Karelian isthmus and Vyborg (Viipuri). Russian casualties totalled 200,000. Finnish losses were 24,900 killed or missing and 43,500 wounded.

MARETH LINE (Tunisia)   Second World War   February–April 1943
Fought between the British under General Sir Bernard Montgomery and the Germans under General Erwin Rommel.

After his defeat at the Second Battle of El Alamein (qv) Rommel retreated 1,500 miles across Libya and halted inside Tunisia where the Panzerarmee Afrika dug in behind the Mareth Line, a defensive fortification originally constructed by the French against a possible Italian attack from Libya. Montgomery, with the British 8th Army, pursued only slowly, hampered by a long and tenuous line of communication.

While awaiting the arrival of the 8th Army, Rommel turned to attack the Allies who lay in the Kasserine Pass (TUNISIA). He defeated the US 1st Armoured and 168th Regimental Combat Team before being driven back to his original lines by a British counter-attack. The British did not pursue, however, and with his rear temporarily safe, Rommel turned to attack the advancing 8th Army. On 6 March Rommel moved the 10th, 15th and 21st Panzers forward, aiming at the British supply dump at Medenine. Montgomery, who had foreseen such a move, had deployed his troops for a defensive action and, having forced Rommel to attack with all three divisions at once (with 140 tanks), he opened fire with 500 anti-tank guns. By nightfall, Rommel had lost 52 tanks and was forced to retire. British losses were 130 men and no tanks. The Desert Fox flew back to Germany six days later.

The 8th Army, resupplied and reinforced by Free French forces under General Jacques Leclerc, now launched its attack on the Mareth Line. On 20 March an artillery barrage was opened all along the 20-mile front of the Mareth Line. A frontal feinting attack by 30 Corps near the coast enabled General Sir Bernard Freyberg's New Zealand Division which formed part of 10 Corps to move south with the 8th Armoured Brigade and the Free French, on a wide flanking movement on the left. After a 200-mile march the Axis position at El Hamma was turned, enabling the British 1st Armoured to move to the German rear around the south end of the Mareth Line. The move was supported by aerial bombardment, and Montgomery, whose first frontal assault had failed, now attacked again. Unable to defend from both front and rear and threatened with encirclement, the Axis were forced to retreat. General Giovanni Messe moved his German-Italian 1st Army north to the Gabes–Gafsa road, having lost 7,000 prisoners during the battle. On 6 April, Montgomery attacked the Gabes position and forced the Axis troops to move farther north to Wadi Akarit. In the first six hours of fighting 2,000 prisoners were taken.

On the following day a British patrol from the 4th Indian Division met a patrol from US 2 Corps. The two Allied forces had moved together from a distance of 2,000 miles and were now ready to launch their final assault in N Africa (TUNISIA).

MARIANA ISLANDS (central Pacific)   Second World War   15 June–31 July 1944

Fought between the Americans and the Japanese.

The American conquest of the Gilbert and Marshall Islands (KWAJALEIN–ENIWETOK) opened the way for an attack on the Mariana Islands, 1,300 miles NW and within the Japanese outer defensive ring of their Pacific bases. Air bases on the islands taken by the Americans would be able to launch B–29 Super-fortress bomber attacks on both Japan itself and the Philippine Islands (qv), two targets which were over 1,500 miles from the Marianas.

The Japanese Central Pacific Fleet under Admiral Chuichi Nagumo, which had attacked Pearl Harbor (qv) in 1941, was also based on the Marianas and an attack here might provoke the Japanese to seek the decisive naval action which Admiral Chester Nimitz wanted. General Hideyoshi Obata's 31st Japanese Army was the military force on the Marianas. On 15 June General Holland Smith's 5 Corps invaded Saipan, the northernmost of the three main islands. Two marine divisions abreast landed along a 4-mile front on the west of the island: General Thomas Watson's 2nd Division on the left, just below the city of Garapan, and General Harry Schmidt's 4th Division, stretching to the south of the island. General Yoshitsugu Saito's 30,000 Japanese troops resisted the landing fiercely, but by nightfall the Americans were about a mile inland. Both divisions continued to move east while, on the night of 16 June, the 27th Infantry Division under General Ralph Smith landed. They took Aslito (Isely) airfield the following day and army P–47 Thunderbolts began to use the strip on 23 June. Although the Japanese continued to fight vigorously, the Americans managed to clear most of the south of the island. The three divisions then moved to the left: the 2nd Marine, forming the left wing, on the west coast, the 27th Infantry in the centre and the 4th Marine on the east coast. The sweep north was begun on 23 June and Japanese resistance continued. The 27th Infantry began to fall back and Ralph Smith was replaced by General Sanderford Jarman and, later, General George Griner. By 1 July the three divisions were in line once more. The 2nd Marine Division stopped to take Garapan while the other two divisions moved towards Marpi Point on the northern tip of the island. Nagumo and Saito killed themselves on 6 July, after which the Japanese troops, now without their High Command, launched suicidal *banzai* attacks in which they lost 2,500 men. On 9 July resistance ended with the mass suicide of Japanese military and civilian personnel off Marpi Point. Only 1,000 Japanese were captured, the sole survivors of the conquest of Saipan. Of 20,000 Americans, 10,347 marines and 3,674 soldiers were casualties, of whom 3,246 died.

On 21 July the Americans switched their attention to the southernmost island of the group, Guam. General Roy Gieger, Commander of the new 3 Amphibious Corps, sent two divisions ashore, the 3rd Marine Division, under General Allen Turnage, north of Apra Harbour, and the 1st Brigade (General Lemuel Shepherd) and 77th Infantry Division (General Andrew Bruce), south of Apra. Both attacks were on the western side of the island where the Japanese had originally conquered Guam (qv) in 1941. The island was defended by 19,000 Japanese under General Takeshi Takashina. By dark of the first day, the southern attack had gained a beachhead a mile deep, but the 3rd Marine Division encountered heavier opposition and it was four days before the two beachheads were linked up a mile inland. On the night of 25 July the Japanese mounted fierce counter-attacks which the Americans pushed back with difficulty. The 1st Brigade cleared the Orote peninsula, between the two landings. On 31 July the 3rd Marine and 77th Infantry Divisions, left and right abreast, moved NE. The 1st Brigade joined the line a week later when the other two divisions had already made steady progress. The attack took the northern end of the island on 10 August, which put Guam into American control. American casualties were 7,800, of which 6,716 were marines,

839 soldiers and 245 sailors, and of these 1,023 were killed.

Tinian, lying between Guam and Saipan, became the next target. Schmidt was now in command of 5 Amphibious Corps vice Holland Smith who had been promoted to Commander of the General Fleet Marine Force Pacific. Tinian lay 3½ miles south of Saipan and contained enough level ground to provide the best B–29 bases in the Pacific Ocean. Defending the island were 9,000 Japanese soldiers under the command of a drunken admiral called Kakuji Kakuda. On 24 July a secondary landing was made by the 2nd Marine Division near the town of Tinian on the SW coast. At the same time the 4th Marine Division landed on the NW of the island, and had created a beachhead a mile deep by nightfall. During the night 1,200 Japanese were killed trying to dislodge the Americans. Watson's 2nd Marine Division landed on the same beach the following day and mopped up the northern end of the island before turning to drive down the east coast, abreast of the 4th Marine Division.

Tinian was overrun by 31 July in the fastest conquest of the war. American casualties were light, being 327 killed and 1,771 wounded. Nearly all the Japanese were killed by the Americans, died in *banzai* attacks or committed suicide. In all, 40,000 Japanese died in the American attack on the Marianas.

The invasion provoked the Japanese into the naval action of the Philippine Sea (qv). On 24 November the first B–29 raid on Japan itself was undertaken from bases on Saipan.

MARSHALL ISLANDS   see KWAJELEIN-ENIWETOK

MATAPAN (Mediterranean)   Second World War   28 March 1941
Fought between the British under Admiral Sir Andrew Cunningham and the Italians under Admiral Angelo Iachino.
Strength: British 3 battleships + 4 cruisers + 1 aircraft carrier; Italians 3 battleships + 6 cruisers + 2 small cruisers + 12 destroyers + surface craft.

In the Greek Peloponnese the Italians attempted to intercept a British convoy off Cape Matapan. The British launched an air attack which slowed the Italians down, and at 10.25 pm on 28 March they opened fire at a range of 3,800 yards. The battleship *Vittorio Veneto* was damaged by air attack, but survived the battle, during which 3 8-inch-gun cruisers, *Zara*, *Fiume* and *Pola* and 2 big destroyers were sunk by the British fleet. British losses totalled 2 aircraft but no seamen. While 900 Italian sailors were rescued from the sea, 2,400 were killed.

The battle guaranteed Allied naval superiority in the Mediterranean, and forcibly demonstrated the superiority of the Royal Navy over its Italian enemies.

MERSA MATRUH (Egypt)   Second World War   25 June 1942
Fought between the Allies under General Sir Claude Auchinleck and the Germans and Italians under General Erwin Rommel.
Strength: Allies 100,000 with 150 tanks; Germans and Italians 113,000 with 60 tanks.

After their defeat at Gazala (qv) the British retreated across the Egyptian frontier, pursued by the Germans. Auchinleck, who had taken personal command of the 8th Army, halted at Mersa Matruh, a British base. The four British divisions were deployed with Lt-General Holmes's 10 Corps in the coastal town itself and Lt-General W. H. E. Gott's 13 Corps 9 miles inland.

On 25 June Rommel pushed through the centre of the British line between the two corps with the German 90th Light Division. The following day, however, they were held by the British. Auchinleck had ordered that the divisions were not to engage in a standing fight, but were to give battle while retreating. Gott, faced with the 21st Panzers in the south, which had only 21 tanks, began to pull back, unaware of the weakness of the Afrika Korps. The rest of the line was therefore also forced to retreat towards the El Alemain–Quattra Depression. In three days the 21st Panzers routed the British force, taking 6,000 prisoners and 40 tanks.

The Axis seemed to be near to capturing both the Nile valley and the Suez Canal.

MIDWAY ISLAND (central Pacific)   Second World War   3–5 June 1942
Fought between the Americans under Admiral Chester Nimitz and the Japanese under First Admiral Isoroku Yamamoto.
Strength: Americans 76 warships including 3 carriers (*Enterprise, Hornet, Yorktown*); Japanese 162 warships and auxiliaries including 12 transports with 5,000 troops + 4 carriers.

The Japanese sought to extend their hold over the chain of islands in the central Pacific which guarded their conquests in the east. Midway Island, 1,000 miles west of Hawaii, was their target and they mounted their biggest-ever naval operation to capture it. Late in May a diversionary force was sent to the Aleutian Islands by Yamamoto while Admiral Chuichi Nagumo made for Midway with a striking force which included 4 carriers. He was followed by an invasion fleet of 88 ships. The Americans had deciphered the Japanese naval code, however, and were aware of their plans to take Midway and destroy the remnants of the US Pacific Fleet by drawing the US fleet north to the diversionary attack in the E and W Aleutians, particularly on Dutch Harbour, while the Japanese themselves took Midway and secured landings, then able to destroy the US fleet piecemeal as it returned from the Aleutians. Nimitz did not rise to the bait, but left the Aleutians to the N Pacific Fleet. The main US force awaiting the arrival of the Japanese NE of Midway, was divided into two task forces, No 16 under Admiral Raymond Spruance and No 18 under Admiral Frank Fletcher. The main US strength lay in her 3 carriers and aircraft based on Midway itself.

An attack on the approaching Japanese fleet by US aircraft from Midway was unsuccessful, and the following morning the Japanese sent 108 aircraft to attack Midway. The raid inflicted much damage and destroyed 15 of the 25 marine fighters which defended the island. An American reconnaissance pilot spotted the Japanese fleet and 10 US torpedo bombers took off from Midway to attack the

Japanese, the first of three waves to do so. No hits were scored and 7 aircraft were lost. In the second wave of 27 bombers again no damage was inflicted, but 8 bombers were shot down. The final attack was made by 15 B – 17s, but these did not cause any damage either. The 3 American carriers then launched their torpedo bombers, but they caused little damage and 35 out of 41 planes were lost. When the Japanese aircraft returned to their ships to refuel and rearm, Nagumo learnt that a fleet of US warships was coming up on them. By midday, 54 dive bombers from the *Enterprise* and *Yorktown* (the *Hornet* planes missed the target), had sunk 3 Japanese carriers, the *Akagi*, *Kaga* and *Soryu*, all with their decks loaded with aircraft ready to take off. They all went down within five minutes, during which time the whole course of the war in the Pacific was changed. During another attack in the afternoon, the fourth carrier, *Hiryu*, was also sunk, but aircraft from this carrier had already attacked the *Yorktown*, which was severely damaged. The Japanese, however, now had no air cover and, deprived of all their carriers, on 5 June they were forced to withdraw. The Americans could not pursue because they too were much weakened by the battle, but they sank the heavy cruiser *Mikuma* on 6 June and, on the same day, in a torpedo attack by Japanese submarines, the *Yorktown* was sunk. American losses during the battle were 150 planes, 307 men, the destroyer *Hammann* and the carrier *Yorktown*. Japanese losses were 275 aircraft, about 4,800 casualties (including many carrier pilots) and 4 carriers (a virtually irreplaceable loss) plus a heavy cruiser.

This action, together with that at Coral Sea (qv), ended the Japanese domination of the Pacific and enabled the Allies to launch their counter-offensive.

MOSCOW (USSR)   Second World War   September 1941–January 1942
Fought between the Germans and the Russians.

After invading the USSR, in September 1941 the Germans halted near Smolensk. General Fedor von Bock's Army Group Centre dispatched two armies during this time to move south as part of a pincer movement around Kiev (qv) with the Army Group South. On 2 October the reassembled force of sixty divisions resumed the attack, their objective being Moscow, 200 miles away, which they wanted to reach before winter. The battle took place in three phases, the first two being German offensives and the third a Russian counter-offensive.

Phase one began when General Heinz Guderian's 2nd Panzer Group ploughed through Orel on 8 October, Chern on 24 October and then moved on Tula which lay 100 miles south of Moscow. Meanwhile, the 3rd and 4th Panzer Groups under Generals Herman Hoth and Erich Hoeppner which had come from the Leningrad (qv) front undertook a pincer movement around Vyazma. Between 2 and 13 October 600,000 Russians were killed or captured in this area, but the Germans broke through and made for the Mozhaisk Line, 50 miles west of Moscow, running from Kalinin to Kaluga. The 3rd Panzer Group, now commanded by General Hans Reinhardt, backed up by the 9th Army, moved north and west of Moscow, taking Kalinin on 15 October, while Guderian, outflanking the Mozhaisk Line, took Kaluga on 21 October. In the centre, General Gunther von Kluge's

Army moved directly on the capital which lay 40 miles away. The Russian government (though not Stalin) moved 550 miles SE to Kuibyshev on the Volga. The first phase petered out at this point, when worsening weather and stiffened Russian resistance slowed the momentum of the German attack.

On 16 November the ground had been hardened by frost and the attack was resumed in the Kalinin–Volokomsk region, and by 22 November, Istra, 15 miles west of Moscow, had been reached. By this time the full force of the Russian winter had almost completely paralysed men and machines, and although on 3 December Tula, 100 miles south of Moscow, was surrounded, it was not taken. The Panzer division under Guderian came to within sight of the Kremlin in the suburbs of the capital and the 258th Infantry Division of the 4th Army fought its way into the suburbs, only to be beaten back by armed factory workers in two days of heavy fighting, during which the Russians suffered heavy casualties. The Russians claimed to have killed 85,000 Germans in the fighting of the second phase.

The cold, lack of petrol, and Russian resistance finally halted the Germans altogether; but Adolf Hitler forbade a withdrawal, which resulted in many casualties from the cold. The German offensive ground to a halt on 5 December, and on the following day Marshal Georgi Zhukov, who had replaced Marshal Semyon Timoshenko–who had gone to the southern front–launched a counter-offensive, thus marking the opening of the third and final phase. Led by ski troops, the Red Army attacked Guderian's salient on 9 December at Tula. The hundred-division Russian army killed 30,000 Germans in five days and captured much heavy equipment. Guderian was replaced by General Rudolf Schmidt. Kalinin, Klin, Istra and Yelets were retaken by 15 December, Kaluga on 26 December (this was lost again, but recaptured four days later), and Mozhaisk on 18 January. By 15 January the Russians had advanced 200 miles in the north and 180 miles in the south. Kluge retired to Vyazma in the south and Rzhev in the north, both lying 125 miles from Moscow. General Gotthard Heinrici now took over the 4th Army. This line, which the Germans had originally broken through at the start of their offensive, was now defended by a series of hedgehog positions that contained the Russians; but the Germans, who suffered so severely from the elements that some corps were reduced to a third of their fighting strength, were more handicapped by the weather than they were by battle casualties and their power had become ineffective in this sector. The Russians had planned to surround and destroy all the Germans between Moscow and Smolensk, but this objective was not achieved.

In this, their first major defeat on land of the war, the Germans lost 55,000 dead, 100,000 wounded, 777 tanks, 297 guns and mortars, 244 machine-guns, according to the Russians, and 192,000 killed and wounded from 30 September to 26 November, according to General Halder. Russian losses were twice as high. Russian Partisans attacking German lines of communications had, for the first time, started to take an important part in the defeat of the German army. The Germans held their ground throughout 1942, but fell back in 1943.

NETHERLANDS   Second World War   10–14 May 1940
Fought between the Dutch under General Henri Winkelman and the Germans under General Fedor von Bock.

After conquering Norway (qv) the Germans turned to the Netherlands, to cover the right flank of the German main attack south against France. The right wing of the huge German army was Bock's Army Group 'B' which moved into Belgium and the Netherlands on the morning of 10 May. Sixteen thousand airborne troops, of whom 4,000 were parachutists, landed in Rotterdam and other important areas and captured key bridges, airfields and other strategic installations. They were commanded by General Kurt Student. On 13 May eleven divisions of General Georg von Küchler's 18th Army linked up with the airborne forces, having advanced 100 miles west to do so. The ten divisions of the Dutch army had therefore already been defeated before Girand, with the French 7th Army in Belgium could come to their aid. On 14 May the government surrendered to Germany, Queen Wilhelmina fled to England and Winkelman surrendered the army.

On the day that the Dutch capitulated, the Luftwaffe attacked Rotterdam, inflicting 30,000 civilian casualties. Excluding prisoners, Dutch military losses totalled about 10,000. German losses were fewer; they lost only 180 in the airborne assault on Rotterdam. The French 7th Army surrendered to the German 18th Army on 17 May before the latter joined the main German forces which were attacking Belgium.

NEW GUINEA (SW Pacific)   Second World War   1942–4
Fought between the Allies and the Japanese.

On 8 March 1942 the Japanese advance through the SW Pacific islands reached New Guinea when Lae and Salamaua on Huon Gulf in NE New Guinea were taken. The capture consolidated the Japanese conquest of the E Indies and placed the town of Port Moresby in SE New Guinea in danger. Port Moresby was the last defensive post held by the Allies to protect Australia. After the Battle of the Coral Sea (qv) a Japanese invasion force making for the port was forced to turn back, after which the Japanese made determined efforts for two and a half years to gain control of the island.

Amphibious troops of General Matazo Adachi's 18th Japanese Army landed at Gona and Buna, 100 miles east of Lae and Salamaua where the chief bridgehead lay, on 21 and 22 July. Gona and Buna lay on the east side of the island, half-way along the N Papuan coast to Milne Bay. From here, a double offensive was launched against Port Moresby. On 26 August 1,900 Japanese stormed ashore at Milne Bay where two Australian brigades and US engineers were constructing airstrips for General George Kenney's newly formed SW Pacific Air Command. Six hundred invaders were killed and the rest forced to evacuate ten days later. At the same time two Japanese regiments, which had begun a southward march from Gona–Buna along the Kokoda Trail on 22 July, occupied Kokoda village on 12 August and, having crossed the Owen Stanley Range which rises to a 6,000-feet pass at Kokoda, had by 17 September reached the village of Ioribaiwa, which lay only 32 miles from Port Moresby. Here the 7th Australian Division, which was defending the trail, halted the Japanese advance and General Edmond Herring then counter-attacked, forcing the Japanese back through the rugged mountain and into the kunai grass swamps around Gona and Buna. The terrain is among the worst in the world and the Australians were joined by the inexperienced US 32nd and later 41st Infantry Divisions.

The Japanese were driven out of Gona on 10 December 1942, and out of Buna on 3 January 1943. The only Japanese resistance left in the sector was at Sanananda Point, and by 23 January this too had been overcome. The liberation of Papua cost the Australians and Americans 8,456 casualties (2,334 Americans were, additionally, incapacitated by disease). The Japanese lost about 12,000 killed and 350 captured, although about 4,000 escaped to New Britain or the Huon Gulf region. This victory enabled General Douglas MacArthur to launch a long-term counter-offensive in the SW Pacific area, of which a major part was contributed by General Robert Eichelberger's US 1 Corps which later grew into the US 6th Army, commanded by General Walter Krueger. During the fighting in New Guinea, Australian Independent Companies, operating against the Japanese communications far in advance of the main Australian/American forces, were one of the main factors contributing to the Allies' success, as the Japanese could not continue resistance to their front whilst their bases at Buna, Gona, Lae and Salamaua were attacked in their rear.

In 1943 Eichelberger, supported by Admiral Thomas Kinkaid's 7th Fleet, began a long drive to wipe the Japanese off the north coast of New Guinea. American and Australian units moved west and north from Gona on the coast and Wau, inland, towards Lae and Salamaua. On the night of 29 June the US 41st Infantry Division landed at Nassau Bay, near Salamaua. Aided by the 5th Australian Division, the unit drove towards Salamaua which they captured on 12 September. Lae was surrounded at the same time. On 4 September the 9th Australian Division, which had been at El Alamein (qv), made an amphibious landing 10 miles east of the village, and the US 503rd Parachute Regiment and the 7th Australian Division flew in and were dropped in the Markham valley, west of the village. Lae fell on 16 September. On 22 September a brigade of the 9th Australian Division landed on the coast at Finschhafen, 50 miles above Lae on the Huon peninsula, and the capture of Finschhafen on 2 October opened the way for the later conquest of the whole area of the Huon Gulf.

On 2 January 1944, 100 miles to the west, the 32nd Infantry landed at Saidor, where they secured an airstrip. Between the two Allied-held positions, there remained 12,000 Japanese who were still on the north coast of the Huon peninsula. No more than 4,400 of them survived. On 5 March the 32nd Infantry moved farther west to take Mindiri. Brigades from the 5th and 11th Australian Divisions moved to the Astrolabe Bay area, moving past the Americans, at the end of April, and taking Bogadjim, Madang and Alexishafen between 24 and 26 April. Krueger's 6th Army moved 400 miles west on 22 April to reach the Hollandia area. The US 24th Infantry disembarked at Tanahmerah Bay while the 41st Infantry landed

25 miles east at Humboldt Bay. The two divisions linked up on 26 April while the 163rd Regiment separated from the 41st Infantry of which it was part, took Aitape, 125 miles east. The three landings marooned over 50,000 Japanese troops of the 18th Army which lay in the Wewak sector. When the Japanese tried to break out of the trap, they were repulsed by troops of the 11 Corps under General Charles Hall. The Japanese lost 8,800 killed. American losses were 450 killed and 2,500 wounded.

On 17 May the 6th Army moved farther west to the Maffin Bay area. They landed at Arara and on Wakde Island which lay off-shore. On Wakde Island the Japanese fought fiercely against the 163rd and 158th Regiments, the 6th Infantry Division and parts of the 31st and 33rd Infantry Divisions. By 21 May the island was secure, though Maffin Bay itself was not taken until the end of June. American losses were 455 killed and 1,500 wounded. The Japanese lost 4,000 killed. During the fighting on Wakde Island the 41st Infantry had advanced another 200 miles on 17 May to Biak Island, which overlooked the entrance to Geelvink Bay, near the western end of New Guinea. Biak Island was held by 10,000 Japanese who were at first successful in resisting American attempts to dislodge them. Early in June 1,000 Japanese reinforcements were landed, but American air and sea attacks inflicted heavy damage on the convoy, sinking 2 destroyers and shooting down 50 aircraft. The landing of further reinforcements for the Japanese became impossible and they began, reluctantly, to give ground to the 41st and 24th Infantry which augmented the American force on the island. By 20 June most of Biak was in American hands, although some pockets of resistance remained until August. The Americans lost 474 killed and 2,400 wounded during the capture. Japanese losses were 6,100 killed and 450 captured.

Noemfoor, a smaller island to the SW, was taken by the 158th Infantry and 503rd Parachute between 1 and 6 July with a loss of 70 killed and 350 wounded. Japanese losses were 2,000 killed and 250 captured. On the NW end of New Guinea, Sansapor and the Vogelkop peninsula were occupied by the 6th Infantry on 30 and 31 July, completing the leap-frogging movement along the northern coast of the island. Within the 1,500-mile stretch, 135,000 Japanese were cut off and left behind.

Although New Guinea was now in Allied control, a strong base had been established by the Japanese on Halmahera Island in the Moluccas during the fighting. Before the liberation of the Philippine Islands (qv) could be undertaken, it was necessary to remove the Japanese from their base. MacArthur accordingly sent Hall's 11 Corps beyond Halmahera to the more northerly island of Morotal. Strong air and naval support was provided by Kinkaid's 7th Fleet and Admiral William Halsey's 5th Fleet during the landing, which took place on 15 September. The 31st and part of the 32nd Infantry dug in in a perimeter behind which airfields could be constructed and used with safety. The base lay midway between the west of New Guinea and Mindanao in the S Philippines. The establishment of this base took place at the same time that Admiral Chester Nimitz was opening a passage east from the Philippines by the conquest of Peleliu-Angaur. American losses on

Morotai were 45 killed and 95 wounded. Japanese losses were 325 killed or captured.

The last action in New Guinea was the capture by Eichelberger of the islands of Asia and Mapia (St David), 150 miles north of the Vogelkop peninsula, for communications bases. It was the first action of the US 8th Army and took place between 15 and 20 November.

The Japanese were an entrenched and numerically superior enemy and therefore difficult to dislodge. The war in New Guinea included the most trying battles in US or Australian history, other factors militating against the Allies being the equatorial climate, the high incidence of disease and the long, tenuous lines of communication. The victory enabled MacArthur to return to the Philippines, and the SW Pacific air forces now had bases from which they could strike deep behind the Japanese lines.

NORMANDY (France)   Second World War   6 June–24 July 1944
Fought between the Allies under Field-Marshal Sir Bernard Montgomery and the Germans under Field-Marshal Erwin Rommel. The overall Commander-in-Chief, West, was Field-Marshal Gerd von Rundstedt, and later (1 July) General Gunther von Klüge. General Dwight D. Eisenhower, the supreme commander of the Allies, did not assume command in France until 1 August.
Strength: Allies rose to 800,000 (47 divisions) + 4,000 ships + 4,900 fighters + 5,800 bombers + an estimated 100,000 French Maquis; Germans 36 infantry divisions + 6 Panzer divisions. In all the Germans had 60 divisions to hold France, Belgium and Holland.

In the greatest amphibious landing in history, five beaches were assaulted by six Allied infantry divisions. From east to west these were: Sword (British 3rd), Juno (Canadian 3rd), Gold (British 50th), Omaha (US 1st and part of 29th) and Utah (US 4th). The immediate objective of the invasion was to establish a second-front beachhead. Ground forces consisted of the 2nd British and 1st US Armies, comprising the 21st Army Group.

In the vicinity of the landings there were only three enemy infantry divisions and one Panzer division: misleading indications given by the British led the Germans to concentrate much of their armour in the Calais area. General Friedrich Dollman with the 7th Army was in charge of this stretch of coast. For a month before D-Day, Allied bombardment had wrecked roads and railways as well as oil depots, hampering enemy communications. Naval minesweepers cleared lanes through the minefields, enabling the invasion force to approach. Three airborne, six infantry, two Commando and three armoured brigades made the first attack. Heavy air bombardment covered the landings, Air Chief Marshal Sir Trafford Leigh-Mallory's air force making 14,600 sorties against German coastal defences during the first twenty-four hours of the invasion. On either flank, airborne troops and parachutists were dropped to secure bridges and exits from the area; the US 82nd and 101st Airborne landed behind Utah Beach to take exits into the Cotentin peninsula and the British 6th Airborne dropped on the eastern end of Sword Beach to take bridges over the Orne River and the Caen Canal.

Operation Overlord began at dawn when the first waves of infantry hit the beaches. With air and naval support, the Allies fought their way ashore through prepared defences while under heavy fire from the Germans. At Utah, the US 4th met heavy German opposition but, after confused fighting, joined up with the 82nd and 101st Airborne, so that by midnight a beachhead 4 miles wide by some 9 miles deep inland had been secured. At Omaha, the 1st and 29th Divisions landed in the wrong place and suffered 3,000 casualties. By midnight they had advanced only a little over a mile inland. The British 50th Division landed at Gold and, against heavy opposition, advanced to take Arromanches and Bayeux. The Canadian 3rd drove inland 7 miles to within sight of the Caen road, but the British 3rd, though they moved inland, were unable to take their objective, Caen, owing to heavy opposition from 21st Panzer Division.

The Germans reacted slowly, fearing the main landing had yet to come in the Pas de Calais and Adolf Hitler refused to launch the reserve Panzers until it was too late. French sabotage of telephone links also helped to create chaos at headquarters. During the next six days the Allies fought their way inland and secured a lodgment 80 miles long by 10 miles deep, while eight more combat divisions landed, thus ensuring the success of the operation. Allied losses in the first phase of the operation totalled 11,000, including 2,500 dead, a very much lower figure than had been forecast.

On the right flank of the lodgment three corps of the US 1st Army held the perimeter from Caumont to Carentan. North of Carentan, General Joseph Collins drove his 7 Corps to the west across the base of the Cotentin peninsula and on 18 June, after five days of skilful and determined fighting, reached the Atlantic coast. The 9th, 79th and 4th Infantry then turned north and made for Cherbourg which they reached in two days. Persistent attacks from 22 to 27 June finally forced the surrender of the garrison 21,000 strong. The unloading piers of the port had been severely damaged by the Germans before they capitulated, but by 7 August they were operable, and a valuable port was thus opened for the landing of supplies.

Elsewhere, the Allies were contained in their beachhead while men and supplies were landed to enable them to break out. The Germans moved Panzer units to this front as fast as they could. On 28 June General Dollman was killed. He was replaced by General Paul Hausser. On 1 July Rundstedt was replaced by von Klüge who had come from the Russian Front. Klüge committed suicide on 19 August, two days after his supersession by Field-Marshal Walter Model. On 3 July the US 1st Army attacked south along most of its front, but it achieved only limited gains. Lessay was taken as an anchor for the right flank and St Lô (qv), near the centre of the American sector, fell on 18 July. Five divisions attacked the town and suffered 11,000 casualties in twelve days.

Meanwhile, still trying to take Caen, Montgomery strove to occupy as many Panzer divisions as possible to give the Americans a chance to break out at St Lô. Concentrating the British 2nd Army's ten infantry, three armoured and one airborne divisions and six armoured brigades (1,350 tanks), he attracted a force of six infantry divisions, seven Panzer divisions and three Nebelwerfer brigades, with a total of 670 tanks. Three battles ensued.

On 10–15 June the British tried to encircle the town, but failed. On 25–29 June 8 Corps attacked German armour and drove it back, enabling it to cut the Caen–Falaise road and finally, after a heavy bombardment, causing many civilian casualties, the British drove their way into Caen and by 18 July occupied most of the town. Continuing to attack east and west of the river, the British kept the Panzers in that sector, so that the Americans, faced with only 100 tanks and nine divisions, were able to take St Lô (18 July) and break out. A further attack (Operation Goodwood) took the British south of Caen but by 20 July three British armoured divisions had been stopped by two German Panzer divisions.

On 15 July Rommel was seriously wounded when fighter aircraft attacked his staff car at Ste Foy de Montgommery.

By 24 July only one-fifth of the assigned area had been taken by the beachhead forces. However, they were now ready to launch a major attack to try to achieve a breakthrough. Of 122,000 losses suffered by the Allies, 6,010 British were killed and 28,690 wounded. Up to 23 July, 116,863 Germans had been killed or wounded.

NORTH-WEST AFRICA   Second World War   8–17 November 1942
Fought between the Vichy French and the Allies.
Strength: Vichy French 60,000; Allies 107,000 + 650 ships.

After the Axis defeat at the Second Battle of El Alamein (qv), on 8 November an Anglo-American force invaded French NW Africa. The invasion was known as Operation Torch and was the biggest amphibious attack ever undertaken up to that time. The Allies were under the overall command of General Dwight D. Eisenhower and three landings were made, at Casablanca on the west coast of Morocco, Oran in W Algeria and Algiers, midway along the Algerian coast.

US General Charles Ryder took the surrender of Algiers from General Alphonse Juin on the evening of the invasion. It was the first city to fall and the force which captured it numbered 32,000 men, including a British unit and regimental combat teams from the US 9th and 34th Divisions. At Oran, the French resisted for two days before the 1st Infantry and 1st Armoured Divisions (31,000 men) under General Lloyd Fredenhall took the city on 10 November. In the Casablanca area resistance by the French under General Auguste Nogues was stronger. The French warships in the harbour engaged the Allied fleet which protected the invaders. The Allies lost 7 ships and 3 submarines and suffered 1,000 casualties. On shore General George Patton's 34,000 men, consisting of the 3rd and 9th Infantry and 2nd Armoured Divisions, strengthened their foothold on the area and took the surrender of the town three days later. A general cease-fire was ordered on 10 November by Admiral Jean François Darlan the most powerful Free Frenchman in N Africa. Although General Henri Giraud, who had escaped German internment in France, had originally been destined to command the French in N Africa, Darlan was the more powerful figure and on 13 November he was made chief French official in N Africa.

Meanwhile, on hearing of the Allied invasion of French NW Africa, the Germans had marched into Vichy France, which had hitherto been unoccupied.

Darlan was assassinated on 24 December and Giraud succeeded him. The force which had landed at Algiers became known as the British 1st Army, although it was more the strength of a division than an army. Commanded by General Sir Kenneth Anderson, this unit occupied Bougie on 11 November and parachutists reached Bone on 12 November. The army was across the Tunisian frontier three days later. Meanwhile, on 15 November, American parachutists took Tebessa, Algeria, and on 17 November arrived at Gafsa in west central Tunisia. The Axis, however, were already arriving in the country, protected by air cover from Sicily. Tunisia was beyond the range of British squadrons at Gibraltar, which had supported the invasion along the NW coast. By the end of November 15,000 Axis troops, including the 10th Panzer Division, were in Tunisia (qv).

NORWAY   Second World War   9 April–9 June 1940
Fought between the Germans and the Allies.

After the conquest of Poland the Germans remained inactive for six months before moving north towards Scandinavia in the first operation which combined land, sea and air forces. Adolf Hitler's objective was to secure the Swedish iron ore for Germany and to stop any Allied design on the Scandinavian countries.

Denmark was occupied on the same day that Norway's six major ports were invaded by parachutists, airborne infantry and troops hidden in the holds of merchant ships. The Norwegian Nazi movement, led by Major Vidkun Quisling, also greatly helped the 25,000 invading troops, since these were well trained and able to operate where the tactic of surprise was not as effective as it had been in the immediate invasion targets. Within two days, the ports along 1,000 miles of coastline–from north to south, Narvik, Trondheim, Bergen, Stavanger, Kristians-and and Oslo–were in German hands. Oslo fell to 1,500 German troops under General Nikolaus von Falkenhorst, overall Norwegian commander, who had landed in Fornebu Field which lay just outside the capital. Part of the Norwegian army surrendered, but some troops under King Haakon VII fled to the forested and mountainous interior to organise resistance from there.

The Allies hastily prepared a counter-attack and between 14 and 19 April three landings were undertaken. The two largest counter-invasion forces landed at the small ports of Namsos and Aandalsnes, either side of Trondheim. The Allies had moved so quickly, however, that they had not organised any port or airfield through which reinforcements or heavy equipment could be landed. There was incessant air attack by the Luftwaffe. The two British brigades, one regular and one territorial (Major-General Bernard Paget), which had landed at Aandalsnes, had been badly mauled by the German forces at Lillehammer, Otta and Dombas, but extensive demolitions carried out by British engineers in the Romsdal Gorge leading to the port ensured that the remnants of the force could be re-embarked successfully by destroyers of the Royal Navy. The Norwegian King, royal family, members of the Norwegian government and much bullion were also successfully evacuated by the Royal Navy from Molde at the entrance to the fjord leading to Aandalsnes.

At Namsos the British forces under Lt-General Carton de Wiart, after a quick thrust to within a few miles of Trondheim, were also evacuated successfully by the Royal Navy. Darkness only lasted about two hours in these latitudes and the navy and army units were under constant attack by Stuka and Heinkel bombers. The only British air effort was by a squadron of 6 Gladiators operating off a frozen lake near Aandalsnes. All but one of these were shot down.

After his evacuation from Molde King Haakon set up his exile government in London where he continued to support Norwegian resistance to the Germans by all the means in his power. General H. R. S. Massey, who was directing the operation from London but who could know little of what was going on, ordered an evacuation of the 30,000 troops, and by 3 May all of central Norway was in the hands of the Germans.

The third of the Allied landings, however, which had taken place near Narvik, was more successful. This landing was commanded by Admiral Lord Cork and Orrery, and his 20,000 troops besieged the port which was defended by 6,000 German soldiers and sailors. On 28 May General Claude Auchinleck's ground troops stormed into the city and drove the Germans into the mountainous terrain inland. At this point, however, the critical state of Allied affairs in N France forced the Allies in Norway to withdraw.

By 9 June the last of the Allies in Narvik had re-embarked. The only area in which the Allies did some lasting damage to the Germans was at sea. The Norwegian fleet, formerly neutral, now joined the Allied side, but other, more direct consequences resulted. Although the Allied losses were heavy and mostly British (the aircraft carrier *Glorious*, the cruisers *Effingham* and *Curlew*, as well as 9 destroyers and 6 submarines), they were replaceable; on the other hand German losses of an 8-inch–gun cruiser, 2 light cruisers, 10 destroyers, 11 transports, 8 submarines and 11 auxiliary vessels seriously weakened Hitler's chances of invading Britain. German manpower losses were 5,300.

The German northern flank was secured, along with Scandinavian resources for German industry. Important sea and air bases were also acquired for attacks on Britain and her shipping. But Britain gained 4 million tons of merchant shipping with their crews as well as an appreciable number of naval vessels and some fine naval officers and ratings.

OKINAWA (Ryukyu Islands, Japan)   Second World War   1 April–2 July 1945
Fought between the Americans and the Japanese.
Strength: Americans 183,000; Japanese 100,000.

The battle for Okinawa was the last and greatest land battle of the Pacific war. The island, 67 miles long by 20 miles wide, is the largest in the Ryukyu chain and lies 400 miles south of Kyshu. It was the last stepping-stone for the Americans before their projected invasion of Japan itself–Kyushu in November 1945 and Honshu in March 1946.

General Mitsuru Ushijima was in charge of defending the island and he deployed the 32nd Army behind the Naha–Shuri–Yonabaru Line which lay across the south of the island, a fifth of the way up it. The Japanese planned to fight to the death behind this line while *kamikaze* pilots destroyed Admiral Raymond Spruance's 5th Fleet which protected the invasion. Admiral Chester Nimitz was in overall command of the invasion, but the amphibious attack was brought into Okinawa by Admiral Richmond Turner who had directed all such operations since Guadalcanal (qv). General Simon Buckner's 10th Army was to undertake the invasion. Meanwhile, on 26 March, the 77th Infantry Division under General Andrew Bruce took the Kerama and Keise Islands which lay off the SW coast of Okinawa. On 1 April the Americans landed on the Hagushi beaches in W Okinawa, 10 miles above the Japanese defence line. The northern wing was made up of General Roy Geiger's 3 Amphibious Corps–the 6th Marine Division of General Lemuel Shepherd on the left, the 1st Marine Division of General Pedro del Valle on the right and the 2nd Marine Division under General Thomas Watson making a feint-landing on the southern tip of the island. The right (S) wing was made up of General Courtney Hodges's 24 Corps–the 7th Infantry under General Archibald Arnold and 96th Infantry under General James Bradley on the left and right respectively. Encountering only light opposition, the invaders had carved out a beachhead 8 miles long and between 3 and 4 miles deep by nightfall. By 3 April the 1st Marine Division had secured a corridor across the island to the east coast. To their left, the 6th Marine Division moved north up both coasts, and on 8 April they reached the Motobu peninsula, a rugged feature which jutted into the E China Sea. At the end of twelve days this area was cleared of Japanese resistance and by 20 April the four-fifths of Okinawa north of the defence line was cleared.

On 16 April the island of Ie Shima, which lies off the Motobu peninsula, was invaded by the 77th Infantry Division. The island took four days of hard fighting to secure and 4,700 Japanese were killed in the process. American losses were 258 dead and 879 wounded. Among those killed (18 April) was the famous American war correspondent Ernie Pyle. 24 Corps, on the southern end of Okinawa, found the going much harder. Having moved across the width of the island in two days, the Americans turned 90 degrees south, the 7th on the left and the 96th Division on the right. By 8 April Japanese resistance had increased greatly, and on 11 April the corps was stopped by the outer defence works of the Naha–Shuri–Yonabaru Line. General George Griner's 27th Infantry was sent in on the west coast next to the 96th Division, and on 19 April 24 Corps launched a major assault, three divisions abreast, along a 5-mile front. In twelve days, however, less than 2 miles of ground was gained. 3 Amphibious Corps was added to the line to form the right wing with the 6th Marine Division on the west coast and the 1st Marine Division inland. On the left, the 7th Division retained its position on the east coast while the 77th Division moved in from Ie Shima on its right, relieving the 27th and 96th Divisions, both of which were much depleted.

On 4 and 5 May Ushijima launched a disastrous counter-attack against the

Americans' left flank. Because the Japanese had to leave their entrenchments to engage the Americans, they suffered heavy losses; 6,227 were killed while 24 Corps suffered not more than 714 casualties. After the 96th Division, now reinforced, had relieved the 7th Division on the far left, Buckner resumed the offensive six days later, despite the spring rains. The Americans ground forward, into and through the Japanese lines. On 23 May the 6th Marines took Naha and turned the left flank of the Japanese line. In the centre, the 1st Marine Division took Shuri Castle on 29 May, while on the right 24 Corps continued to move south, outflanking the east end of the line. On 4 June the 6th Marine Division made a shore-to-shore assault on the Oroku peninsula in the SW; it was reduced after ten days of fighting. The 8th Regiment under Colonel Clarence Wallace from the 2nd Marines joined the main thrust to the south of Okinawa. During this last advance General Buckner was killed. His place was taken by Geiger. On 21 June the 10th Army reached the south coast and turned to wipe out remaining pockets of resistance. The battle ended officially on 2 July. Over 90,000 Japanese were killed (Ushijima committed *hara-kiri*) and 7,400 were taken prisoner. American casualties were 2,938 marines killed or missing and 13,708 wounded. Army casualties were 4,675 dead and 18,099 wounded.

At sea and in the air the battle raged just as furiously. A force of Japanese warships, the giant battle-cruiser *Yamato*, a light cruiser and 8 destroyers, coming to the aid of the embattled forces on Okinawa, was intercepted by US aircraft in the Van Diemen Strait. The *Yamato*, 1 cruiser and 4 destroyers were sunk and 9 other Japanese vessels were also sunk while the battle for Okinawa raged, virtually destroying their navy. Japanese bombers harassed the 10th Army and its protective fleet during the invasion. Their bombs did little damage, but *kamikazes* made 1,900 attacks, sinking 36 American ships and damaging 368: 4,907 seamen were killed and 4,824 were wounded. Altogether, 7,800 Japanese planes were destroyed at a cost of 763 US aircraft. As a result Japanese air power was nullified.

Okinawa now became the base for the projected invasion of Japan. General Joseph (Vinegar Joe) Stilwell took over the 10th Army which, with the 1st Army from Europe, came under the command of General Douglas MacArthur. Admiral Chester Nimitz continued to have control of all naval units. Six weeks after the end of the Battle of Okinawa, however, two atomic bombs were dropped on Japanese cities, forcing the unconditional surrender of the Japanese forces and rendering the invasion unnecessary (JAPAN, AERIAL BOMBARDMENT).

During the Okinawa operation the British Far East Fleet under Vice-Admiral Sir Bernard Rawlings and consisting of 4 fleet carriers (the *Indomitable*, *Indefatigable*, *Illustrious* and *Victorious*), 2 battleships, 5 cruisers (1 New Zealand) and 11 destroyers (2 Australian) co-operated with the US 5th Fleet by neutralising neighbouring airfields with air raids and naval bombardment. The British lost 160 aircraft and were attacked by *kamikaze* pilots. But as the British carriers had armoured flight decks they did not suffer as badly as the US carriers.

ORAN II (Algeria)   Second World War   3 July 1940

Fought between the British under Admiral Sir James Somerville and the pro-Vichy French under Admiral Marcel-Bruno Gensoul.

Strength: British 6 capital ships + 11 destroyers; French 2 battle-cruisers + light cruisers, destroyers, submarines and auxiliary vessels.

Aim: The French fleet was the fourth largest in the world and, after the surrender of France (qv) to the Nazis, the Allies sought to prevent the fleet from being used by the Germans.

Battle: A large part of the French fleet lay in the Algerian port of Mers-el-Kebir at Oran and the British Naval Task Force H under Somerville approached the harbour to deliver an ultimatum. The fleet had been ordered by the Vichy government to join the Nazis, but Somerville told Gensoul either to sail to N America with the Allied fleet or to scuttle. The ultimatum was rejected and the British opened fire. In ten minutes, naval and aerial bombardment practically destroyed the French fleet, the only large ships to escape destruction being the battle-cruiser *Strasbourg*, sister ship to the *Dunkerque*. In this bombardment 1,000 French sailors were killed.

Result: Britain was thus able to maintain naval supremacy in the W Mediterranean. The rest of the French fleet was scuttled at Toulon on 27 November 1942 to prevent its being taken over by the Nazis.

PEARL HARBOR (Hawaii, central Pacific)   Second World War   7 December 1941

Fought between the Americans under Admiral Husband Kimmel and General Walter Short, and the Japanese commanded by Vice-Admiral Chuichi Nagumo.

Strength: Americans 8 battleships + 12 cruisers + many destroyers and other vessels; Japanese 360 bombers and fighters + 6 fleet carriers and battleships + 2 light carriers + 6 cruisers + many destroyers and submarines.

While negotiations between the Americans and Japanese were continuing to keep the peace, a fleet of 6 Japanese aircraft carriers under Nagumo with supporting battleships and cruisers set sail from the Kurile Islands on 26 November. Their target was Hawaii, which they approached undetected through fog and gales, and 275 miles north of the islands they launched their bombers and fighters. These reached their objective, Pearl Harbor on Oahu Island, at 7.55 am, the first wave of 183 planes striking a nearby airfield where training aircraft were lined up and the harbour itself where the American fleet lay. A second wave of 170 planes attacked at 8.40 am. Five midget submarines also penetrated the harbour, but they did little damage and were all destroyed. There were 8 American battleships in the harbour and it was on these that the Japanese concentrated their attack. The *Arizona* was blown up, the *Oklahoma* capsized, the *West Virginia* sank at her moorings, as did the *Calfornia*. The remaining 4 battleships all suffered damage and 11 other vessels were sunk or crippled. The US aircraft carriers were all out on exercise and were therefore not touched. The virtual destruction of the rest of the US Pacific Fleet forced the Americans, in subsequent hostilities, to fight in the Pacific in a new fashion, employing carriers and aircraft instead of battleships and cruisers. Besides the ships, 247 US planes were destroyed at a cost to the Japanese of 29 aircraft and 5 midget submarines. American casualties were 2,330 killed and 1,145 wounded. The US commanders, Kimmel and Short, were relieved.

Simultaneous with their attack on Pearl Harbor, the Japanese bombed the Philippine Islands and Hong Kong (qqv) and made several landings in and around the Malay peninsula (MALAYA). The Japanese were now the dominant power in the W Pacific.

The Americans at once declared war on the Japanese and then Germany and Italy.

PELELIU-ANGAUR (central Pacific)   Second World War   15 September-25 November 1944
Fought between the Americans under Vice-Admiral Theodore S. Williams III and the Japanese under General Sadae Inoue.
Strength: Americans 25,000; Japanese 10,000 (Peleliu) + 1,400 (Angaur).

Having conquered the Mariana Islands (qv), only one more base was needed in the central Pacific before Admiral Chester Nimitz would be able to attack the Philippines. This was the Palau Islands in the W Carolines, 550 miles east of the Philippines. General Roy Geiger's 3 Amphibious Corps (under the temporary command of General Julian Smith) was to undertake the assault of Peleliu, Angaur, a smaller island 8 miles south, and Ulithi. Peleliu, 6 miles long and 2 miles wide, was defended by the Japanese under Inoue, strongly entrenched in 500 fortified caves, mostly interconnected. General William Rupertus's 1st Marine Division landed on the SW corner of the island on the morning of 15 September, three regiments abreast. Although the landing was accompanied by heavy naval and air bombardment, the Japanese fought back fiercely and it was only after four days of fighting that the southern end of the island was cleared. The airfield in this area was opened for Allied use on 26 September.

The force then moved north to assault the other end of the island but were stopped by heavy resistance, artillery and small-arms fire from Umurbrogol Mountain, later known as Bloody Nose Ridge. On 17 September General Paul Mueller's 81st Infantry Division assaulted Angaur, which was more or less overrun in three days. Some resistance remained in the west until 13 October. Geiger, by now in charge of 3 Corps again, ordered the 321st Regiment to move to Peleliu while the 323rd occupied Ulithi without encountering any resistance. On 24 September the 321st Regiment joined the attack on Bloody Nose Ridge by assaulting from the west. By nighfall on 27 September the Japanese at the top of the ridge had been surrounded. Peleliu came under Mueller on 15 October, but the last pockets of resistance on Bloody Nose Ridge were not wiped out until 25 November, by which time both the 321st and the 323rd Regiments were engaged in the struggle for possession of the height.

The operation produced the highest casualty rate ever recorded for an amphibious assault in American history–almost 40 per cent of the force was lost. The 1st Marine Division lost 6,526 men, of whom 1,252 were killed; the 81st Infantry Division lost 208 dead out of 1,393 casualties. Japanese casualties were 13,600 killed and 400 captured, one of the prisoners being Inoue.

Morotai was captured simultaneously with the assault on the Palaus, giving the Americans a southern entrance to the Philippines. The capture of Peleliu, Angaur and Ulithi secured the Allied right flank.

PHILIPPINE ISLANDS   Second World War   8 December 1941–18 May 1942
Fought between the Americans and Filipinos under General Douglas MacArthur, and the Japanese under General Masaharu Homma.
Strength: Americans/Filipinos 11,000 US soldiers and marines + 8,000 air corps personnel + 12,000 Filipino scouts + 100,000 Filipino soldiers + US Asiatic Fleet (Admiral Thomas Hart) + US Army Air Corps (General Lewis Brereton) 35 B – 17s and 107 P – 40s; Japanese 43,000 men (main assault only).

Luzon, the largest island in the Philippine archipelago, was one of the chief objectives of the Japanese invading force in the W Pacific. The main body of the US Far East forces was stationed here, including the large Filipino army, which was for the most part untrained and poorly equipped. The Asiatic Fleet lay in Manila Bay and the Air Corps was also present, although of its 275 aircraft only 35 Flying Fortresses and 107 Tomahawks and Kittyhawks could be considered as modern combat planes.

The key air base, Clark Field, which lay 50 miles NW of Manila, was attacked at noon on 8 December and 15 out of 17 Flying Fortresses on the ground were knocked out. Admiral Thomas Hart, withdrew his naval force to Borneo in order to take it out of the range of Japanese bombers. On 10 December the Japanese then began to land troops on the island, 4,000 of them landing at the northern end of Luzon at Aparri and Vigan. On 14 December another landing took place at Legaspi on the southern end of the island. The main invasion took place on 22 December when Homma's 14th Army landed at Lingayen Gulf on the west coast, 125 miles from Manila. The Japanese had complete superiority of the air and quickly joined forces with the invaders who had landed on the north of the island. The main force then moved south towards the plains, beyond which lay Manila. MacArthur ordered a withdrawal to the Bataan peninsula on the west coast between Manila Bay and the S China Sea.

The following day 9,500 Japanese landed at Lamon Bay, 60 miles SE of Manila, thus placing the capital within a pincer movement. In order to get all Allied forces safely into the Bataan peninsula, the Americans and Filipinos fought delaying actions for the next week until all combatants had withdrawn from north to south. Manila was heavily bombed for two days and on 26 December it was declared an open city to prevent further destruction (it was occupied on 2 January 1942). By 1 January the northern force under General Jonathan Wainwright and the southern force under General George Parker–later replaced by General Albert Jones–were in Bataan and the two Calumpit bridges over the Pampanga River were destroyed before the Japanese reached them. MacArthur and the Philippine President, Manuel Quezon (Manuel Luis Quezon y Molina), set up headquarters on Corregidor Island (BATAAN–CORREGIDOR) with 19,000 US troops and 21,000 Filipinos on half rations, scant ammunition and lack of medical supplies. The island, known as the 'Rock', lay off the south coast of Bataan at the mouth of Manila Bay. The withdrawal was accomplished with the loss of 13,000, many of whom were Filipino deserters. On 20 December, during the early part of the Japanese invasion, 5,000 troops had landed on Mindanao, on the south of the archipelago. Moving south, they took the strategic port of Davao that day and moved on to Jovo Island and N Borneo, thus cutting the Allies in the Philippines from their ever-strengthening base in Australia.

The Japanese continued to drive back the US forces in Bataan, and on 10 January Franklin D. Roosevelt ordered MacArthur to embark on a torpedo boat which took him to Australia as Commander of the SW Pacific Area. He was evacuated safely via Mindanao. The Japanese were thwarted in their aim to conquer any further part of the Philippines because of the strength of the defence at Luzon. However, they broke through the lines on Bataan on 31 March, and General Edward King ordered the evacuation of the peninsula. After this, the Japanese quickly occupied strategic coastal points throughout the Visayan Islands, meeting little opposition. King's men, 12,000 Americans and 55,000 Filipinos, surrendered and were sent on a death march to the north of Luzon.

On Corregidor, Wainwright held out until 6 May when he was forced to surrender (BATAAN–CORREGIDOR). General William Sharp, in Malaybalay, Mindanao, surrendered on 10 May, and Colonel John Horan capitulated with his guerilla force on 14 May in N Luzon. On 18 May, Panay, the last of the Visayan forces under General Bradford Chynoweth, surrendered.

The Filipino and American forces had now all officially surrendered, but guerilla activity never ceased, and the mounting counter-offensive in the SW Pacific under MacArthur in Australia was continuously supplied with information from Allied underground movements.

PHILIPPINE SEA   Second World War   19–20 June 1944
Fought between the Japanese under Vice-Admiral Jisaburo Ozawa and the Americans under Admiral Raymond Spruance.
Strength: Japanese 9 carriers + 5 battleships + 13 cruisers + 28 destroyers + 473 aircraft; Americans 15 fast carriers + 7 battleships + 21 cruisers + 69 destroyers + 956 aircraft.

The American invasion of the Mariana Islands (qv) induced the Japanese fleet to seek a pitched naval battle with the Americans for the first time since Guadalcanal (qv) in 1942. Admiral Sormu Toyoda, deciding to force a showdown battle, sent out a force of carriers under Ozawa and battleships and cruisers under Admiral Matomu Ugaki to attack the American fleet protecting the invasion force on Saipan. Spruance, in command of the 5th Fleet, organised a defence and sent Admiral Marc Mitscher with Task Force 58 to intercept the Japanese fleet

90 miles away.

The interception took place in the Philippine Sea, between the Marianas and the Philippines, and early on 19 June Japanese aircraft from Guam and Truk attacked Task Force 58, in response to which Hellcat fighters from the US carriers destroyed 35 planes. Following this, 430 Japanese carrier aircraft pitted themselves against 450 American carrier-based aircraft in a battle which fell into four separate waves. At the end of eight hours, 330 Japanese aircraft had been destroyed in the most decisive air battle in history. The Americans lost 30 aircraft in what became known as 'The Marianas Turkey Shoot'. The 5th Fleet itself suffered no serious damage. Two American submarines managed to get through the screen protecting the Japanese carriers. The *Albacore* sank the 33,000-ton *Taiho*, Japan's biggest flat-top, with a single torpedo, costing 1,650 men. The *Cavalla* launched 3 torpedos against the 22,650-ton *Shokaku*, which exploded with heavy loss of life. On the night of 19 June the Japanese fled to the NW, pursued by the American carriers. On the evening of 20 June 209 aircraft were launched against the Japanese, although they were now 300 miles away. This force was intercepted by 75 Japanese aircraft, but 40 of these were shot down and the carrier *Hiyo* was destroyed. The Americans lost 20 aircraft during the battle and 80 more during the flight back to base after dark, although 51 pilots were picked up from the sea. The action marked the end of the battle.

Ozawa escaped with 6 of his carriers, but nearly all his trained carrier pilots had been lost and the invasion of the Marianas had not been halted.

POLAND   Second World War   1–27 September 1939
Fought between the Poles under Marshal Edward Smigly-Rydz and the Germans under General Fedor von Bock and General Gerd von Rundstedt. The Russians made a separate invasion.

The Germans invaded Poland without prior warning on 1 September. They had forty-four infantry divisions and fourteen armoured (Panzer) or motorised divisions to Poland's thirty infantry and cavalry divisions and one motorised brigade. The Germans employed a new method of warfare, the Blitzkrieg, whereby Polish forces were attacked piecemeal wherever they were found. Consequently the whole of Poland became a battlefield. The 1,400 planes of the Luftwaffe destroyed the 900 aircraft–mostly obsolete–of the Polish air force, mainly on the ground, within the first two days of hostilities.

The German forces advanced from three directions and amounted to five separate armies. The 3rd (General Georg von Küchler) moved in from E Prussia in the north, the 4th (General Gunther von Klüge) from Pomerania in the west and the 8th (General Johannes von Blaskowitz), 10th (General Walther von Reichenau) and 14th (General Wilhelm List) from Silesia in the SW. Bock commanded the northern armies and Rundstedt the southern. The Germans reached Warsaw, having penetrated 140 miles in one week. They began to bombard the city by land and air. The 10th Army, the first to arrive on the SW front, was joined by the 3rd on the northern on 14 September, and the Polish capital was surrounded by

17 September when the 4th and 14th Armies closed in from west and east.

The Russians marched into Poland the same day and advanced 110 miles in two days to reach the Curzon line of 1919. Warsaw fell on 27 September and Poland was divided between Russia and Germany the following day. Some Polish leaders escaped to Paris and thence to London, where they set up an exile government under General Wladyslaw Sikorski; but 450,000 Poles became prisoners of war. German losses were 10,600 killed, 30,300 wounded and 3,400 missing.

Russia now turned on Finland and Germany feinted in the west to attack Norway (qv) the next spring. In June 1941 the Nazis overran Russian Poland.

The Polish Home Army continued the war under General Rowecki and his Second in Command (and successor in 1943) General Tadeusz Bor-Komorowski.

POLAND–EAST PRUSSIA   Second World War   July 1944–April 1945
Fought between the Allies and the Germans.

The Russian offensive in the winter of 1943–4 pushed the Germans back to the 1939 border of Poland. The offensive was renewed in the summer of 1944 on two fronts: the north between the Baltic and the Pripet Marshes, and in the south between the Pripet Marshes and the Carpathian Mountains.

The northern front, known to the Germans as the Fatherland Line, since it protected Germany itself, was manned on the Russian side by General Ivan Chernyakhovsky's 3rd White Russian Army. This group forced three crossings of the Nieman (Nemunas) River in Lithuania–White Russia. The northern force captured Kaunas (Kovno) on 1 August and drove on towards the E Prussian border. The centre prong, having bridged the river on 26 July at Grodno, moved towards Suwalki and the SE of E Prussia. The left (S) flank of the Russian force joined with General T. Zakharov's 2nd White Russian Army to take Bialystok on 18 July. Zakharov moved NW towards E Prussia as well. Field-Marshal Ernst Busch, in charge of German defences in Prussia, set up a stiff resistance to the Russian attack. South of this, General Konstantin Rokossovsky's 1st White Russian Army crossed the Bug River on 11 July and, turning north, took Brest-Litovsk six days later. Wheeling west, Rokossovsky unexpectedly moved on Warsaw and, going through Siedlce, reached the eastern suburb of Praga on 31 July.

The arrival of the Russians on the Vistula sparked off an uprising in the Polish capital which Germans ruthlessly quelled, while three corps of the SS were moved to Warsaw to throw back the Russian force. Meanwhile, however, Marshal Georgi Zhukov, who had taken over the 1st White Russian Army, came up the line of the Vistula on this front to support the spearhead at Praga. South of the Pripet Marshes, the Russian left had launched its summer offensive on 16 July. General Ivan Konev's 1st Ukrainian Army attacked along a 125-mile front stretching between Luck (Lutsk) and Tarnopol. Rawa Ruska was taken on 20 July and the German forces in this sector, commanded by Field-Marshal Walther Model, were routed. South of this front, General Ivan Petrov took Stanislav and moved west. L'vov, caught between the two drives, fell on 27 July. The two forces foined up and pressed on west, crossing the San at Jaroslaw and Przemsyl on 28 July. By 1 August the 1st Ukrainian Army had secured a bridgehead across the Vistula at Baranow, south of Warsaw. Having pushed 450 miles in five weeks, the Soviet offensive stalled as the German forces rallied to hold the line of the Vistula for six months. Fighting now shifted to a front south of the Carpathians.

On 12 January 1945 the Russians launched their last great offensive along a 750-mile front. Stalin tanks, mounting 122mm cannon, were being brought to the front in great numbers and these spearheaded the attack. To the south, Konev's three armies, the strongest Russian force, consisting of thirty-two infantry divisions and eight armoured corps, broke out of the Vistula bridgehead. The left wing moved SW towards Krakow and the centre moved west on Oppeln. Averaging 18 miles per day, the two cities were reached on 19 and 26 January respectively. The objective of the drive was the Upper Oder and, in the process of attaining it, the important industrial centre in Upper Silesia was cut off. The right flank of Konev's force moved north from the Vistula bridgehead to enflank the German forces which faced Zhukov's force in the centre. On 14 January Zhukov had launched his attack across the Vistula. Bypassing Warsaw, which fell on 17 January, the Russian armour moved 150 miles in six days between the Vistula and Warta Rivers, avoiding the strongly held communication centres of Thorn (Torun) and Posen (Poznan). General Heinrich Himmler took command of the crumbling German forces in the area. By 30 January Zhukov's force was crossing the Brandenburg frontier, under 100 miles from Berlin. To Zhukov's left, Konev drew abreast, so that within three weeks the Russians had advanced 300 miles as far as German pre-war territory. To the right, Rokossovsky, who was now commanding the 2nd White Russian Army Group, moved NW and reached the Baltic west of Danzig (Gdansk) on 26 January.

The drive blew a great hole in the German front and isolated the German defenders in E Prussia. Turning east, Rokossovsky entered Cdynia on 28 March and Danzig two days later. The E Prussian pocket, pressurised by Rokossovsky on the SW, was also under siege from the south and east by the 3rd White Russian Army Group. On 1 February Chernyakhovsky split the pocket in two by driving through to the Baltic between Elbing (Eldlag) and Königsberg (Kaliningrad). When Chernyakhovsky was killed in action on 18 February, his replacement, Marshal Alexander Vasilievsky, continued to press relentlessly on the German defensive line. On 20 March a German bridgehead at Braunsberg collapsed, and on 9 April the garrison of 90,000 at Königsberg capitulated.

Although this battle was now over, the battle for E Germany (qv) had just begun.

PO VALLEY (N Italy)   Second World War   9 April–8 May 1945
Fought between the Allies and the Germans.
After the winter stalemate of five months, General Mark Clark's 15th Army Group resumed the offensive against General Heinrich von Vietinghoff-Scheel's

10th and 14th Armies with the aim of breaking through the mountainous defences of the Gothic Line (qv) and destroying the German forces in the Po valley beyond.

The attack opened on the east (Adriatic) flank on 9 April when three corps of the British 8th Army moved north. General Sir Richard McCreery's 5 Corps moved up Highway 16 to the Argenta Gap on the right, and on 14 April the Polish 2 Corps on the left took Imola on the road to Bologna. General Truscott's US 5th Army took up the attack on that day, 2 Corps moving north towards Bologna while 4 Corps drove west of the city (the 92nd Infantry held a long front stretching west from here to the Ligurian Sea). The 10th Mountain Division led the Americans into the open country NW of Bologna on 20 April and the city, half surrounded, fell to the Poles the next day. Both Allied armies moved north so fast that thousands of Germans were trapped in the rear. By 23 April the 10th Mountain Division faced the Po to the SE of Mantua.

As the rest of the Allied forces closed up, the German armies retreated across the Po and the Allies subjected the Germans to such intense bombardment that they lost most of their heavy equipment. The pursuit became a rout north of the river as the Allies sped towards the foothills of the Alps. Italian Partisans revolted in the wake of the Allied advance and seized control of Genoa, Milan and Venice (on 28 April, Benito Mussolini and his mistress were captured and mercilessly slain). On 26 April the 5th Army entered Verona and on 29 April Milan. To the right, the 8th Army moved round the head of the Adriatic and linked with Marshal (Josep Broz) Tito's Yugoslav Partisans on 1 May. The collapse of the German armies was completed on 29 April when Vietinghoff-Scheel formally surrendered all his forces in Italy to Field-Marshal Sir Harold Alexander, effective as from 2 May. Nearly 1 million men were included in the surrender: the first of a series of large-scale capitulations which concluded the war in Europe.

After the Normandy landings the Italian theatre diminished in importance. Still it held divisions which the Germans needed elsewhere and stimulated the guerilla resistance on other fronts. Allied casualties suffered on this front amounted to 350,000, but the German losses were higher.

PRINCE OF WALES and *REPULSE* (China Sea)   Second World War
10 December 1941
Fought between the British under Admiral Sir Tom Phillips and the Japanese under General Tomoyuki Yamashita.
Strength: British 1 battleship (*Prince of Wales*) + 1 battle-cruiser (*Repulse*) + 4 destroyers (*Electra, Express, Tenedos, Vampire* [RAN]); Japanese 84 aircraft.

The British sent 2 capital ships to Singapore (qv), the 35,000-ton battleship *Prince of Wales* and the 33,000-ton battle-cruiser *Repulse*, when the outbreak of war in the Pacific became imminent.

When the Japanese invaded the Malay peninsula on 8 December (MALAYA) Admiral Phillips took the *Prince of Wales, Repulse* and 4 destroyers into the China Sea to try and defend the area against the Japanese invasion. On 10

December the Japanese launched an attack of bombers and torpedo bombers from their base near Saigon. The 84 aircraft attacked in waves of about 9 planes and, as the warships had no fighter cover of their own, the Japanese enjoyed complete superiority of the air. The *Repulse* went down in an hour and a half, the *Prince of Wales* an hour later. Phillips and 1,000 men were lost.

The Japanese were now the supreme naval power in the W Pacific Ocean.

RABAUL (New Britain, S Pacific)   Second World War   22 June 1943–20 March 1944

Fought between the Allies and the Japanese.

Early in 1942 the Japanese turned their attention on the Australian base of Rabaul which lies in northern New Britain in the Bismarck archipelago. Aircraft from Truk in the Carolines and from Admiral Chuichi Nagumo's fleet back from Pearl Harbour (qv) opened the attack and on 23 January, Japanese troops landed at Rabaul and Kavieng, a base on the nearby island of New Ireland. Both garrisons were overrun and the conquerors proceeded to develop Rabaul and, to a lesser extent, Kavieng, into formidable air and naval stations, anchoring their SW Pacific line.

The Allies did not counter this move until 1943 when an offensive was launched in the area. Rabaul was bypassed, the intention being to isolate the base. On 22 June the US 112th Cavalry and 158th Infantry took Woodlark and Trobriand Islands in the Solomon Sea in the south. These bases, plus others gained by Allied successes in the Solomon Islands (qv), enabled the Allies to make repeated air attacks on Rabaul, carrier-based planes from Admiral William Halsey's 3rd Fleet joining in the assaults. On 15 December the 112th Combat Team made a landing on New Britain at Arawe on the SW coast. A major amphibious landing was then made by the US 1st Marine Division under General William Rupertus at Cape Gloucester, 75 miles NW, on 26 December. By 30 December the airstrip at Cape Gloucester had been captured, and by 16 January an impregnable perimeter around it had been constructed, opening it for the use of Allied aircraft. The 1st Marine Division moved northward up the coast from here to take Talasea between 6 and 8 March. American losses were 310 dead and 1,083 wounded, and Japanese casualties totalled 5,000 killed and 500 captured out of General Iwao Matsuda's 10,000-man force. The SW Pacific Fleet now had access to the straits between New Britain and New Guinea. (During this battle, Major Boyington became the top marine ace of the war, shooting down 28 aircraft before he was captured near Rabaul on 2 January after his plane had been shot down.)

The Allies continued to encircle Rabaul. The 3rd New Zealand Division took the Green Islands, 115 miles east of Rabaul, on 15 February, the US 1st Cavalry overran Los Negros in the Admiralties to the west and when, in March, the 1st Cavalry occupied Manus and gained control of the Admiralties, they effectively shut off all Japanese communications with Rabaul. In the Admiralties, 3,300 Japanese and 300 Americans were killed. On 20 March the US 4th Marine Regiment landed on Emirau Island in the Bismarcks, lying 70 miles north of Kavieng. Having built and operated airfields on all these conquests, the Allies neutralised the bases at Rabaul and Kavieng, which were now completely cut off.

The Allied offensive now moved west and north, leaving 100,000 Japanese on the islands to 'wither on the vine'.

RHINELAND (Germany)   Second World War   8 February–24 March 1945
Fought between the Allies under General Dwight D. Eisenhower and the Germans under General Gerd von Rundstedt.
Strength: Allies 85 divisions; German 60 (weak) divisions.

Before the end of the fighting in the region of the Ardennes (qv) bulge, fighting all along the front to break through to the Rhine valley was resumed. The Allies advanced so slowly, however, that it became necessary to undertake a major offensive in order to effect the breakthrough required.

Operation Veritable was launched by General Henry Crerar's Canadian 1st Army on 8 February (500,000 men). Under the overall command of Field-Marshal Sir Bernard Montgomery, the force drove SE from Nijmegen between the Meuse and the Rhine, through and around the Reichswald via Goch to Geedern. The Canadians reached the Rhine on 14 February. Meanwhile, a converging thrust, to be made from the south by General W. H. Simpson's 9th Army, had been held up by floods caused by the destruction of the Roer River Dam by the Germans. The German 1st Parachute Division faced the British and Canadians in the north where the latter experienced bad weather, extensive minefields and stiff German resistance. When the 9th Army crossed the Roer River on 23 February, however, it advanced so rapidly that the Germans were threatened with encirclement and were forced to withdraw. The two armies joined forces at Geldern on 3 March and together they drove the Germans back across the Rhine. By 5 March the armies had reached the Rhine, having driven north from Düsseldorf. The only German bridgehead remaining in the sector at Xanten–Wesel was wiped out by the British on 10 March. To the south, General Courtney Hodges's US 1st Army had advanced with Simpson to cover his right flank, and while this drive swept across the Rhine Plain, General George Patton's US 3rd Army drove through the Siegfried Line north of the Moselle.

Operation Lumberjack was launched by the 1st and 3rd Armies on 5 March. This was a drive towards the middle Rhine and on 10 March they reached the river, having moved through Koblenz and north through Bonn and Cologne (Köln). A link was then made with the British/Canadians at Wesel. The rapid advance brought the Allies to the railway bridge at Remagen, the only bridge across the Rhine which the Germans did not destroy. Advance units crossed the bridge and created a bridgehead on the east bank and reinforcements were sent to the area by Eisenhower to exploit the opening. The Germans counter-attacked fiercely and made determined attempts to blow the bridge up, but three corps (3, 5 and 7) were ferried across the river by bridge, pontoon and ferry. By 21 March, a bridgehead 20 miles long and 8 miles deep had been established.

On the strength of this unexpected find, the main weight of the attack was shifted from Montgomery's army group in the north to General Omar Bradley's in the centre. During this activity, Operation Undertone was launched by General Jacob Devers's group in the south. A pincer movement was undertaken against General Paul Hausser's 7th and 1st German Armies. On 15 March the right wing of Patton's 3rd Army attacked south across the Moselle into the Saar, and on 17 March Patch's 7th Army began to drive through the Siegfried Line, bearing NE. By 21 March all German opposition west of the Rhine had been eliminated, except for an ever-decreasing bridgehead around Landau. On 22 March Patton's 5th Infantry swung east and crossed the river at Oppenheim. Finding little opposition, 8 Corps bridged the river at Boppard, 40 miles north, on 24 March.

Three crossings of Germany's last natural defensive line had now been made on the centre. All three German army groups, General Johannes von Blaskowitz in the north, Field-Marshal Walther Model in the centre and Hausser in the south, were severely defeated. 60,000 Germans were killed or wounded, 250,000 captured. Much of the Germans' heavy equipment was lost. American losses were 6,570 killed in action. The other Allies lost fewer men.

RUHR POCKET (Germany)   Second World War   25 March–18 April 1945
Fought between the Germans under Field-Marshal Albert Kesselring and the Allies under General Dwight D. Eisenhower.
Strength: Germans 317,000; Allies 1 million.

The Allied armies in the Ruhr area–which was one of the prime objectives in the advance on the Rhine–were deployed as follows: Lt-General W. H. Simpson's US 9th Army in the south, between Worringen, 12 miles south of Düsseldorf, and the Lippe River, just north of the vital communications centre at Wesel; the British 2nd Army from the Lippe to the Dutch frontier, 8 miles south of Emmerich; and the Canadian 1st Army from there to the North Sea, securing the left (N) flank.

The main crossing of the Rhine was to take place north of the Ruhr between Rheinberg and Rees where the river was about 500 yards wide at low water. The German forces opposing the Allies were: the 25th Army from Emmerich to the North sea; the 1st Parachute Army from near Krefeld to west of Emmerich; four parachute divisions from near Krefeld to Essen; and four infantry divisions from Essen to Cologne. The 47th Panzer Corps and 116th and 15th Panzer Grenadier Divisions were in reserve. The British 2nd Army comprised four armoured, two airborne and eight infantry divisions with five independent armoured brigades and one Commando brigade and an independent infantry brigade. The US 9th Army had nine infantry and three armoured brigades. The Lippe River separated the two forces. At 3.30 pm, Field-Marshal Sir Bernard Montgomery launched an artillery barrage of 900 guns to cover the crossing of the Rhine, an operation which was successful and with only light casualties being suffered. Airborne landings followed, and east of the river German resistance crumbled.

Meanwhile, the US 15th Army under General Leonard Gerow had been assigned the task of holding the west bank of the river from Bonn north to Duisberg. General Courtney Hodges's US 1st Army at Remagen now moved east from there on 25 March, reaching Marburg, 75 miles east, on 28 March–which was the same day that the Rhine crossings were completed. From there, 7 Corps swung north towards Lippstadt while 19 Corps of Simpson's 9th moved along the Lippe with the same destination. On 1 April the two corps linked up–the 9th Army's 2nd Armoured Division and the 1st Army's 3rd Armoured Division–and in so doing they completed the encirclement of the Ruhr pocket, trapping Field-Marshal Walther Model inside with the 5th and 15th Panzer Armies and 100,000 other soldiers. Although their position was hopeless, the Germans resisted fiercely, hoping to block the Allied advance; but General Omar Bradley, now commanding both the 1st and 9th Armies, ordered the drive east to continue and left only two corps from each army to reduce the pocket. Simpson's 16 Corps and part of 19 Corps moved south on the Ruhr River and Hodges's 3 and 18 Corps moved on the east and south sides. A north–south attack on 14 April split the pocket in two and the Germans surrendered wholesale during the next four days. Model committed suicide. Resistance finally ended on 18 April when 317,000 prisoners were taken, including 30 generals.

ST LÔ BREAKTHROUGH (Normandy, France)   Second World War   25 July–8 August 1944
Fought between the Allies and the Germans.

After the D-Day landings (NORMANDY) the invasion troops built up as planned, but the beachhead had been contained on a line stretching from Caen through Caumont and St Lô to Lessay, 20 miles inland. In order to break out of the position which was too enclosed for the effective use of armour, General Sir Bernard Montgomery and General Omar Bradley launched Operation Cobra.

Fourteen divisions of the British 2nd Army were already engaging fourteen German divisions in the region of Caen. On 25 July 4,200 tons of bombs were dropped in an area 2,500 yards by 6,000 yards in ninety minutes. The target was so close to the American lines that 558 casualties were caused by bombs which fell short. General Joseph Collins's 7 Corps launched the assault west of St Lô, and although only 1,000 casualties were suffered the first day, two mobile columns were committed on 26 July, the American 1st Infantry and 3rd Armoured Divisions, while six 2nd Army divisions moved south towards the German rear. The left-hand column held off fierce counter-attacks by the Germans, while on 28 July the right fought its way into Coutances and on 30 July into Avranches. On 1 August General George Patton's 3rd Army came into operation, moving through the gap at Avranches into Brittany. 8 Corps penetrated into the region and cut it off by reaching Nantes on 10 August. Brest, Lorient and St Nazaire held out and were bypassed. Three other corps of Patton's army moved south and east to the rear of the 7th Army. On 6 August Adolf Hitler ordered five Panzer divisions to reinforce General Paul Hausser's 7th Army with the aim of breaking through the Avranches gap and driving to the coast, cutting off the American forces in Brittany. The attack drove west from Mortain, but Hodges's 1st Army contained the attack after two days of fighting and Allied air attacks fragmented the German columns. On 8 August Patton turned his 15 Corps north towards

Argentan, threatening to drive the whole of General Guther von Klüge's army group into the British 2nd and Canadian 1st Armies which still held the original line from Caen to Caumont. German armour and troops at Mortain were surrounded and destroyed in the Mortain–Falaise pocket (FALAISE–ARGENTAN POCKET) and the US 3rd Army moved west on the Seine from Dreux, Orléans and Chartres.

ST NAZAIRE (France)　Second World War　28 March 1942
Fought between the British and the Germans.
Strength: British 1 destroyer (*Campbeltown*), 1 motor gunboat (headquarters), 16 motor launches; Germans 10,000 in the area.

In order to prevent the battleship *Tirpitz* from joining her sister ship, the *Bismarck*, raiding in the Atlantic, it was resolved to destroy the gates of the Forme Écluse in the port of St Nazaire. This was the only dry dock on the Atlantic coast big enough to take the vessel, and it was hoped that the action would prevent the *Tirpitz* from putting to sea. An old, expendable American destroyer, the *Campbeltown*, was lightened so that she could sail up the Loire, her bows packed with explosives which, when the ship rammed the outer dock gates, would explode and destroy the gates. Men of the No 2 Commando under Lt-Colonel Charles Newman accompanied the naval force in order to carry out demolition work. The naval force was under Commander R.E.D. Ryder.

Leaving Falmouth on 26 March the destination was approached on 28 March, the force still undetected. The Germans eventually illuminated the ships but fake identification signals made them slow to open fire. The *Campbeltown* (Lt-Commander S. H. Beattie) rammed the dock gates and stuck fast, the Commandos on board getting off successfully, while the smaller craft found the Old Mole too strongly held, and only 3 landed their soldiers as planned.

In the confusion of the withdrawal, some commandos were left behind. At midday the following day the *Campbeltown* exploded while being inspected by a party of German officers. The lock gates were completely destroyed and the dock was not used for the rest of the war, thus achieving the major objective of the operation. Casualties numbered 397. The German losses were also heavy. This has been called 'the greatest raid of all'. Five Victoria Crosses were won.

SALERNO (Italy)　Second World War　9–16 September 1943
Fought between the Allies under General Dwight D. Eisenhower and the Axis under Field-Marshal Albert Kesselring.

The Allied invasion of S Italy (qv) on 3 September was really only a secondary thrust, the main attack being directed at Salerno on the west coast, where the ultimate objective was Naples. When, on 8 September, Marshal Pietro Badoglio surrendered the Italian government to the Allies, Kesselring immediately seized strategic points in Italy and poured German troops south to stem the Allied advance.

At dawn on 9 September Operation Avalanche was launched when the 5th Army under General Mark Clark made an amphibious assault on Salerno. General Ernest Dawley's–later General John Lucas's–US 6 Corps landed on the right (S) flank. During the first three days, the 36th and 45th Infantry took Paestum and moved 10 miles inland. On the left (N), the British 10 Corps of General Sir Richard McCreery captured Battipaglia near the centre of the beachhead and Salerno itself on the north flank. On 12 September, however, the Germans counter-attacked strongly. Armour recaptured Battipaglia, and on 14 September the Germans reached to within 2 miles of the coast. On that day the Allies made 2,000 sorties against the Germans and naval guns added to the aerial bombard-ment. General Sir Harold Alexander, in command of ground forces, moved in the US 82nd Airborne Division and the British 7th Armoured Division. By the evening of the following day, the counter-attack had been halted and Kesselring had begun to pull back. General Sir Bernard Montgomery's 8th Army, moving up from the south, made contact with the Allied landing, finally securing the beachhead. Clark's 5th Army, reinforced by the US 3rd Division, broke out of the beachhead towards Naples, which fell on 1 October. It became the main supply base for the Allied drive north towards the Gustav-Cassino Line (qv) and Rome.

SANGRO (Italy)   Second World War   19 November–3 December 1943
Fought between the British under General Sir Bernard Montgomery and the Germans under General Heinrich von Vietinghoff-Scheel.

During the drive north of the Allied armies, the British 8th Army en-countered a German force in the Sangro valley, 80 miles east of Rome in the Abruzzi Mountains. Three British infantry divisions and an armoured brigade attacked and defeated two infantry divisions and one Panzer group of the German 10th Army and proceeded to force a crossing of the Sangro while under heavy fire.

The British were unable to advance much farther and a joint Allied offensive the following year was needed to break the Gustav-Cassino Line (qv).

SCHARNHORST, GNEISENAU and *PRINZ EUGEN*–ENGLISH CHANNEL
Second World War   11 February 1940
Fought between the Germans and the British.

When Adolf Hitler became convinced that it was Britain's intention to invade Norway (qv), he ordered the squadron which had been raiding in the Atlantic and was then in Brest to return to Germany. The force included the battle-cruisers *Scharnhorst* and *Gneisenau* and the heavy cruiser *Prinz Eugen*. General Adolf Galland provided air cover for the force which, in order to preserve the element of surprise, was to leave at night. Vice-Admiral Ciliax planned to move, swept the minefields in the Channel and marked the passages so that the squadron could move as fast as possible.

The British were aware that something was afoot and had equipped 3 Hudson coastal patrols with radar. When, however, the squadron set sail from Brest at 10.45 pm on 11 February, none of the patrols picked it up on their radar and the British did not know for certain what was happening until a Spitfire patrol was debriefed the following morning. All available aircraft were sent to attack as soon as they were ready and the Royal Navy 825 Squadron attacked, losing all its aircraft. Further air attacks, supported by destroyers and motor torpedo boats, proved futile, and although the *Gneisenau* was hit once by a mine and the *Scharnhorst* twice, all ships managed to reach German ports by 13 February.

SCHARNHORST VERSUS *DUKE OF YORK* (Barent Sea)   Second World War   25–6 December 1943

Fought between the Allies under Rear-Admiral R. L. Burnett and Admiral Sir Brian Fraser, and the Germans under Rear-Admiral Erich Bey.
Strength: Allies 1 battleship (*Duke of York*) + 4 cruisers (*Belfast, Sheffield, Norfolk, Jamaica*) + 4 destroyers; Germans 1 battle-cruiser (*Scharnhorst*) + 5 destroyers.

On 25 December the *Scharnhorst* left Altenfjörd to intercept the eastbound Convoy JW 55B, which was escorted by 14 destroyers, her cover under Burnett who was guarding this convoy and the westbound Convoy RA55A. Fraser's force provided distant cover. At 7.30 am on 26 December Bey ordered his destroyers to fan out and search for the convoy, leaving himself with the *Scharnhorst* undefended. The *Belfast* sighted the *Scharnhorst* on her radar about an hour later and, having illuminated her with a starshell, she and the *Sheffield* and *Norfolk* opened fire at 9.29 am.

The *Scharnhorst* immediately turned south to avoid the cruisers before moving NE. As she moved faster than the British ships, Burnett resolved not to chase her, but to keep between the estimated position of the *Scharnhorst* and the convoy itself. The *Scharnhorst* did reappear on *Belfast*'s radar and the two sides engaged, both inflicting damage before the *Scharnhorst* once again broke away to the south. This time, however, Fraser's force (the *Duke of York, Jamaica* and four destroyers) was there to meet her. The *Duke of York* picked her up on her radar at just after 4.15 pm and the *Belfast* illuminated her at 4.50 pm. The battleship and the *Jamaica* then opened fire. The *Scharnhorst* was now trapped between Burnett and Fraser and could not escape: 14-inch shells from the *Duke of York*, fired at long range, ripped through the deck plating and the ship sank at 7.45 pm that evening, ending the threat to the Arctic convoys.

'SHANGRI-LA', JAPAN   Second World War   18 April 1942

Fought between the Americans under Admiral William Halsey and the Japanese.
Strength: Americans 16 B–25s with 80 airmen.

Following the unbroken string of Japanese successes in the Pacific, Halsey decided to take the initiative, however briefly, in what was really only a morale-boosting exercise. Naval Task Force 16 crossed the N Pacific to within 650 miles of Japan and then Lt-Colonel James H. Doolittle, with 15 others, took off in B–25 Mitchell bombers to attack Japanese targets. They left the carrier *Hornet* and 13 aircraft attacked Tokyo while the remaining 3 each attacked Nagoya, Osaka and Kobe, inflicting little damage, but alarming the Japanese and raising the spirits of the Allies. One aircraft landed in Vladivostock, where it was impounded by the Russians. The other 15 were abandoned in mid-air or crashed in China. The Americans lost 3 men killed and 8 captured. The captive airmen were tried for 'inhuman' acts and all were found guilty: 3 were beheaded and the remaining 5 were given life sentences.

In order to keep the carrier-launching secret, the US announced that the aircraft had been based at Shangri-La, which does not exist.

SICILY (Italy)   Second World War   10 July–17 August 1943
Fought between the Allies and the Axis.
Strength: Allies 160,000 + 2,700 ships and craft + 14,000 vehicles + 600 tanks + 1,800 guns + 3,680 aircraft; Axis 350,000, including 75,000 Germans + 1,400 aircraft.

After the conquest of N Africa by the Allies, Operation Husky was launched against Sicily.

Preceded by a week of heavy bombing by the Allies, elements of the British 1st Airborne and the US 82nd Airborne Divisions parachuted into the island in advance of the amphibious assault and proceeded to wreak havoc among the defenders which consisted of two German infantry, four Italian infantry and six Italian coast defence divisions, all commanded by General Alfredo Guzzoni. Allied air superiority allowed air cover during the amphibious landing, which took place at dawn on 10 July on a front of 100 miles. General Sir Bernard Montgomery's 8th Army landed on the SE coast, Lt-General Sir Miles Dempsey's 13 Corps (5th and 50th Infantry Divisions) on the right and Lt-General Sir Oliver Leese's 30 Corps (51st Infantry, 1st Canadian Divisions) on the left. West of them, on the south coast, came General George Patton's 7th Army (1st, 3rd, 45th Infantry and 2nd Armoured Divisions). Commando and Ranger units spearheaded both landings.

By dark, all seven assault infantry divisions had established their assigned beachheads. To the right, the 8th Army took the ports of Syracuse (Siracusa) on 12 July and Augusta on 14 July. Commandos and parachutists, by securing bridges near Lentini and at Primosole, gave the British access to the plain of Catania half-way along the east coast. The troops then encountered strong Axis defences on the south of Mount Etna, including the Hermann Göring Division, which blocked any further advance for three weeks. German reinforcements were being rushed into Sicily at this time, General Hans Hube taking command of all Nazi troops. The Allied 7th Army took the port of Licata on D-Day and, with the help of naval gunfire from Admiral Sir Andrew Cunningham's Allied fleet, beat back a strong armoured attack by the Germans at Gela. A provisional corps under General Geoffrey Keyes, consisting of the US 3rd Infantry, the 82nd Airborne and the 2nd Armoured Divisions, then cleared the SW coast and then moved to the centre of the island to San Stefano whence the main American drive turned east in a two-pronged offensive. The thrusts, one along the coast and the other 20 miles inland along the Nicosia–Randazzo road, squeezed out the

German defences on Mount Etna, enabling the British to capture Catania on 5 August. Bradley took Troina on 6 August and Randazzo on 13 August and then moved on Messina at the NE end of the island, which he reached on 17 August. The 8th Army was not long behind him. The Axis fought a rearguard action while 40,000 German (including the crack 1st Parachute) and 60,000 Italian troops were evacuated across the straits of Messina to Italy. The campaign ended with the capture of Messina. Axis losses totalled 167,000, of whom 37,000 were Germans. Allied losses were 31,158 killed, wounded or missing, 11,923 of whom were Americans. Malaria in the plain of Catania decimated the British forces.

The Allied invasion of Sicily brought the threat of invasion too close to the Italians for comfort. The fascist government fell when Benito Mussolini resigned on 25 July, and he was succeeded by Marshal Pietro Badoglio. The Germans now moved into Italy in force to take over its defence, ensuring that the Allies would have to fight for its capture.

SIDI BARRANI (Egypt)   Second World War   9–12 December 1940
Fought between the British and the Italians.
Strength: British 36,000 + 120 tanks; Italians 75,000 + 275 tanks.

The war in the desert began when the Italians invaded Egypt from Libya with the 10th Army which set up a series of seven fortified camps at Sidi Barrani, 60 miles inside Egypt. The British Western Desert Force (known also as the Army of the Nile, renamed 13 Corps and, later, the 8th Army) lay 80 miles east at Mersa Matruh, at the end of the road and railway which led from Alexandria. The British force, consisting chiefly of the 4th Indian Infantry and the 7th Armoured Division, marched round the Italian camp which was defensible only from the east, and attacked from the flank and rear (W), through a 20-mile gap between forts. In three days the Italians were routed, losing 38,000 prisoners. British losses were 600.

Lt-General Richard O'Connor now moved west with the 7th Armoured Division to cross the Libyan border and make for Bardia (qv). The 4th Indian Infantry was ordered by General Sir Archibald Wavell, head of Middle East Command, to Eritrea.

SIDI REZEGH (Libya)   Second World War   18 November 1941–6 January 1942
Fought between the British under General Sir Claude Auchinleck and the Germans under General Erwin Rommel.
Strength: British 118,000; Germans and Italians 100,000.

The British launched their second offensive in Libya, ordered by Auchinleck and directed by General Sir Alan Cunningham, in November 1941. The recently formed 8th Army was pitted against the Axis Panzergruppe–the three divisions of the German Afrika Korps and eight Italian divisions.

A two-pronged attack, known as Operation Crusader, was launched on 18 November. General A. R. Godwin-Austen's 13 Corps (infantry) thrust along the coast and General Willoughby Norrie's 30 Corps (armour) moved south into the desert. The armour reached Sidi Rezegh, the key to Tobruk (qv) which was besieged, on 19 November, but an attempt to link up with the garrison was beaten back by Rommel who then counter-attacked on 22 November. In a fierce tank battle the British were driven back from Sidi Rezegh, which fell on 23 November. The Panzers then attacked the British rear with two divisions. Fighting was confused, but the Germans reached back to the Egyptian frontier within three days of the start of their attack. Cunningham wanted to withdraw to Mersa Matruh, whereupon Auchinleck relieved him, putting General Neil Ritchie in his place as commander of the 8th Army. The British held their ground for two weeks and managed to open a corridor to Tobruk on 29 November (TOBRUK II). On the night of 7 December Rommel, short of supplies, began to withdraw across Cyrenaica. The British pursued, occupying Gazala on 15 December and Benghazi on 25 December. At El Agheila on 6 January the pursuit was called off. Tobruk had been relieved. Axis casualties totalled 24,500 killed or wounded and 36,000 prisoners. The British lost 18,500 men.

Rommel attacked again two weeks later.

SIEGFRIED LINE (Germany)   Second World War   17 September – 22 November 1944
Fought between the Germans and the Allies.

The advance of the Allies across France brought them swiftly to the German frontier and the Siegfried Line – or Westwall. This was a line of defensive positions prepared in 1939/40 by the Todt organisation, which was repaired and occupied by the retreating German army as well as by Nazi units from inside Germany. The Allied advance lost its momentum as it met stiffened enemy resistance and over-extended its own tenuous supply lines. General Dwight D. Eisenhower, head of SHAEF (Supreme Headquarters Allied Expeditionary Force), now had seven Allied armies stretching in a line from the North Sea to the Swiss border: Field-Marshal Sir Bernard Montgomery's 21st Army Group, consisting of the Canadian 1st (Lt-General Henry Crerar) and the British 2nd (General Sir Miles Dempsey); General Omar Bradley's 12th Army Group comprising the Us 9th (General W. H. Simpson) and US 1st (General Courtney Hodges) and the US 3rd (General George S. Patton); and General Jacob Devers's 6th Army Group consisting of the US 7th (Lt-General Alexander Patch) and French 1st (General Jean de Lattre de Tassigny). Field-Marshal Gerd von Rundstedt, German Commander in the west, opposed this force with sixty-three divisions divided into six armies: the 15th (General G. von Zangen), the 1st Parachute (Colonel General Kurt Student), and the 7th (General Ernst Brandenberger) under Field-Marshal Walther Model, stretching from the North Sea to the Moselle River; and to the south, below the Siegfried Line in Alsace and Lorraine, the 1st (General von Knobelsdorff), 5th Panzer (General Hasso von Manteuffel) and 19th (General W. Wiese) under General Hermann Balck. The battle along this front continued for three months and included some of the fiercest fighting of the war.

In the north, Montgomery sought to establish a bridgehead over the lower Rhine and outflank the northern end of the Siegfried Line. In Operation Market-Garden, three airborne divisions, the US 82nd and 101st and British 1st, were dropped in an area stretching from Nijmegen to Arnhem on 17 September. They were to open a corridor 60 miles long into Holland and to capture seven bridges over the Rhine. At the same time, Lt-General Brian Horrocks's 30 Corps drove north to link up with the airborne troops. While the American landings at Eindhoven and Nijmegen secured bridges over the Maas and Waal Rivers, the British 1st were dropped too far from the bridge at Arnhem and could not take it immediately.

The German 9th SS Panzer Division counter-attacked fiercely, and bad weather prevented the airlifting of ammunition, supplies and reinforcements. The Guards Armoured Division (30 Corps of the British 2nd Army) made slow progress north, hampered by German resistance, chiefly from the 1st German Parachute. On 21 September the weather lifted sufficiently to allow two-thirds of the Polish Parachute Brigade to be dropped in the Arnhem area, on the other side of the Rhine near Elst, but they did not make contact before, on 25 September, British resistance collapsed before relentless German attacks. On the night of 25 September 2,400 survivors crossed the river in assault boats. A quarter of the 10,000 British troops returned safely, but 1,130 were killed and 6,450 captured. German losses were 3,300 killed or wounded.

Although the major objective of Arnhem was not achieved, the bridges over the Waal and Maas were held. Arnhem itself was not taken for another seven months.

To the left, the Canadian army had more success. On 30 October they seized S Beveland, and on 3 November Walcheren Island, both at the mouth of the Scheldt River. By 9 November the area around the port of Antwerp was cleared at a cost to the Canadians of 27,633 casualties: 12,500 Germans were taken prisoner, and from 26 November onwards the city became a key source of supplies for the Allies, despite Nazi V–1 and V–2 flying-bomb attacks lasting four months (GERMAN VENGEANCE-WEAPON BOMBARDMENT).

In the centre, the US 1st Army reached the Siegfried Line at Aachen on 12 September. 19 and 7 corps fought their way into the town after a hard struggle on 13 September, and after eight days the streets were cleared and the German city became the first to fall into Allied hands. In November the 9th Army, which had moved up on the left, joined the 1st in an attack on the German defences along a 25-mile front east of Aachen. 5 Corps became engaged in a fight through Hürtgen Forest, which was one of the costliest actions in the campaign. The advance had reached the Roer River, 25 miles from Cologne, by 1 December. To the south, the 3rd Army under Patton had repulsed a counter-attack made by the 5th Panzer and 1st Armies south of Metz between 18 September and 1 October. Taking the offensive, Patton encircled Metz on 18 November and pivoted to the north, forcing the Germans back to the Siegfried Line along the Saar River.

The biggest advance was made by the Allies in the south during this period. The US 7th Army moved into the Vosges Mountains, took the Saverne Gap and went on to Strasbourg on 23 November. The army also wheeled north, putting pressure on the Siegfried Line from Strasbourg via Karlsruhe to the junction with Patton's forces near Bitche. The French 1st moved through Belfort and Mulhouse on 22 November to reach the Rhine at the Swiss border. The German 19th Army resisted strongly against the French advance, however, and continued to hold a salient which stretched as far as Colmar. In the autumn of 1944 75,000 Germans were taken prisoner, but although the Allies advanced closer to the Rhine, the skilful German defence prevented them from making any large gain and the broad-fronted attack had left the line very weak in places, particularly in the Ardennes (qv).

SINGAPORE I (SE Asia)   Second World War   31 January–15 February 1942
Fought between the British, Indians and Australians under Lt-General A. E. Percival, and the Japanese under General Tomoyuki Yamashita.
Strength: Allies 107,000 (of whom only 80,000 were armed, combat soldiers); Japanese 2 divisions (about 40,000 men).
The Japanese victory in the Malay peninsula (MALAYA) forced the Allied troops to evacuate it altogether. On 31 January the last of these men crossed the Johore Strait into Singapore and the 70-feet-wide causeway was then blown up and partially destroyed. There were 30 miles of perimeter defences to man and the fortress of Singapore was designed to repulse naval attack rather than threats from across the strait which now menaced the unfortified northen end of the island. The city of Singapore was full of 'useless mouths'. The Japanese brought heavy guns to the southern tip of the Malay peninsula and began to pound the island on 5 February. Throughout this battle the British artillery capable of being used against the attack from the north outnumbered the Japanese by 50 per cent and was about equal in calibre. On the nights of 8 and 9 February amphibious landings established bridgeheads on the NW and north of the island. The causeway was swiftly repaired by Japanese engineers after which tanks and 25,000 reinforcements poured across the strait. There was no serious counter-attack. As the ground troops moved towards the city of Singapore, they were supported by artillery and air cover. On the night of 13 February 3,000 specialist troops and non-combatants left Singapore for Java in small boats. Many of them were killed or captured by the Japanese fleet which was sent to intercept them, but a number were rescued and collected from Java by British and Australian destroyers. Japanese spearhead thrusts drove deep into the British lines, isolating the defenders, and capturing the reservoirs. With the water supply cut off, and food, petrol and ammunition running low – as was morale – Percival decided on 15 February to surrender.

In the battles for Malaya and Singapore British losses were 138,000, of whom 130,000 were captured. By nationalities these losses were comprised of 67,000 Indians, 38,000 British, 18,500 Australians and 14,400 local militia. Japanese losses were 9,800.

The fall of Singapore opened the Japanese way to the Indian Ocean. The Dutch E Indies were also now doomed. Lt-General Renya Mutaguchi, who commanded the Japanese 18th Division, was named the victor of Singapore.

It is worth noting that a total of 50,016 British servicemen (army, navy and air force) were captured by the Japanese between 1941 and 1945, of whom 12,433 died or were killed in captivity. This total is 37 per cent of the total of 36,220 British servicemen killed and missing during the whole war with Japan. The chances of dying of disease or being killed after surrender was 1 in 4.

SINGAPORE, SMALL-BOAT RAIDS (SE Asia)   Second World War   September 1943 and July 1945
There were two small-boat raids launched from Australia against Japanese shipping in Singapore harbour.

The first, called Jaywich, entailed a voyage of 2,000 miles in an old Japanese fishing boat, the *Kofuku Maru*, renamed the *Krait*, with a crew of 14 (4 soldiers, 10 sailors) from Exmouth Gulf in W Australia, through the Lombok Straits, across the Java Sea to the Rhio archipelago, just off Singapore. From a rear base at Pandjang a 3-canoe attack was made on 26 September 1943 on Japanese shipping. A total of about 40,000 tons of shipping was sunk or damaged, including the 10,000-ton oil tanker *Sinkoku Maru*. The raiding force under Major Ivan Lyon, Gordon Highlanders, and navigated by Lieutenant Carse, RANVR, returned safely after forty-seven days.

Operation Rimau under Lt-Colonel Ivan Lyon was a failure. The raiding party was carried to the scene of operations by HMS Submarine *Porpoise*. From Pejantan Island in the S China Sea, the 22-man raiding force first sailed in the captured junk *Mustika* on 1 October 1944 to Merapas Island, their rear base, and then on to Pulau Laban, an island opposite Singapore harbour. There they were discovered. After a short retreat Lyon ordered the *Mustika* with its cargo of explosives to be destroyed, and for the crew to make their way back to Merapas Island by canoe. Although a number of men were known to reach their rendezvous with the submarine at Merapas, for some reason the *Porpoise* failed to keep its rendezvous with the raiders. Lyon and five survivors were rounded up, court-martialled on 5 July 1945, executed by the Japanese with full military honours and buried on 7 July alongside the graves of some of the Japanese sailors killed in their 3 midget-submarine raid on Sydney harbour on 31 May 1942.

SMOLENSK (USSR)   Second World War   16 July–6 August 1941
Fought between the Russians and the Germans.
Strength: Russians 26½ infantry divisions + 7 armoured divisions + 1 cavalry division; Germans 42 infantry divisions + 9 armoured divisions + 7 motorised divisions + 1 cavalry division.
General Fedor von Bock's Central Army Group surrounded Smolensk on 16 July. On 18 July the 10th Panzer Group fought its way into the town, but strong Russian counter-attacks in the south against this salient enabled several Russian

divisions to escape encirclement. The Russians continued their counter-offensive and stepped up its intensity so that, even though the Germans committed some of their reserves, the Russians still succeeded in cutting their way out of the trap at Yeremolino.

Although Smolensk itself fell on 6 August, fighting to the east continued for a further two weeks and the Germans were finally held at a line 25 miles east of Yartsevo–Yelna–Desna. The Russians lost heavily: 100,000 killed or wounded, 150,000 taken prisoner and thousands of tanks and guns taken. But they had halted the German offensive for the first time, enabling the defences of Moscow, Adolf Hitler's main objective, to be built up.

SOLLUM-HALFAYA PASS (Libya)   Second World War   15–17 June 1941
Fought between the British under General Sir Henry Beresford-Pierse nd the Germans under General Erwin Rommel.

Rommel's initial offensive in N Africa began from El Agheila on 24 March and moved across Cyrenaica–missing out Tobruk (qv), which the Afrika Korps besieged–until by April they had reached Egypt. General Sir Archibald Wavell, at Winston Churchill's insistence, launched a counter-attack to try and stem the German advance. Operation Battleaxe was carried out by two divisions under Beresford-Peirse which launched two attacks, one at the coastal town of Sollum and one inland at Halfaya Pass in NW Egypt. Between 15 and 17 June the British armour was decisively beaten in the first action in which the Germans used their 88mm anti-tank gun. It caused the destruction of 100 British tanks and 1,000 British casualties.

Wavell was replaced four days after the battle and sent to India. He was replaced by General Sir Claude Auchinleck, whose job he took over.

SOLOMON ISLANDS (S Pacific)   Second World War   1942–4
Fought between the Allies and the Japanese.

By March 1942 the Japanese conquest of islands in the W Pacific stretched as far as north New Guinea (qv). Their next objective was the Solomon Islands which, along with New Guinea, enclosed the Coral Sea NE of Australia. The Solomon Islands as a group stretches 600 miles NW–SE in two parallel chains, consisting of seven large and many small islands.

On 13 March the battle opened with the seizure by the Japanese of Buka, at the northern end of the archipelago. They moved on to Bougainville on 7 April and Tulagi on 3 May. On 6 July the Japanese landed on Guadalcanal (qv), near the southern end of the islands. Here they began to construct an airfield, later to be known as Henderson Field. This was the turning point in the SW Pacific theatre. After eight months of defeat–except the Battle of Midway (qv)–the Allies were ready to launch a counter-offensive, and on 7 August the US 1st Marine Division landed on Guadalcanal and Tulagi. The Japanese navy reacted strongly to both incidents, leading to the six naval actions known collectively as the Guandalcanal Naval Actions (qv). The US S Pacific Fleet of Admiral William

Halsey suffered heavily but succeeded in preventing the Japanese from retaking Guadalcanal, while marines at Henderson Field also resisted stubbornly.

Two weeks after the conquest of Guadalcanal, the US 43rd Infantry Division took Russell Island to the NW. It was the first attack in the campaign to regain the Solomon chain for the Allies. On 18 April the Japanese Supreme Commander in the Pacific, First Admiral Isoroku Yamamoto, was shot down and killed over Bougainville by P–38s. He was succeeded by Admiral Mineichi Koga. On 30 June the US 43rd Infantry captured Rendova Island off the New Georgia coast in the central Solomons. On 2 July New Georgia itself was invaded, the immediate objective being control of the Munda airfield. The Japanese stepped up their runs of supplies and reinforcements, made down the 'Tokyo Express' under cover of darkness, to the Japanese on the island who were under General Noboru Sasaki.

The US 3rd Fleet sought to prevent this and clashed with the Japanese between New Georgia and Kolombangara Island in Kula Gulf on 6 and 12 July. The Americans lost the cruiser *Helena* and 2 destroyers. The Japanese lost 3 warships, but they landed their troops. The 25th and 37th Infantry Divisions and two marine Raider battalions plus a brigade of New Zealanders were then put on to the island. Known as 14 Corps, the force was under General Oscar Griswold and it captured Munda airfield on 5 August, completing the conquest of New Georgia within the following two months, also overrunning Kolombangara and Vella Lavella nearby. During naval actions in the central Solomons, the Japanese lost 3 destroyers in Vella Gulf on 6 and 7 August, 2 more being sunk later by Allied aircraft, and a further 2 during the evacuation of Vella Lavella on 6 and 7 October. In the latter action the Allies lost the destroyer *Chevalier*, while on the ground Allied losses were 1,150 killed and 4,100 wounded. Japanese losses were about 10,000.

Moving north once more, the 3rd New Zealand Division landed on the Treasury Islands on 27 October and had secured them at the end of eleven days. To the east, a US amphibious marine battalion made a feint-attack against Choiseul Island. On 1 November General Allen Turnage's 3rd Marine Division bypassed the Shortland Islands to land at Empress Augusta Bay on the west coast of Bougainville. A beachhead large enough to hold an airfield was quickly established. The Japanese 17th Army counter-attacked fiercely, but the US 37th Infantry Division began to land on 8 November to help defend the beachhead, now stretching 10 square miles and held by General Alexander Vandegrift's 1 Marine Corps. Japanese counter-attacks by land, sea and air became increasingly savage. By 10 December an airstrip had been built by Navy Seabees (a construction battalion), and on 28 December the Americal (American/Allied) Infantry Division arrived to relieve the marines. American losses were 423 killed and 1,418 wounded, but the Americans had destroyed a force of 4,000 Japanese.

Between 8 and 25 March 1944 the Japanese made their last attempt to dislodge the Americans from their enlarged beachhead, now of 11 square miles. 14 Corps under Griswold repulsed the attack with a loss of 263 men, inflicting losses of 5,000 on the Japanese. By now the Allies had air and sea superiority and the

Japanese were unable to supply or reinforce their troops, who soon became too weak to threaten the Allied position. The last naval action in the Solomons had taken place on 25 November between Buka and Rabaul. Captain Arleigh A. Burke sank 3 out of 5 Japanese destroyers with a force of 5 'Little Beaver' destroyers. It was the last Japanese convoy of the Tokyo Express out of Rabaul.

The Allied victory at Empress Augusta Bay ended the Battle of the Solomon Islands, and elsewhere in the Pacific the Allied offensive had gained a great deal of ground.

SOUTHERN PHILIPPINES–BORNEO Second World War 28 February–1 July 1945
Fought between the Allies under General Douglas MacArthur, and the Japanese.

The Allied victory on Leyte (qv) and the assurance of victory on Luzon (qv), both in the Philippines, enabled MacArthur to organise the liberation of the S Philippines through General Robert Eichelberger's 8th Army. Thirty-eight landings were to be made, most of them by Regimental Combat Teams (RCTs), to be undertaken by Admiral Daniel Barbey's 7th Amphibious Force.

On 28 February the first of these attacks were made by the 186th RCT of the 41st Infantry which landed on Palawan, an island on the west of the archipelago. Panay, to the NE, was taken by the 40th Infantry on 18 March and this division then moved east to N Negros on 29 March. The 503rd Parachute RCT joined them on 8 April, but Japanese resistance continued until the middle of May. The Americal (American/Allies) Infantry Division took Cebu between 26 March and 2 May. By the end of May the central Philippines were all in Allied hands, their troops being greatly helped by Filipino guerillas. On 10 March Mindanao was invaded by the 41st Infantry (less the 186th RCT), which landed at Zamboanga in the SW. Shore-to-shore landings in April liberated the Sulu archipelago, allowing the Allies access to Borneo. On 17 April 10 Corps (24th and 31st Infantry) landed on Mindanao, and although the force was joined by the 108th RCT of the 40th Infantry and parts of the 41st Infantry, elements of the Japanese 35th Army were still resisting on 15 August when the war ended. The last Mindanao landings in July were the fifty-second amphibious assault made by Eichelberger's 8th Army since December 1944.

When Japan surrendered, 100,000 of their garrison of 450,000 were still free. The liberation of the Philippines cost the Americans 62,143 casualties, including 13,700 killed. The Australian General, Thomas Blamey, was assigned the invasion of Borneo which would stop the Japanese supply of oil from the E Indies. American and Australian air and sea forces supported the 1 Australian Corps (Lt-General Morshead), when, on 1 May, they took the island of Tarakan. The Japanese lost 1,540 dead and 852 prisoners. Australian casualties were 225 killed and 669 wounded.

On 10 June 29,000 Australian troops under Major-General Wootton landed at Brunei Bay, losing 114 killed and 221 wounded, but killing 1,400 Japanese. The Japanese continued a guerilla resistance in N Borneo which accounted for further Australian casualties. Eventually about 1,800 more Japanese were killed.

The assault on Balikpapan on 1 July by the Australian 7th Division under Major-General Milford with a total strength of 33,446 army and air force, was the largest Australian amphibious operation. In this, about 1,800 Japanese were killed.

The Japanese surrender on 15 August ostensibly brought operations in Borneo to an end, but the Japanese in the jungles needed more convincing. Some refused to surrender for another twenty-five years.

SOVIET UNION   Second World War   1941–4
Fought between the Russians and the Germans.
Strength: Russians 148 divisions; Germans 138 divisions.

Having conquered all W Europe except Britain, against whom only sea and air forces could initially be employed, the Germans turned to Russia in their *Drang nach Osten,* the drive to the east, which had long been planned. Operation Barbarossa was launched on 22 June 1941 and was the greatest ground attack ever undertaken. Nineteen of the German divisions were armoured. On the left was General Wilhelm von Leeb's Army Group 'C', which consisted of thirty divisions. These attacked from E Prussia across the Baltic states to Leningrad (qv). To the right was General Gerd von Rundstedt's Army Group 'A', whose fifty-seven divisions drove SE from S Poland and Romania into the Ukraine. The centre group, 'B', had the biggest concentration of armour. General Fedor von Bock advanced from Warsaw with his fifty-one divisions, moving north of the Pripet Marshes towards Moscow. From the Baltic Sea to the Black Sea, the Russians deployed 148 divisions along their 1,500-mile frontier. From north to south, the Russian army groups were commanded by Generals Kliment Voroshilov, Semyon Timoshenko and Semyon Budënny. The greatest land battle in history was to follow.

Germany's aim was to surround parts of the Russian force with Panzer groups and then to annihilate them with the slower-moving infantry. It was thought that the Russian army could thus be destroyed before it reached the comparative safety of the Ural Mountains. Most of the Russian divisions along the frontier were dealt with in this manner during the early stages of the battle, and the Germans were aided by their great superiority in the air, both in numbers and type of aircraft. In the first two months of the battle 4,500 Russian aircraft were destroyed by the Luftwaffe, as against 2,000 Nazi aircraft. By the end of September 1 million Russians had been taken prisoner, and although the Germans had penetrated deep into Russia on all fronts, none of their objectives had been reached and the Russians committed a further 210 divisions from the reserves to slow the Nazi attack still more. Leningrad was approached by Army Group 'C' after ten weeks of the invasion to the north. In the centre, the Germans advanced through Russian Poland and into White Russia (Byelorussia), north of the Pripet Marshes, and by 2 July Generals Heinz Guderian's and Hermann Hoth's Panzers had passed round a large force of Russians in the area around Bialystok and

Slonim. The Panzers went on to form a pincers at Minsk on 27 June, and the German infantry swept after them, killing or capturing 300,000 Russians in six days. However, many Russians escaped the movement and retreated east, where they formed up once more. The Germans moved along the Minsk–Moscow road, and on 10 July the Panzers crossed the Dnieper River, reaching Smolensk six days later. At the end of this, a further advance of 200 miles, another pincer movement closed in, and by 6 August 100,000 Russians were killed or captured in the vicinity.

The Russians built up defences along the Desna River, however, with those men who had once again escaped the German net, and at this point, 200 miles from Moscow, Bock was ordered to halt his central thrust with Army Group 'B' while Guderian with the 2nd Panzer Group and General Maximilian von Weichs with the 2nd Army turned south to attack Kiev (qv). The advance on Moscow was not resumed until 2 October. Rundstedt, with three armies and General Paul von Kleist's 1st Panzer Group to the south, moved across Russian Poland to the SE into Ukraine. The Russian commander in this sector was Budënny, and by the end of July his numerically superior Russian forces had been routed completely south of Kiev and were being pushed towards the Black Sea. Rundstedt's attack reached the mouths of the Bug and Dnieper Rivers two weeks later and, in so doing, trapped a large Russian force on the Prut and Dniester Rivers which had been defending against the advance from Romania that moved more slowly. Many entrapped Russian forces took to banditry to live and were later organised into most effective Partisan groups all over conquered Russia, numbering over 750,000 men, and played a major part in the eventual German defeat.

At the same time that Guderian and Weichs moved south from the Desna River, Kleist moved his Panzers north from the southern attack. The two forces made a huge pincer movement in the Kiev area on both sides of the Dnieper. By 26 September over 600,000 Russians had been killed or captured, Kiev itself having fallen on 19 September. This defeat was the worst suffered by Russia during the war. The German forces then returned to their respective army groups.

On the return of Kleist, Rundstedt launched a complex offensive in the south, where Timoshenko had taken over the Russian command. General Walther von Reichenau's 6th Army on the left moved towards Voronezh in the west but was blocked by stubborn Russian resistance at Kursk. The 17th Army in the centre moved to the Donets, and Kharkov fell to this force on 29 October, although the Don, which was their objective, was still 125 miles away. General Erich von Manstein's 11th Army in the south had moved down from the Leningrad sector and was the most successful, taking Odessa on the Black Sea on 16 October and advancing into the Perekop isthmus of the Crimea (Krym) (qv). Kleist moved his Panzers on the Maikop oilfields beyond the Don River. Rostov, the gateway to the Caucasus, which lies on the Lower Don, was captured on 22 November, but the Russians counter-attacked across the frozen river and retook the city a week later. Adolf Hitler insisted that the Germans hold Rostov, and Rundstedt resigned on 1 December as a result. Under Reichenau, the Germans in the southern sector fell back to the Mius River, 50 miles away. Here they remained throughout the winter, preparing for a spring offensive into the Caucasus. At this point in the invasion, six months after its start, the Germans had penetrated 550 miles into Soviet territory and had occupied more than 500,000 square miles of the country. Germany reported the loss of 770,000 killed, wounded or missing, though their losses were probably higher. Russian casualties alone were three times as high and did not include over 1 million prisoners.

The major German offensive of 1942 took place in the south. Beginning in June, sixty-six German and seventeen other (Italian, Romanian and Hungarian) divisions took the offensive and by the end of July had cleared the Crimea. The Cauasian oilfields proved more elusive, however, their drive being stopped at Stalingrad, which was one of the decisive battles of history. The German drive was finally halted by a Russian winter offensive and by then the Wehrmacht had suffered about 1,200,000 casualties as well as the loss of a great many aircraft, tanks and guns. Russian losses were probably less severe. The Russian attacks gained momentum throughout 1943 and the Germans suffered increasingly severely from them. The heaviest fighting occurred in the south where the Russians started to push the invaders out of the Ukraine (qv). The front at Leningrad was quiet during this time but in the centre, where Timoshenko had just taken command, four Russian armies were massed to strike west towards the main German advance along the Minsk–Moscow road. General Gunther von Klüge, who had taken over command of this sector from Bock after the attack on Moscow, retired from the Rzhev–Vyasma salient and concentrated instead around the vital position of Smolensk, a key road and rail centre. Two hundred miles SE of this, the German Army Group Centre attacked the 150-mile salient at Kursk which penetrated 100 miles into Nazi lines. For eight days, beginning on 5 July, Klüge's thirty-eight German divisions, of which seventeen were armoured, attacked. The two-pronged attack came from north and south against General Konstantin Rokossovksy to the north and General Nikolai Vatutin to the south. The Russians managed to annihilate 40 per cent of the German armour, which included new Mark VI Tiger tanks.

On 12 July General Markian Popov's army attacked to the north, where the Germans had driven a wedge into the Russian line at Orel. This advance, which took place 100 miles north of the main battle, and the fierce Russian resistance within the salient, forced Klüge to call off the attack on 13 July. This tank attack, the largest in history, involving nearly 3,000 vehicles, was the last major German offensive on the east front and it cost them 100,000 men, crippling most of the Panzer and motorised divisions. Popov's attack gradually spread all along the front, which stretched 1,000 miles, and the Orel salient became untenable. It was abandoned on 5 August. By 20 September Popov had reached Bryansk, 75 miles west, and he moved on into White Russia. To the north, Generals Vasily Sokolovsky and Andrei Yeremenko drove into Smolensk on 25 September and then divided in a two-pronged offensive in which Sokolovsky moved on Vitebsk, while Yeremenko to his right (N) moved on

Polotsk via Velikie Luki and Nevel (which he reached on 5 October). Rokossovsky reached Gomel in the south late in November.

During 1944 the Russians liberated the rest of their country from Crimea (S), Ukraine, White Russia and Russia itself (N). On 27 August Russian troops liberated Bessarabia and moved on Galati, Romania, and by this time only the Baltic states remained in Nazi hands. The Germans did not surrender here until the spring of 1945. It had been estimated that 6,750,000 Russians died during the German offensive.

On 8 August Russia declared war on Japan and began mobilising to march into Manchuria. Six days later, however, Japan surrendered, which brought the war to an end.

STALINGRAD (VOLGOGRAD) (USSR)   Second World War   24 August 1942–31 January 1943
Fought between the Russians and the Axis.
Strength: Russians 1,050,000 + 900 tanks + 13,000 guns + 1,100 aircraft, Axis about 1,050,000 + 700 tanks + 10,000 guns + 1,200 aircraft.

The Germans' offensive in Russia of 1942 was concentrated in the south where General Fedor von Bock's Army Group 'B' on the left aimed for Stalingrad (Volgograd) and, south of him on his right, Army Group 'A' had for its objective the rich oilfields of the Caucasus. Bock's attack was launched on 22 June from the German position on the line of the Upper Donetz (running through Izyum, Kharkov and Kursk). The left wing had advanced to the Don at Voronezh by 1 July, but was unable to hold the city. Bock was replaced by General Weichs on 13 July. To the south, General Hermann Hoth's Panzers quickly reached the Don, 100 miles from their starting point, and turned SE to move down the corridor formed by the Donetz and Don. General Paul von Kleist's Panzers, heading for the Caucasus, were aided in crossing the Lower Don by Hoth's drive. General Friedrich von Paulus, with the German 6th Army, moved east from the bend in the Don towards Stalingrad which lay on the right (W) bank of the Volga. German ground forces reached the suburbs to the west of the city on 24 August, where they encountered the 62nd Red Army, under General Vassili Chuikov, which fought the invaders every step of the way. Artillery bombardment had reduced the centre of the city to rubble by the time that the Germans reached it on 22 September. Meanwhile, Marshal Georgi Zhukov reinforced the Stalingrad garrison from across the river (to the east) so that the Germans were prevented from reaching the river in force. The flanks of the Russian forces above and below the city were also strengthened, and on 19 November, when frost had hardened the ground, the Russians under General Konstantin Rokossovsky attacked north of the city, and on 21 November their armour crossed the Don and Kalach. From this point, General Nikolai Vatutin routed three Axis armies, the 3rd Romanian, 8th Italian and 2nd Hungarian. Panzer Corps 'H', consisting of two armoured divisions, tried a counter-attack, but it was beaten back.

Meanwhile, south of the city, General Andrei Yeremenko moved forward on 20 November and routed the fifteen divisions of the Romanian 4th Army in five days. The Russians took 65,000 prisoners. Adolf Hitler refused to allow the 6th Army to retire, and by 23 November the two Russian forces had surrounded 300,000 men (twenty-two divisions), Rokossovsky having broken through to General Goronkhov's bridgehead on the Volga north of Stalingrad. The German forces were in an area 25 miles long, east to west, and about 21 miles deep. Their only means of communication with the German headquarters was by radio and aircraft. Field-Marshal Hermann Göring promised to airlift an average of 300 tons of supplies to the beleaguered troops each day, but bad weather and Russian anti-aircraft defences meant that the actual amount flown in was well below this quantity, which was the subsistence minimum. Hitler continued to be adamant that the 6th Army must not leave the Volga, but he consented to the formation of Army Group Don under General Erich von Manstein to act as a relief force.

Hoth's 4th Panzer Army led the attack which was to break the Russian line. It was launched on 12 December 60 miles SW of Stalingrad and advanced steadily until by 21 December it was only 30 miles from the encircled Germans. At this point, however, German progress halted, and on 23 December the three tank and three infantry divisions were recalled. The Russians at once renewed the offensive and in three weeks the Germans lost 300,000 men, 2,000 tanks and 4,000 guns. On 8 January the Russians demanded the surrender of the German 6th Army, which was doomed in any case. Paulus refused to submit because Hitler would not allow him to do so. On 10 January the Russians launched an artillery and mortar barrage of 7,000 guns and mortars and attacked on three sides, splitting the Germans into isolated groups. The last airfield was taken on 16 January, and the German enclave reduced to 15 miles long by 9 miles deep. On 25 January the Russians crossed the Volga and joined the western force of the 62nd Army. The German force was now completely split into two halves. The Russians again demanded the Germans to surrender, but Hitler ordered them to fight to the last man. The Germans were by now dangerously short of supplies and the Russians continued to attack them relentlessly. At last, on 31 January, General Seydlitz's 51st Corps surrendered, and Paulus capitulated with the rest of the 6th Army later that day. The last formation to surrender was the 11th Panzer Corps. By the end of the battle, only 91,000 men remained alive.

The surrender took so long that it saved Kleist's army in the Caucasus from a similar fate, because the Russians had so many men tied up in the Stalingrad sector. The German forces were, however, drastically weakened by the defeat, and they never again launched a major offensive on the Eastern Front.

This decisive battle was the great turning point of the Second World War and it changed the course of military history.

TARANTO (Italy)   Second World War   11 November 1940
Fought between the British under Admiral Sir Andrew Cunningham and the Italians under Admiral Domenico Cavagnari.

Aim: The British sought to control the E Mediterranean and the first major engagement took place when Cunningham ordered an attack on the Italian fleet which lay in the spacious harbour of Taranto, in the heel of Italy.

Battle: On the evening of 11 November 1940 20 ancient Swordfish from the carrier *Illustrious* were dispatched against the Italians and these made a torpedo attack which crippled 3 out of 6 battleships, and 2 cruisers and sank 2 auxiliaries, putting much of the fleet out of action for four months. The British lost 2 aircraft, with 1 officer killed and 3 men taken prisoner.

Result: The disaster cost the Italian fleet Commander, Cavagnari, besides his fleet, his job. This was the first of many overwhelming victories by aircraft from carriers, which was to prove that battleships were becoming obsolescent.

TARAWA – MAKIN (central Pacific)   Second World War   20–4 November 1943

Fought between the Americans under General Holland Smith and the Japanese under Admiral Keiji Shibasaki.

Strength: Americans 5,000; Japanese 4,800.

The American offensive against Japan began in the Gilbert Islands, 2,400 miles SW of Hawaii, where Shibasaki had heavily strengthened the Tarawa chain of atolls, particularly the islets of Betio and Makin, 100 miles north. Holland Smith's 5 Amphibious Corps began the attack when the 2nd Marine Division under General Julian Smith landed at Betio. The attack was preceded by aircraft strikes and heavy naval shelling, but the Japanese were well protected by pillboxes, blockhouses and ferro-concrete bombshelters. The Japanese subjected the invaders to a hail of artillery, machine-gun and small-arms fire. In the first day 1,500 Americans were killed or wounded while two small beachheads were secured, neither of which was more than 250 yards deep. Casualties continued to run high, but the Americans fought their way across the island through a corridor and captured the airstrip which later became known as Hawkins Field.

The next four days were simply a struggle to clear the rest of Betio of Japanese. The 291-acre islet was won at a cost of 991 killed and 2,311 wounded. Nearly 4,700 Japanese were killed. At the same time as this assault was taking place, Major-General Ralph Smith with the 27th Infantry Division had taken Makin Island, manned by 900 Japanese troops and workers. The main island of Butaritari was taken by the 165th Regiment, who lost 66 dead and 152 wounded in the process; while 440 Japanese were killed. The supporting US fleet suffered more heavily, the carrier *Liscome Bay* being sunk by torpedo attack with a loss of 650 of her complement of 900. Air bases captured here and in the Gilberts enabled the Americans to attack the Marshalls (KWAJALEIN–ENIWETOK), their next target.

TIMOR (Indonesia)   Operations of Sparrow Force, Second World War   18 February 1942–2 February 1943

Fought between the Japanese 228th Infantry Regiment and Australian Independent Companies with some Dutch guerillas under command of Lt-Colonel Spence and Lt-Colonel Callinan.

The 2/2nd Australian Independent Company had been landed on Timor Island on 8 December 1941 to defend it by defensive guerila tactics. When the Japanese 228th Regiment from Amboina landed, the Australians, with the help of a few Dutch troops, resisted and then retired slowly into their sanctuaries in the hills. The 2/2nd was reinforced later by the 2/4th Independent Company. These two specially trained companies, totalling less than 500 men, carried out offensive guerila warfare for a period of nearly twelve months, tying up over 10,000 Japanese troops which could have operated elsewhere, or could have used Timor as an invasion base for an attack on Darwin.

The Australian force, which became known as Sparrow Force, lost contact with Army Headquarters in Melbourne and for four months was considered overrun and destroyed. But a radio set was eventually improvised. Further contact was then made by submarine. Finally, resupply of this force became uneconomic and evacuation was ordered. This was achieved with the loss of 1 transport, in January/ February 1943. The Australians suffered less than 50 casualties to the Japanese 1,200.

This operation is a classic example of economy of force, in which quality trained troops were used for a special purpose. Colonel Callinan was the main leader of the resistance throughout the whole period.

TOBRUK I (Libya)   Second World War   21 January 1941
Fought between the British under Lt-General Richard O'Connor and the Italians under General Petassi Manella.
Strength: British 30,000; Italians 32,000.

During the first British offensive in Libya, O'Connor moved west from Bardia with the 13 Corps on 4 January. They reached Tobruk, 70 miles from the Egyptian frontier, three days later. The town, which guarded the best harbour in Libya, was held by an Italian force under Manella which formed part of Marshal Rodolpho Graziani's Italian 10th Army. The Allies besieged the town at once, and on 21 January the 6th Australian and 7th Armoured Divisions assaulted the fortress. The perimeter defences were breached during the initial attack and Tobruk fell on the evening of the following day at small cost to the British. 25,000 Italians, including Manella, were captured and a large quantity of stores were taken.

O'Connor pressed on towards Benghazi.

TOBRUK II (Libya)   Second World War   8 April–29 November 1941
Fought between the Germans under General Erwin Rommel and the Allies.
Strength: Germans 90,000; Allies 23,000.

The Germans began their drive in N Africa from El Agheila on 24 March. Rommel moved east quickly, finding little Allied resistance. Lt-General Philip Neame evacuated Benghazi, which was occupied by the Germans on 4 April.

Rommel reached Tobruk, garrisoned chiefly by the 9th Australian Division under General Morshead, which made up 15,000 of the garrison strength.

With one German and four Italian divisions Rommel stormed the city between 10 and 14 April and again on 30 April, being repulsed each time. The Germans attacked the British relieving force at Sidi Rezegh (qv) and subsequently drove east to the Egyptian border. The garrison held out for 240 days, being supplied by the Royal Navy from the sea. The RN also relieved the garrison personnel, replacing them with the 70th Infantry. On 29 November, at the end of the Battle of Sidi Rezegh, the British managed to open a corridor to Tobruk, thus relieving the siege.

TOBRUK III (Libya)   Second World War   17–19 June 1942
Fought between the Allies under Major-General Klopper and the Germans under General Erwin Rommel.

After the Germans had beaten the Allies at Gazala (qv) at the start of their second offensive, the main British force retreated beyond the Egyptian frontier and Rommel pushed on to Tobruk, 40 miles east, where Lt-General Neil Ritchie had unwisely left 35,000 men, chiefly the 2nd S African Division. Sidi Rezegh (qv) was captured on 17 June and the Germans then turned NW to Tobruk itself.

On 20 June Stuka dive bombers and artillery bombarded the defences of the town. German infantry and the tanks of the 15th and 21st Panzers made assaults and at the end of the day Klopper surrendered 25,000 men and a vast quantity of stores. Part of the Coldstream Guards refused to surrender and successfully broke out in their transport.

The British defeat opened the way for an Axis invasion of Egypt. Ritchie was relieved by General Sir Claude Auchinleck who took personal command of the 8th Army. When the Germans were defeated at El Alamein (qv), they retreated across Libya and passed through Tobruk without stopping. The town thus fell once more into Allied hands.

It has been alleged that one reason for Klopper's surrender was that he saw no reason why many white South Africans should be killed in a war against Germany when every one of them would be required in Africa after the war. It is more likely that the neglected defences were no longer tenable.

TRUK (central Pacific)   Second World War   17 February–19 April 1944
Fought between the Americans and the Japanese.
Strength: Americans 5 fast carriers (with 72 Hellcat fighters) + 2 battleships + 2 cruisers + 4 destroyers; Japanese 2 light cruisers + 4 destroyers + 9 other naval vessels + 24 merchantmen + 365 aircraft.

After the attack on Pearl Harbor (qv) the Japanese seized the island of Truk and made it into an important air and naval base. The island, one of the Caroline group, lying 1,500 miles west of Tarawa and 800 miles north of Rabaul, became one of Admiral Chester Nimitz's objectives during his drive across the central Pacific.

On 17 February Admiral Raymond Spruance's 5th Fleet arrived in the Caroline group with the battleships *New Jersey* and *Iowa*, the cruisers *Minneapolis* and *New Orleans* and 4 destroyers. Heavy naval guns bombarded Japanese ships outside the lagoon while 72 Hellcat fighters from Admiral Marc Mitscher's Task Force 58 attacked inside the harbour. The craft listed above were all destroyed as well as most of the aircraft, for a loss of 25 US aircraft. The US carrier *Intrepid* was damaged. On 28 and 29 April a further attack was made on the base, 'the Gibraltar of the Pacific'. For two days carrier bombers and fighters bombarded Truk and sank every Japanese vessel in sight: 93 planes were destroyed, 59 in the air and 34 on the ground. In the attack 46 American planes were shot down, but more than half of the pilots were recovered.

Truk was now obliterated, and the Mariana Islands (qv) were now next in line.

TUNISIA (N Africa)   Second World War   November 1942–13 May 1943
Fought between the Allies and the Axis.

Three Allied landings were made in NW Africa (qv), aimed ultimately to take Tunis and Bizerta and trap General Erwin Rommel's Afrika Korps in retreat after their defeat at the Second Battle of El Alamein (qv). The landings provoked a swift reaction from the Axis, however, and German and Italian forces arrived by air and sea to capture French military and naval sites in Tunisia. German bombers and fighters were flown into Tunisian airfields while General Jürgen von Arnim concentrated most of the troops in Tunis and Bizerta themselves, thus preventing the Allies from making a swift end of the Afrika Korps. By the end of November 15,000 men were in the two cities, including the 10th Panzers with 100 tanks.

The Allies moved into Tunisia during November. Lt-General K. A. N. Anderson, with the British 1st Army in the north, reached Jefna, 32 miles SW of Bizerta and Tebourba, 12 miles from Tunis, by 28 November, but the Axis launched fierce counter-attacks which forced the British back 20 miles in a week. To the south, General Lloyd Fredenhall's American 2 Corps was blocked in the Sbeitla–Gafsa sector in central Tunisia. Both offensives were now stopped and between these two attacking wings lay the Free French corps of General Georges Barre. On 24 December General Dwight D. Eisenhower ordered all the Allied forces to assume defensive positions in front of the Axis bridgehead which stretched south from the coast through Medjez-al-Bab, Ousseltia and Faïd to the Mareth Line in the SE. Anderson was given command of the front on 24 January to speed up the operation. Two weeks later Eisenhower became Supreme Commander of all Allied forces in Africa, with General Sir Harold Alexander, who commanded the British force pursuing the defeated Germans through Libya, as his deputy and in charge of ground forces, now designated the 18th Army Group.

There was a lull in the fighting throughout the winter, but in February Rommel launched an attack from behind the Mareth Line where his Panzers were re-equipped with Mark VI Tiger tanks, 56-ton machines with 4 inches of armour,

88mm cannon and 2 heavy machine-guns. The attack was begun on 14 February when the 10th and 21st Panzers of the Afrika Korps moved out of Faïd towards the Kasserine Pass which led to the communications centre at Tebessa. The pass was held by part of Fredenhall's 1st Armoured Division and 168th Regimental Combat Team. The Americans were driven back 21 miles in nine days with a loss of 192 killed, 2,624 wounded and 2,459 missing or captured. The Axis thrust was checked, however, by stiffened American resistance and a strong counter-attack from the north by the British 6th Armoured Division. The German forces suffered casualties about equal in number to the Allies before they began to draw back. By 23 February they had reached their original positions. General George Patton took command of 2 Corps two weeks later and built its strength up to include the 1st Armoured and 1st, 9th and 34th Infantry Divisions. The Axis attack on Kasserine was the last successful offensive made by them in Africa.,

On 6 March three Panzer divisions attacked the British 8th Army at Medenine, but they were repulsed with the loss of 52 tanks. On 26 March General Sir Bernard Montgomery's 8th Army breached the Mareth Line and on 6 April took Gabes. On 7 April a patrol from Montgomery's 4th Indian Division met a patrol from the 9th US Division and the ground forces were thus linked up, ready to undertake a final offensive against the Axis.

The 8th Army continued to move up the east coast, taking Sfax on 10 April, Sousse on 12 April and attacking Axis positions at Enfidaville on 13 April. Here the 8th Army fought a diversionary action while the main Allied thrust moved north. 2 Corps, now under General Omar Bradley, moved up from the south to form the left (N) flank (the 7th Army was being organised for the invasion of Sicily (qv) by Patton). Bradley's 1st Armoured took Mateur on 3 May and the 9th Infantry took Bizerta on 7 May. South of them, elements of the British 1st Army and three divisions of the 8th Army moved towards Tunis on 6 May, the 7th Armoured Division moving 30 miles in thirty-six hours to capture the city on 7 May. Three Axis divisions, trapped between Tunis and Bizerta, surrendered on 9 May, while the rest of the Axis forces retreated to the Cape Bon peninsula, a natural fortress. The British 6th Armoured moved across the base of the peninsula on 10 May and on 12 May it was joined by the 8th Army and the 19 French Corps from the south. The Axis forces, in an untenable position, surrendered piecemeal, the last of them capitulating on 13 May.

Air assaults by Air Marshal Arthur Tedder's Mediterranean air force had been incessant throughout the Battle of Tunisia. Axis aircraft and troops were bombarded and General Carl Spaatz's tactical aircraft flew as many as 2,500 sorties a day. At the end of the battle, 250,000 Axis forces surrendered, including the Afrika Korps, the 5th Panzer Army of Arnim and General Giovanni Messe's 1st Italian Army. Messe had been in nominal charge of operations in Tunisia. Axis battle casualties were about 40,000 killed or wounded. British 1st Army losses totalled about 23,000 casualties, 8th Army losses were about 10,000. American losses were 2,184 killed out of 18,500 casualties.

The battle of Tunisia ended the N African campaign and helped to open the

Mediterranean as a shipping lane to the east. Without it the invasion of Sicily, two months later, would have been impossible. For Adolf Hitler it was a disaster comparable with that of Stalingrad (qv).

UKRAINE   Second World War   23 July 1943 – 17 July 1944
Fought between the Russians and the Germans.

The German defeats at Stalingrad and in the Caucasus (qqv) enabled the Russians to launch an offensive SW towards the Ukraine along 500 miles, a front which stretched from the Pripet Marshes to the north to the Black Sea in the south. The Russian armies which lay south from Orel were commanded by Generals Markian Popov, Konstantin Rokossovsky, Nikolai Vatutin, Ivan Konev Rodion Malinovsky, Fedor Tolbukhin and Ivan Petrov.

The attack began on 23 July after the Germans had been defeated in their attempt to take the Russian-held salient at Kursk in a massive attack involving eighteen infantry, two motorised and seventeen armoured divisions. The Russians advanced using tanks, aircraft and massed artillery to good effect. The Germans resisted only sporadically, their defences crumbling before the weight of the Russian advance, and from the operations of 100,000 partisans on their communication in their rear. Following their victory at Kursk, the Russians at Orel attacked the salient held by the Germans around the city and broke through the Nazi defences with the help of a massive artillery bombardment, greater than anything yet experienced by the Germans. After fierce house-to-house fighting, Orel fell on 5 August. Russian casualties were very heavy, owing to the minefields with which the Germans had ringed the city.

On the same day Vatutin took Belgorod, 200 miles south, before pressing southwards to support Konev's attack on Kharkov, a vital communications centre and former capital of the Ukraine. The town had changed hands several times already during the year: the Russians had taken it when General Erich von Manstein had withdrawn to the Donets and Mius Rivers with the Army Group Don in February, but the Germans had retaken the town in March before going on to attack the Russian salient at Kursk. After the Germans were defeated there, the Russians surrounded Kharkov on three sides during their broad advance on the Dnieper, and the town finally fell to them on 23 August, although Adolf Hitler had ordered the town to be held at all costs. Vatutin then turned NW to link up with Rokossovsky and both forces reached Konotop, well inside the Ukraine, during September.

To the south of this drive, 200 miles from Kharkov, Tolbukhin moved forward between Stalino (Donetsk) and the Sea of Azov on 22 August. Russian tanks routed the Germans and reached Taganrog on 30 August while the supporting army under Malinovsky took Stalino on 7 September. South again, Petrov moved against the last German bridgehead in the Caucasus, from the Taman peninsula south to Novorossisk. The latter town was taken after a year of siege on 15 September. The survivors from eight German and six Romanian divisions retreated across the Kerch Strait to the Crimea where the German 17th Army held out until the spring of 1944. The Russians continued to advance on the central and southern fronts, forcing the Germans back towards the Pripet Marshes which were impassable. The Germans knew that if the retreat continued, their army would be divided and it was therefore necessary to stall the Russians while the two groups withdrew around the marshes. A rearguard action was fought, costing the Germans many casualties, but allowing major units to retreat northwards into White Russia (Byelorussia) (qv) and southwards into the Ukraine. An effort was then made to stabilise the line for the winter and the Germans, under General Gunther von Klüge in the centre and General Manstein in the south, were ordered to stand along the line of the Dnieper. The Russians, however, made advances on four Ukrainian fronts, forcing the Germans back.

First Front: The Russian objective was Kiev. On 23 September Rokossovsky crossed the Desna River and took Chernigov, 75 miles NE of Kiev, while early in October Vatutin, on his left, crossed the Dnieper north and south of Kiev. The city was recaptured from the Germans from the rear on 6 November. Vatutin advanced 100 miles in a week and took Korosten and Zhitomir, losing them almost immediately to a strong counter-attack by Manstein's Panzers under General Hasso von Manteuffel.

Second Front: Down-stream, Konev created a bridgehead across the Dnieper at Kremenchug and proceeded to advance SW across the salient formed by the river's bend to the east.

Third Front: The advance on the second front opened the way for Malinovsky to cross the river on 25 October and take Dnepropetrovsk from Kleist's Army Group 'A' before pushing on towards Krivoi Rog.

Fourth Front: The former three advances had caused most of the German reserves to move north so that the most southerly thrust met with less opposition. From Zaporozhe southwards, Tolbukhin moved his force across the top of the Perekop isthmus, to reach the mouth of the Dnieper on the Black Sea by the beginning of November. The German forces in the Crimea (Krym) (qv) were now isolated.

The Germans still held a 30-mile salient on the Dnieper 50 miles south of Kiev and this they held grimly, apparently on the orders of Hitler. Meanwhile, with no cogent German front to contend with, the Russians moved across the west of the Ukraine. Vatutin launched a winter offensive on 24 December, thrusting out of the Kiev salient. He had recaptured Korosten and Zhitomir before the end of the year and on 4 January he crossed the 1939 Polish frontier. Lutsk (Luck) was taken on 5 February, while a southern thrust from Vatutin's force joined with Konev's army at Zvenigorodka. The German salient between Korsun and Shevchenkovo was now encircled. Manstein sought to relieve the ten trapped divisions and suffered 20,000 casualties, having committed most of his reserves, before the hopeless fight was over. The Germans surrendered on 17 February. Eighteen thousand men were captured as well as 500 tanks and 300 aircraft and other equipment. German casualties totalled 55,000. During the battle and as a result of it, Nikopol, in the eastern bend of the Dnieper, fell to Tolbukhin on 8 February and he went to carry out a mopping-up operation south of the Dnieper before moving south into the Crimea via the Perekop isthmus.

The third front took Krivoi Rog on 22 February. Early in March Vatutin was mortally wounded. His command was taken over by General Khukov in time to launch a spring offensive. On 4 March Khukov moved past the Upper Bug, to reach Tarnopol on 9 March. Despite stiff resistance, Rovko was taken and L'vov became the next objective.

On the second front Konev routed a Panzer force near Uman on 6 March and reached the Bug, which he crossed on 15 March. Moving 70 miles west, he captured the German pontoon bridge over the Dnieper at Mogilev while, behind him, Hitler's former headquarters at Vinnitsa were taken on 20 March. Malinovsky moved across the mouths of both the Dnieper and the Bug, taking Kherson on 13 March and Nikolayev on 28 March. Khukov was in Romania by the end of March, having crossed the Upper Dnieper and Prut.

Konev reached the Prut near Jassy (Iasi) on March, bringing the first and second fronts to the base of the Carpathian Mountains. Khukov reached the Jablonica Pass on 1 April. Passage through this would bring the Russians out into the Hungarian plain. Hitler therefore occupied Hungary. Meanwhile, Khukov's van was thrown back by a German counter-attack from L'vov, directed by Field-Marshal Walther Model, who had replaced Manstein. It was Model's first major action. Kleist was replaced by General Ferdinand Schoerner at about the same time. The second front under Konev had also been blocked by the German drive along the N Romanian frontier. He now swung his left wing south to move down the Dnieper, thus threatening the rear of the Germans who were in turn menacing Malinovsky, who was driving along the northern shore of the Black Sea. The Germans were forced to withdraw and Malinovsky went on to liberate Odessa on 10 April.

A lull ensued; the battle was almost over, and when the offensive was resumed in July, the last major city in German hands, L'vov, fell in two weeks–27 July. The Russians were by then marching through the Balkans (qv) and Poland.

WAKE ISLAND (central Pacific)   Second World War   8–23 December 1941
Fought between the Americans under Commodore Winfield Cunningham and the Japanese under Admiral Sadamichi Kajioka.
Strength: Americans 449 combat marines + 69 naval personnel + 6 army signalmen; Japanese 2,000.

The US held a tiny atoll 2,000 miles west of Hawaii. This was one of Japan's targets at the start of her big Pacific offensive in December 1941. Besides the military presence, there were also 1,216 civilians in the island, nearly all construction workers from Guam (qv).

On 8 December 34 bombers from Japanese aircraft carriers attacked the island and destroyed 8 of Major Paul Putnam's 12 Wildcat fighter aircraft. On 11 December the Japanese attempted a landing, but were beaten off, chiefly by

Major James Devereaux's marines. On 23 December the Japanese made a second landing with specially trained seamen who overwhelmed the defenders. Cunningham, Commander of the island, surrendered the same day to Kajioka. Japanese losses totalled 820 killed and 335 wounded. American losses were 50 marines and 70 civilians killed, the rest being taken prisoner.

The Japanese now pushed on into the central Pacific.

WARSAW (Poland)   Second World War   31 July–2 October 1944
Fought between the Poles under General Tadeusz Bor-Komorowski and the Germans under the Governor-General, Hans Frank.
Strength: Poles 40,000; Germans 100,000.

When, on 31 July, General Konstantin Rokossovsky's spearhead reached the Warsaw suburb of Praga on the Vistula, the Polish underground army within the city responded to calls made to them on Moscow radio. Believing that the Russians would soon be inside the city, the Poles revolted at 5 pm on 1 August, attacking the Germans with small arms and home-made grenades. It was a gamble; they had food and weapons for only seven days and the success of their venture depended on Russian relief and supplies airlifted by the Allies.

SS Gruppenführer von dem Bach-Zelewski was sent to quell the rising and he was reinforced by units of the Hermann Göring Division of the SS, two whole SS divisions, the Kaminisky Brigade of turncoat Russian prisoners and the Dirlewanger SS Brigade of German convicts. The Poles were successful only at first; brutal street fighting ensued, in which neither women nor children were spared. Food, medical supplies and water all gave out and disease spread. The superior weapons of the German forces began to tell; the Polish forces were fragmented and annihilated in cold blood by German tanks and ceaseless air raids. Fighting soon spread to the sewers. During the fighting, two Russian bridgeheads over the Vistula were made, but no aid was sent to the Poles within the city. Marshal Joseph Stalin refused Winston Churchill's and Franklin D. Roosevelt's pleas for aid to be flown in, calling the Polish leaders 'criminals' and refusing Allied aircraft landing rights after they had flown supplies to the city. On 4 August 15 RAF Halifaxes and Liberatórs, 7 with Polish crews, flew from Brindisi and dropped supplies. Six were lost and the remainder damaged. Between 8 August and 13 September well over 100 sorties were made, for the purpose of delivering supplies to Bor-Komorowski's forces, but at least 50 per cent of the supplies went astray and about 50 per cent of the aircraft, which were manned by British, Polish and S African crews, were lost or badly damaged.

On 2 October the last of the Poles surrendered, including Bor-Komorowski. The Poles lost 15,000 troops killed. German losses were also high: 10,000 killed, 7,000 missing and 9,000 wounded. In addition, 200,000 civilians died during the fighting. The German counter-insurgent commander, General Kaminiski, was executed by the Germans for committing alleged atrocities.

Military action on this front now lay dormant until the great Russian offensive in

January 1945. Warsaw was bypassed by the Russian advance, and when it finally fell on 17 January, it had, under Hitler's orders, been razed to the ground.

WHITE RUSSIA (BYELORUSSIA) (USSR) Second World War 25 September 1943–14 July 1944

Fought between the Russians and the Germans.

After their defeat at Kursk (UKRAINE), the Germans retreated from both the Kursk front and in the centre and south where General Paul von Kleist, withdrawing from the Caucasus (qv), moved towards the Dnieper. Kharkov was retaken on 23 August, Poltava on 22 September and Smolensk on 25 September. Marshal Semyon Timoshenko, Commander of the Russian centre in the vicinity of Moscow, launched an offensive in July 1943 which drove General Gunther von Klüge's German forces back west and opened the way for a Russian offensive into White Russia complementary to the southward drive into the Ukraine (qv). The retreating Germans crossed the Dnieper, followed by the Russians who took Zaporozhe on 14 October, Melitopol on 23 October and Kiev on 6 November. Three million Germans now faced 5,700,000 Russians, who reorganised before their spring offensive. Four armies, 146 infantry and forty-three armoured divisions, moved into White Russia (Byelorussia/Byelo-russiyan SSR): Generals Andrei Yeremenko moved to Polotsk, Vasily Sokolovsky to Vitebsk, Markian Popov to the area around Orsha–Mogilev and Konstantin Rokossovsky to Gomel. As on the Ukraine front, the Russians moved relentlessly forward before the winter. Popov bridged the Dnieper, a line which the Germans tried desperately to hold, above and below Mogilev, while Rokossovsky, on Popov's left, took Gomel on 25 November and moved along the NE edge of the Pripet Marshes, his left wing having aided General Nikolai Vatutin in the capture of Kiev in the Ukraine.

In 1944 the German Central Army Group in White Russia was commanded by Field-Marshal Ernst Busch. On 22 June the Russians resumed their offensive, and all along the 350-mile front German resistance crumbled. To the north, on the Russian right, Generals Ivan Bagramian's 1st Baltic Army and Ivan Chernyakhovsky's White Russian Army attacked north and south of Vitebsk. The pincer movement caused the city to fall on 27 June. Five German divisions went with it. Chernyakhovsky's left wing took Orsha on the same day. Mogilev was captured by General T. Zakharov's 2nd White Russian Army on 28 June, and on 29 June Rokossovsky's 1st White Russian Army destroyed a German force of 33,000 at Brobruisk. During this main advance, equipped with 31,000 guns and mortars, 5,200 tanks and self-propelled guns and 6,000 planes, 140,000 Partisans systematically destroyed the railway communications supplying the Germans. The attack was soon through White Russia. The Moscow–Smolensk road was cut in two places west of Minsk, which fell on 3 July with 50,000 Germans inside it. In the centre, Baronowicze fell on 8 July and Grodno on 16 July. To the north, Bagramian moved west into the Baltic states to take Vilnius (Wilno) in Lithuania and Daugavpils (Dvinsk) in Latvia on 13 July. The right wing of the

German Army Group 'N' was burst open and the front was split into two sectors: the Upper Baltic states, occupied by the Germans who had besieged Leningrad, and the E Prussia–Poland area where the Russians now stood, having conquered White Russia.

Twenty-five German divisions were knocked out by the battle. Busch was replaced by Field-Marshal Walther Model as Commander of the German Army Group Centre, which was now very scattered.

YUGOSLAVIA   Second World War   7–17 April 1941

Fought between the Yugoslavians under General Dusan Simovic and the Germans.

On 27 March 1941 the pro-German government of Prince Paul was overthrown and Peter II was installed as ruler. Ten days later the German Wehrmacht marched on the country, simultaneously with their advance into Greece.

The German army, thirty-three divisions strong, marched into Yugoslavia from four countries. From Austria and Hungary the German 2nd Army under General von Weichs moved on Zagreb in the north and Belgrade in the NE, while from Romania and Bulgaria General Siegmund List's 12th Army of fifteen divisions moved into the centre and south of the country towards Belgrade and Bitolj (Monastir). Although Yugoslavia had twenty-eight divisions (three being cavalry), she was unable to mobilise because of the speed of the German advance. Moreover, her formations were all deployed on the frontier with only one in strategic reserve. German armour moved swiftly to fragment the Yugoslavian army, and an Italian advance from the west combined with a Hungarian thrust from the north caused the quick destruction of the ill-equipped Yugoslav army. The Luftwaffe met with no opposition. Belgrade was bombed incessantly for three days on 6–8 April, causing 17,000 deaths. On 12 April the city was occupied by the German columns, which linked there. King Peter fled to London. Sarajevo fell on 14 April and on 17 April Yugoslavia capitulated. Six thousand Yugoslavian officers and 335,000 men surrendered at a cost to the Germans of 558.

Five of List's divisions which had moved on Bitolj in the SE to prevent a possible link between Yugoslavian and Greek forces now turned south to Athens.

YUGOSLAV WAR OF NATIONAL LIBERATION   Second World War
April 1941–May 1945

The Yugoslav guerillas were divided into the Chetniks under General Mihailovitch and the Communist Partisans under Tito (Josip Broz). The Germans stirred up rivalry between these two until the Chetniks made a secret non-intervention treaty with the Germans, and Tito's partisans were the only forces operating against the occupying Italian and German armies. A number of British missions were sent out, and eventually one under Brigadier Fitzroy MacLean reported back to Winston Churchill. The British then decided to support only Tito. Tito fought long, hard and well against the Germans, Italians and Croat 'Ustasi' to the north, in spite of drastic retaliation. In 1943 he supervised the disarming of ten Italian divisions, which were sent back to Italy.

Guerilla warfare continued, supported by the British both by sea and by air and by Commandos based on the island of Vis until Tito was tying down almost as many divisions as were operating against the British-American forces in Italy. As the Red Army advanced in 1945 contact was made, but Tito declined to take orders from the Russians and maintained his authority over the liberated areas, where stern retribution was inflicted against the Ustasi and others who had aided the Germans.

In this war Yugoslavia lost 1,700,000 killed out of a population of less than 17 million, a percentage which was the highest of any country in the war. Such was the price of resorting to guerilla warfare and internecine strife.

The war finished with tension mounting as to who should occupy Gorizia and Trieste, and fire was exchanged between a New Zealand Division and Tito's partisans before General Sir William Morgan, Field-Marshal Sir Harold Alexander's Chief of Staff, met Tito. Together they drew up a demarcation zone, known as the Morgan Line. Full settlement between Yugoslavia and Italy over the exact boundary was not reached until 1975, after an uneasy period from 1945 to 1955 during which Trieste was recognised as a free state.

SECTION TWELVE

OTHER EUROPEAN CONFLICTS
OF THE TWENTIETH CENTURY

See Map Section, nos 35–7

BARCELONA II (Spain)   Spanish Civil War   23 December 1937–5 February 1938

Fought between the Nationalists under General Gastone Gambara, General José Solchaga and General Juan de Yagüe, and the Republicans under General Hernández Sarabia.

When the Nationalists had cut Republican Spain into two, General Francisco Franco launched a massive offensive against the eastern pocket of Catalonia. Six Nationalist armies advanced on a wide front which stretched from the Pyrenees south to the Ebro River. The Republicans, already exhausted by the Battle of the Ebro River (qv), were driven back all along the line. Four Italian divisions under Gambara and the Army of Navarre under Solchaga crossed the Segre River, a northern tributary of the Ebro. The Republicans retreated steadily towards Barcelona. Borjas Blancas fell on 4 January and in the face of a relentless Nationalist advance the Republican retreat soon became a rout. De Yague's Moroccans seized Tarragona across the Lower Ebro on 14 January. Barcelona was being bombed by the Nationalists when on 24 January they reached the line of the Llobregat River 3 miles from Barcelona, and the government of Juan Négrin was forced to flee to Gerona. On 26 January the Nationalists entered the city, meeting almost no resistance.

A wholesale flight now began, and by 10 February 230,000 civilians, 10,000 wounded and 250,000 Republican troops had crossed the Pyrenees into France. The Nationalists occupied Gerona on 5 February and by 10 February had reached the frontier. Négrin and other leaders arrived in Toulouse and flew back to the Madrid–Valencia area, the last government-held area in Spain.

The number killed on either side in the Civil War totalled some 500,000.

BILBAO (Spain)   Spanish Civil War   31 March–19 June 1937

Fought between the Nationalists under General Emilio Mola and General Fidel Davila, and the Republicans under General Francisco Llano de la Encomienda.

Strength: Nationalists 50,000; Republicans 40,000.

Aim: While the siege of Madrid dragged on, General Francisco Franco ordered an offensive on the industrial city and Basque stronghold of Bilbao.

Battle: Mola began his offensive striking NW towards Bilbao on 31 March, and Llano de la Encomienda, whose troops were but poorly armed, was forced to give ground. Durango and Guernica were both yielded on 28 April after suffering heavy bombing by the Nationalists. Mola was killed in an air crash and was succeeded by Dávila, who pressed on with the attack. By 11 June the Nationalists had reached the Ring of Iron defences which encircled Bilbao. Dávila ordered a heavy artillery bombardment, under cover of which the Nationalists penetrated the outer defences: the Ring of Iron collapsed. Civilians were evacuated from the town on the night of 13 June, and on the night of 18 June the survivors of the Basque army, now under General Mariano Gamir Ulibarri, abandoned Bilbao which was entered by the Nationalists next day.

Result: The Basque independence movement, which had been aligned with the Republicans, collapsed.

CYPRUS, CIVIL WAR AND TERRORISM   1952–63

Fought between the Greek and Turkish Cypriots.

1952-4: The Greek population of Cyprus (about 80 per cent) wanted *Enosis* (union with Greece), but the Turks feared that this would deny them the rights they enjoyed under British rule. Accordingly, both sides engaged in guerilla warfare and terrorism. Field-Marshal Sir John Harding and Sir Hugh Foot represented Britain in this conflict and did much to keep it at a reasonable level of political armed dispute. General George Grivas was the outstanding leader on the Greek side. Archbishop Makarios III, who supported union with Greece, was exiled for a time by the British to the Seychelles. On 13 March 1959 there was a cease-fire in Cyprus following an agreement with all parties that Cyprus should be granted independence with the rights of the Turkish minority ensured. Britain continued to hold two military bases on the island at Limassol and Famagusta. On 14 December 1959 Makarios was elected President. British army casualties in the period 1955-8 were 79 killed and 414 wounded.

1960-3: The Greeks continued to press for *Enosis* with Greece, thus causing friction between the Greek and Turkish communities. On 21 December 1963 conflict broke out after Makarios tried to alter the constitution and reduce the rights of the Turks. Britain sent in soldiers to restore order, but fighting spread. Efforts by Britain and the United States to mediate in early 1964 were rejected by Makarios who continued to build up his military strength. On 4 March the United Nations intervened, sending in a peace-keeping force and appointing a mediator. The UN peace force became operational on 27 March. Following Greek attacks on Turkish Cypriot villages, the Turks bombed Greek positions and the two countries came close to war. Once again the UN was able to organise a cease-fire.

Stalemate then ensued until the Turkish invasion of Cyprus in 1974, which forced the temporary exile of Makarios. On his return, however, he was re-elected President.

Turkish forces remain on the north of the island in the Kyrenia–Famagusta area, holding far more territory than was formerly theirs. The maximum British forces on the island during the trouble was 20,000.

EBRO RIVER (Spain)   Spanish Civil War   24 July–18 November 1938

Fought between the Nationalists under General Juan de Yague and the Republicans under General Juan Modesto.

Strength: Nationalists 60,000; Republicans 100,000.

Aim: The Republicans sought to launch an offensive which would take the pressure off Madrid (qv) and would, if successful, restore communications between Catalonia and the rest of Republican Spain.

Battle: The Republican attack was made across the Lower Ebro River and was undertaken by the newly formed Army of the Ebro. The Republicans crossed the river to the west side under cover of darkness and surprised the Moroccan troops of de Yague, taking 4,000 prisoners and forcing the Nationalists back, and creating a bulge in their line. The republican General Enrique Lister advanced 25 miles into Nationalist territory before being checked short of Gandesa. The advance halted here and the Republicans began to dig in to protect themselves from the air attacks which the Nationalists now began, along with a series of relentless counter-attacks on the ground. An average of 10,000 bombs were dropped each day. The Republicans gave up only a quarter of the territory they had gained. In late September the last of the International Brigades was withdrawn from the Republican army, though 6,000 men chose to stay, claiming Spanish citizenship. Twenty-nine nationalities were represented in the Brigade. On 30 October the strengthened Nationalists launched a massive counter-offensive, and by 18 November the last of the Republicans withdrew to the east bank of the Ebro. The Nationalists suffered 33,000 casualties and lost 200 aircraft during the four-month battle. Republican losses were 30,000 dead, 20,000 wounded and 20,000 captured. The International Brigades lost three-quarters of their men, some being shot by the Communists and others deserting.

Result: The Army of the Ebro was now crushed, and the Republican movement lost its last striking force.

GIJÓN (Spain)   Spanish Civil War   1 September – 21 October 1937
Fought between the Republicans and the Nationalists under General Antonio Aranda and General José Solchaga.

Aim: The Nationalists sought to reduce Asturias, the only Republican stronghold left in N Spain after the fall of Bilbao and Santander (qqv).

Battle: The Nationalists launched an offensive northward through the Mountains of Léon towards Gijón on the Bay of Biscay. The Asturians held the mountain passes until 15 October when, at the village of Infiesto, Aranda linked up with a Navarrese force under Solchaga which was on its way west along the coast. Thereupon Asturian resistance collapsed, and on 21 October Aranda and Solchaga entered Gijón.

Result: The entire north coast of Spain was now in Nationalist control and thousands of executions and imprisonments followed (16 Basque priests were executed among the victims).

GREEK CIVIL WAR   May 1946 – October 1949
Fought between the Communist rebels under General 'Markos' Vaphiades, and the Greek government.

Supported by Albania, Yugoslavia and Bulgaria, Greek Communists under Vaphiades took control of the northern border regions while fighting broke out all over Greece. The government received help from Britain, but her hold on some major cities and parts of the countryside was only tenuous. British troops were stationed at Athens and Salonika, which were therefore secure.

The Vardar valley saw the fiercest fighting. On 10 December 1946 the United Nations Security Council began to look into Greek charges that the rebels in their country were being aided by guerillas from Albania, Yugoslavia and Bulgaria. On 23 May 1947 the Balkans Investigating Committee found that such aid had been rendered. On 12 March Britain had been forced to suspend her aid to Greece because she was herself in economic difficulties.

President Harry S. Truman then offered aid to both Greece and Turkey to hold off the Communist threat and, having poured aid into Greece and trained her army—a task well begun by the British—helped the country to regain the initiative and put down the revolt everywhere except in the northern border regions. On 1 January the siege of Koritsa was brought to an end when the town was relieved by government troops. Rebel guerillas retired into Albania and their effort to capture the town on 25 January was repulsed. On 19 June 1948 the Greek government launched a drive to capture Vaphiades's headquarters. In this they were partially successful, but severe fighting continued in the Mount Grammos region. On 27 November the UN condemned Greece's neighbours for rendering assistance to the rebels, but the decline of Yugoslav aid had greatly eased the Greek government's task. In 1949 Vapiades was replaced by John Ioannides. The Bulgarians were condemned on 25 June 1949 for allowing their men to build strongpoints from which to fire across the border into Greece. Mount Grammos was cleared on 28 August. When on 29 September 1949 the Yugoslavs broke with the Russians, denounced the Treaty of Friendship (1945) and closed the frontier with Greece, the last hope of the Greek Communists was gone. The Civil War ended on 16 October 1949.

GUADALAJARA (Spain)   Spanish Civil War   8–18 March 1937
Fought between the Nationalists and Italians under General José Moscardó and General Mario Roatta, and the Republicans under Colonel Jurado.
Strength: Nationalists 52,000; Republicans 100,000.
Aim: The Nationalists launched an attack NE of Madrid (qv) which aimed at the complete encirclement of the city.
Battle: On 8 March two Nationalist armies moved towards Guadalajara, 34 miles from Madrid. The right (W) column, led by Moscardó, was composed of 22,000 Moroccans, Legionaries and Carlists, and the left (E), under Roatta, was made up of 30,000 Italians. The inexperienced Republicans gave ground before the Nationalist advance. On 10 March Brihuega, half-way to Guadalajara, fell to the Italian column, but after that resistance began to stiffen and, when Roatta paused between 15 and 17 March, the Republicans organised a counter-attack. Two divisions, aided by Russian aircraft and tanks, surprised the Italians on 18 March, and their retreat soon became a rout. Their withdrawal compelled Moscardó to fall back. Brihuega was retaken. Roatta lost 2,200 killed, 4,000 wounded and 300 captured, and was replaced by General Ettore Bastico. Republican losses were comparable.

Result: Some ground was gained by the Nationalists, but their designs on Guadalajara were frustrated.

The defeat of the Italians led some observers to undervalue the usefulness of motorised transport–a view the Germans did not share.

IRELAND   SEE NORTHERN IRELAND

KRONSTADT (Kotlin Island, USSR)   18 August 1919

In 1919 a British fleet under Rear-Admiral Sir Walter Cowan, Commander of the British Baltic Force, accompanied by US, French and Italian warships, was dispatched to the Baltic to support the Baltic states of Lithuania, Latvia and Estonia in their efforts to attain independence, and ostensibly to continue the blockade on Germany. Cowan's fleet reached a maximum of 88 ships in the summer when the Baltic was unfrozen. The Bolsheviks countered with mines and submarines from their base at Kronstadt off Petrograd (Leningrad) and sunk 17 ships including the *Curaçao, Gentian, Myrtle, Cassandra* and a fleet auxiliary. The *Vindictive* ran aground off Revel. The Russian Baltic Fleet, consisting of 39 ships, had 2 battleships. Cowan had none. So Cowan decided to counter-attack.

At 1 am on 18 August 1919 8 British coastal motor boats, each armed with 2 18-inch torpedoes, crept out of the naval base at Björkö Sound in S Finland. Their destination was the 'impregnable' Kronstadt harbour on Kotlin Island which barred the entrance to Petrograd. The CMBs under Commander C. C. Dobson bypassed 20 forts, each armed with 16 11-inch guns, 10 9-inch guns and 6 6-inch guns. By 4.25 am the battleships *Petropaveovsk* (23,370 tons) and *Andrei Pervozranni* (17,680 tons) and the submarine depot ship *Pamyat Azova* (12,000 tons) had been sunk by Dobson's naval raiders. Three CMBs were sunk by coast defence guns, and also the destroyer *Gavrill.* Six officers and 9 ratings were killed, and 3 officers and 6 ratings were taken prisoner. Lieutenant A. Agar, who had previously sunk the cruiser *Oleg* (6,650 tons)–for which he was awarded the Victoria Cross–helped guide the CMBs into the harbour. The embryo RAF with 12 Sopwith Camels led by Major G. Donald assisted the raid by carrying out two bombing attacks which confused the defence, and later photographed the sunken ships so that the rather startled British public, who had little knowledge of these hostilities, could see the results. Commander Dobson and Lieutenant Gordon Steel were both awarded the Victoria Cross, and all surviving members of the raid were decorated for bravery.

As a result of this action the Russian fleet ceased to be a menace to Britain and her Allies, and the Baltic states were helped towards attaining their freedom. Freedom of access to and from the Baltic was given to all naval and mercantile marine of the Allies.

British left-wing politicians disapproved of the raid.

MADRID (Spain)   Spanish Civil War   6 November 1936 – 31 March 1939

Fought between the Nationalists under General Francisco Franco and the Republicans under General José Miaja.

While the Nationalists fought the Civil War throughout Spain, Madrid was under siege the whole time.

Aim: On 19 July a body of Nationalists moved south from Pamplona under Colonel Francisco Garcia Escámez, intending to occupy Madrid. The Republicans held the passes in the Sierra de Guadarrama which protected the capital.

Battle: On 22 July the Nationalists captured Alto de León, NW of Madrid, and on 25 July they took Somosierra Pass, to the north. Despite these successes, the Republicans still blocked the road to the capital, but when Toledo fell on 27 September the Nationalists under General Emilio Mola marched on Madrid from the south, SW and west. By 6 November four columns of the Nationalist army were deploying for an assault on the city, claiming that supporters within gave them a fifth column. The Republican Prime Minister, Francisco Largo Caballero, quitted the city and went to Valencia, leaving the defence to Miaja. On 7 November Mola sent General José Varela with 20,000 men—chiefly Moroccans and Legionaries—to the SW side of the city. He was supported by Italian armour and the aircraft of the German Condor Legion. The ill-trained Republican forces comprised badly armed urban militia and the 11th International Brigade, consisting of Germans, Poles, French and others, and commanded by the Hungarian Lazar Stern, who called himself Emilio Kléber. (Five other such brigades supported the government during the war.) Miaja also had Russian tanks and aircraft. On 16 November, after fierce fighting, Varela forced a crossing of the Manzanares River and, in the following week, captured three-quarters of the University City. Buenaventura Durruti, the last of the classical Spanish anarchists, was killed during the fighting while leading a column of 3,000 Republicans. By 23 November both sides had exhausted themselves and turned to digging trenches and building fortifications. The Nationalists now hemmed in the city on the north and west and German, Italian and Nationalist aircraft bombed it constantly.

On 13 December Varela launched an offensive aimed at tightening the siege. The objective was the Corunna road which runs to El Escorial, 25 miles north of the city. 3 to 15 January 1937 saw the climax of the fighting when the Nationalists took a 7-mile portion of the road and held it during a fierce action. Both sides lost some 15,000 men in this inconclusive operation which merely confirmed the military stalemate. The next Nationalist offensive was aimed at cutting the Valencia road, SE of the city in the Jarama valley. On 6 February the Nationalists under General Luis Orgaz began the drive which, by 11 February, had driven the Republicans under General Sebastian Pozas east of the river. On 15 February Miaja took command in this sector and when at the end of the month the fighting died down, the Republicans, despite a bulge in their line, still held the Valencia road. Republican losses were 20,000 to Nationalist 25,000.

Another Nationalist offensive at Guadalajara was contained by the Republicans who now launched a counter-attack. On 6 July 50,000 Republicans thrust south and took Brunete, creating a 5-mile salient in the Nationalist lines before Varela managed to rally his troops and launched a counter-offensive which, by 25 July, had driven the Republicans almost back to their start line. The attack was a costly one, the Republicans suffering 25,000 casualties and losing 100 of their 150 aircraft; and the Nationalists 10,000 men and 23 aircraft.

There was now a lull on this front. Franco being content to maintain his position outside the city itself while his forces subdued northern Spain and the eastern region, including Aragón and Catalonia. In January 1939 Barcelona fell, and with it the chances of a Republican victory became minimal. In February Britain and France recognised Franco's régime as the legitimate government of Spain. Meanwhile, in the closely beleaguered city 400 people were dying of starvation each week. Late in February, the commander of the Republican army in Madrid, Colonel Segismundo Casado, led a revolt against the Communist administration of Miaja and Juan Négrin. The latter were unable to prevent the outbreak of violence between the factions, and on 6 March Négrin and others fled to France. While the Nationalists looked on, the Republicans battled with each other until, after six days of internecine strife, the Communists were defeated. On 19 March Franco agreed to begin peace negotiations with Casado, but when the Republicans hesitated to accept Franco's demand for unconditional surrender, on 26 March the Nationalists resumed the offensive after two years. There was little resistance, 30,000 people south of the city capitulated on the first day, while many others laid down their arms and departed.

Result: The Nationalists entered the capital on 31 March, putting Franco in power and ending the Civil War.

MÁLAGA III (Spain)   Spanish Civil War   17 January–3 February 1937
Fought between the Nationalists and Italians under General Gonzalo Queipo de Llano, Colonel Antonio Muñoz and General Mario Roatta, and the Republicans under Colonel Villalba.
Strength: Nationalists–?; Republicans 40,000.

Three Nationalist columns converged on Málaga, 66 miles NE of Gibraltar, while the main scene of activity was Madrid. From the west, the Army of the South advanced under Queipo de Llano, while from Granada, to the NE, came a column under Muñoz, and between these two forces were nine mechanised battalions of Italian Blackshirts under Roatta. The offensive began on 17 January.

The Republican-held city was heavily defended, but by badly organised militia, and the troops retreated before the Nationalist advance which reached Málaga by 3 February. By 6 February, all Republican resistance had collapsed and the survivors fled north towards Almería, pursued and harassed by the victors.

The Nationalists now held Málaga.

NORTHERN IRELAND   IRA Rebellion   August 1969–
Fought between the Provisional Branch (Provos) of the Irish Republican Army (IRA) in Ulster, supported by the IRA in Eire and NORAID (Northern Irish Aid Committee) in the USA, and the security forces of the United Kingdom and Northern Ireland.

In 1969 the IRA, a movement emerging from the Civil War in 1922, split into two factions, the 'Officials' and 'Provisionals' (Provos). The Official IRA is the military wing of the Southern Irish political movement, Sinn Fein, whose aim is a Marxist socialist republic embracing the whole of Ireland. In 1974 its strength was about 1,000 led by Cathal Goulding. The Provisional IRA is the military wing of the Provisional Sinn Fein. Their aim is a Catholic, nationalist, socialist (but not Communist) republic for the whole of Ireland. Their strength in 1975 was about 1,300, mostly under training or resting in Eire, while about 300 were on active operations in N Ireland. In 1976 their main leaders were Seamus Twomey and David O'Connell. Other leaders have included Joe Cahill, Sean MacStiofain (an Englishman, John Stephenson, who was imprisoned in 1973) and Ivor Bell.

Weak handling of the rebellion at the outset, both by the British government and the security forces, led in 1971 to the creation of a Protestant counter-insurgency force called the Ulster Volunteer Force (UVF), with a strength of about 400. Allied to them are the more extreme Ulster Defence Association (UDA), and the Ulster Freedom Fighters (UDF). Total Loyalist groups number about 4,000. In 1975 these groups converted the IRA rebellion against the British into an inter-communal fight between the extreme Catholics and Protestants, with reprisals and counter-reprisals causing the majority of casualties. Ninety-nine sectarian murders were reported in the last six months of 1975. A further 15 casualties occurred when terrorists inadvertently blew themselves up.

COURSE OF OPERATIONS

The rebellion started with a pre-planned protest movement by 'civil rights' marchers and, on 14 August 1969, major riots in Belfast and Londonderry. On the same day the government of N Ireland asked for the use of troops. On 15/16 August 'freedom fighters' set up barricades in the streets of Belfast and Londonderry, which the troops removed. On 20th August the British government ordered the Army to take over the responsibility for security from the police. The government, at the instigation of the Hunt Committee (under Lord Hunt, of Mount Everest fame), abolished the only effective paramilitary force trained and equipped to deal with IRA insurgency, the B-Specials of the Ulster Police, without putting in its place any force, other than the army, ill-trained for this rôle, and lacking the B-Specials' intelligence organisation and knowledge of the people and terrain. This amounted to a great victory for the insurgents.

From that time onwards attacks on property, British troops and civilians escalated. In 1972 497 people were killed, of whom 323 were civilians. On 13 January 1972 a banned and provocative civil rights march took place in Londonderry, under cover of which the IRA fired on the troops. During the exchange of fire 13 civilians, some of them known IRA members or sympathisers, were shot dead. This became known as 'Bloody Sunday'. On 22 February 1972 7 civilians were killed by a bomb in a barracks at Aldershot, England, bringing the war home to the British. On 8 March the first of a number of car bombs was exploded in London. On 21 July 19 bombs in Belfast killed 9 and wounded 130 civilians, which proved a turning point in public opinion against the Provos. On

31 July in Operation Motorman, security forces entered the 'no-go' districts of Creggan and Bogside in Londonderry. An all-party conference was held at Darlington on 25 September. On 28 March the Irish Navy found arms and explosives on the SS *Claudia*.

On 16 July 1973 Irish police found a quantity of ammunition, destined for the Provos, aboard the British ship, *Manchester Vigour,* docked in Dublin. The Provos were still obtaining 85 per cent of their weapons and ammunition from the USA from such organisations as NORAID.

From May 1972, mainly in response to Republican violence, cross-border incidents and car-bomb explosions in the Irish Republic increased and from July 1972 to October 1974 it was estimated that there were 251 sectarian killings.

Casualties in the period August 1969–23 February 1976 were as follows:

	Killed	Wounded
Civilians	1,089	11,707* from June 1970
Army and UDR	300	2,786.
RUC and RUCR (police)	76	2,468
TOTAL	1,465	16,961

* Figures for civilian casualties do not include those suffered in England at Birmingham, Guildford, London, Woolwich which total over 150.

Casualties of IRA, UDA, UVF and UFF are not issued by the British government, but are said to be very much higher than security forces' estimates or the figures released to the press by these clandestine organisations.

Property damage in N Ireland to March 1976 totalled £137,028,027.

POLISH WAR WITH THE UKRAINE   November 1918–May 1919
The Ukrainians entered Galicia with the aim of setting up a W Ukrainian Republic at L'vov (Lemberg). After six months' fighting the Poles compelled the invaders to withdraw.

RUSSIAN CIVIL WAR   1917–22
Following the Bolshevik Revolution in November 1917, when Vladimir Lenin overthrew the government of Alexander Kerensky in Petrograd (Leningrad) and established a Soviet government, unrest spread to many areas within Russia and unco-ordinated counter-revolutionary movements sprang up. Poland, Finland, S Russia and the Ukraine, White Russia (Byelorussia), the Baltic states and Siberia were the chief regions of conflict. The major campaigns of the Civil War in S Russia and the Ukraine were fought in an area from the Black to Caspian Seas, encompassing Odessa on the west, Kiev, Orel, Voronezh, Tsaritsin (Stalingrad/Volgograd) and Astrakhan and the Volga estuary.

9 December 1917: The Don Cossacks rebelled against a Bolshevik decree expropriating their lands. Generals Alexei Kaledin and Lavr Kornilov headed the northward march of the Cossacks through the Kuban and the Don basin. Several indecisive actions took place between this force and the Bolshevik militia. Kaledin and Kornilov strove to turn their force into an effective army while at the same time Leon Trotsky was transforming the Bolshevik militia into the Red Army.

April–May 1918: On 22 April and 26 May Georgia, Armenia and Azerbaydzhan declared their independence and Bolshevik attempts to secure the oil-rich lands in the region brought open revolt.

November–December 1918: In the Ukraine, German-backed General Pavel Skoropadsky was overthrown by socialists under General Simon Petlyura when the Germans withdrew on 15 November. France put a garrison in Odessa to aid the counter-revolution on 18 December.

3 February 1919: As German forces withdrew, Bolsheviks moved in and, on 3 February, they took Kiev. Moving down the Bug, they spread west and on 8 April drove the French out of Odessa.

January 1919: Bolshevik efforts to secure the oilfields in the Caucasus turned insurrection into war: white counter-revolutionaries under General Anton Denikin massed and drove the Bolsheviks out. The war now spread to the whole of S Russia. Kaledin committed suicide on 13 February and Kornilov was killed in action on 13 April, so Denikin came out of the Caucasus to assume nominal command of the White Russians in the area. He was supported by General Petr Krasnov, hetman of the Don Cossacks.

May 1919: The White Russians now had four armies in the field. From left to right these were: the Kiev, Volunteer, Don and Caucasus. Opposed to them were the 12th, 14th, 13th, 9th and 10th Red Armies. Trotsky had now to contend with White Russians who were active on several fronts. Admiral Alexander Kolchak, advancing along the Trans-Siberian Railway, had reached the Urals as far as the Ufa-Perm line. General Nikolai Yudenich was assembling a White Army in the Baltic provinces and Allied forces were landing in strength in N Russia, at Archangel, and in E Siberia, with the apparent intention of helping the Whites. It was correctly decided that Kolchak posed the most pressing problem and General Mikhail Tukhachevsky was sent east to deal with him, while elsewhere the Bolsheviks went on to the defensive.

May–October 1919: Denikin now launched a White offensive from the south. His four armies moved north on an ever-diverging course. Kiev was retaken on 2 September and General Pëtr Nikolaevich Wrangel's army made for Tsaritsin, hoping to join hands with Kolchak. Bad supply lines delayed Wrangel, however, and by the time he had taken Tsaritsin (17 June), Kolchak had been rolled back through the Urals by Tukhachevsky's offensive. The Red Army now turned on Wrangel, who was also forced back. The Don Army under Krasnov had got as far as Voronezh (6 October) but on 24 October Tukhachevsky's advancing Red Army hit the White force in the flank and rolled it back. Tukhachevsky's next objective was the Volunteer Army, which had reached Orel on 13 October. This, too, collapsed and the Kiev Army abandoned Kiev on 17 December. The White Armies then withdrew to the Black Sea, and were evacuated (27 March 1920), chiefly by British ships from Novorossisk. Only a small force under Wrangel remained in the Crimea.

April 1920: The Bolsheviks penetrated the Crimea, reaching Baku on 28 April. For a time British ships based in Persian Caspian Sea ports prevented the Red Armies from gaining control of the Caspian Sea.

June–November 1920: The Russo-Polish War gave Wrangel the opportunity to launch an offensive. But when he pushed north from the Sea of Azov, he found that the war with the Poles was already over and the Red forces, concentrating in his path, pushed him back into the Crimea (1 November). This last White force was evacuated to Constantinople by the British on 14 November.

SIBERIA AND E RUSSIA

June 1918: About 100,000 Bohemian (Czecho-Slovakian) prisoners of war from the Austro-Hungarian army took control of the Trans-Siberian Railway when the Bolsheviks interfered with their proposed repatriation programme. The Czechs captured arms from local Bolshevik units and, organising themselves into an efficient army, they marched west into E Russia where they captured Ekaterinburg (Sverdlovsk) on 26 July, just after the massacre there of the Czar and his family. Negotiations were then begun between this force and the Soviets as well as the anti-Bolshevik government which had been set up at Omsk.

18 November 1918: Admiral Kolchak took control of the Omsk government, proclaiming himself 'Supreme Ruler of Russia'. He formed an alliance with the Czechs and advanced from Siberia into E Russia, taking Perm and Ufa in December.

1919–20: Under Trotsky, the Bolsheviks launched a counter-offensive, attacking Kolchak's army and recapturing Ekaterinburg on 27 January. Kolchak was slowly driven back into Siberia, and Omsk was taken on 14 November. Kolchak himself was captured and executed by the Soviets on 7 February 1920. After this, the Czechs retreated east along the Trans-Siberian Railway until they reached the area controlled by an American expeditionary force. Transported to Vladivostock, they were evacuated by ship. Fighting continued, but the Bolsheviks consolidated their position in Siberia except in those areas held by American and Japanese troops.

ALLIED INTERVENTION

June 1918: A Japanese force under General Otani landed and occupied Vladivostock. Their apparent intention to annex the Russian province caused alarm in Washington, London and Paris.

1918–19: A British, French and American expeditionary force under British command took Murmansk on 23 June 1918, occupying Archangel on 1–2 August. Their stated aim was to recover supplies and munitions supplied to the

Czarist government, although it was secretly hoped that these small forces would move south and east to join the Czech legion in the Urals. After a year of undeclared war along the Vologda River, however, the forces were withdrawn, the Americans in August and the French and British during September and October.
August 1918: The Americans launched a Siberian expedition of two regiments under General William Graves in order to prevent the Japanese from annexing the Russian Maritime Provinces and also to aid the Czech legion, though without meddling in Russian internal affairs. The Americans soon fell out with the British and French military missions, as well as with the Bolsheviks and the White Russians, and friction between the Americans and Japanese came close to hostilities. Britain, France and Japan all expected the Americans to support Kolchak, but Graves held to his brief. The Americans guarded the Trans-Siberian Railway from Lake Baikal to Vladivostock and were attacked by both White and Red Russian forces, but they kept control of the railway. They maintained their hold until the Czechs were evacuated after the collapse of Kolchak's régime, when they themselves left Siberia (April 1920). E Siberia was now in Soviet control except for the vicinity of Vladivostock, which the Japanese evacuated on 25 October 1922.

FINLAND

6 December 1917: Finland became independent.
18 January 1918: Baron Carl von Mannerheim, a former Russian cavalry general, was put in command of the Finnish army. Helsingfors (Helsinki) had already been taken by the Bolsheviks and a Finnish Red Guard was in the process of formation. Vasa (Vaasa), where Mannerheim's headquarters was situated, contained a Russian garrison.
28 January 1918: Despite Russian opposition, a revolution broke out through the country. Mannerheim seized the Russian garrison and armed his levies from the plentiful supply of munitions left there. Moving south, he took Tammerfors (Tampera), but a large Red Guard army blocked him on 16 March.
3 April 1918: Ten thousand Germans under General Count Rüdiger von der Göltz surprised the Red Guard by landing unexpectedly at Hanko (Hangö). The force seized Helsingfors on 18 April, cutting the Bolshevik force in half. Mannerheim moved east on 19 April and cut off the Karelian isthmus from Russia. Russian forces attempted to break out at Vyborg (Viipuri), but the attempt ended in surrender. On 29 April 12,000 Reds capitulated with much booty. Fighting continued along the border.
14 October 1920: Finnish independence was finally secured by the Treaty of Dorpat (Tartu).

ESTONIA

1917–18: Estonia declared its independence on 28 November 1917 and was swiftly occupied by the Bolsheviks and the Germans. The Germans were in occupation when the Treaty of Litovsk came into operation.

22 November 1918: The German evacuated the country on 11 November and it was reoccupied by the Bolsheviks. They withdrew, however, in face of Estonian resistance, supported by a British squadron in the Baltic (KRONSTADT).
October 1919: The White Russian General, Nikolai Yudenich, gathered a counter-revolutionary army in NE Estonia and crossed the Russian border near Narva in an attempt to seize Petrograd (Leningrad) on 6 October. With only 20,000 men, he reached the edge of the city on 19 October and Trotsky rallied the panic-stricken Bolsheviks to drive Yudenich back. Yudenich withdrew to Estonia.
2 February 1920: By the Treaty of Dorpat Estonia's independence was recognised.

LATVIA

January 1919: The Latvian declaration of independence brought with it a Russian invasion after 18 November 1918. Riga fell on 4 January and a Soviet government was set up. German and Latvian forces drove the Bolsheviks back in March, following which the Germans attempted to take over the government. This resulted in confused fighting, the occupation of Riga and an armistice, lasting from 16 April to 22 May. On 20 October fighting broke out anew between the Latvians and Germans and Russians. The Germans were forced to withdraw in accordance with the Treaty of Versailles (20 November).
January 1920: The Russians withdrew from Latvia and an armistice with Russia came into effect on 1 February.
11 August 1920: Latvian independence was recognised by The Treaty of Riga.

LITHUANIA

1918: As soon as the Lithuanians declared independence on 16 February they were attacked by the Bolsheviks, who were, however, driven out by the Germans. But when they in turn withdrew, the Bolsheviks invaded once again (11 November).
5 January 1919: The Russians captured Vilna, which led to Polish intervention and the outbreak of the Russo-Polish War.
12 July 1920: The Treaty of Moscow ended hostilities, with Russian recognition of Lithuanian independence.
9 October 1920: The Poles seized Vilna, and when the League of Nations attempted to hold a plebiscite, they were unable to do so. Peace was not re-established until seven years later.
11 January 1923: Memel (Klaipeda), a mainly German town, was the scene of an insurrection when the French garrison, put in during 1918, was forced by Lithuanian troops to withdraw. The Allies recognised the *fait accompli*.

SAKARYA RIVER (Turkey)   Turko-Greek War II   24 August–26 September 1921
Fought between the Greeks and the Turks under Mustafa Kemal (Kemal Atatürk).
    Greek troops, supported by the Allies of the First World War, occupied Smyrna (Izmir) on 15 May 1919. Because Turkey now seemed to be in danger of being

carved up between the victors, a strong Nationalist movement grew up under Mustafa Kemal and in 1920 established a provisional government in Angora (Ankara).

The Greeks advanced on 22 June and occupied Alasehir on 24 June. The offensive was halted during peace negotiations which were held in Constantinople, but the nationalists refused to agree to the concessions which the Sultan (Mohammed VI) had made to the Greeks. The Greeks renewed their advance on 23 March 1921. They were checked by a force under Ismet Pasha at Inönü, 150 miles west of Angora, but by 24 August they had reached the Sakarya River, 70 miles from Angora. The Turks under Ismet Pasha and Mustafa Kemal put up a stout defence and by 16 September the Greeks had been repulsed. On 18 August 1922 the Turks launched a counter-offensive which drove the Greeks back until, by 9 September, Smyrna had been liberated and the Greeks had retired in disorder from the mainland of Asia.

In 1923, by the Treaty of Lausanne, Greek claims to Anatolia were rejected, and the European border with Turkey was fixed at the Maritsa River. Meanwhile, Mohammed VI abdicated and Mustafa Kemal became the first President of the Republic.

SANTANDER (Spain)   Spanish Civil War   14–25 August 1937
Fought between the Nationalists under General Fidel Dávila and the Republicans under General Mariano Gamir Ulíbarri.
Aim: After the capture of Bilbao (qv) the Nationalist army sought to take Santander, west of the city.
Battle: On 14 August 106 Nationalist battalions began to move west through the Cantabrian Mountains. Ulíbarri commanded about 50,000 troops in Santander, but they were badly trained and poorly armed. Bombarded by land and air, the Republicans fell back without making any stand at all. On 23 August the Basque forces withdrew from the campaign altogether, and surrendered to General Ettore Bastico.
Result: Dávila entered Santander on 25 August, while Ulíbarri and other leaders fled by air to France.

SARAGOSSA III (Spain)   Spanish Civil War   24 August–September 1937
Fought between the Nationalists under General Miguel Ponte and the Republicans under General Sebastian Pozas.
The Republican Army of the East under Pozas launched an offensive from Catalonia into Aragón, aiming at Saragossa on the river Ebro. Advancing on a wide front from the French border south to Teruel, the attackers gained some initial success north and south of the Ebro, but the Nationalist centre held firm, and both Huesca to the north and Teruel to the south remained in their hands. By the end of September the Republican army in Aragón had practically ceased to exist and the offensive had collapsed. Heavy casualties had been sustained to little purpose.

TERUEL (Spain)   Spanish Civil War   15 December 1937–20 February 1938
Fought between the Nationalists under General José Varela and General Antonio Aranda, and the Republicans under General Hernández Sarabia and General Leopoldo Menéndez.

When the Nationalists had completed their conquest of N Spain, they turned their attention to Madrid (qv) and the territory in the east and south still held by the Republicans. The Republican government, however, moved from Valencia to Barcelona and launched an offensive before the Nationalists could do so. On 15 December two armies under Sarabia and Menendez marched on Teruel, 138 miles east of Madrid, and by nightfall Sarabia's troops had surrounded the city. The weather was very cold. The garrison, commanded by Colonel Rey d'Harcourt, consisted of 4,000 men, half of whom were civilians, and these held out in the southern part of the town. Two weeks later, General Francisco Franco sent Varela and Aranda to try and relieve the city. The Nationalists launched a counter-attack which dented the Republican lines but did not break them. The bad weather hindered both sides and d'Harcourt, his force much diminished, surrendered on 8 January.

The Republicans now found themselves besieged in Teruel, and the fierce fighting continued. On 7 February the Nationalist cavalry drove the Republicans back to the north of the city, taking 7,000 prisoners and inflicting 15,000 casualties. On 17 February General Juan de Yagüe's Moroccan troops crossed the river Alfambra and marched south along the east bank to cut the town off from the north. The city was encircled by 20 February with the exception of the Valencia road to the SE. Sarabia withdrew, leaving 10,000 dead in the city and 14,500 prisoners.

The Republican offensive had failed.

TOLEDO (Spain)   Spanish Civil War   20 July–27 September 1936
Fought between the Nationalists under Colonel José Moscardó and Colonel José Varela, and the Republicans.

When the Republican militia thought they had routed the Nationalist garrisons in Madrid, on 20 July, they moved 40 miles SW and took the town.

Moscardó with about 1,300 men, members of the Civil Guard, army officers and Falangists as well as cadets of the Military Academy, held out in the commanding fortress of the Alcázar. The Republicans, unable to dislodge them, sat down to besiege the place. Two months later two columns of Varela's army moved up the Tagus to relieve the Alcázar before moving on Madrid. On 26 September Varela moved northwards and cut the road to Madrid. The following day the Nationalists stormed the town; the Moroccan troops, who were better trained than the Republicans, routed the militia and relieved the Alcázar. All suspected Republicans were massacred. The Nationalists resumed their march on Madrid (qv).

VINAROZ (Spain)   Spanish Civil War   9 March–23 July 1938
Fought between the Nationalists under General Fidel Dávila and the Republicans under General Leopoldo Menéndez.

When the Republican attack on Teruel (qv) was repulsed, General Francisco Franco launched an offensive designed to cut the Republican-held area of Spain into two parts. The attack was ordered east into Aragón and Levante on a broad front. Preceded by heavy air and artillery bombardment, the Nationalists advanced on 9 March with five columns on a wide front. The government troops fell back before the superior armament of the Nationalists and in some places yielded 60 miles in eight days. General Juan de Yagüe's column penetrated Catalonia on 25 March Lérida fell on 3 April. On 15 April General Camilo Alonso Vega, with a Navarrese division, took the fishing village of Vinaroz, about midway between Barcelona and Valencia. Republican Spain had been cut in two. Turning south, Vega met increasing opposition but Castellón de la Plana, 40 miles north of Valencia, fell on 14 June. Varela set out from Teruel marching SE in order to support the attack, but Menéndez put up a strong defence and between 18 and 23 July the Nationalists sustained some 20,000 casualties. The attack petered out with Valencia still in government hands.

VYBORG (VIIPURI) (USSR)   Russo-Finnish War   29 April 1918
Fought between the Finnish White Army, under General Baron Carl Gustav von Mannerheim, supported by a German force, commanded by General Count Rüdiger von der Göltz, and the Reds.

During the Communist revolution in Russia the grand duchy of Finland proclaimed its freedom (20 July 1917). The Russian Civil War (qv) spread to Finland and early in 1918 Finnish Communists and Bolsheviks overran much of S Finland. Mannerheim and von der Göltz liberated Helsingfors (Helsinki) on 13 April and two weeks later they had reached Vyborg (Viipuri), 70 miles NW of Leningrad, where on 29 April the Whites defeated the Reds and drove them out of Finland.

Finland became an independent republic the following year.

WARSAW IV (Poland)   Russo-Polish War   31 July–25 August 1920
Fought between the Russians under Trotsky and General Mikhail Tukhachevsky and the Poles and Ukrainians under Marshal Jozef Pilsudski, advised by General Maxime Weygand.

On 9 November 1918, during the final stages of the First World War, Poland was proclaimed a republic, and an alliance was formed between the Poles and the Ukrainians under Simon Petlyura who was directing the independence movement of Ukraine during the Russian revolution. The Poles helped to seize Kiev on 7 May 1920 and then moved eastwards against the Red Armies. On 18 May the Russians launched a counter-offensive north and south of the Pripet Marshes, making the line which the Allies had to hold over 800 miles long. The Poles and Ukrainians were soon driven back.

To the south, General Semyon Budënny led Russian cavalry in an advance of 200 miles which reached L'vov (Lemberg) by the end of July, while to the north the Russians moved 300 miles to the Bug River and were at the outskirts of

Warsaw by the end of July. With their capital thus threatened, the Poles launched a counter-attack on the south flank of the Russian force in front of Brest-Litovsk. On 15 August Pilsudski, with the 4th Army (consisting of five divisions), led an attack which after three days broke through the Russian lines. The Russian army to the south was blocked by the Pripet Marshes and this factor, combined with bad leadership, brought its collapse, so that by 25 August the Poles had advanced 200 miles. As a consequence 70,000 Russians were captured, of whom 35,000 had fled to E Prussia, where they were interned.

An armistice was signed on 12 October at Riga. This defined the boundary between Poland and Russia, which lasted until September 1939.

MAP SECTION

575

1   Western Europe (*Section One*)

2   Spain: The Carlist Wars (*Section One*)

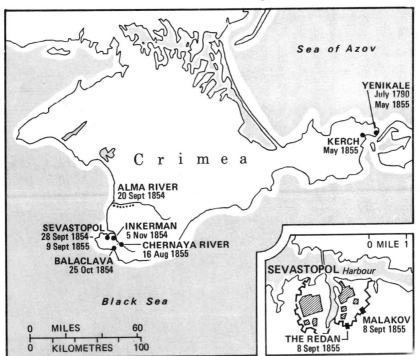

3   The Crimean War (*Section One*)

Map 1 labels:
- ALSEN ISLAND 29 June 1864
- DENMARK
- DYBBOL 30 Mar - 18 Apr 1864
- BALLYMORE 3 June 1798
- IRELAND
- GREAT BRITAIN
- ARKLOW 9 June 1798
- London
- ANTWERP Nov - 23 Dec 1832
- GISIKON 23 Nov 1847
- SWITZ.
- 0 MILES 300
- 0 KILOMETRES 500

Map 2 labels:
- FRANCE
- SAN SEBASTIAN Feb - June 1836
- IRUN 18 May 1837
- BILBAO 9 Nov - 25 Dec 1836
- PENA CERRADA 21 June 1838
- PUENTE DE LA REYNA 6 Oct 1872
- HERNANI 29 Aug 1836 15-16 Mar 1837
- MORELLA 23 May 1840
- Madrid
- SPAIN
- PORTUGAL
- SANTAREM 18 Feb 1834
- Lisbon
- ALCOLEA 28 Sept 1868
- 0 MILES 200
- 0 KM. 300

Map 3 labels:
- Sea of Azov
- YENIKALE July 1790 May 1855
- Crimea
- KERCH May 1855
- ALMA RIVER 20 Sept 1854
- SEVASTOPOL 28 Sept 1854 - 9 Sept 1855
- INKERMAN 5 Nov 1854
- CHERNAYA RIVER 16 Aug 1855
- BALACLAVA 25 Oct 1854
- Black Sea
- 0 MILES 60
- 0 KILOMETRES 100
- 0 MILE 1
- SEVASTOPOL Harbour
- MALAKOV 8 Sept 1855
- THE REDAN 8 Sept 1855

MORAZZONE
1848

VARESE
25 May 1859

BRESCIA
31 Mar - 1 Apr 1849

TURBIGO
3 June 1859

MAGENTA
4 June 1859

MELEGNANO
8 June 1859

NOVARA
23 Mar 1849

CUSTOZZA
24-25 July 1848

SOLFERINO
24 June 1870

GOITO
8 Apr 1848

VENICE
20 July - 28 Aug 1849

Trieste

Fiume

PALESTRO
30 May 1859

MONTEBELLO
20 May 1859

Po

MORTARA
21 Mar 1849

MODENA
Feb - Mar 1831

I

ANCONA
19-29 Sept 1860

CASTELFIDARDO
18 Sept 1860

T

VIS
20 July 1866

CORSICA

RIETI
7 Mar 1821

MENTANA
3 Nov 1867

PALESTRINA
9 May 1849

A

ADRIATIC SEA

ROME
30 Apr - 2 July 1849

VELLETRI
19 May 1849

GARIGLIANO RIVER
1850

VOLTURNO RIVER
26 Oct 1860

L

GAETA
Nov 1860 - Feb 1861

SARDINIA

Y

SAPRI
28 June 1857

MEDITERRANEAN

SEA

PALERMO
27 May - 7 June 1848

MILAZZO
20 July 1860

ASPROMONTE
29 Aug 1862

CALATAFIMI
15 May 1860

SICILY

0   MILES   200

0   KILOMETRES   300

4   The Italian Wars of Liberation (*Section One*)

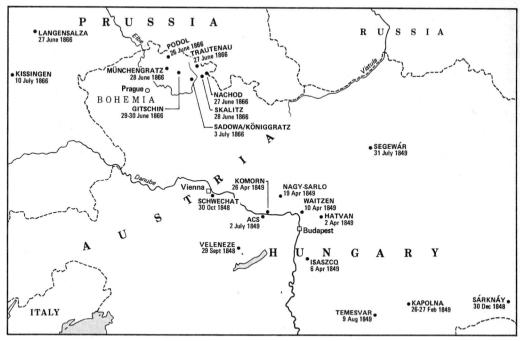

5 The Hungarian Uprising and the Austro-Prussian War (*Section One*)

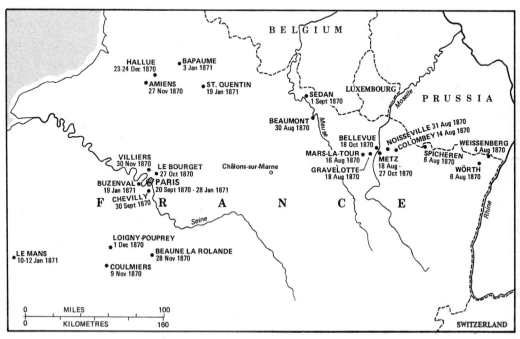

6 The Franco-Prussian War (*Section One*)

578

7   The Balkans: Ottoman Wars, Balkan Wars, Greek War of Independence, World War I (*Sections One and Nine*)

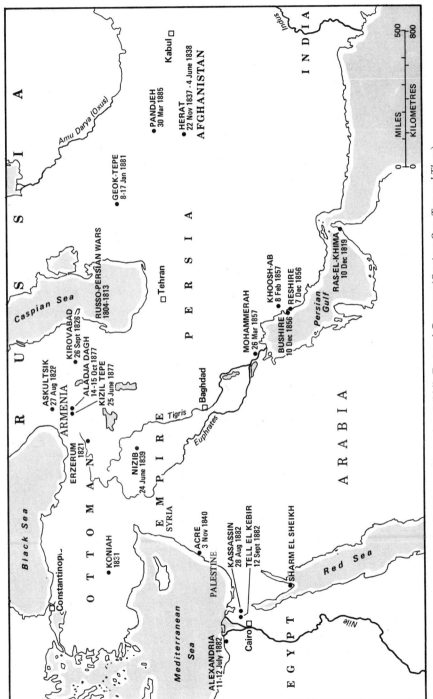

8 Western Expansion: Middle East and Caucasus (*Sections One, Two and Three*)

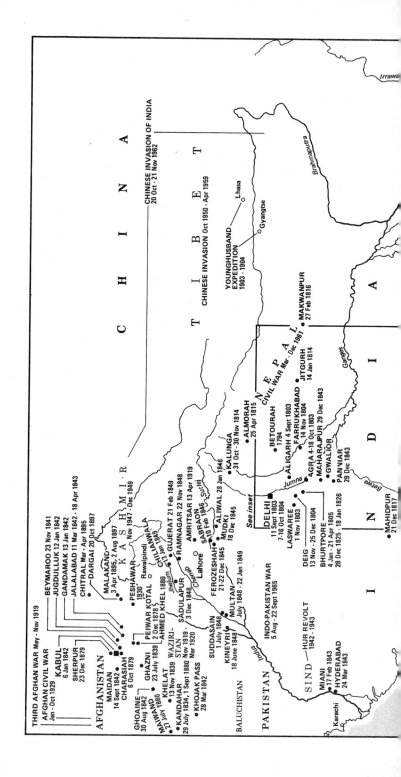

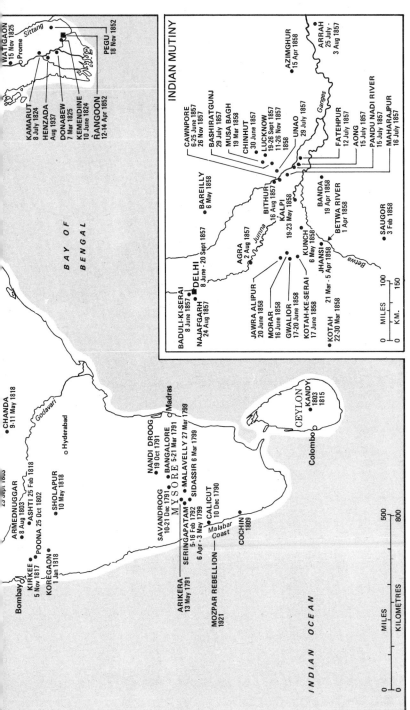

9   India and Ceylon: Expansion of Empire, Indian Mutiny, Wars in Tibet (*Section Two*)

582

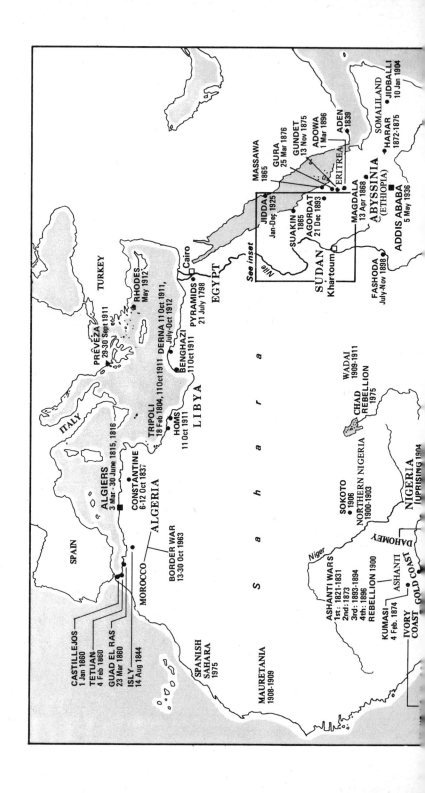

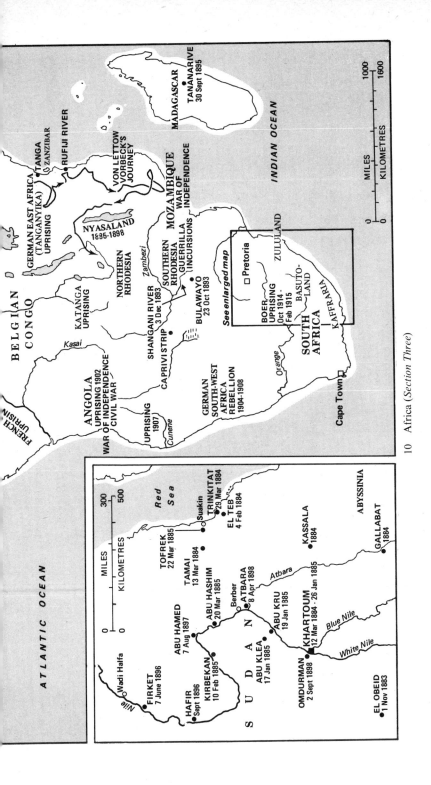

10 Africa (Section Three)

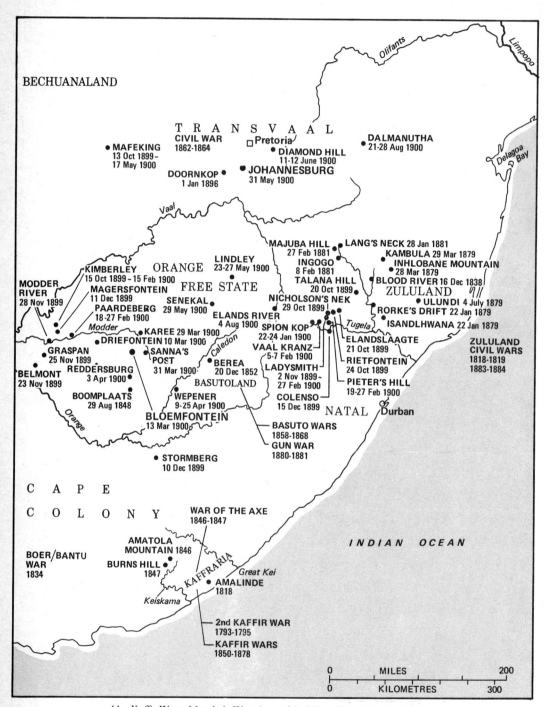

BECHUANALAND

TRANSVAAL

CIVIL WAR
1862-1864

□ Pretoria

● MAFEKING
13 Oct 1899–
17 May 1900

● DIAMOND HILL
11-12 June 1900

● DALMANUTHA
21-28 Aug 1900

DOORNKOP ●
1 Jan 1896

● JOHANNESBURG
31 May 1900

Vaal

ORANGE

LINDLEY
23-27 May 1900

MAJUBA HILL
27 Feb 1881

LANG'S NECK 28 Jan 1881

KAMBULA 29 Mar 1879

KIMBERLEY
15 Oct 1899–15 Feb 1900

FREE STATE

INGOGO
8 Feb 1881

INHLOBANE MOUNTAIN
28 Mar 1879

MODDER
RIVER
28 Nov 1899

MAGERSFONTEIN
11 Dec 1899

SENEKAL
29 May 1900

TALANA HILL
20 Oct 1899

BLOOD RIVER 16 Dec 1838

PAARDEBERG
18-27 Feb 1900

NICHOLSON'S NEK
29 Oct 1899

ZULULAND

ELANDS RIVER
4 Aug 1900

ULUNDI 4 July 1879

Modder

● KAREE 29 Mar 1900

RORKE'S DRIFT 22 Jan 1879

● DRIEFONTEIN 10 Mar 1900

SPION KOP
22-24 Jan 1900

ISANDLHWANA 22 Jan 1879

GRASPAN
25 Nov 1899

SANNA'S
POST
31 Mar 1900

Caledon

VAAL KRANZ
5-7 Feb 1900

Tugela

ELANDSLAAGTE
21 Oct 1899

ZULULAND
CIVIL WARS
1818-1819
1883-1884

REDDERSBURG
3 Apr 1900

BEREA
20 Dec 1852

RIETFONTEIN
24 Oct 1899

BELMONT
23 Nov 1899

LADYSMITH
2 Nov 1899–
27 Feb 1900

PIETER'S HILL
19-27 Feb 1900

BASUTOLAND

BOOMPLAATS
29 Aug 1848

WEPENER
9-25 Apr 1900

COLENSO
15 Dec 1899

NATAL

◊ Durban

BLOEMFONTEIN
13 Mar 1900

Orange

BASUTO WARS
1858-1868
GUN WAR
1880-1881

● STORMBERG
10 Dec 1899

C A P E

C O L O N Y

WAR OF THE AXE
1846-1847

INDIAN OCEAN

BOER/BANTU
WAR
1834

AMATOLA
MOUNTAIN 1846

BURNS HILL ●
1847

KAFFRARIA

Great Kei

● AMALINDE
1818

Keiskama

2nd KAFFIR WAR
1793-1795

KAFFIR WARS
1850-1878

Olifants

Limpopo

Delagoa Bay

0	MILES	200
0	KILOMETRES	300

11   Kaffir Wars, Matabele War, 1st and 2nd Boer Wars (*Section Three*)

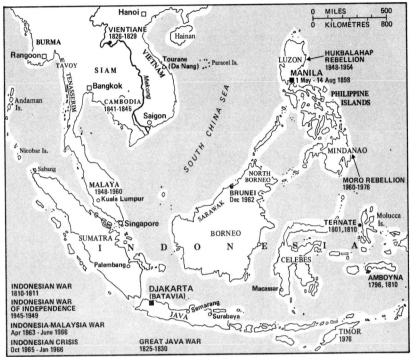

12 South East Asia (*Sections Four and Six*)

13 New Zealand: Maori Wars (*Section Four*)

586

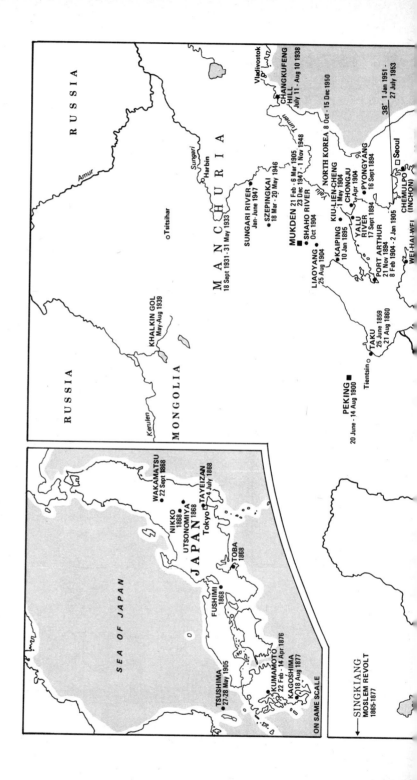

RUSSIA

MANCHURIA
18 Sept 1931 - 31 May 1933

Amur

Sungari

Harbin

Tsitsihar

SUNGARI RIVER
Jan - June 1947

SZEPINGKAI
18 Mar - 20 May 1946

MUKDEN 21 Feb - 6 Mar 1905
23 Dec 1947 - 1 Nov 1948

SHAHO RIVER
Oct 1904

LIAOYANG
25 Aug 1904

Vladivostok

CHANGKUFENG
HILL
July 11 - Aug 10 1938

Tumen

NORTH KOREA 8 Oct - 15 Dec 1950

KIU-LIEN-CHENG

CHONGJU
1 May 1904

KAIPING
10 Jan 1895

YALU
RIVER
Apr 1904

PORT ARTHUR
21 Nov 1894
8 Feb 1904 - 2 Jan 1905

PYONGYANG
16 Sept 1894

WEI-HAI-WEI

38° 1 Jan 1951 -
27 July 1953

Seoul

CHEMULPO
(INCHON)

TAKU
25 June 1859
21 Aug 1860

Tientsin

PEKING
20 June - 14 Aug 1900

RUSSIA

KHALKIN GOL
May-Aug 1939

Kerulen

MONGOLIA

WAKAMATSU
22 Sept 1868

NIKKO
1868

UTSONOMIYA
1868

TAYEIZAN
4 July 1868

Tokyo

TOBA
1868

FUSHIMI
1868

JAPAN

SEA OF JAPAN

TSUSHIMA
27-28 May 1905

KUMAMOTO
22 Feb - 14 Apr 1876

KAGOSHIMA
18 Aug 1877

ON SAME SCALE

SINGKIANG
MOSLEM REVOLT
1865-1877

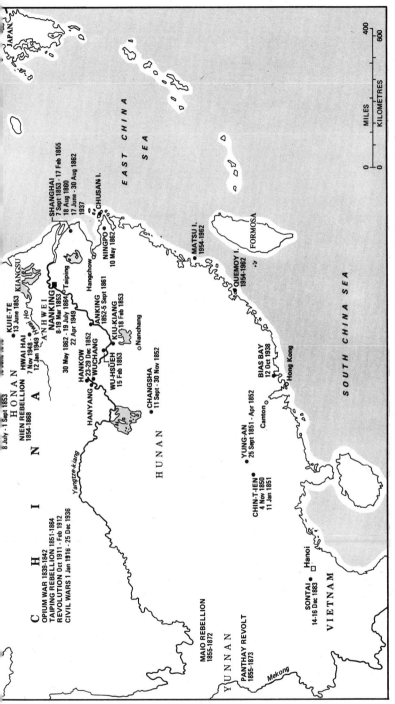

14   China and Japan: T'ai P'ing Rebellion, Opium Wars, Civil Revolts, Civil War (*Section Four*)

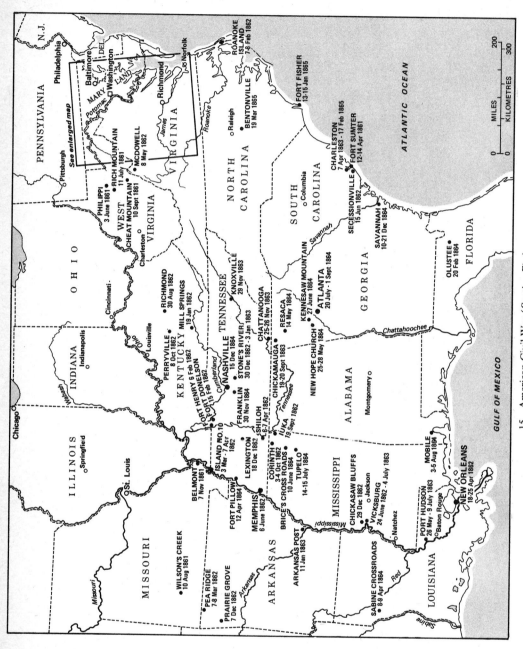

15　American Civil War (*Section Five*)

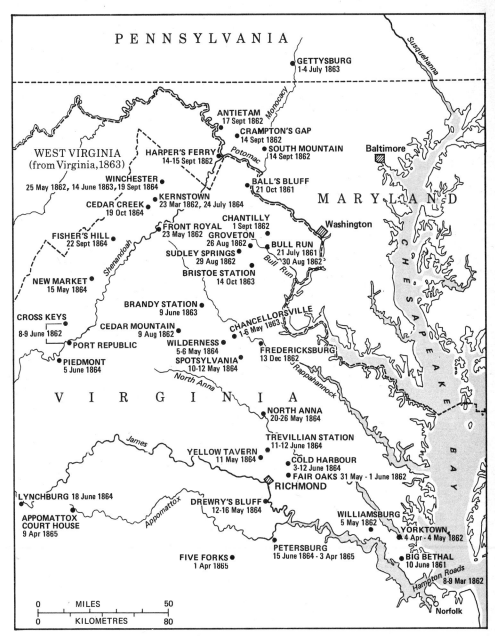

16   American Civil War: Eastern Seaboard (*Section Five*)

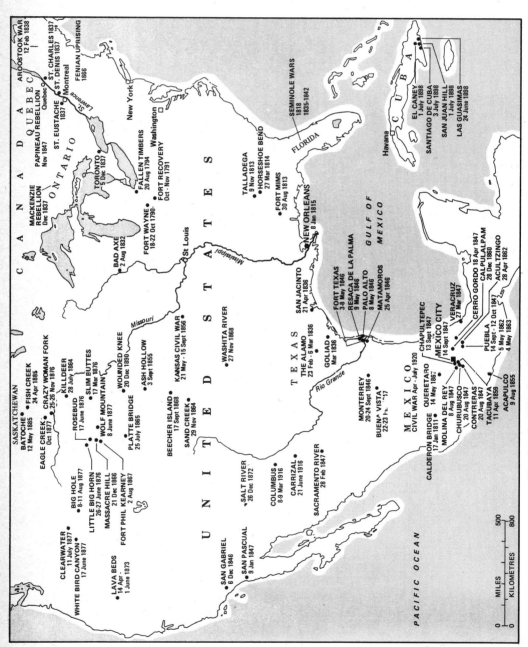

17 Canada, USA (less Civil War), Cuba and Mexico (*Section Six*)

591

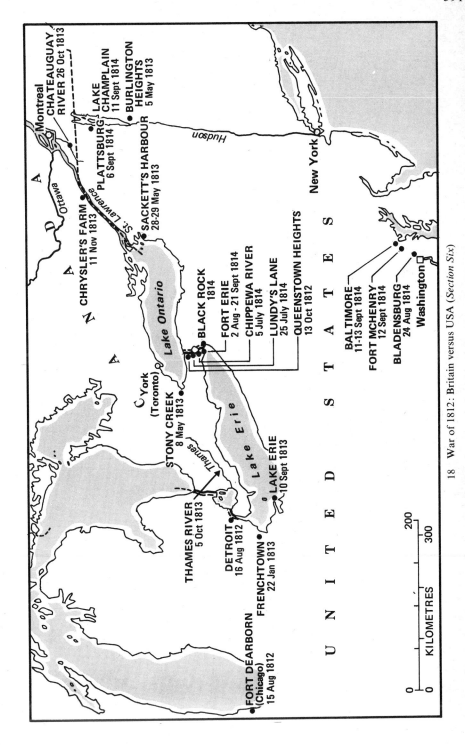

CHATEAUGUAY RIVER 26 Oct 1813
Montreal
LAKE CHAMPLAIN 11 Sept 1814
BURLINGTON HEIGHTS 5 May 1813
Ottawa
PLATTSBURG 6 Sept 1814
St. Lawrence
CHRYSLER'S FARM 11 Nov 1813
SACKETT'S HARBOUR 28-29 May 1813
Hudson
New York
C A N A D A
Lake Ontario
York (Toronto)
BLACK ROCK 1814
FORT ERIE 2 Aug - 21 Sept 1814
CHIPPEWA RIVER 5 July 1814
LUNDY'S LANE 25 July 1814
QUEENSTOWN HEIGHTS 13 Oct 1812
BALTIMORE 11-13 Sept 1814
FORT McHENRY 12 Sept 1814
BLADENSBURG 24 Aug 1814
Washington
STONY CREEK 8 May 1813
Thames
Lake Erie
LAKE ERIE 10 Sept 1813
THAMES RIVER 5 Oct 1813
DETROIT 16 Aug 1812
FRENCHTOWN 22 Jan 1813
U N I T E D   S T A T E S
FORT DEARBORN (Chicago) 15 Aug 1812
200
300
KILOMETRES
0
0

18   War of 1812: Britain versus USA (*Section Six*)

HAITI - WAR OF INDEPENDENCE
1794 - 1804

SOUTH AMERICAN WARS OF INDEPENDENCE
1806 - 1824

CUBA - TEN YEARS' WAR
1868 - 1878

CUBA - WAR OF INDEPENDENCE
1895 - 1898

NICARAGUA - HONDURAS WAR
Feb - Dec 1907

HONDURAS - CIVIL WAR
1909 - 1911

NICARAGUA - CIVIL WAR
July 1912

EL SALVADOR - HONDURAS FOOTBALL WAR
July 1969

Havana
BAY OF PIGS
17 - 19 Apr 1961
CUBA
SIERRA MAESTRA
1956 - 1959
HAITI
DOMINICAN
REPUBLIC
Apr 1965

Caribbean Sea

U.S./FRANCE
QUASI WAR
1798-1800
GUADELOUPE
ST. LUCIA
4 Apr 1794

GUATEMALA HONDURAS
CHALCHUAPA
2 Apr 1885
EL SALVADOR NICARAGUA

CANAL ZONE
1964
Panama

TOBAGO
15 Apr 1793

CARABOBO
24 June 1821 Caracas
Orinoco

NIQUITAO
1 July 1813 VENEZUELA

BOYACA
7 Aug 1819
BOGATAZO BOGOTA
Apr 1948 10 Aug 1819
COLOMBIA

ATLANTIC
OCEAN

Negro

PICHINCHA
24 May 1822 Quito
ECUADOR
Guayaquil

Amazon

ECUADOR - PERU WAR
July 1941

Maranon

JUNIN
6 Aug 1824
Lima
LIRCAY Apr 1830
AYACUCHO
9 Dec 1824

INGAVI
18 Nov 1841

B R A Z I L
UPRISING 1922 - 1924

CALLAO
5 Nov 1820
2 May 1866
MIRAFLORES
15 Jan 1881
CHORRILLOS
13 Jan 1881

LA PAZ Jan 1865

BOLIVIA
ORURO CHACO WAR
1862 1932 - 1935

TACNA
26 May 1880

WAR OF THE PACIFIC
1878 - 1883

TUMUSLA
1 Apr 1825

Pilcomayo

Rio de Janeiro

PACIFIC
OCEAN

AQUIDABAN RIVER
1 Mar 1870

Asuncion

PARAGUAYAN CIVIL WAR
30 Mar - 20 Aug 1947

ITUZAINGO
20 Feb 1827

MONTE CASEROS
3 Feb 1852

CONCON
21 Aug 1891
Valparaiso
CHACABUCO
12 Feb 1817
Santiago
PLACILLA
28 Aug 1891
CANCHA RAYADA
16 Mar 1818
RANCAGUA
1 Oct 1814
MAIPO RIVER
5 Apr 1818
Buenos
Aires
YUNGAY
20 Jan 1839

URUGUAY
ARROYO GRANDE 1842
MONTEVIDEO
16 Feb 1843 - 8 Oct 1851
Aug 1863

OBLIGADO
Nov 1845
CEPEDA
1 Feb 1820
23 Oct 1859

CHILOE ISLAND
19 Jan 1826

FALKLAND
IS.

MILES
0   1000
0   1600
KILOMETRES

LOMAS VALENTINAS
21 Nov - 7 Dec 1868
Asuncion
AVAY
Dec 1868
YTORORO
Dec 1868

PARAGUAY

HUMAITA
16 July 1868
CURUPAITI
22 Sept 1866
TUYUTI
24 May 1866
3 Nov 1867
ESTERO-BELLACO
2 May 1866

Resistencia
Corrientes

A R G E N T I N A

RIACHUELO RIVER
June 1865

MILES
0   80
0   120
KM.

19 South America (*Section Seven*)

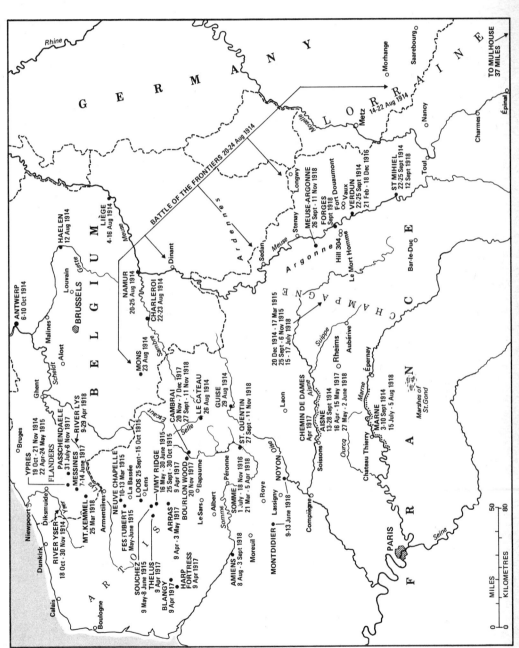

20 World War I: Western Front (Section Eight)

GERMANY

Rhine

Morhange ○   ○ Saarebourg

LORRAINE

TO MULHOUSE
37 MILES

Moselle

Metz ○
14-22 Aug 1914

Nancy ○

Charmes ○   ○ Épinal

Longwy ○

MEUSE-ARGONNE
26 Sept - 11 Nov 1918

Stenay ○

FORGES
Sept 1918
Fort Douaumont
VERDUN Vaux ○
22-25 Sept 1914
21 Feb - 18 Dec 1916

ST MIHIEL
22-25 Sept 1914
12 Sept 1918

Toul ○

Sedan ○

Argonne

Hill 304 ○
Le Mort Homme

Bar-le-Duc ○

BELGIUM

HAELEN
12 Aug 1914

LIÈGE
4-16 Aug 1914

Louvain ○
⊗ BRUSSELS
Malines ○   ○ Alost

Ghent ○

Scheldt

Gette

Meuse

NAMUR
20-25 Aug 1914

Dinant ○

CHARLEROI
22-23 Aug 1914

Sambre

MONS
23 Aug 1914

Ardennes

Meuse

BATTLE OF THE FRONTIERS 20-24 Aug 1914

CHAMPAGNE

20 Dec 1914 - 17 Mar 1915
25 Sept - 6 Nov 1915
15 - 17 July 1918

Suippe

Laon ○

CHEMIN DE DAMES
Apr 1917

Aisne

Soissons ○

AISNE
13-28 Sept 1914
16 Apr - 15 May 1917
27 May - 2 June 1918

Rheims ○
Aubérive ○

Épernay ○

Marne

Marshes of
St. Gond

ANTWERP
6-10 Oct 1914

Bruges ○

FLANDERS

YPRES
19 Oct - 21 Nov 1914
22 Apr-24 May 1915

PASSCHENDAELE
31 July-6 Nov 1917

RIVER LYS
9-29 Apr 1918

MESSINES
7-14 June 1917

NEUVE CHAPELLE
10-13 Mar 1915

LOOS 25 Sept - 15 Oct 1915

La Bassée

Lens ○

VIMY RIDGE
16 May - 30 June 1915
25 Sept - 30 Oct 1915
9 Apr 1917

ARRAS
9 Apr - 3 May 1917

BOURLON WOOD
20 Nov 1917

CAMBRAI
20 Nov - 7 Dec 1917
27 Sept - 11 Nov 1918

Selle

LE CATEAU
26 Aug 1914

GUISE
29 Aug 1914

ST. QUENTIN
27 Sept - 11 Nov 1918

Péronne ○

Bapaume ○

Le Sars ○

Somme

SOMME
1 July - 18 Nov 1916
21 Mar - 5 Apr 1918

Albert ○

Roye ○

MONTDIDIER
9-13 June 1918

Lassigny

NOYON
27 May - 2 June 1918

Oise

Compiègne ○

Ourcq

Château Thierry

MARNE
3-10 Sept 1914
15 July - 5 Aug 1918

FRANCE

PARIS ⊗

Seine

Nieuwpoort ○
Diksmuide ○

RIVER YSER
18 Oct - 30 Nov 1914

MT. KEMMEL
25 Mar 1918

Armentières

FESTUBERT
May-June 1915

SOUCHEZ
9 May-8 June 1915
THELUS
9 Apr 1917
BLANGY
9 Apr 1917
HARP
FORTRESS
9 Apr 1917

AMIENS
8 Aug - 3 Sept 1918

Moreuil ○

Calais
Boulogne ○
Dunkirk ○

Yser

Lys

MILES   50
KILOMETRES   80

0

Map 21 (Eastern Front):

BALTIC SEA

RIGA
1 Sept 1917

Königsberg

GUMBINNEN
20 Aug 1914

STALLUPONEN
17 Aug 1914

VILNA
19 Sept 1915

LAKE NAROCH
18 Mar 1916

ORLAU/FRANKENAU
24 Aug 1914

MASURIAN LAKES
9-14 Sept 1914
7-21 Feb 1915

GRODNO
2 Sept 1915

G E R M A N Y

TANNENBERG
26-31 Aug 1914

R U S S I A

Vistula

VISTULA RIVER
28 Sept - 3 Oct 1914

BOLIMOV
31 Jan 1915

WARSAW
4-7 Aug 1915

BREST LITOVSK
25 Aug 1915

P O L A N D

LODZ
11-25 Nov 1914

Bug

BRUSILOV
OFFENSIVE I
4 June 1916
20 Sept 1916

KRASNIK
23-24 Aug 1914

ZAMOSC
26 Aug - 1 Sept 1914

KOMAROV

Vistula

RAVA RUSKA
3-11 Sept 1914 Lemberg

BRUSILOV
OFFENSIVE II
July 1917

TARNOW
2 May - 27 June 1915

GORLICE

PRZEMYSL
22 Mar 1915

GNILA LIPA RIVER
26-30 Aug 1914

Dniester

A U S T R I A – H U N G A R Y

CZERNOWITZ
17 Feb 1915

RUMANIA

MILES 150
KILOMETRES 250

21 World War I: Eastern Front (*Section Nine*)

Map 22 (Austria-Hungary and Italy):

AUSTRIA–HUNGARY

CAPORETTO
24 Oct - 12 Nov 1917

ISONZO
23 June - 7 July 1915
18 July - 3 Aug 1915
18 Oct - 4 Nov 1915
10 Nov - 2 Dec 1915
11-29 Mar 1916
6-17 Aug 1916
14-26 Sept 1916
10-12 Oct 1916
1-14 Nov 1916
12 May - 8 June 1917
18 Aug - 15 Sept 1917

TRENTINO

Isonzo

Gorizia

ASIAGO
11-29 May
1916

VITTORIO
VENETO
Oct - Nov 1918

PIAVE
June 1918

Piave

ITALY

WIEN
9 Dec 1917

Trieste

Venice

Fiume

Po

Adriatic
Sea

Pola

VIVIBUS UNITAS
1 Nov 1918

MILES 60
KILOMETRES 100

SZENT ISTVAU
10 June 1918

22 World War I: Austria-Hungary and Italy (*Section Nine*)

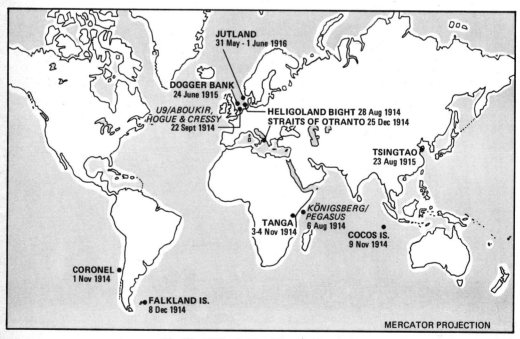

Map 23 (Naval Battles):

JUTLAND
31 May - 1 June 1916

DOGGER BANK
24 June 1915

U9/ABOUKIR,
HOGUE & CRESSY
22 Sept 1914

HELIGOLAND BIGHT 28 Aug 1914
STRAITS OF OTRANTO 25 Dec 1914

TSINGTAO
23 Aug 1915

KÖNIGSBERG/
PEGASUS
6 Aug 1914

TANGA
3-4 Nov 1914

COCOS IS.
9 Nov 1914

CORONEL
1 Nov 1914

FALKLAND IS.
8 Dec 1914

MERCATOR PROJECTION

23 World War I: Naval Battles (*Section Nine*)

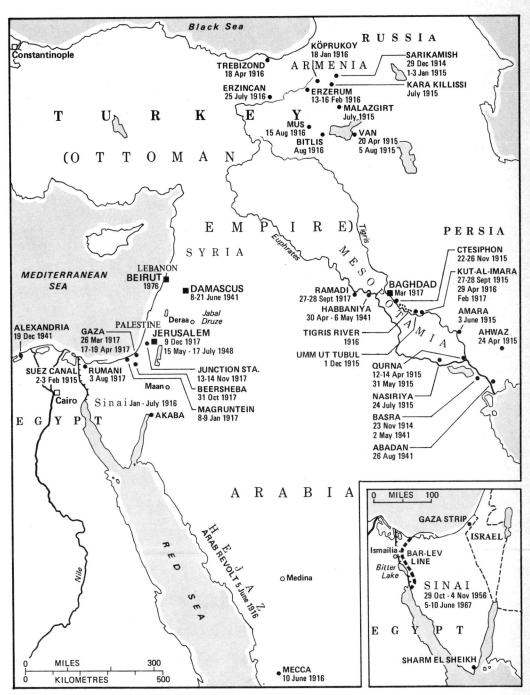

Black Sea

Constantinople

RUSSIA

KÖPRUKOY
18 Jan 1916

SARIKAMISH
29 Dec 1914
1-3 Jan 1915

TREBIZOND
18 Apr 1916

ARMENIA

KARA KILLISI
July 1915

ERZINCAN
25 July 1916

ERZERUM
13-16 Feb 1916

MALAZGIRT
July 1915

T U R K E Y

MUS
15 Aug 1916

VAN
20 Apr 1915
5 Aug 1915

BITLIS
Aug 1916

(O T T O M A N

PERSIA

E M P I R E)

Euphrates

Tigris

CTESIPHON
22-26 Nov 1915

S Y R I A

KUT-AL-IMARA
27-28 Sept 1915
29 Apr 1916
Feb 1917

LEBANON
BEIRUT
1976

RAMADI
27-28 Sept 1917

BAGHDAD
Mar 1917

DAMASCUS
8-21 June 1941

HABBANIYA
30 Apr - 6 May 1941

AMARA
3 June 1915

**MEDITERRANEAN
SEA**

Deraa

Jabal
Druze

TIGRIS RIVER
1916

AHWAZ
24 Apr 1915

PALESTINE

ALEXANDRIA
19 Dec 1941

GAZA
26 Mar 1917
17-19 Apr 1917

JERUSALEM
9 Dec 1917
15 May - 17 July 1948

UMM UT TUBUL
1 Dec 1915

QURNA
12-14 Apr 1915
31 May 1915

SUEZ CANAL
2-3 Feb 1915

RUMANI
3 Aug 1917

JUNCTION STA.
13-14 Nov 1917

NASIRIYA
24 July 1915

Cairo

Maan

BEERSHEBA
31 Oct 1917

BASRA
23 Nov 1914
2 May 1941

E G Y P T

S i n a i Jan - July 1916

MAGRUNTEIN
8-9 Jan 1917

AKABA

ABADAN
26 Aug 1941

Nile

A R A B I A

0   MILES   100

GAZA STRIP

ISRAEL

Ismailia

BAR-LEV
LINE

Bitter
Lake

**H
E
J
A
Z**

ARAB REVOLT 5 June 1916

S I N A I
29 Oct - 4 Nov 1956
5-10 June 1967

RED

Medina

SEA

E G Y P T

MILES   300

KILOMETRES   500

SHARM EL SHEIKH

MECCA
10 June 1916

24   Middle East and Caucasus: 1914 – present day (*Section Nine*)

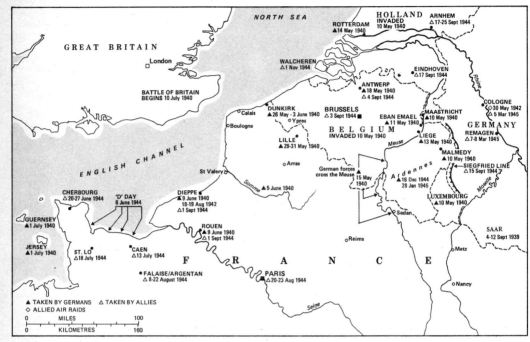

GREAT BRITAIN

London

NORTH SEA

ROTTERDAM
▲14 May 1940

HOLLAND
INVADED
10 May 1940

ARNHEM
△17-25 Sept 1944

BATTLE OF BRITAIN
BEGINS 10 July 1940

WALCHEREN
△1 Nov 1944

EINDHOVEN
●17 Sept 1944

ANTWERP
▲18 May 1940
△4 Sept 1944

COLOGNE
◇30 May 1942
△5 Mar 1945

Calais

Boulogne

DUNKIRK
▲26 May - 3 June 1940
●Ypres

BRUSSELS
△3 Sept 1944 ■

EBAN EMAEL
▲11 May 1940

MAASTRICHT
△10 May 1940

GERMANY

REMAGEN
△7-8 Mar 1945

ENGLISH CHANNEL

Arras

LILLE
▲29-31 May 1940

BELGIUM
INVADED 10 May 1940

LIEGE
▲13 May 1940

MALMEDY
▲10 May 1940

SIEGFRIED LINE
△15 Sept 1944

St Valery

Somme

▲5 June 1940

German forces
cross the Meuse
15 May
1940

Meuse

Ardennes
16 Dec 1944
28 Jan 1945

Moselle

CHERBOURG
△20-27 June 1944

'D' DAY
6 June 1944

DIEPPE
▲9 June 1940
18-19 Aug 1942
△1 Sept 1944

Sedan

LUXEMBOURG
△10 May 1940

GUERNSEY
▲1 July 1940

ROUEN
▲9 June 1940
△1 Sept 1944

Reims

SAAR
4-12 Sept 1939

Metz

JERSEY
▲1 July 1940

ST. LO
△18 July 1944

CAEN
△13 July 1944

F   R   A   N   C   E

Nancy

FALAISE/ARGENTAN
△8-22 August 1944

PARIS
▲△20-23 Aug 1944

▲ TAKEN BY GERMANS   △ TAKEN BY ALLIES
◇ ALLIED AIR RAIDS

Seine

0   MILES   100
0   KILOMETRES   160

25   World War II: Western Front (*Section Eleven*)

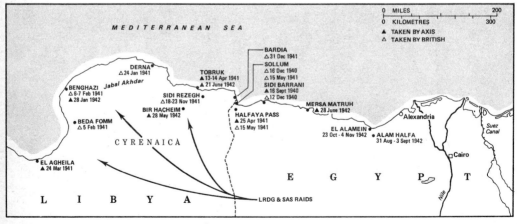

0   MILES   200
0   KILOMETRES   300

▲ TAKEN BY AXIS
△ TAKEN BY BRITISH

MEDITERRANEAN SEA

BARDIA
△31 Dec 1941

SOLLUM
△16 Dec 1940
△15 May 1941

DERNA
△24 Jan 1941

TOBRUK
▲13-14 Apr 1941
△21 June 1942

SIDI BARRANI
▲16 Sept 1940
△12 Dec 1940

BENGHAZI
△6-7 Feb 1941
▲28 Jan 1942

Jabal Akhdar

SIDI REZEGH
△18-23 Nov 1941

BIR HACHEIM
▲28 May 1942

MERSA MATRUH
▲28 June 1942

BEDA FOMM
△5 Feb 1941

HALFAYA PASS
△25 Apr 1941
△15 May 1941

Alexandria

Suez
Canal

CYRENAICA

EL ALAMEIN
23 Oct - 4 Nov 1942

ALAM HALFA
31 Aug - 3 Sept 1942

Cairo

EL AGHEILA
▲24 Mar 1941

E   G   Y   P   T

Nile

L   I   B   Y   A

LRDG & SAS RAIDS

26   World War II Desert Campaign: North Africa (*Section Eleven*)

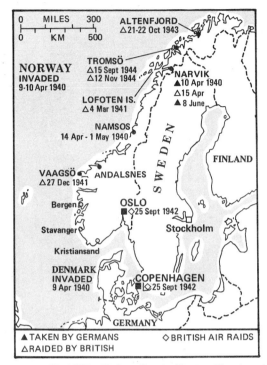

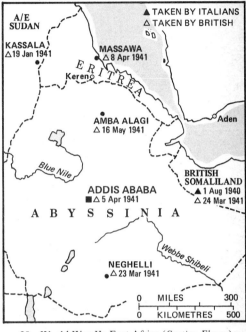

Map 27 (Scandinavia):

0 MILES 300
0 KM 500

NORWAY
INVADED
9-10 Apr 1940

ALTENFJORD
△21-22 Oct 1943

TROMSÖ
△15 Sept 1944
△12 Nov 1944

NARVIK
▲10 Apr 1940
△15 Apr
▲ 8 June

LOFOTEN IS.
△4 Mar 1941

NAMSOS
14 Apr - 1 May 1940

SWEDEN

FINLAND

VAAGSÖ
△27 Dec 1941

ANDALSNES

Bergen

OSLO
◇25 Sept 1942

Stockholm

Stavanger

Kristiansand

DENMARK
INVADED
9 Apr 1940

COPENHAGEN
◻◇25 Sept 1942

GERMANY

▲ TAKEN BY GERMANS   ◇ BRITISH AIR RAIDS
△ RAIDED BY BRITISH

27   World War II: Scandinavia (*Section Eleven*)

Map 28 (East Africa):

A/E
SUDAN

▲ TAKEN BY ITALIANS
△ TAKEN BY BRITISH

KASSALA
△19 Jan 1941

MASSAWA
△8 Apr 1941

ERITREA

Kereno

Aden

AMBA ALAGI
△16 May 1941

Blue Nile

ADDIS ABABA
◼△ 5 Apr 1941

BRITISH
SOMALILAND
▲ 1 Aug 1940
△ 24 Mar 1941

A B Y S S I N I A

Webbe Shibeli

NEGHELLI
● △23 Mar 1941

0   MILES   300
0   KILOMETRES   500

28   World War II: East Africa (*Section Eleven*)

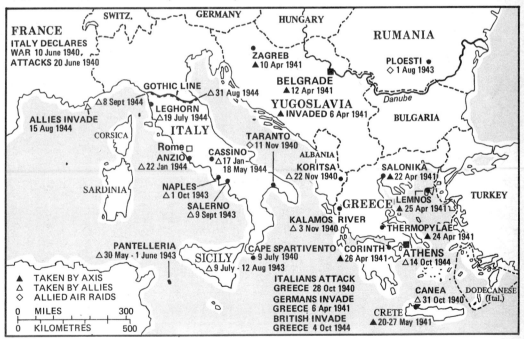

Map 29 (Mediterranean and Balkans):

FRANCE
ITALY DECLARES
WAR 10 June 1940,
ATTACKS 20 June 1940

SWITZ.   GERMANY   HUNGARY

RUMANIA

ZAGREB
▲10 Apr 1941

PLOESTI ●
◇ 1 Aug 1943

GOTHIC LINE
△31 Aug 1944

BELGRADE
▲12 Apr 1941

YUGOSLAVIA
▲ INVADED 6 Apr 1941

Danube

△8 Sept 1944

LEGHORN
△19 July 1944

BULGARIA

ALLIES INVADE
15 Aug 1944

CORSICA

ITALY

TARANTO
◇ 11 Nov 1940

Rome ◻

ANZIO
△ 22 Jan 1944

CASSINO
● 17 Jan-
18 May 1944

ALBANIA

KORITSA
△ 22 Nov 1940

SALONIKA
▲22 Apr 1941

TURKEY

SARDINIA

NAPLES
△1 Oct 1943

SALERNO
△ 9 Sept 1943

GREECE

LEMNOS
▲ 25 Apr 1941

KALAMOS RIVER
△ 3 Nov 1940

THERMOPYLAE
▲ 24 Apr 1941

PANTELLERIA
△ 30 May - 1 June 1943

CAPE SPARTIVENTO
● 9 July 1940

CORINTH
△ 26 Apr 1941

ATHENS
◼△ 14 Oct 1944

SICILY
△ 9 July - 12 Aug 1943

ITALIANS ATTACK
GREECE 28 Oct 1940
GERMANS INVADE
GREECE 6 Apr 1941
BRITISH INVADE
GREECE 4 Oct 1944

CANEA
△ 31 Oct 1940

CRETE
▲20-27 May 1941

DODECANESE
(Ital.)

▲   TAKEN BY AXIS
△   TAKEN BY ALLIES
◇   ALLIED AIR RAIDS

0   MILES   300
0   KILOMETRES   500

29   World War II: Mediterranean and Balkans

30 World War II: Eastern Front and Winter War in Finland (*Section Eleven*)

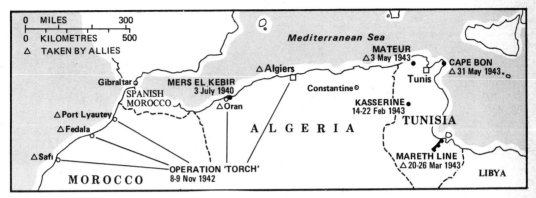

31   World War II: North African Campaign (*Section Eleven*)

32   World War II: Naval and Air Operations (*Section Eleven*)

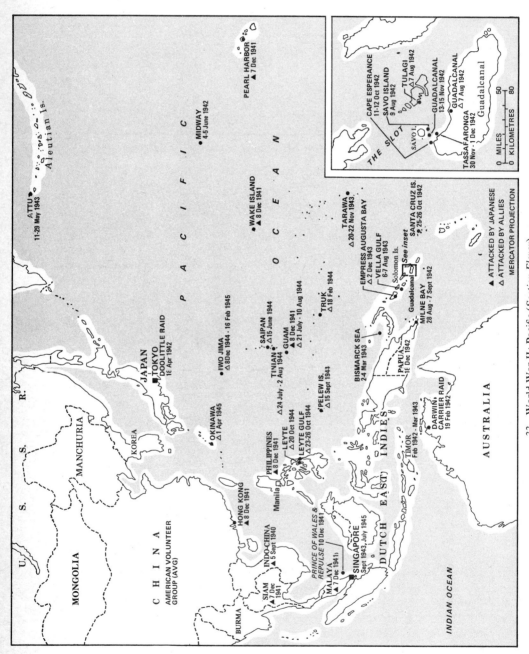

33 World War II: Pacific (*Section Eleven*)

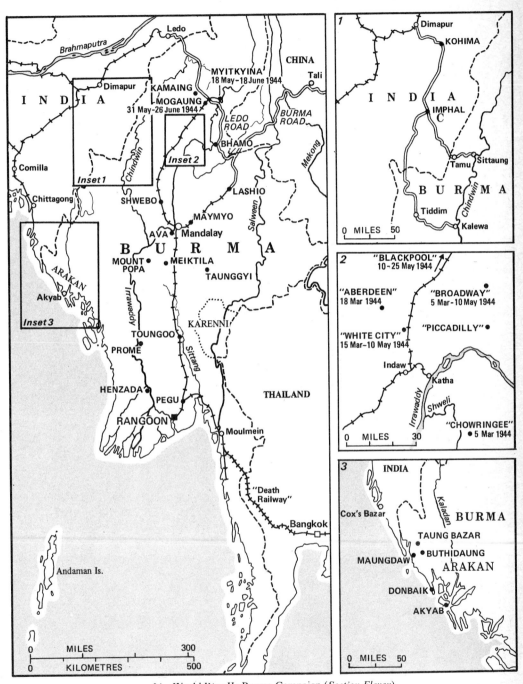

34 World War II: Burma Campaign (*Section Eleven*)

FRANCE

EL FERROL
19-20 July 1936

CORUNNA
3-15 Jan 1937

GIJON
1 Sept - 21 Oct 1937

SANTANDER
14-24 Aug 1937

GUERNICA
26 Apr 1937

IRUN
26 Aug - 4 Sept 1937

ASTURIAS

BILBAO
31 Mar - 19 June 1937

BASQUE
PROVS.

VILLARREAL
DE ALAVA
30 Nov - 5 Dec

Sept 1937

Andorra

TARDIENTA
Mar 1938

HUESCA
22 Mar 1938

TREMP
8 Apr 1938

10 Feb 1939

VALLADOLID
19 July 1936

ALCUBIERRE
Mar 1938

PINA
Mar 1938

CAMARASA
8 Apr 1938

SARAGOSSA
26 Aug - 4 Sept 1937

LERIDA
3 Apr 1938

CATALONIA

SOMOSIERRA PASS
20-25 July 1936

A R A G O N

FRAGA
25 Mar 1938

BARCELCNA
19 July 1936
26 Jan 1939

BOADILLA
DEL MONTE

BELCHITE
24 Aug - 6 Sept 1937
10 Mar 1938

TARRAGONA
17 Jan 1939

ALTE DE LEON PASS
21-22 July 1936

GUADALAJARA
8-18 Mar 1937

CASPE
17 Mar 1938

GANDESA
3 Apr 1938 1 Aug - 3 Sept 1938

BRUNETE
6-26 July 1937

MONTALBAN
13 Mar 1938

CHAPINERIA
18-19 Oct 1936

MADRID
6 Nov 1936 - 27 Mar 1939

VINAROZ
15 Apr 1938

TORTOSA
18 Apr 1938

S P A I N

TERUEL
15 Dec 1937 - 21 Feb 1938

JARAMA
6-27 Feb 1937

TALAVERA DE LA REINA
2-3 Sept 1936

TOLEDO
20 July - 27 Sept 1936

ILLESCAS
17-23 Oct 1936

CASTELLON DE LA PLANA
14 June 1938

MERIDA
10 Aug 1936

Valencia

MAJORCA
16 Aug - 3 Sept

Lisbon

MEDELLIN
Aug 1936

Ibiza

P O R T U G A L

BADAJOZ
14-15 Aug 1936

SANTA MARIA
DE LA CABEZA
July 1936 - 1 May 1937

POZOBLANCO
18 July - 18 Aug 1936

Cordoba

LOPERA
28-29 Dec 1936

M E D I T E R R A N E A N   S E A

CARTAGENA
6 Mar 1938

MALAGA
17 Jan - 8 Feb 1937

A T L A N T I C

Gibraltar

O C E A N

Tangier

CEUTA
17 July 1936

TETUAN
17 July 1936

LARACHE
18 July 1936

S P A N I S H   M O R O C C O

MELILLA
17 July 1936

MILES		150
KILOMETRES		250

35 The Spanish Civil War (*Section Twelve*)

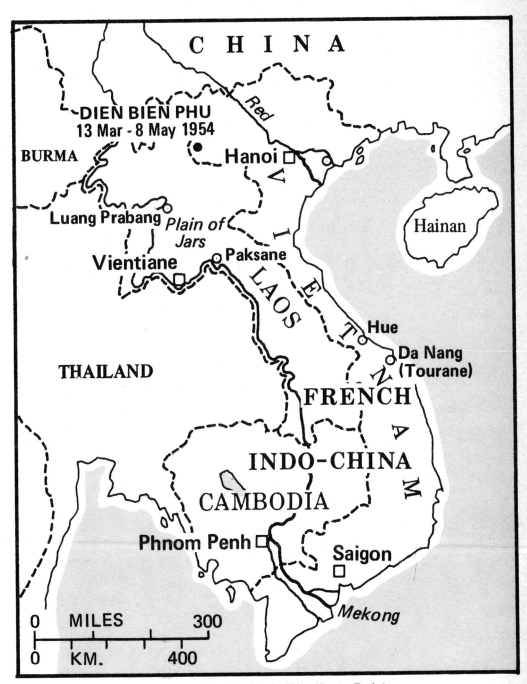

C H I N A

DIEN BIEN PHU
13 Mar - 8 May 1954

Red

BURMA

Hanoi

Hainan

Luang Prabang *Plain of Jars*

Vientiane Paksane

LAOS

V I E T N A M

Hue

Da Nang
(Tourane)

THAILAND

FRENCH

INDO-CHINA

CAMBODIA

Phnom Penh

Saigon

Mekong

0 MILES 300

0 KM. 400

36   French Indo-China (*Section Twelve*)

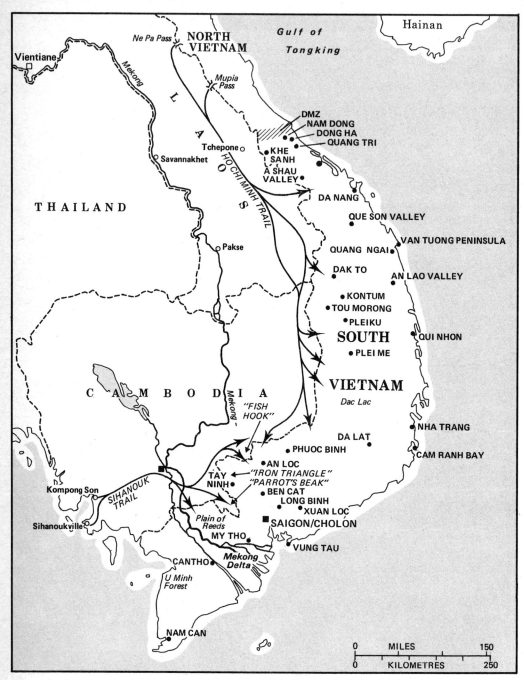

37 South Vietnam War (*Section Twelve*)

Select Bibliography

Allen, and Muratoff. *Caucasian Battlefields* (1953)

Almirante, J. (ed). *Bosquejo de la Historia Militar de España* (1923), 3 vols

Bleiberg, Germán (ed). *Diccionario de Historia de España* (1968)

Boatner III, Lt-Colonel Mark Mayo. *The Civil War Dictionary* (1959)

Bruce, George. *The Burma Wars, 1824–1886* (1973)

Chandler, D. G. (ed). *A Traveller's Guide to the Battlefields of Europe* (1965), 2 vols

Claridge, W. Walton. *History of the Gold Coast and Ashanti* (1964)

Churchill, Winston S. *The World Crisis* (1923–27), 3 vols

De Wet, Christiaan. *Three Years War* (1903)

Dictionary of National Biography

Dulles, Foster J. *The United States since 1865* (1959)

Dupuy, Ernest and Trevor. *The Encyclopaedia of Military History* (1970)

Edmunds, Brigadier-General Sir James E. *History of the Great War. Military Operations* (1922 *et seq*)

Edwardes, Michael. *Battles of the Indian Mutiny* (1963)

Ellis, Major L. F. *Victory in the West* (1962), 2 vols

Encyclopaedia Brittannica (1911 edition)

Falls, Captain Cyril (ed). *Great Military Battles* (1964)

Fisher, H. A. L. *A History of Europe* (1936)

Fortescue, Sir John. *History of the British Army* (1900 *et seq*)

Fuller, Major-General J. F. C. (ed John Terraine). *The Decisive Battles of the Western World and their Influence upon History* (1970), 2 vols

Furneaux, Rupert. *Massacre at Amritsar* (1963)

Grun, Bernard. *The Timetables of History* (1975)

Harrison, James P. *Communist and Chinese Peasant Rebellions* (1970)

Hodge, Fredrick W. *Handbook of American Indians* (1959)

International Institute for Strategic Studies (I.I.S.S.). *Adelphi Papers and Strategic Surveys* (1966–76)

Institute for the Study of Conflict. *Annual of Power and Conflict* (1972–76)

Jenkins, E. H. *History of the French Navy* (1973)

Kaye, and Mallcson. *Indian Mutiny* (1889), vols I–IV (1889)

Macrory, Patrick. *Signal Disaster. The Retreat from Kabul, 1842* (1966)

Marshall, Brigadier-General S. L. A. *The American Heritage History of World War I* (1964)

Martin, K. L. and Lovett, G. H. *Encyclopaedia of Latin-American History* (1964)

Mason, Francis K. *Battle over Britain* (1969)

Milford. *Dictionary of American History* (1940)

Mordal, Jacques. *25 Centuries of Sea Warfare* (1959)

Richardson, H. E. *Tibet and its History* (1962)

Sterneggs, General-Major von. *Schlachten-Atlas des XIX Jahrhunderts*

Stewart, A. T. Q. *The Pagoda War. Lord Dufferin* (1972)

Story, Norah. *The Oxford Companion to Canadian History and Literature* (1967)
Teng, S. E. *The Tai Ping Rebellion and the Western Powers* (1971)
Thomas, Hugh. *Cuba or the Pursuit of Freedom* (1971)
Vives, J. Vicens (ed). *Historia de España y América* (1961), 5 vols
Wavell, Colonel A. P. *The Palestine Campaign* (1928)
Webster's Biographical Dictionary (1972)
Wolf, Professor Eric. *Peasant Wars of the Twentieth Century* (1971)
Woodburn Kirby, S. *The War against Japan* (1957–65) 5 vols
Young, Brigadier Peter and Natkiel, Richard, *Atlas of the Second World War* (1973)
Young, Brigadier Peter. *History of the British Army* (1967)
—— *World War, 1939–1945* (1966)
—— *The Israeli Campaign, 1967* (1967)